D1119863

BOTTOM LINE YEAR BOOK 2013

BY THE EDITORS OF
Bottom Line PERSONAL
www.BottomLinePublications.com

Bottom Line Year Book 2013

First Printing

10 9 8 7 6 5 4 3 2 1

ISBN 0-88723-681-2

Bottom Line Books® publishes the advice of expert authorities in many fields. These opinions may at times conflict as there are often different approaches to solving problems. The use of a book is not a substitute for legal, accounting, investment, health or any other professional services. Consult competent professionals for answers to your specific questions.

Offers, prices, rates, addresses, telephone numbers and Web sites listed in this book are accurate at the time of publication, but they are subject to frequent change.

Bottom Line Books® is a registered trademark of Boardroom® Inc.
281 Tresser Boulevard, Stamford, CT 06901

www.BottomLinePublications.com

Bottom Line Books® is an imprint of Boardroom® Inc., publisher of print periodicals, e-letters and books. We are dedicated to bringing you the best information from the most knowledgeable sources in the world. Our goal is to help you gain greater wealth, better health, more wisdom, extra time and increased happiness.

Printed in the United States of America

Contents

Preface xi

PART ONE: YOUR HEALTH

1 • HEALTH UPDATES

Salt! Not So Bad After All? 1
Statin Alert 3
Omega-3 Fish Oil Cautions 3
Promising News on New Drug 3
Keep Still 4
Better Blood Pressure Drug 4
Better Blood Pressure Readings 4
Exercise Not Enough to Keep Your Heart Healthy 4
Insomnia Raises Heart Disease Risk 5
Hidden Heart Problem 5
Help for Angina 5
Alcohol More Dangerous for Women 5
Calcium Concerns 5
Exposure to Cold Increases Heart Attack Risk 6
Did You Have a Heart Attack—and Not Know It? 6
Smoking Danger 7
Heart-Breaking Loss 8
Family Heart Risk 8
Drug Alert 8
Safer Way to Detect Blood Vessel Blockages 8
NSAIDs Linked to Risk for Second Heart Attack ...8
Better Heart Attack Care 8
Aspirin Before Heart Surgery a Lifesaver 9
Pacemaker Safety 9
Tall People at Higher Risk for Blood Clots 9
Depression and Stroke 9
Is It a "Wake-Up" Stroke? 10
Antidepressants Speed Stroke Recovery 10
Mini-Stroke Increases Risk for Heart Attack 10
One in Three US Adults Could Have Diabetes by 2050 11
Statins May Raise Risk for Diabetes 11
Women at Risk 11
Heat Hurts Diabetes 11
Blood Sugar Dangers 11
Potent Cancer Drug on the Way 12
Is Sweetener Safe? 12
Cancer Caution 12
Aluminum Bottles—More BPA Than Plastic? 12
BPA Concern from Canned Soup 12
Cell Phones and Brain Tumors—Steps to Protect Yourself 13

Radiation Concern 14
Early Detection..15
Another Aspirin Benefit 15
Drivers' Danger..15
Exfoliate!..15
HPV May Raise Heart Risks 15
Nicotine Replacements..16
Buy Organic Milk..16
Help a Smoker Quit..16
Danger in the Attic 16
New Device Eases Chronic Pain..16
Antibiotic Creams May Increase MRSA Resistance..17
Chemo Without Hair Loss?..17
Thinning Eyebrows May Signal Disease..17
Iced Tea Raises Kidney Stone Risk 17
Simple Urine Test for Kidney Disease 18
Good News..18
Boomers, Beware 18
Reflux Drugs May Deplete Magnesium 18
Cell-Phone Radiation Warning..18
Hip Replacement Warning..19
Help for Fibromyalgia 19
Troubling New Statistics..19
Maternal Link to Alzheimer's 19
Marital Link 20
Hearing Loss Raises Dementia Risk 20
Cholesterol Warning..20
Better Brain Health..20
Cold Sores May Link to Alzheimer's 20
Cancer Drug Shows Promise 21
Antidepressant for Older Adults..21
Violent Dreams?..21
Ibuprofen Lowers Parkinson's Risk 21
Fast Food Warning..21
Mental Health Alert..21
Help for OCD..22
Belly Fat and Osteoporosis 22
Aspirin Caution 22
More Aspirin Caution 22
Nearsightedness Increases Glaucoma Risk..23
Sepsis—the Little-Known Killer of Up to 375,000 Americans a Year 23
Seek Care Right Away 25
Melon Rx 25
When to Buy Organic..25
Better Canned Tuna..25
Too Much TV Shortens Life Span..25

2 • DOCTORS, HOSPITALS & YOU

Stop Paging Dr. Google!...End Unreasonable Health Worries..26
How to Get Exactly What You Need from Your Doctor 28
Don't Die of a Misdiagnosis..30
How to Get an Oncologist Appointment..31
Is Your Doctor Suffering from Burnout? 32
Don't Forget Your Nurse..34
A Bigger, Better MRI 34
Medical Tests and Treatments You Really Don't Need 35
Not So Fast! When It Comes to CT Scans 36
The Stats on Scans 37
Cut Down Radiation Risk..37
The Deadly Dangers of Off-Label Drugs 38
Common Medication Mistakes Can Be Deadly....40
Prescription Errors 41
Swallow Pills More Easily 42
OTC Alert..42
Walking Reduces Hospital Stays 42
Steroid Concern 42
Seniors at Risk..42
Age Matters..43
Paging Dr. Mozart... 43
Hospital Self-Defense 43
Patient Alert..43
Better Postsurgical Pain Relief..43
Faster Recovery from Orthopedic Surgery 44
Maggots Can Speed Wound Healing 44
Best Ways to Prevent Hospital Infections..44
Better Inhaler Use..45
Germs Galore..45
Hospitals Make Misleading Claims About Robotic Surgery 45

3 • FAST HEALTH FIXES

Stress Raises Blood Pressure, Right? Wrong! Health Myths Debunked..46
Rx: Belt One Out! 47
Surprising Conditions That Chiropractors Can Treat..48
Herbal Cold Remedies..50
The 100-Day Cough..50
Surprising Sinus Help..51
Asthma Relief..51
It's True..51
Better Posture Eases Pain..51
The Fascinating Science Behind Cracking Joints, Whistling Noses... 51
You Can Prevent Texting Tendonitis..53
Cluster Headache Relief 53
New Treatment for Severe Migraines..54
Migraines and Stroke..54
Prevent Hair Loss..54

Do-It-Yourself Face-Lift—Look Years Younger in Just 20 Days 54
Help for Badly Chapped Lips 55
Easy Reading Help....56
Cleaning Your Contacts....56
Anti-Cavity Strategy....56
Hand-Drying Smarts 56
Heel Pain 56
Better Treatment for Hamstring Injury 57
Bunion Relief 57
Fun Way to Cut Stress 57
Share the Work 58
All-Natural Mood Booster 58
Feeling Blue? Try Bananas....58
Don't Fall Asleep With the TV On....58
Cool Brain, Better Sleep....59
The Simplest Prescription of All....59
Got Insomnia? Go to Bed Later 60
Avoid Mosquitoes 60
First Aid Basics....61
Tetanus Booster 61
More Veggies, Less Infection 61

4 • FITNESS FOCUS

How to Lose 12 Pounds…in Just 17 Days....62
Pepper Helps Burn More Calories 64
Grapefruit Does Aid Weight Loss....64
Blueberries to the Rescue—Again!....64
Healthful Chinese Food....64
If You Think a Food Is Filling, It Will Be....65
Better Portion Control....65
How to Stop Craving the Foods That Make You Fat 65
Dig In! 67
Sweet Suppressor....67
Surprise Finding....67
Anyone Can Have an Eating Disorder 67
Less Protein, More Weight Gain....69
Burn Calories While Watching TV....69
Get Off the Plateau....70
Surprise About Swimming 70
Extra Benefits from Bypass Surgery....70
Cool Tip for Weight Loss 70
Walk It Off....70
Get More Exercise…By Acting Like a Kid!....71
Ice Bath Prevents Soreness After a Run....72
How to Relieve Muscle Aches 72
The Best Energy Bars....72
Got Chocolate Milk?....73

5 • NATURAL HEALERS

Put Down That Slice of Bread! 74
Work Out!....76
Laughing As Good for You As Exercise 76
Omega-3s May Slow Aging....76
High-Fiber Diet May Lead to Longer Life 76
Live Longer the Nordic Way 77
Reset Your "Body Clock" 77
Don't Let Stress Harm Your Health....79
20-Minute Way to Fight Heart Disease 80
Purple Potatoes for Blood Pressure 82
Olive Oil for Arthritis and Other Amazing Food Cures 82
Apples Lower Cholesterol....85
OJ for the Heart?....85
Try Cranberry Juice....85
Melon Medicine....85
Lower Blood Pressure Naturally....85
Fiber Helps You Live Longer....86
You Can Pedal While You Work 86
Black Tea Lowers Blood Pressure....86
Chew Gum and Other Simple Ways to Prevent Heart Disease 87
Fight Killer Blood Clots—Reduce Your Risk For Heart Attack and Stroke....89
Coffee Reduces Stroke Risk 90
Fruits Fight Stroke 91
30-Day Diabetes Cure—You May Even Be Able to Throw Away Your Meds!....91
Leafy Greens Lower Diabetes Risk....93
Magnesium-Rich Foods Reduce Stroke Risk 93
Beware Fish-Oil Contaminants 93
Dark Leafy Greens Protect Eyes....93
Fight Cancer with This Formula....93
Spicy Foods Boost Broccoli's Cancer-Fighting Effect....95
Chinese Cancer-Fighter 95
Tomato Juice Helps Prevent Bone Loss....96
Prunes Help Prevent Osteoporosis 96
Vitamin K Strengthens Bones 96
Foods that Fight Inflammation 96
Spice Eases Arthritis 96
Don't Wear Thick-Soled Sneakers and Other Surprising Ways to Prevent Falls....97
Get Rid of Back Pain in Just 7 Minutes a Day....98
Coffee Fights Depression 100
Disease-Fighting Berries....100
Eat Vegetables, Live Longer....100
Spices With Surprising Health Benefits 101

6 • VERY PERSONAL MATTERS

Best Ways to Increase a Woman's Libido....103
Satisfaction Leads to Happiness 105
Fantasies Help Analytical Thinking....105

Proud Men Attract Women 105
Special Needs Dating Sites 105
Meeting Online 106
Can You Have Sex After Heart Disease? 106
Lovers May Make Better Athletes 106
Sex May Be Risky for Sedentary People 106
Infidelity May Be Genetic 106
Dramatic HIV Finding 106
HPV Affects Half of All Men 107
New HPV Test Catches Cancer Earlier 107
Hair-Loss Treatment Can Have Sexual Side Effects 107
Kegel Exercises Not Just for Women 107
Pain Relievers Linked to Erectile Dysfunction 109
New ED Drug 109
Blood Test for ED 109
Estrogen—The Rest of the Story 109
Soy Does Not Ease Menopause 111
Hysterectomy May Raise Kidney Cancer Risk 111
Aspirin Fights Breast Cancer 112
Hot Flashes Reduce Breast Cancer Risk 112
Too Many Biopsies? 112
Breast Cancer Blood Test 112
Help for Chemo Hair Loss 112
Surgery Reduces Cancer Risk 113
Better Breast Cancer Treatment 113
Better Ovarian Cancer Detection 113
IUDs Reduce Cervical Cancer Risk 113
Mammogram May Find Other Health Problems 114
The Perfect Colonoscopy Prep 114
Coffee Benefits 116
Diabetes and Colon Growths 116
Warning on Colon Cleanses 116
Right Diet for Men 117
Early Hair Loss Links to Prostate Cancer 117
Better Colonoscopy Prep 117
Smarter PSA Testing 117
New Prostate Test 118
Rising PSA 118
Enlarged Prostate 118
Shorter Treatment 118
Improved Radiation 119
Music Eases Prostate Biopsy 119
The Truth About Life After Prostate Cancer 119
Cancer Recurrence Linked to Weight 121
Vitamin D 121
Prunes Better Than Psyllium 122
Natural Remedy for IBS 122
NSAIDs Linked to Diverticulitis 122
Vegetarian Advantage 122
Lack of Sleep Linked to Colon Cancer 122
New Tests on the Horizon 123

PART TWO: YOUR MONEY

7 • MANAGE YOUR MONEY

Better Than Banks—Credit Unions 124
Get to the Point 125
What to Do When Interest Rates Are Low 126
Safeguards When You Switch Bank Accounts 127
Less Expensive Check Cashing 128
Avoid Those Nasty New Bank Fees 128
"Joint" Account Self-Defense 129
No More Paper Savings Bonds 130
Best Order to Pay Debts 130
Check for Clarity 130
Best Credit Cards Now 130
Be Careful with Prepaids 132
Gold Cards Not So Elite 133
Lower Credit Card Fees 133
Check Credit Card Refunds 133
Easier Loans Now 133
Little-Known Ways to Boost Creditworthiness 133
Free Credit Scores Easier to Obtain 134
New Reporting 134
The Credit Score Myth 134
Now Is the Time to Buy a House! Here's Why... 135
Buy Real Estate Where the Best Bargains Are Already Gone 136
Buying a Home? Tricky Traps to Avoid Now 137
Check Your Insurance 138
Larger FHA Loans 138
Shop Carefully for a Mortgage 138
Older Homes Preferred 138
Low Appraisals Prevent Home Sales 139
Simpler Way to Weigh Refinancing 139
Mortgage Lenders Cutting Fees 139
Sale Strategy 139
Estimate College Costs 140
Education Accounts 140
Get More College Financial Aid with This Simple Strategy 140
Leftover Money in a 529 College Savings Plan? 141
529 Tax Loophole 141
The Student Loan Crisis—What to Do If You Or Your Child Can't Make the Payments 141
If You Divorce After 50—Watch Out for the Big Financial Traps 143
Watch Your E-Mail 145

Beware Promise of Unclaimed-Property..........145
Identity Scams..........145
Don't Send Money..........145
Ads That Infect Computers Turn Up on Legitimate Web Sites..........146
Bar Code Alert..........146
New Twist on Internet Car Scams..........146
Protect Your Social Security Identity..........146

8 • YOUR INSURANCE

What Health Insurance Companies Don't Want You to Know..........147
Some Good News On Insurance..........149
What Does "Explanation of Benefits" Really Mean?..........149
Latest Trend in Coverage..........150
HSA Loophole..........150
Choosing a Medicare Advantage Plan? Common Mistakes Can Be Very Costly..........151
Understanding Medicare Options..........152
Unraveling the Medicare Insurance Maze..........152
Medicare Covers More Screening Tests..........153
How to Research Costs..........153
Less Disability Insurance..........154
Manage Disability Payments..........154
Earthquake Insurance Loopholes..........154
Do the Research Yourself..........155
Don't Be Fooled..........155
Accident Scams..........155
Car Insurance Discounts..........155
Customers Rate Insurers..........156
Ways to Save..........156
Life Insurance Warning—Your Paid-Up Policy May *Not* Be Paid Up After All..........156

9 • TAX TUNE-UP

These Taxpayers Fought the IRS...and Won! Loopholes for Us All..........158
What to Do Now to Cut Your Bill..........160
Seniors, Take Note..........161
Friendlier Tax Brackets for 2012..........162
Correct Filing Errors..........162
Education Rules..........162
Tax Deductions for Damage from Natural Disasters..........163
Domestic Matters..........163
IRS Cracks Down on Rental Losses..........164
Audit Rates Have Risen for the Wealthy..........164
Careful With Charities..........164
Protect Yourself..........164
Tax Talks May Not Be Confidential..........164
When You Inherit an IRA...Avoid These Mistakes That Can Cost You Big..........165
New Gift Tax Rules Can Save You Big..........167
Tax Stats..........168
Small Businesses..........168
Federal Tax Credit for Hiring Veterans..........168
New Scam..........168

10 • INVESTMENT INSIGHTS

Stocks Under $10 That Are Worth Much More..........169
The Shrewdest Money Moves You Can Make Now..........171
More Ways to Get a 7% Yield...or Even 9%..........173
Secrets of a Bargain Hunter..........175
Get a Better Yield—Secrets of America's "Dividend Detective"..........176
How to Find Insider Information..........178
Expert's Stock Strategy..........178
Software Stock Opportunity..........178
Pawn Stores..........179
Computer Security Stocks..........179
Less Risky Investment Idea..........179
Investment Opportunity..........179
Bank Stocks..........179
Investment Opportunity..........180
Spin-Off Boom..........180
Use "Loss Robots" to Offset Capital Gains, Save on Taxes..........180
Is It Time to Ditch Your Ailing Mutual Funds?..........180
Bank Loan Mutual Funds..........183
New Predictive Tool..........183
"Ladder" Your Bond Mutual Funds..........183
Higher Yields from Emerging-Market Bond Funds..........183
Copper Could Rise 50%—How to Invest..........184
Protect Yourself Against Investment Fraud..........184
Advisor Check-Up..........184
Tricky Scams Even Smart Investors Fell For..........185

11 • CONSUMER SMARTS

Sneaky Ways Companies Trick You Into Buying..........188
Paying Extra for Better Service..........190
Keep It Confidential..........190
How to Tell an Honest Evaluation from a Phony One..........190
Layaway Rules..........193
Downside of a Digital Wallet..........193
Search for Savings..........193
Always Compare..........193

The Dark Side of Coupons 193
How America's Cheapest Family Eats Great Food on $12 a Day....................195
Get the Most Savings....................196
Consumer Alert on Beef Prices....................197
Save Money by Buying Grocery Basics at the Best Times....................197
House Brands Rising....................197
Small Fast-Food Chains Rank Higher....................197
Save on Wine 197
New Homes to Have Energy Labels....................198
Compare Your Energy Usage 198
Save on Winter Heating Bills....................198
Cut Costs with Wind Turbine?....................198
Before You Travel Overseas....................198
Mobile Phone Alert....................199
Save Money by Unplugging Appliances 199
Power Savings....................199
Rabbit Ears?....................199
Every Man Can Pick the Perfect Perfume....................200
Vintage Values 200
Electronic Textbook Rentals 201
Don't Get Taken by One of These Health Scams....................201
Clark Howard Shows How to Save on Doctor Bills...Prescription Drugs...Phone Bills...More....................202
Compare Medical Costs....................204
Considering Pet Insurance?....................204
Beware Online Pet Meds 204
Online Help with Consumer Complaints....................204
Robocalls Rules Getting Tougher....................204
Watch Care 205
Shopping May Be Healthy 205

PART THREE: YOUR FINANCIAL FUTURE

12 • RICHER RETIREMENT

How to Spend More in Retirement Without Running Out of Money 206
Trade Annuities? 208
Are These Retirement Mutual Funds Right For You? 208
Review Target Date Funds....................210
Appeal Social Security Decisions Within 60 Days....................210
Social Security Scam Warning....................211
The COLA Increase....................211
What Your Employer Doesn't Want You to Know About Your Retirement Benefits....................211
Know Your Plan 213
Sneaky Fees Can Reduce Your 401(K) by 10%—But These New Rules Will Help You Fix That....................213
401(K) Plan Participants Gaining More Access to Cost Details and Options 215
When to Consider a Roth....................216
IRA Limits....................216
Reverse Mortgage?....................216
New Rules 216
Elder Abuse 217
Tax Deduction....................217
Amazing Discounts If You're 50 or Older 217
Senior Fare Savings....................219
How to Enjoy Life Until 100 (and Beyond!)....................220
The Easiest Computers Ever—Simple to Use, Right Out of the Box 221
Your Heirs Will Lose Money If You Don't Take These Steps Now....................223
Plan Carefully....................224
Establish Trust....................224

PART FOUR: YOUR LEISURE

13 • TRAVEL SECRETS

The Secrets Hotels Don't Want You To Know....................225
Luxury Camping for Nature Lovers....................227
City Discount Cards 229
For Group Travel 229
New Travel Web Sites 229
Free Travel Apps....................229
Fliers' Favorites 230
Watch Your Miles 230
How to Get More Mileage from Your Frequent-Flier Miles....................230
Don't Let Your Frequent-Flier Miles Expire....................231
Best Ticket Shopping 232
Fly in Style....................232
For the Best Seats 232
Airline Customer Favorites....................233
Protect Your Luggage....................233
Lock It Up!....................233
For Weather Alert 233
Turn It Off! 233
Don't Drink the Water....................234
Health Precaution 234
Free Apps for Air Travelers....................234
Healthy Airport Eating....................234
Need a Nap? 234
Best Tech Airports 235
Crime Rates Higher Near Big Airports....................235

Renters' Picks....235
Best Car Rental Rates in Europe....235
Car Rental Safety....235
Consider Travel Insurance....236
Big City Savings....236
Gas Discounts....236
Late-Breaking Bargains....236
Clean It Yourself....236
Don't Be Tempted to Take a Souvenir....237
Chemicals That Kill Bedbugs Can Cause Illness....237
Hotel Safety Tip....237
At Your Service....237
New Program....237
Who Needs a Hotel? Swap Homes Instead....238
Room Reservation Up for Bids....240
Hidden Cruise Costs....240
Safety on Board....240
Cruise Ship Illnesses....240
Safe Travel in Risky Times....240
Free Language Translation App....241
Charge It Wisely Overseas....241
Taking Your Smartphone Abroad?....241

14 • TIME OFF TIPS

Tricks to Improve Your Golf Game (Without Leaving Home)....242
Dining Tip....243
Casinos You Can Bet On....244
Cook the Perfect Burger....246
Borrow eBooks....247
Hidden Treasures at Yard Sales....247
Planting Help....249
No More Slugs....249
Lyme Disease Alert....249

PART FIVE: YOUR LIFE

15 • CAR CARE

How to Beat a Traffic Ticket....250
Emergency Move....251
Stuck-in-Snow Strategy....251
Mechanics' Pick....251
Easy Way to Save on a New Car....251
Trading in Your Car?....251
Leasing a Car May Be Better Than Buying If You Avoid These Traps....252
The Best Used Cars Under $6,000....253
Car Shoppers: 31,000 Miles Better Than 29,000....255
Your Used Car Could Be Worth Big Bucks....255
Best Rated....257
Dangerous Trend....257
Save $150 (or More) a Year on Gas With the Right Credit Card....257
Buy Groceries, Save on Gas....259
Share Your Car to Make Money....259
Most Likely...to be Stolen....259
Tell Your Auto Mechanic "NO" When He Tells You This....260

16 • FAMILY LIFE

Are You Parenting Your Parents?....263
Stay Connected to a Loved One with Alzheimer's....265
Advice for Caregivers....266
Social Networking for Elder Care....266
Spouses Affect Each Other's Health....266
Don't Like Your Child's Friends?....266
Lack of Sun Hurts Young Eyes....267
"Green" Danger....267
Croup Can Be Fatal....267
Radiation Concern for Children....267
Rx Not Necessary....267
Meningitis Shots for Teens....268
Teen Hearing Loss....268
Depression on the Net....268
Life After High School....268
Top Colleges for Kids with Learning Disabilities or ADHD....269
Back Home....271
Natural Flea Control for Dogs and Cats....271
Keep Your Puppy Calm....272
Dental Disease in Dogs Is on the Rise—And It Can Kill Your Pet....272
More Dognapping....274
Pet Precautions....274
Coyote Alert....274
Missing Pet Registry....275
Best Toys for Your Cat....275
Shelter Dog Help....275
Your Medications Can Poison Pets....275

17 • HOUSEHOLD HELPERS

Quick Cures for Clutter—All You Need Is 10 Minutes or Less....276
Cheaper Way to Enlarge Your Home....278
Save When You Remodel....278
Moldy Basement....278
Home Repairs You Should Not Put Off....279
Dishwasher Danger....279
Radiation from Your Washing Machine? Hair Dryer? These Secrets Will Help Keep You Safe....279

For Cleaner Dishes 282
Cookware Care....282
Secrets from America's Lawn Geek....282
Clean Crystal Candleholders 284
"Nutty" Solution to Cover Scratches....284
Beautiful Houseplants That Clean Indoor Air....285
7 Things to Do with Dental Floss (Besides Floss) 287

18 • WINNING WAYS

How to Get Anyone to Like You in Two Minutes or Less 288
Go With the Flow 290
To Boost Happiness, Grab a Pen and Paper....290
How to Complain to People You Know… So That You Get Results 290
Secrets of People Who Excel Under Pressure 292
How to Get a Yes from Anyone…Fast 294
The Prophetic Power of Your Dreams 296
Connect! Social Networking Fosters Stronger Friendships 298
How to Gracefully End a Bad Relationship....298
Banish Guilt!....300
Multitasking May Hurt Your Self-Control 300
Creativity Boosters....301
New Type of Translator 301
Clever Phone Tricks to Get Through to Anyone 301
Memory Aid....302
For a Sharper Memory....302
Break Free from Habits That Hold You Back 303

19 • WORKING LIFE

Good Professions for People Without a Degree 305
Where the Jobs Are....307
Some Industries Eager to Hire....309
Don't Let Interviewers Steal Your Ideas Or Your Clients....309
LinkedIn Basics....311
LinkedIn Strategy....311
Where to Look for Jobs....311
Facebook Strategy....311
Bad News 311
For People with Disabilities....312
Smokers, Beware....312
Salary Strategy....312
Beauty Does Pay....312
Good Investments....312
What to Ask a Job Candidate....313
Consider Paying Your Interns 313
Easier Transition for Veterans....313
Are You Using 'QR' Codes?....313
Get the Word Out....314
Business Owner Concerns 314
Clever Ways to Make Money on the Internet (Anyone Can Do It!)....314
Borrowing Basics....316
"Crowdfunding" for New Projects....316
The Amazing Things Humble Jobs Can Teach....317
How to Enchant Others with Your Ideas, Plans or Products....319
Five Things Never to Say at Work....321
Easier E-mails 322
Don't Waste Time Organizing E-mail....322
Get Better Voice-Mail Messages....322
Productivity Booster 322
Keep a Young Outlook 322
Extra Perks 323
On the Move 323
Read the Fine Print....323
Protect Yourself 323
Criticism of Bosses May Be Protected Speech 324
Apologies Can Help Mend Fences 324
Be Mindful....324
Business Travel Hurts Your Health....324
On the Rise....324
Long Work Hours May Harm Your Heart 325
Be Healthy....325
Home Work Attractive....325
More Bikes 325

20 • SAFETY MATTERS

The Whistle-Blower's Guide to Doing What's Right While Protecting Yourself....326
Early Warning System 328
Protect Your Documents....329
If Your Home Phone Is Wireless....329
Ordinary People Who Foiled Terrorists....329
Be Careful in Big Crowds 330
Involved in a Lawsuit?—Watch Out For These Attorney Tricks 330
Beware of Free Charging Stations....331
Invisible Stalkers Track Your Online Moves 331
Cyber Bandits Could Strike Anytime....333

Index 335

Preface

We are happy to bring you our *Bottom Line Year Book 2013*. You will find numerous helpful and practical ideas for yourself and for everyone in your family.

At Bottom Line Publications, it is our mission to provide all of our readers with the best information to help them gain better health, greater wealth, more wisdom, extra time and increased happiness.

The *Year Book 2013* represents the very best and the most useful *Bottom Line* articles from the past year. Whether you are looking for ways to get the most from your money or land a job in this tough economy...reduce your blood pressure naturally or assert your rights in the hospital...revive the romance in your marriage or get more organized, you'll find it all here...and so much more.

Over the past 30 years, we have built a network of thousands of expert sources.

When you consult the *2013 Year Book*, you are accessing a stellar group of authorities in fields that range from natural and conventional medicine...to shopping, investing, taxes and insurance...to cars, travel, security and self-improvement. Our advisers are affiliated with the premier universities, financial institutions, law firms and hospitals. These experts are truly among the most knowledgeable people in the country.

As a reader of a *Bottom Line* book, you can be assured that you are receiving reliable, well-researched and up-to-date information from a trusted source.

We are very confident that the *Bottom Line Year Book 2013* can help you and your family have a healthier, wealthier, wiser life. Enjoy!

The Editors, *Bottom Line/Personal*
Stamford, CT

1

Health Updates

Salt! Not So Bad After All?

For years, we've been told that people who consume a lot of sodium (primarily in the form of dietary salt) are at increased risk for high blood pressure (hypertension).

Now: *The Journal of the American Medical Association* recently published a European study that suggests the issue may be more complex than previously believed—a finding that may mean that many of us can safely use more salt.

Recent finding: In an eight-year study, which followed more than 3,600 men and women ages 60 and younger (all of whom had normal blood pressure at the start of the research), researchers found that the one-third of study participants who had the highest sodium intake experienced only a slight rise in systolic (top number) blood pressure and no rise in diastolic (bottom number) blood pressure.

Those in the highest intake group consumed an average of 6,000 mg of salt daily, which is more than twice the daily recommendation for adults in general. Even more surprising, the research found that the one-third of study participants with the lowest salt intake (an average of 2,500 mg daily) were 56% more likely to suffer a heart attack or stroke than the group consuming the most salt.

Lower sodium levels reduce blood pressure but also increase resistance to insulin and sympathetic nervous system activity, including heart rate. If sodium levels fall too much, it can damage the cardiovascular system.

What does this research mean for people who are concerned about controlling their blood pressure...and avoiding heart attack and stroke?

Michael Alderman, MD, distinguished emeritus professor of medicine and population health at Albert Einstein College of Medicine in New York City and editor of the *American Journal of Hypertension*. Dr. Alderman has authored more than 270 scientific papers, book chapters and textbooks describing his research on hypertension.

The results of the European study are controversial—some scientists point out that many of the people with low-sodium intake had preexisting health problems that caused them to curtail their salt intake. The findings also call into question one of the most basic premises of good medicine—that a low-sodium diet helps prevent high blood pressure, which is itself a significant risk factor for heart attack and stroke.

In fact, the CDC urges adults in general to not exceed 2,300 mg of sodium per day (about one teaspoon of salt). If you have hypertension or are among those at increased risk for it—such as adults ages 51 and older and African-Americans of any age—the CDC recommends no more than 1,500 mg per day.

As a physician and researcher who has closely followed the scientific evidence on sodium consumption for the past 35 years, I believe this latest study simply confirms that the salt issue is not as straightforward as it might seem. In fact, there have been mixed results from about 15 major studies conducted over the past several years on the health effects of sodium consumption. Roughly one-third of those studies found no association between salt intake and mortality...one-third found that people who consumed more sodium (6,000 mg to 8,000 mg per day) were more likely to die...and one-third found, like the recent European study, that high salt intake does not increase one's risk for death.

Also recently, a review prepared by The Cochrane Collaboration of existing research involving 6,250 people found that cutting salt intake lowered blood pressure but had no effect on cardiovascular deaths. In fact, lower sodium increased risk for those with congestive heart failure.

It's important to remember that none of this research is definitive—all of the studies are observational, which means that researchers draw inferences about behaviors of people in the general population without creating a controlled environment. This type of research is limited in its ability to reveal a causal relationship between a biological factor—in this case, sodium intake—and a complex condition with many contributing factors, such as heart attack or stroke.

Bottom line: Since there is currently no definitive evidence showing that reducing sodium saves lives or prevents heart attack and stroke among healthy adults—and a number of studies suggest that sodium restriction actually may be dangerous to at least some people's health—there still are many unanswered questions.

So, what should you do about salt? *Important points to consider...*

1. Sodium intake is not the only factor that contributes to high blood pressure and related ailments. Over the past two decades, the percentage of American adults with high blood pressure has risen from one in four to about one in three—a trend that sodium-reduction advocates blame on our increased sodium intake from processed and fast foods.

Problem with this theory: A recent analysis by Harvard nutritionist Walter Willett, MD, based on 24-hour urine samples (the best way to measure sodium consumption), found that US average sodium intake has remained quite steady over the past 50 years, at around 3,500 mg per day. This suggests that sodium is not the main reason for the higher incidence of hypertension and that other factors, such as rising rates of obesity and diabetes—both of which harm cardiovascular health in other ways—may be more to blame.

2. Sodium has many important functions in the body. Most people are well aware of the research suggesting that reducing sodium intake lowers blood pressure—mainly by decreasing fluid retention, which in turn decreases blood volume.

What is less well-known is that reducing sodium intake increases insulin resistance, triglycerides and sympathetic nervous system activity, all of which are harmful to the cardiovascular system. Reducing sodium also activates the renin angiotensin system, a network of hormones that controls blood pressure and fluid balance in the body. When this system is activated, it triggers the release of substances that cause the blood vessels to constrict and blood volume to increase—both of which promote increased blood pressure. This explains why blood pressure goes up in some people when they cut back on salt.

3. People react to sodium differently. A significant percentage of people (including many with high blood pressure) are "salt-sensitive"—meaning that their blood pressure reacts more strongly than does the average person's to increases in sodium. Others, however, are "salt-resistant" and need higher levels of sodium to maintain normal, healthy physiological functions.

At present, we have no good way of determining which individuals are salt-sensitive or salt-resistant, though genetics, age, race and body mass all appear to play a role. People who are salt-sensitive tend to have relatively low levels of potassium in their diets, are over age 55, are obese, have hypertension or a family history of hypertension and/or are African-American.

Research suggests that there is likely a range of healthy sodium intake that we instinctively aim for in our individual diets—and that if your sodium intake is either above or below this range, health problems, such as dehydration, high blood pressure and fluid retention, can occur. The health risks tend to occur when the kidneys are unable to excrete excess salt (for example, in people with kidney disease), so it accumulates in the blood, causing fluid buildup. This range will vary among individuals—it's most likely about 2,000 mg to 4,000 mg a day for individuals who are not salt-sensitive—making it impossible to come up with a "one-size-fits-all" recommendation on sodium intake.

Very important: There's enough evidence to show that a low-sodium diet should be tried as part of any treatment plan for the one-third of Americans with hypertension (blood pressure of 140/90 mmHG and above) and the one-quarter of Americans with prehypertension (systolic pressure of 120 mmHG to 139 mmHG and/or diastolic pressure of 80 mmHG to 89 mmHG).

But right now, there's no good scientific evidence to suggest that people with normal blood pressure who are not at risk for hypertension should reduce sodium intake to a certain predetermined number—this practice may do more harm than good. Ask your doctor what your target sodium levels should be based on your personal medical profile.

Statin Alert

Zocor should not be taken in an 80-milligram dose. The FDA says that the 80-mg dose of the statin drug *simvastatin* (Zocor) can cause a myopathy, a potentially severe muscle disorder. A patient taking the 40-mg dose who still has not reached his/her cholesterol goal should be switched to another statin, such as *atorvastatin* (Lipitor) or *rosuvastatin* (Crestor).

Caution: Never change your medication or dose without your doctor's OK.

Steven E. Nissen, MD, chairman of cardiovascular medicine, Cleveland Clinic, Ohio.

Omega-3 Fish Oil Cautions

In people who take blood thinners (such as Coumadin), omega-3 fish oil supplements can cause internal bleeding. In people who are immunocompromised, supplements totaling more than 3,000 milligrams a day can suppress the immune system. In people who are allergic to seafood, they may cause allergic reactions...and in people taking blood pressure medications, they may lower blood pressure too much.

Best: Before starting omega-3 fish oil supplements, check with your physician.

Environmental Nutrition, PO Box 8535, Big Sandy, Texas 75755. *www.environmentalnutrition.com*

Promising News on New Drug

Benefits of new anticlotting drug outweigh the risks for most patients. *Dabigatran* (Pradaxa) has been shown to prevent stroke in patients with atrial fibrillation. There was concern that Pradaxa raised the risk for heart attack or acute coronary syndrome, but the actual risk is small for most patients—although it can be significant for patients with other heart disease risk factors. Talk to your doctor.

Ken Uchino, MD, director of Vascular Neurology Fellowship Training Program, Cleveland Clinic Cerebrovascular Center, Ohio, and coauthor of an analysis of data on seven clinical trials that included 30,514 patients.

Keep Still

For an accurate blood pressure reading: Empty your bladder because a full bladder can affect the reading. Avoid smoking, drinking anything caffeinated and exercising 30 minutes before the test. Keep your feet flat on the floor for five minutes prior to checking your blood pressure. During the reading, keep still and rest your arm on a table so that it is at heart level.

Consumer Reports on Health, 101 Truman Ave., Yonkers, New York 10703. *www.consumerreports.org/health*

Better Blood Pressure Drug

In a study, 33,000 adults with high blood pressure took the generic diuretic *chlorthalidone* or one of two newer, brand-name drugs—the calcium channel blocker Norvasc or the ACE inhibitor Lisinopril—for nine years, on average.

Result: Compared with those taking a diuretic, those taking Norvasc were 12% more likely to have died from or been hospitalized for heart failure, and those taking Lisinopril were 20% more likely to have died from stroke.

When exercise and diet changes don't lower blood pressure: Ask your doctor about diuretics.

Paul Whelton, MD, former president and CEO, Loyola University Health System, Chicago.

Better Blood Pressure Readings

Recent study: Researchers performed automatic 24-hour blood pressure monitoring on 3,344 men and women (average age 52) for two days, then checked their health outcomes after five years.

Result: Patients whose systolic (top number) blood pressures dipped significantly during sleep were 25% less likely to suffer a heart attack, stroke or other cardiac event.

Theory: Blood pressure during sleep seems to be more predictive of cardiovascular risk than daytime blood pressure, which can vary with activity.

If you take a hypertension medication: Talk to your doctor about taking it at bedtime.

Ramon Hermida, PhD, director, bioengineering and chronobiology laboratories, University of Vigo, Spain.

Exercise Not Enough to Keep Your Heart Healthy

Key: Avoid sitting for long periods of time as well.

Recent finding: People who sat at a computer or in front of a TV screen for four or more hours a day were 48% more likely to die during the four-year study regardless of how much they exercised. Also, some type of cardiovascular event, such as a heart attack, was twice as likely in those who spent at least two hours a day sitting in front of a screen—compared with those who had less than two daily hours of screen time.

Self-defense: Take frequent breaks from the computer or TV to get up and walk around.

Study of 4,512 adults by researchers at University College London and University of Queensland, Baker IDI Heart and Diabetes Institute and Edith Cowan University, all in Australia, published in *Journal of the American College of Cardiology.*

Insomnia Raises Heart Disease Risk

Recent finding: People who have trouble falling asleep most nights have a 45% higher risk for heart disease than people who don't have trouble falling asleep. Those who have trouble staying asleep have a 30% higher risk.

Possible connection: Insomnia may be linked to increased stress hormones, blood pressure and inflammation, all of which increase the risk for heart disease.

Lars Erik Laugsand, MD, public health researcher and internist at Norwegian University of Science and Technology, Trondheim, and lead author of a study of 52,610 people, published online in *Circulation*.

Hidden Heart Problem

Restless legs may be a sign of hidden heart problems. People whose legs move very frequently during sleep (more than 35 times per hour) are almost twice as likely to have a thickened heart muscle as people whose legs move less frequently. Thickening of the heart muscle can increase the risk for arrhythmias, heart attack or heart failure.

Self-defense: If you have been diagnosed with restless legs, ask your physician about cardiac testing.

Arshad A. Jahangir, MD, heart rhythm specialist at Mayo Clinic Arizona, Scottsdale, and leader of a study of 584 people with restless legs syndrome, presented at a recent American College of Cardiology conference.

Help for Angina

Angina sufferers may benefit from gout medication.

Recent study: Among 65 adults with heart disease and stable angina (chest pain that occurs with activity or stress), those who took 600 mg of the gout medication *allopurinol* (Aloprim) daily for six weeks could exercise longer before chest pain occurred than those who took a placebo.

Theory: Allopurinol blocks a crucial enzyme, reducing oxygen demand during exercise.

If you have stable angina: Ask your doctor about allupurinol. Side effects may include upset stomach, diarrhea and drowsiness.

Allan D. Struthers, MD, professor of cardiovascular medicine, Centre for Cardiovascular & Lung Biology, University of Dundee School of Medicine, Dundee, UK.

Alcohol More Dangerous For Women

Women who drink to excess are at much greater risk for liver, brain and heart damage than men who drink to excess. Women have more body fat than men, less water in their systems and lower levels of an enzyme that breaks down alcohol, so the effects of alcohol are more acutely concentrated in women. Excessive drinking is an average of four or more drinks within two hours for women and five or more drinks within two hours for men.

Deidra Roach, MD, program director, division of treatment and recovery research, National Institute on Alcohol Abuse and Alcoholism, Bethesda, Maryland. *www.niaaa.nih.gov*

Calcium Concerns

Calcium supplements may increase risk for cardiovascular disease.

Recent finding: People who take 1,000 milligrams of calcium per day have a 25% higher risk for heart attack and 15% higher risk for stroke than people who do not take the supplements.

Possible connection: The supplements may increase the blood calcium level rapidly, contributing to arterial disease.

Best: Get calcium naturally from food.

Ian Reid, MD, professor of medicine and endocrinology at University of Auckland, New Zealand, and senior author of a study published in *British Medical Journal*.

Exposure to Cold Increases Heart Attack Risk

For every one-degree Celsius drop in temperature, heart attack risk increased by 2%. Risk was highest among people ages 75 to 84 and those with a history of coronary heart disease. Cold weather may make blood vessels work harder to regulate body temperature... and strenuous cold-weather tasks such as shoveling snow may put stress on the heart.

Krishnan Bhaskaran, PhD, lecturer, statistical epidemiology, London School of Hygiene & Tropical Medicine, and leader of a study of 84,010 hospital admissions, published in *BMJ.*

Did You Have a Heart Attack—and Not Know It?

Wilbert Aronow, MD, professor of medicine in the divisions of cardiology, geriatrics and pulmonary/critical medicine, and chief of the cardiology clinic at Westchester Medical Center/New York Medical College in Valhalla, New York. Dr. Aronow has edited numerous books and is author or coauthor of more than 2,250 scientific papers, abstracts and commentaries that have appeared in *The Lancet, The New England Journal of Medicine, Circulation* and other medical journals.

When you have a heart attack, you know it, because the main symptom—crushing chest pain—is overwhelmingly obvious. That's what most of us believe about heart attacks. But it's not always true.

What few people realize: Studies show that 20% to 60% of all heart attacks in people over age 45 are unrecognized or "silent." And the older you are, the more likely it is that you've already had a silent heart attack. In a study of 110 people with a mean age of 82, an astounding 68% had suffered a silent heart attack.

What happens during a silent heart attack? You may have no symptoms at all. Or you may have symptoms that are so mild—for example, a bout of breathlessness, digestive upset or neurological symptoms such as fainting—that neither you nor your doctor connects them with a heart attack.

Scientists don't know why some people have unrecognized heart attacks. But they do know that a silent heart attack is a real heart attack and can cause as much damage to heart muscle as a nonsilent heart attack. And just like a person with a known heart attack, anyone who has had a silent heart attack is at higher risk for another heart attack, heart failure, stroke...or sudden death from an irregular heartbeat.

Recent scientific evidence: In a six-year study by cardiologists from the University of California in San Diego and San Francisco—published in *Clinical Research in Cardiology* in April 2011—people who were diagnosed with a silent heart attack at the beginning of the study were 80% more likely to have another "cardiovascular event," such as a heart attack or stroke, by the end of the study period.

In a five-year study by cardiologists at the Mayo Clinic, people with an unrecognized heart attack were seven times more likely to die of heart disease than people who didn't have an unrecognized heart attack.

If you have risk factors for heart disease, it is vitally important to your health that you find out if you have had a silent heart attack. *Here's how...*

THE KEY TO DETECTION

If you're at high risk for heart disease, your primary care physician should perform an electrocardiogram (EKG)—a test that checks for problems with the electrical activity of your heart—every year during your regular checkup. If the EKG reveals significant "Q-waves"—markers of damaged heart tissue—you have had a silent heart attack.

"High risk" means that you have two or more risk factors for heart disease. These risk factors include a family history of heart disease (in a first-degree relative such as a sibling or parent)...high blood pressure...smoking... inactivity...obesity...high LDL "bad" cholesterol...low HDL "good" cholesterol...high triglycerides...and type 2 diabetes.

The groups at highest risk for having an unrecognized heart attack are adults over age 65...women...and people of any age with type 2 diabetes.

THE TREATMENT YOU NEED

If your EKG reveals a previously unrecognized heart attack, it's wise to see a cardiologist and receive the exact same treatment that you would get if you had a recognized heart attack. *Elements of that treatment should include...*

• **Treadmill stress test.** The cardiologist will check for and interpret many variables, such as your symptoms (if any), the electrical patterns of your heart rhythms and your blood pressure while you are on a treadmill.

Important: Be sure to get your cardiologist's advice on special steps to take to ensure accurate results. For example, you should have no caffeine within 24 hours of the test.

If the results of the stress test indicate "severe myocardial ischemia"—poor blood flow to the heart muscle—it may be necessary to have a coronary angiogram (X-rays of the heart's arteries) to accurately diagnose the degree of blockage and decide whether you should pursue such options as angioplasty (in which a balloon is inserted into the coronary artery and inflated to restore normal blood flow) or coronary bypass surgery (in which a blood vessel is grafted from another part of the body to give blood a new pathway to the heart).

However, in most cases, heart disease that is associated with a silent heart attack can be managed with lifestyle changes, such as not smoking...losing weight if you're overweight... and getting regular exercise. *In addition, medications may include...*

• **Aspirin.** A daily dose of 81 mg of aspirin is the best choice for an antiplatelet drug to reduce the risk for blood clots.

Very important: A higher dose does not increase the cardiovascular benefit—but does increase the risk for gastrointestinal bleeding.

• **Beta-blocker.** This class of drugs slows the heart rate, relaxing the heart and helping to manage high blood pressure.

• **Angiotensin-converting enzyme (ACE) inhibitor.** These drugs expand blood vessels, improving blood flow and lowering blood pressure—thus allowing the heart to work less.

• **Statin.** If you have heart disease, this cholesterol-lowering medication reduces your risk for another heart attack or dying from heart disease—regardless of whether your levels of LDL "bad" cholesterol are high or low.

In addition, statin use should be accompanied by a diet that is low in cholesterol (less than 200 mg per day) and low in saturated fat (less than 7% of total calories).

Also important: It's crucial that people with diabetes maintain tight control of their HbA1C levels. This measure of long-term blood sugar control should be less than 7%.

However, HbA1C levels should not be aggressively lowered below 6.5% in diabetes patients with cardiovascular disease, according to the Action to Control Cardiovascular Risk in Diabetes study—that increases the risk for death because it would indicate that blood glucose is at times too low.

In general, the best way for people with diabetes to protect against heart attacks and strokes is to give up cigarettes if they smoke... lose weight if necessary...reduce blood pressure to 130–139/80–89 mmHg...and reduce LDL cholesterol to less than 70 mg/dL.

If these lifestyle measures do not also sufficiently lower the person's HbA1C level, standard antidiabetes medication can be used.

Smoking Danger

One cigarette can trigger a heart attack in someone with underlying heart disease. Cigarettes damage cells, inflame tissue and harm DNA.

Regina Benjamin, MD, Surgeon General of the United States, Rockville, Maryland. *www.surgeongeneral.gov*

Heart-Breaking Loss

Recent study: The risk for heart attack increases about 21 times in the first day after the death of a loved one.

Reason: Grief-related changes affect heart rate, blood pressure and blood clotting.

Circulation

Family Heart Risk

Parental history significantly boosts heart attack risk.

Recent study: An analysis of nearly 30,000 adults found that an individual's parental history of heart attack increased his/her likelihood of having a heart attack over and above other risk factors, including smoking, high blood pressure, elevated cholesterol or diabetes. Adults whose parent had a heart attack before age 50 were 2.5 times more likely to have one. When both parents suffered heart attacks before age 50, personal risk increased sixfold. Parental heart attack after age 50 was not studied.

Clara Chow, PhD, assistant clinical professor of medicine, McMaster University, Ontario, Canada.

Drug Alert

Smoking-cessation drug is linked to heart attack.

Recent finding: Smokers who took Chantix to help them quit smoking had a slightly higher risk for heart attack and other heart problems than people taking a placebo.

Alternative: Nicotine-replacement therapy has not been shown to increase heart disease risk.

Sonal Singh, MD, assistant professor of medicine, Johns Hopkins University School of Medicine, Baltimore, and leader of a study of 8,216 smokers, published in *Canadian Medical Association Journal.*

Safer Way to Detect Blood Vessel Blockages

In conventional catheterization, a thin plastic tube is inserted through the groin and advanced to the heart to detect blood vessel blockages and to insert stents to hold vessels open.

New method: Now most patients can have the tube inserted through the wrist instead of the groin—resulting in a better-than-70% reduction in bleeding risk...faster recovery time...and less pain.

Sunil V. Rao, MD, associate professor, department of medicine, Duke University Medical Center, and director of the Cardiac Catheterization Laboratories, Durham VA Medical Center, both in Durham, North Carolina.

NSAIDs Linked to Risk For Second Heart Attack

Recent study: Researchers examined data on 83,677 heart attack survivors (average age 68) to study the effects of nonsteroidal anti-inflammatory drugs (NSAIDs), such as *ibuprofen* (Advil), *diclofenac* (Voltaren) and *celecoxib* (Celebrex).

Result: Regularly taking NSAIDs after a heart attack increased the risk for a second heart attack or death by 45% after just one week, and by up to 55% after three months.

If you've had a heart attack: Talk to your doctor before regularly using an NSAID. Earlier research has linked regular use of an NSAID to an increased risk for a first heart attack.

Anne-Marie Schjerning Olsen, MD, research fellow, Copenhagen University Hospital, Hellerup, Denmark.

Better Heart Attack Care

Records of 104,622 heart attack patients (average age 68) showed that about 60% waited longer than two hours after symptoms began to go to the hospital. Such delays increase risk for death or heart damage.

Self-defense: Call 911 immediately if symptoms last for more than five minutes. These include pressure, squeezing or pain in the chest, shortness of breath and/or sudden, profuse sweating. Women may have additional or different symptoms, including extreme fatigue, clammy skin and/or upper abdominal pain or pressure.

Henry Ting, MD, professor of medicine, Mayo Clinic College of Medicine, Rochester, Minnesota.

Aspirin Before Heart Surgery a Lifesaver

Cardiac patients on aspirin therapy who continued taking aspirin—instead of stopping one week before surgery, as many doctors recommend—had a significantly lower risk for death in the month after surgery than patients who stopped taking aspirin. The aspirin users had a lower risk for kidney failure and major postsurgical cardiac problems, and they spent less time in intensive care.

Jian-Zhong Sun, MD, associate professor of anesthesiology at Thomas Jefferson University Hospital, Philadelphia, and leader of a study of cardiac patients published in *Annals of Surgery.*

Pacemaker Safety

Unlike other imaging tests, magnetic resonance imaging (MRI) creates magnetic fields that can damage or interfere with pacemakers.

Recent development: The FDA approved a pacemaker (Revo MRI SureScan) that is unaffected by MRI.

Recent study: When 211 patients implanted with the new pacemaker had an MRI, not one suffered complications—which ordinarily may include device malfunction.

The new pacemaker can be switched into "safe" mode during an MRI.

If you need a pacemaker: Ask your doctor about this device, especially if you have a chronic condition requiring frequent MRI scans.

Richard Sutton, DScMed, consultant cardiologist, St. Mary's Hospital, London, UK.

Tall People at Higher Risk for Blood Clots

In taller people, blood must be pumped a longer distance, so there may be reduced blood flow in the legs—raising clot risk. Clot risk is greatest in men who are tall and heavy. Obese men who are five feet, 11 inches tall have five times the risk of normal-weight men who are about five feet, seven inches tall or less. In obese, tall women—more than five feet, six inches—the risk is 2.9 times greater than in normal-weight women, who are five feet, 2.6 inches tall or less.

Sigrid Braekkan, PhD, researcher, Hematological Research Group, University of Tromsø, Norway, and investigator of a study of 26,714 Norwegian people, published by the American Heart Association in *Arteriosclerosis, Thrombosis and Vascular Biology.*

Depression and Stroke

Depressed women have a 29% greater stroke risk than women who are not depressed, according to a recent study.

Possible reason: Depression is linked to increased inflammation, which raises stroke risk.

Also: People with depression may not exercise regularly, use prescribed medications consistently or take other steps that help prevent strokes. The study looked only at women, but the findings likely apply to men as well.

Kathryn Rexrode, MD, associate professor of medicine at Harvard Medical School and associate physician at Brigham and Women's Hospital, both in Boston. She is senior author of a study of 80,574 women, published in *Stroke.*

Is It a "Wake-Up" Stroke?

Rebecca Shannonhouse, editor, *Bottom Line/Health*, Boardroom Inc., 281 Tresser Blvd., Stamford, Connecticut 06901.

In a recent study that looked at 1,854 ischemic (clot-related) strokes, 273 (14%) were "wake-up" strokes, in which patients had a stroke during sleep and then woke up with symptoms.

It's likely that many of these patients suffered their strokes just before they woke up, according to Jason Mackey, MD, a stroke research fellow at the University of Cincinnati College of Medicine and lead author of the study. Identifying these patients, he explains, would improve recovery by increasing the use of the clot-busting drug tPA.

Treatment guidelines state that tPA can be used only within three hours after a patient develops symptoms of an ischemic stroke. Some patients may benefit up to 4.5 hours after stroke onset.

It's possible that imaging studies, such as MRI or CT scans, will help determine the time that symptoms began in patients who were asleep when they had a stroke. It's not yet known if this approach will be effective. Clinical studies are under way.

For now: Anyone with stroke symptoms morning, noon or night—particularly facial drooping on one side, arm or leg weakness or difficulty with speech—should call 911 immediately.

Don't delay by calling a friend or family member. A recent study found that more than 70% of patients hospitalized with stroke called one of these people first. Even if a friend or family member gets you to the emergency room quickly, the staff won't be prepared to give tPA right away. A 911 call will alert doctors ahead of time so that you get the fastest treatment possible.

Antidepressants Speed Stroke Recovery

Recent finding: Both depressed and nondepressed stroke patients who were given antidepressant medication daily for three months following their strokes showed greater physical recovery than patients given a placebo.

And: Improvements continued even nine months after they stopped taking the medication.

Theory: Antidepressants may block inflammatory proteins released during a stroke that inhibit cellular growth and can promote growth of new cells in the brain.

Robert Robinson, MD, professor of psychiatry at University of Iowa City and leader of a study published in *American Journal of Geriatric Psychiatry.*

Mini-Stroke Increases Risk for Heart Attack

A mini-stroke, or transient-ischemic attack (TIA), occurs when a blood clot temporarily blocks a blood vessel to the brain. Symptoms include sudden weakness or numbness of the face, arm or leg...sudden confusion...trouble seeing...and sudden dizziness. Symptoms generally disappear in 24 hours.

Recent finding: Patients who have suffered a mini-stroke are twice as likely to suffer a heart attack within the next five years.

If you have had a mini-stroke: Reduce your risk for heart attack by maintaining healthy blood pressure and cholesterol levels.

Robert D. Brown, Jr., MD, MPH, chair of neurology, Mayo Medical School, Mayo Clinic, Rochester, Minnesota, and leader of a study of 456 TIA patients, published in *Stroke.*

One in Three US Adults Could Have Diabetes By 2050

Currently one in nine people has the disease. The predicted increase in cases is attributable to aging of the population, obesity, sedentary lifestyle, people with diabetes living longer and an increase in the population of minority groups that are at higher risk for type 2 diabetes.

Ann Albright, PhD, RD, director, Division of Diabetes Translation, Centers for Disease Control and Prevention, Atlanta. *www.cdc.gov*

Statins May Raise Risk for Diabetes

Recent findings: People taking high doses of the cholesterol-lowering drugs had a 12% higher risk for diabetes than those taking moderate statin doses. And users of high doses had a 20% higher risk for diabetes than people who do not take statins at all. But doctors say these statistics may be misleading. Statins increase blood sugar only a little, which may push a few patients over the threshold for diagnosis of diabetes. Most experts agree that the cardiovascular benefits of statin use far outweigh the increase in diabetes risk.

Steven E. Nissen, MD, chairman of cardiology, Cleveland Clinic.

Women at Risk

Statins raise diabetes risk in postmenopausal women.

Recent finding: Postmenopausal women who took cholesterol-lowering statin drugs had a 48% higher likelihood of developing type 2 diabetes than women who did not take statins. Statins lower risk for cardiovascular disease in people who already are at risk for cardiovascular disease.

Caution: Talk to your doctor about the risks and benefits. Do not stop taking statins on your own.

Yunsheng Ma, MD, PhD, epidemiologist and associate professor of medicine, University of Massachusetts Medical School, Worcester, and leader of a study of 153,840 postmenopausal women, published in *Archives of Internal Medicine.*

Heat Hurts Diabetes

Extreme heat is more dangerous for people with diabetes.

Recent finding: People who have type 1 or type 2 diabetes often have difficulty adjusting to rises in temperature. Also, due to nerve damage associated with diabetes, their sweat glands may not produce enough perspiration to cool them down. This may explain why people with diabetes have higher rates of hospitalization, dehydration and death in warmer months. Winter also can be a problem for diabetics because poor circulation increases the likelihood of skin damage in the cold weather.

Jerrold S. Petrofsky, PhD, professor of physical therapy, School of Allied Health Professions, Loma Linda University, Loma Linda, California, and coauthor of a study published in *The Journal of Applied Research.*

Blood Sugar Dangers

High blood pressure, memory problems and fatigue can be linked to insulin-resistance. People who are insulin-resistant have an impaired ability to control their bodies' blood glucose levels. In addition to diabetes, the condition can lead to cardiovascular disease, decreased immunity, depression, increased inflammation, weight gain and breast and colon cancers.

Self-defense: Ask your doctor about getting tested for insulin-resistance.

Allan Magaziner, DO, founder and director of Magaziner Center for Wellness, Cherry Hill, New Jersey, and author of *The All-Natural Cardio Cure* (Avery). *www.drmagaziner.com*

Potent Cancer Drug On the Way

Researchers have found that many cancer cells contain a faulty version of the gene WWP2, which attacks an inhibitor protein that otherwise would keep cancer cells from metastasizing. A potent drug that stops the activity of WWP2 could be available within the next decade to help fight the spread of most cancers.

Andrew Chantry, PhD, senior lecturer in cell biology, department of biological sciences, University of East Anglia, UK, and coauthor of a study of WWP2, published in *Oncogene*.

Is Sweetener Safe?

Saccharin is no longer considered a cancer cause. The EPA recently announced there is insufficient evidence that saccharin causes cancer. The EPA is following in the FDA's footsteps, which gave the sweetener approval as safe in 2000. Saccharin was linked to cancer in rats in the 1970s.

Tufts University Health & Nutrition Letter, 50 Broadway, New York City 10014.

Cancer Caution

A common home-building material may cause cancer. Formaldehyde typically is found in plywood, particleboard and other wood composites, such as medium-density fiberboard (MDF) used to make furnishings and in housing construction. It has been officially identified by the National Institutes of Health as a possible cause of cancer.

Self-defense: Buy formaldehyde-free products, such as ones made of solid wood, or products labeled ULEF (ultra-low-emitting formaldehyde). The half-life of formaldehyde emissions is about one year, so if products have been in your home for many years, current off-gassing may be negligible.

Richard J. Shaughnessy, PhD, program manager, The University of Tulsa Indoor Air Program, Oklahoma.

Aluminum Bottles—More BPA Than Plastic?

Some reusable aluminum bottles release up to five times as much bisphenol A (BPA) as older, polycarbonate bottles. Aluminum bottles can have plastic or epoxy resin liners that contain BPA, a hormone-disrupting chemical that is associated with impeded brain and nervous system function, and can cause birth defects, reproductive problems and some types of cancer.

Self-defense: If you opt for aluminum bottles, choose ones that are labeled BPA-free.

Scott Belcher, PhD, associate professor of pharmacology and cell biophysics, University of Cincinnati, and leader of a study of aluminum bottles, published in *Chemosphere*.

BPA Concern from Canned Soup

Bisphenol A (BPA) is an endocrine-disrupting chemical that may increase risk for heart disease, diabetes and obesity. BPA is used in the linings of many metal cans.

Recent finding: People who ate just 12 ounces of canned vegetable soup every day for five days had more than 1,000% more BPA in their urine than people who ate soup made from fresh ingredients.

Karin Michels, ScD, PhD, associate professor at Obstetrics and Gynecology, Brigham and Women's Hospital, associate professor, department of obstetrics, gynecology and reproductive biology, Harvard Medical School, both in Boston.

Cell Phones and Brain Tumors—Steps to Protect Yourself

Magda Havas, PhD, associate professor of environmental and resource studies at Trent University in Peterborough, Ontario, Canada. She is a leading expert in radiofrequency radiation, electromagnetic fields, dirty electricity and ground current. She is coauthor, with Camilla Rees, of *Public Health SOS: The Shadow Side of the Wireless Revolution* (CreateSpace). *www.magdahavas.com*

About nine out of 10 US households now have at least one cell phone—and that doesn't include other wireless devices, such as cordless phones, iPads, baby monitors and computers.

Result: The average adult (and child) is flooded with nonionizing radiation, a form of energy that—for the first time—has been officially linked to cancer. In May, a panel of the World Health Organization (WHO) listed cell phones as a class 2b carcinogen, which means that it's "possible" that cell phones, like some industrial chemicals, increase the risk for cancer.

This conclusion has been disputed by many scientists. But careful analysis of the best studies to date indicate that people who log the most cell-phone minutes are more likely to develop tumors on the same side of the head that they hold the cell phone, compared with those who use cell phones less often.

DISTURBING RESEARCH

The largest study of cell-phone use, known as INTERPHONE, was conducted in 13 countries over a 10-year period. The study, published in *International Journal of Epidemiology*, found that people who used cell phones for at least 1,640 hours over the 10-year period—that comes to about 30 minutes a day—had a 40% higher risk of developing a glioma, a deadly type of brain tumor.

Disturbing: The development of a brain tumor to the point that it can be detected often takes 20 to 30 years. The fact that these tumors are showing up after 10 years of exposure is disturbing because it is much faster than expected.

Previous studies have linked frequent or prolonged cell-phone use to an increase in parotid (salivary gland) and auditory nerve tumors.

The actual risk probably is higher than the studies indicate. The INTERPHONE study defined "heavy use" as using a cell phone for about 30 minutes a day. That's a fraction of the time that many people currently spend on their cell phones.

Also, the study looked only at adults, even though young people are frequent users of cell phones and the ones who face the highest cancer risks from decades of radiation exposure.

In addition, the study "diluted" the data by identifying people as regular cell-phone users who may have used their phones only once a week for at least six months. These light users were obviously exposed to far less radiation than heavy users. Including them in the study caused the cancer percentages to appear artificially low. For example, we would not expect someone who smoked one cigarette a week for at least six months to develop lung cancer.

SAFER USE

Skeptics of cell-phone dangers argue that nonionizing radiation is too weak to heat tissues or break chemical bonds, factors that are known to increase cancer risks. But recent studies indicate damage to DNA in rat brains exposed to cell-phone radiation, and this type of damage can lead to cancer.

Ways to stay safe...

- **Hold the phone away from your ear.** The fine print in cell-phone manuals usually advises users to hold the phone at least 7/8 of an inch away from the ear. Farther is better. Use speakerphone mode.

• **Wait for good reception.** Cell phones emit much higher levels of radiation when the antenna is sending out signals to search for a tower or satellite. These signals can travel hundreds of miles—and the poorer the reception, the greater the radiation emitted by your cell phone.

• **Use a hollow-tube headset.** This is the safest type of headset because the last few inches, those closest to the ear, consist of a hollow tube. This hollow tube transmits sound like a stethoscope. Wired headsets need to be kept away from the body because the continuous wire that runs from the phone to the earpiece will expose you to some unnecessary radiation. Hollow-tube headsets can be purchased at *www.mercola.com* or *www.waveshield.com.*

• **Use "airplane mode."** Even when you're not talking on a cell phone, the phone is sending out signals every few minutes to search for the nearest tower. Turn off the phone when you're not using it. Or switch it to airplane mode so that it can't send or receive signals, but you still can use the phone to listen to music, watch videos and check your calendar.

• **Keep the phone on your desk when working.** When the phone is switched on, don't keep it in your pocket or attached to your belt. This is particularly important for men. Preliminary research indicates that men who keep their phones close to their bodies (often in holsters or pockets) have lower sperm counts and poorer sperm quality than those without this exposure. We do not know the effects on egg cells because they are more difficult to harvest.

Caution: The worst way to use a Bluetooth wireless headset is to place it on your ear with the cell phone in your pocket. This way, your head and lower body are both being irradiated. A better way to use a Bluetooth is to keep the cell phone on a table several feet away from all body parts and to periodically move the earpiece from one ear to the other to minimize one-side radiation exposure.

• **Text instead of talk.** There's a burst of radiation when you send or receive a text message, but the intensity and duration of the radiation are lower than when you talk. Texting is a better alternative to talking on your cell phone, but keep the phone as far away from your body as possible. Normal clothing, including leather, will not reduce your exposure.

• **Don't use your phone in a car, train or bus.** Using a cell phone inside a metal vehicle can increase levels of radiation due to reflection and the fact that your cell-phone signal has to be higher to exit the vehicle. The best practice is to keep the phone off or in airplane mode and to check it periodically for messages. Then return messages by text or use a landline phone later.

Radiation Concern

Radiation may be a concern with iPads or other e-tablets

No one has studied cancers of the abdomen from iPads or laptops. But an iPad is a wireless device, and there is some evidence, though not definitive, that holding a cell phone to your head may increase risk for brain cancer on the side of the head where it is used intensely for many years. But if the iPad or the cell phone is held away from your body, it will not give significant exposure. Holding an e-tablet on your lap will expose your pelvis, and research shows that men who wear cell phones on their belts in the "on" mode have lowered sperm counts and reduced bone density in the hip bone where the phone is placed. Until we have more information, it is best not to hold an e-tablet or a laptop on your lap for long periods.

David O. Carpenter, MD, director, Institute for Health and the Environment, University at Albany-SUNY, Rensselaer, New York.

Early Detection

Pancreatic cancer can sometimes be stopped before it starts. Most pancreatic cysts are benign—but up to 20% become malignant. The cysts usually are detected when CT or other scans are performed for other reasons. Additional testing can help determine whether surgery is indicated. Patients who have a cyst and/or a strong family history of pancreatic cancer—for example, a parent or sibling who has or had the disease—should have regular imaging tests.

Christopher Wolfgang, MD, PhD, director of pancreatic surgery at The Johns Hopkins Hospital and associate professor of surgery and oncology at The Johns Hopkins University School of Medicine, both in Baltimore.

Another Aspirin Benefit

Aspirin may reduce risk for pancreatic cancer, says a recent study.

Recent finding: Men and women who took aspirin at least once a month had a 26% lower risk for pancreatic cancer than those who did not take aspirin.

Caution: People should not take aspirin for this purpose without first talking to their doctors.

Xiang-Lin Tan, MD, PhD, research fellow at Mayo Clinic, Rochester, Minnesota, and leader of a study presented at a recent meeting of the American Association for Cancer Research.

Drivers' Danger

Skin cancers are more common on the left side of the face.

Possible reason: When people drive, the left side of the face is exposed to more sunlight than the right.

Self-defense: Even when you are in the car, wear sunscreens that block both UVA and UVB rays.

Susan Butler, MD, dermatologic surgeon, California Skin Institute, San Mateo, California, and coauthor of a study of 1,047 Americans, published in *Journal of the American Academy of Dermatology.*

Exfoliate!

Exfoliating helps prevent skin cancer. Exfoliants that contain glycolic acid have been shown to reduce the number of actinic keratoses—skin lesions that can develop into squamous cell cancer.

Best: Creams and gels with up to 20% glycolic acid, available online and at some cosmetics stores.

Neal Schultz, MD, cosmetic dermatologist in private practice in New York City and associate clinical professor of dermatology at Mount Sinai School of Medicine, New York City. He is coauthor of *It's Not Just About Wrinkles* (Stewart, Tabori and Chang). *www.dermtv.com*

HPV May Raise Heart Risks

Several types of the human papillomavirus cause cervical cancer—and new evidence suggests that women with certain strains of HPV are more than twice as likely to have a heart attack or stroke as women not infected with the strains. The HPV vaccines, which protect against certain cancers, have not yet been proven to have cardiovascular benefits.

Hsu-Ko Kuo, MD, MPH, medical resident, University of Texas Medical Branch, Galveston, and leader of a study of 2,450 women, ages 20 to 59, published in *Journal of the American College of Cardiology.*

Nicotine Replacements

Quit-smoking aids can be used for longer than 12 weeks. The Food and Drug Administration is considering eliminating the current warning on most nicotine-replacement gum, lozenges and patches recommending that people stop using them after 12 weeks. Use of these medications beyond 12 weeks may help some people abstain from smoking. And nicotine itself is not believed to raise the risk for cancer, though it can elevate heart rate, raise blood pressure and may cause adverse skin reactions.

K. Michael Cummings, PhD, chair, department of health behavior, division of cancer prevention and population sciences, Roswell Park Cancer Institute, Buffalo.

Buy Organic Milk

Cow's milk sold in the US often is produced from cows injected with the synthetic hormone recombinant bovine growth hormone (rBGH), also known as recombinant bovine somatotropin (rBST), which increases milk production. The hormone may be linked to cancer and antibiotic resistance in humans. It is banned in Canada, Australia, Japan, New Zealand and the European Union.

Unfortunately, there is no uniform labeling rule.

Best: Buy organic milk, or look for labels such as, "This milk is from cows not treated with rBGH"..."rBGH-free"..."rBST-free"...or "no artificial hormones."

Suzanne Havala Hobbs, DrPH, licensed, registered dietitian and clinical associate professor in the departments of health policy and management and nutrition in the Gillings School of Global Public Health, University of North Carolina at Chapel Hill. She is author of *Living Vegetarian for Dummies* and *Living Dairy-Free for Dummies* (both from Wiley).

Help a Smoker Quit

Smokers are twice as likely to quit if they receive supportive text messages. People who had been sent five motivational texts a day for five weeks and then three texts a week for 26 weeks were twice as likely to be smoke-free after six months as people who had received texts thanking them for participating in the study.

Caroline Free, PhD, clinical lecturer in epidemiology, nutrition and public health interventions research department, London School of Hygiene & Tropical Medicine, and lead researcher of a study of 5,800 smokers, published online in *The Lancet.*

Danger in the Attic

Attic insulation may cause cancer. From the 1960s to the 1990s, about 30 million homes were insulated with Zonolite, an asbestos-contaminated brand of vermiculite. It was used mainly to retrofit or add to attic insulation in existing buildings. Photos of Zonolite are available at *www.thescottlawgroup.com/zonoliteatticinsulation.* If you suspect Zonolite, have the insulation tested by a trained professional. Do not attempt to remove or repair it yourself.

Devra Davis, PhD, MPH, epidemiologist, toxicologist and founder of the Environmental Health Trust, Teton Village, Wyoming. She is author of *Disconnect* (Dutton) about cell-phone radiation and is producing a film based on it. *www.disconnectfilm.com*

New Device Eases Chronic Pain

The Calmare pain therapy treatment relieves chronic neuropathic pain from diabetes, shingles, herniated disks, chemotherapy, reflex sympathetic dystrophy (RSD) and other causes. The FDA-approved device uses electrodes applied to the skin to transmit "no-pain" messages to the brain. Patients usually undergo 10 to 12 daily treatments, each lasting less than one hour. For a list of centers that offer Calmare therapy, go to *www.calmarett.com/locations.html.*

C. Evers Whyte, MS, DC, pain expert and founder and director of the New England Center for Chronic Pain, Stamford, Connecticut. *www.neccp.com*

Antibiotic Creams May Increase MRSA Resistance

Over-the-counter triple-antibiotic creams and ointments, such as Medi-Quik and Neosporin, seem to be leading to the emergence of a form of methicillin-resistant Staphylococcus aureus (MRSA) that resists bacitracin and neomycin—two of the antibiotics found in the creams.

Self-defense: Washing with soap and water is all that many scrapes and cuts require. If you do use an antibiotic cream, apply only a small amount and use it for as short a time as possible.

William Schaffner, MD, professor of preventive medicine, Vanderbilt University School of Medicine, Nashville, commenting on a study by Japanese researchers, published in *Emerging Infectious Diseases.*

Chemo Without Hair Loss?

A "cold cap" allowed breast cancer patients to undergo chemo without losing their hair. During chemo sessions, patients wore the silicone cap, which circulates a coolant that brings the scalp's temperature down to 42°F.

Theory: The cap constricts blood flow to hair follicles and reduces exposure to the chemo chemicals. More than 3,000 women in Europe and Asia have used the cap, and about 80% did not suffer significant hair loss. The cap has not yet been approved in the US. However, the Penguin Cold Cap, which uses frozen packs to cool the scalp, can be rented for about $500 a month (316-243-4946, *www.MSC-Worldwide.com/indexusa.html*). Insurance does not cover the cost.

Susan Melin, MD, associate professor of hematology and oncology, Wake Forest University School of Medicine, Winston-Salem, North Carolina.

Thinning Eyebrows May Signal Disease

Brows tend to thin naturally with age, but if the outer third of the brows (closest to your ears) starts to disappear without plucking or waxing, consult your doctor. This may be a sign of hypothyroidism (underactive thyroid gland).

Reason: Thyroid hormones are critical to hair production. There usually is a loss of hair elsewhere on the body, too, but it is more noticeable on the brows first.

Richard L. Shames, MD, thyroid specialist, Preventive Medical Center of Marin, San Rafael, California. *www.thyroidpower.com*

Iced Tea Raises Kidney Stone Risk

The tea contains high concentrations of oxalate—a chemical that contributes to the formation of kidney stones. Hot tea also contains oxalate, but it is rarely drunk in large enough quantities to have an effect on kidney stone formation. People often drink large amounts of iced tea during hot weather, but iced tea should not be the drink of choice for anyone with a personal or family history of kidney stones.

Better: Water—plain or flavored with a slice of lemon.

John Milner, MD, assistant professor, department of urology, Stritch School of Medicine, Loyola University, Maywood, Illinois.

Simple Urine Test for Kidney Disease

Recent finding: The dipstick urine protein test identified 90.8% of people with rapid kidney-function decline—whose symptoms often do not appear until later stages, when the condition is less treatable and can lead to kidney failure. The test, which costs less than $1, should be given every year to people who have diabetes, hypertension or a family history of kidney disease.

William F. Clark, MD, nephrologist and professor, division of nephrology, Schulich School of Medicine & Dentistry, University of Western Ontario, Canada, and leader of a study of 2,574 people, published in *Journal of the American Society of Nephrology.*

Good News

New drugs for hepatitis C boost cure rate. Either *boceprevir* (Victrelis) or *telaprevir* (Incivek) is taken with two other drugs—*pegylated interferon alpha* and *ribavirin.*

Recent finding: The three-drug combination effectively cured more than 70% of patients in clinical trials, compared with 20% to 40% cured by the two-drug treatment. The treatments are expensive, and insurance coverage varies.

Robert G. Gish, MD, professor of clinical medicine, director of hepatology, University of California, San Diego School of Medicine.

Boomers, Beware

Everyone born between 1945 and 1965 should be tested for hepatitis C. Most people with the virus acquire the infection 20 to 40 years before having any symptoms. If an infection is detected, drug treatment reduces the likelihood of serious consequences, such as cirrhosis and liver cancer, by about 97%. Universal testing would detect 800,000 new cases of hepatitis C and prevent 82,000 deaths.

One reason baby boomers are at increased risk: They may have had transfusions before the blood supply was fully monitored.

Robert G. Gish, MD, professor of clinical medicine, director of hepatology, University of California, San Diego School of Medicine.

Reflux Drugs May Deplete Magnesium

The FDA has issued a warning about proton pump inhibitors (PPIs), which are often used for gastroesophageal reflux disease (GERD). Taking PPIs, such as *omeprazole* (Prilosec) or *esomeprazole* (Nexium), regularly for a year or more may lower levels of magnesium, which may increase the risk for leg spasms, arrhythmias and seizures. The risk for this effect may be higher in people who also are taking diuretics or the heart medicine *digoxin* (Lanoxin).

If your doctor prescribes a PPI: Have your magnesium levels checked—especially if you're taking digoxin or a diuretic. The magnesium depletion may occur in prescription or over-the-counter PPIs when taken for more than a year.

Lisa Kubaska, PharmD, LCDR, US Public Health Service, FDA Center for Drug Evaluation and Research, Silver Spring, Maryland.

Cell-Phone Radiation Warning

Recent study: Researchers examined the bones of 48 healthy men who carried cell phones.

Result: Men who carried cell phones on their hips were more likely to have lower mineral content and density in the upper thigh bones where the phones were placed.

Theory: Over time, the low levels of electromagnetic radiation emitted by cell phones appear to degrade the bone in the hip.

Self-defense: Avoid carrying your cell phone against any part of your body.

Fernando D. Saravi, MD, PhD, professor, department of morphology and physiology, National University of Cuyo, Mendoza, Argentina.

Hip Replacement Warning

Metal-on-metal hip replacements may shed chromium and cobalt particles as they wear. Tissue damage caused by the shedding of these tiny particles is not life-threatening. Some patients with tissue damage have no symptoms, while others experience pain, rashes and inflammation. In either case, the device may need to be removed. Patients should have routine annual follow-up visits and X-rays.

Geoffrey H. Westrich, MD, orthopedic surgeon at Hospital for Special Surgery, New York City.

Help for Fibromyalgia

SHINE stands for Sleep, Hormones, Infections, Nutritional supplements and Exercise—and this approach has led to improvements in 91% of fibromyalgia patients. Patients should get eight to nine hours of sleep a night...be tested for hormone deficiency and treated if necessary...get treated for any symptoms of infections...have nutritional supplementation, such as B-12 and magnesium...and exercise as much as possible.

Also effective: Taking 5,000 milligrams of *ribose* (Corvalen), a nonprescription medical food, twice a day increased energy by an average of 61%.

Jacob Teitelbaum, MD, medical director at Fibromyalgia & Fatigue Centers, Addison, Texas. *www.endfatigue.com*

Troubling New Statistics

New diagnosis guidelines for Alzheimer's may double the number of people defined as having the disease. The guidelines create two new stages—the preclinical stage, when there are no symptoms but brain changes are occurring...and mild cognitive impairment (MCI), with mild symptoms.

Guy M. McKhann, MD, professor of neurology and neuroscience, department of neurology, Johns Hopkins University, Baltimore, and coauthor of new Alzheimer's diagnostic guidelines, published in *Alzheimer's & Dementia.*

Maternal Link to Alzheimer's

Alzheimer's disease is inherited from mothers more often than from fathers. People with a mother or father with Alzheimer's are four to 10 times more likely to develop Alzheimer's than people with no family history of the disease. Among that group, those whose mothers had the disease had twice as much gray-matter shrinkage and one-and-a-half times as much total brain shrinkage as people whose fathers had the disease. Shrinking of the brain occurs with Alzheimer's.

Robyn Honea, DPhil, assistant professor of neurology, University of Kansas School of Medicine, Kansas City, Kansas, and leader of a study published in *Neurology.*

Marital Link

Spouses of people with dementia are six times more likely to develop the illness according to recent research. Increased risk may be caused by the stress associated with caring for a loved one struggling with dementia. Shared environmental factors such as diet also may be responsible.

Maria C. Norton, PhD, associate professor, department of family, consumer and human development, Utah State University, Logan, and leader of a study of 1,221 couples, published in *Journal of the American Geriatrics Society.*

Hearing Loss Raises Dementia Risk

A recent study that tracked more than 600 adults for approximately 12 years found that every 10 decibels of hearing that is lost made participants 20% more likely to develop cognitive problems associated with dementia and Alzheimer's. Researchers are trying to determine whether hearing loss is really a cause of dementia or a symptom.

Frank R. Lin, MD, PhD, assistant professor, division of otology, neurotology and skull base surgery, Johns Hopkins School of Medicine, Baltimore.

Cholesterol Warning

High cholesterol is linked to Alzheimer's disease. People with high cholesterol are significantly more likely to have brain plaques associated with Alzheimer's than people with low cholesterol levels.

Recent study: 86% of people with high cholesterol had brain plaques, compared with 62% of people with low cholesterol.

Kensuke Sasaki, MD, PhD, assistant professor, department of neuropathology, Kyushu University, Fukuoka, Japan, and leader of a study of 2,734 people, ages 40 to 79, published in *Neurology.*

Better Brain Health

When researchers examined clinical records of 211 adults diagnosed with probable Alzheimer's disease, those who spoke multiple languages over their lifetimes showed initial Alzheimer's symptoms an average of five years later than those who spoke one language.

Theory: Bilingual people build concentration skills by focusing on the language they are speaking while minimizing interference from a second language.

If you are bilingual: It's not enough to hear or read a second language—contact libraries, universities and cultural centers to find groups that converse. If you are not bilingual, learning a second language can help promote brain health.

Fergus Craik, PhD, senior scientist, The Rotman Research Institute, Toronto, Canada.

Cold Sores May Link to Alzheimer's

Research has shown that a herpes simplex infection—the virus that causes cold sores—increases the amount of amyloid precursor protein, the parent protein of the plaque associated with Alzheimer's disease.

Self-defense: Treat cold sores quickly with an antiviral agent to minimize the amount of time that the virus remains active.

Elaine Bearer, MD, PhD, Harvey Family Professor and vice-chair for research, departments of pathology and neurosurgery, University of New Mexico School of Medicine, Albuquerque, and principal investigator in a study published in *PLoS One.*

Cancer Drug Shows Promise

The skin cancer drug *bexarotene* (Targretin) was shown in animal studies to promptly stimulate the removal of amyloid plaques that can lead to the cognitive and memory deficits of Alzheimer's disease. Research to confirm these findings in humans is under way.

Science

Antidepressant for Older Adults

Researchers analyzed the use of antidepressants in 60,746 depression patients (age 65 and older).

Result: Those who took selective serotonin reuptake inhibitors (SSRIs), such as *citalopram* (Celexa), were at increased risk for several adverse events (including death, stroke, falls and fractures) compared with those who took older tricyclic antidepressants (TCAs), such as *amitriptyline* (Elavil).

If you're 65 or older and your doctor prescribes an SSRI: Be sure to ask about the risks and benefits—and discuss perhaps taking a lower dose.

Carol Coupland, PhD, associate professor, medical statistics, The University of Nottingham, UK.

Violent Dreams?

Adults with REM sleep behavior disorder, characterized by violent dreams, often develop neurodegenerative disorders, including dementia. Catching warning signs could lead to earlier treatment.

Neurology

Ibuprofen Lowers Parkinson's Risk

Recent finding: People who take *ibuprofen*, such as Advil or Motrin, at least twice a week are about 40% less likely to develop Parkinson's disease than people who do not. Regular use of other painkillers, such as aspirin and *acetaminophen*, was not associated with lowering Parkinson's risk.

Xiang Gao, MD, assistant professor of medicine at Harvard Medical School and research scientist at Harvard School of Public Health, both in Boston, and leader of a study of 136,197 people, published in *Neurology*.

Fast Food Warning

People who ate the highest levels of trans fats were 48% more likely to be depressed than those who consumed the lowest levels. Trans fats are typically in fast foods, baked goods and margarine. Depression risk went down among people consuming higher levels of monounsaturated and polyunsaturated fats. Monounsaturated fats are in olive oil and avocado...and polyunsaturated fats are in fish, nuts, seeds and vegetable oils.

Not known: Whether trans fats raise depression risk—it could be that the factors causing depression may also raise people's tendency to consume trans fats.

Miguel Martínez-González, MD, PhD, chair, department of preventive medicine and public health, University of Navarra, Pamplona, Spain, and leader of a study of 12,059 people, published online in *PLoS One*.

Mental Health Alert

Marijuana is linked to early onset of mental illness.

Recent finding: Among people diagnosed with mental illness, those who had smoked marijuana when they were younger developed symptoms of mental illness nearly three years earlier than those with mental illness who had not used marijuana at all.

Matthew Large, MBBS, clinical senior lecturer, School of Psychology, University of New South Wales, Sydney, Australia, and leader of a study that included results from more than 80 studies and more than 20,000 people, published in *Archives of General Psychiatry.*

Help for OCD

Obsessive-compulsive disorder (OCD) can be helped by electrical brain stimulation. It can make treatment far more effective in patients with the most severe form of OCD. Doctors insert electrodes deep into the brain. The electrodes are attached to a pacemaker-like device to deliver electrical current in a way that makes OCD symptoms less severe and helps patients respond better to conventional therapy. The treatment is appropriate for only a very small subset of OCD patients who have severe, chronically disabling illness despite at least five years of aggressive treatment by doctors who are experts at OCD treatment.

Benjamin Greenberg, MD, PhD, psychiatrist, Butler Hospital, associate professor of psychiatry and human behavior, Brown University, both in Providence, and a pioneer in the use of brain stimulation to treat severe OCD. He is leader of a study presented at a recent meeting of the American Association for the Advancement of Science.

Belly Fat and Osteoporosis

Recent finding: Obese women with more fat around the waist were more likely to have low bone-mineral density—a risk factor for osteoporosis—than similar women with less fat around the waist. Earlier studies suggested that excess body fat might protect against bone loss and osteoporosis—but not all fat is the same. Women with excessive subcutaneous fat (just below the skin surface) show normal bone structure, but women with deep belly fat, who often have applelike figures, are more likely to have lower bone-mineral density.

Miriam Bredella, MD, assistant professor of radiology, Massachusetts General Hospital, Boston, and leader of a study of 50 premenopausal women, presented at a meeting of the Radiological Society of North America.

Aspirin Caution

Daily aspirin use may be linked to vision loss. Wet late-stage aging macular disorder (AMD)—also called age-related macular degeneration—is twice as common in people who take aspirin daily as in people who never use aspirin.

Caution: Do not stop aspirin therapy without talking with your physician. Eat a healthful diet, rich in vitamins C and E, beta-carotene and omega-3 fatty acids.

Paulus de Jong, MD, PhD, emeritus professor of ophthalmic epidemiology at the Netherlands Institute for Neuroscience and Academic Medical Center, Amsterdam, and first author of a study of 4,691 people, age 65 and older, published in *Ophthalmology.*

More Aspirin Caution

High doses of aspirin can cause hearing loss and tinnitus (ringing, clanging or whistling in the ears). Aspirin's active ingredient, salicylic acid, can cause changes in the inner ear when eight to 12 tablets are taken in a day. Even only occasional high doses may result in hearing loss.

At highest risk: The elderly and people who suffer from kidney problems, have a family history of hearing loss or are regularly exposed to loud noises. Symptoms often disappear after treatment is stopped or the dose is reduced. If you take aspirin and develop hearing problems, talk to your doctor.

UC Berkeley Wellness Letter, 500 Fifth Avenue, New York City 10110. *www.wellnessletter.com*

Nearsightedness Increases Glaucoma Risk

Recent finding: Nearsighted people are about 90% more likely to develop open-angle glaucoma than people who are not nearsighted. Glaucoma damages the optic nerve, causing gradual loss of vision. Treatments, including drugs and surgery, are available but cannot restore sight once it has been lost.

Self-defense: Regular eye exams are recommended for all adults age 40 and older.

Study by University Medical Center Groningen, the Netherlands, published in *Ophthalmology*.

Sepsis—the Little-Known Killer of Up to 375,000 Americans a Year

Derek C. Angus, MD, MPH, professor of critical care medicine, health policy and management, and clinical and translational science at the University of Pittsburgh School of Medicine, where he is also chair of the department of critical care medicine. His research has been published in dozens of professional journals, including *Critical Care Medicine, The Journal of the American Medical Association* and *Annals of Surgery*.

Sepsis kills up to 375,000 Americans each year—more than breast cancer, prostate cancer and AIDS combined. *But there are steps you can take to reduce your risk of developing this life-threatening condition...*

WHAT CAUSES SEPSIS?

Inflammation is one of the body's defenses. When you develop an infection—such as the flu, a urinary tract infection or even an infected cut—the immune system releases inflammatory mediators and other substances that destroy pathogens, increase blood flow to the area and initiate healing.

Sepsis occurs when this normal local response goes awry, for reasons that still aren't clear. Inflammation rapidly spreads throughout the body, disturbing normal physiologic processes and compromising function of vital organs, such as the heart and kidneys. Organ failure and death can quickly result.

Sepsis is always an emergency. A 2006 study in *Critical Care Medicine* found that the risk of dying from sepsis increased by 7.6% with every hour that passed without treatment. Those who survive still face serious risks.

Recent finding: A report in *The Journal of the American Medical Association* found that the risk of developing moderate-to-severe cognitive impairment, including memory loss and confusion, was 3.3 times higher in patients who had recovered from sepsis. It is estimated to contribute to 20,000 new cases of long-term cognitive impairment in the US annually.

WHO'S AT RISK

Hospitalized patients—particularly those in intensive care units who have invasive devices, such as urinary catheters—have a high risk of developing sepsis. But at least half of all cases occur in nonhospital settings.

Any bacterial or viral infection can progress to sepsis. In general, bacterial infections that are easily (and quickly) treated with antibiotics, such as bladder or skin infections, are unlikely to lead to sepsis. The viruses that cause the common cold rarely cause it, but the flu virus can.

Less common triggers: Other syndromes, such as severe trauma or pancreatitis, can cause similar activation of the body's inflammatory processes and lead to acute organ dysfunction. These syndromes, as well as sepsis itself, then can leave the body weakened and less able to resist secondary infections, which, in turn, can precipitate further bouts of sepsis, leading to a vicious circle of debilitation and critical illness. People with artificial joints also are at higher risk for sepsis—the devices can harbor an undetected infection. Both lingering and acute infections can lead to sepsis.

DIAGNOSIS AND TREATMENT

Sepsis is diagnosed according to clinical signs that accompany an infection, such as fever (above 101.3°F), rapid heart rate (higher than 90 beats/minute) and rapid breathing. In severe cases, patients may have decreased urine output and platelet counts, difficulty breathing, heart irregularities, including arrhythmias (abnormal heart rhythms) and sometimes mottled skin due to decreased circulation. Although sepsis tends to occur in people who are hospitalized, if you suffer any of the signs described above and have an infection or recently had surgery, seek immediate medical care.

When sepsis is suspected, a culture is typically performed to identify the organism causing the patient's infection. If it's a bacterial infection, the culture helps doctors identify the most effective antibiotic. Treating the underlying infection helps curb the inflammatory process that led to sepsis.

Because it usually takes a few days to get the results of a culture, at-risk patients are immediately given a broad-spectrum antibiotic, which is effective against a wide range of organisms. The drug may be changed later, depending on the results of the culture and/or blood tests. If the underlying infection triggering sepsis is viral, antiviral medication may be given.

Regardless of its cause, sepsis is life-threatening, so it is always treated in the hospital. In addition to antibiotics or antiviral medication, a person with sepsis is usually given intravenous fluids and vasopressors, medications that raise blood pressure and help prevent/reverse septic shock (a condition marked by life-threatening low blood pressure). Other treatments may include supplemental oxygen, mechanical ventilation or kidney dialysis.

Important: Everyone who has recovered from sepsis should ask his/her doctor about rehabilitation, such as speech therapy and exercises to improve motor skills and memory, to help prevent cognitive decline.

PREVENTING SEPSIS

Since there's no way to predict who will get sepsis, prevention is important. *Best approaches...*

• **Clean cuts and burns thoroughly.** Wash them one to three times daily using soap and water, followed by a dab of antibacterial ointment. If the wound is particularly large, doesn't seem to be healing or gets very red and continues to produce pus, see your doctor.

• **Don't ignore mucus.** You're unlikely to get sepsis from a mild upper-respiratory infection, but it's not impossible—particularly if you develop a secondary bacterial infection in the sinuses, lungs, etc. See your doctor if you're producing foul-smelling mucus—a telltale sign of a more serious infection.

• **Ask about preventive antibiotics.** People who have had joint replacement surgery have a higher-than-average risk for infection because bacteria can proliferate on foreign matter in the body, including the materials used to make artificial joints. For about two years after the surgery, your doctor may advise you to take antibiotics prior to any invasive procedure, such as dental work, to help prevent an infection that could lead to sepsis.

• **Be sure to get the flu vaccine in the fall.** According to the CDC, annual flu vaccination is particularly important for adults age 65 and older...people with chronic medical conditions, such as diabetes, heart disease or asthma...pregnant women...health-care workers...and those who care for or live with people at risk for flu-related complications, such as those with compromised immunity. If you're traveling this summer to a destination south of the equator (to parts of Africa or South America, for example) and did not receive a flu vaccine in the fall, ask your doctor about getting one before you go.

Also important: The pneumonia vaccine is recommended for all adults age 65 and older...those with chronic health problems or who are taking medications that lower immunity...and smokers or those with asthma. The vaccine is usually given once every five years.

More from Dr. Angus...

Seek Care Right Away

Sepsis can occur within hours of an infection developing—in some cases, patients may be fighting for their lives within 24 hours. Call a doctor right away if you develop any of the symptoms described in the accompanying article or if you feel like you're too sick to "just" have the flu, for example. If you can't see your doctor immediately, go to the emergency room.

Melon Rx

Wash a melon's rind with running water before cutting into the fruit—to prevent the knife from transferring surface bacteria to the flesh inside. Unlike most fruits, melon is not acidic, so bacteria thrive when the fruit is cut and not kept cold.

Self-defense: Refrigerate melon within two to four hours of cutting it. If you buy precut melon, be sure it is refrigerated.

UC Berkeley Wellness Letter, 500 Fifth Ave., New York City 10110. *www.wellnessletter.com*

When to Buy Organic

Apples top the "Dirty Dozen." Apples are number one on the list of the produce that is most contaminated with pesticides, followed by celery, strawberries, peaches and spinach. The "Clean 15," which are lowest in pesticides, include onions, sweet corn, pineapples, avocado and asparagus.

Self-defense: Buy organic if choosing from the "Dirty Dozen." For a complete list, go to *www.ewg.org/foodnews.*

Sonya Lunder, MPH, senior analyst, Environmental Working Group, a public health advocacy group, Washington, DC.

Better Canned Tuna

Recent study: When researchers measured levels of mercury in about 300 samples taken from three top-selling brands of canned tuna, 55% exceeded amounts declared safe by the EPA for commercially sold fish (0.5 parts per million). "Light" tuna contained more than three times less mercury than albacore ("white" tuna).

Shawn Gerstenberger, PhD, professor and chair, department of environmental and occupational health, University of Nevada, Las Vegas.

Too Much TV Shortens Life Span

Researchers studied lifestyle and health data on 11,000 adults (ages 25 and older) and found that for every hour of sedentary TV-watching per day, life expectancy was reduced by 22 minutes, on average. A six-hour daily TV habit after age 25 reduced life expectancy by nearly five years.

Surprising: Watching TV may be as dangerous as cardiovascular risk factors such as smoking and obesity.

Lennert Veerman, MD, senior research fellow, The University of Queensland, Brisbane, Australia.

2

Doctors, Hospitals & You

Stop Paging Dr. Google! ...End Unreasonable Health Worries

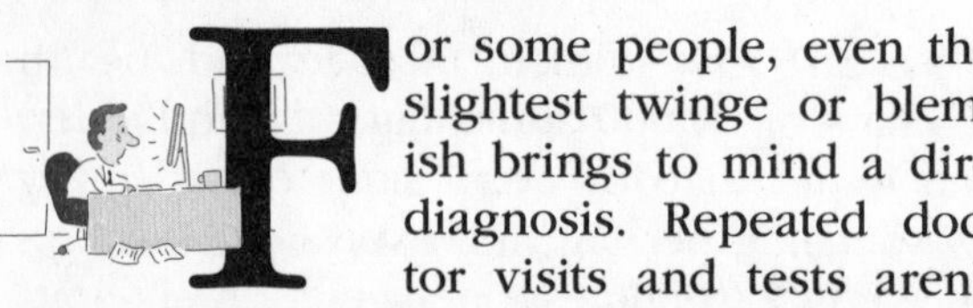

For some people, even the slightest twinge or blemish brings to mind a dire diagnosis. Repeated doctor visits and tests aren't reassuring, and the preoccupation becomes so consuming that it's difficult to enjoy one's good health. The term for this form of excessive anxiety is hypochondriasis, also known as hypochondria or illness anxiety disorder. As many as 24 million Americans may suffer from it.

Now: The Internet has made life even more complicated for many such sufferers. Mountains of information—and misinformation—that are just a few clicks away can turn a smoldering worry into a roaring blaze. The problem has often been referred to as cyberchondria.

If such troubles sound familiar, here's what you need to know...

WHAT ARE YOU THINKING?

No one knows for sure why some people worry more about health than others—genetics, upbringing and life experience are all believed to play a role. But what does seem clear is that habitual thought and behavior patterns can worsen and sustain health anxiety.

What happens: You notice, say, a tight feeling in your upper abdomen and begin to worry, "What if it's something serious?" Focusing attention on any sensation makes it seem stronger, so you start to feel that it's getting worse. Monitoring symptoms can be useful or problematic, depending on how often it's done. People with elevated health anxiety tend to overmonitor their symptoms, which can lead to a tendency to focus on symptoms that

---

Martin M. Antony, PhD, professor and chair of psychology at Ryerson University in Toronto. He is author of many books, including *Overcoming Health Anxiety: Letting Go of Your Fear of Illness* (New Harbinger), which he coauthored with Katherine M.B. Owens, PhD.

are not important and ultimately result in an increase in symptoms. As anxiety builds, you think about it more often...and soon you're convinced that you have a dread disease.

To break this cycle, begin by becoming aware of the type of thoughts that magnify health anxiety. *Common traps to avoid...*

• **Overestimating probability.** Do those recurrent headaches mean a brain tumor? Once you start to worry, you overlook the fact that many problems, including stress, lack of sleep and other, mostly benign, conditions, are far more likely than a brain tumor to be the cause of headaches.

• **Confirmation bias.** We all tend to remember things that confirm our beliefs and to ignore information that contradicts them. If you're prone to health anxiety, you can easily accumulate a file of "evidence" to justify your worries. For example, you remember reading that excess thirst is a symptom of diabetes and then notice all the times when you're thirsty—even though it is no more frequent than before.

ANXIOUS ACTIONS

Surprisingly, many of the actions that people take to ease their health fears may, in fact, sustain and magnify them. "Safety behaviors," such as repeated doctor visits or continual pulse checks, make you feel better momentarily, but the reassurances never seem quite sufficient to eliminate the constant fear. To distinguish appropriate doctor visits from excessive visits that fuel anxiety, talk to your doctor about how to evaluate the intensity, duration and context of symptoms to determine which are problematic and which probably are not.

"Safety" behaviors that actually can make things worse...

• **Seeking excessive reassurance.** You share every worry with friends and family. Responses such as "You look fine" or "I'm sure it's nothing serious" make you feel better—but not for long.

• **Repeating medical tests.** Seeing the doctor (or doctors) repeatedly and having multiple tests for the same symptoms—despite reassurances and negative test results—is a hallmark of heightened health anxiety.

• **Self-monitoring.** Have you gained (or lost) another pound since yesterday? Your blood pressure was OK this morning, but now you feel tense—maybe you ought to take it again? People with elevated health anxiety feel compelled to excessively monitor their health.

• **Gathering information.** Reading self-help books and/or scanning newspapers and magazines for information on your "problem"—these behaviors can take up increasing amounts of time but fail to ease your health worries. Using the Internet to research can create its own set of problems.

All of these activities can be helpful—in moderation. Of course, you should see your doctor for an annual checkup and have unusual, prolonged or intense symptoms checked out. It's also fine to read up on health news and sometimes seek out second opinions.

But when is it too much? If you're doing the same things over and over again and it never seems to put your worries to rest, you are most likely engaging in unhelpful, repetitive safety behaviors. The only real solution is to simply stop them. Don't ask friends for reassurance. Don't repeat medical tests on the off-chance that negative results were a mistake or make a habit of seeking multiple medical opinions when your doctor says it isn't necessary.

If you have health anxiety, it will be a struggle to overcome such habits and you'll experience more anxiety than usual for a while. The best thing to do when the anxiety kicks in is to challenge your anxious thoughts and wait it out, rather than falling into old habits of seeking reassurance. If your anxiety is affecting your day-to-day life, seeking professional help, such as cognitive behavioral therapy or taking medications to reduce anxiety, may be useful. But if you can hold out, it does get easier over time.

CONQUERING CYBERCHONDRIA

As stated earlier, the Internet is a great source of health information—but it also can fuel health anxiety.

Important finding: A survey by researchers at Microsoft found that more than one-third of those who searched for medical information online said that it made them feel more anxious some of the time.

What's more, 90% of those surveyed reported times when their searches "escalated"—they started out with a general medical question and proceeded to research serious illnesses. One in five people reported that this happened frequently.

It's easy to see why. Information is often presented on the Internet in a way that fuels the thought patterns that promote hypochondria, such as overestimating the probability of a particular condition.

Examples: An online search for "headache" found "brain tumor" on 26% of sites—the same proportion that mentioned "caffeine withdrawal." Yet while headaches are common, a brain tumor occurs in only one of every 10,000 Americans.

What's more, because there's no quality control on the Internet, even a slick, professionally produced Web site may be filled with misinformation and highlight frightening reports. A person who has complications with a colonoscopy, for example, is more likely to write about it online than the thousands for whom the procedure goes well. *To protect yourself from cyberchondria...*

- **Keep Internet information in perspective.** Bear in mind that it may be biased toward dramatic, if rare, conditions and mishaps.

- **Don't research symptoms online.** Once you've been given a diagnosis, use the Internet to educate yourself so that you can participate intelligently in decisions about treatment. But be careful and skeptical. Don't believe everything you read. If you find that you're spending more and more time searching health topics online and it magnifies your anxiety, stay away from it altogether—unless you have a specific diagnosis.

- **Be highly selective online.** Internet sites published by government health agencies, major medical institutions, nonprofit foundations or professional medical organizations are most likely to have reliable information. But, again, use them only when you really need to.

Good choices: National Institutes of Health, *www.nih.gov*...National Library of Medicine, *www.medlineplus.gov*...National Cancer Institute, *www.cancer.gov*...American Heart Association, *www.heart.org*...Cleveland Clinic, *www.clevelandclinic.org*...Mayo Clinic, *www.mayoclinic.org*...and MD Anderson Cancer Center, *www.mdanderson.org*.

How to Get Exactly What You Need From Your Doctor

Robert M. Arnold, MD, professor and director of palliative care services and the Leo H. Criep chair in patient care at the University of Pittsburgh School of Medicine. His research focuses on helping doctors communicate better with patients with life-threatening illnesses. He has written numerous articles for professional journals, including *The Journal of the American Medical Association* and *Annals of Internal Medicine*.

How many times have you left a doctor's appointment and realized that you forgot to ask an important question or didn't fully understand your physician's instructions?

It happens to everyone. Fortunately, there are simple steps you can take to avoid the common mistakes that keep you from getting exactly what you need at the doctor's office...

Mistake 1: **Making your list too long.** Most people know to write down their concerns and bring the list to their appointment. But many people make the mistake of trying to include every question they may have. The average doctor's appointment lasts only about 15 minutes, so you'll probably get to cover only a few issues in a single appointment.

What works best: Edit your list, and be sure that the problems that trouble you the most are the ones you bring up first. If you can't decide what's most important, hand your list to your doctor and say, "I'd like you to help me figure out which of these we should discuss today." If you believe all the issues are crucial, consider booking a double appointment, but be aware that insurance may not cover the extra cost.

Mistake 2: **Diagnosing, not describing.** If you tell your doctor that you have "neuropathic pain," he/she will have no idea whether you are knowledgeable enough to make that judgment. Instead, be descriptive. Say, "I have burning pain, numbness and tingling." What helps doctors make the best diagnosis is your data—unfiltered. Even if another doctor has given you a diagnosis, describe your problem to your current doctor in your own words.

What works best: Think like a reporter. Interview yourself before your appointment, and write down your answers. When did the problem start? How does it feel? Where does it hurt? What makes it better? What makes it worse?

Mistake 3: **Being on a different page from the person who accompanies you to your visit.** As we all know, bringing a friend or family member to your appointment can help you remember crucial information and remind you of details you wanted to share with your doctor. But if your companion's agenda is different from yours, it can interfere with your care.

What works best: Let your companion know ahead of time what your goals are for the visit and how he can help you reach them. Also ask about his concerns, and if he has questions for the doctor, tell that to the doctor at the beginning of the appointment.

Mistake 4: **Letting your doctor cut you off.** The widely publicized studies that showed doctors interrupt patients within 18 seconds are misleading. The researchers counted anything the doctor said—including "uh-huh" or "go on"—as interruptions. That said, doctors often don't let patients finish, mostly because they are thinking ahead to what the problem might be and they jump in with questions.

What works best: Say, "What I need to tell you will take only about another 30 seconds. May I finish telling you what's going on? Then I'll answer your questions." Similarly, some doctors appear distracted—for example, he may be talking to you and taking notes on the computer at the same time. Of course, you do want him to take good notes, but if you're truly bothered, you can move your chair or otherwise position yourself so the doctor can see you and the screen. Or simply say, "You know, doctor, having your full attention would really help me."

Mistake 5: **Thinking your doctor is "dismissing" you.** Sometimes your doctor won't agree with you. If you think that you have a certain condition but he doesn't agree, don't assume that he hasn't considered what you said. It probably just means that based on your symptoms and his experience, he disagrees.

What works best: Ask yourself if your theory about your ailment could be wrong and what harm there would be in trying your doctor's advice. If you don't want to take the chance or still believe the doctor was dismissive of your concern, get a second opinion.

Mistake 6: **Not being completely honest.** In an ideal world, patients would be comfortable telling their doctors anything, but in reality, some things are embarrassing. Doctors know this—that's why many will say things like, "How are you doing with your medicines? It must be hard to remember to take them all." This is their way of letting you know it's OK to be honest.

What works best: Be straight with your doctor about your habits—good and bad. If you say you're taking your blood pressure medicine and your blood pressure is still high, the doctor may increase the dose or add another drug. That's bad because it may expose you unnecessarily to side effects.

But if you are honest and tell your doctor that you haven't been taking the medication as directed, you can talk to him about the reason. Maybe you can't afford a certain drug or it's causing side effects. In many cases, there are alternatives that will work for you.

Mistake 7: **Forgetting the wrap-up.** At the end of every doctor's appointment, summarize the conversation and be sure that you understand what to expect and what your next steps are.

What works best: Write down what's new from your appointment. Are there new medicines? How will you know if they are working? Do you need tests? How do you schedule them? And always ask, "When do you want to see me again?"

Mistake 8: **Being afraid to "break up" with your doctor.** It's important to find a doctor who fits your personality. But in order to do that, you must know yourself and your needs. Do you want a doctor who's always on time and is all about the facts? Or is it more important that your doctor be soothing and responsive to your emotional needs? Should he be someone who worries about unusual things and will order tests that other doctors normally wouldn't?

What works best: Ask friends or family for recommendations, but realize that it often takes a visit or two to find out if you're in sync with a particular doctor. If not, don't be embarrassed to move on to someone else. It's OK to say: "I like you, but I think I need a doctor who is more like X. Can you recommend someone?" Most doctors know their colleagues well enough to give you the right referral.

Don't Die of a Misdiagnosis

Joe Graedon, MS, consumer advocate and cofounder of The People's Pharmacy, based in Durham, North Carolina. He first published the book *The People's Pharmacy* in 1976 with his wife, Teresa Graedon, PhD. Since then, they have written "The People's Pharmacy," a syndicated newspaper column discussing issues related to drugs, herbs and vitamins. One of their most recent books is *Top Screwups Doctors Make and How to Avoid Them* (Crown Archetype).

Millions of patients each year are misdiagnosed and treated for the wrong disease. A report in *The Journal of the American Medical Association* estimated that between 40,000 and 80,000 hospital deaths a year in the US are due to misdiagnosis. In autopsy studies, researchers have found that doctors misdiagnosed illnesses between 20% and 40% of the time.

WHAT GOES WRONG?

According to the International Disease-Classification System, there are more than 13,600 possible diagnoses. It's impossible for any human being to consider—or even remember—that many possibilities.

Medical students are taught to play the odds—to think of the most obvious diagnosis rather than something more rare. This approach is useful for narrowing the list of possibilities, but it invariably means that some conditions will be overlooked.

Example: For a sore throat, your doctor probably will tell you to wait it out. Or if the pain is extremely severe, he/she might recommend a rapid throat culture to test for strep throat.

However, there is another bacterial infection that is at least as common as strep throat but not as well-known called F-throat (the organism is F. necrophorum). It doesn't show up on rapid-culture tests. It doesn't respond to the same antibiotics, and it can be much more dangerous.

Why do doctors miss it? Because they aren't looking for it.

HOW TO PROTECT YOURSELF

Here's what you can do to help your doctor diagnose you properly...

- **Encourage your doctor to repeat what you've said.** Studies have shown that doctors tend to listen to patients for only 18 seconds or less before interrupting. Much of what patients say after that is overlooked or ignored.

A doctor who doesn't listen may miss important information about symptoms, the history of the problem, etc. To make sure this doesn't happen, ask your doctor to repeat back all of the key information. This allows you to verify that nothing important has been confused or left out. A nice way to say this is, "Doctor, can you please summarize what I have told you? I want to make sure that I didn't forget anything important."

- **Ask, "How sure are you about the diagnosis?"** You always should ask this question. Doctors routinely take a mental shortcut known as anchoring. They quickly latch onto an idea about what's causing your symptoms. Once this occurs, they stop thinking about other possibilities.

Example: In the book *How Doctors Think*, Dr. Jerome Groopman recounts a case in which a woman went to the emergency room because of a fever and difficulty breathing. The ER doctor had recently treated dozens of patients with pneumonia and assumed that she had the same thing. The doctor anchored this conclusion even though tests didn't indicate pneumonia. It turned out that the woman's symptoms were due to an aspirin overdose, a possibility that the doctor hadn't considered.

Asking the doctor to confirm his confidence in the diagnosis provides an opportunity for him to at least consider other possibilities.

- **Ask, "Could something else be causing my symptoms?"** This is another important question that pushes the doctor to keep an open mind. Make sure that your doctor takes at least some time to consider other conditions that could be causing your symptoms.

- **Prioritize your discussion.** In many HMOs and other busy practices, doctors try to limit patient visits to as little as seven minutes. That's not enough time to hear a patient's whole story and discuss diagnostic possibilities, tests, medications, etc.

Before you arrive at the doctor's office, jot down a list of your most important issues. It might include new symptoms, where in your body you've experienced discomfort, when the problem started, etc.

In a short office visit, you'll be lucky to get the doctor's undivided attention for the top three issues, let alone more than that, so it's important to discuss the most important issue first.

Example: If you're having chest discomfort, don't start the discussion by talking about knee pain.

If you have a lot to discuss, you may also want to let your doctor know this at the start of the visit.

- **Follow up on tests.** One study found that doctors mistakenly failed to report abnormal test results to patients one out of 14 times. In some practices, about 25% of abnormal reports aren't passed on to patients.

Failing to tell patients about unusual results can be dangerous or even deadly. Terry, my wife and colleague, had a glucose-tolerance test because her doctor suspected that her fatigue was due to a form of hypoglycemia. The doctor never called back, so we assumed that the test was normal. It was not. She only discovered this months later when another physician looked at her chart and saw the test result.

Important: If your doctor orders tests, ask the doctor—or the nurse or lab technician—when the results will be ready. Call then and ask about the results and for a written report.

- **Always get a second opinion if you've been diagnosed with something serious or if your doctor is uncertain about the diagnosis.** A second opinion often differs significantly from the first diagnosis—so sometimes a third opinion is needed before you can make a wise decision about treatment.

Example: We knew a young woman who had a suspicious-looking mole. The biopsy report said that it was the very serious skin cancer melanoma, and she was scheduled for surgery immediately. Her parents insisted that she get a second opinion. A leading expert looked at the biopsy and concluded that it was not melanoma but a benign growth and that surgery was not necessary. A third opinion confirmed the second opinion.

Getting additional opinions saved her from unnecessary worry and an unnecessary surgery.

How to Get an Oncologist Appointment

Marjory Abrams, president, *BottomLine* newsletters, Boardroom Inc., 281 Tresser Blvd., Stamford, Connecticut 06901.

In a recent study conducted by the University of Pennsylvania Perelman School of Medicine, researchers contacted cancer centers around the US posing as people with newly diagnosed, inoperable liver cancer. Though the condition merits timely treatment, a mere 22% of the callers received appointments—and often only after multiple calls. The others were turned down because of referral requirements and other reasons... or never reached a scheduler. This confirms what friends have told me—you can leave lots of messages for doctors and never get a call back.

Consumer health advocate Charles Inlander wasn't surprised by the data. He advises asking the diagnosing physician to make an appointment for you—preferably right after the diagnosis, while you still are in the room. Specialists get patients through referrals, and they don't want to antagonize the people who send business their way.

If you do end up having to make an appointment yourself, Inlander suggests calling the chief of oncology at the nearest hospital. You may not be able to reach him/her personally, but ask the assistant for a referral to one of the oncologists. Then call that oncologist's office and say, "Dr. X, the chief of oncology at Hospital Y, asked that I call to set up an appointment as soon as possible."

Another tactic to get an earlier appointment is to ask to be put on the cancellation list. About 10% to 20% of all appointments get canceled or changed each week. Also, call on Mondays around 10 am to see if there are any cancellations for the week. Most cancellation calls come in after the weekend when the office has been closed.

Is Your Doctor Suffering From Burnout?

Robert M. Stark, MD, preventive cardiologist and internist in private practice in Greenwich, Connecticut. He is also an adjunct assistant professor of medicine at New York Medical College in Valhalla, New York, and medical director of the Cardiovascular Prevention Program at Greenwich Hospital (affiliated with the Yale New Haven Health Heart Institute). A Fellow of the American College of Cardiology, Dr. Stark has written on burnout in physicians and served as media expert for the *Psychology Today* blog on the topic "On Being a Physician."

The word "burnout" probably calls to mind air-traffic controllers, emergency room personnel and other people who work at a rapid pace under relentless pressure. But burnout also strikes people you might not expect—like your doctor. And this could be very hazardous to your health.

A MEDICAL EPIDEMIC

Exact statistics are hard to come by, but repeated studies in the US, Canada and Europe have found symptoms of burnout in 40% to 60% of doctors. And no one is exempt—the problem affects doctors who are fresh out of medical school and old-timers...generalists and specialists...men and women.

Shocking finding: A 2011 study published in *Archives of Surgery* found that one of every 16 surgeons in the US had thought about suicide in the prior year—often due to burnout. *Burnout has three main characteristics...*

- **Emotional and physical exhaustion.** The stress of work and its demands on attention and energy leave the sufferer mentally drained and often physically fatigued.
- **Depersonalization.** Those who are approaching burnout may feel detached from themselves and others. They begin to see people less as individuals and may show a lack of enthusiasm and perform their work in a more impersonal manner.
- **Lack of a sense of achievement.** Burnout robs people of the satisfaction they need from their work. They may believe that they're doing a poor job or that their work is less meaningful than they would like.

Why has physician burnout increased so much in recent years? Many experts believe that the rapid changes in the health-care system are largely to blame.

For example, doctors have less control over their work than they once did—a known risk factor for burnout. They may be unable to order certain tests or use treatments that they believe their patients need because an HMO or insurer has said "no."

Pressed by managed care systems to see more patients in less time, doctors are often working harder and faster—overwork is another risk factor for burnout—and are unable to practice medicine in the way they feel is best. The threat of malpractice lawsuits, pressure to rein in costs and more frequent Medicare/Medicaid audits also add to the stress.

BURNOUT TAKES ITS TOLL

Burnout doesn't affect only the doctor, it can impact the patient as well. A 2010 study of 188 primary care physicians published in the journal *Family Practice* found that on days when doctors felt anxious, fatigued and stressed, they wrote more prescriptions and ordered more tests (some of them unnecessary, the researchers suggested) and spent less time talking with patients. More errors in diagnosis and treatment also have been linked to physicians who suffer from burnout than among doctors who do not, according to research.

Less easily measured, but at least as important, is the impact on the doctor-patient relationship. A common consequence of burnout is loss of empathy—the doctor's ability to care about others, including his patients. It shows up in lapses in attention and failure to respond with displays of concern when patients express worry or distress.

This lack of feeling on the doctor's part affects the patient's care because a person who senses that his doctor is listening sympathetically is likely to go into more detail about symptoms and other problems such as side effects of drugs. A doctor's apparent lack of empathy can mean this information is withheld by patients, often leading to errors in diagnosis and treatment.

IS YOUR DOCTOR BURNED OUT?

The signs of burnout can be missed if you're not looking for them—even in a longtime family doctor whom you feel you know well. *Be alert for these red flags...*

- **Shorter office visits could mean your doctor is under increased financial and insurance company pressure or simply overeager to get through the day.**

One tip-off: If visits used to last, say, 15 minutes, but your doctor now heads for the door in five, something may be amiss.

- **An air of distraction suggests that the doctor is having difficulty maintaining focus.** This could lead to cutting corners in decision-making and making snap judgments.

One tip-off: Is your doctor quicker than he/she used to be in diagnosing your health problem?

- **Lack of empathy due to burnout may be apparent if you tell your doctor about something that's worrying you.**

One tip-off: Your doctor may fail to express concern and probe further if you reveal that you're, say, having marital difficulties. If he just goes on to the next topic—and says something like "and how is your stomach doing?"—then he may be suffering from burnout.

It's harder to recognize burnout in a specialist you're seeing for the first time, but just as important. You need him to be alert and fully involved when dealing with a problem that demands expert care.

Main clue: Does the specialist know who you are and why you're there, what tests have been done and what treatments have been tried? Your regular doctor should have sent information about you along with lab and radiology results—has the specialist taken the time to look at them?

HOW TO LOOK FOR ANSWERS

If you suspect burnout in your doctor, what should you do? There's always the option of finding another doctor. But if it's someone you've been seeing for years and know to be essentially competent and compassionate, such a switch may not be best for you or your doctor.

Ask your doctor: "How are you? Is everything OK?" You may learn that today's inattention is due to the kind of passing stress or disruption that can affect anyone, such as a poor night's sleep or an office crisis. Or you may get an inkling that problems run deeper.

At the very least, showing your concern will strengthen your relationship and may even encourage him to recognize that pressure and stress are taking their toll. This may well help to persuade him to do some introspection, consult with a colleague or seek needed help. If your visits continue to leave you dissatisfied, however, it may be time to look for a new doctor.

Don't Forget Your Nurse

Rebecca Shannonhouse, editor, *Bottom Line/Health*, Boardroom Inc., 281 Tresser Blvd., Stamford, Connecticut 06901.

Nurses are the health-care professionals most likely to help prevent the 44,000 to 98,000 deaths that occur in hospitals every year because of medical errors, according to the Institute of Medicine. If a doctor writes an incorrect drug dose or schedules you for the wrong test, nurses are in the best position to catch the mistake.

Unfortunately, heavy workloads and inadequate staffing make their jobs difficult. A survey of 2,203 nurses found that 92% say they're unable to spend enough time with patients to provide optimal care.

But patients can help nurses help them, I was told by Dorie Byers, RN, a clinical instructor at the Indiana University School of Nursing in Indianapolis. One important—but often overlooked—way to do this is to engage nurses. *Here's how...*

- **Get personal.** Nurses are trained to treat everyone the same, but you'll get more attentive care when you're not just another face. Introduce yourself to the nurses—and get to know them.

Also helpful: Introduce frequent visitors—your spouse, children, etc.—to the nurses. You'll get better care when everyone is working together.

- **Ask how you can help them.** Nurses love it when patients do things for themselves that their condition permits. An assertive, can-do attitude will earn respect from all the members of your health-care team.
- **Ask detailed questions about drug doses, tests, etc.** Nurses enjoy using their knowledge, particularly when it helps them catch errors that others might have missed.

Lesson: Don't be passive. Patients who take the initiative tend to have better health outcomes.

A Bigger, Better MRI

Rebecca Shannonhouse, editor, *Bottom Line/Health*, Boardroom Inc., 281 Tresser Blvd., Stamford, Connecticut 06901.

A good friend of mine recently had an MRI, and it was definitely not a pleasant experience!

It's true that magnetic resonance imaging (MRI) can reveal tumors and other abnormalities with tremendous clarity, often at a very early stage. However, up to 30% of people who undergo MRIs experience some degree of anxiety and/or claustrophobia.

If you or a loved one needs an MRI but is anxious about the procedure, ask whether the imaging center has a large-bore machine, suggests James Borgstede, MD, a radiologist at the University of Colorado Hospital in Aurora.

These machines, which produce high-quality images, can be used to diagnose abnormalities in many parts of the body and have extra-large (more than two feet across) openings, which help patients with anxiety/claustrophobia feel less confined. The machines can also more easily accommodate obese individuals.

Other options...

- **Open-field MRIs are more spacious than traditional, tube-like models.** However, the image quality isn't as good and, as a result, may not be acceptable for all purposes.
- **Prism glasses, available at most centers, allow you to see out the opening** and watch a movie while lying on your back in a traditional machine. This is also useful for those who are claustrophobic.

Also helpful: Tell your doctor when scheduling your test if confined spaces make you nervous. That way, sedation can be used to ease your discomfort.

Medical Tests and Treatments You Really Don't Need

Stephen R. Smith, MD, MPH, professor emeritus of family medicine and former associate dean of The Warren Alpert Medical School of Brown University in Providence. Based in New London, Connecticut, he is on the executive committee and board of directors of the National Physicians Alliance, a group of 22,000 members that advocates for affordable, evidence-based health care. *www.npalliance.org*

If you're like most people, you assume that you need the tests and treatments that your doctor orders.

But that's not always true. According to a report from the National Physicians Alliance, some of the most frequently used tests and treatments often are unnecessary—and may be harmful. Even the common PSA test to detect prostate cancer has come under scrutiny recently.

The excessive use of tests and treatments adds billions of dollars to the nation's spiraling health-care costs. And these can lead to further—and also unnecessary—testing if there's a false-positive, a reading that indicates an abnormality when everything actually is normal.

Why do doctors order questionable tests and treatments? One reason is habit. Doctors tend to do things the way they were taught in medical school even though new evidence shows that something isn't helpful. Also, many doctors practice "defensive medicine" to reduce the risk for lawsuits, assuming that a physician is unlikely to get sued for giving too much care.

If your doctor recommends any of the following tests and treatments, ask him/her whether they are really necessary and why...

UNNECESSARY TESTS

1. Imaging for low-back pain. Pain in the lower back is the fifth-most-common reason for doctor visits. Doctors routinely order MRIs of the lumbar spine when patients complain about back pain.

The problem: In the vast majority of cases, imaging tests are unnecessary. Low-back pain typically clears up without treatment in six weeks or less.

Exceptions: MRIs or other imaging tests may be needed for severe low-back pain or pain that lasts longer than six weeks...or when the symptoms include fever, incontinence, numbness and tingling.

2. Blood tests/urinalysis. When you have an annual exam, your doctor might order urine and/or blood tests. A urine test typically is used to check for diabetes. Blood chemistry panels are used to screen for diseases of the kidneys, liver and parathyroid gland, among many other things.

The problem: These tests rarely reveal anything in patients without symptoms who generally are healthy—and they often lead to false-positives.

Exceptions: Patients with specific symptoms—such as a persistent fever or tenderness in the abdomen—probably will need to have blood tests to determine the cause. A blood test also is recommended for checking cholesterol levels.

Urinalysis can be used to identify diabetes in patients who already have symptoms, such as frequent urination and/or increased thirst.

There may be other good reasons your doctor wants to order blood and/or urine tests, but he should be willing to explain to you exactly what those reasons are.

3. Cardiovascular screening. You don't need an annual electrocardiogram (EKG) if you don't have symptoms of, or risk factors for, heart disease (such as smoking, diabetes or a family history of cardiovascular disease).

The problem: Many doctors advise patients to have an EKG every year. My doctor used to recommend it for me, but in patients without symptoms, an EKG rarely reveals useful information. It may show a minor abnormality in the heartbeat that will lead to further tests, such as an echocardiogram or a stress test, even though these abnormalities rarely are important.

Exceptions: Patients who have been diagnosed with heart disease or who have significant risk factors for it probably will need an annual EKG or other cardiac tests.

4. Bone-density scan. More than 28 million Americans have osteoporosis, the leading cause of weak bones and fractures. A test called dual energy X-ray absorptiometry (DEXA) can detect bone weakness before a fracture occurs. This gives patients time to increase bone strength with exercise and vitamin D/calcium supplements.

The problem: The test doesn't make sense for younger patients with a low risk for osteoporosis. If you're a woman under age 65, you routinely should be taking calcium and vitamin D supplements and exercising to increase bone strength. The test itself won't change the treatment recommendations even if you test positive.

Exceptions: Women who are younger than 65 who have osteoporosis risk factors, such as smoking, a slight build, hyperthyroidism or a history of bone fractures, should have this test. So should men younger than age 70 with the same risk factors.

Women age 65 and older and men age 70 and older should have the DEXA screening even if they don't have risk factors. The DEXA test is important for these groups of people because they have a high risk for fractures and might benefit from medications.

UNNECESSARY TREATMENTS

• **Antibiotics for sinus infections.** Patients don't realize that any upper-respiratory infection, including a cold, will cause infection and inflammation throughout the area, including in the sinuses. They often ask their doctors for antibiotics to clear up postnasal drip, congestion or other sinus symptoms.

The problem: About 98% of sinus infections are caused by viruses. Antibiotics do nothing for viral infections. Even when a sinus infection is caused by bacteria, it usually will clear up without antibiotics.

Exception: Antibiotics should be considered for a sinus infection if the symptoms are severe, such as high fever and severe pain and tenderness over the sinuses. Antibiotics also should be considered when the symptoms last for one week, improve briefly and then get worse—this may indicate that a bacterial infection has developed on top of the initial viral infection.

• **Brand-name statins to lower cholesterol.** The statin class of medications is among the best ways to lower cholesterol and reduce the risk for heart attack and stroke among people who can't achieve these goals with diet and exercise. All statins have these benefits, including the generic versions.

The problem: Many doctors routinely prescribe expensive brand-name statins, such as Crestor or Lipitor, rather than the cheaper generics *lovastatin, simvastatin, pravastatin or atorvastatin.* A generic statin costs about $4 a month. A brand-name medication such as Lipitor, depending on the dose, costs about $150.

Between 75% and 80% of patients can achieve the recommended levels of LDL cholesterol (below 130 mg/dL is typical) by taking generic statins.

Not So Fast! When It Comes to CT Scans

Charles B. Inlander is a consumer advocate and health-care consultant based in Fogelsville, Pennsylvania. He was the founding president of the nonprofit People's Medical Society, a consumer advocacy organization credited with key improvements in the quality of US health care in the 1980s and 1990s, and is author of 20 books, including *Take This Book to the Hospital With You: A Consumer Guide to Surviving Your Hospital Stay* (St. Martin's).

During a recent visit to my primary care doctor, he suggested that I take a decongestant for the postnasal drip that I had been suffering—and he urged me to get a CT scan of my sinuses just to "cover all the bases." I promptly said "no"—I wanted to go only "one base at a time." It turned out that the pills worked, and I saved myself some unneeded radiation, not to mention hundreds of dollars in insurance copayments for the test.

Certainly, CT scans and PET scans, which may be used to detect extremely small tumors, have helped diagnose diseases at early stages in tens of millions of people and saved countless lives. But some scientists are becoming increasingly alarmed by the total amounts of radiation that many Americans are getting. This radiation comes from CT or PET scans (and, to a lesser extent, X-rays, which produce far less radiation) that are used to diagnose such conditions as tumors, fractures and blood clots, and radiation therapy that is used to treat certain diseases, including most types of cancer. In fact, a study published in *Archives of Internal Medicine* estimated that up to 15,000 people worldwide die each year as a result of cancers caused by medical radiation.

So should you refuse to get scans or X-rays? Of course not. *But there are some key questions you should ask before you agree to the test...*

• **Do I really need this scan?** Studies have reported that one-third of all radiation-producing tests are unnecessary.

My advice: Don't be afraid to talk to your doctor about taking it one step at a time. Or, if an imaging test is necessary, ask whether an MRI scan (magnetic resonance imaging uses magnets that produce no radiation) or ultrasound (which also produces no radiation) can be used.

• **Does the doctor own his/her own scanning machines?** Studies published in the journal *Health Affairs* have found that doctors who own their own CT or PET machines order far more scans than doctors who do not have a financial interest in this type of equipment. And the patients who receive these scans don't have better outcomes, on average, than those who don't get the tests.

My advice: Ask your doctor whether he has a financial interest in the scanning equipment. If so, consider getting a second opinion on your need for the test.

• **What's the age of the scanner?** Your reasonable goal should be to avoid exposure to any unnecessary medical radiation. Researchers recently noted that the average total dose of medical radiation that Americans are exposed to today is double what we received 30 years ago. What's more, older equipment emits a greater radiation dose per scan than that from newer machines.

My advice: Before you go to an imaging center, call and ask the radiologist or technician for the approximate age of their CT and PET machines. Try to go to centers that have equipment no more than eight to 10 years old.

The Stats on Scans

Doctors who own or lease MRI equipment order more scans for low-back pain. The scan rate is 13% higher for patients of orthopedists and 32% higher for patients of primary care doctors who own the machines, compared with the rate for patients of doctors who don't own or lease the equipment.

Caution: There is no strong evidence that an MRI for nonspecific low-back pain improves long-term patient outcomes.

Jacqueline Baras Shreibati, MD, resident physician, Stanford University School of Medicine, California, and leader of a study published in *Health Services Research*.

Cut Down Radiation Risk

There is a high radiation risk from post–heart attack cardiac imaging. Cancer risk rises with cumulative exposure to radiation from catheterization, angioplasty and nuclear scans—and some of these tests may not be necessary.

Self-defense: Ask your doctor which tests you really need.

Louise Pilote, MD, PhD, MPH, professor of medicine—James McGill Chair and director, division of general internal medicine, McGill University, Montreal. She led an analysis of data on 82,861 people, published in *Canadian Medical Association Journal*.

The Deadly Dangers of Off-Label Drugs

Randall S. Stafford, MD, PhD, director of the Program on Prevention Outcomes and Practices at the Stanford Prevention Research Center and associate professor of medicine at Stanford University. He is author or coauthor of more than 120 scientific papers—including several on studies of off-label drugs—that have appeared in *Annals of Internal Medicine, The New England Journal of Medicine, The Journal of the American Medical Association* and other leading medical journals.

At least 21% of prescriptions written by American doctors are written for medical conditions that the drugs have not been proven to treat. The prescriptions are "off-label," which means that the drugs are being used in ways that have not been formally tested or approved by the Food and Drug Administration (FDA) as safe and effective.

A drug also is considered off-label if it's used...

- **For a type of person that the drug has not been tested on** (such as children or the elderly).
- **At a dosage not approved by the FDA.**
- **By itself, when labeling specifies it should be used with other drugs.**
- **With other drugs, when labeling specifies it should be used alone.**

Key finding: A study in *Archives of Internal Medicine* showed that 73% of off-label prescriptions do not have good scientific evidence justifying their use.

OFF-LABEL, ON TRIAL

It is illegal for pharmaceutical companies to promote their drugs for off-label use, but billions of dollars in possible profits are a strong incentive to circumvent the law. In a study recently published in *PLoS Medicine*, researchers from Harvard Medical School analyzed 18 cases where drug companies were prosecuted for off-label marketing that resulted in $7.9 billion in judgments against the companies.

The researchers found that the drug companies tried to expand the use of the drugs to unapproved diseases...to unapproved disease subtypes (such as prescribing an antidepressant for mild depression when it has been approved only for severe depression)...and to unapproved drug doses.

They also found that the drug companies used marketing schemes to influence doctors, including "direct financial incentives" (85% of the time)..."self-serving presentations" of the scientific literature about the drug (76%)...sponsorships of teaching (54%) and research (20%)...and free drug samples (20%).

In other words, doctors were essentially being bribed and duped by drug companies to prescribe drugs off-label.

My colleagues and I conducted research to identify the most problematic off-label drugs, publishing the results in *Pharmacotherapy*. *Each of the riskiest drugs had one or more of the following problems...*

1. It lacked scientific evidence for off-label use.

2. It raised safety concerns.

3. It was newer to the marketplace, meaning that rare or long-term adverse effects were less likely to be known.

4. It cost more than FDA-approved drugs for the same problem.

5. It was marketed heavily by drug companies.

Most of these drugs fall into three classes of medications...

ATYPICAL ANTIPSYCHOTICS

This new generation of medicines is now the top-selling class of drugs in the US, replacing cholesterol-lowering agents as number one. They're called "atypical" to distinguish them from older antipsychotics. The drugs are approved to treat the psychosis of schizophrenia and bipolar disorder.

Main off-label uses: In 2008, there were nine million off-label prescriptions written for antipsychotic drugs in the US, more than double the amount in 1995. They are used for a wide range of psychiatric conditions, including the behavioral problems of dementia, such as severe agitation (the most common use)... depression...long-term maintenance in bipolar disorder (the drugs are approved only for short-term use)...obsessive-compulsive disorder...and post-traumatic stress disorder (PTSD).

Biggest risks: With long-term use, the drugs tend to cause weight gain and the subsequent development of type 2 diabetes. And in the elderly with dementia, they are linked to an increased incidence of heart problems and a higher death rate.

The drugs: *Quetiapine* (Seroquel), *risperidone* (Risperdal), *olanzapine* (Zyprexa), *aripiprazole* (Abilify) and *ziprasidone* (Geodon).

Shocking finding: Researchers in the department of psychiatry at the University of Pennsylvania studied 2,597 people with Parkinson's disease and psychosis (hallucinations and delusional thinking), a common symptom of the disease. Fifty percent of the patients were prescribed antipsychotic drugs. Of those, most received off-label atypical antipsychotics—in spite of the fact that there are no scientific studies showing that the prescribed drugs work for psychosis in Parkinson's...that two of the drugs (Zyprexa and Risperdal) have been shown to worsen Parkinson's symptoms...and that there is a "black box" warning on these antipsychotics alerting doctors that they increase the risk for death in those patients who have been studied. Less than 2% of the patients received *clozapine* (Clozaril)—an older atypical antipsychotic that scientific studies show does improve psychosis in Parkinson's. The study was reported in the July 2011 issue of *Archives of Neurology*.

ANTIDEPRESSANTS

This is another top-selling class of drugs, approved for major depression and a few other conditions.

Main off-label uses: In a study of Medicaid patients, 75% of prescriptions for antidepressants were off-label. Off-label uses include treating mild depression (dysthymia)...bipolar disorder...insomnia...hot flashes...urinary incontinence and bladder infections...diabetic neuropathy...and chronic pain.

Biggest risks: Antidepressants don't pose the same level of health risk as antipsychotics. But while they may have a low risk of harming you, there is little scientific evidence showing that their off-label use helps the conditions for which they are being prescribed. Why spend money on a drug with potential side effects and no proven benefit?

The drugs: *Escitalopram* (Lexapro), *bupropion* (Wellbutrin), *sertraline* (Zoloft), *venlafaxine* (Effexor) and *duloxetine* (Cymbalta).

ANTISEIZURE DRUGS

These drugs are approved to treat epilepsy.

Main off-label uses: They're commonly prescribed for chronic pain—in fact, they're often used without making certain that other approaches have been tried.

Biggest risks: When an off-label drug replaces approved therapies for chronic pain and when there's evidence that the pharmaceutical industry is promoting that particular use, then there's a serious question as to whether that drug is the best treatment for chronic pain.

The drugs: *Gabapentin* (Neurontin) and *pregabalin* (Lyrica).

QUESTIONS TO ASK YOUR DOCTOR

If you or a family member is prescribed an antipsychotic, antidepressant or antiseizure drug, ask your doctor the following question...

- **Could you give me more background on the evidence that this drug will work for the condition I have and be beneficial for me?**

Best answer: The drug is FDA-approved for the condition and has been recommended by an expert group based on a review of the available scientific literature.

If that's not the answer, consider other treatment options.

Also, many doctors tend to prescribe new, expensive, brand-name drugs over tried-and-true drugs.

Example: The newer diabetes drug *sitagliptin* (Januvia) is often prescribed over the generic drug *metformin*—even though Januvia has not been proven to work better than metformin.

This practice is widespread for both off-label and FDA-approved drugs, so ask your doctor...

- **What's the rationale for putting me on this expensive new drug?**

Best answer: The newer drug was proven in clinical studies to work better than the older drug. (This is rarely the case.) If that's not the answer, consider the older, safer, proven drug.

WHEN OFF-LABEL IS GOOD

There are several situations where off-label drugs may be helpful: Your doctor has tried FDA approved drugs for your condition and they haven't worked...or there are no approved drugs for your condition. Using an off-label drug allows the doctor to explore other options that might work. The drug is moving through the process of FDA approval for your condition. An off-label prescription for that drug gives you early access to a valuable medication.

Common Medication Mistakes Can Be Deadly

Matthew Grissinger, RPh, director of Error Reporting Programs at the Institute for Safe Medication Practices. He is clinical analyst for the Pennsylvania Patient Safety and Reporting System and served on the US Pharmacopeia's Safe Medication Use Expert Committee. He is adjunct assistant professor at Temple University School of Pharmacy and clinical assistant professor for the University of the Sciences, both in Philadelphia. *www.consumermedsafety.org*

Nearly two million Americans are hurt every year by the medication mistakes of others, such as being given the wrong drug or the wrong dose. But this total includes only the errors that are caused by doctors or in hospitals. It doesn't include the mistakes that many of us make on our own, such as forgetting to take a pill or accidentally double dosing.

Thankfully, most of these errors are not fatal, but they can be. Common mistakes—and how to avoid them...

Mistake: Taking two different products with the same ingredient. Suppose that you normally take *acetaminophen* several times a day to reduce pain from arthritis. Each dose contains 325 milligrams (mg). Then you get a cold. So you take an over-the-counter cold remedy such as NyQuil. Many cold medications contain about 650 mg of acetaminophen per dose.

You could wind up getting 2,500 mg of acetaminophen from several doses of the cold remedy...in addition to the acetaminophen that you're taking for arthritis. You could exceed the maximum safe dose of 4,000 mg a day without even knowing it.

Self-protection: Always read labels. Don't take any medication without knowing what it contains. Many have more than one active ingredient. If a new medication contains an ingredient that you're already taking, ask your doctor or pharmacist if the combined dose is safe.

Also, drugs can have similar actions even if the active ingredients are different. Some antidepressants, for example, lower blood pressure as a side effect. Your pressure could drop too low if you're also taking medication for hypertension. Again, never take any combination of drugs without consulting your doctor first.

Mistake: Assuming two doses are better than one. Many people think that more is better. For example, if one dose of a painkiller gives some relief, they tell themselves that a double dose will be even more effective.

Not true. For example, you'll get the same relief from 400 mg of *ibuprofen* (the usual adult dose for mild-to-moderate pain), taken every four to six hours, as you would from one dose of 800 mg—with less risk for side effects.

Most of the common painkillers, such as aspirin and ibuprofen, take time to work. You might not notice much improvement in the first hour or two. After that, the medication gets more effective as it changes your body's chemistry. Be patient.

Self-protection: Take the recommended dose for at least a few days. If your problem still isn't under control, ask your doctor if you should take a higher dose—or if another painkiller might be more effective.

Mistake: Missing a dose. Everyone forgets to take medication sometimes. It rarely matters, particularly if a drug is used for treating a long-term condition such as hypertension or high cholesterol. Just take your next scheduled dose.

Exception: Medication that you need for an acute problem, such as an infection. If you're taking an antibiotic four times daily and you miss the morning dose, you usually can take a double dose at lunchtime, then return to the normal schedule.

But check with your doctor or pharmacist because doubling up is dangerous with some medications.

Examples: Patients taking Coumadin, a blood thinner, could experience excessive bleeding if they take a double dose. With blood pressure drugs, you could suffer from hypotension, pressure that falls too low.

Self-protection: When you get a new prescription, ask your doctor or pharmacist what to do if you miss a dose. The rules are different depending on the medication.

Mistake: Using a regular spoon to measure medications. People routinely use kitchen spoons to measure their liquid medications. Don't do it. A study in *Annals of Internal Medicine* found that participants who used kitchen spoons to measure medications wound up taking either too much or too little.

Self-protection: Some liquid or powder medications are packaged with a measuring device, such as a graduated cap. These devices are far more accurate than a kitchen spoon. Or you can buy dosing syringes or other appropriate measuring devices at pharmacies.

Mistake: Unsafe splitting. In an effort to save money, many patients ask their doctors to prescribe a higher-strength pill, which they split in two to get the correct dose.

This isn't necessarily a bad idea. The cost of a 5-mg dose usually is about the same as you would pay for 10 mg. You'll probably get the right dose if the pill is scored for easy cutting. But if it is not scored for cutting and you cut it anyway, you could get uneven doses.

Self-protection: To split tablets that are hard, very small or have an unusual shape, use a pill splitter, available at pharmacies. They have sharp blades and are designed to hold pills in the correct position when cut.

Never split or separate capsules—and don't split medications that have a time-release mechanism. Breaking the coating could cause the medication to be absorbed too quickly—or even, in some cases, not absorbed at all.

Mistake: Buying or taking the wrong drug. This happens more often than you might think. Name confusion is among the most common types of drug errors. The US Pharmacopeia, an organization that sets drug standards, estimates that more than 1,400 commonly used medications have names that are so similar that people often confuse them.

Examples: It would be easy to confuse the osteoporosis medication Fosamax with Flomax (used to treat an enlarged prostate gland). Are you supposed to take Lamictal to prevent seizures or Lamisil to treat a fungal infection? Even names that don't sound alike, such as Avandia and Coumadin, may look similar on handwritten prescriptions.

Self-protection: Know the correct name of every drug that you're taking and why you're taking it. Never take pills in a dark room.

Helpful: When your doctor is writing a prescription, ask him/her to jot a note on the prescription saying what the drug is for. If the prescription is for Coumadin, for example, the note might read "to thin the blood." The pharmacist will be less likely to make a mistake. Also, confirm with the pharmacist what the drug is for when you pick up your prescription.

Prescription Errors

Computerized prescriptions are not always accurate. More than 10% of computer-generated prescriptions that were printed or faxed to a pharmacy contained errors, according to a review of 3,850 computerized prescriptions received over four weeks. About one-third of these computerized errors could have caused potentially serious side effects.

Self-defense: Carefully review your prescriptions, and talk to your physician or pharmacist if you suspect that anything is amiss.

Karen C. Nanji, MD, MPH, resident physician, department of anesthesia, critical care and pain medicine, Massachusetts General Hospital, Boston.

Swallow Pills More Easily

Before putting the pill in your mouth, take a deep breath and exhale to help you relax and reduce your gag reflex. Swallow some water, then place the pill far back on your tongue, and swallow it with another sip of water. Don't throw your head back when swallowing—it is better to tilt it forward and toward your chest. If you still have trouble—and if your doctor and pharmacist say it is OK—open capsules or crush pills and add to applesauce, chocolate pudding or other foods that go down easily. Or ask if there are easier-to-swallow versions available, such as liquids, powders or chewables.

UC Berkeley Wellness Letter, 500 Fifth Ave., New York City 10110. *www.wellnessletter.com*

OTC Alert

Painkillers may make antidepressants less effective. Selective serotonin reuptake inhibitor (SSRI) antidepressants, such as *fluoxetine* (Prozac) and *citalopram* (Celexa), are 25% less effective when the patient also is taking a painkiller, such as *acetaminophen* (Tylenol), *ibuprofen* (Advil) or aspirin. Talk to your doctor about switching to another type of antidepressant, such as *amitriptyline* (Elavil) or *buproprion* (Wellbutrin) if you take painkillers regularly, for example, for arthritis.

Jennifer Warner-Schmidt, PhD, research associate in Dr. Paul Greengard's Laboratory of Molecular and Cellular Neuroscience, The Rockefeller University, New York City, and leader of a study published in *Proceedings of the National Academy of Sciences.*

Walking Reduces Hospital Stays

Recent finding: Hospital patients who were mobile and who walked around their rooms or wards at least once a day shortened their hospital stays by an average of one day, compared with patients who remained in bed or seated. Patients who started walking the same day they were hospitalized had even shorter stays.

Efrat Shadmi, PhD, department of nursing, University of Haifa, Israel, and leader of a study of 485 people age 70 and older, published in *Archives of Internal Medicine.*

Steroid Concern

Oral steroids may lead to vitamin D deficiency. These anti-inflammatory medicines, such as *prednisone* and *dexamethasone*, often are prescribed for asthma, certain types of arthritis and autoimmune diseases such as lupus and multiple sclerosis.

If you take steroids: Have your doctor check your vitamin D level regularly. Vitamin D deficiency can lead to softening of bones, muscle pain and other health problems.

Amy L. Skversky, MD, assistant professor of pediatrics, Albert Einstein College of Medicine, New York City, and leader of an analysis of data on 22,650 people, published in *The Journal of Clinical Endocrinology & Metabolism.*

Seniors at Risk

Home health care has been linked to unsafe medication use.

Recent study: A review of 3,124 adults ages 65 and older receiving home health care (from visiting nurses, for example) found that nearly 40% were taking at least one drug considered inappropriate for seniors—twice as high as older adults who did not receive home health care.

Possible reason: Home-health-care patients tend to take more drugs than similarly aged adults. These drugs are often prescribed by a variety of doctors, with little coordination regarding the drugs taken by a patient.

Yuhua Bao, PhD, assistant professor of public health, Weill Cornell Medical College, New York City.

Age Matters

A recent study of more than 3,500 operations found that surgeons who were between ages 35 and 50 had better results than younger and older colleagues.

BMJ.com

Paging Dr. Mozart...

Doctors who listen to Mozart when performing colonoscopies are more likely to find precancerous polyps.

Possible reason: Previous research shows that listening to Mozart's music boosts spatial skills needed to perform colonoscopies.

American College of Gastroenterology.

Hospital Self-Defense

Print your name on a large piece of brightly colored poster board, and hang it over your hospital bed so that everyone who enters can easily identify you. Bring antiseptic wipes or sprays, and use them from time to time on everything you touch. Bring shoes or slippers with rubber soles to use when walking to the bathroom or into the hall. Take a cell phone programmed with the number for the hospital's front desk or emergency department—if you need urgent help and your call button does not produce a response, you can use the phone.

Trisha Torrey, hospital advocate, Baldwinsville, New York, and author of *You Bet Your Life! The 10 Mistakes Every Person Makes: How to Fix Them to Get the Health Care You Deserve* (Langdon Street). *www.everypatientsadvocate.com*

Patient Alert

All hospital patients should have their blood glucose levels checked, according to new guidelines issued by the Endocrine Society.

Reason: Between 32% and 38% of hospitalized patients have hyperglycemia (high blood glucose), which increases risk for longer hospital stays, infections and death in those who are not critically ill.

If you are hospitalized: Be sure to get this test.

Guillermo E. Umpierrez, MD, professor of medicine, division of endocrinology, metabolism, Emory University School of Medicine, Atlanta.

Better Postsurgical Pain Relief

In a study of 40 adults being prepared for spinal surgery, half gargled with a diluted licorice solution and half gargled with water five minutes before receiving anesthesia via an airway tube.

Result: Two hours after surgery, about 25% of the licorice group had a sore throat, compared with 75% of those who gargled with water. Licorice group members also were less likely to develop postoperative cough.

Theory: Licorice contains active ingredients that have anti-inflammatory, anti-irritant and anticough effects.

Self defense: If you are scheduled to undergo surgery requiring general anesthesia with an airway tube, ask your surgeon about using a licorice gargle.

Anil Agarwal, MD, professor, department of anesthesiology and biostatistics, Sanjay Gandhi Post Graduate Institute of Medical Sciences, Lucknow, India.

Faster Recovery from Orthopedic Surgery

Vitamin D speeds recovery from orthopedic surgery by promoting the formation of bone tissue.

Recent study: When researchers studied preoperation charts of 723 patients scheduled for orthopedic surgery (such as fracture repair or spine surgery), 43% had insufficient vitamin D levels (low levels were defined as less than 32 ng/mL).

Self-defense: Ask your doctor to measure your vitamin D level four to six weeks before surgery. If low, ask about taking 1,000 international units (IU) to 2,000 IU of vitamin D-3 daily.

Joseph Lane, MD, orthopedic surgeon, Hospital for Special Surgery, New York City.

Maggots Can Speed Wound Healing

Recent finding: Maggot therapy healed wounds more quickly than surgical wound cleaning. Maggots may secrete substances that fight infection.

Study by researchers at Université de Caen Basse-Normandy, Caen, France, and Regional Center Léon Bérard, Lyon, France, published in *Archives of Dermatology.*

Best Ways to Prevent Hospital Infections

Charles B. Inlander is a consumer advocate and health-care consultant based in Fogelsville, Pennsylvania. He was the founding president of the nonprofit People's Medical Society, a consumer advocacy organization credited with key improvements in the quality of US health care in the 1980s and 1990s, and is author of 20 books, including *Take This Book to the Hospital With You: A Consumer Guide to Surviving Your Hospital Stay* (St. Martin's).

We all know that infection is a very real risk during a hospital stay. And the numbers are staggering—at least 1.7 million Americans develop a hospital-acquired infection each year, and 99,000 people die from it. But aside from being vigilant about asking medical staff to wash their hands, is there really anything a patient can do to prevent infection? Absolutely! *There are several additional—and, in some cases, surprising—approaches...*

• **Start the conversation.** Many doctors never raise the subject of hospital-acquired infection unless the patient brings it up. So, bring it up! Ask your doctor what the overall infection rate is at the hospital where you are going to be treated. If he/she doesn't know, call the facility and ask for the infection control officer (required at every hospital). The infection rate should be below 6%. If it's above that, talk to your doctor about using a different hospital. But keep in mind that your overall medical status is an important factor. For example, people with diabetes are at higher risk for postsurgical infections, but if presurgical blood glucose levels are well-controlled, infection rates drop. Cancer patients having surgical procedures have been found to have a higher risk of developing pneumonia after surgery. But getting a presurgical pneumonia vaccine or, in some cases, taking a presurgical antibiotic can lower that risk.

My advice: If you are being hospitalized for a specific health problem, be sure that your doctor is aware of any other medical conditions you may have.

• **Beware of certain procedures.** Research shows that certain procedures have relatively high risks for infection. For example, close to 10% of colorectal surgical patients develop surgical site infections (at the incision). Other procedures with high risks for infection include bladder catheterizations and the use of a breathing tube or intravenous (IV) line. But studies have found that, in some cases, wearing special surgical blankets and hats before—and sometimes during—surgery can help your body fight infection.

My advice: Ask your doctor about steps that can be taken to keep you warm during surgery and/or when you are given IVs.

• **Check out the latest research.** Numerous medical studies have been published on just about all medical procedures. And most discuss infection risk.

My advice: Ask your doctor to discuss what the studies show are the infection risks associated with your procedure. Also ask about infection risks for other procedures that might be appropriate. For example, an open surgical gallbladder removal has a higher infection risk than laparoscopic gallbladder removal.

• **Be alert at home.** Many infections do not become apparent until after you get home. An infection may also be contracted when a nurse or other health-care provider administers care in your home.

My advice: Be watchful for signs of infection, including increasing tenderness, redness or pus at an incision site, unexplained fever or internal pain that was unexpected in the course of your healing. When in doubt, immediately call your doctor.

Better Inhaler Use

Researchers asked 100 hospital patients with asthma or another lung disease, such as emphysema, to demonstrate using their inhalers.

Finding: Patients misused them up to 86% of the time—often forgetting to exhale completely before inhaling. People with poor vision, who had trouble reading the directions, were most likely to misuse inhalers.

If you use an inhaler: Read the instructions or ask a friend to read them to you. Also ask your doctor to demonstrate how to use your inhaler.

Valerie Press, MD, instructor of medicine, The University of Chicago Medical Center, Illinois.

Germs Galore

Swabs taken from the sleeves, pockets and mid-sections of nurses' uniforms and doctors' white coats and clothing showed that more than 60% were contaminated with dangerous bacteria.

American Journal of Infection Control

Hospitals Make Misleading Claims About Robotic Surgery

Researchers studied 400 randomly chosen hospital Web sites to scrutinize their claims about robotic procedures, typically used in minimally invasive gynecological, heart and prostate surgeries.

Result: Most sites (89%) that made claims about robotic surgery cited clinical superiority over traditional surgery even though there is no scientific evidence that robotic surgery is always better than conventional surgery. No sites mentioned any risks. Most (73%) used promotions from the robots' manufacturers.

Martin A. Makary, MD, associate professor of surgery, Johns Hopkins University School of Medicine, Baltimore.

3

Fast Health Fixes

Stress Raises Blood Pressure, Right? Wrong! Health Myths Debunked

"Don't cross your eyes—they'll get stuck that way." That's what my mother used to tell me. Of course, though my mother was right about many things, she was wrong about that.

Many of the things that we hear about our bodies just aren't true. The result is that we may be worrying about stuff that we don't need to worry about or doing things that we think will help our health but won't.

Here, six common health myths and the truth behind them...

Myth: Airplane air makes you sick.

Reality: There's nothing inherently more risky about airplane air. Multiple studies do show that if you're sitting within two rows of a sick passenger, you're likelier to catch what he/she has. But the danger is no greater than if you were to encounter that person on a train or bus, in an office or at the mall.

In fact, research shows that airplanes are cleaner than land-bound sites for three reasons...

- **The air circulated is drawn from outside,** where the high altitude means few bacteria or viruses.
- **Cabin air is exchanged about 20 times an hour,** more frequently than the air in most office buildings.
- **Bacteria and viruses like moist air, and airplanes typically are quite dry.** (The lack of moisture may irritate mucous membranes, and some researchers speculate that this could increase vulnerability to infection, but there's no backup for this yet.)

Aaron E. Carroll, MD, associate professor of pediatrics and director of Center for Health Policy and Professionalism Research at Indiana University School of Medicine, Indianapolis. He is coauthor, with Rachel C. Vreeman, MD, of *Don't Cross Your Eyes...They'll Get Stuck That Way! And 75 Other Health Myths Debunked* (St. Martin's).

One real risk of air travel is that of developing deep vein thrombosis (DVT), or a blood clot in your leg, from sitting still for long periods. Avoid DVT by stretching and walking around once an hour or so.

Myth: Cheese makes you constipated.

Reality: This bad rap probably started with the apparent connection between infant dairy intake and firmer stools, but it's not true. According to a study by the National Center for Health Statistics, which looked at data from more than 15,000 people ages 12 to 74, the 13% reporting constipation actually ate less cheese, not more. They also took in less high-fiber food, such as legumes, fruits and vegetables.

Myth: If you're ill, dairy products increase congestion.

Reality: Once again, cheese—and milk and other dairy products—have been unfairly accused. Numerous studies have not found any link between milk products and phlegm production or an increase in coughing, congestion or a runny nose. In one study, people with colds were given milk but produced no more mucus than the control group.

Some people, though, are extra sensitive to how milk feels in the mouth. Milk hits the mouth in something called droplet flocculation, spreading out as tiny droplets over saliva and creating a mucus-like sensation. But there isn't truly any more phlegm—it just may feel that way to some people.

Myth: Tilting your head back stops a nosebleed.

Reality: Think about it. How could this possibly work? It can't help the blood to clot or put pressure on the source of the flow. What it does do is send blood down your throat, which could cause choking or vomiting.

Instead, keep your head above your heart by standing or sitting upright...lean your body forward...and squeeze just below the bony bridge of your nose for five to 15 minutes until the bleeding has stopped. If the bleeding doesn't stop after 20 minutes or is the result of an injury that could involve a broken nose, seek medical help right away. The same is true, too, if you have frequent incidents.

Myth: Eating lots of protein after a workout builds muscles.

Reality: There are studies showing that some protein eaten after exercise helps build muscles. But loading up is a bad idea, because taking in excess protein can dehydrate the body, make the kidneys work harder and cause gas, indigestion and heartburn. Worse, there's some evidence that eating a high-protein diet is connected with a greater risk for heart disease. So a little protein goes a long way.

Myth: Stress causes high blood pressure.

Reality: Increased blood pressure is one aspect of the fight-or-flight response to stress, but there is no apparent connection between chronic stress and high blood pressure. A study that followed 36,530 people for 11 years detected no connection between anxiety and the development of high blood pressure. In fact, people who tended to be anxious actually had lower blood pressure, which could not be explained by other known factors such as medication, age and gender.

It may be that people who are under stress don't take as good care of themselves—eating or drinking too much, using recreational drugs or not sleeping enough—and increase their risk that way. If this describes you, you know what to do.

Rx: Belt One Out!

Rebecca Shannonhouse, editor, *Bottom Line/Health,* Boardroom Inc., 281 Tresser Blvd., Stamford, CT 06901.

Can't carry a tune? It doesn't really matter. Go ahead and sing or hum something anyway. It could make you healthier.

New finding: Researchers who looked at members of a choral group (average age 80) found that they took fewer medications, were less likely to be depressed and made fewer doctor visits than a comparison group of nonsingers.

What's going on?

Because singing stimulates multiple parts of the brain and can improve lung function, it can help...

• **Asthma and chronic obstructive pulmonary disease.** Singing helps strengthen chest muscles and increases peak respiratory flow rate, a measure of lung health.

• **Depression...and agitation in Alzheimer's patients.** Both can be eased by singing and other forms of music therapy.

• **Infections.** Regular singers have been shown to experience a temporary increase in disease-fighting antibodies.

Unfortunately, many adults feel too self-conscious to sing, explains Barbara Reuer, PhD, a San Diego–based music therapist and researcher who has published extensively on music therapy and health. *To incorporate singing into your daily routine...*

• **Start by humming your favorite tunes.** Then sing along with music from your iPod or the radio. (If you're alone in the car, no one can hear you!)

• **Consider taking a few lessons from a voice coach.** Even if you can't carry a tune, this will teach you proper breathing techniques, improve your singing—and perhaps even better your health.

Surprising Conditions That Chiropractors Can Treat

James N. Dillard, MD, DC, LAc, a pain and integrative medicine specialist in private practice in New York City and East Hampton, New York, *www.drdillard.com.* Trained as a medical doctor, chiropractor and acupuncturist, he was an assistant clinical professor at the Columbia University College of Physicians and Surgeons and was medical director of Columbia University's Rosenthal Center for Complementary and Alternative Medicine, both in New York City. Dr. Dillard is coauthor of *The Chronic Pain Solution* (Bantam).

If you were asked to name a condition commonly treated by chiropractors, chances are neck and back pain would come to mind. But the list could be much longer.

Even though 11% of Americans seek the services of a chiropractor each year, most people are unaware that chiropractic care—a more than 100-year-old hands-on discipline that focuses primarily on manipulation of the spine—can be used to treat discomfort in many parts of the body.*

To learn more about the surprising conditions that chiropractors can help relieve, we spoke with James N. Dillard, MD, DC, CAc, a medical doctor, chiropractor and acupuncturist who specializes in treating chronic pain. *For example...*

• **Asthma.** The goal of treating people with asthma is to stimulate the rib cage muscles to ease breathing, optimize blood and lymph flow and enhance nervous system activity, all of which help reduce symptoms such as chest tightness and shortness of breath. In treating asthma, chiropractors typically use not only spinal manipulation but also other modalities such as stretching and/or trigger-point massage. Exercise, good eating habits and meditation also may be discussed. Additionally, chiropractic and acupuncture can be an effective combination for asthma.

Scientific evidence: A 2010 study in *The Journal of the Canadian Chiropractic Association,* which compiled data from eight scientific articles, showed improvements, based on pulmonary function tests, in 5,882 asthma patients who underwent chiropractic care.

• **Carpal tunnel syndrome (CTS).** This condition, which causes shooting pain and numbness in the hand (usually the thumb, index and middle fingers), often occurs in people who have poor posture while performing repetitive tasks, such as working with small hand tools or typing at a keyboard.

Chiropractors can improve CTS by doing stretching and manipulation at the wrist, guiding physical therapy exercises and counseling patients on how they position their hands at

*Chiropractic care is safe for most people. However, people who have osteoporosis or take blood-thinning medications could be at increased risk for bone fractures and/or internal bleeding, while in extremely rare cases, those with a history of stroke may have an increased risk for a subsequent stroke. If you have these conditions or any other chronic health problem, consult your doctor before seeking chiropractic care.

the computer or while using hand tools. Wrist splints, worn at night, also may help.

Scientific evidence: Two studies support the use of chiropractic for CTS, including one reporting significant progress in strength, range of motion and pain after several chiropractic sessions. Most improvements were maintained for at least six months.

• **Fibromyalgia.** Characterized by chronic pain and tenderness in joints and muscles, fibromyalgia is a diagnosis of exclusion, meaning other illnesses must first be ruled out, since no laboratory tests can identify it.

Chiropractors can help relieve symptoms by focusing on the tender points—and relaxing these areas as well as the patient's entire frame. They can also apply heat, ice or electrostimulation, which uses electric current to promote muscle contractions, improving blood flow.

A diet that reduces the systemic inflammation that fibromyalgia patients typically have also may be recommended. Such a diet emphasizes fish, fresh vegetables and fruit and discourages fatty meat, fried food and dairy products.

Scientific evidence: A 2009 study of fibromyalgia patients in *The Journal of Alternative and Complementary Medicine* tested the effects of resistance training—including chest presses and leg extensions—combined with chiropractic care. It found that the resistance training's positive impact on patient strength was enhanced by the addition of chiropractic, which improved flexibility, balance and coordination.

In addition to the healing effects of chiropractic's hands-on approach, chiropractors tend to excel at listening to their patients, which also provides comfort.

• **Headache.** Many of the up to 45 million Americans affected by chronic headache (occurring at least 15 days a month) try one drug after another to find relief. While headache pain obviously manifests in the head, a significant number of headaches are related to the alignment of the cervical spine (neck).

Scientific evidence: Research has found chiropractic care to be especially useful for tension headaches, the most common type experienced by adults in the Western world. Chiropractic may also help with migraines. A 2009 study in the *Journal of Manipulative and Physiological Therapeutics* suggested that the combination of spinal manipulation and *amitriptyline* (Elavil), an antidepressant also used for migraine pain, produced stronger results than either alone.

The hand movements chiropractors use to stretch the neck, which often include manual traction to increase space between the vertebrae and/or side-to-side stretches of the neck, may relax the muscle tension at the root of tension headaches in ways that can't necessarily be achieved with drugs.

• **Temporomandibular joint disorder (TMD).** This refers to a variety of conditions marked by intermittent pain in the jaw joints and surrounding tissues, making it difficult to chew or yawn. Many patients have a genuine mechanical malfunction in the jaw, but in my experience, the majority who think they have TMD simply have too much tension in their jaws. They're holding their jaws too tightly and/or grind their teeth at night.

Chiropractic, which may involve manually stretching the jaw and the surrounding muscles, can be enormously helpful for jaw pain. Spinal adjustments to the upper neck and jaw can properly realign the joints, and exercise and lifestyle changes can prevent a relapse. Mouth guards also can be used by people who grind their teeth at night.

Scientific evidence: Research published in 2003 in the *Journal of Manipulative and Physiological Therapeutics* tracked nine TMD patients who suffered pain while opening their mouths. After eight weeks of chiropractic therapy, all of the patients were able to open their mouths more widely and with less pain.

To find a chiropractor near you: Consult the American Chiropractic Association, 703-276-8800, *www.acatoday.org.*

Herbal Cold Remedies

Rosemary clears congestion. Place one-half cup of crushed leaves in the toe of hosiery, and put it in a tub of warm water. Soak the stocking in the tub for 20 minutes. Sage relieves a sore throat. Make a tea by steeping two teaspoons of crushed leaves in eight ounces of hot water for 20 minutes. Strain, and add one teaspoon of sea salt. Gargle with the liquid for 30 seconds, then spit it out. Repeat as necessary. Thyme unplugs sinuses. Pour three cups of boiling water over two tablespoons of crushed thyme leaves in a bowl. Cover your head with a towel, and lean over the bowl. (Don't let the steam burn you.) Close your eyes, and breathe in deeply for eight to 10 minutes.

Stephanie Tourles, licensed holistic esthetician, Orland, Maine, and author of *Organic Body Care Recipes: 175 Homemade Herbal Formulas for Glowing Skin & a Vibrant Self* (Storey).

The 100-Day Cough

Richard O'Brien, MD, is an attending emergency physician at Moses Taylor Hospital and an associate professor of emergency medicine at The Commonwealth Medical College of Pennsylvania, both in Scranton. He is also a spokesperson for the American College of Emergency Physicians. *www.acep.org*

Last winter, I met Jeannette and Phil, who were both in their 60s. They did almost everything together, including going to the gym. Cold and flu season had set in, and both were pleased that they had already received their seasonal flu vaccinations. Within a short time, some of the regulars at the gym started coughing. Two weeks later, despite vigorous hand-washing and other precautions, Jeannette began to cough as well. She did not get terribly ill—she had only a low-grade fever and, except for the annoyingly regular dry cough, largely went about her business.

The cough gradually worsened, and she was convinced that she had pneumonia. After a visit to her family doctor, however, she learned that her lungs sounded "clear," and her chest X-ray was normal. Jeannette was told she had a cold. But after two full weeks, she had had enough and returned to her doctor, who then prescribed an antibiotic to try to knock out what he probably guessed was bacterial bronchitis. When Jeannette's cough did not improve, her doctor prescribed two different classes of antibiotics. But her cough persisted, and she had begun to suffer more frequent spells of coughing to the point of occasionally vomiting and experiencing sharp chest pains. She was becoming concerned that she had something far worse than pneumonia—perhaps even lung cancer. Jeannette then underwent a CT scan of her chest that showed no pneumonia, evidence of a tumor or other lung problem. It was normal.

When I met Jeannette in the emergency department, she had been coughing for three months and could not stand it any longer. As she waited to be seen, I could hear her cough incessantly—10 to 15 extremely rapid and short, dry coughs in a row, followed by a quick inhalation that sounded like she was gasping for air after holding her breath for too long. Based on the pattern of her coughing, I tested her for pertussis, more commonly known as "whooping cough" in children who contract the infection. The test result confirmed Jeannette's diagnosis. Because pertussis tends to linger, doctors often call it the "100-day cough." Antibiotics do kill the bacteria that cause the illness but don't eliminate the cough-producing toxins secreted by pertussis. That just takes time. Antibiotics also can prevent the spread of pertussis to loved ones—the bacteria travel via air droplets.

What do I want readers to learn from Jeannette's cough? That you should always see a doctor—more than one if you have to—to get a firm diagnosis for a cough that goes on for more than a week. This is also true if the cough is severe, accompanied by a fever, you're coughing up blood or have shortness of breath and/or chest pain—symptoms that could indicate a clot in the lung, tuberculosis or cancer. Even if you may have received a pertussis vaccination early in life, also talk to your doctor about getting a "Tdap" vaccination, recently recommended for all adults. It protects against tetanus, diphtheria—and pertussis. If you've received a tetanus shot alone at any time, Tdap is still a good idea. This is a onetime vaccination. It may be time to protect yourself against this 100-day cough.

Surprising Sinus Help

Humming may reduce risk for sinus infections. More than 37 million Americans suffer the pain, headaches and congestion caused by sinus infections each year.

Recent finding: Humming increases airflow between the sinus and nasal cavities, keeping the sinuses healthy and reducing the likelihood of infection.

Jon O. Lundberg, MD, PhD, professor, department of physiology and pharmacology, Karolinska Institute, Sweden, and coauthor of a study published in *The European Respiratory Journal.*

Asthma Relief

Indian frankincense may relieve asthma. A white resin from the frankincense tree is a potent anti-inflammatory that may make breathing easier for people with asthma.

Recent finding: Breathing eased and frequency of attacks dropped in 70% of asthma patients who took boswellia daily for six weeks. Ask your doctor about taking 300 milligrams (mg) to 400 mg of a standardized extract with at least 60% boswellia acids three times a day.

Laurie Steelsmith, ND, naturopathic doctor and acupuncturist in private practice, Honolulu. *www.drsteelsmith.com*

It's True

Thunderstorms worsen asthma and sleep apnea. The storms' winds cause pollen to rupture into fragments that can get into the lungs easily, worsening asthma. Falling atmospheric pressure can cause soft tissue in the back of the throat to relax and block the flow of air, increasing the number of apnea events.

Harvard Health Letter, 10 Shattuck St., Boston 02115. *www.health.harvard.edu/health*

Better Posture Eases Pain

Recent finding: People feel more powerful, in control and able to tolerate pain when they stand tall. Better posture may increase levels of testosterone, which improves pain tolerance and decreases stress hormones.

Vanessa Bohns, PhD, assistant professor, department of management sciences, University of Waterloo, Ontario, Canada, and Scott Wiltermuth, PhD, assistant professor of management and organization, USC Marshall School of Business, Los Angeles, and leaders of a study of 129 people, published in *Journal of Experimental Social Psychology.*

The Fascinating Science Behind Cracking Joints, Whistling Noses...

Roshini Rajapaksa, MD, an attending physician at New York University Langone Medical Center and an assistant professor of medicine at the New York University School of Medicine, both in New York City. The coauthor of *What the Yuck?: The Freaky & Fabulous Truth About Your Body* (Oxmoor House), Dr. Rajapaksa has published several research articles on colon cancer screening.

A noisy nose or cracking and popping joints may make you want to crawl under a rock from embarrassment. Thankfully, these peculiar noises and other sounds your body makes are typically benign. Unless they're accompanied by pain, inflammation or a fever, body noises are usually just evidence of your body functioning in all of its natural glory. *How to tell the difference...*

WHISTLING NOSE

Why it happens: In a healthy nose, air passes through fairly undisturbed. But any type of obstruction in the nasal passage narrows the space through which air can travel, which can result in a whistling sound. That obstruction may be mucus from a virus or allergies, a deviated septum (when one side of the nose is narrower than the other) or nasal polyps.

To quiet things down: If the whistling is occurring during a cold, use an over-the-counter antihistamine to dry up mucus. Allergy sufferers should see their physicians to discuss long-term allergy treatment. For chronic congestion, your doctor may recommend a saline nasal spray to clear excess mucus.

When to seek help: If you don't have a cold or allergies and the whistling persists, visit an ear, nose and throat (ENT) doctor. You may have a deviated septum—particularly if you have trouble breathing—and may need corrective surgery. If the whistling is accompanied by yellow or green mucus, lasts more than five to seven days or is accompanied by a headache or pain in the cheeks or face, you may have a sinus infection and need antibiotics. Rarely, a perforated nasal septum may be at fault, resulting from such causes as trauma or an infection.

CRACKING JOINTS

Why it happens: Don't believe the old wives' tale that cracking your knuckles leads to arthritis! The cracking noise is simply the result of air bubbles popping in the synovial fluid that surrounds the joints. Motion can create these tiny bubbles, which make noise when popped. If other joints, such as your shoulder or knee, make noise when you simply move, and it's accompanied by pain and/or swelling, it could be arthritis.

To quiet things down: Not necessary—you won't hurt yourself if you crack away!

When to seek help: If the cracking is a sign of arthritis, your doctor may prescribe pain relievers, physical therapy, exercise or cortisone injections. And, of course, if you have arthritis in your knuckles, you should stop cracking them to avoid putting stress on weak joints.

HICCUPS

Hiccups are the result of an involuntary contraction of the diaphragm, which causes sudden closure of the vocal cords. This sudden closure creates the "hiccup" sound.

Why it happens: Hiccups are usually triggered by eating too much, drinking carbonated beverages and/or alcohol, as well as by stress.

To quiet things down: Home remedies generally work—eat a teaspoon of sugar... gargle with ice water...breathe into a paper bag...hold your breath for as long as you can.

When to seek help: See your doctor if hiccups persist for more than two days—it could be a sign of many conditions, including gastroesophageal reflux disease (GERD), laryngitis, tumors, etc.

POPPING EARS

Why it happens: Popping ears can happen in an airplane, an elevator or while diving underwater—a difference in air pressure inside and outside of the eardrum forces it to equalize the stress. The popping you "hear" is actually a sensation. An ear infection or fluid behind the eardrum from a cold, sinus infection or allergies may prompt popping as well.

To quiet things down: Yawning or swallowing should equalize the pressure—both actions cause your Eustachian tubes (which connect the back of the nose with the middle ear) to open, allowing air to flow in or out of the middle ear, equalizing pressure. Sucking on candy or chewing gum can help by promoting swallowing. If you're flying while congested, take an antihistamine or decongestant an hour before takeoff or landing to help shrink the membranes and let ears pop more easily. As for the old "hold your nose and blow" trick, I recommend avoiding it. Most people blow too hard, which causes too much pressure and can lead to pain or even damage your ear.

When to seek help: Normally, popping ears are healthy ears. But if the popping is not occurring in response to a change in air pressure or is not accompanied by a cold, see an ENT.

You may have a perforated eardrum or fluid behind the ear, both of which require treatment.

You Can Prevent Texting Tendonitis

Marjory Abrams, president, *BottomLine* newsletters, Boardroom Inc., 281 Tresser Blvd., Stamford, Connecticut 06901.

Soon after I purchased a smart-phone, I developed "texting tendonitis." (It's also called "BlackBerry thumb," although it's not just my thumb that hurts.) The pain started after I began checking e-mail and typing out long responses on my smartphone in the evenings instead of on my computer.

Physical therapist Mitchell Yass, DPT (*www.mitchellyass.com*), author of *Overpower Pain,* told me that tendonitis from cell-phone overuse—or misuse—can affect arms and shoulders as well as fingers and hands. But exercise can help. Below are his two favorite exercises to help prevent and relieve smart-phone-induced pain. *For each, work both hands and do three sets of 10 repetitions twice weekly...*

- **Strengthen the opposing muscles—the ones on the back of the hand.** To do this, close your fingers as if to grab an envelope between your thumb and other fingers. Then gently cup your hand (so your thumb and forefinger form an oval), and wrap a rubber band around all your fingers at the knuckle. Open your hand to stretch the rubber band.
- **Wrist extensions with a dumbbell.** Start with a three- or four-pound weight. Holding the weight, place your forearm on a surface so that only your hand hangs over the edge. Relax your wrist so that it bends down. Then raise the weight, keeping your forearm on the surface. If this amount of weight feels uncomfortably heavy, start with a one- or two-pound weight. Gradually add more weight to be sure that you continue to exert yourself slightly.

Yass's strategies to use smart-phones smarter...

- **Don't always type with the same fingers.** This is easier to do if you rest the phone on another surface—say, a table—rather than holding it in your hands while you type. Resting the phone on a table also places less stress on your shoulders. These strategies may not sound practical, but doing them as often as you can will make a big difference to minimize pain. (I can personally vouch for this.)
- **Don't text for more than a few minutes without taking a break**—and text with your elbows mildly extended.
- **Keep messages brief.** If you have a lot to say, do it at your desktop computer on a full keyboard.
- **Choose a phone cover that adds bulk,** which makes the phone easier to hold and manipulate.
- **When buying a new phone, opt for one with a "virtual keyboard" on the screen** (it requires less force than physical keyboard buttons) or one with dictation technology.

Cluster Headache Relief

Michael H. Bennett, MD, associate professor, department of anesthesia, The Prince of Wales Hospital, Randwick, Australia.

Cluster headaches, which are among the most painful type of headache, usually occur in cycles (clusters) during which patients may experience frequent attacks over a period of weeks or months.

Recent advance: Breathing 100% oxygen from a tank at the beginning of a cluster attack may help. In research conducted in the US, Sweden and Italy, 50% to 60% of patients who breathed 100% oxygen at the beginning of a cluster attack reduced or eliminated their pain within 30 to 60 minutes. Because oxygen causes blood vessels to constrict, this therapy appears to help some patients with migraines, too.

Patients who use this treatment, which requires a prescription, keep an oxygen tank at home. When an attack starts, they put on a face mask to inhale the oxygen.

Caution: Breathing pure oxygen can cause lung scarring with prolonged use, so limit treatments to five to 10 minutes.

New Treatment for Severe Migraines

An implanted device called Genesis uses mild electrical impulses to stimulate the occipital nerves, just beneath the skin at the back of the head, and block pain transmission in the brain stem. Genesis already is in use in the US for chronic back pain and is approved for migraine treatment in Europe. Some US doctors prescribe it for migraine on an off-label basis.

Stephen D. Silberstein, MD, professor of neurology and director of Jefferson Headache Center, Thomas Jefferson University, Philadelphia, and past president of the American Headache Society.

Migraines and Stroke

Migraines increase risk for stroke in women by 25% to 50%. The increased stroke risk may be linked to the vascular spasms that occur during a migraine, which constrict the blood vessels and limit oxygen delivered to the brain. Studies have shown this effect only in women. Women who suffer from migraines should control blood pressure, weight and blood sugar levels...and should not smoke.

Frederick Nahm, MD, PhD, medical director at Greenwich Hospital Stroke Program, Greenwich, Connecticut, and a neurologist with Neurology of Greenwich, PC. He is assistant clinical professor of neurology at Yale University, New Haven, Connecticut.

Prevent Hair Loss

People who want to prevent hair loss should avoid smoking—a major risk factor—and wear a hat as much as possible to protect hair from the sun. For men, it also is advisable to reduce stress and reduce alcohol consumption. For women, drinking one to two cups of coffee a day and controlling high blood pressure were found to help prevent hair loss.

Bahman Guyuron, MD, chair, department of plastic surgery, University Hospitals Case Medical Center, Cleveland, and leader of a study of male and female identical twins, presented at the American Society of Plastic Surgeons' annual meeting in Denver.

Do-It-Yourself Face-Lift—Look Years Younger In Just 20 Days

Shellie Goldstein, LAc, a licensed acupuncturist, esthetician and certified Chinese herbologist who maintains a private practice in New York City and Amagansett, New York (*www.hamptonsacupuncture.com*). One of the first acupuncturists to work in hospitals and healthcare facilities in New York state, Goldstein is author of *Your Best Face Now: Look Younger in 20 Days with the Do-It-Yourself Acupressure Facelift* (Avery).

If you've got facial wrinkles that you would like to reduce but you don't want to get Botox injections or a surgical face-lift, there's a do-it-yourself option that's far less invasive and far less expensive.

With a technique known as facial acupressure (similar to acupuncture but performed without needles), you can take up to five to 10 years off your appearance—and perhaps even improve your overall health in the process.

Sound far-fetched?

I've treated hundreds of patients who were contemplating face-lifts but found success with acupressure.

Bonus: Unlike Botox or surgery, acupressure won't give you a tight, frozen or pulled-back appearance. The results are softer and more natural.

WHY ACUPRESSURE?

Acupressure is based on a Chinese healing technique that involves pressing or kneading key points on the body to stimulate energy flow, known as Qi (pronounced chee), through invisible pathways called meridians. It can be used to relax or tone muscles, boost circulation and even improve digestion.

The conventional view: From the Western medical perspective, wrinkles are formed by changes in the skin's composition, thickness and elasticity as well as continuous muscle activity—for example, forehead wrinkles may appear after years of furrowing your eyebrows or squinting. As a result, the skin covering the muscle creases, eventually creating a wrinkle.

Chinese medicine has a different perspective. For example, specific meridians (that correspond to organ systems, such as those for the "Liver" and "Gallbladder") are believed to affect certain body parts, but they don't always seem to correlate. For instance, a meridian located at the junction between your thumb and index finger corresponds to the head—rubbing that area can reduce headaches and, yes, wrinkles.

DO-IT-YOURSELF ROUTINES

To help reduce wrinkles and puffiness, use the following routines each day until you are satisfied with the results and then as needed...

- **Forehead wrinkles.**

What to do: Begin at the top of your right foot, in the junction between your big and second toes. Using medium to firm (but not painful) pressure, massage the point in a clockwise circle 10 times. (If you have arthritic fingers, use your knuckle instead.) Repeat on left foot.

Next, move to the back side of your right hand between your right thumb and index finger. In a clockwise circular motion, massage this point for 10 rotations. Repeat on the left hand.

Then, move to the back of your neck. Place both thumbs where your spine meets the base of your skull and move them two inches to either side until they each land in an indentation. Massage clockwise with firm pressure for 10 rotations.

Lastly, move to your face. Place the pad of each index finger a half inch above the center of each eyebrow. Massage with medium pressure in 10 clockwise (right to left) circles.

Repeat the entire sequence three times in a single session each day. For deeper wrinkles, do the sequence several times throughout the day. You should notice a reduction in forehead wrinkles within 20 days.

- **Under-eye puffiness** (due to age or allergies).

What to do: Place your index finger two inches above the inside of your right ankle between the bone and muscle. Do 10 clockwise rotations using medium to firm pressure. Repeat on left leg.

Next, move to the back of your right hand, as described earlier, and perform 10 clockwise rotations. Repeat on the left hand.

Then, with your arm at your side, bend your left elbow to make a 90° angle. Pinpoint the area located at the outside edge of the elbow crease, between the bend and the bone. Use your index finger to massage 10 times in a clockwise rotation using medium to firm pressure. Repeat on your right elbow.

Lastly, move to your face. Place your right index finger just to the side of your right nostril. Move the finger laterally to a spot directly underneath the center of your eye, in your sinus area. Press in and slightly upward, performing 10 clockwise rotations. Repeat on the left side.

Do the entire sequence three times daily. You should notice a reduction in puffiness under your eyes after a few days.

Help for Badly Chapped Lips

Over-the-counter 1% hydrocortisone reduces the swelling, soreness and flaking of severely chapped lips. Use it three or four times a day for one week. After applying the cortisone cream, use an unflavored lip balm containing a moisture-locking agent, such as petrolatum or beeswax, to seal in the moisture better. If symptoms continue for more than one week, contact your dermatologist. The steroid cream does not have a good taste, but it shouldn't harm you if you taste some.

Kathleen Welsh, MD, dermatologist in private practice and medical staff member of the California Pacific Medical Center, San Francisco. *www.weloveskin.com*

Easy Reading Help

To determine which reading glasses you need, hold printed material about 14 to 16 inches away from your eyes and test different glasses. When you find a pair that allows you to read the print comfortably, that is the power you need. You will need prescription reading glasses if each eye requires a different power.

Mayo Clinic Health Letter, 200 First St. SW, Rochester, Minnesota 55905.

Cleaning Your Contacts

Rub contact lenses to clean them, even when using a "no rub" solution.

Reason: No-rub solutions kill bacteria, but they don't clear away the buildup on the surface that can lead to eye irritation and infection.

Best: After placing the lens in your palm, rub with solution for five seconds and then rinse with more solution for five seconds.

Men's Health, 400 S. 10th St., Emmaus, Pennsylvania 18098. *www.menshealth.com*

Anti-Cavity Strategy

To protect teeth from cavities, don't eat one piece of candy or sweets now, then another piece an hour later and so on.

Reason: After eating just one piece of candy, your mouth becomes acidic and it can take up to an hour for the mouth's pH balance to return to normal. The longer the teeth are exposed to acid, the greater the chance of cavities.

If you choose to eat sweets: Limit treats to one after-meal serving—the increased production of saliva during and after a meal helps to wash away acidity. Also, try to brush your teeth or at least rinse your mouth with water after eating sweets.

Mark Helpin, DMD, acting chair, pediatric dentistry, Temple University's Maurice H. Kornberg School of Dentistry, Philadelphia.

Hand-Drying Smarts

Readers often want to know the most hygienic way to dry their hands—air dryers or paper towels?

Either method can be effective. What's key is to completely dry your hands—water is a breeding ground for bacteria.

A Mayo Clinic study involving 100 adults who dirtied, washed and then dried their hands, either with paper towels for 15 seconds or under an air dryer for 30 seconds, found the methods equally reduced residual bacteria. With dryers, avoid rubbing your hands together—a recent study found that this undoes the germ removal of hand washing, likely because the friction releases bacteria deep in your pores. Place your palms so they face the dryer for at least 30 seconds.

Important: Turn off the tap with a paper towel, and keep purses and bags off floors. In one study, traces of feces were found on one-third of purses placed on bathroom floors.

Charles Gerba, PhD, professor of microbiology, University of Arizona, Tucson.

Heel Pain

About 90% of people with heel pain (plantar fasciitis) recover—but healing takes time. This overuse injury develops gradually, as repetitive stress (often from running or cycling) tears the tissue band along the bottom of the foot.

What to do: Ice the heel for 15 minutes three times a day—and after any exercise. Sleep wearing a padded night splint with straps (found at doctors' offices or online), loosely, at first—tightly pulled straps can worsen pain.

Also, try this five-minute stretch after waking, prolonged sitting or standing: Plant your good foot on the ground. Cross your bad foot over the opposite knee, perpendicular to the ground. Pull your toes back with one hand while massaging the bottom of the foot with the other hand. If you have pain in both heels, perform the stretch on each foot. Cross-train with bike riding, water-running and, if your doctor approves, elliptical trainers.

Mark Klion, MD, clinical instructor of orthopedics, The Mount Sinai Medical Center, New York City.

Better Treatment for Hamstring Injury

Among 42 patients with small tears of the hamstring or tendon, those who received injections of their own blood, known as autologous blood injection (ABI), along with a local anesthetic and an anti-inflammatory steroid reported an almost 90% improvement in pain and function. Other study subjects, who received only the anesthetic and steroid or an anesthetic and ABI, reported less improvement.

Theory: Blood contains many factors that can promote healing in degenerative injuries such as hamstring microtears, which are painful and slow to heal.

Waseem Bashir, MD, radiologist, Ealing Hospital, London, UK.

Bunion Relief

Michael J. Trepal, DPM, vice president for academic affairs and dean, New York College of Podiatric Medicine.

A bunion (an enlarged joint at the base of the big toe) typically results from a weak foot structure that tends to be hereditary, and the only way to correct it is with surgery.

If your bunion is not too painful, relieve pressure on it by wearing shoes with wide, deep toe boxes and low or flat heels. Your podiatrist can prescribe orthotic shoe inserts that correctly position your feet. Moleskin patches can protect the bunion from being rubbed by shoes.

Toe stretches may help ease the ache of the bunion.

What to do: While slightly lifting your foot off the ground, point it straight ahead and hold for five seconds. Then curl your toes under for five seconds. Repeat 10 times daily.

Generally, surgery is needed when pain or limitation of function significantly affects one's quality of life. The more severe the deformity, the more aggressive and involved the surgery. Recuperation times will vary depending on the procedure but could take several weeks or months.

Fun Way to Cut Stress

Tango dancing lowers stress and makes dancers feel sexier and more relaxed and thus has a positive effect on their emotional state. The tango requires intense focus to learn the footwork, and that focus interrupts negative thoughts that can bring on anxiety and depression. The physical expressiveness of the tango helps people release pent-up feelings so that they can start to deal with them. The high levels of communication required and the close embrace during the dance contribute to the highly positive feelings and good connection that a tango couple feels.

Cynthia Quiroga Murcia, MSc, psychologist, department of psychology, Goethe University, Frankfurt am Main, Germany, and leader of a study of emotional and hormonal responses to tango dancing, published in *Music and Medicine*.

Share the Work

Women's stress levels drop most when men help out around the house.

Recent finding: Women had healthier levels of the stress hormone cortisol when their husbands helped with housework. Men's cortisol levels were healthier when their wives devoted more time to housework, child care and other work at home.

Darby Saxbe, PhD, NRSA postdoctoral fellow, department of psychology, University of Southern California, Los Angeles. She led a study of stress hormones among dual-earner couples, published in *Journal of Family Psychology.*

All-Natural Mood Booster

A moderate 20-minute workout can boost your mood for up to 12 hours—much longer than previous research had suggested. Consider riding a stationary bike or walking on a treadmill for 20 minutes most mornings.

Study of 48 people by researchers at University of Vermont, Burlington, presented at a meeting of the American College of Sports Medicine in Seattle.

Feeling Blue? Try Bananas

Ara DerMarderosian, PhD, is professor of pharmacognosy (the study of natural products used in medicine) and Roth chair of natural products at the University of the Sciences in Philadelphia. He is coeditor of *The Review of Natural Products* (Lippincott Williams & Wilkins).

You may already know that bananas are chock-full of potassium (one ripe banana supplies more than 10% of an adult's daily requirement). It's crucial to get enough potassium because people with a low dietary intake of the mineral are 28% more likely to suffer a stroke than those who consume higher levels, probably because adequate potassium levels help control blood pressure.

The other health benefits of bananas are less well-known. For example, as a good source of tryptophan (a precursor to serotonin, a brain chemical that helps regulate mood), bananas help fight depression. Bananas also are rich in the B vitamin folate—several epidemiological studies have linked low blood levels of folate and vitamins B-6 and B-12 to an increased risk for depression.

Research has not identified the optimal daily intake of bananas to fight depression, but anecdotal evidence suggests that eating two to three bananas (or other tryptophan sources, such as turkey and cottage cheese) daily—while maintaining a well-balanced diet and getting regular exercise—may help prevent mild-to-moderate depression.

In addition, bananas help fight heartburn by neutralizing acidity and soothing and coating esophageal tissue with pectin.

Important: In rare cases, bananas may cause an allergic reaction. Overly ripe bananas with blackened skin can increase blood sugar levels. People with kidney problems should check with their doctors before eating this potassium-rich fruit.

Don't Fall Asleep With the TV On

Marjory Abrams, president, *BottomLine* newsletters, Boardroom Inc., 281 Tresser Blvd., Stamford, Connecticut 06901.

A recent survey found that 95% of Americans between the ages of 13 and 64 watch TV or use other electronic devices in the hour before going to bed. However, the National Sleep Foundation, which conducted the survey, advises people to turn off TVs, computers and other electronic media at least one hour before going to sleep. That would be a big change for a lot of people.

Sleep expert Lawrence Epstein, MD, explained that light from the devices, or from lamps and overhead lighting, serves as a stimulus, shifting the circadian rhythm and delaying the sleep cycle. Even when your eyes are shut, light perceived through your eyelids suppresses your production of melatonin, the hormone that helps regulate the sleep cycle. Not everyone's sleep is disrupted by this, but if you are having trouble with your sleep, think about changing your routine.

Dr. Epstein, chief medical officer of Sleep Health Centers in Brighton, Massachusetts, and author of *The Harvard Medical School Guide to a Good Night's Sleep,* suggests a sleep routine that includes avoiding caffeine after 12 noon...keeping the bedroom dark and cool... maintaining a standard bedtime even on weekends...taking a warm shower or bath before bed...reading, deep breathing or practicing progressive relaxation or meditation once in bed.

To go beyond the basics, here are some fall-asleep methods that work well for people I know...

- **Doing crossword puzzles or Sudoku before bed.** It's absorbing without being stress-inducing.
- **Listening to frogs, crickets or other outdoor sounds through an open window.** Or using a sound machine. One friend likes white noise...another, the sound of rain or even a heartbeat.
- **Listening to music**—especially music intended to help you sleep.

Example: Steven Halpern's *Sleep Soundly.*

- **Putting lavender oil on your pillowcase or using an aroma diffuser.** Research shows that lavender has a slight calming and soothing effect when inhaled.
- **Visualization.** One woman imagines herself floating on a "comfort cloud." Another visualizes herself slowly drifting in a kayak on a mountain lake, recapturing the sight of the rocks beneath the surface, the smell of the cedars, the feel of the lapping water, the sound of the wind. One friend mentally replays a round of golf.

Cool Brain, Better Sleep

A refrigerated cap worn by insomnia patients caused them to fall asleep in 13 minutes (faster than those who also wore caps but didn't have insomnia). Cooling the frontal cortex, an overactive area in those with insomnia, restores restful sleep—a finding that may lead to the development of brain-cooling caps.

University of Pittsburgh School of Medicine.

The Simplest Prescription of All

Jamison Starbuck, ND, is a naturopathic physician in family practice and a guest lecturer at the University of Montana, both in Missoula. She is past president of the American Association of Naturopathic Physicians and a contributing editor to *The Alternative Advisor: The Complete Guide to Natural Therapies and Alternative Treatments* (Time Life).

Do you really drink enough water? Most of my new patients do not—and they often are shocked to learn about the health problems associated with chronic low-level dehydration (a condition many people don't even know they have). *It's linked to surprising health problems, such as high blood pressure, as well as...*

- **Irritability, depression and lack of focus.**
- **Pain, stiff joints, muscle spasms and headache.**
- **Sugar and carbohydrate cravings, and weight gain.**
- **Indigestion, heartburn and constipation.**

Despite the strong, science-based association between inadequate water consumption and common ailments, most conventional doctors fail to "prescribe" sufficient water intake for their patients. But in my opinion, a prescription for an individualized, correct amount of daily water should be at the top of any treatment plan for most conditions.

Water is absolutely critical for the normal functioning of our bodies. First, it is an integral part of our blood and carries nutrients to tissues throughout the body and to the brain. Among other things, water also lubricates joints, carries oxygen throughout our bodies, and allows us to eliminate waste via the kidneys, bowels, skin and lungs.

Many people are confused about the amount of water they should drink each day.

So I recommend a simple formula: Weigh yourself and divide that number in half. This is the base amount, in ounces, of plain water you should drink in a day. (I do not count other fluids—even green tea—toward this total because they contain compounds that reduce the net amount of water that is bioavailable.) Consume 80% of your water intake at least 30 minutes before or after meals. (*Example*: A 150-pound woman should have at least 75 ounces of water a day, with 60 ounces consumed away from food). *Then add more water based on such factors as...*

- **Eight ounces for every 30 minutes of activity that promotes sweating** (such as strenuous exercise or use of a sauna or hot tub).
- **Four ounces for every 30 minutes spent outdoors in temperatures above 80°F...**in low-humidity (less than 45%) winter outdoor activity...or at an altitude above 8,000 feet (as can occur with skiing or flying).
- **An amount equal to the coffee, black tea or caffeinated soda you consume.**

People with fever, diarrhea and/or vomiting also need to replenish water that is lost from their bodies. Check with your doctor on the amount you need if you have one of these health concerns.

Alcohol and several medications, including antihistamines, diuretics, blood pressure drugs, antidepressants and antipsychotic medicines, contribute to dehydration. If you drink alcohol, drink twice as much water as the amount of alcoholic beverages you consume. If you take a prescription drug, ask your pharmacist about increasing your daily water intake.

Caution: If you have heart failure or a kidney, liver or adrenal disorder, speak with your doctor before changing your water-drinking habits—these conditions increase water retention.

Got Insomnia? Go to Bed Later

Recent study: Researchers gave 79 women with insomnia (average age 72) printed material on good sleep habits or four weeks of behavioral therapy that included in-person counseling.

Result: Those who received therapy significantly improved sleep by going to bed later, waking up at the same time each morning and limiting time in bed.

Theory: Turning in later increases one's natural sleep drive.

If you have insomnia: Go to bed later, when sleepy, and get up at your usual time each day. Your total time in bed should equal your average amount of actual sleep plus no more than 30 minutes.

Daniel Buysse, MD, professor of psychiatry, Sleep Medicine Institute, University of Pittsburgh School of Medicine.

Avoid Mosquitoes

Mosquitoes lay eggs in undisturbed standing water, and the eggs hatch in 24 to 48 hours. Four to 10 days later, the mosquitoes are mature. So if you have torrential rain, expect a big upsurge in the mosquito population seven to 10 days later—especially if the temperature is above 80°F.

Also: Mosquitoes prefer shade to direct sun and calm conditions to strong winds.

Outside, 400 Market St., Santa Fe, New Mexico 87501. *www.outsideonline.com*

First Aid Basics

Treat cuts with water, not hydrogen peroxide. Hydrogen peroxide can damage healthy tissue. (The same is true of alcohol and iodine.) Rinsing with water first, then cleaning the surrounding area with mild soap and water is sufficient for most cuts.

Richard O'Brien, MD, attending emergency physician, Moses Taylor Hospital, and associate professor of emergency medicine at The Commonwealth Medical College of Pennsylvania, both in Scranton.

Tetanus Booster

Tetanus shots are not just for puncture wounds. Tetanus bacteria live in dirt and can get into the body through cuts—although it is harder for them to grow in an open scrape than in a deep puncture wound.

Self-defense: If you have not had a tetanus booster in 10 years, you are due one, even if you are not injured.

William Schaffner, MD, professor and chair of the department of preventive medicine, Vanderbilt University School of Medicine, Nashville.

More Veggies, Less Infection

Broccoli and other cruciferous vegetables increase levels of intra-epithelial lymphocytes, immune cells in the skin and intestines that inhibit microbes and assist in wound repair.

Cell

4

Fitness Focus

How to Lose 12 Pounds...in Just 17 Days

According to conventional wisdom, anyone who loses weight rapidly (more than a pound or two a week) will invariably regain the lost pounds because the diet will be too strict to maintain. But some researchers are now finding evidence that slow isn't necessarily better when it comes to weight loss.

Recent research: A 2010 study in the *International Journal of Behavioral Medicine* analyzed data from 262 middle-aged obese women.

Result: The fast weight losers dropped more pounds overall and maintained their weight loss longer than the gradual weight losers.

Good news: With rapid weight loss, most people can boost their metabolism, combat fat storage and help prevent obesity-related diseases, such as diabetes and certain types of cancer—all without feeling deprived of satisfying food.

Sound impossible? I've seen thousands of people lose weight by following what I call the 17 Day Diet.*

Why 17 days? This is roughly the amount of time it takes for your body's metabolism to adapt to a change in calories. By varying your diet at 17-day intervals, you "trick" your metabolism into functioning at its maximum efficiency to help you reach your target weight. *Four simple cycles to follow...*

*Be sure to check with your doctor before you start this or any other weight-loss program.

Mike Moreno, MD, physician in charge of primary care and coordinator for new physician education at Kaiser Permanente in San Diego. Dr. Moreno is author of *The 17 Day Diet* (Free Press) and sits on the board of the San Diego chapter of the American Academy of Family Physicians. In 2008, Dr. Moreno launched "Walk with Your Doc," a program that involves walking with his patients every Tuesday and Thursday morning before his workday begins to promote the benefits of exercise.

CYCLE 1: CLEANSE YOUR SYSTEM

For the first 17 days, the goal is to "cleanse" your system by eating lots of lean protein, such as poultry and fish. Lean protein requires more energy to digest than carbohydrates, so it burns additional calories and helps control your blood sugar. Because it's satisfying, protein also fights food cravings.

During this cycle, you're also allowed as many vegetables as you like. You will need to temporarily cut out all grains, potatoes, pasta and desserts. Doing this helps you avoid the dramatic fluctuations in blood sugar that fuel binge eating.

Note: Use olive oil for cooking during this cycle.

Fruit is allowed but only before 2 pm—when sugar (including natural sugar from fruit) is less likely to be stored as fat.

Good fruit choices: Apples, berries, oranges, pears, plums and red grapes. These fruits are relatively low in sugar and high in fiber, which slows digestion and helps you feel full. Avoid bananas and pineapple—both contain too much natural sugar.

During this 17-day cycle, people lose an average of 10 to 12 pounds (depending on their starting weights) while eating three to four meals daily plus snacks (for a total of 1,300 calories per day for men and women). Some of this weight loss will be due to water loss—but this is also beneficial because fluid retention can contribute to fatigue.

Sample day's meals: Breakfast—two scrambled egg whites...one-half grapefruit or other fresh fruit...one cup green tea. Lunch—fish, poultry or eggs...vegetables...one cup green tea. Dinner—fish or chicken ...vegetables...one cup green tea. Snack—raw, cut-up veggies.

CYCLE 2: RESET YOUR METABOLISM

During the second 17-day cycle, the goal is to reset the metabolism by alternating higher calorie intake (1,500 to 1,700) on even days with lower calorie intake (1,300) on odd days. Switching back and forth stimulates fat burning because it prevents your body from adapting to a certain level of daily calories.

Slow-digesting complex carbs, such as oatmeal, sweet potatoes and brown rice, are reintroduced during this cycle.

CYCLE 3: GOOD EATING HABITS

By now, a little more than a month since you started, your body has undergone a significant metabolic shift that will allow you to reintroduce moderate portions—and no more than two to three servings per day before 2 pm—of carbohydrates such as whole-grain breads and pastas that may have made you feel sluggish or heavy before.

If you've reached your target weight, you may proceed to cycle 4, the maintenance cycle. If not, be sure to focus on portion control and continue to emphasize lean protein and nonstarchy vegetables, limiting carbohydrates after 2 pm until you reach cycle 4.

CYCLE 4: WEIGHT MAINTENANCE

During this cycle, which is followed indefinitely to maintain your weight loss, you are more strict with yourself throughout the workweek but relax your eating habits on the weekends. From 6 pm Friday to 6 pm Sunday, you can enjoy your favorite indulgences, such as pizza or hamburgers, as long as you maintain portion control and enjoy no more than three indulgences over a single weekend. This approach allows you to eat some favorite foods in moderation while also giving your metabolism the variety it needs to function efficiently.

Rule of thumb: Weigh yourself on weekends. If you gain five pounds or more over a week's time, return to any of the earlier cycles.

OTHER SECRETS TO WEIGHT LOSS

In addition to following the cycles described earlier...

- **Get more probiotics.** New research suggests that people who have an overabundance of "bad" bacteria in the intestinal tract are more susceptible to weight gain. But healthful bacteria, known as probiotics (found in such foods as certain yogurts, sauerkraut and miso soup), control the proliferation of bad bacteria and help fight infection—and ensure that your metabolism functions effectively.

My advice: Aim to consume two daily servings of foods containing probiotics.

Examples of one probiotic serving: Six ounces of fat-free plain yogurt or one-half cup of Breakstone LiveActive cottage cheese (which includes added probiotics).

Or: Take probiotic supplements, following label instructions.

• **Don't forget to exercise.** To avoid getting run down while you're scaling back on calories (especially the first few days of cycle 1), do only 15 to 20 minutes of walking a day.

Thereafter, aim for at least 30 minutes of aerobic exercise five days a week. Walking is a good choice, as is jogging, swimming, or using a stationary bicycle or an elliptical machine. For strength training, make the exercises as aerobic as possible using lighter weights and more repetitions.

Pepper Helps Burn More Calories

Recent finding: People who ate about one-half teaspoon of cayenne pepper in foods had higher core body temperatures and burned more calories than people who did not eat cayenne pepper. Being able to taste the pepper in the foods resulted in greater appetite suppression and boosted energy...and the effects were greater in people who did not regularly eat spicy foods.

Mary-Jon Ludy, PhD, researcher, and Richard Mattes, PhD, distinguished professor of nutrition science, department of nutrition science, Purdue University, West Lafayette, Indiana, and coauthors of a study published in *Physiology & Behavior.*

Grapefruit Does Aid Weight Loss

Remember the grapefruit diet? There may be some validity to it.

Recent finding: Study participants lost an average of three-and-a-half pounds in 12 weeks by eating one-half a grapefruit with each meal, versus a group who followed the same diet but without the grapefruit.

Theory: Grapefruit lowers insulin levels, which helps prevent sugar from being stored as fat.

Caution: Grapefruit and grapefruit juice may interfere with some medications, such as statin drugs, so check with your doctor.

Ken Fujioka, MD, director, Center for Weight Management, Scripps Clinic Nutrition and Metabolic Research Center, San Diego, and leader of a study published in *Journal of Medicinal Food.*

Blueberries to the Rescue—Again!

The polyphenols in blueberries do more than protect the heart. They also reduce the development of fat cells. Animals given high doses of blueberry polyphenols had a 73% decrease in fat cells, compared with those on a normal diet.

Federation of American Societies for Experimental Biology.

Healthful Chinese Food

Chinese food can be nutritious and low-calorie. It generally contains high amounts of dietary fiber, vitamins, minerals and phytochemicals but also can have a lot of sodium, corn starch, sugar and monosodium glutamate (MSG), a flavor enhancer that is associated with headaches in some people.

Avoid fried foods and dishes that contain fatty pork, beef or chicken.

Better: Hot tea, soup, salad, steamed vegetable dumplings, vegetable or shrimp stir-fries and steamed brown rice. Ask that MSG not be added to your entrée.

Suzanne Havala Hobbs, DrPH, RD, associate professor of health policy and management, The University of North Carolina at Chapel Hill.

If You Think a Food Is Filling, It Will Be

Recent study: Forty-six volunteers tested a 380-calorie vanilla milkshake in two different packages. One was labeled "heaven in a bottle," a high-fat "indulgent" 620-calorie shake. The other, supposedly containing only 140 calories, was called a "sensi-shake."

Results: The participants' levels of ghrelin—a hormone that sends hunger signals to the brain—remained flat or only slightly higher when drinking the sensi-shake, suggesting that participants had little physiological satisfaction with the drink. When they drank the "indulgent" beverage, ghrelin levels steeply increased, showing that they craved the beverage, and then the levels quickly decreased after drinking the milkshake, showing satisfaction.

Studies by researchers at Yale University, New Haven, Connecticut, on the effects of mind-set on ghrelin levels, published online in *Health Psychology*.

Better Portion Control

Recent study: Researchers asked 60 adults to serve equal amounts of white-sauce or red-sauce pasta on either red or white dinner plates.

Result: When study participants served food on a dinner plate whose color contrasted with the sauce, they portioned out 21% less than participants whose plates matched their food.

Theory: The "Delboeuf illusion" tricks the mind into overestimating the size of a small circle that is surrounded by a slightly larger circle in a contrasting color.

If you're watching your weight: Eat from a plate that contrasts with the color of your food.

Koert van Ittersum, PhD, associate professor of marketing, Georgia Institute of Technology, Atlanta.

How to Stop Craving the Foods That Make You Fat

Mike Dow, PsyD, clinical director of therapeutic and behavioral services at The Body Well integrative medical center in Los Angeles and host and psychotherapist of the TLC series *Freaky Eaters.* He is a member of the California Psychological Association and the International Society of Eating Disorder Professionals. He is author of *Diet Rehab: 28 Days to Finally Stop Craving the Foods That Make You Fat* (Avery). *www.drmikedow.com*

How often have you heard people say that they're addicted to certain foods? They very well might be. Food addictions are just as real as addictions to drugs or alcohol, just not as obvious. The reason that most diets fail is that they don't address the changes in brain chemistry caused by food that can be more powerful than the effects of cocaine.

Last year, the Scripps Research Institute released a groundbreaking study that found that rats given diets of bacon, sausage, chocolate and cheesecake had sharp rises in dopamine and serotonin, neurochemicals that affect the brain's pleasure centers.

Later, when the researchers withheld these foods and tried to put the rats on a nutritious diet, the rats refused to eat, almost to the point of starvation. The rats even chose to endure painful shocks to get the sweet and fatty foods. They were literally addicted—and it took two weeks for their brains to return to normal. Rats addicted to cocaine, on the other hand, recovered normal brain functions in just two days.

Bottom line: An addiction to food can be harder to overcome than drug addiction.

CHEMISTRY AND WEIGHT GAIN

Most people who are overweight don't experience more hunger than anyone else. *They eat too much as a form of self-medication, unconsciously trying to balance levels of the two brain chemicals that are disrupted by unhealthy foods...*

• **Dopamine is the neurochemical that produces excitement and other high-energy feelings.** When you eat foods that are high in fat, such as red meat, french fries and cheesecake, you experience a surge of dopamine. It feels good, but the "high" is short-lived. As dopamine levels decline, you may feel listless, sad or depressed. The quickest way to offset the negative feelings is to eat more high-fat foods...and the up-and-down cycle continues.

• **Serotonin is somewhat different, but just as addictive.** It's a "calming" neurochemical that promotes feelings of optimism and hope. It's the primary target of most antidepressant medications. People who consume a lot of sugar or carbohydrates made primarily from white flour (pasta, crackers, white bread) or a combination of sugar and white carbs (cookies, cakes, doughnuts) have increases in serotonin that make them feel good. But, as with dopamine, the effects are temporary unless you keep eating these foods.

BREAK THE CYCLE

Traditional diets mainly deal with calorie restriction. They rarely work because they fail to address the addiction that causes people to overeat in the first place. *Important steps...*

• **Know your pitfalls.** These are the thoughts and activities (and foods) that ultimately lower levels of dopamine and/or serotonin and make you crave another "fix."

Examples: A stressful meeting at work that makes you anxious will increase cravings for sugar or carbohydrates (for the serotonin boost). Spending the night alone in front of the television can lead to loneliness that makes you crave both sugar (for the serotonin boost) and fat (for the dopamine).

Just about everyone with a weight problem engages in what's known as emotional eating. When you realize that you're eating ice cream every night because you're lonely or that you're digging into bags of chips or other snacks when you get anxious or frustrated, you'll be less likely to indulge in this behavior.

• **Increase "booster activities."** These are activities that increase and help maintain healthier levels of serotonin and dopamine. You can tailor these activities to increase levels of either one of these substances. *Examples...*

• For more dopamine. Being active and social are the best ways to boost dopamine. Go to a museum or an art opening. Clean the house while listening to loud music that makes you want to dance. Cook a new, healthful dish. Go dancing.

• For more serotonin. Cultivating relationships and being kind help increase serotonin. Ask a coworker how he/she is feeling. Call a friend or loved one just to say "I'm thinking about you." Give someone a compliment. Play with your dog or cat.

• **Detox gradually.** Just as smokers are more likely to successfully quit when they use nicotine patches or gum, you'll find it easier to give up addictive, high-calorie foods when you replace them with healthier foods that also help balance brain chemistry.

Many of the foods that you already know are healthy will increase serotonin and dopamine. *These include...*

• **Whole grains**

• **Beans**

• **Lean meats, such as chicken and turkey**

• **Low-fat dairy, such as cottage cheese and yogurt**

• **Healthy snacks, such as unsalted nuts, popcorn and fresh fruits.**

Important: It takes at least 10 "exposures" to a healthy food before you'll start to crave it in the same way that you once craved unhealthy choices.

• **Identify risk times.** How many times have you sat down in front of the TV with a full bowl of snacks and emptied it by the end of the show—without even being fully aware that you were eating? Most food addicts snack or binge after 6:00 pm, when they are relaxing at home. This is known as mindless eating, and it's a common behavior of food addicts. People often eat mindlessly in the car as well.

Important: Plan other activities during your own high-risk times. If you tend to snack in the evening, use that time for something else, such as straightening the house or calling friends. It also is helpful to have ready-to-go healthy snacks, such as air-popped popcorn or sliced fruit, for quiet nights when you're reading or watching TV.

- **Allow occasional "slips."** We all have special treats that we don't want to give up. For me, it's buttery movie-theater popcorn. For someone else, it might be ice cream or soft drinks.

In my experience with thousands of patients, those who achieve a healthy relationship with food—those who eat when they're hungry or simply to enjoy a particular food, rather than to fulfill emotional needs—can enjoy up to two servings daily of a pitfall food and still maintain a healthy weight.

To be safe: Don't exceed 300 calories per serving. This might be, for example, half a Big Mac or a small order of fries.

It's not weak to occasionally give in to cravings. As long as your life is full of healthy serotonin- and dopamine-boosting foods and activities, you'll have these cravings only occasionally.

Dig In!

Researchers have discovered that taking big bites with large forks may help people to eat less when dining out.

Journal of Consumer Research

Sweet Suppressor

Curb your appetite by smelling vanilla before a meal. The aroma is satisfyingly rich and tricks your brain into thinking you are eating more than you actually are, so your body feels content sooner and needs less food.

Alan Hirsch, MD, founder, Smell & Taste Treatment and Research Foundation, Chicago. *www.smellandtaste.org*

Surprise Finding

Yo-yo dieting is better than no dieting. Mice that repeatedly lost then gained weight lived more than 30% longer than those that remained obese.

Edward List, PhD, scientist, Ohio University, Athens, and principal investigator of a dieting study of mice presented at The Endocrine Society's annual meeting.

Anyone Can Have an Eating Disorder

Cynthia M. Bulik, PhD, director of The University of North Carolina (UNC) at Chapel Hill Eating Disorders Program. She is also a distinguished professor of eating disorders at UNC as well as a professor of nutrition in the university's Gillings School of Global Public Health. She has written more than 400 scientific papers and chapters on eating disorders and is author of *Crave: Why You Binge Eat and How to Stop* and the forthcoming *The Woman in the Mirror: How to Stop Confusing What You Look Like with Who You Are* (both published by Walker & Company).

Until recently, eating disorders have been primarily associated with adolescent girls who don't eat enough—or eat far too much.

Now: The landscape of these disorders has changed. More and more women (and men) in their 40s, 50s, 60s and beyond are struggling with these sometimes life-threatening conditions.

Most of the 11 million Americans—10 million women and one million men—who struggle with an eating disorder, such as anorexia nervosa, bulimia nervosa or binge-eating disorder (a condition that's only recently been recognized by health professionals), are under age 30.

However, in the last 10 years, there has been a substantial increase in the number of women over age 30 who seek treatment for an eating disorder. There are no up-to-date data to tell us whether eating disorders are increasing in men, but clinical experience suggests that they are.

WHAT IS AN EATING DISORDER?

Scientists aren't sure exactly what causes an eating disorder, but research shows that genetics play a role. People who have a first-degree relative, such as a parent or sibling, with an eating disorder are generally at greater risk themselves. When this genetic predisposition is combined with certain psychological and emotional triggers, an eating disorder may result.

Older adults battling an eating disorder fall into three categories—those who have struggled their entire lives…those who struggled as adolescents, recovered to some degree, then relapsed…and those who have recently developed the problem for the first time. *Eating disorders can be divided into the following categories…*

• **Anorexia nervosa is characterized by low weight (typically less than 85% of normal weight for one's age and height),** fear of weight gain, denial of illness and distorted body image—typically, thinking you are overweight when you are not. Anorexia nervosa can lead to a number of complications, such as hair loss, osteoporosis, electrolyte imbalances, cardiac problems and organ failure.

• **Bulimia nervosa occurs in people at all weights and is marked by binge eating—** uncontrolled consumption of unusually large amounts of food—accompanied by purging that seeks to "undo" the binge in the form of vomiting, unnecessary use of laxatives or excessive exercise. Bulimia causes many of the same health consequences as anorexia.

• **Binge-eating disorder (BED) is similar to bulimia but without the purging.** BED differs from simple overeating in that sufferers feel a loss of control over what they eat. The condition can lead not only to obesity but also to problems such as insomnia and body aches.

AREN'T I TOO OLD FOR THIS?

Older women (and men) face a number of situations that can trigger an eating disorder…

• **Hormonal changes.** At menopause, most women are unprepared for the physical changes, including a hormonally driven redistribution of fat from other parts of the body to the abdomen. This can result in extreme weight-loss strategies to try to retain a youthful body. Hormonal changes also can lead to mood swings and sleep disturbances that often trigger cravings and increase appetite, setting the stage for binge eating. In men, decreases in testosterone and age-related changes in their bodies can trigger eating disorders.

• **Divorce.** Following a breakup, women may seek a new mate and want to appear as physically attractive as possible. This can prompt some women to take extreme measures to lose weight. If a man's wife initiates the divorce, he can feel lost and abandoned and turn to food for comfort.

• **Empty-nest syndrome.** A mother who has spent many years attending to her children can experience a sense of loneliness, uselessness and boredom when they leave home. This is a classic set-up for binge eating—often seen as a desperate attempt to find a sense of "fullness" in the pantry.

• **Depression.** Older women and men must contend with the deaths of friends and other life events that can trigger depression. Reduced appetite is a common symptom of depression and can lead to anorexia in some cases.

• **Overdoing fitness regimens.** Anorexia can develop in people who are overly zealous in diet and fitness regimens. Their good intentions can quickly cross the line from healthful to obsessive.

HOW TO GET HELP

One of the challenges of treating older adults is that, unlike a teenager, a 60-year-old woman or man cannot be compelled to enter treatment. It's crucial that women or men who experience thoughts and behaviors that characterize eating disorders (such as distorted body image, irrational fears of being overweight and an inability to control bingeing) realize that it may not be just a passing phase, and the earlier they seek help, the better.

In the case of anorexia, inpatient treatment is often necessary. With anorexia, the brain is unable to function properly because of malnutrition (decision-making can be impaired and brain shrinkage may occur). About 10% of patients with anorexia die from medical complications of starvation, such as heart failure, or suicide.

Insurance companies often cover inpatient treatment for anorexia but tend to deny coverage for inpatient treatment of bulimia and BED.

For anyone struggling with bulimia or BED...

- **Find the right professional.** The most effective treatment includes a therapist (a psychiatrist, psychologist, social worker or other experienced health professional) with a background in treating eating disorders. To find a practitioner in your area, consult the National Eating Disorders Association, *www.nationaleatingdisorders.org*...or the Binge Eating Disorder Association, *www.bedaonline.com.* A registered dietitian should be consulted to offer advice on proper nutrition and healthful eating habits.

Also, be sure that the symptoms—mental and physical—are discussed with the patient's primary care physician. This is important to ensure that the doctor takes the patient's eating disorder into account when offering medical advice.

Caution: Some doctors are not educated about the growing prevalence of eating disorders among older patients. If you believe that you or a loved one has symptoms of one of these conditions but your doctor doesn't agree, get help from a therapist on your own and seek a second medical opinion.

- **Start therapy.** Cognitive behavioral therapy, a form of psychotherapy that teaches patients how to understand their own patterns of thinking and behavior, is the most effective treatment for eating disorders. With the help of a therapist, you will explore why you starve yourself and when you're more likely to binge so you can work to change these habits.

- **Consider medication.** The only FDA-approved medication for eating disorders is the antidepressant *fluoxetine* (Prozac), which is approved for the treatment of bulimia. This drug can decrease the frequency of binge eating and purging but does not offer a permanent solution.

If you suspect that a loved one may have an eating disorder: Have a conversation that begins with a loving message such as "I care about you, and I care about your health. And I worry about how much you seem to be struggling with your eating."

Try to persuade your loved one to at least undergo a professional evaluation (with a dietitian or psychologist or psychiatrist) and to then think through the options. Point out that it's always better to have information and an expert's opinions than to make decisions in a vacuum.

Less Protein, More Weight Gain

Recent finding: People whose diets were 10% protein took in 1,000 more calories in a four-day period than those who consumed 15% protein.

Possible reason: The lower protein group may not have felt as full.

Study by researchers at University of Sydney, Australia, Medical Research Council, Cambridge, UK, and Institute for Natural Sciences, Massey University, Auckland, New Zealand, published in the online journal *PLoS One.*

Burn Calories While Watching TV

Step in place as the commercials air during a one-hour program to burn almost 150 calories.

Study of people ages 18 to 65 by researchers at University of Tennessee, Knoxville, published in *Medicine & Science in Sports & Exercise.*

Get Off the Plateau

Lost weight and feel like you've hit a plateau? Make a few changes in your exercise routine to "surprise" your body's metabolism. Also, stay hydrated—drink six to eight eight-ounce glasses of water a day, and limit alcohol and caffeine. Although fruit is a good source of vitamins, minerals and fiber, it can be high in sugar and other carbs. Limit fruit to two pieces each day. Check your portion sizes—no more than five ounces each of protein and whole grains a day for women ages 31 and older and six ounces each for men ages 31 and older. A serving is about the size of your palm.

Never eat carbs (including fruit) after 2 pm, since it is harder for your body to burn them off. For dinner, emphasize lean protein and vegetables.

And keep moving! You need at least 30 minutes of exercise every day, but the more you do, the more weight you will lose. Take the stairs, walk after lunch and dinner and/or try a new form of exercise, such as water aerobics or karate, to get other muscles moving.

Mike Moreno, MD, a family physician based in San Diego and author of *The 17-Day Diet* (Free Press).

Surprise About Swimming

Swimming in cold water results in less weight loss than other aerobic activities, such as running and cycling.

Reason: Cold water pulls more heat from the body than air does—and that energy loss stimulates the appetite.

Also: Regular exposure to cold water may encourage the body to increase fat stores under the skin as insulation.

UC Berkeley Wellness Letter, 500 Fifth Ave., New York City 10010. *www.wellnessletter.com*

Extra Benefits from Bypass Surgery

Family members of gastric bypass patients lose weight, too. They often improve their diets and exercise more frequently.

Recent finding: Obese spouses and other obese adult family members of gastric bypass patients lost an average of nearly 10 pounds in the year following the patient's surgery. The gastric bypass patients lost an average of 100 pounds.

John Morton, MD, director of bariatric surgery, Stanford School of Medicine, Stanford, California, and author of a study published in *Archives of Surgery.*

Cool Tip for Weight Loss

People who set the thermostat higher than 68°F are more than twice as likely to become obese than those in cooler homes.

Possible reason: Warm bodies burn fewer calories.

International Journal of Obesity

Walk It Off

Walk three times more to lose weight. Sedentary Americans walk an average of 2,000 to 3,000 steps a day. But 6,000 steps a day significantly reduces risk for death and 8,000 to 10,000 steps a day promotes weight loss.

Best: Buy a pedometer, and gradually increase your steps by 200 to 300 each week.

Ann Yelmokas McDermott, PhD, associate professor, kinesiology department, California Polytechnic State University, San Luis Obispo, California.

Get More Exercise...By Acting Like a Kid!

Toni Yancey, MD, MPH, *www.toniyancey.com*, a professor of health services at the University of California, Los Angeles, School of Public Health, and co-director of the UCLA Kaiser Permanente Center for Health Equity. She is author of *Instant Recess: Building a Fit Nation 10 Minutes at a Time* (University of California).

Do you get at least 30 minutes of moderate to vigorous exercise most days of the week? That's the amount of physical activity recommended by most major health groups. But according to the latest statistics published in *Medicine & Science in Sports & Exercise*, fewer than 5% of people over age 20 consistently reach this goal. In fact, the average American engages in just six to 10 minutes of moderate-to-vigorous activity each day.

With all the well-known life-saving benefits conferred by exercise, why is it so difficult for us to follow this one powerful health recommendation?

The reasons are complex, but based on my more than 20 years of research on the subject, there are ways to give yourself the best possible odds of successfully incorporating physical activity into your daily life. *My secrets for creating an exercise plan that you can stick to...*

Secret 1: **Think like a kid.** A daily exercise program will never be effective if it involves doing activities that you find tedious or uncomfortable. That's why it helps to think like a kid. Perhaps you enjoyed playing catch, jumping rope, throwing a Frisbee or using a Hula Hoop.

If you draw a blank, make a list of types of physical activity you enjoy or find relaxing.

Examples: Dancing, gardening, strolling through an art museum, or activities such as washing the car or dog or raking leaves or cutting the grass. Be sure to include the locations (at home, in a park, etc.) and times of day that work best for your schedule.

Secret 2: **Lower your expectations.** Rather than telling yourself you're going to start exercising 30 minutes a day, set your sights a little lower in the beginning. If, like the majority of Americans, you're currently getting at most only about 10 minutes of activity per day, adding just 10 minutes of daily exercise will double your activity level.

Once you settle into this routine, start working on adding another daily activity break. If you can get in a total of two additional 10-minute daily activity sessions, you'll be getting about 30 minutes daily.

Secret 3: **Plan activities that don't require a change of clothes.** It's risky, in my opinion, for your exercise plan to depend on a single window of opportunity, such as getting to the gym at a certain time of day. Give yourself multiple options—some of which don't require special clothing or equipment.

Good choices: Do a short aerobics session when you wake up...cycle on a stationary bike during your favorite TV show or while reading...take a walk in your neighborhood after dinner. If you work in an office, do some mid-morning calisthenics instead of taking a coffee break...take a brief walk with colleagues at lunchtime...schedule a "walking meeting" in the midafternoon.

Free-form dancing is another excellent activity that can be done in street clothes. If you're in a place where the music might disturb others, use headphones with an iPod. If possible, have a short group session with a leader everyone can follow—and choose energizing music with 100 to 120 beats per minute.

Fun options: Highly energetic forms of Latin dance provide excellent aerobic exercise, as do ballroom, square dancing or line dancing. All are widely available in most parts of the country. Check your local fitness or community center.

Secret 4: **Remove the loophole.** Structure your day so that you don't have the option of not exercising. *For example...*

- When paying bills...stand at the kitchen counter.

• When surfing the Internet or checking e-mail…sit on an inflatable therapy ball.

• If you regularly go places within walking distance…such as a mall or drugstore, tell yourself that driving is no longer an option.

• If you take public transportation…buy a monthly pass that drops you off five to 10 minutes from your destination.

• If you regularly go out to eat…choose a diner or sandwich shop that's a five- to 10-minute walk.

• If you use a computer at work…connect it to a printer at the other end of the office so you'll have to take a short walk anytime you need to retrieve printed materials.

Secret 5: **Make it social.** Studies show that social interaction is among the most important factors in determining whether adults perform regular physical activity. When people view exercise as a social activity, they're much more likely to do it.

Cultivating opportunities to meet up with regular exercise companions—from your neighborhood, place of work, etc.—should be a key part of your exercise menu.

Examples: Use a Nintendo Wii Fit at a community center, organize walking tours of museums or go antiquing.

Ice Bath Prevents Soreness After a Run

The cold slows blood flow, which reduces inflammation and speeds recovery of muscles.

What to do: Put enough cold water in your bath to cover your legs, add ice and sit for 10 to 15 minutes.

Editor's note: Recommended water temperature is between 53°F and 59°F.

Runner's World, 33 E. Minor St., Emmaus, Pennsylvania 18098. *www.runnersworld.com*

How to Relieve Muscle Aches

Ice the muscles for at least 10 minutes immediately after you are done exercising. Later, apply heat, either with a heating pad or by taking a warm bath—but not until 24 hours later, because heat can increase inflammation if applied too soon. Do 20 to 30 minutes of low-impact exercise, such as walking, to enhance the blood flow to the area and facilitate healing. Do some gentle stretching, holding each stretch for about 30 seconds at a time. Use a nonsteroidal anti-inflammatory drug (NSAID), such as aspirin, ibuprofen or naproxen, sparingly, because it actually slows the body's muscle-repair process.

Allan Goldfarb, PhD, professor, department of kinesiology, School of Health and Human Performance, University of North Carolina at Greensboro.

The Best Energy Bars

Carolyn Brown, RD, a nutritionist and registered dietician with Foodtrainers, a private nutrition consulting company based in New York City. She holds a masters degree in clinical nutrition. *www.foodtrainers.net*

Energy bars are supposed to provide a quick-yet-nutritious boost. But while certain bars are tasty and good for you, others are unpleasant to eat or not healthful.

Some contain more calories than we really need—often upward of 300. Many have excessive sugars—anything above 15 grams is too much.

You'll find heavily processed and artificial ingredients in some, including aspartame, soy protein isolates, whey concentrate, isoflavones, hydrolyzed collagen and hydrolyzed gelatin, which don't deliver as much nutritional value as unprocessed and natural ingredients.

The most healthful and delicious energy bars, all of which generally cost between $1.40 and $3 per bar…

Best high-fiber bar: **Gnu Bar.** One bar has 12 grams of fiber—almost half of our daily fiber needs. Unlike many high-fiber snacks, it doesn't have a "cardboardy" consistency. Gnu is among the lowest-calorie full-sized energy bars on the market—130 to 140 calories per bar. *www.gnufoods.com.*

Drawbacks: Going from a low-fiber diet directly to a high-fiber diet can cause digestive distress. Start with just half a Gnu Bar a day if you do not currently eat many high-fiber foods.

Best meal-replacement bar: **ProBar.** These taste great, and they're made from healthful ingredients such as dried fruits, nuts, seeds and rolled grains. At 370 to 390 calories, they're much too filling for a snack, but they occasionally can replace part of breakfast or lunch when you are in a hurry. *www.theprobar.com.*

Downside: ProBar's eight to 12 grams of protein are low for a full meal. If possible, supplement a ProBar with a few spoonfuls of Greek yogurt.

Best pre- or postworkout bar: **Picky Bar.** This has the ideal ratio of carbs to protein—4:1—to prepare the body for a strenuous workout or help it recover. *www.pickybars.com.*

Downside: Picky Bar's 22 to 23 grams of sugar are acceptable before or after a workout—our bodies consume simple sugars when we exercise—but excessive at other times.

Best energy bar that tastes like dessert: **Kookie Karma.** A cross between a cookie and a bar, this round-shaped snack is made from healthful ingredients such as nuts, seeds and fruit. *www.kookiekarma.com.*

Downside: Some varieties contain xylitol, a natural sugar alcohol that can cause gastrointestinal distress.

Best savory energy bar: **Savory Bar.** While most bars strive to taste like dessert, Savory Bar comes in grown-up flavors such as Rosemary, Sesame, Spicy and Everything (which features sesame, poppy, onion and garlic flavors). Savory Bars have a crunchy, cracker-like consistency. *www.sheffafoods.com.*

Downside: With just four grams of protein and only 140 to 150 calories, a Savory Bar might not be sufficient to tide you over until mealtime. Consider pairing one with a healthful protein such as cottage cheese.

Best energy bar that's very widely available: **Kind Bar.** This simple, healthful, nut-based bar can be found in many convenience stores, supermarkets and Starbucks. With as much as seven grams of protein and five grams of fiber, and 10 to 13 grams of sugar for most varieties, it's a healthier choice than other very widely distributed bars, including PowerBars, which have as much as 30 grams of sugar, and Luna Bars, which feature heavily processed ingredients such as soy protein isolates. *www.kindsnacks.com.*

Got Chocolate Milk?

B***est drink after a workout:*** Chocolate milk. When consumed immediately after a workout, low-fat chocolate milk helps athletes build more muscle than a comparable high-carbohydrate sports drink. Drinking chocolate milk also leads to faster muscle recovery and better subsequent workouts.

Also: Individuals who drank chocolate milk immediately after cycling five days a week over four weeks had twice as much improvement in their maximum oxygen uptake—an indicator of cardiovascular fitness—as individuals who drank calorie-free beverages or a carbohydrate sports drink.

John Ivy, PhD, professor of kinesiology and health education, University of Texas at Austin and leader of a study published in *Journal of Nutrition and Metabolism.*

---

5 Natural Healers

Put Down That Slice Of Bread!

What could possibly be more wholesome than whole-wheat bread? For decades, nutritionists and public health experts have almost begged Americans to eat more whole wheat and other grains.

It's bad advice.

Most of us know that white bread is bad for us, but even whole-wheat bread is bad, too. In fact, on the Glycemic Index (GI), which compares the blood sugar effects of carbohydrates, both white bread and whole-wheat bread increase blood glucose more than pure sugar. Aside from some extra fiber, eating two slices of whole-wheat bread is little different from eating a sugary candy bar.

What's particularly troubling is that a high-wheat diet has been linked to obesity, digestive diseases, arthritis, diabetes, dementia and heart disease.

Example: When researchers from the Mayo Clinic and University of Iowa put 215 patients on a wheat-free diet, the obese patients lost an average of nearly 30 pounds in just six months. The patients in the study had celiac disease (a form of wheat sensitivity), but I have seen similar results in nearly everyone who is obese and gives up wheat.

NEW DANGERS FROM A NEW GRAIN

How can a supposedly healthy grain be so bad for you? Because the whole wheat that we eat today has little in common with the truly natural grain. Decades of selective breeding and hybridization by the food industry to increase yield and confer certain baking and aesthetic characteristics on flour have created new proteins in wheat that the human body isn't designed to handle.

William Davis, MD, a preventive cardiologist and medical director of Track Your Plaque, an international heart disease prevention program. Based in Fox Point, Wisconsin, he is author of *Wheat Belly: Lose the Wheat, Lose the Weight, and Find Your Path Back to Health* (Rodale). *www.wheatbellyblog.com*

The gluten protein in modern wheat is different in structure from the gluten in older forms of wheat. In fact, the structure of modern gluten is something that humans have never before experienced in their 10,000 years of consuming wheat.

Modern wheat also is high in amylopectin A, a carbohydrate that is converted to glucose faster than just about any other carbohydrate. I have found it to be a potent appetite stimulant because the rapid rise and fall in blood sugar causes nearly constant feelings of hunger. The gliadin in wheat, another protein, also stimulates the appetite. When people quit eating wheat and are no longer exposed to gliadin and amylopectin A, they typically consume about 400 fewer calories a day.

NOT JUST CELIAC DISEASE

Celiac disease, also known as celiac sprue, is an intense form of wheat sensitivity that damages the small intestine and can lead to chronic diarrhea and cramping, along with impaired absorption of nutrients. But wheat has been linked to dozens of other chronic diseases, including lupus and rheumatoid arthritis. *It also has been linked to...*

- **Insulin resistance and diabetes.** It's not a coincidence that the diabetes epidemic (nearly 26 million Americans have it) parallels the increasing consumption of modern wheat (an average of 134 pounds per person per year) in the US. The surge in blood sugar and insulin that occurs when you eat any kind of wheat eventually causes an increase in visceral (internal) fat. This fat makes the body more resistant to insulin and increases the risk for diabetes.

- **Weaker bones.** A wheat-rich diet shifts the body's chemistry to an acidic (low-pH) state. This condition, known as acidosis, leaches calcium from the bones. Grains—and particularly wheat—account for 38% of the average American's "acid load." This probably is the reason that osteoporosis is virtually universal in older adults.

- **More heart disease.** A diet high in carbohydrates causes an increase in small LDL particles, the type of cholesterol that is most likely to lead to atherosclerosis and cardiovascular diseases. Studies at University of California, Berkeley, found that the concentration of these particles increases dramatically with a high-wheat diet. The increase in small-particle LDL, combined with diabetes and visceral fat, increases the risk for heart disease.

A WHEAT-FREE LIFE

People who crave wheat actually are experiencing an addiction. When the gluten in wheat is digested, it releases molecules known as exorphins, morphinelike compounds that produce mild euphoria. About one-third of people who give up wheat will experience some withdrawal symptoms, including anxiety, moodiness and insomnia. *My advice...*

- **Go cold turkey.** It's the most effective way to break the addiction to wheat. The withdrawal symptoms rarely last more than one week. If you're really suffering, you might want to taper off. Give up wheat at breakfast for a week, and then at breakfast and lunch for another week. Then give it up altogether.

- **Beware of gluten-free products.** People who give up wheat often are tempted to satisfy their craving by buying gluten-free bread or pasta. Don't do it. The manufacturers use substitutes such as brown rice, rice bran, rice starch, corn starch and tapioca starch, which also increase blood glucose and cause insulin surges. Even oatmeal can cause blood sugar to skyrocket.

- **Switch grains.** Small supermarkets now stock quite a few nonwheat grains, such as millet, quinoa, buckwheat and amaranth. They're easy to cook, and they taste good—and they don't have the gluten and other wheat proteins that trigger weight gain, inflammation and insulin resistance.

Helpful: If you aren't willing to give up wheat altogether, you can substitute an older form of wheat, such as spelt or kamut. These grains haven't undergone all of the genetic modifications, so they're somewhat better for you than modern wheat. Any form of wheat can be a problem, however. You'll want to limit yourself to small servings—say, a few ounces once or twice a week.

- **Get plenty of protein.** Protein satisfies the appetite more effectively than carbohydrates.

Eat eggs for breakfast and chicken salad for lunch. For dinner, you can have fish or even steak.

Recent finding: Research has shown that people who eat a reasonable amount of saturated fat in, say, red meat (about 10% or a little more of your total fat calories) have a reduction in small LDL particles, as well as an increase in protective HDL cholesterol.

Work Out!

Even 15 minutes of daily exercise can lengthen life.

Recent study: Researchers administered an exercise questionnaire to 416,175 adults, then followed their health outcomes for an average of eight years.

Result: Those who reported exercising (taking a brisk walk, for example) for only 15 minutes per day extended their expected life spans by three years, compared with those who did not exercise. While the study established that a better target is 30 minutes per day, the benefits of 15 minutes were significant.

Xifeng Wu, MD, chair, department of epidemiology, The University of Texas MD Anderson Cancer Center, Houston.

Laughing As Good for You As Exercise

Laughing lowers stress hormones and cholesterol…enhances the immune system…and releases hormones and other chemicals that make you feel good. Watching 20 minutes of a funny video can provide these benefits.

Lee S. Berk, DrPH, director, molecular research laboratory, School of Allied Health Professions, Loma Linda University, Loma Linda, California, and leader of a laughter study published in *FASEB Journal.*

Omega-3s May Slow Aging

Theory: The faster the ends of cellular chromosomes (telomeres) shorten, the shorter a person's life span may be.

Recent study: Researchers measured blood levels of the omega-3 fatty acids docosahexaenoic acid (DHA) and eicosapentaenoic acid (EPA) in 608 heart disease patients and the effect of those levels on the patients' telomeres over five years.

Result: Telomeres of patients with higher omega-3 levels shortened more slowly than telomeres of those with lower levels.

Theory: Fatty acids may slow telomere shortening by reducing inflammation and blood pressure.

Self-defense: Eat at least two 3.5-ounce servings of oily fish (such as salmon and sardines) weekly or ask your doctor about omega-3 supplements.

Mary Whooley, MD, physician investigator, VA Medical Center, San Francisco.

High-Fiber Diet May Lead to Longer Life

People who ate a diet rich in fiber—including whole grains, beans, fruits and vegetables—were 22% less likely to die during a nine-year study period than those who ate the least fiber. They also were less likely to die from cardiovascular disease, infectious diseases or respiratory disease. And men who ate a high-fiber diet had reduced risk for death from cancer.

Theory: Fiber has anti-inflammatory properties, which lower blood lipids and improve blood glucose levels, reducing the likelihood of disease.

Yikyung Park, ScD, staff scientist, National Cancer Institute, Bethesda, Maryland, and leader of a study of 388,122 people, published in *Archives of Internal Medicine.*

Live Longer the Nordic Way

Researchers monitored the diets of 57,053 people living in Denmark for 12 years. Participants were scored according to how closely they adhered to a "Nordic" diet high in cabbage, root vegetables (such as carrots) and 100% rye bread. Among those who closely adhered to the diet, men were 36% less likely to die during the study period than those who did not regularly eat such foods and women were 25% less likely.

Possible reason: Those foods are rich in dietary fiber and micronutrients.

Anja Olsen, PhD, project office manager, Danish Cancer Society, Copenhagen, Denmark.

Reset Your "Body Clock"

Steve A. Kay, PhD, dean and Richard C. Atkinson Chair in the division of biological sciences at the University of California, San Diego, where he is also a Distinguished Professor of Cell and Developmental Biology. He directs the Kay Laboratory, also at the University of California, San Diego, which investigates the role of circadian disorders in regulating sleep-wake cycles, glucose stability and weight control.

Chronobiology is the study of circadian rhythms—the body's 24-hour cycles of physical, mental and behavioral changes. Light and darkness are the main factors that influence one's circadian rhythms, affecting the body's temperature, sleep-wake cycles, hormone release and other key bodily functions.

For most of us, our bodies need a day or two to adjust when we travel across time zones or change the clock (for example, daylight saving time).

But increasing evidence now shows that chronic (or even occasional) interruptions in our circadian rhythms—the 24-hour cycles that regulate sleep and wakefulness—may affect our health more than we thought.

What's new: The brain used to be considered the body's only biological "clock." Now researchers are finding that many cells in the body have "clock genes" that regulate their activity—for example, organs such as the liver also have cycles.

WHEN BODY CLOCKS FALTER

Exposure to light is one of the main factors for maintaining, or changing, our daily rhythms. And our modern society has essentially turned night into day with near-constant exposure to lights, TVs, computers and other electronic gadgets. In many cases, our bodies haven't adapted, and it's putting us at increased risk for health problems.

- **Age is also a factor.** Older adults tend to have a weaker circadian orchestration of physiology, which means the body's clocks are less able to work together—a problem that has been linked to heart disease.

What you can do: Here's how to help manage your body's internal clocks so that you minimize your risk for health problems, such as...

DEPRESSION

Seasonal affective disorder (SAD), in which episodes of depression increase in the fall and winter when there are fewer hours of daylight, is thought to be caused in part by changes in the circadian cycles.

Simple self-defense: Light therapy, which involves the use of indoor light that mimics sunlight.

Light boxes, available at many pharmacies and online retailers for about $100 to $400, are typically used for a half hour or longer each morning. Exposure to the light increases alertness, and repeated exposure can help fight SAD.

Caution: If you have cataracts, glaucoma or another eye condition...or take medications that increase your skin's sensitivity to light, be sure to consult a doctor before using a light box. In addition, light boxes may trigger mania in people with bipolar disorder.

HEART ATTACK

More than half of heart attacks occur in the six hours between about 6 am and noon. The greater frequency probably is due to several circadian factors, including body position—most people experience about a 10-to-25-point increase in systolic (top number) blood pressure when they rise from bed in the morning. What's more, people who have a heart attack in the morning are likely to suffer more damage to the heart than those who have heart attacks later in the day.

Recent finding: In a study published in *Heart*, researchers analyzed data from 811 patients who had suffered heart attacks. Those whose attacks occurred in the morning were found to have about a 20% larger infarct, an area of dead tissue, than those whose attacks happened later in the day. It's not known why morning heart attacks are more severe.

Caution: In most people, blood pressure rises in the morning, then dips slightly in the afternoon and falls during sleep. However, some people don't have these periodic declines. Known as "non-dippers," they're more likely to have a heart attack than those who experience normal cycling.

Simple self-defense: Get out of bed slowly. In addition, because high blood pressure is a leading risk factor for heart attack, people who take blood pressure–lowering medication may benefit from timing it so that they get the greatest reduction in the morning.

Example: The blood pressure medication *verapamil* (such as Verelan PM) is meant to be taken at bedtime. The active ingredient isn't released during the first hours of sleep (when blood pressure is already low)—more is released in the morning, the time when blood pressure rises. Other drugs that are designed to provide greater benefit when taken at night include timed-release versions of *diltiazem* (Cardizem LA) and *propranolol* (InnoPran XL). If you take blood pressure medication, ask your doctor about timed-release drugs—or if you could take your current medication at night.

ASTHMA

People with asthma are more likely to need emergency treatment between 10 am and 11 am than at other times of the day, research has shown. The use of rescue inhalers also increases during the morning.

Reason: Lung movements are reduced during sleep and soon after waking up. This impairs the elimination of mucus, which can lead to congestion and difficulty breathing several hours later.

Simple self-defense: If you have asthma and use a bronchodilator, such as one containing *theophylline* (Uniphyl), talk to your doctor about taking your last dose of the day a few hours before bedtime. This allows the active ingredients to increase through the night and reach peak levels in the morning.

DIABETES

Several studies have shown that people with poor sleep habits (especially those who sleep five or fewer hours per night) are more likely to be overweight—and have a higher risk for diabetes. Now researchers are speculating that disruptions in circadian rhythms may be to blame.

Recent research: In lab studies, mice with a genetic mutation in the part of the brain that synchronizes circadian rhythms ate all day instead of just in the evening, the time that they're normally active. They were more likely to be obese and also had high blood sugar.

Why does this occur? A protein called *cryptochrome* stimulates the production of hepatic glucose, a sugar used for energy. In humans, cryptochrome is normally suppressed during the day, when energy is supplied by eating, and increased at night to provide energy while we're sleeping. Research has shown that a disruption in sleep-wake cycles causes a prolonged elevation of cryptochrome and an increased risk for obesity and diabetes.

Simple self-defense: To help minimize your risk for weight gain and diabetes, be sure to keep a regular sleep schedule. Go to bed at the same time every night, and get up at the same time in the morning. Aim for seven to eight hours' sleep each night, and don't change your routine on weekends. If you work at night, use heavy curtains to block sunlight, and turn off telephones so that you can sleep during the day.

DROWSINESS

Feel drowsy after lunch? Blame your circadian rhythms. It's normal for body temperature, blood pressure, metabolism and cognitive abilities to decline in the afternoon.

The peak mental hours for most adults are from about 7 am or 8 am until early afternoon. This is followed by a brief (one- to two-hour) dip, after which energy rises again until later in the evening.

Simple self-defense: If your job and lifestyle allow it, take a brief (20- to 30-minute) nap in the afternoon. Or, if that's not possible, try to schedule less demanding tasks during the "dip" period.

Don't Let Stress Harm Your Health

Irene Louise Dejak, MD, an internal medicine specialist who focuses on preventive health, including counseling patients on the dangers of chronic stress. She is a clinical assistant professor at the Cleveland Clinic Lerner College of Medicine of Case Western Reserve University in Cleveland and an associate staff member at the Cleveland Clinic Family Health Center in Strongsville, Ohio.

It's widely known that acute stress can damage the heart. For example, the risk for sudden cardiac death is, on average, twice as high on Mondays as on other days of the week, presumably because of stress many people feel about going back to work after the weekend. People also experience more heart attacks in the morning because of increased levels of cortisol and other stress hormones.

Important research: In a study of almost 1,000 adult men, those who had three or more major stressful life events in a single year, such as the death of a spouse, had a 50% higher risk of dying over a 30-year period.

But even low-level, ongoing stress, such as that from a demanding job, marriage or other family conflicts, financial worries or chronic health problems, can increase inflammation in the arteries. This damages the inner lining of the blood vessels, promotes the accumulation of cholesterol and increases risk for clots, the cause of most heart attacks.

Among the recently discovered physical effects of stress...

- **Increased blood sugar.** The body releases blood sugar (glucose) during physical and emotional stress. It's a survival mechanism that, in the past, gave people a jolt of energy when they faced a life-threatening emergency.

However, the same response is dangerous when stress occurs daily. It subjects the body to constantly elevated glucose, which damages blood vessels and increases the risk for insulin resistance (a condition that precedes diabetes) as well as heart disease.

What helps: Get regular exercise, which decreases levels of stress hormones.

- **More pain.** Studies have shown that people who are stressed tend to be more sensitive to pain, regardless of its cause. In fact, imaging studies show what's known as stress-induced hyperalgesia, an increase in activity in areas of the brain associated with pain. Similarly, patients with depression seem to experience more pain—and pain that's more intense—than those who are mentally healthy.

What helps: To help curb physical pain, find a distraction. One study found that post-surgical patients who had rooms with views of trees needed less pain medication than those who had no views. On a practical level, you can listen to music. Read a lighthearted book. Paint. Knit. These steps will also help relieve any stress that may be exacerbating your pain.

Also helpful: If you have a lot of pain that isn't well-controlled with medication, ask your doctor if you might be suffering from anxiety or depression. If so, you may benefit from taking an antidepressant, such as *duloxetine* (Cymbalta) or *venlafaxine* (Effexor), which can help reduce pain along with depression.

- **Impaired memory.** After just a few weeks of stress, nerves in the part of the brain associated with memory shrink and lose connections with other nerve cells, according to laboratory studies.

Result: You might find that you're forgetting names or where you put things. These lapses are often due to distraction—people who are stressed and always busy find it difficult to store new information in the brain. This type of memory loss is rarely a sign of dementia unless it's getting progressively worse.

What helps: Use memory tools to make your life easier. When you meet someone, say that person's name out loud to embed it in your memory. Put your keys in the same place every day.

Also: Make a conscious effort to pay attention. It's the only way to ensure that new information is stored. Sometimes the guidance of a counselor is necessary to help you learn how to manage stress. Self-help materials, such as tapes and books, may also be good tools.

- **Weight gain.** The fast-paced American lifestyle may be part of the reason why two-thirds of adults in this country are overweight or obese. People who are stressed tend to eat more—and the "comfort" foods they choose often promote weight gain. Some people eat less during stressful times, but they're in the minority.

What helps: If you tend to snack or eat larger servings when you're anxious, stressed or depressed, talk to a therapist. People who binge on "stress calories" usually have done so for decades—it's difficult to stop without professional help.

Also helpful: Pay attention when you find yourself reaching for a high-calorie snack even though you're not really hungry.

Healthy zero-calorie snack: Ice chips.

Low-calorie options: Grapes, carrots and celery sticks. Once you start noticing the pattern, you can make a conscious effort to replace eating with nonfood activities—working on a hobby, taking a quick walk, etc.

STRESS-FIGHTING PLAN

There are a number of ways to determine whether you are chronically stressed—you may feel short-tempered, anxious most of the time, have heart palpitations or suffer from insomnia.

However, I've found that many of my patients don't even realize how much stress they have in their lives until a friend, family member, coworker or doctor points it out to them. Once they understand the degree to which stress is affecting their health, they can explore ways to unwind and relax.

In general, it helps to...

- **Get organized.** Much of the stress that we experience comes from feeling overwhelmed. You can overcome this by organizing your life.

Examples: Use a day calendar to keep your activities and responsibilities on-track, and put reminder notes on the refrigerator.

- **Ask for help.** You don't have to become overwhelmed. If you're struggling at work, ask a mentor for advice. Tell your partner/spouse that you need help with the shopping or housework.

Taking charge of your life is among the best ways to reduce stress—and asking for help is one of the smartest ways to do this.

- **Write about your worries.** The anxieties and stresses floating around in our heads often dissipate, or at least seem more manageable, once we write them down.

- **Sleep for eight hours.** No one who is sleep-deprived can cope with stress effectively.

20-Minute Way to Fight Heart Disease

Norman E. Rosenthal, MD, clinical professor of psychiatry at Georgetown University School of Medicine, who maintains a private practice in the Washington, DC, area. He has conducted research at the National Institutes of Mental Health and is a recipient of the Anna-Monika Foundation Prize for his contribution to research in treating depression. He is author of *Transcendence: Healing and Transformation Through Transcendental Meditation* (Tarcher). *www.normanrosenthal.com*

Wouldn't it be great if there were a simple way to lower blood pressure, reverse heart disease and sharpen your brain? There is! It's called transcendental meditation, or TM for short.

Many people think of TM as a vestige of the 1960s, a vaguely religious practice that was popularized when the Beatles went to India to study with Maharishi Mahesh Yogi.

- **TM is not a religious practice.** It does not involve immersing yourself in a particular belief system. It's a mental technique that changes brain wave patterns and alters, in beneficial ways, physiological processes, such as blood pressure, heart rate and hormone levels.

Bonus: TM is easier to do than many other forms of meditation and relaxation therapy. And beginners exhibit the same brain wave changes as long-time practitioners, sometimes within just a few weeks after starting TM.

WHAT IT INVOLVES

Various relaxation techniques require you to sit with your eyes closed, focus on your breathing and/or visualize a particular scene. TM requires the repetition of a mantra, a meaningless word that you mentally focus on.

There's nothing mystical about the mantra. It's simply a tool for quieting the mind and "transcending" stressful thoughts, worries and concerns.

Most people who practice TM do so twice a day for 20 minutes each time. During a session, the breathing slows and the brain (as measured on an EEG) produces a preponderance of alpha waves, slow frequency signals (eight to 12 cycles per second) that indicate deep relaxation. There's also an increase in brain wave coherence, in which activity in different parts of the brain is roughly synchronized.

TM has been studied more than most other forms of meditation and relaxation—and, in some cases, appears to have more pronounced health effects. Researchers have published approximately 340 peer-reviewed articles on TM, many of which appeared in respected medical journals. *Important benefits...*

LOWERS BLOOD PRESSURE

A University of Kentucky meta-analysis that looked at data from 711 participants found that those who practiced TM averaged a five-point reduction in systolic pressure (top number) and three points in diastolic (bottom number). This might sound like a modest benefit, but it's enough to potentially reduce the incidence of cardiovascular disease by 15% to 20%.

Scientists speculate that TM lowers blood pressure by reducing the body's output of hormones, such as epinephrine, that accompany and stimulate the natural stress response. People with hypertension who meditate twice a day for more than three months require, on average, 23% less blood pressure medication.

Other nondrug treatments for hypertension, including biofeedback, progressive relaxation and stress-management training, don't have these same effects.

REVERSES HEART DISEASE

Researchers divided participants with hypertension into two groups. Those in one group were given health education (the control group), while those in the second group practiced TM for six to nine months. The thickness of the intima (inner lining) of the carotid artery was measured at the beginning and end of the study.

Result: The intima thickened slightly in the control group, indicating that cardiovascular disease had progressed. In the TM group, the thickness of the intima decreased. This study, published in *Stroke*, indicates that TM actually can reverse cardiovascular disease.

It's not known why TM has this effect. We suspect that it's more effective in patients with early-stage disease. In those with advanced atherosclerosis, which is accompanied by calcification of plaques (fatty deposits) in the coronary arteries, TM might slow disease progression but is unlikely to remove plaque that has already accumulated.

REDUCES PAIN

I sometimes recommend TM for patients who suffer from chronic-pain conditions, such as arthritis. We know that pain tends to be more severe in patients with high levels of anxiety and stress—and TM is very effective at reducing stress.

In one study, participants dipped their fingers into painfully hot water, then rated the pain. Those who practiced TM rated their pain exactly the same as those who didn't use TM, but they were less bothered by it. Interestingly, participants who practiced TM for just five months achieved the same results as those who had meditated for decades.

SHARPENS YOUR BRAIN

When people meditate, the coherence of alpha brain waves throughout the brain is accompanied by slightly faster beta waves in the prefrontal region of the brain, behind the forehead. The alpha waves produce relaxation, while the beta waves increase focus and decision-making.

Brain studies of top-level managers show that they have higher levels of both alpha and beta coherence than lower-level workers. A similar thing occurs in elite athletes.

Practice helps: Some of the physiological changes produced by TM occur immediately, but people who keep doing it for several months tend to have better results, probably because of increased synaptic connections (connections between brain cells). The brain may literally rewire itself, with practice.

HOW TO START

During a TM session, you'll achieve a state of restful alertness, during which your thoughts are clear but without the distractions of the internal noise that we live with. How people achieve this is highly individual. I like to relax in a comfortable chair in a quiet room. I dim the lights, turn off the telephones and start repeating my mantra. A friend of mine who has practiced TM for 40 years can enjoy a brief session in the back of a taxi.

You might find it tricky to keep mentally repeating the mantra. You might be distracted by physical sensations, outside sounds, etc. All of this is natural and expected. At some point during the session, you'll feel mentally silent. You will be present in the moment but removed from it.

Important: TM is easy to practice but difficult to learn on your own. People start with one-on-one sessions with an instructor. In general, each teaching session lasts about 90 minutes. Your instructor will assign a mantra and give instructions for using it. Sometimes people wonder why they can't pick their own mantras. One reason is that it is a tradition not to. Another is that someone who chooses his/her own mantra might do so because of underlying meanings or associations. A mantra from a teacher won't have this baggage.

You will work with the instructor once a day for four consecutive days. After that, you might return once every month to make sure that your technique is working. The Web site *www.tm.org* can provide referrals to instructors in your area.

Purple Potatoes for Blood Pressure

Recent study: Eighteen overweight people with high blood pressure ate about seven golf ball–sized purple potatoes twice daily for a month. The potatoes with skins were cooked in a microwave.

Result: The study participants' diastolic (bottom number) blood pressure readings dropped 4%, on average, and their systolic (top number) readings were 3.5% lower. None of the participants gained weight. Purple potatoes are available at specialty-food stores and some supermarkets.

Joe Vinson, PhD, professor of chemistry, The University of Scranton, Pennsylvania.

Olive Oil for Arthritis And Other Amazing Food Cures

Stephen Sinatra, MD, cardiologist and founder of Heart MD Institute, an educational platform that promotes complementary treatments for heart disease, Manchester, Connecticut. He writes the monthly newsletter *Heart, Health & Nutrition* and lectures worldwide about natural and nutritional remedies. He is coauthor of *The Healing Kitchen* (Bottom Line Books). *www.drsinatra.com*

Exciting news: Certain foods have been proven to work better than standard medical treatments—and they are safer, too. *Here, top food cures...*

SLEEP BETTER WITH HONEY

This natural sweetener can help you get more of the sleep you need.

What research shows: Recent research at the Massachusetts Institute of Technology shows that honey increases the activity of serotonin, a "calming" neurotransmitter in the brain. It also sends a signal to the brain to curtail the release of orexin, a substance that promotes alertness during the day and can interfere with falling asleep at night.

How much: One-half teaspoon to one teaspoon 45 minutes to one hour before bed. I like to add it to a sliced banana and one-quarter cup of plain yogurt.

More sweet news: A study of more than 900 people found that a dab of honey was more effective than some standard dressings at helping small burns heal more quickly. Cover with gauze, and change the dressing every day. Any type of honey will work.

SPINACH IMPROVES MOOD

It's estimated that 15% of Americans eventually will suffer from depression that is severe enough to require medical attention...a higher percentage will experience milder forms.

What research shows: Up to 38% of people with depression are deficient, or borderline low, in the B vitamin folate. Folate is thought to increase levels of serotonin, the same brain chemical that is boosted by the most widely used antidepressant medications.

How much: The recommended daily amount of folate is 400 micrograms (mcg). That's about the amount in one cup of raw spinach or any dark green leafy vegetable, such as kale, Swiss chard and mustard greens. You also can get generous amounts of folate in other fresh vegetables, fortified fruit juices and pumpkin and sunflower seeds.

LOWER BLOOD PRESSURE WITH CELERY

Celery contains the compound apigenin, which dilates blood vessels and can help prevent and treat hypertension. Another chemical in celery, 3-n-butylphthaide, not only relaxes arteries but also reduces levels of adrenaline and other hormones that cause blood pressure to rise.

What research shows: A laboratory study at the University of Chicago found that animals given purified 3-n-butylphthaide for eight weeks had drops in systolic (top number) blood pressure of 12 points.

How much: Four or five stalks of celery daily. That's enough to reduce blood pressure in most people—it can shift a patient with mild hypertension into the safety zone.

MORE ROSEMARY, LESS CANCER

Any form of high-heat cooking for meats, including broiling and grilling, produces heterocyclic amines (HCAs), carcinogens that may increase the risk for breast and colon cancers.

What research shows: Marinating or seasoning meat with rosemary produces two natural antioxidants, carnosol and rosemarinic acid, that destroy HCAs. Studies at the University of Illinois at Urbana-Champaign found that animals given rosemary extract after being exposed to a carcinogen had less DNA damage and fewer tumors.

How much: Add rosemary, fresh or dried, to marinades and stews...sprinkle it on roasted potatoes and meats.

OLIVE OIL FOR ARTHRITIS

The omega-3 fatty acids in fish are among the best-known anti-inflammatory agents. Many people don't realize that olive oil has similar effects.

What research shows: People who consume extra-virgin olive oil have less arthritis-related inflammation. This is important because inflammation is what causes pain and stiffness—and, in many cases, subsequent joint damage.

Olive oil contains the naturally occurring chemical compound oleocanthal, which blocks the activity of an inflammatory enzyme. A report in *Nature* showed that extra-virgin olive oil's anti-inflammatory effects were similar to those of the drug *ibuprofen*.

How much: One to two tablespoons of olive oil daily (in place of other fats).

Also helpful: Two oranges. A Boston University School of Medicine study found that people with a vitamin C intake of 120 milligrams (mg)—about the amount in two oranges—were three times less likely to have a progression of osteoarthritis of the knee, compared with those with lower levels.

HELP DIABETES WITH CHROMIUM

Up to 90% of Americans are deficient in chromium, a mineral that makes the body's cells more responsive to insulin's effects.

What research shows: People with diabetes who eat more onions, which are high in chromium, typically have lower fasting blood glucose levels. They also have lower triglycerides and LDL cholesterol. High levels of triglycerides and LDL increase the risk for heart disease—a serious threat for diabetics.

How much: Aim for one to two servings of chromium-rich foods a day. In addition to onions, other high-chromium foods include brewer's yeast, sweet potatoes, oysters, beef and tomatoes.

Also helpful: A sprinkle of cinnamon. One study found that people who used cinnamon had blood sugar levels that averaged 20% lower than people who didn't use it. A compound in cinnamon mimics the effects of insulin even in amounts as small as one-quarter teaspoon two to three times daily.

SEXY ARGININE

Drugs such as Viagra have revolutionized the treatment of erectile dysfunction in men, but these drugs are expensive and can be dangerous for those with heart disease. Foods containing the amino acid arginine can promote better erections but without the dangers of medications.

What research shows: Arginine stimulates the release of nitric oxide, a chemical that dilates blood vessels and improves blood flow to the penis. This is the same chemical that is affected by Viagra and related drugs.

How much: Aim for one to two daily servings of foods high in arginine, such as milk, chickpeas, coconut and soybeans (edamame, tofu, soy milk). A few hours before intimacy, take an arginine supplement in a dose of four to six grams. Before taking any supplement, it's best to check with your doctor.

Caution: This dose of arginine should not be taken if you have had a heart attack within the past six months.

NUTS FOR THE HEART

Nuts are among the most potent remedies for heart health.

What research shows: People who eat nuts up to five times a week can reduce their risk for heart disease by 30% to 50%, according to the Harvard Nurses' Health Study and other medical trials. People who eat nuts regularly have better heart health even when they eat unhealthy amounts of saturated fat or consume few fruits or vegetables.

The omega-3 fatty acids in nuts reduce arterial inflammation and the risk for clots. Nuts also contain oleic acid, which improves cholesterol.

How much: One small handful of nuts daily. Any kind of nut is fine (including peanuts, which actually aren't a nut), roasted or raw (no salt).

MAGNESIUM FOR MIGRAINES

People who suffer from migraines typically have lower-than-normal amounts of magnesium in the brain. Those who increase their consumption of magnesium-rich foods can dramatically reduce these painful headaches.

What research shows: German researchers gave one group of migraine patients magnesium supplements for 12 weeks. Those in a second group were given a placebo. Those taking magnesium had a 41.6% reduction in migraines, compared with a 15.8% reduction for those in the control group.

How much: Try to get 400 mg of magnesium from food daily. Magnesium-rich foods include nuts (one ounce of almonds, 80 mg)...spinach (one-half cup cooked, 78 mg)...and oatmeal (one cup cooked, 58 mg).

Caution: If you have kidney disease or kidney stones, check with your doctor before loading up on magnesium.

Apples Lower Cholesterol

R*ecent study:* Among 160 women ages 45 to 65, half ate about three-quarters cup of dried apples (equal to two fresh apples) daily for a year, while the other half ate eight to 10 prunes. The women who ate apples had an average drop in LDL "bad" cholesterol of 23% and a 4% increase in HDL "good" cholesterol. The women also lost an average of 3.3 pounds.

Theory: Pectin and polyphenols in apples improve lipid metabolism and reduce inflammation.

Bahram Arjmandi, PhD, RD, director, Center for Advancing Exercise and Nutrition Research on Aging, The Florida State University, Tallahassee.

OJ for the Heart?

Drinking orange juice made from concentrate lowers cholesterol levels. A recent study of people with both high and normal cholesterol found that those who drank three cups of orange juice from concentrate daily had a significant improvement in HDL "good" cholesterol levels. Those with high cholesterol also had a drop in their LDL "bad" cholesterol levels. Other types of orange juice besides concentrate were not studied.

Thaïs B. César, PhD, associate professor, food and nutrition department, São Paulo State University, Brazil, and leader of the study published in *Nutrition Research.*

Try Cranberry Juice

Cranberry juice may be good for your heart. The healthful polyphenols in cranberry juice have been found to improve blood vessel function. When study participants were tested immediately after drinking cranberry juice and then again 12 hours later, they showed a decrease in arterial stiffness, a risk factor for heart disease.

Beware: Some cranberry juice products are blends of multiple fruit juices and may not have enough cranberry content to achieve this benefit.

Best: Because of the natural tartness of 100% cranberry juice, stick with "cranberry juice cocktail." Low-calorie versions contain less sugar and calories than 100% grape juice and 100% pomegranate juice.

Jeffrey B. Blumberg, PhD, director, HNRCA Antioxidants Research Laboratory, Tufts University, Boston, and coauthor of a study published in *The American Journal of Clinical Nutrition.*

Melon Medicine

In an eight-week study, animals given watermelon juice in place of water lost weight and had a drop in cholesterol. They also showed a reversal of atherosclerosis, the cause of most heart attacks.

Theory: Watermelon is a rich source of the antioxidant lycopene.

University of Kentucky.

Lower Blood Pressure Naturally

Mark Houston, MD, associate clinical professor of medicine at Vanderbilt University School of Medicine and director of the Hypertension Institute at Saint Thomas Hospital, both in Nashville.

The supplemental form of melatonin, the "sleep" hormone, may alleviate nocturnal hypertension (a form of high blood pressure that occurs during sleep). In most people, blood pressure drops by 10% to 20% during sleep. But about one-quarter of people with prehypertension or hypertension are "non-dippers"—their sleeping pressure is about as high as or higher than their waking pressure.

High blood pressure during sleep (which is diagnosed by a 24-hour blood pressure monitor) is particularly common among blacks and people with chronic kidney disease, and it worsens their risk for heart attack, stroke and kidney failure. Researchers at Boston's Brigham and Women's Hospital have found that 2.5 mg of melatonin, taken one hour before bedtime, may lower systolic (top number) pressure by an average of 6 mm Hg and diastolic (bottom number) pressure by 4 mm Hg during sleep.

My advice: If you know that you have nocturnal hypertension, or if you have hypertension plus insomnia or chronic kidney disease, ask your doctor about taking melatonin. At the very least, it may help you sleep better.

Fiber Helps You Live Longer

In a recent study, researchers followed more than 388,000 volunteers, ages 50 to 71, and found that men and women who consumed the most fiber were 24% to 59% less likely to die from infections, heart disease or respiratory illness than those who did not.

Possible reason: Fiber may steady blood sugar, lower blood lipids and control inflammation.

Recommended: 21 to 25 grams of fiber daily for women and 30 to 38 grams for men from naturally occurring plant-based sources, such as grains, legumes, vegetables and fruits. Commercially made foods that are fortified with fiber were not studied.

Yikyung Park, ScD, staff scientist, National Cancer Institute, Bethesda, Maryland, and leader of a study of more than 388,000 people, published in *Archives of Internal Medicine.*

You Can Pedal While You Work

Recent study: For four weeks, 18 mostly overweight office workers were given portable pedal machines to use while seated at their desks. Study participants pedaled 23 minutes daily, on average—enough time to improve heart health if performed regularly.

If you sit for extended periods: Consider using a pedal machine, such as the MagneTrainer for $149 (*www.magnetrainer.com*, 877-426-3292) or Medline for $240 (*www.amazon.com*).

Lucas Carr, PhD, assistant professor of exercise and sport science, East Carolina University, Greenville, North Carolina.

Black Tea Lowers Blood Pressure

Recent study: Among 95 tea drinkers (average age 56.5), those who drank three cups of black tea daily for six months saw their systolic (top number) and diastolic (bottom number) blood pressure readings drop by three and two points, respectively. Even such small drops in blood pressure translate into a 7% to 10% drop in risk for cardiovascular disease.

Theory: Flavonoids in black tea may improve the functioning of endothelial cells that line the blood vessels.

Jonathan Hodgson, PhD, research professor, The University of Western Australia, Perth.

Chew Gum and Other Simple Ways to Prevent Heart Disease

Barry A. Franklin, PhD, director of Cardiac Rehabilitation and Exercise Laboratories at William Beaumont Hospital, Royal Oak, Michigan. He has served as president of the American Association of Cardiovascular and Pulmonary Rehabilitation and the American College of Sports Medicine. He is coauthor, with Joseph C. Piscatella, of *109 Things You Can Do to Prevent, Halt & Reverse Heart Disease* (Workman).

Everyone knows the "big" things that can damage the heart. These include smoking, high cholesterol, hypertension, diabetes, obesity and/or a sedentary lifestyle. Coping with these factors can be difficult—and, for certain patients, even can be overwhelming.

What people don't realize is that there are small steps anyone can take to reduce the risk for a heart attack...

TAKE TWO BABY ASPIRIN

Millions of Americans take a daily aspirin to reduce the risk for a heart attack. In the past, doctors typically advised taking one "baby" aspirin (81 mg) daily—a conservative dose that minimizes the risk for the gastrointestinal bleeding that aspirin can cause.

Latest recommendation: A review of studies, published in *The American Journal of Medicine,* concluded that the optimal dose is 162 mg (two baby aspirin or half an adult aspirin) daily. Aspirin therapy reduces the risk for a first cardiovascular event (heart attack or stroke) in men and women by 30%. (Aspirin appears to be more protective in preventing heart attacks in men and strokes in women.) In those who already have had a cardiovascular event, it reduces the risk for a second event by about the same amount.

Patients who take 162 mg of aspirin daily have about the same bleeding risks as those taking the lower dose (and in both cases, the risk for bleeding is very low).

Important: Aspirin is not recommended for everyone. In addition to increasing the risk for gastrointestinal bleeding, it can lead to severe allergic reactions and other problems in some patients. Talk to your doctor before using aspirin at any dose for cardioprotection.

CHEW GUM AND FLOSS

People with gum disease are two to three times more likely to have a heart attack than those without it.

Reason: Plaque, the sticky film that accumulates on teeth, can damage gums and create small pockets that harbor bacteria. The bacteria then enter the bloodstream and cause chronic inflammation that increases the risk for clots and other heart attack risk factors.

What to do: Chew sugarless gum that contains xylitol, a natural sweetener that suppresses mouth bacteria.

Also, be sure to floss every day. A study in *The New England Journal of Medicine* found that people who take care of their gums with regular flossing and brushing and regular visits to their dentists have improved function of the arteries—the ability of blood vessels to expand and contract normally.

DRINK A CUP OF TEA

A heart specialist at Brigham and Women's Hospital looked at the tea-and-coffee drinking habits of 340 men and women who had suffered heart attacks. He compared them with people in a control group who hadn't had heart attacks.

Conclusion: People who drank one or more cups of black tea daily were 44% less likely to have heart attacks than people who didn't drink tea.

Flavonoids in tea are strong antioxidants that protect blood vessels from injury and inflammation. Tea also contains compounds that improve blood vessel function in as little as 30 minutes.

Choose black or green teas, whichever you prefer. They have similar properties. Herbal teas are not recommended for heart health.

EAT A BOWL OF CEREAL

A study of more than 1,700 people found that those with low levels of vitamin D had double the risk for a cardiovascular event—such as a heart attack, heart failure or stroke—in the next five years than those with higher levels.

Vitamin D deficiency also is linked with insulin resistance, metabolic syndrome and diabetes, as well as hypertension. And it appears to increase inflammation throughout the body, including in artery walls.

Vitamin D is produced in the skin after exposure to sunlight. But in many parts of the US, there simply isn't enough sunshine to produce sufficient levels of vitamin D. It's estimated that about two-thirds of Americans don't get enough vitamin D.

Recommended: I advise patients to eat vitamin D–fortified cereal daily.

Bonus: Cereal also can provide heart-healthy fiber. According to recent research from Northwestern University, people who consume more than 22 grams of dietary fiber a day are more likely to have a lower lifetime risk for cardiovascular disease. One-half cup of 100% ready-to-eat bran cereal typically provides nine grams of fiber.

Other food sources of vitamin D include fatty fish, such as herring, wild salmon and mackerel. Fortified juices are good sources as well. And try to get 15 minutes of direct sunshine two to three days a week. If necessary, you can take a vitamin D supplement of 500 international units (IU) to 1,000 IU daily.

GET YOUR ZZZZZS

People who don't get enough sleep are more likely to develop hypertension and diabetes. Blood tests show that they have an increase in C-reactive protein and interleukin-6, inflammatory markers that are linked to heart disease.

Sleep deprivation also can lead to weight gain, in part because it disrupts leptin and ghrelin, hormones that regulate appetite.

Recommended: Six to eight hours of sleep per night. A recent study in *European Heart Journal* found that people who sleep less than six hours per night are 48% more likely to get heart disease and 15% more likely to have a stroke than those who sleep more.

If you have trouble sleeping, a short nap during the day can help increase alertness and productivity. Also, 30 to 40 minutes of daily exercise can help some people fall asleep more easily.

DON'T GET ANGRY

Emotional stress simulates the release of epinephrine and norepinephrine, potent hormones that elevate blood pressure and heart rate and increase the risk for clots, the cause of most heart attacks.

I strongly advise patients to identify the sources of stress in their lives—rude drivers, an angry boss—and remind themselves not to react. When you get really angry, the risk for a heart attack is two to three times higher in the hour afterward than it was before.

Both stressful events and chronic, long-term stress can damage the heart.

Example: Doctors sometimes refer to the first day of the workweek as blue Monday because people stressed about returning to work have twice as many heart attacks on that day than on any other day of the week.

Everyone has his/her own way of dealing with stress. It could be playing with your dog, doing volunteer work, taking vacations or exercising. In fact, a 15-minute walk can reduce tension as effectively as a prescription tranquilizer.

STAY CLOSE TO FAMILY AND FRIENDS

In the mid-1960s, researchers noticed that the death rate from heart disease in a close-knit Italian-American community in Roseto, Pennsylvania, was much lower than in neighboring towns. An analysis of medical records over a six-year period showed that Roseto had had 157 cardiovascular deaths per 100,000 residents. In adjoining communities, the number was nearly four times higher.

The difference: Most families in Roseto had multiple generations living at home. People knew their neighbors. They went to church together, joined social clubs and chatted during strolls together.

People with strong social networks and/or family ties tend to be healthier than those without these connections. They're more likely to follow up on doctors' appointments and orders. They tend to eat healthier foods.

Researchers at Duke University Medical Center studied survival rates of more than 1,300 cardiac patients. The five-year survival rate of unmarried patients who didn't have close ties to family or friends was 50%, compared with 82% for those with a spouse, close friend or both.

There is a lot to Barbra Streisand's contention that "people who need people are the luckiest people in the world."

Fight Killer Blood Clots—Reduce Your Risk for Heart Attack and Stroke

Decker Weiss, NMD, a naturopathic medical doctor who specializes in integrative cardiology. He is the founder and owner of Weiss Natural Medicine, in Scottsdale, Arizona, *www.weissnaturalmedicine.com*, and author of *The Weiss Method: A Natural Program for Reversing Heart Disease and Preventing Heart Attacks* (Shannake).

Millions of Americans take anticlotting medications, or "blood thinners," including aspirin and *warfarin* (Coumadin), to prevent clots and reduce the risk for such conditions as heart attack and stroke.

These drugs are extremely effective. Daily aspirin, for example, can reduce the risk for a first heart attack by 44%, according to data from the Physicians' Health Study.

The downside: Even at low doses, every anticlotting agent can cause bleeding—often from the stomach, gums or intestines—as a side effect. Sometimes, gastrointestinal bleeding can occur even without causing noticeable symptoms.

In addition, warfarin, one of the leading blood thinners, doubles the risk for intracerebral hemorrhage (bleeding in the brain).

NATURAL BLOOD THINNERS

The good news is that certain herbs and other supplements can be used for their anticlotting properties—and may have a reduced risk for side effects, such as bleeding.

This approach is not intended to replace medications—patients with a high risk for clotting need to take such drugs. Under a doctor's supervision, these supplements can be combined with blood-thinning medications to boost the drugs' effectiveness and potentially allow you to take a lower dose, thus reducing the risk for bleeding.

Those with only a slight risk for clots (due to family history, for example) may want to consider using natural anticoagulants alone, under a doctor's supervision, to promote better circulation.

Bonus: Natural blood thinners usually have anti-inflammatory properties. This is important because most chronic diseases, including heart disease, rheumatoid arthritis and stroke, are caused in part by inflammation.

The supplements below can be taken alone or in combination, depending on the degree of protection that's required.

Some of these supplements may interact with prescription medications, so consult a doctor who is knowledgeable about supplement use.* *Best choices...*

- **Fish oil.** Studies of large populations show that people who eat a lot of cold-water fish, such as salmon and mackerel, tend to have lower heart attack death rates than people who don't eat fish.

The omega-3 fatty acids in cold-water fish are strong anticlotting agents. Fish oil is thought to inhibit platelet aggregation (clumping), part of the clotting process. One report, published in *The Annals of Pharmacotherapy,* found that taking fish oil along with warfarin caused an increase in anticlotting activity.

Typical dose: Depending on other risk factors, such as elevated cholesterol and high blood pressure, one tablet twice daily of Vectomega's Whole Food Omega-3 DHA/EPA Complex—it provides 292 mg of omega-3s (DHA and EPA balanced) in a phospholipid peptide complex, in which the fish oil is bound to peptides to increase absorbability. Or one teaspoon twice daily of Nordic Naturals' Ultimate Omega Liquid, which provides 1,626 mg of EPA and 1,126 mg of DHA.

- **Ginger and curcumin.** Ginger reduces levels of fibrinogen, a precursor to fibrin, a

*To find a doctor who has experience treating patients with supplements, consult the American Association of Naturopathic Physicians, 866-538-2267, *www.naturopathic.org*.

protein that is a major component of blood clots. Curcumin has only modest effects on coagulation but is a stronger anti-inflammatory agent. That's why I advise patients to take these herbs together. Studies have shown that both ginger and curcumin can reduce inflammation in the body. An Australian study found that substances in ginger inhibited the activity of arachidonic acid, part of the chemical sequence involved in clotting. In the study, ginger compounds were more effective than aspirin at blocking platelet activity.

Typical dose: Twice daily, 50 mg to 100 mg of ginger and one or two 375-mg capsules of curcumin.

Good products: Gaia Herbs' Ginger Supreme Phyto-Caps and EuroPharma's CuraMed curcumin complex.

• **Nattokinase.** Extracted from soybeans, nattokinase is an enzyme that helps prevent clot formation—it also makes platelets less likely to clump together. Unlike warfarin, which only prevents clots, nattokinase appears to break down clots that already have formed.

Typical dose: Depending on other risk factors, one to two capsules or tablets (2,000 fibrin units per 100 mg) twice daily.

Important: I recommend taking nattokinase between meals. The anticlotting properties are strongest when it is taken without food.

• **Vinpocetine.** This supplement is extracted from periwinkle. It's extremely important to take vinpocetine under a doctor's supervision. Vinpocetine is the most potent natural substance for preventing clots—and, like prescription anticlotting agents, it can cause internal bleeding in some patients. For this reason, I recommend it mainly for high-risk patients who are unable to take warfarin because of side effects and/or complications.

Typical dose: 2 mg total—in divided doses twice daily. Higher doses (5 mg total in divided doses) might be needed, but don't increase from the starting dose without talking with your doctor. Vinpocetine should be taken without food.

• **Ginkgo.** The extract from the dried leaves of the ginkgo biloba tree has traditionally been used to treat intermittent claudication, leg pain caused by insufficient blood flow, as well as cognitive impairments (such as memory problems) due to poor blood circulation in the brain.

Ginkgo is effective at reducing clots and also acts as a vasodilator that helps improve blood flow to the brain, heart and other parts of the body. I don't recommend it as often as other anticoagulants because it has little effect on inflammation. If you use ginkgo, ask your doctor about combining it with curcumin or other anti-inflammatory herbs/supplements.

Typical dose: About 40 mg, three times daily.

• **Garlic.** Studies have shown that patients who take garlic supplements have a lower risk for clots. Use only those products that list a high allicin content—the main active ingredient in garlic. This can be found frequently in fresh garlic supplements.

Typical dose: The optimal dose for garlic hasn't been definitively established. However, some studies indicate that you need at least 180 mg of allicin twice daily.

Good brand: Allimax.

Important: In general, natural therapies should be started at low doses that are slowly increased, under a doctor's supervision, over time. I recommend that the supplements described in this article be used at least twice daily to ensure that adequate levels of the therapeutic compounds are maintained in the body.

Coffee Reduces Stroke Risk

Recent finding: Drinking one or more cups of coffee daily was associated with a 22% to 25% reduction in stroke risk.

Theory: Coffee beans contain antioxidants and other disease-fighting chemicals that reduce inflammation and improve insulin activity. Moderate coffee consumption also has been linked to decreased risk for diabetes, colon cancer, heart disease, liver disease and Parkinson's disease.

Susanna Larsson, PhD, division of nutritional epidemiology, Institute of Environmental Medicine, Karolinska Institute, Stockholm, Sweden. She was lead researcher of a study of 34,670 women, published in *Stroke.*

Fruits Fight Stroke

White-fleshed fruits and vegetables may protect against stroke.

Recent finding: The more apples, bananas, cauliflower, cucumbers, pears and other white-fleshed produce people ate, the more their stroke risk was reduced—by up to 52%. Other fruits and vegetables did not affect stroke risk, but they have health benefits as well.

Linda Oude Griep, MSc, postdoctoral fellow in human nutrition at Wageningen University, the Netherlands, and lead author of a study of 20,069 people, published in *Stroke.*

30-Day Diabetes Cure—You May Even Be Able to Throw Away Your Meds!

Stefan Ripich, ND, a naturopathic physician based in Santa Fe, New Mexico. He practiced for 10 years at the Palo Alto Veterans Administration Medical Center and established the first holistic clinic in the VA system. He is coauthor, with Jim Healthy, of *The 30-Day Diabetes Cure* (Bottom Line Books). *www.bottomlinepublications.com/diabetes*

In the US, a new case of diabetes is diagnosed every 30 seconds. And many of those people will be given drugs to treat the disease.

You can control high blood sugar with medications, but they aren't a cure and they can have side effects. They also are expensive, costing $400 or more a month for many patients.

Much better: Dietary remedies that have been proven to reduce blood sugar, improve the effects of insulin (a hormone produced by the pancreas that controls blood sugar), promote weight loss and, in many cases, eliminate the need for medications. A UCLA study found that 50% of patients with type 2 diabetes (the most common form) were able to reverse it in three weeks with dietary changes and exercise.

How you can do it, too...

- **Eliminate all HFCS.** A 2010 Princeton study found that rats given water sweetened with high-fructose corn syrup (HFCS) gained more weight than rats that drank water sweetened with plain sugar, even though their calorie intake was exactly the same.

Reasons: The calories from HFCS fail to trigger leptin, the hormone that tells your body when to quit eating. Also, HFCS is more likely than natural sugar to be converted to fat...and being overweight is the main risk factor for diabetes.

What to do: Read food labels carefully. HFCS is the main sweetener in soft drinks and many processed foods, including baked goods such as cookies and cakes.

- **Don't drink diet soda.** If you give up HFCS-laden soft drinks, don't switch to diet soda. Diet sodas actually cause weight gain by boosting insulin production, leading to excessively high insulin in your blood that triggers greater fat accumulation and even more cravings for sugar.

A study published in *Diabetes Care* found that drinking diet soda every day increased the risk for type 2 diabetes by as much as 67%.

If you crave sweet bubbly beverages, pour one inch of pure fruit juice into a glass and then top it off with carbonated water.

- **Eat barley.** I advise patients to eat foods that are as close to their natural state as possible—whole-grain cereals and breads, brown rice, etc. These "slow carbohydrates" contain fiber and other substances that prevent the spikes in glucose and insulin that lead to diabetes.

Best choice: Barley. Researchers at the Creighton Diabetes Center in Omaha compared the effects of two breakfasts—one consisting of oatmeal (one of the best slow carbohydrates) and the other consisting of an even slower breakfast cereal made from barley. Participants who ate barley had a post-meal rise in blood sugar that was significantly lower than participants who ate the oatmeal breakfast.

You can eat cooked barley as a side dish...sprinkle it on salads...or mix it into tuna, chicken, tofu or lentil salad.

• **Season with cinnamon.** About one-quarter teaspoon of cinnamon daily reduces blood sugar, improves insulin sensitivity and reduces inflammation in the arteries—important for reducing the risk for heart disease, the leading cause of death in diabetics.

Research published in *Diabetes Care* found that people with type 2 diabetes who ate at least one-quarter teaspoon of cinnamon daily reduced fasting blood sugar levels by up to 29%. They also had up to a 30% reduction in triglycerides (a blood fat) and up to a 27% drop in LDL (bad) cholesterol.

• **Eat protein at breakfast.** Protein at breakfast stabilizes blood sugar and makes people feel satisfied, which means that you'll consume fewer calories overall. Lean protein includes eggs, chicken and fish.

• **Eat more meat (the good kind).** We've all been told that a diet high in meat (and therefore saturated fat) is inherently unhealthy. Not true. Other things being equal, people who eat more saturated fat actually tend to weigh less and have smaller waist measurements than similar adults who eat less.

The real danger is from processed meats, such as bacon, hot dogs and many cold cuts. These foods have more calories per serving than natural meats. They're higher in sodium. They have a lower percentage of heart-healthy omega-3 fatty acids and other beneficial fats that lower inflammation.

A large study that looked at data from 70,000 women found that those who ate processed meats with every meal were 52% more likely to develop diabetes than those who ate healthier meats and other foods.

I advise people to look for grass-fed beef. It's lower in calories and fat than industrialized grain-fed factory feedlot beef and higher in omega-3s.

• **Snack on nuts.** Healthful snacking between meals keeps blood sugar stable throughout the day. Nuts are the perfect snack because they're high in fiber (which reduces abrupt increases in glucose and insulin) and protein (for appetite control). They also are good sources of important nutrients and antioxidants.

A Harvard study of 83,000 women found that those who frequently ate almonds, pecans or other nuts were 27% less likely to develop diabetes than those who rarely ate nuts. A small handful every day is enough.

Caution: "Roasted" nuts usually are a bad choice because they often are deep-fried in coconut oil. They also have added salt and/or sugar. "Dry-roasted nuts" have not been fried in fat but usually have salt and sugar.

If you like roasted nuts, it's best to buy organically grown raw nuts and lightly toast them in a dry fry pan over very low heat (or in your oven).

• **Supplement with vitamin D.** In theory, we can get all the vitamin D that we need from sunshine—our bodies make it after the sun hits our skin. But about 90% of Americans don't get adequate amounts—either because they deliberately avoid sun exposure or because they live in climates without much sun.

A Finnish study found that participants with high levels of vitamin D were 40% less likely to develop diabetes than those with lower amounts. Vitamin D appears to improve insulin sensitivity and reduce the risk for diabetes-related complications, including heart disease.

Recommended: Take 1,000 international units (IU) to 2,000 IU of vitamin D-3 daily.

• **Remember to exercise.** It's just as important as a healthy diet for preventing and reversing diabetes. The Diabetes Prevention Program (a major multicenter clinical research study) found that people who walked as little as 17 minutes a day, on average, were 58% less likely to develop diabetes.

Walking for 30 minutes most days of the week is optimal.

Leafy Greens Lower Diabetes Risk

Recent study: People who ate the most greens, such as Chinese cabbage, kale and spinach, had a 14% lower risk for type 2 diabetes than those who ate the least.

Possible reason: Leafy greens have magnesium, an antioxidant involved with glucose metabolism. And the alpha-linoleic acid in leafy greens helps increase insulin sensitivity.

Patrice Carter, PhD candidate, research nutritionist, University of Leicester, England, and leader of an analysis of six studies, published online in *British Medical Journal.*

Magnesium-Rich Foods Reduce Stroke Risk

A recent analysis of studies showed an 8% reduction in risk for each additional 100 milligrams (mg) of magnesium eaten daily.

Possible connection: The mineral is known to decrease blood pressure, cholesterol levels and the tendency toward diabetes, all of which affect stroke risk. Magnesium-rich foods include nuts...leafy greens...whole grains...and dried beans.

Jeffrey Saver, MD, director of the UCLA Stroke Center and professor of neurology at David Geffen School of Medicine at UCLA.

Beware Fish-Oil Contaminants

In a test of 13 brands, all had their labeled amounts of the omega-3 fatty acids EPA and DHA, but four brands also contained trace amounts of polychlorinated biphenyls (PCBs) —CVS Natural...GNC Triple Strength...Nature's Bounty Odorless...and Sundown Naturals. The PCB levels met federal safety standards but would require warning labels under stricter California law.

Supplements that passed all quality standards: Walmart Spring Valley...Walgreens Finest Natural...Walgreens Omega-3 Fish Oil Concentrate...Barleans Organic Oils EPA-DHA...Nature Made 1,200 mg...The Vitamin Shoppe Meg-3 EPA-DHA...Carlson Super Omega-3 Gems...Norwegian Gold Ultimate Critical Omega...Nature's Way Fisol.

Consumer Reports, 101 Truman Ave., Yonkers, New York 10703. *www.consumerreports.org*

Dark Leafy Greens Protect Eyes

The compounds lutein and zeaxanthin found in dark leafy greens can reduce the risk for cataracts and advanced macular degeneration.

Best sources (for one-half cup cooked): Kale, 11.9 milligrams (mg)...spinach, 10.2 mg... Swiss chard, 9.6 mg...collard greens, 7.3 mg.

Julie Mares, MSPH, PhD, professor of ophthalmology, University of Wisconsin School of Medicine and Public Health, Madison, quoted in *Nutrition Action Healthletter. www.cspinet.org*

Fight Cancer with This Formula

Raymond Chang, MD, a faculty member at Weill Cornell Medical College, New York City, and a pioneer in the use of complementary and alternative treatments in oncology. He is founder and medical director of Meridian Medical Group, New York City, and founder of the Institute of East-West Medicine, a nonprofit organization devoted to preserving traditional healing arts and integrating them with modern medicine. He is author of *Beyond the Magic Bullet—The Anti-Cancer Cocktail: A New Approach to Beating Cancer* (Posters Please).

Researchers are discovering that multiple treatments given simultaneously can be far more effective at fighting cancer than any single treatment. That's because a typical cancer involves an average of 63 genetic mutations, each of which works in different ways. A single treatment is unlikely to affect more than a few of these processes.

Better approach: Cancer "cocktails" that simultaneously attack abnormal cells in a multitude of ways.

Examples: A deadly form of blood cancer, multiple myeloma, now is routinely treated with drug combinations that have doubled survival rates. A French study, published in May 2011 in *The New England Journal of Medicine,* found that patients with pancreatic cancer who were given a combination of four drugs lived about 60% longer than those given standard chemotherapy.

For the most part, the conventional treatment strategy for cancer involves using one or two traditional treatments—surgery, radiation, chemotherapy or hormone therapy—one after the other. Only on occasion are different treatments used in combination simultaneously such as when radiation and chemotherapy are administered following a patient's surgery.

Many oncologists now believe that it's better to hit cancers all at once with a barrage of treatments—including, in some cases, unconventional treatments, such as vitamins, herbs, supplements and medications typically prescribed for other health problems.

Example: I might advise a cancer patient getting conventional treatments to include the arthritis drug *celecoxib* (Celebrex), which makes cancer cells more sensitive to radiation...the hormone melatonin (which decreases the growth of some cancers)...and vitamin D-3 (which may reduce cancer recurrence).

GETTING STARTED

Here's how to make this approach work for you...

• **Keep an open mind.** Ask your doctor if there are safe and effective treatments that he/she recommends that may be unconventional, including "off-label" drugs—medications that haven't been approved by the FDA specifically for your type of cancer.

Doctors often know about new treatments that seem to work for a given cancer. They share stories with their colleagues about treatments that appear to be effective but that haven't yet been completely validated. When you have cancer, there's no reason not to try innovative approaches as long as they are safe.

Important: Don't try any treatment without first checking with your doctor to make sure that it is safe for you. If it is, he can recommend the right dose and tell you when you should take it.

• **Start with conventional care.** I never advise patients to forgo appropriate standard cancer treatments such as chemotherapy and/or radiation. These approaches have been proven to improve survival. You can then supplement these approaches with off-label medications, herbs and/or supplements to help increase effectiveness.

• **Define your goals.** A cure isn't the only reason to use a medley of treatments. The right cocktail also can reduce treatment side effects and improve your quality of life.

Example: Patients with breast cancer may be given hormonal treatments that reduce tumor growth, but in premenopausal women, these treatments also induce early menopause—and the accompanying hot flashes, night sweats and "brain fog." To be more comfortable during the posttreatment period, you can take vitamin E to reduce hot flashes...ginkgo to improve memory...and herbs such as black cohosh to reduce vaginal dryness and night sweats.

INGREDIENTS TO CONSIDER

Ask your doctor what you can add to your current treatments to increase their effectiveness. Some of the most common medications in the US have been shown to help cancer patients, as have supplements. *Here, some unconventional treatments that can help...*

• **Vitamin D.** Studies have shown that vitamin D induces apoptosis, the death of cancer cells. This is important because one of the characteristics of cancer cells is the ability to avoid cell death. Using vitamin D along with chemotherapy, surgery and/or radiation could improve your outcome.

•**The ulcer medication *cimetidine* (Tagamet)** strengthens the immune system so that it can fight cancer cells. Studies have shown that patients who start taking cimetidine a few days before colon cancer surgery may be less likely to have a recurrence of the cancer.

•**Aspirin.** An analysis of data from the Harvard Nurses' Health Study found that breast cancer patients who took aspirin reduced the risk of the cancer spreading (metastasis) by nearly 50%.

•**Curcumin,** the active compound in the spice turmeric. Like aspirin, it's an anti-inflammatory that can reduce the invasion and spread of cancer cells. It also can inhibit angiogenesis, the development of blood vessels that nourish tumors.

•**Green tea.** This is one cancer-cocktail ingredient that everyone can "take." One cup of green tea has approximately 45 milligrams (mg) of epigallocatechin 3-gallate (EGCG), a compound that appears to reduce the growth of cancer cells. Dozens of studies have shown that green tea may be effective.

Example: A Mayo Clinic study found that the majority of leukemia patients who took EGCG showed clear improvement. Other studies have shown that it can reduce prostate-specific antigen (PSA), a substance that is elevated in patients with prostate cancer.

I recommend eight cups of green tea a day to fight cancer.

•**Red yeast rice.** This type of yeast, taken in supplement form, contains monacolin K, the same active compound that is used in *lovastatin*, one of the cholesterol-lowering statins. Red yeast rice is an anti-inflammatory that also affects immune response and cell signaling—actions that can help prevent and possibly treat some cancers.

Laboratory studies indicate that red yeast rice (as well as statins) might increase the effectiveness of radiation and chemotherapy.

As for statins, in studies involving nearly a half-million patients, the drugs have been shown to significantly reduce the incidence and recurrence of colon, breast, lung and prostate cancers.

GO SLOW

Mix the cocktail slowly. It's not good to start many treatments at the same time. You need to know if a particular ingredient is causing side effects.

Example: I might advise a patient to use Chinese herbs for a week. If he/she is doing well, I might add a second ingredient and then a third.

Spicy Foods Boost Broccoli's Cancer-Fighting Effect

Researchers found in a small human study that combining broccoli powder with a spicy food, such as mustard, horseradish or wasabi, boosts the cancer-fighting properties of each food and helps ensure optimal absorption.

Theory: The spicy foods contain myrosinase, an enzyme needed to form sulforaphane, broccoli's main cancer-fighting component.

Less spicy options: Cabbage, arugula and Brussels sprouts also contain myrosinase. The enzyme may be destroyed by cooking, so eat these foods raw or steam them for two to four minutes.

Elizabeth H. Jeffery, PhD, professor of nutritional sciences, University of Illinois at Urbana-Champaign.

Chinese Cancer-Fighter

A Chinese herbal remedy, Dang Gui Long Hui Wan, appears to inhibit the growth and spread of glioblastoma multiforme, a deadly brain cancer.

Cancer Research

Tomato Juice Helps Prevent Bone Loss

Tomatoes contain the antioxidant lycopene, which reduces harmful oxidative stress that causes the body to resorb bone and damage cells responsible for bone formation.

Recent finding: Postmenopausal women who got at least 30 milligrams daily of lycopene through tomato juice or supplements showed improved bone health.

Leticia Rao, PhD, director, Calcium Research Laboratory, St. Michael's Hospital, and associate (adjunct) professor of medicine, University of Toronto, Canada, and leader of a study of 60 postmenopausal women, published in *Osteoporosis International.*

Prunes Help Prevent Osteoporosis

As we age, our bones break down faster than they are built. Prunes suppress the rate at which people's bones break down.

Recent finding: Women who ate about 10 prunes per day for 12 months had higher bone mineral density than women who ate dried apples. These women also took 500 milligrams of calcium and 400 international units of vitamin D daily.

Bahram H. Arjmandi, PhD, RD, chair, department of nutrition, food and exercise sciences, The Florida State University, Tallahassee, and leader of a study published in *British Journal of Nutrition.*

Vitamin K Strengthens Bones

Recent finding: Older people who consumed the most broccoli, spinach and other leafy green vegetables rich in vitamin K had higher bone mineral density than those who consumed the least vitamin K. Supplements of vitamin K also improve bone quality, but it is best to get the vitamin from food sources, which have other nutrients as well.

Caution: If you are taking a blood-thinning medication, such as *warfarin,* talk to your doctor before increasing your intake of vitamin K.

Study of 365 people by researchers at Universitat Rovira i Virgili, Reus, Spain, published in *Bone.*

Foods that Fight Inflammation

Inflammation is linked to heart disease, diabetes, arthritis and cancer.

The following foods may reduce inflammation in the body: Cabbage—the sulforaphane in this cruciferous vegetable wards off inflammation-related diseases, such as cancer...artichokes—the antioxidants in this cactus reduce cholesterol, boost immunity and prevent premature aging...tart cherries—anthocyanins and quercetin in tart cherries are natural inflammation fighters...pistachios—these have lutein, resveratrol and other antioxidants that fight free-radical damage, and they have more cholesterol-lowering plant sterols than any other tree nuts...onions—sulfur compounds and quercetin in onions prevent inflammation and reduce blood pressure and cancer risk.

Best: Aim for at least one serving of one of these foods daily.

Jackie Newgent, RD, CDN, culinary and nutrition communications consultant, New York City, and author of *Big Green Cookbook: Hundreds of Planet-Pleasing Recipes & Tips for a Luscious, Low-Carbon Lifestyle* (Wiley). *www.jackienewgent.com*

Spice Eases Arthritis

Frankincense is a traditional arthritis treatment that blocks the production of inflammatory molecules and helps protect joint cartilage.

Cardiff University.

Don't Wear Thick-Soled Sneakers and Other Surprising Ways to Prevent Falls

Hylton Menz, PhD, deputy director of the Musculoskeletal Research Center at La Trobe University in Victoria, Australia. He is author of the textbook *Foot Problems in Older People: Assessment and Management* (Churchill Livingstone) and coauthor of *Falls in Older People: Risk Factors and Strategies for Prevention* (Cambridge University).

Each year, about one in every three people over age 65 suffers a fall, a mishap that is far more dangerous than most people realize.

Important research: In a 20-year study of nearly 5,600 women ages 70 and older, breaking a hip doubled the risk for death in the following year. Men who suffer a broken hip after a fall are also at increased risk for an untimely death.

Most people know the standard recommendations to reduce their risk for falls—get medical attention for balance and vision problems...improve the lighting in and around their homes...and eliminate loose carpets, cords and other obstacles.

What often gets overlooked: Painful feet...foot deformities such as bunions...weak foot and ankle muscles...and improper footwear also can significantly increase one's risk for falls.

Recent scientific evidence: In a 2011 study in the *British Medical Journal*, a comprehensive program of foot care reduced falls by one-third among a group of older people with assorted foot problems.

GET A FIRM FOUNDATION

With age, the muscles that support our ankles and feet often become weak—a common problem that contributes to foot pain and reduced activity levels. Structural abnormalities in the feet, such as bunions and hammertoes, undermine stability. And conditions that blunt sensations in the feet, such as nerve damage commonly caused by diabetes, may impair the ability of one's feet to react quickly and adjust to potentially hazardous conditions.

BASIC FALL-PREVENTION WORKOUT

Stretching and strengthening exercises can reduce foot pain—and lower your risk for falls. *Basic exercises to perform daily...*

To increase your ankles' range of motion: Sit in a chair with one knee extended. Rotate your foot in a clockwise, then counterclockwise direction. Repeat 10 times with each foot, in each direction.

To strengthen your toe muscles: Place small stones or marbles on the floor in front of you. While seated, pick up the stones with your bare toes and place them in a box, one by one. Pick up 20 stones with each foot, then repeat.

To stretch your calf muscles: Stand about two feet from a wall, then lean into it with one leg slightly bent at the knee about three inches in front of the other. Then reverse the position of your feet and lean forward to stretch the muscles of the other calf. Hold the stretch for 20 seconds, three times for each leg.

PROPER FOOTWEAR

The right shoes are essential for everyone, but especially those with problem feet.

Most women know to avoid high heels, which make it more difficult to maintain balance. But many people opt for flimsy slip-on footwear, such as flip-flops, which may be comfortable but often become loose or come off the foot altogether, creating a balance hazard. It's far better to wear shoes that fasten to your feet with laces, Velcro or buckled straps.

Surprising fact: Most people assume that thick, cushiony soles, such as those found on most sneakers, help prevent falls because they tend to provide good support for your feet. But thinner, harder soles, such as those on some walking shoes, are safer because thin-soled shoes allow your feet to feel the sensations that help you maintain balance. A trade-off between comfort and safety may be necessary—you may have to wear less cushiony shoes that optimize balance.

Also, be sure that your shoes are the right size. Your feet may slide around in shoes that are too loose, while tight footwear won't allow your toes to respond to variations in the ground to help maintain stability while walking.

Remember: Shoe size often changes with age, as feet swell and spread. So have your feet measured every time you buy shoes.

Slightly more falls occur indoors than outdoors, and the proportion increases with age. Therefore, even when you're at home, proper footwear is crucial.

Important recent finding: When researchers at Harvard's Institute for Aging Research followed a group of older adults for more than two years, they found that more than half of those who fell indoors were barefoot, in their stocking feet or wearing slippers. These injuries tended to be more serious than those of people who were wearing shoes when they fell.

Best to wear at home: Sturdy, thin-soled shoes that have more structural integrity than the average slipper.

DO YOU NEED ORTHOTICS?

Many adults over age 65 could benefit from wearing orthotics—inserts that fit inside the shoe—to help prevent falls by providing additional support.

Properly made orthotics may improve the way your feet move as you walk, distribute your weight more broadly to reduce pressure on sensitive spots and help convey sensory information to your feet, all of which may lessen the risk for falls.

If you have structural foot problems due to diabetes or rheumatoid arthritis, you may need customized orthotics from a podiatrist.

Typical cost: About $400. Insurance coverage varies. But over-the-counter versions (made with firm material, not just a soft cushion) may work as well if your feet are relatively normal and your foot pain is fairly mild. Good brands include Vasyli and Langer. Usually, you will be able to transfer orthotics between shoes.

Most people find that full-length orthotics are less likely to slip inside the shoe than the half-length variety. Full-length orthotics also may feel more comfortable, especially if you have corns or calluses under the toes or on the ball of your foot.

GETTING HELP

If you have foot problems, seek care from a podiatrist or other health professional—and be sure to mention any concerns about falling. Also ask for exercises, in addition to the ones described here, to address your specific foot issues.

Get Rid of Back Pain in Just 7 Minutes a Day

Gerard Girasole, MD, orthopedic spine surgeon at The Orthopaedic & Sports Medicine Center in Trumbull, Connecticut. He is coauthor, with Cara Hartman, CPT, a Fairfield, Connecticut–based certified personal trainer, of *The 7-Minute Back Pain Solution—7 Simple Exercises to Heal Your Back without Drugs or Surgery in Just Minutes a Day* (Harlequin).

Of the 30 million Americans who suffer from low back pain, only about 10% of the cases are caused by conditions that require surgery, such as pinched nerves or a slipped disk.

For the overwhelming majority of back pain sufferers, the culprit is tight, inflamed muscles.

Surprising: This inflammation usually is not caused by strain on the back muscles themselves, but rather a strain or injury to the spine—in particular, to one of five "motion segments" in the lower back.

Each segment, which is constructed to bend forward and back and side to side, consists of a disk (the spongy cushion between each pair of spinal vertebrae)...the two vertebrae directly above and below it...and the facets (joints) connecting the vertebrae to the disk.

Unfortunately, the segments' disks or facets can be injured in a variety of ways—by lifting something the wrong way, twisting too far, sitting too long or even sneezing too hard—causing the surrounding muscles to contract in order to protect the spine from further damage.

This contraction and the muscle inflammation that it produces is what causes the intense lower back pain that so many Americans are familiar with.

WHEN BACK PAIN STRIKES

Low back pain caused by inflammation usually subsides on its own within three to six weeks.* However, the healing process can be accelerated significantly by taking over-the-counter *ibuprofen* (Motrin) for several days after injury to reduce inflammation if you don't have an ulcer (follow label instructions)...and getting massage therapy to help loosen knotted muscles and increase healing blood flow to them.

Also important: Perform the simple stretching routine described in this article. In my more than 16 years of practice as an orthopedic spine surgeon, it is the closest thing I've found to act as a "silver bullet" for back pain.

How it works: All of the muscles stretched in this routine attach to the pelvis and work in concert to stabilize the spine. Stretching increases blood flow to these specific muscles, thereby reducing the inflammation that leads to painful, tightened back muscles.

GETTING STARTED

In preparation for the back stretch routine described here, it's important to learn a simple approach that systematically stimulates and strengthens your core (abdominal, back and pelvic muscles). This is one of the best ways to protect your spine. Although there are many types of exercises that strengthen the core, abdominal contractions are the easiest to perform.

What to do: Pretend that you have to urinate and then stop the flow—a movement known as a Kegel exercise. Then while lying on your back, place your hands on your pelvis just above your genitals. Now imagine that someone is about to punch you in the stomach, and feel how your lower abdomen tightens protectively.

To do a full abdominal contraction, combine these two movements, holding the Kegel movement while tightening your lower abdomen. Then, continuously hold the full abdominal contraction during all of the stretches shown here.

*If you suffer from severe back pain or back pain accompanied by fever, incontinence or weakness or numbness in your leg, see a doctor right away to rule out a condition that may require surgery, such as serious damage to disks, ligaments or nerves in the back.

7-MINUTE STRETCHING ROUTINE

Do the following routine daily until your back pain eases (start out slowly and gently if you're still in acute pain). Then continue doing it several times a week to prevent recurrences. Regularly stretching these muscles makes them stronger, leaving your lower spine less prone to painful, back-tightening strains.

1. Hamstring wall stretch. Lie face-up on a carpeted floor (or on a folded blanket for padding), positioning your body perpendicular inside a doorframe. Bend your right leg and place it through the door opening. Bring your buttocks as close to the wall as possible and place the heel of your left foot up against the wall until it is nearly straight. Next, slide your right leg forward on the floor until it's straight, feeling a stretch in the back of your left leg. Hold for 30 seconds. Repeat twice on each side.

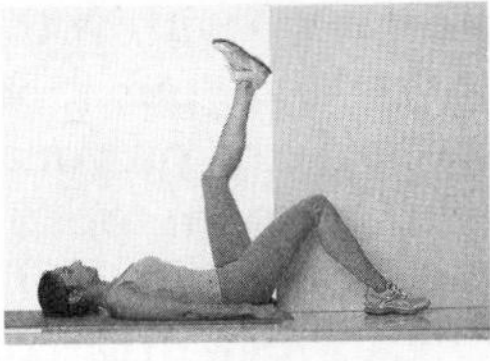

2. Knees to chest stretch. Lie on your back with your feet flat on the floor and your knees bent. Use your hands to pull your right knee to your chest. Next, try to straighten your left leg on the floor. While keeping your right knee held to your chest, continue the stretch for 20 seconds, then switch sides and repeat. Finally, do the stretch by holding both knees to your chest for 10 seconds.

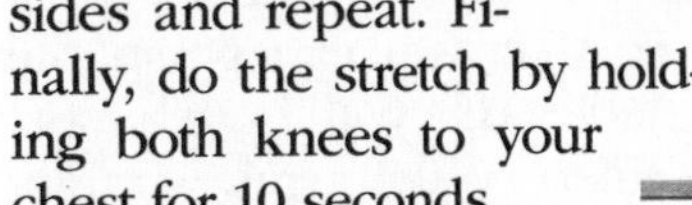

3. Spinal stretch. While on the floor with your left leg extended straight, pull your right knee to your chest (as in stretch #2), then put your right arm out to the side. Next, use your left hand to slowly pull your right knee toward your left side so that your right foot rests on the back of your left knee. Finally, turn your head toward your right side.

Hold for 20 seconds, then reverse the movements and repeat.

4. Gluteal (buttocks) stretch. Lie on your back with your feet flat on the floor and your knees bent. Cross your right leg over your left, resting your right ankle on your left knee. Next, grab your left thigh with both hands and bring both legs toward your body. Hold for 30 seconds, then switch sides and repeat.

5. Hip flexor stretch. Kneel on your right knee (use a thin pillow for comfort) with your left leg bent 90° in front of you and your foot flat on the floor. Place your right hand on your waist and your left hand on top of your left leg. Inhale and then, on the exhale, lean forward into your right hip, feeling a stretch in the front of your right hip. Hold for 30 seconds, then switch sides and repeat.

6. Quadriceps stretch. While standing, hold on to the back of a sturdy chair with your left hand for balance. Grasp your right foot with your right hand and gently pull your right leg back and up, with your toes pointing upward. Be sure to keep your right knee close to your left leg. Hold for 30 seconds, then switch sides and repeat.

7. Total back stretch. Stand arm's length in front of a table or other sturdy object and lean forward with knees slightly bent so that you can grasp the table edge with both hands. Keep your arms straight and your head level with your shoulders. Hold for 10 seconds.

Next, stand up straight with our left hand in front of you. Bring your right arm over your head with elbow bent, then bend your upper body gently to the left. Hold for 10 seconds, then switch sides and repeat.

Photos by Scott Wynn.

Coffee Fights Depression

Recent study: Researchers examined health and lifestyle data on 50,739 women (average age 63) for more than 10 years.

Finding: Women who drank two to three cups of coffee per day were 15% less likely to develop clinical depression than those who drank one or fewer cups daily. Decaffeinated coffee had no effect on depression.

Theory: Caffeine increases production of dopamine and other neurotransmitters in the brain that help regulate moods.

Alberto Ascherio, MD, professor of epidemiology and nutrition, Harvard School of Public Health, Boston.

Disease-Fighting Berries

Berries lower Parkinson's disease risk. A recent study found that men who ate the most berries—along with tea, apples, oranges and other major sources of healthful flavonoids—were about 40% less likely to develop Parkinson's than men who ate the least amount. Women and men appear to have a lower risk for the disease mainly due to anthocyanins, a type of flavonoid found in berries.

Xiang Gao, MD, PhD, research scientist at Harvard School of Public Health and assistant professor of medicine at Harvard Medical School, both in Boston, and leader of a study presented at the American Academy of Neurology's 63rd Annual Meeting.

Eat Vegetables, Live Longer

People with the highest blood levels of alpha-carotene were 39% less likely to die from all causes over 14 years.

Foods with the most alpha-carotene: Pumpkin, carrots, winter squash, plantains, vegetable juice cocktail, tangerines, collard greens, snap beans, tomatoes, cornmeal and corn, peas, raspberries, sweet potatoes, bell peppers and mangoes.

Chaoyang Li, MD, PhD, epidemiologist, division of behavioral surveillance, Centers for Disease Control and Prevention, Atlanta, and leader of a study of 15,318 people, published in *Archives of Internal Medicine.*

Spices With Surprising Health Benefits

James A. Duke, PhD, an economic botanist retired from the USDA, where he developed a database on the health benefits of various plants. He is author of numerous books including, most recently, *The Green Pharmacy Guide to Healing Foods: Proven Natural Remedies to Treat and Prevent More Than 80 Common Health Concerns* (Rodale).

You may already know that sprinkling cinnamon on your food helps control blood sugar levels and using ginger can ease nausea.

What fewer people realize: There are several lesser-known spices that not only give foods wonderful flavors, but also offer significant health benefits.* In some cases, spices can be just as helpful as medication for people with certain conditions—and safer.

Common medical conditions that you can help prevent—or improve—with the use of spices...

OREGANO FOR ARTHRITIS

Oregano helps alleviate osteoarthritis and other inflammatory conditions, such as rheumatoid arthritis. You might be surprised to learn that this favorite spice of Italian cooking contains natural compounds that have many of the same effects as the powerful anti-inflammatory COX-2 inhibitor drug *celecoxib* (Celebrex).

In addition, oregano contains dozens of other anti-inflammatory compounds that act as muscle relaxants and pain relievers. Unlike celecoxib, which may increase heart attack risk in some people, oregano actually protects the heart by helping to prevent blood clots and irregular heart rhythms.

Best uses: Use oregano liberally on salads or on pizzas. Oregano also can be mixed with peppermint and/or spearmint for a hot or iced mixed-herb tea. If you prefer to take an anti-inflammatory supplement, oregano is one of the half dozen spices in a product called Zyflamend (its ingredients also include rosemary and turmeric). The herbs in Zyflamend act synergistically to provide a more powerful effect than each would when used individually. Zyflamend can be purchased in health-food stores and online. Follow label instructions.

CALENDULA FOR CATARACTS

Calendula, or marigold, contains powerful plant-based carotenoids—particularly lutein and zeaxanthin—that help protect the eyes. In addition to being powerful antioxidants, these two compounds absorb damaging blue-light wavelengths from the sun. Increased intake of lutein and zeaxanthin has been associated with reduced risk for cataracts.

Best uses: Calendula makes an excellent addition to homemade vegetarian soup. If you prefer to use calendula in supplement form, follow label instructions.

ONION FOR HIGH BLOOD PRESSURE

Onion contains blood-thinning compounds, all of which have a blood pressure–lowering effect. One of the most potent of these compounds is the flavonoid quercetin. Onion also acts as a natural diuretic, which lowers blood pressure by helping the body excrete excess fluids and salt.

Best uses: If possible, use a full onion (all types contain some blood pressure–lowering compounds) in onion soup, for example.

Reason: The onion's thin outer skin is the plant's best source of quercetin. Onion powder and cooked onions are not as effective as fresh onion.

Research shows that people who take quercetin as a supplement can lower their blood pressure in less than a month. In a 2007 double-blind study, people with hypertension who took 730 mg of quercetin daily for 28

*Check with your doctor before using any of the spices mentioned in this article for medicinal purposes. The natural compounds found in spices may interact with some prescription drugs. Pregnant and nursing women should avoid using spices medicinally.

days lowered their systolic (top number) blood pressure by an average of 7 mm HG and diastolic (bottom number) by 5 mm HG.

FENNEL SEED FOR INDIGESTION

Fennel seed is surprisingly effective at relieving indigestion. If I get indigestion, I pick some fennel seeds from the fennel plant in my garden. Fennel is easy to grow, and it keeps coming back year after year. In my experience, it can settle the stomach as well as many over-the-counter products.

Fennel seed relaxes the smooth muscles that line the digestive tract, relieving flatulence, bloating and gas, as well as nausea and vomiting, motion sickness and abdominal pain. If you don't want to grow your own, store-bought fennel seed also works well.

Best uses: Fennel seed can be eaten whole (it tastes and smells similar to anise) or made into a tea by pouring boiling water over it (use one gram to three grams of fennel seed—about one-half to one and one-half teaspoons—per cup). To sweeten the tea, molasses or honey is the best choice.

Caution: Because fennel seed can increase estrogen levels, it should be avoided by women who are pregnant or breast-feeding or who have an estrogen-sensitive medical condition, such as estrogen-responsive breast cancer.

GARLIC FOR THE COMMON COLD

While the research on garlic's positive effect on cardiovascular health is perhaps most widely known, this popular allium also boosts immunity, helping to prevent and treat the common cold.

In one study of nearly 150 people who took a garlic supplement or placebo for 12 weeks during cold season, those taking the garlic had significantly fewer colds (or symptoms that eased more quickly in cold sufferers) than those taking a placebo.

Best uses: To help cure or prevent a cold, add a clove or two of garlic to all soups... sprinkle garlic powder on toast...and/or mix diced raw garlic with olive oil and vinegar.

SAFFRON FOR DEPRESSION

Saffron, a spice derived from a small, blue crocus, acts as a potent antidepressant and has been used for centuries in traditional medicine for this purpose. No one is sure how it works, but its active ingredient, crocetin, appears to enhance blood flow to the brain.

Research conducted in Iran has shown that 30 mg per day of saffron powder (about one-tenth of a teaspoon) relieved mild-to-moderate depression as effectively as standard doses of the antidepressant medications *fluoxetine* (Prozac) and *imipramine* (Tofranil).

Best uses: One of the world's most expensive spices, saffron can be used in herbal tea or chicken paella. A five-gram bottle of Exir Pure Saffron Powder is $41 at *www.amazon.com.*

6

Very Personal Matters

Best Ways to Increase A Woman's Libido

Ever since an FDA advisory panel rejected the approval of a so-called "female Viagra" last year—the drug was deemed no more effective at increasing libido than a placebo—there's been a lot of debate on the female libido.

Key issue: If a woman's desire for sex is low, is that necessarily a "dysfunction" that should be treated? *What women—and their partners—need to know...*

IS THERE A PROBLEM?

When it comes to libido, medical experts agree that there is no "normal" or "abnormal." Doctors diagnose a libido dysfunction only when there is a recurrent or persistent problem with libido that causes personal distress to the woman.

Therefore, if a woman has no sexual desire but is undisturbed by this fact, then no dysfunction exists. Alternatively, if a woman wants to have sex twice a week but is distressed because she used to want it more often than that, then the decrease in libido is a dysfunction for her.

To diagnose low libido: A woman needs to answer just one basic question—do you think you have a problem with your level of sexual desire?

Note: When a man and woman's desire don't match, it's called "desire mismatch," which is not truly a sexual dysfunction, though the partners may benefit from sex therapy.

CAUSES OF LOW LIBIDO

Not all doctors ask about their patients' sexual health, so any woman who experiences chronic or recurrent low libido should tell her

Leah Millheiser, MD, clinical assistant professor in the department of obstetrics and gynecology and director of the Female Sexual Medicine Program at Stanford University School of Medicine in Stanford, California.

gynecologist and/or primary care physician. *Most common causes...*

• **Health problems.** Some chronic diseases, such as diabetes and atherosclerosis (clogged arteries), can decrease blood flow—including that feeding the sex organs. Without proper blood flow, sex can feel uncomfortable, and orgasm may be impossible—both of which may negatively impact a woman's libido. And because sexual desire starts in the brain, doctors shouldn't ignore the possibility that low desire could be a side effect of a brain injury from, say, a fall, car wreck or stroke.

• **Medication use.** The side effects of many drugs may include a change in sexual desire and/or difficulty reaching orgasm.

Common culprits: Antidepressant drugs known as selective serotonin reuptake inhibitors (SSRIs), such as *fluoxetine* (Prozac) and *sertraline* (Zoloft)...and cholesterol-lowering statin medications, such as *atorvastatin* (Lipitor) and *simvastatin* (Zocor).

• **Psychosocial factors.** If a woman is in a relationship that is physically, emotionally or verbally abusive, her sexual desire can diminish. Past physical or sexual abuse can also lower libido. Any woman experiencing abuse should work with her doctor to create a plan to improve the relationship or leave it. Those experiencing current or past abuse may also benefit from therapy.

• **Partner's health issues.** If a woman with low libido has a partner who has a sexual dysfunction—such as low sex drive, erectile dysfunction or inability to orgasm—both partners can drag each other's desire down even further. Therefore, both people should be evaluated by a sex therapist.*

• **Hormone levels.** The primary male hormone (testosterone), which is also present in females, plays a crucial role in women's libido. Postmenopausal women, in particular, have decreased testosterone, which lowers libido and makes it more difficult to have an orgasm. Premenopausal women may experience lowered testosterone levels if they take birth control pills.

While it might seem that taking testosterone would be an easy fix for libido, research has been mixed. Some studies have shown a benefit, while others have shown no or only slight improvement in sexual desire. Because the potential side effects (such as excessive body hair and acne) are serious, women taking testosterone need to be carefully monitored with blood tests every three to six months.

WHAT YOU CAN DO

It's important to work with your doctor to rule out underlying physical problems that may be leading to your low libido. *In the meantime, simple therapies may help...*

• **Reduce vaginal dryness.** Vaginal moisturizers—which are different from lubricants in that they are used two to three times a week, not just before sex—add moisture barriers in the vagina. This helps provide a layer of protection and comfort so that sex is not painful—a common complaint among women who experience vaginal dryness.

Recommended: KY Silk-E or Replens.** Follow label instructions.

Important: You must use such vaginal moisturizers for at least two months before judging results.

• **Masturbate.** Yes, this simple action can be a powerful libido booster for women—partly because it turns out that sexual desire really is a "use it or lose it" function.

• **Use lubricants.** Sexual lubricants help make sex more comfortable—painful sex is a common cause of low libido.

Recommended: Pjur Eros Bodyglide, which is a silicone-based, glycerin-free product. This combination offers several advantages, including a reduced risk for yeast infections or vaginal inflammation, compared with products that contain glycerin.

• **Increase stimulation before and/or during sex.** When testosterone drops, some women need more stimulation to become aroused and to have an orgasm. The best method is to

*To find a sex therapist or MD in your area who specializes in treating sexual dysfunction, consult the International Society for the Study of Women's Sexual Health, *www.isswsh.org*.

**All the products mentioned in this section can be purchased from *www.drugstore.com*, which ships its orders in a plain box labeled only with the company name.

use a vibrator for clitoral stimulation. My sexual dysfunction patients report that the best vibrator is the Hitachi Magic Wand—it provides a very strong vibration.

Helpful: Using an over-the-counter botanical oil with a vibrator has been shown in studies to increase a woman's ability to have an orgasm.

Recommended: Zestra Essential Arousal Oils.

• **Exercise.** We know that exercise elevates mood, improves blood circulation and general health, and helps enhance body image. All of these factors can improve sex drive.

Recommended: Any aerobic exercise, but especially walking and dancing because they are low-impact, low-stress exercise and can be fun to do. Aim to get out and walk (or dance) every day for at least 20 minutes.

Satisfaction Leads to Happiness

Happier older women are more satisfied with their sex lives. Researchers studied data on 1,235 women (ages 60 to 89, some of whom were sexually active and some not) to measure their quality of life, including sexual satisfaction.

Finding: High sexual satisfaction was closely correlated with overall quality of life. Among women ages 80 to 89, 61% reported being moderately or very satisfied with their sex lives, a decline of only 6% from age 60. Men are now being studied.

Wesley Thompson, PhD, assistant professor of psychiatry, Stein Institute for Research on Aging, University of California, San Diego, School of Medicine.

Fantasies Help Analytical Thinking

People who thought about casual sex with someone they did not love did better on a test filled with analytical questions and worse on a creativity test. People who thought about taking a long, loving walk with their partner were more creative and less analytical.

Possible reason: Love is a broad, long-term emotion that may help people make big-picture associations and connect differing ideas. Sex is more intensely connected to a focus on details.

Jens Förster, PhD, social psychologist, University of Amsterdam, the Netherlands, and senior author of a study published in *Personality and Social Psychology Bulletin.*

Proud Men Attract Women

Participants viewed images of people who displayed happiness (smiles), pride (puffed-up chests) and shame (lowered heads). Women preferred men who looked proud, reflecting gender norms—male displays of pride imply status and the ability to provide for a partner.

Jessica Tracy, PhD, associate professor, department of psychology, University of British Columbia, Vancouver, and coauthor of a study of 1,041 people, published online in *Emotion.*

Special Needs Dating Sites

Dating4disabled.com is a community site and dating service for people with disabilities. Nolongerlonely.com is for adults with mental illnesses. Pozpersonals.com is for people who are HIV positive. Prescription4love.com has communities dedicated to sexually transmitted diseases, physical disabilities and even diseases such as diabetes and Parkinson's. All these sites are free.

The New York Times

Meeting Online

Facebook works as a dating Web site. Roughly 50% of Americans who use Facebook disclose whether they are single or in a relationship on their Facebook pages. In addition, nearly 75% of those who are single use Facebook as a way to find out about people they might be interested in dating.

USA Today Magazine, The Society for the Advancement of Education, 500 Bi-County Blvd., Farmingdale, New York 11735. *www.usatodaymagazine.net*

Can You Have Sex After Heart Disease?

Patients recovering from stroke or heart disease can safely enjoy sex as long as their cardiovascular disease is stable and they experience minimal or no symptoms, such as chest pains or shortness of breath, during routine activities. Sex with a familiar partner in a familiar setting is generally no more strenuous than an activity that requires moderate exertion, such as golf—and resuming sexual activity can be an important part of healing.

John Moran, MD, professor of medicine, Loyola University Chicago Stritch School of Medicine.

Lovers May Make Better Athletes

Being in a long-term, loving relationship improves athletic performance. Passionate love—typical in earlier relationship stages—has a smaller effect than committed, compassionate love but still is a positive influence. This runs counter to the idea that relationships drain us of energy. Brain scans of people in love show increased blood flow to the areas associated with motivation—the same areas activated when athletes focus on winning.

Kelly Campbell, PhD, assistant professor, department of psychology, California State University, San Bernardino, and leader of a study presented at a recent meeting of the American Psychological Association in Washington, DC.

Sex May Be Risky for Sedentary People

Recent finding: Any burst of activity, including sex, increases risk for heart attack by up to 3.5 times for sedentary people, compared with people who usually are active. The increased risk can be significantly reduced through walking or any kind of physical activity done on a regular basis.

Meta-analysis of 14 studies by researchers from Tufts Medical Center, Boston, published in *The Journal of the American Medical Association*.

Infidelity May Be Genetic

Recent finding: People with a variation of the DRD4 gene were more likely to have a history of uncommitted sex, including one-night stands and acts of infidelity.

Justin Garcia, postdoctoral fellow, The Kinsey Institute for Research in Sex, Gender and Reproduction, Indiana University, Bloomington and leader of a study of 181 people, published in *PLoS One*.

Dramatic HIV Finding

Recent study: If antiretroviral treatment (ART) is begun when a person first tests positive for the virus, the risk of transmission to a partner is cut by 96% (versus a reduction of 80% to 85% when only condoms are used).

Important: As a precautionary measure, people with HIV should always practice safe sex even if ART is started early on.

Myron S. Cohen, MD, J. Herbert Bate Distinguished Professor of Medicine, Microbiology and Immunology and Public Health, University of North Carolina at Chapel Hill, and director of the UNC Institute for Global Health & Infectious Diseases. He is leader of a study presented at the 2011 International AIDS Society conference.

HPV Affects Half of All Men

Most don't know that they have the sexually transmitted disease because men usually don't have symptoms and doctors rarely test men for it. While most of the 40 strains of HPV affecting the genital areas aren't harmful, several strains can lead to a variety of cancers in men and women, as well as genital warts.

Anna Giuliano, PhD, chair of the department of cancer epidemiology at the H. Lee Moffitt Cancer Center & Research Institute, Tampa, and leader of a study of 1,159 men, published in *The Lancet.*

New HPV Test Catches Cancer Earlier

The FDA-approved Cobas test is the only HPV test able to determine whether a woman has HPV types 16 and 18—the forms that are most likely to lead to cervical cancer. Women age 30 and older should have an HPV test along with a Pap test—usually every three years. Ask your doctor for details.

Health, 2100 Lake Shore Dr., Birmingham, Alabama 35209. *www.health.com*

Hair-Loss Treatment Can Have Sexual Side Effects

Finasteride, the treatment for male-pattern hair loss sold as Proscar or Propecia, can cause reduced sexual desire, erectile dysfunction, decreased arousal and problems with orgasm. The effects usually reverse when finasteride is no longer taken—but in some cases, they can persist for three months or more.

Michael S. Irwig, MD, assistant professor, department of medicine, The George Washington University, Washington, DC, and coauthor of a study published in *The Journal of Sexual Medicine.*

Kegel Exercises Not Just for Women

Jonathan M. Vapnek, MD, a urologist and an associate clinical professor of urology at Mount Sinai School of Medicine in New York City. He has published more than 25 articles in medical journals, including *Urology, The Journal of Urology, The Annals of Pharmacotherapy* and *Geriatrics.* A member of the American Urological Association, he's been named by *New York Magazine* as one of New York City's best urologists.

Just about every woman who has experienced childbirth or gone through menopause has heard of "Kegels." These simple exercises are widely used to treat and prevent urinary leaks.

What you may not realize: Kegels, named after the American gynecologist Arnold Henry Kegel, are also useful for men—not just for reducing urinary and bowel incontinence but also for easing prostate discomfort and relieving premature ejaculation.

Bonus: Many men and women report that these exercises enhance sexual pleasure as well.

Good news: You don't have to set aside a specific time to do these exercises. Because no one can see what you're doing, you can exercise the muscles almost any time—when you're standing in line, driving your car or watching TV.

But even people who have heard of Kegels—or perhaps tried them—may not be getting all the possible benefits if they're making some common mistakes while performing the exercises.

WHAT GOES WRONG

The goal of Kegel exercises is to strengthen the pelvic floor—a group of muscles that control urination and defecation and help support pelvic organs, such as the bladder (and uterus in women).

In women, pregnancy and vaginal childbirth can stretch and weaken the pelvic floor, leading to urinary incontinence. Women who haven't had children can also suffer from incontinence, in part because age-related declines in estrogen may weaken the urinary sphincter.

In men, urinary incontinence is usually due to prostate enlargement or prostate surgery. Prostate enlargement causes the bladder muscle to become overactive, resulting in urinary incontinence. Prostate surgery can damage the sphincter or nerves that control the sphincter.

HOW TO DO KEGELS PROPERLY

Kegels are simple—they involve contracting and relaxing your pelvic-floor muscles. *Yet many women and men make these mistakes when performing the exercises...*

Mistake 1: **Not identifying the pelvic-floor muscles.** Some people simply can't "feel" these muscles. When contracting them, there should be no movement of the abdominal muscles and minimal movement of the buttocks. Men can see a "shortening" of the base of the penis, and women should feel a "lifting or narrowing" of the vagina.

Solution: The next time you urinate, try to stop the flow in midstream. If you can do this, you're contracting all of the right muscles. You can also tighten the muscles that prevent you from passing intestinal gas. (Once the proper muscles have been located, do not do Kegels while urinating or defecating.)

If you still can't locate the muscles: A woman can insert a finger into her vagina and tighten the muscles to squeeze her finger. A man can place a finger in his anus. If he is tightening the correct muscles, he will feel a contraction on his finger.

A physical therapist trained in pelvic-floor rehabilitation can also teach you where the muscles are. He/she may use biofeedback, which involves placing electrodes on the abdomen or in the vagina or anus. A machine can then monitor the contraction/relaxation of the appropriate muscles and alert patients when they're doing it right. This procedure is painless.

Mistake 2: **Stopping too soon.** It's common for women and men to do a few Kegels then stop.

Solution: Make sure you know how to correctly count your repetitions. To begin, squeeze the muscles as hard as you can for three to five seconds. Then relax for five seconds. This is one Kegel. Start with five or 10 repetitions. As your muscles get stronger, you'll easily be able to do 20 in a row and hold each Kegel for about 10 seconds.

Mistake 3: **Not doing the exercises often enough.** Until you've incorporated Kegels into your daily schedule, it's easy to try the exercises a few times, then forget about them for several days.

Solution: As with any exercise, Kegels are more effective when you do them regularly. To get the most benefit, do 10 or 20 Kegels, relax for a minute, then do 10 or 20 more. Repeat this three times daily. Be patient. It may take six to 12 weeks to see any benefits, but many people report beneficial effects earlier.

For improved sexual function: Men who experience premature ejaculation can learn to delay their orgasms by squeezing the muscles, hard, during masturbation or intercourse. Women can use Kegels to create more friction during intercourse and reach orgasm sooner.

Important: Avoid devices sold online that claim to strengthen pelvic-floor muscles—they aren't necessary and often don't work.

Pain Relievers Linked to Erectile Dysfunction

Recent *study:* Men who regularly used nonsteroidal anti-inflammatory drugs (NSAIDs), such as aspirin or *ibuprofen*, were about 40% more likely to have erectile dysfunction (ED) than other men. The reason for the link is unknown.

Caution: If you use an NSAID for heart protection or other benefits, do not stop taking it without first consulting your physician.

Steven J. Jacobsen, MD, PhD, director of research at Kaiser Permanente Southern California, Pasadena, and research professor of preventive medicine, Keck School of Medicine, University of Southern California, Los Angeles. He is senior author of a study of 80,966 men, published in *Journal of Urology*.

New ED Drug

A new erectile dysfunction drug works faster than Viagra or Cialis. *Avanafil* (Stendra), made by Vivus, is effective in as little as 15 minutes and works for up to eight hours. Viagra takes an hour to work...Cialis, two hours. The FDA approved Stendra in April 2012.

Irwin Goldstein, MD, director, San Diego Sexual Medicine at Alvarado Hospital, San Diego, and editor in chief of *The Journal of Sexual Medicine*.

Blood Test for ED

Erectile dysfunction (ED) may be caused by low blood levels of certain vitamins and minerals.

Especially important: Magnesium (deficiency hinders blood flow)...vitamin D (involved in magnesium absorption and behavioral responses)...vitamin B-12 (behavioral responses)...zinc (testosterone and sperm production). If you have ED, ask your physician whether your vitamin and mineral levels should be tested.

Barbara Bartlik, MD, sex therapist, psychiatrist and assistant clinical professor of psychiatry at Weill Cornell Medical College, New York City.

Estrogen—The Rest of The Story

John E. Morley, MD, a gerontologist and endocrinologist who is the Dammert Professor of Gerontology and director of the division of geriatric medicine at Saint Louis University School of Medicine. Dr. Morley is also director of geriatric research at the St. Louis VA Medical Center and coauthor, with Sheri R. Colberg, PhD, of *The Science of Staying Young* (McGraw-Hill).

Until about 10 years ago, menopausal women were routinely advised to take hormone replacement therapy (HRT), including estrogen, to prevent heart disease, strengthen bones and improve mental and emotional health.

Then women began avoiding HRT when an important study announced in 2002 that it increased the risk for heart disease, stroke, pulmonary embolism and breast cancer.

Recent development: An analysis of data from the same study indicates that for the estimated one-third of women over age 50 who have had a hysterectomy, using estrogen alone actually reduces breast cancer risk, while among the younger study participants, risk for heart disease was reduced. These new findings were reported in *The Journal of the American Medical Association*.

To help readers make sense of the latest research on estrogen, we spoke with John E. Morley, MD, a leading gerontologist who also specializes in the study of hormones.

- **Why has hormone replacement therapy for menopausal women become so controversial?** A decade ago, more than one-third of postmenopausal American women were taking estrogen, alone or with other hormones, to help fight hot flashes, vaginal dryness and other menopausal symptoms.

HRT was assumed to be both effective and safe—but this assumption had never been tested in a large-scale clinical trial.

In 1991, the National Institutes of Health launched the Women's Health Initiative study to investigate the long-term health effects of HRT. The study, which included more than 160,000 women, was stopped early when investigators concluded that study participants on HRT with estrogen and the hormone progestin had a higher risk for stroke, breast cancer and other health problems than participants taking placebos.

Reports of the study had an immediate effect—the number of prescriptions for HRT decreased by 50% almost overnight. Today, millions of menopausal women refuse any form of HRT, even though this decision greatly increases their risk of getting osteoporosis.

- **Based on the original findings, aren't women correct in refusing HRT?** In the original study, for every 100,000 women treated with estrogen and progestin, we would expect to see about seven additional cases of heart disease and about eight additional cases of cancer. It's a concern, but the risk for a particular woman is, on average, small.

Remember, these complications occurred only in women taking the two hormones.

- **Why is the new analysis important?** The conclusions are different from the earlier ones, but only because the analysis looked at a different group of women—those who had previously had a hysterectomy (which surgically induces menopause with removal of the uterus) and were taking only estrogen (or a placebo), rather than the estrogen-progestin combination.

The results were striking. Women taking estrogen alone had a 23% lower risk of developing breast cancer than those in the placebo group. We don't know why estrogen was protective in this group.

No one is recommending that women take estrogen solely for breast cancer prevention. However, this finding should be reassuring to the women who have had hysterectomies and are using estrogen therapy for relief from hot flashes or other menopausal symptoms.

- **Why were postmenopausal women historically instructed to take progestin if it's dangerous?** Supplemental estrogen increases the risk for endometrial cancer. The addition of progestin mitigates that risk. It's not a perfect solution because progestin/estrogen has been linked to a slight increase in breast cancer. In the past, many doctors routinely prescribed the two hormones together. This was not the right approach for all women.

A woman who has had a hysterectomy obviously can't get endometrial cancer because she doesn't have a uterus. In these women, as the new analysis has shown, taking estrogen without progestin actually reduces breast cancer risk.

Important: Some types of breast cancer proliferate in the presence of estrogen. Women who have had estrogen-dependent cancers, or have a high risk of getting them due to such factors as obesity, also need to be cautious about estrogen-only therapy.

Women who still have their uteruses and are suffering from severe menopausal discomfort will be advised to continue using the combination treatment at the lowest possible dose and for the shortest period of time—say, for three to five years.

- **Does estrogen help or hurt the heart?** While the original study found an increase in heart problems in women using a combination of estrogen and progestin, the new analysis found that the increase applied to only the older women who had had hysterectomies and took estrogen alone.

The researchers estimate that for every 10,000 women age 70 or older who are taking estrogen, there would be 16 additional heart attacks. It's possible that women in this age group already have advanced atherosclerosis.

Estrogen causes the coronary arteries to relax excessively. With existing atherosclerosis, this could dislodge unstable plaques (deposits) in the arteries and trigger a heart attack.

For younger women (generally age 59 or younger), the situation was the opposite. The analysis found that participants who had undergone a hysterectomy and started taking estrogen in their 50s had nearly 50% fewer heart attacks compared with those taking placebos.

My advice: It's clear from this study that older women who have had a hysterectomy probably should not start taking estrogen—the risks are likely to outweigh the benefits. Younger women without uteruses, on the other hand, can clearly benefit.

• **How young should a woman be to consider HRT?** A woman without a uterus who is age 59 or younger and is experiencing moderate-to-severe menopausal symptoms or has a high risk of developing osteoporosis—due, for example, to low body weight—could benefit from estrogen.

We advise women who do use HRT to not exceed 10 years of use. The risks rise with longer use, with the highest risk for those who take it for 15 years or longer.

• **Are bioidentical forms of estrogen safer than prescription versions?** This topic is controversial. One criticism of the Women's Health Initiative study is that the participants were given prescription Prempro or Premarin, conjugated estrogens made from mare's urine. However, study skeptics argue that estradiol, a so-called bioidentical hormone that's touted as being more similar to the estrogen produced by a woman's ovaries, is a safer choice.

Bioidentical forms of estrogen are typically synthesized from soy or yams, foods that contain estrogen-like compounds. Despite the fact that many women use bioidentical hormones, there's no clear evidence, in my opinion, that they're safer or more effective than traditional hormone therapy. Estrogen (traditional or bioidentical) in nonpill forms, such as creams or patches, may have fewer side effects because they are metabolized differently than the oral form. Ask your doctor for advice.

Women in my practice who have added soy and yams to their diets weren't able to get enough of the hormonelike substances from these foods to significantly improve menopausal symptoms.

• **Do men ever need estrogen?** Men's bodies naturally produce small amounts of estrogen, just as women produce small amounts of testosterone. In general, men never need to take estrogen for health maintenance.

Soy Does Not Ease Menopause

Soy contains a plant form of the hormone estrogen that researchers had hoped would prevent bone loss and reduce menopause symptoms.

Recent study: There was no significant difference in bone density between women who took 200 milligrams of soy isoflavone daily and women who took a placebo.

And: The women who took soy isoflavone actually had more hot flashes.

Silvina Levis, MD, director, Osteoporosis Center, Miller School of Medicine, University of Miami, and leader of a study of 248 women, ages 45 to 60, over two years, published in *Archives of Internal Medicine.*

Hysterectomy May Raise Kidney Cancer Risk

Recent study: Researchers compared rates of a common kidney cancer in about 185,000 women who had undergone hysterectomies with about 657,000 who had not.

Result: Those who had undergone hysterectomies were up to 50% more likely to develop kidney cancer—with women age 44 or younger when they had the hysterectomy at highest risk.

Theory: Hysterectomy may alter urine flow, setting the stage for kidney cells to become cancerous.

If a doctor recommends hysterectomy for a noncancerous condition: Discuss kidney cancer risk and other nonsurgical options for treating your problem.

Daniel Altman, PhD, associate professor of medical epidemiology, Karolinska Institute, Stockholm, Sweden.

Aspirin Fights Breast Cancer

After breast cancer patients receive standard treatment, taking aspirin at least two days a week reduces the risk for having the disease spread by as much as 60%...and risk for death from the disease by as much as 71%. Aspirin and other nonsteroidal anti-inflammatory drugs (NSAIDs) block Cox-2, which has been linked to metastasis of the disease. Further clinical trials are needed to confirm the results.

Michelle D. Holmes, MD, DrPH, associate professor of medicine at Harvard Medical School and associate physician at Brigham and Women's Hospital, both in Boston, and leader of a study of 4,164 women, published in *Journal of Clinical Oncology.*

Hot Flashes Reduce Breast Cancer Risk

Recent finding: Women who experience intense hot flashes that wake them up at night and other severe symptoms of menopause, such as night sweats, vaginal dryness, bladder problems and depression, have up to 50% lower risk for breast cancer than women who don't have such symptoms. The protective effect increases with the number and severity of menopausal symptoms.

Possible reason: The symptoms occur as hormone levels fluctuate and drop. Women who have the intense symptoms may have lower levels of estrogen. High levels of estrogen are linked to breast cancer.

Christopher I. Li, MD, PhD, breast cancer epidemiologist, Fred Hutchinson Cancer Research Center, Seattle, and leader of a study published in *Cancer Epidemiology, Biomarkers & Prevention.*

Too Many Biopsies?

Surgical breast biopsies are overutilized. Researchers analyzed data on 172,342 breast biopsies of women with and without breast cancer.

Finding: Thirty percent of the biopsies were surgical as opposed to the less invasive needle biopsy, in which a tissue sample is obtained via a needle and syringe. Current guidelines recommend that only 10% of biopsies should involve surgery.

Theory: Doctors who overrely on surgery, which has a greater risk for infection than needle biopsy, might not have the resources to perform needle biopsies.

If you need a breast biopsy: Seek a doctor who is knowledgeable about surgical and needle biopsy.

Stephen Grobmyer, MD, associate professor of surgical oncology, University of Florida, Gainesville.

Breast Cancer Blood Test

Breast cancer may be detected by a blood test that detects prostate cancer in men.

Recent finding: Levels of prostate-specific antigen (PSA) are more than three times higher in women who have breast cancer than in women who do not have the disease.

Chien Chou, PhD, professor, Graduate Institute of Electro-Optical Engineering, Chang Gung University, Taiwan, and leader of a study published in *Analytical Chemistry.*

Help for Chemo Hair Loss

Breast cancer patients are more likely to keep their hair when scalp-cooling caps are worn during chemo sessions. The Penguin Cold Cap contains a frozen gel that cools the scalp, reducing blood flow to the area and minimizing chemo's effect on the scalp. The cap requires changing every 20 minutes (more convenient models are under development).

Information: *www.msc-worldwide.com.*

Hope Rugo, MD, codirector of the breast oncology clinical trials program and clinical professor of medicine, Helen Diller Family Comprehensive Cancer Center, University of California, San Francisco.

Surgery Reduces Cancer Risk

There is now more evidence that breast and ovary removal reduces cancer risk for women at high risk for breast and ovarian cancer. For women with the BRCA-1 or BRCA-2 mutations, which increase risk for both types of cancer, surgery is more effective than rigorous screening.

Recent study: Four years after preventive double mastectomy, none of the high-risk women developed breast cancer...but 7% who had intensive screening without surgery did. Only 1% of women at high risk for ovarian cancer who had at least one ovary and fallopian tube removed developed the disease, versus 6% of women who did not have the surgery.

Claudine Isaacs, MD, medical director of cancer assessment and risk evaluation program, Georgetown Lombardi Comprehensive Cancer Center, Washington, DC, and coauthor of a study of 2,482 women at 22 cancer centers in the US and Europe, published in *The Journal of the American Medical Association.*

Better Breast Cancer Treatment

An analysis of 17 randomized trials involving 10,801 women found that those who had breast-conserving surgery plus radiation had a 10-year recurrence rate of 19.3%, compared with 35% in the group that received surgery but no radiation. Risk for death after 15 years was 21.4% in the radiation group and 25.2% in the nonradiation group. This means that one death is prevented for every four recurrences.

Sarah C. Darby, PhD, professor of medical statistics, University of Oxford, UK.

Better Ovarian Cancer Detection

Recent finding: Among 37,000 healthy women (average age 57) who took part in studies to investigate the effectiveness of transvaginal ultrasound screening, 72 ovarian cancers were detected. Of these, 70% were early stage, and 88% of these women had a five-year survival rate, compared with about 50% of unscreened women who were diagnosed with ovarian cancer.

Theory: Ultrasound detects changes in size and structure of the ovary. Women at risk for ovarian cancer (due to family history, for example) should discuss transvaginal screening with their doctors.

Edward J. Pavlik, PhD, director, Ovarian Screening Research Program, University of Kentucky, Lexington.

IUDs Reduce Cervical Cancer Risk

Women who used an intrauterine device (IUD) for birth control had only about half the risk for cervical cancer, compared with women who had not used one. Research suggests that IUDs—possibly because they cause chronic low-grade inflammation—may boost a woman's immune system, helping to fight off human papillomavirus (HPV) infections that can progress to cancer.

Xavier Castellsagué, MD, PhD, unit chief, Institut Català d'Oncologia, Barcelona, Spain, and leader of an analysis of 26 studies of a total of more than 20,000 women, published in *The Lancet Oncology.*

Mammogram May Find Other Health Problems

When 71 women with advanced kidney disease had routine mammograms, the images from 63% of them showed signs of calcification in breast artery tissue. This is a marker of vascular disease, which is common in people with kidney disease. By comparison, only 17% of a matched group of women without kidney disease showed calcification.

When having a mammogram: Ask the radiologist to look for breast tissue calcification. If spotted, talk to your doctor about screening for undetected vascular disease and kidney disease.

W. Charles O'Neill, MD, professor of medicine, Emory University School of Medicine, Atlanta.

The Perfect Colonoscopy Prep

Douglas K. Rex, MD, professor of medicine at Indiana University School of Medicine in Indianapolis. Dr. Rex has authored hundreds of papers and book chapters on colonoscopy and was a member of the committee that wrote the guidelines, Screening and Surveillance for the Early Detection of Colorectal Cancer and Adenomatous Polyps, 2008.

It's widely known that colonoscopy is the most effective way to help prevent cancer of the colon and rectum.

What you may not know: The results of some colonoscopies are more accurate than others.

Important recent finding: When researchers reviewed the medical records of nearly 5,000 people diagnosed with colorectal cancer, 8% of the cases—or about one in 13—had malignancies that were not detected during colonoscopies performed within the prior three-year period.

Of course, the skill of the doctor you choose to perform your colonoscopy affects whether polyps (growths that are typically benign and can be removed before they turn malignant) and/or cancers are found. But to a surprising extent, the steps you take before your colonoscopy also greatly affect the test's accuracy.

SECRETS TO A GOOD BOWEL PREP

For most people over age 50, colonoscopy should be performed every three to five years if polyps have been found and up to every 10 years if no polyps have been found.* Perhaps the most dreaded part of the test, however, is the bowel prep.

If the bowel is not cleansed properly, it increases the likelihood that growths will be missed and that the procedure will take longer than it should, thus increasing the possibility of complications, such as perforation of the colon or rectum wall and post-procedure abdominal discomfort. If the test results are questionable, you may also need to repeat the test sooner.

To give yourself the best odds of an accurate colonoscopy...

Secret 1: **Start preparing early.** Review your doctor's instructions on bowel prep one week before the procedure, if possible. You may be told to temporarily avoid certain medications, such as iron-containing drugs or supplements that can color the intestines and make preparation more difficult. If you are taking medications that increase bleeding risk—for example, blood thinners such as *clopidogrel* (Plavix) or *warfarin* (Coumadin)—you should contact your doctor or the colonoscopist for instructions.

If you take medication for a chronic illness such as heart disease, ask your doctor whether you should take it up to and including the day of the procedure. People with diabetes may need to adjust their medication to keep their blood sugar levels normal while they are following dietary restrictions.

Beginning two to three days before the colonoscopy, many doctors advise you to avoid undigestible fiber from foods such as nuts, seeds, corn and bran cereal. Little pockets of

*Some people, including those with a family history of colorectal cancer, may be advised to begin regular colonoscopies sooner or get them more often—speak to your doctor.

residue from such foods may linger in the intestine, obscuring the doctor's view.

Secret 2: **Be clear on what foods you can eat.** For years, the standard instruction was to take nothing but clear liquids by mouth the day before a colonoscopy. But there is increasing evidence that a diet that includes fiber-free solid foods is not only easier to follow, but also may result in better cleansing.

A 2010 study in the journal *Endoscopy* found that patients tolerated the laxative better and the bowel was cleaner when they followed a fiber-free diet that included scrambled eggs, cheese and white bread, compared with a clear-liquid diet.

Theory: A liquid diet may decrease intestinal contractions and slow down bowel activity, while a bit of solid food keeps the bowel active so it can empty more completely.

Don't take this step on your own, though—ask your doctor if it's OK to eat light, fiber-free meals the day before your colonoscopy.

Secret 3: **Discuss your options for a laxative.** The most important part of bowel prep is taking a strong laxative, usually starting the afternoon or evening before you're scheduled for the procedure.

This is typically an unpleasant-tasting prescription preparation, such as polyethylene glycol (PEG), dissolved in an electrolyte solution containing sodium, potassium and other minerals. You may also be instructed to take laxative pills, usually *bisacodyl* (Dulcolax), at some time during the prep.

Not long ago, the standard approach called for a "high-volume" solution—four liters (more than a gallon) of liquid consumed over a period of several hours. Now, many doctors prescribe a "low-volume" solution—two liters versus four—that most people find easier to consume.

Caution: The low-volume approach usually works well but may fail to cleanse the bowel adequately if you are prone to constipation or take medication that slows down digestion, such as an opioid for pain or a tricyclic antidepressant, such as *amitriptyline* (Elavil).

If you are still passing brown stool when it's time to leave home for your colonoscopy, let the nurse know when you arrive at the colonoscopy center. The doctor may ask you to use an enema for further cleaning before starting the colonoscopy.

Secret 4: **Ask your doctor about splitting the laxative dose.** Whether you go the high-volume or low-volume route, when you take the purgative can make a crucial difference.

Most doctors used to advise drinking all the solution the night before the procedure. But many now counsel dividing the dose—half the night before and half four to five hours prior to the colonoscopy, even if you have to drink it at 3 am. A 2009 study rated the bowel significantly cleaner when less time elapsed between preparation and procedure.

Here's why: The laxative cleans fecal matter out of the colon, but over time, thick digestive mucus will descend from the small intestine, accumulate and obscure the doctor's view of the part of the large intestine where many cancers develop. Studies have shown that seven to eight hours after taking the laxative, the ascending bowel starts to become obscured by mucus. By 15 to 16 hours, it's often covered with mucus.

Secret 5: **Make sure you're not alone during a bowel prep.** It's rare, but some people get shaky or pass out during bowel prep. This may result from the abdominal cramping, vomiting, diarrhea and/or dehydration that can occur in some patients, so have someone with you overnight, particularly if you're an older adult and/or frail. Drink plenty of fluids to help prevent dehydration. Your doctor will tell you when to stop drinking and eating prior to the colonoscopy.

Secret 6: **Schedule early in the day, if possible.** Several studies have shown that some physicians detect fewer polyps as the day wears on, possibly due to fatigue. For this reason, you may want to schedule the procedure for earlier in the day, although time of day makes far less difference than the doctor's skill.

CHOOSE THE RIGHT DOCTOR

Gastroenterologists as well as some family physicians and internists perform colonoscopies, but gastroenterologists typically have more training and experience doing the procedure.**

However, the number of polyps a doctor detects in his patients is a much better measure of competence than his specialty. Look for a doctor who finds growths in 20% or more of patients.

If a doctor does not find precancerous polyps in this percentage of his screening patients, these patients are up to 10 times more likely to develop cancer before their next colonoscopy. If your doctor can't or won't tell you the number of growths he finds in his patients, consider looking elsewhere.

Research also shows that doctors who spend more time find more growths. For example, doctors should take at least six minutes to withdraw the scope (that's when the actual inspection takes place). Although taking more time doesn't guarantee a quality examination, it's fair for patients to tell a doctor that they've heard that taking longer increases polyp detection and that they're expecting a slow, careful exam and documentation of how long the procedure took.

**To find a gastroenterologist near you, consult the American College of Gastroenterology at *www.acg.gi.org* (click on the "Patients" tab).

Coffee Benefits

Coffee protects against aggressive cancers of the prostate and breast.

Recent finding: Women who drank more than five cups of coffee a day had a 57% lower risk for ER-negative breast cancer—the most aggressive subtype—than women who drank less than one cup a day. Men who consumed six or more cups of coffee daily had a 60% lower risk for lethal prostate cancer. The coffee in the women's study was caffeinated...in the men's study, both regular and decaffeinated coffee reduced the risk for cancer.

Michael F. Roizen, MD, chief wellness officer and chair, Wellness Institute, Cleveland Clinic.

Diabetes and Colon Growths

Diabetes increases risk for precancerous colon growths called adenomas.

Recent finding: Twenty-nine percent of adults with diabetes had at least one adenoma, versus 21% of those without diabetes. People with diabetes also tended to have more advanced adenomas.

Possible reason: High levels of insulin may cause the growth of precancerous and cancerous cells.

Self-defense: Diabetics should follow guidelines for colon cancer screening, which should begin at age 50.

Study of 556 people by researchers at James J. Peters Veterans Affairs Medical Center, New York City, presented at the American College of Gastroenterology 76th Annual Scientific Meeting, Washington, DC.

Warning on Colon Cleanses

Colon cleansing can cause serious side effects. Also known as colonic irrigation, it has been promoted as a way to lose weight, eliminate toxins from the body, enhance immunity and treat a host of conditions, including allergies, arthritis and depression. The practice involves flushing the colon with a mixture of herbs and water through a tube inserted in the rectum. Over-the-counter alternatives include laxatives, teas and capsules that can be taken orally or inserted in the rectum.

Recent finding: There is no evidence to back up any of the purported claims. Moreover, colon cleansing can cause vomiting, diarrhea, electrolyte imbalance, kidney failure, abdominal cramping, bloating and even injury to the lining of the colon, including outright perforation, which can lead to death.

Ranit Mishori, MD, assistant professor, department of family medicine, Georgetown University School of Medicine, Washington, DC, and leader of a literature review, published in *The Journal of Family Practice.*

Right Diet for Men

Men should not change their diets despite recent findings that omega-3 fatty acids increase risk for aggressive prostate cancer…and trans-fatty acids reduce risk. These findings are contrary to what researchers would have expected, because omega-3 fatty acids typically are good for the heart…and trans-fatty acids are linked to inflammation and heart disease.

Reality: Men's risk of dying from heart disease is so much greater than their risk of dying from aggressive prostate cancer that a diet high in omega-3s and low in trans-fatty acids still is best for most men.

Theodore M. Brasky, PhD, cancer epidemiologist in the Public Health Sciences Division of the Fred Hutchinson Cancer Research Center, Seattle, and leader of a study published in *American Journal of Epidemiology.*

Early Hair Loss Links to Prostate Cancer

Men who start to go bald at age 20 are more likely to develop prostate cancer in later life than men who start to lose their hair at age 30 or older.

Possible reason: Men who start balding earlier may have more testosterone or be more sensitive to testosterone.

Philippe Giraud, MD, PhD, professor of radiation oncology, Paris Descartes University, France, and leader of a study of 669 men, published in *Annals of Oncology.*

Better Colonoscopy Prep

Recent study: Researchers administered either a full-liquid diet (including ice cream and creamed soup) or a clear-liquid diet (including clear broth and gelatin) to 34 volunteers (average age 53) before they had colonoscopies.

Result: The adequacy of bowel cleansing and the number of patients with detected polyps did not differ between the two groups.

Theory: The liquids in both diets were low residue and adequately washed away with laxatives.

If you are planning a colonoscopy: Talk to your doctor about the possibility of a full-liquid diet that includes milk-based foods, which are more filling than clear liquids.

Ellen Gutkin, DO, researcher, division of gastroenterology, New York Hospital Queens, Flushing, New York.

Smarter PSA Testing

Rebecca Shannonhouse, editor, *Bottom Line/Health,* Boardroom Inc., 281 Tresser Blvd., Stamford, Connecticut 06901.

The US Preventive Services Task Force's recommendation that healthy men should not receive the prostate-specific antigen (PSA) test to screen for prostate cancer has generated a lot of controversy.

What was the panel's rationale? It concluded that the PSA test doesn't save enough men from dying of prostate cancer to justify the risk that they'll receive biopsies or other procedures—sometimes unnecessarily—that may cause incontinence or impotence.

Unfortunately, the panel, which was comprised of primary care doctors—but no urologists or oncologists—identified the wrong culprit, says Mark Scholz, MD, an oncologist and executive director of the Prostate Cancer Research Institute, *www.prostate-cancer.org.* PSA testing is not perfect, he explains, but it is essential—doctors just need to be smarter in using it. *Common mistakes…*

- **Rush to biopsy.** A single positive PSA should be repeated to ensure that the results are accurate…repeated again over time to look for changes…and combined with other tests, such as urine PCA3 and ultrasound, to confirm the presence/size of a tumor. A man should have a biopsy only if all of the tests point to a possible malignancy.

• **Not enough discussion.** Men should be told before the PSA test that a positive result doesn't always indicate cancer or a cancer that's worrisome.

Rather than following blanket recommendations, men should ask their own doctors if—or when—they should receive the PSA test. Insurance companies will probably continue to pay for it.

New Prostate Test

New prostate cancer test helps some men avoid biopsy.

Recent study: Doctors examined urine samples from 1,312 men (average age 62) who showed elevated levels of prostate-specific antigen, an indicator of increased risk for prostate cancer. A new test was then used to analyze the urine for a fusion of two genes thought to cause prostate cancer.

Result: Biopsy indicated cancer in 69% of those found by the gene fusion test to be at high risk. This new test may allow some men to avoid or delay a painful needle biopsy. The test will likely become widely available within the next year.

Arul Chinnaiyan, MD, director, Michigan Center for Translational Pathology, University of Michigan Medical School, Ann Arbor.

Rising PSA

Rising PSA is not a good prostate cancer predictor. When a man has a normal prostate-specific antigen (PSA) count of four nanograms per milliliter (ng/mL) or below, many doctors look at how quickly his PSA rises as a disease indicator.

Recent finding: A rising PSA indicates only a slight increase in risk for prostate cancer—and not the aggressive, dangerous kind of cancer.

Andrew Vickers, PhD, associate attending research methodologist, department of epidemiology and biostatistics, Memorial Sloan-Kettering Cancer Center, New York City, and leader of a study of 5,519 men, published in *Journal of the National Cancer Institute.*

Enlarged Prostate

Treatment for enlarged prostate reduces cancer risk. Roughly 16% of men will be diagnosed with prostate cancer. Men who take *dutasteride* (Avodart) or *finasteride* (Proscar, Propecia) for benign enlarged prostate are 26% less likely to develop prostate cancer.

But: Men taking either drug who do develop prostate cancer are slightly more likely to have a more dangerous form of the disease.

J. Stephen Jones, MD, FACS, professor and chairman, department of regional urology, and Leonard Horvitz and Samuel H. Miller Distinguished Chair in Urological Oncology Research, Cleveland Clinic.

Shorter Treatment

A five-week course of radiation for prostate cancer works as well as the traditional seven-and-a-half-week course. It also costs less and is more convenient for patients. The shorter approach, called *hypofractionation*, primarily is for men who have intermediate or high-risk prostate cancer and good pretreatment urinary function. Standard fractionation—the longer approach—is better for men with poor pretreatment urinary function.

Alan Pollack, MD, PhD, chairman of radiation oncology, Miller School of Medicine, University of Miami, and leader of a study of 303 men with prostate cancer, presented at a recent meeting of the American Society for Radiation Oncology.

Improved Radiation

New radiation treatment for prostate cancer has fewer side effects. Intensity-modified radiotherapy lowers the incidence and severity of gastrointestinal problems, such as rectal pain and bleeding, associated with traditional three-dimensional conformal radiotherapy. The new therapy facilitates the shaping of the beam to the target area and delivers a more consistent dose of radiation. It costs about $1,800 more than traditional treatment and may not be covered by insurance. Ask your doctor for details.

Silvia Hummel, MSc, senior analyst, School of Health and Related Research, University of Sheffield, UK, and leader of a review of data from 13 studies, published in *Health Technology Assessment.*

Music Eases Prostate Biopsy

Recent study: Eighty-eight men (average age 62) undergoing a prostate biopsy were assigned to three groups—one with noise-cancelling headphones...one with headphones that played Bach concertos...and one without headphones. Compared with the other two groups, the men who listened to music reported less pain and had lower diastolic (bottom number) blood pressure, which often rises due to anxiety.

Theory: Music stimulates the frontal cortex of the brain, which modulates perceived pain and anxiety.

If you need a prostate biopsy: Listen to classical music on an iPod or other device during the procedure. Music may also help with other minor procedures.

Matvey Tsivian, MD, postdoctoral associate, division of urology, Duke University Medical Center, Durham, North Carolina.

The Truth About Life After Prostate Cancer

Arnold Melman, MD, professor of urology at Albert Einstein College of Medicine in New York City, where he also has a private practice. A former president of the Society for the Study of Impotence, he specializes in prostate surgery and the diagnosis and treatment of male sexual dysfunction. He is author, with Rosemary E. Newnham, of *After Prostate Cancer: A What-Comes-Next Guide to a Safe and Informed Recovery* (Oxford University).

Roughly two million American men are now living with prostate cancer or the aftereffects of treatment.

That's largely because the ability to detect and treat prostate cancer has greatly improved. Now, about 90% of the nearly 250,000 American men who are diagnosed with the disease each year are alive at least 15 years after treatment.

The downside: Surgery and radiation, the main treatments, can cause serious side effects, including erectile dysfunction (ED) and incontinence.

Important recent study: Nearly half of men who had surgery for prostate cancer expected to have a better recovery than they actually did.

WHAT TO REALLY EXPECT

The complications of surgery (which typically involves total removal of the prostate gland) and radiation vary widely, depending on a man's age, the presence of other diseases (such as diabetes) and the specific type of treatment he receives. For example, a 50-year-old who had good erections prior to surgery will probably have them again within a year or two. An older man with a history of health problems won't do as well.

COPING WITH ED

Some of the nerves that control erections are invariably damaged during prostate removal surgery. This occurs even with so-called nerve-sparing procedures that are designed to minimize damage to nerves that supply the penis. In many cases, a man's ability to have erections can return within about 18 months, but there's no guarantee of a full recovery. In fact, recovery varies widely depending on the age and health of the patient—overall, 50% to 60% have permanent ED.

Men who are treated with radiation may retain their ability to have erections initially, but damage to nerves and blood vessels from radiation increases in the weeks and months after treatment.

Even so, prostate cancer survivors and their partners can still have satisfying sex lives (though the man may have a somewhat lower level of performance). *Here's how...*

• **Consider injections.** The average man is unwilling to stick a needle in his penis when he wants to have sex. But I encourage my patients to consider this treatment because it is the most effective—and always the least expensive—approach.

The drugs that are injected, *papaverine*, *prostaglandin* and *phentolamine*, are often combined in one solution. The injection usually produces an almost immediate erection even when a man isn't sexually aroused. The erection can last anywhere from about 10 minutes to four hours, depending on the dose.

The needle is so small that the injections are virtually painless. Once a man learns how to inject himself, he's given a prescription for enough medication to provide at least 50 doses.

Cost per shot: About $3.

Drawbacks: Apart from the fear of injections, the only likely side effect is an erection that lasts too long. This might not sound like a problem, but an overly persistent erection is painful and dangerous, potentially leading to permanent dysfunction. It can be prevented by reducing the dose.

• **Take a pill.** For those patients who are unwilling to try injections, *sildenafil* (Viagra), *vardenafil* (Levitra) and *tadalafil* (Cialis) promote blood flow to the penis when a man is sexually aroused and improve erections in about 60% of prostate cancer survivors who use the medications.

These medications work best in men who are in relatively good physical shape, don't have other serious health problems and have had nerve-sparing surgery or radiation alone. They're least effective in older men or men with low testosterone or complications from diabetes—and usually not effective at all for men who have had total removal of the prostate and surrounding tissue because they may have suffered nerve damage. Viagra, Levitra and Cialis can produce an erection in 30 to 60 minutes, and it typically lasts two to four hours.

Drawbacks: The medications cost $12 to $20 per pill (sometimes covered by insurance) and often cause headaches, dizziness, nasal congestion and other side effects. These drugs can also be dangerous or even deadly when combined with nitroglycerine medications, taken for heart problems.

• **Use a vacuum device.** This can be a good choice for men in long-term relationships who are comfortable "tinkering" before intercourse.

What happens: Just before intercourse, a man places a plastic sheath over his penis. Then, a motor (or a plastic crank, in less expensive models) creates a vacuum inside the sheath, which pulls blood into the penis. Once a man has an erection, he slips a rubber band around the base of the penis to hold the blood in place for 30 minutes.

Cost: $95 to $550, depending on the model.

Important: Use a vacuum device that has FDA approval and is prescribed by a doctor—the devices sold at "adult" stores may lack safety controls and generate too much pressure.

Drawbacks: Some men experience bruising on the penis. Also, many couples find the mechanical aspect of the devices unromantic.

• **Ask your doctor about surgical implants.** Men who can't get an erection any other way or prefer not to use the ED treatments described earlier may opt for a surgical implant.

Main choices: Semirigid, rodlike devices that are implanted in the penis and can be bent, like a pipe cleaner, into the proper position for intercourse...or a hydraulic device, controlled by a small bulb implanted in the scrotum, that pushes fluid into hollow tubes in the penis, causing them to inflate.

Most men who have these devices like them because they don't need pills or injections or require the steps that are necessary to use a vacuum device. As a result, they can have sex whenever they want.

Drawbacks: Postsurgical infection is the main risk. This occurs in about 3% of nondiabetic men. In men with diabetes, the infection rate is about 8%. The devices are expensive but often partially covered by insurance. Out-of-pocket costs are about $5,000 for the semirigid device and $8,000 for the inflatable one.

URINARY INCONTINENCE

Lack of urinary control is the second most common complication of prostate cancer treatments.

Reason: The prostate gland helps control/block the flow of urine. When the gland is removed or damaged, the urinary sphincter (the muscle that controls urine) has to work alone—and often fails. Most men eventually regain bladder control, but this can take two years or more.

Surgery—to implant an artificial sphincter, for example—may be needed if a man accidentally voids or "leaks" large amounts of urine. *My advice...*

• **Expect some leakage.** Most men who are treated with surgery and/or radiation for prostate cancer will experience some degree of stress incontinence—the leakage of a few drops of urine when they cough, sneeze, laugh, etc. It can be embarrassing, but as long as the amounts of urine are small, it's usually nothing to worry about. It will probably improve with time. Some men who have radiation may also have urge incontinence—a strong, sudden need to urinate.

When men are leaking large amounts of urine or when they're so embarrassed that they feel they can't leave the house, over-the-counter pads can help.

• **Do Kegel exercises.** Apart from surgery, this is the most effective way for men to regain bladder control. (Kegel exercises probably won't help men who are leaking large amounts of urine, but it doesn't hurt for these men to try them.) Start doing them every day after a diagnosis—before cancer treatments begin—to prevent future problems.

What to do: First, identify the pelvic-floor muscles. They're the muscles that you contract to hold urine in the bladder—or to stop the flow of urine in midstream.

Several times a day, squeeze the muscles as hard as you can. Hold for about five seconds, then relax. Repeat this sequence a few times. As the muscles get stronger, try to do 20 or more contractions at a time. Do them a few times a day.

Cancer Recurrence Linked to Weight

Prostate cancer patients who gain weight have a higher risk for recurrence.

Recent finding: Men who gained five or more pounds between five years before and one year after surgery for prostate cancer were twice as likely to experience a recurrence, compared with men who maintained their weight or lost weight.

Corinne E. Joshu, PhD, MPH, teaching assistant, department of epidemiology, Bloomberg School of Public Health, Johns Hopkins University, Baltimore, and leader of a study of 2,498 men, presented at the 101st annual meeting of the American Association for Cancer Research.

Vitamin D

Vitamin D protects against urinary tract infections by promoting the body's production of the antimicrobial peptide cathelicidin.

Recent finding: When exposed to E. coli bacteria that causes urinary tract infections, bladder tissue taken from women given 2,000 international units (IU) of vitamin D daily for

12 weeks showed an increase in infection-fighting cathelicidin.

Annelie Brauner, MD, PhD, professor, department of microbiology, tumor and cell biology, division of clinical microbiology, Karolinska Institute and Karolinska University Hospital, Sweden, and leader of a study published in *PLoS One.*

Prunes Better Than Psyllium

Recent *finding:* Daily consumption of five or six prunes relieved constipation more effectively than daily use of a tablespoon of a psyllium laxative, such as Metamucil. Psyllium is mostly soluble fiber, while prunes contain both soluble and insoluble types of fiber, as well as a sugar alcohol called sorbitol that has a laxative effect. These differences may account for prunes' greater effectiveness. There also is a psychological component—prunes have been used for so long as a constipation remedy that study participants may have expected them to be effective, making them work better.

Satish Rao, MD, PhD, professor of medicine, Carver College of Medicine, University of Iowa, Iowa City, and leader of a study published in *Alimentary Pharmacology & Therapeutics.*

Natural Remedy for IBS

Peppermint oil can alleviate the gastrointestinal symptoms associated with Irritable Bowel Syndrome, including flatulence and abdominal pain and distension, by blocking the flow of calcium into muscle cells in the intestines, which in turn reduces muscle contractions.

Best: When symptoms are present, take two coated capsules of peppermint oil three times daily.

Alexander Ford, MD, senior lecturer, section of molecular gastroenterology, Leeds Institute of Molecular Medicine, Leeds University, UK.

NSAIDs Linked to Diverticulitis

Researchers who examined 22 years' worth of data on 47,275 men (ages 40 to 75) found that men who took nonsteroidal anti-inflammatory drugs (NSAIDs), such as aspirin and *ibuprofen* (Motrin), two or more times weekly were significantly more likely to develop diverticulitis (inflamed pouches in the colon) than men who did not take NSAIDs. The finding is believed to also apply to women.

Theory: NSAID use may damage the colon, allowing for the influx of bacteria and other toxins. Earlier research has linked regular NSAID use to stomach upset and bleeding.

Lisa L. Strate, MD, assistant professor of gastroenterology, University of Washington, Seattle.

Vegetarian Advantage

Vegetarians are 30% less likely to develop diverticular disease than meat eaters. And those who ate a high-fiber vegetarian diet (more than 25 grams a day) were 41% less likely to be diagnosed with the disease than vegetarians who ate less than 14 grams. Diverticular disease includes diverticulosis (small pouches in the colon) and diverticulitis (inflamed or infected pouches).

Francesca Crowe, PhD, nutritional epidemiologist, Cancer Epidemiology Unit, University of Oxford, UK, and leader of a study of 47,033 adults, published in *BMJ.*

Lack of Sleep Linked to Colon Cancer

Recent *study:* Prior to having colonoscopies, 1,240 patients were surveyed about their sleep habits.

Finding: Those who slept fewer than six hours nightly, on average, were 50% more likely to have adenomatous polyps (precancerous lesions) in the colon and/or rectum than those who slept at least seven hours nightly.

Theory: Lack of sleep can lower production of melatonin, a hormone shown in animal studies to help repair DNA damage, a critical step to preventing cancer.

Li Li, MD, PhD, associate professor of family medicine, Case Western Reserve University School of Medicine, Cleveland.

New Tests on the Horizon

Colonoscopy may be replaced by a DNA test. Two noninvasive DNA tests that are effective at finding abnormalities in the colon may be available within two years. One test looks at stool samples...the other looks for changes in a gene in the blood. A colonoscopy would be needed if a DNA-based test found abnormalities.

David A. Ahlquist, MD, colon cancer expert, Mayo Clinic, Rochester, Minnesota, and adviser to DNA-test developer Exact Sciences, Madison, Wisconsin.

7

Manage Your Money

Better Than Banks—Credit Unions

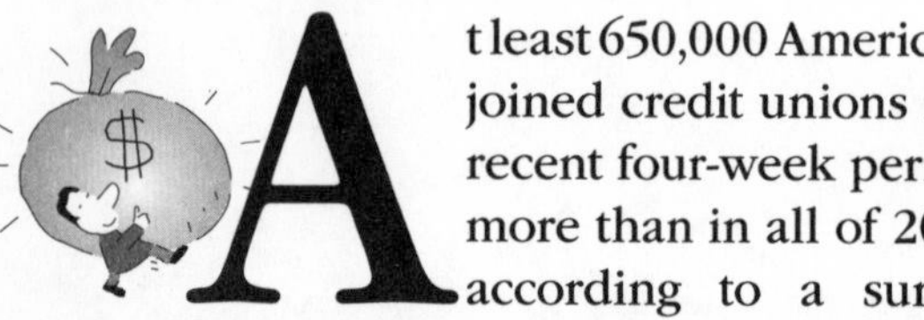

At least 650,000 Americans joined credit unions in a recent four-week period, more than in all of 2010, according to a survey by the Credit Union National Association. Many of them have shifted to credit unions in disgust over what has been happening at their banks—namely, higher fees, new fees and new requirements to avoid fees, even though several major banks have backed off from plans to charge up to $5 each month for the use of a debit card. And people who switched have been happy to find that in many cases, credit unions have become as easy to join and use as banks.

Here are some of the most convenient ways to take advantage of better rates and fewer fees at credit unions...

ATM AND BRANCH NETWORKS

In the past, credit union members were limited to a few locations when they wanted to make transactions, especially deposits. *That has changed dramatically...*

- **The Co-Op Network.** More than 1,400 of the 7,200 credit unions in the US belong to this network, which gives credit union members surcharge-free access to more than 28,000 ATMs across the US and Canada, including machines at retailers such as 7-Eleven, Costco and Walgreens. About 9,000 of these ATMs allow members to make deposits, too.
- **The Credit Union Service Center Network.** If you join a credit union that belongs to this network, you can walk into any of more than 6,700 branches of other credit unions

Allan S. Roth, CFP, CPA, president of Wealth Logic, LLC, a financial advisory firm in Colorado Springs that serves clients with investments ranging from $10,000 to $50 million. He has kept a portion of his own assets and those of many of his clients in credit unions for the past decade. He is author of *How a Second Grader Beats Wall Street: Golden Rules Any Investor Can Learn* (Wiley). *www.daretobedull.com*

and use them as though they were your home branch, including making deposits and withdrawals. To locate participating branches, go to *www.cuswirl.com.*

• **Other ATMs.** In addition to the credit unions that belong to one of the networks above, most credit unions belong to bank ATM networks such as STAR, Pulse, Cirrus and NYCE, which allow access to tens of thousands of ATMs around the country. However, when you use one of these ATMs, you may be charged a fee by your credit union, as well as a surcharge by the owner of the particular ATM that you use. But some credit unions don't charge a fee and reimburse you in full or in part for ATM fees that you are charged by other institutions.

DEPOSITS BY COMPUTER

Some credit unions make it easy to make deposits by allowing you to scan a check into your personal computer.

Example: If you become a member of Digital Federal Credit Union (*www.dcu.org*), whose branches are in Massachusetts and New Hampshire, you can deposit your checks by scanning them into your computer with a scanner or digital camera, or scan them into an iPhone or Android smartphone. Membership is open to anyone who has worked for, or is related to someone who has worked for, one of several hundred participating employers...or you can become a lifetime member by joining an organization such as Reach Out for Schools or American Association of People with Disabilities (membership fees range from $10 to $29).

HOW TO FIND THEM

To search for credit unions by location or by the organizations that they are affiliated with, including companies, schools or places of worship, go to *www.creditunion.coop.*

To search by the best rates on certificates of deposit (CDs), high-yield checking accounts or savings and money-market accounts, go to *www.depositaccounts.com.*

Credit unions that are easy to join...

• **Pentagon Federal Credit Union.** This credit union, which serves US government employees, also is open to people who make a onetime tax-deductible $20 donation to the nonprofit National Military Family Association or who are employees or volunteers of the American Red Cross. It also is open to relatives of anyone who is eligible to join. PenFed has more than one million members and more than $15 billion in assets. The yields on its CDs are among the highest in the nation—for instance, 2.4%* annually on a seven-year CD recently. And it recently offered four-year new-car loans at an annual interest rate of 1.99% (*www.penfed.org*).

• **Alliant Credit Union.** This credit union, which serves residents of the Chicago area and has more than 300,000 members, also is open to US citizens who make a onetime donation of $10 to a charity called Foster Care to Success, which serves foster teens across the US. The yields on its accounts—recently 0.89% on a savings account...0.75% on a high-yield checking account...and 1.65% on a five-year CD of at least $25,000—top those at most banks. And its Visa Platinum credit card charges no fee for balance transfers (*www.alliantcreditunion.org*).

Get to the Point

Overdraft fees still cost consumers heavily despite new rules requiring banks to get customer permission before enrolling them in a standard overdraft plan for ATM and debit cards.

Reason: Disclosures are complex, with much of the text densely printed, difficult to decipher and highly technical and legalistic. In fact, the median length of bank disclosures for checking accounts is 111 pages.

Example: A disclosure may not make clear that the median overdraft-protection fee is $35, but the median charge to transfer funds from savings to cover an overdraft is only $10.

What to do: Take a one-page disclosure form to your banking institution, and ask a representative there to fill it out. You can

*All rates and prices in this chapter are quoted as of July 2012, and are subject to change.

download a form that has blank spaces for all the key terms and conditions of your account at *www.pewtrusts.org/safechecking* (click "Checking Accounts: Long on Words, Short on Protections—the Need for a Disclosure Box").

Susan K. Weinstock, director, Pew Safe Checking in the Electronic Age Project, Washington, DC. *www.pewtrusts.org/money*

What to Do When Interest Rates Are Low

Whether you are a saver, an investor, a borrower, a credit card user—or even a traveler—here, eight personal finance experts give their recommendations on what to do now...

SAVINGS

Richard Barrington, CFA
moneyrates.com

• **Upgrade to an online savings account.** This is more important now than ever. The average yield on savings and money market accounts offered by banks is about 0.15%, and even less for money market mutual funds offered by brokerage firms. You can improve that by up to one full percentage point—an extra $1,000 a year on a $100,000 balance—and do so risk-free by opening an FDIC-insured savings account over the Internet.

Examples: Sallie Mae Bank High-Yield Savings Account, recent yield: 0.75%, *www.salliemae.com*...Discover Bank Online Savings, 0.8%, *www.discover bank.com*...American Express Bank High-Yield Savings Account, 0.85%, *www.personalsavings.americanexpress.com.*

Richard Barrington, CFA, personal finance expert at moneyrates.com. He is based in Macedon, New York.

Allan S. Roth, CPA, CFP
Wealth Logic, LLC

Look for five- or 10-year certificates of deposit (CDs) with low early-withdrawal penalties and relatively high yields. You will benefit if interest rates in general stay low for many years—but you can cash out and reinvest without too much pain if interest rates go up before your CDs mature.

Allan S. Roth, CPA, CFP, president of Wealth Logic, LLC, a financial advisory firm in Colorado Springs. He is author of *How a Second Grader Beats Wall Street: Golden Rules Any Investor Can Learn* (Wiley).

BONDS

Russ Koesterich, CFA
iShares, BlackRock

Consider a municipal bond exchange-traded fund (ETF). While states and municipalities face tough fiscal challenges, they still can be viewed as a safe haven for jittery investors seeking a tax break. Muni defaults lately have been minimal and state tax revenues are rebounding. Many governors are cutting spending by pushing unions to accept contracts with multiyear wage freezes. Moreover, munis are cheap relative to US Treasuries now, and their yields can be much better after considering taxes. (Municipal bond interest is exempt from federal and possibly state and local tax depending on where you live, while Treasuries are exempt from state and local tax.) The recent average yield on 10-year AAA-rated municipal bonds is 1.85%. For a 10-year Treasury, the yield is about 1.66%.

Russ Koesterich, CFA, managing director and chief investment strategist of the San Francisco–based iShares division of BlackRock, an asset-management firm with more than $3.5 trillion in assets. He is author of *The Ten Trillion Dollar Gamble: The Coming Deficit Debacle and How to Invest Now* (McGraw-Hill).

Robert M. Brinker
Brinker Fixed Income Advisor

Invest with a proven intermediate-bond fund manager. The current environment calls for a nimble bond fund manager who has proved his skills in the face of many varied challenges and is great at balancing risks with the potential for higher rewards.

My favorite fund now: Doubleline Total Return Fund (DLTNX) is an intermediate-term bond fund whose recent annual yield was 7.3%—among the highest in the category. This was achieved by mixing risky and conservative investments, including more than 60% of its assets held in AAA-rated bonds. It gained 8.9% over the past year as of June 28, putting it in the top 8% of its category. Although the fund is new, it is run by Jeffrey Gundlach, one of the most talented bond fund managers anywhere, who had a stellar record for 16 years at TCW Total Return Bond. (He was ousted from TCW in December 2009 over a dispute with management.) *www.doubleline funds.com.*

Robert M. Brinker, editor of *Brinker Fixed Income Advisor*, a monthly investment letter covering Treasuries, municipal bonds and no-load bond funds, Littleton, Colorado. *www.brinkeradvisor.com*

BORROWING/SPENDING

Keith Gumbinger
HSH Associates

Look into a 15-year mortgage. Many home owners who are refinancing have been abandoning traditional 30-year fixed-rate loans for shorter-term loans. Of course, a shorter-term loan requires a higher monthly payment, but interest rates on 15-year loans are so low—recently averaging 3.0% versus 3.7% for a 30-year mortgage—that these payments can be surprisingly affordable, allowing you to pay off your mortgage faster and save tens of thousands of dollars over the long run. For example, someone with $200,000 left on a 30-year mortgage who refinances to a 15-year mortgage may see monthly payments go up by just $100 to $150. The strategy is especially attractive at this time when there are few attractive options for investing any extra money that would be saved in monthly payments by choosing a 30-year mortgage.

Keith Gumbinger, vice president of HSH Associates, the nation's largest publisher of mortgage and consumer loan information, Pompton Plains, New Jersey. *www.hsh.com*

Ben Woolsey
CreditCards.com

Grab lower interest rates on credit cards. With the Fed pledging low short-term interest rates for many months to come and with a drop in the rate of delinquencies on credit card payments, expect to see credit card issuers compete more aggressively by offering lower interest rates. This could help you if you must maintain a credit card balance.

Recommended no-fee cards: Chase Freedom Credit Card (800-432-3117, *www.chase.com*) offers a 0% introductory rate for the first billing cycles on balance transfers and six months on purchases, with a variable rate as low as 12.99% after the introductory period, plus a $100 cash-back bonus if you spend $500 in the first three months...Capital One Platinum Prestige Credit Card (800-955-7070, *www.capitalone.com*) offers a 0% introductory rate on balance transfers and purchases until September 2013, with a variable rate as low as 10.9% afterward.

Ben Woolsey, director of marketing and consumer research, CreditCards.com, Austin, Texas.

Jesse Toprak
TrueCar.com

Expect more 0% to 1.9% financing on new-car loans in the next several months even from manufacturers such as Toyota that have rarely offered these kinds of deals in the past. Rates are typically based on a tiered structure, such as 0% for up to 36 months...0.9% for 48 months...and 1.9% for 60 months.

Jesse Toprak, vice president of industry trends at TrueCar.com, which tracks new-car pricing and trends, Santa Monica, California.

Tom Parsons
BestFares.com

Don't rush to lock in airfares right away. The cost of airline travel may very well drop in coming months, due to sagging demand from worried consumers scaling back in case of another recession. Look for the biggest bargains to certain places in the US (such as Florida and Las Vegas), Mexico and the Caribbean (such as Aruba). Unfortunately, Europe will remain very expensive because fuel surcharges have more than doubled in the past four years.

Tom Parsons, cofounder and CEO of BestFares.com, Arlington, Texas.

Safeguards When You Switch Bank Accounts

Many big-bank customers are shifting their accounts because of new fees and requirements. Of course, shifting your account from one financial institution to another can be a hassle, which is why many customers are reluctant to do so, and mistakes can lead to bounced checks and overdrawn accounts. But many local banks now offer online "switch kits" that streamline the process and paperwork. Just be sure to redirect your automatic bill-paying setups and direct deposit of your paycheck or Social Security check from one account to the other...maintain your old checking account for a few billing cycles in case billers are slow to make the switch...obtain written confirmation when you do close your old account.

Ken Tumin, founder, DepositAccounts.com, Sanford, Florida, a Web site for consumer information on small financial institutions.

Less Expensive Check Cashing

Large retail chains, such as Kmart, Sears and Walmart, have been expanding into check-cashing services, and some offer fees that are lower than those of traditional check-cashing stores.

Example: Walmart charges $3 to cash checks up to $1,000 and $6 for checks up to $5,000. That compares with a typical cost of 2% to 4% of a check's face value to cash it at a check-cashing store.

Also: Walmart will cash checks from a variety of sources, including checks from the government, payroll checks, money orders and others.

Caution: Check cashing at retail stores is still higher than the free check cashing typical at banks—if you have an account. Consider using these services only if you do not have a bank account and the store is convenient for you.

DailyFinance.com

Avoid Those Nasty New Bank Fees

Ken Tumin, founder of DepositAccounts.com, a site for consumer information about small financial institutions, based in Sanford, Florida. It monitors interest rates, financial health and new developments at more than 8,000 banks and credit unions.

Many angry checking-account customers are searching for new options as some of the biggest US banks are slapping higher fees on more accounts. Hundreds of small banks across the US are offering an attractive alternative—no-fee checking accounts that pay big monthly rewards for using your debit card to make many of your purchases. Many banks pay between 2% and 4% on balances, typically up to $15,000 or $25,000. The high-yield checking account at Southern Bank in Arkansas and Missouri pays 4.01% up to a balance of $15,000. That's a lot more generous than online accounts from national financial institutions such as Bank of Internet USA or Flagstar Direct, which pay about 1% or less.

Big fees at big banks: Some banking giants appear to be penalizing rather than rewarding customers. For example, to avoid a $20 monthly fee on a mid-tier checking account at Citibank, you will have to keep a combined minimum average balance in your accounts of at least $15,000, up from $6,000, or meet other conditions. Even if you meet the new requirements for avoiding fees at the big banks, they pay you little or no interest. And in a survey of the largest banks in 25 major markets by Bankrate.com, just 45% still are offering free no-interest checking accounts, down from 76% in 2009.

The big banks blame the federal government, which has set new restrictions and requirements on their activities, including limits on how much debit card issuers can charge merchants for transactions—limits that the banks say cut into their profits. But the little banks fall under different rules. They are able to reward you for debit card transactions because the new federal rules exempt financial institutions with assets totaling less than

$10 billion from the limits on how much they can charge merchants for debit card transactions, giving those institutions greater incentives to attract checking-account customers.

The fine print: You typically must be a resident of the state where the small bank operates to open one of these no-fee, high-interest accounts. Most of the banks don't require a minimum balance or they require a minimum opening balance of just $100 to get the high yields, but you often must meet the following requirements in addition to making a certain number of debit card transactions (typically, 10 to 15 per month)...

- **Have at least one direct deposit per month made into your account,** such as a paycheck or a Social Security or pension check...or make one electronic payment of a bill each month.
- **Agree to accept online bank statements instead of hard copies.**

Fail to meet these conditions, and your interest rate falls to as low as 0.1% for that month.

Also, the bank may not have many, or any, branches or ATMs near where you live or work, so you may end up doing a lot of your banking online. But many of these banks will reimburse you for fees that you are charged for using ATMs of other institutions, up to certain limits (typically, $10 to $25 per month).

You can look for banks in your state at my Web site, *www.depositaccounts.com.*

Alternative: High-yield checking accounts at credit unions. There often are restrictions regarding who is eligible to join, but not always. For example, Beacon Credit Union in Lynchburg, Virginia, offers 5.05% on checking accounts for anyone who lives, works, worships or goes to school in the Lynchburg area. However, Consumers Credit Union based in Waukegan, Illinois, which pays 4.09% on balances up to $10,000, allows anyone to join for a onetime fee of $5.

Credit unions, which, like banks, have insurance protection for accounts, usually have the same monthly requirements to earn high-yield rates as small banks. To find a credit union near you, go to *www.creditunion.coop* or *www.depositaccounts.com.*

"Joint" Account Self-Defense

Marjory Abrams, president, *BottomLine* newsletters, Boardroom Inc., 281 Tresser Blvd., Stamford, Connecticut 06901.

I recently tried to cash in rewards points on our American Express card, but I couldn't because my husband is the primary cardholder and I was not authorized for the particular offering. I ran into a similar trap when I tried to cancel our second phone line, but I couldn't because that account is in my husband's name, too.

This swings both ways. For example, my husband couldn't add another cell-phone line to our family plan because I am the primary person on that account.

For anyone like me who has had "joint" household accounts for a long time, these restrictions may come as a surprise. After we got married, I thought we were combining our AmEx accounts, not simply canceling mine...and I had previously "spent" some of our AmEx points on hotel reservations.

As frustrated as I felt, I understand the rules from the providers' perspective—they're trying to protect themselves from nasty divorces and finger-pointing of responsibility on delinquent accounts. When there's one key person, there is no confusion as to who is responsible for a bill.

The remedy—and I suggest you do this before you have a problem—is for the primary person to make the spouse an authorized user on the account. Such a designation gives additional, albeit limited, abilities to manage the account. So, for example, my husband now can authorize most types of changes to our cell-phone plans.

When you sign up for a new service, be sure to make the person who is most likely to deal with any problems the primary and assign your "secondary" at the same time. These simple steps will save you time and frustration down the road.

No More Paper Savings Bonds

US Savings Bonds are now sold only electronically, through the Treasury Department's Treasury Direct Web site (*www.treasurydirect.gov*). Banks and credit unions no longer sell savings bonds. Electronic bonds will be easier to keep track of and are automatically redeemed when they reach final maturity and are no longer earning interest.

However, if you already own paper bonds, you can still keep them and redeem them at financial institutions whenever you choose to.

Tom Adams, publisher of the Web site Savings Bond Advisor, New York City. *www.savings-bond-advisor.com*

Best Order to Pay Debts

If you are overburdened with debt, you may have to choose which debts to pay first. Start with those that can land you in jail if left unpaid, such as taxes and child support. Next, figure out which have the worst terms. Compare interest rates and whether there are tax benefits (mortgage interest can be deducted, for example). Then decide which debts will hurt the least if they must go unpaid. Walking away from unsecured debt, such as hospital or credit card bills, will hurt your credit score but probably won't result in you losing any assets, such as a home. If you owe more on your home than it is worth, defaulting on your mortgage can make sense in some cases, even though it will heavily damage your credit score and you will lose the home. Consult the National Foundation for Credit Counseling (*www.nfcc.org*) for advice.

SmartMoney.com

Check for Clarity

Some credit card applications bury important information. In his firm's ranking of the 10 largest card issuers for clarity of information on application forms, Capital One came out on top, followed closely by Bank of America, while Citigroup—whose disclosures don't make clear how much its "Thank You" rewards points are worth, for example—was at the bottom and Discover next to the bottom. For the full list, go to ***http://education.cardhub.com/credit-card-application-study-2011.***

Odysseas Papadimitriou, founder and CEO of Evolution Finance, parent of CardHub.com, a Web site for credit card information.

Best Credit Cards Now

Bill Hardekopf, CEO of LowCards.com, a Web site based in Birmingham, Alabama, that helps consumers compare credit cards and provides rankings and reviews. He is coauthor of *The Credit Card Guidebook* (Lulu).

Credit card issuers have been rolling out an array of attractive incentives to get consumers to choose and use their cards. That's partly because credit cards still are very profitable for the issuers despite new federal regulations that try to protect consumers from credit card issuers' worst practices, such as imposing harsh penalties for late payments and jacking interest rates way up. The incentives include cash bonuses of as much as $300 to sign up for cards with rewards programs that offer as much as 5% cash back.

Caution: Many of the best credit card offers are available only to consumers who have very good credit scores. If your credit score is below the mid-700s, your options for a new card will be more limited, but there still are some good ones available.

Today's best credit card offers...*

CASH BACK

While cards that offer rebates of 1% cash back on purchases are common, those that offer much more for many types of purchases are harder to find. Keep in mind that some cash-back cards have higher interest rates, so they may not be appropriate for people who carry balances.

• **Best all-purpose cash-back card.** Fidelity Investment Rewards American Express offers a flat 2% cash back on all purchases. While some cards offer higher cash-back levels after you have spent a certain amount each year, no other card currently open to new customers can match the 2% rate for all purchases right from the start each year. The rebates automatically are deposited into a Fidelity brokerage, retirement or college savings account. 866-598-4971, *www.fidelity.com.*

Alternative: Capital One Cash. It offers 1% cash back on all purchases, but there also is an annual bonus equal to 50% of the cash back earned during the year, for the equivalent of 1.5% cash back. Capital One Cash also has been offering new cardholders a $100 cash bonus for spending $500 on the card within three months and a 0% interest rate on purchases and balance transfers until December 2012. 800-410-0020, *www.capitalone.com.*

• **Best cash-back card with higher rewards for rotating categories.** Chase Freedom Visa offers 5% on purchases totaling up to $1,500 per quarter in specific spending categories that change quarterly...and 1% on all other purchases. Grocery stores and movie theaters are the current 5% cash-back categories...then gas stations and restaurants in the next quarter...and hotels, airlines and purchases from Best Buy and Kohl's in the final quarter of 2012.

Chase Freedom Visa offers new cardholders a bonus of $100 to $300 for spending $500 within three months of opening the account. 800-432-3117, *www.chase.com.*

*Cards in this article carry no annual fee unless otherwise indicated. Be aware that card features and availability change frequently.

Downside: You must call Chase or visit its Web site each quarter to activate those 5% rotating category rewards, then remember which are current.

TRAVEL REWARDS

Travel rewards credit cards let cardholders earn airline frequent-flier miles or hotel loyalty program points when they make purchases.

• **Best airline card linked to a particular airline.** United MileagePlus Explorer Card offers 25,000 bonus miles the first time you use the card—enough for a round-trip ticket in the US or Canada, excluding Hawaii. The card also offers two miles for each dollar spent on United flights, plus one mile per dollar spent on everything else. Cardholders earn an additional 10,000-mile bonus for spending at least $25,000 on the card in a calendar year. Additional perks include priority boarding on United flights, two complimentary passes to United's Airport Club lounges each year and free baggage check for your first piece of luggage on each flight. 866-652-3261, *www.theexplorercard.com.*

Downside: A steep $95 annual fee, although it's waived in the first year.

• **Best travel card not linked to a particular airline.** Capital One Venture Rewards Visa offers cardholders two frequent-flier miles for each dollar spent. Those miles can be used on any airline, and there are no blackout dates, seat restrictions or expiration dates. But unlike with traditional frequent-flier programs, there is no set number of miles required for a rewards ticket. Instead, add two zeroes to the purchase price of the ticket you want in order to get the number of miles needed. For example, a $480 ticket requires 48,000 miles. 800-417-0090, *www.capitalone.com.*

Downside: There's a $59 annual fee after the first year.

Alternative: Venture Rewards' sister card, Capital One VentureOne Rewards Visa, has no annual fee and offers 1.25 miles per dollar spent on all purchases.

LOW INTEREST RATES

If you carry a balance on your credit card, low interest rates matter much more than rewards programs.

• **Low-rate cards.** Simmons First Visa Platinum and IberiaBank Visa Classic both offer variable interest rates as low as 7.25%. That's about the lowest you can find these days, aside from limited-time introductory rates. *Simmons*: 800-272-2102, *www.simmonsfirst.com. IberiaBank:* 800-217-7715, *http://creditcards.iberiabank.com.*

Downside: If your credit score is below 680, your application probably will be either rejected or approved only for a higher rate.

BALANCE TRANSFERS

Lots of cards offer 0% introductory rates on balance transfers—but how long does that 0% rate last? And what rate applies when it expires? *Recent deals...*

• **Longest 0% introductory balance-transfer-rate card.** Citi Platinum Select Visa Cards offers a 0% introductory rate on balance transfers and purchases for 18 months, much longer than the typical six- to-12-month introductory rate period. After that, your interest rate could climb to between a reasonable 11.99% and a steep 21.99%, depending on your creditworthiness. 800-311-9098, *www.citicards.com.*

Downside: Although the card's 3% balance transfer fee is at the low end of the 3% to 4% typically charged, it still adds up to $300 for every $10,000 transferred. A single late payment could replace your 0% introductory rate with the ongoing interest rate.

• **Lowest balance-transfer fee.** Slate from Chase charges no transfer fee for balances transferred to the card within 60 days of opening the account. It also offers a 0% annual percentage rate on balance transfers and purchases for 15 months. Rates then climb to between 11.99% and 21.99%, depending on your creditworthiness. 800-432-3117, *www.chase.com.*

SMALL-BUSINESS PERKS

Several credit card issuers have begun marketing attractive new cards to small-business owners. *Examples...*

• **Best small-business card.** Chase Ink Cash offers a 0% interest rate for the first 12 months and a higher rate thereafter, recently 10.24%. Cardholders earn a $250 cash bonus if they spend $5,000 in the first three months, and there's a cash-back rewards program that features 5% cash back on the first $25,000 spent each year at office-supply stores and on wireless, cable and landline services...2% cash back on the first $25,000 spent at restaurants and gas stations...and 1% cash back on all other purchases. 800-432-3117, *www.chase.com.*

FOR WEAK CREDIT

Consumers whose credit scores are below 680 or whose credit histories are limited still have some reasonable credit card options...

• **Best student credit card.** Discover Student Card combines competitive rates—0% for the first nine months, then ongoing rates as low as 12.99%—with cash-back bonuses. Users earn 5% cash back on purchases in rotating categories and 1% cash back on everything else. 800-347-2683, *www.discover.com.*

Downside: By law, students younger than 21 must provide proof of income or a co-signer to qualify for a card.

• **Best card for those with middling credit scores (620 to 679).** Capital One Classic Platinum MasterCard is a straightforward card for those with middling credit scores. It offers a 0% interest rate on purchases until March 2013, then 17.99% to 22.99% thereafter, depending on your credit score. 800-410-0020, *www.capitalone.com.*

Downside: A $39 annual fee.

Be Careful With Prepaids

Prepaid credit cards are loaded with fees and don't always help rebuild credit scores. Fees may include activation fees as high as $19.95...monthly or annual fees...and fees for inactivity, transactions, closing the account, adding cash to the account, using an ATM and running low on your balance. If your goal is to rebuild your credit score, pick a card with reasonable fees that reports to a credit-reporting agency, such as AccountNow Prepaid Visa or Public Savings Open Sky Secured Visa.

Bill Hardekopf, CEO of LowCards.com, which compares credit cards, Birmingham, Alabama, and coauthor of *The Credit Card Guidebook* (Lulu). *www.lowcards.com*

Gold Cards Not So Elite

Almost one-third of credit card offers mailed in the second quarter of this year were for premium cards. Many of the offers targeted consumers with credit scores in the 600s—not the scores of 760 and above at which these offers used to aim.

Reason: People who get premium cards tend to charge more on them—and many card issuers charge merchants more to process premium-card payments.

What to do: Consider the value to you of premium cards (some of which charge hefty fees)—not in terms of status but strictly financially.

Example: Some of the cards offer benefits such as priority boarding and/or no foreign currency transaction fees.

Curtis Arnold, founder, CardRatings.com, Little Rock, Arkansas.

Lower Credit Card Fees

Discover Financial and Citigroup (for the ThankYou Premier and ThankYou Prestige cards) have dropped their foreign-transaction fees. JPMorgan Chase has eliminated that fee on its Sapphire Preferred card. Some lenders also are charging less, or nothing, for balance transfers—for example, Chase waives the 3% transfer fee for balances switched within the first 30 days of opening the Chase Slate credit card.

The Wall Street Journal

Check Credit Card Refunds

If retailers do not accept a return, most Gold, Platinum, World and World Elite MasterCards will refund up to $250 within 60 days of an item's purchase, and some Visa cards will reimburse up to $250 within 90 days of purchase. American Express offers all cardholders up to $300 back for up to 90 days. Discover does not offer return protection.

Remember: Read your credit card agreement carefully, or contact the issuer to find out what your card provides. Restrictions on refund offers differ, too—ask about them.

Bankrate.com

Easier Loans Now

Unsecured personal loans are easier to get now. Lenders including Capital One, SunTrust, TD Bank and Wells Fargo have loosened the reins on loans that require no collateral. These loans can help consumers with emergency expenses or to consolidate credit card debt, although their interest rates average a steep 11%.

John Ulzheimer, president of consumer education at SmartCredit.com, a credit-monitoring site, and president of The Ulzheimer Group, a consulting firm that specializes in credit scoring, Atlanta. *www.johnulzheimer.com*

Little-Known Ways to Boost Creditworthiness

Insurance and utility payments, rent and any other regular payments can help increase the likelihood that you can get a loan. The Equal Credit Opportunity Act (ECOA) requires lenders to consider these credit references if the consumer asks them to.

What to do: Gather proofs of payment in these areas, and give them to the lender. Say that you want them considered as credit references under Regulation B of the ECOA. Lenders who refuse to do so violate federal law and may be subject to punitive damages.

John Ulzheimer, president of consumer education, SmartCredit.com, Costa Mesa, California.

Free Credit Scores Easier to Obtain

The law that set up the Consumer Financial Protection Bureau requires banks and other companies to disclose credit scores to consumers whenever the scores are used to deny credit or set less advantageous credit terms, such as higher interest rates. The disclosures must provide consumers with the exact credit score used by the financial institution in making the decision.

What to do: If you receive a notice, ask the lender what score is required to either be approved or get a better interest rate.

John Ulzheimer, president of consumer education, SmartCredit.com, Costa Mesa, California.

New Reporting

New type of credit report tracks more of your financial life. CoreLogic, a company whose database includes property tax liens, evictions, child-support judgments, applications for payday loans and missed rental payments that go to collection, will use the data to formulate the new reports and sell them to mortgage, auto and other lenders. CoreLogic already helps lenders gather traditional credit reports from credit bureaus Equifax, Experian and TransUnion, so lenders are highly likely to use the new reports, called "CoreScore," as well. The reports could affect—either negatively or positively—the ability of consumers to obtain loans and/or the interest rates they pay. Check your report's accuracy when it comes online—or call 877-532-8778 to request a copy.

John Ulzheimer, president of consumer education, SmartCredit.com, Costa Mesa, California

---

The Credit Score Myth

John Ulzheimer, president of consumer education for SmartCredit.com, a credit-information Web site based in Costa Mesa, California. He formerly worked at Fair Isaac and Equifax.

When consumers hear the term "FICO credit score," they often are confused as to where that credit score comes from. It is important because the score can determine whether you get a mortgage, auto loan or credit card with attractive terms.

Despite a common misconception, Fair Isaac, the company behind FICO, does not actually calculate anyone's credit score. It simply developed the software that is used to calculate credit scores and licenses its software to the three credit-reporting agencies—Equifax, Experian and TransUnion.

Although all three credit-reporting agencies use FICO scoring software, each tends to produce slightly different FICO credit scores. This is because each agency compiles its own credit history for each individual and inevitably misses certain credit accounts and events. Which of the three scores should you care about? It depends on which of the three credit reports a lender happens to check—only mortgage lenders check all three.

Some organizations calculate non-FICO credit scores—these tend to be the scores offered for free on the Internet—but those non-FICO scores are rarely checked by lenders.

Now Is the Time to Buy A House! Here's Why...

Mike Castleman, Sr., CEO and cofounder of Metrostudy, a Houston-based consulting company that has tracked and analyzed housing-market information for more than 35 years. The company has 500 inspectors monitoring housing projects in nearly 50,000 subdivisions across the country. Metrostudy maintains the largest database of primary housing-market information in the US. *www.metrostudy.com*

Yes, there are plenty of skeptics today when it comes to talk of a housing recovery, and granted, they have a lot of evidence to fuel their doubts.

US housing prices continue to slide and are falling to levels that are one-third lower than the peak in July 2006 and wiping out gains for nearly the past decade, according to a survey of 20 major metro areas.

This persistent and frightening trend has encouraged many would-be home buyers to postpone their purchases until the real estate market stabilizes. It has driven the percentage of home owners down to 65.4%, compared with a peak of 69.2% in 2004, a big drop for that industry. And it has led many housing analysts to urge caution because they expect home values to drop by as much as another 8% or more this year.

But the naysayers are making a mistake—and I can prove it. *This is a great time to buy, and here's why...*

CONSTRUCTION PLUMMETS

The housing market, like all markets, is based on supply and demand. And while foreclosed homes and short sales (sales of homes for prices below the homes' outstanding mortgage amounts) do continue to create a well-publicized supply glut in certain areas, that's a regional problem, not a national one.

Meanwhile, there's an aspect of today's housing supply story that is true in most of the US and that is being ignored—construction of new homes has fallen to historic lows. Recently, there were fewer than 80,000 new homes either under construction or vacant and for sale in the 19 states that my company covers, a fraction of the more than 340,000 new homes five years ago.

With so few new homes coming onto the market, most regions are not suffering from what would normally be considered an oversupply of housing—they're suffering from tremendous underdemand, which puts downward pressure on prices. *Potential home buyers aren't buying for three reasons...*

- **They have lost their jobs and can't afford to buy now...**or they are concerned about their job security.
- **They worry that home prices will continue to fall** and don't want to tie themselves to a declining asset.
- **They want to buy but can't get a mortgage** because lenders have tightened their requirements.

The first of those reasons already is easing—the job market is, very slowly, starting to trend back up.

There are good reasons to be optimistic about the second as well—for one, rents are rapidly climbing relative to home-ownership costs. In an increasing number of regions, the monthly cost of renting now exceeds the cost of owning, which makes buying a house more attractive. Real estate might no longer be widely regarded as a guaranteed source of investment profits, but most people still conclude that owning makes sense, once they see that the cost of renting nears or exceeds the cost of owning.

The big sticking point inhibiting a home-price rebound is the availability of mortgages. Lenders currently are offering attractive terms to only extremely qualified borrowers with credit scores of 740 and higher. The reason isn't the lenders—it's the government. My firm has heard the same message again and again from mortgage lenders across the country—federal bank regulators are warning them to be stingy with mortgage loans. Government-subsidized programs such as Fannie Mae and Freddie Mac have severely tightened their lending policies as well.

MORTGAGES ARE KEY

The housing market will rebound strongly when the federal government starts to encourage rather than discourage making mortgage loans. Despite the government's current policies, I think that there's an excellent chance that that will happen within the coming months. Why? This year is an election year. The most effective way to significantly reduce unemployment is to increase home construction, which in normal times provides huge numbers of jobs...and the most effective way to boost home construction is to make it easier for would-be buyers to obtain mortgages.

Besides, even if the bears are right and home values have an additional 10% or so to fall, this still is a good time to buy—at least for those who can obtain attractive mortgages in today's tight lending environment. Mortgage rates currently are so low that locking them in likely will offset any remaining real estate price declines, assuming that you intend to live in the home for five years or longer.

Let's say you decide not to buy a home this year because you are afraid that real estate values will continue to decline...and let's say you're right, and prices drop by another 10%. If today's extremely low interest rates climb by just one percentage point, your monthly mortgage payment on a 30-year fixed-rate loan won't be any lower despite the 10% lower purchase price. If interest rates climb significantly more than one percentage point, your monthly mortgage payments will be higher—even if you are correct and home prices do continue to fall.

SOME REGIONS REBOUND

The real story in real estate is regional.

Best bets: According to a study that my firm conducts, home prices already have stopped falling and even have begun rising in numerous markets, including Charlotte, North Carolina...South Florida...Austin, Houston, Dallas/Fort Worth and San Antonio, Texas... Nashville...Boise, Idaho...and Phoenix.

Homes in southern California and the Virginia/Maryland suburbs of Washington, DC, appear poised to skyrocket. Demand for homes in those regions is virtually guaranteed to exceed supply once the current difficult lending environment is behind us because of their excellent long-term employment prospects and tight land-development restrictions.

However, in individual neighborhoods still burdened with large numbers of short sales and foreclosures, any significant housing rebound still could be a ways off.

Buy Real Estate Where The Best Bargains Are Already Gone

Robert Irwin, a real estate broker and investor with more than 40 years of experience. Based in Westlake Village, California, he is author of numerous real estate books, including *Tips & Traps When Buying a Home* (McGraw-Hill). *www.robertirwin.com*

While this is a very good year to buy property—mortgage rates are very low, and real estate prices have essentially bottomed out in many areas—the real estate market has divided into two very different segments. In some areas, the recovery already is well under way, while in others, home prices continue to languish as heavy foreclosure activity continues. Resist the urge to buy in regions where the housing recovery has not yet begun. Homes there might seem like once-in-a-lifetime bargains, but these areas actually are where the risk of continued losses or years of languishing prices are highest. They tend to be places where problems run very deep—perhaps jobs are scarce, and residents are moving away. It is better to buy where a rebound has already begun, even if that means you don't get the lowest possible price.

Two statistics that suggest a neighborhood falls into this category: A shortage of inventory—ask your real estate agent to check the multiple listing service (MLS) to find out how many months of inventory are on the market in the town or neighborhood (less than four months suggests a strong market)...and price appreciation—confirm that the Case-Shiller Home Price Index is showing appreciation in the area (go to *www.standardandpoors.com*, and search for "Case-Shiller").

Buying a Home? Tricky Traps to Avoid Now

Robert Irwin, who has more than 40 years of experience as a real estate broker and investor. Based in Westlake Village, California, he is author of numerous real estate books, including *Tips & Traps When Buying a Home* and *Home Buyer's Checklist: Everything You Need to Know But Forget to Ask—Before You Buy a Home* (both from McGraw-Hill). *www.robertirwin.com*

Prices aren't the only thing that have changed about home buying in the past four years. Mortgages have become much more difficult to obtain...property values have become much harder to evaluate... and some sellers and real estate agents have adopted new strategies that could trap unwary buyers into expensive losses.

Here is what you need to know to overcome these challenges if you want to buy a house this year...

THE MORTGAGE MESS

Advertised mortgage rates are low these days, but good luck obtaining one of those mortgages. *To have a reasonable shot at the lowest rates...*

- **Your down payment must be at least 20% and preferably 25% or more.**
- **Your credit score must be at least 740, preferably upward of 780 or even 800.**
- **Your overall debt-to-income ratio must be below 45%.** This includes all debt, not just the mortgage.

These lending criteria make it more important than ever to pay down debts, save up for a substantial down payment and scan your credit report for errors in the months before applying for a mortgage.

Apply for a mortgage with a few banks—especially ones you do other business with—in addition to a mortgage broker. Banks often offer the most competitive deals these days, something that didn't used to be true.

HIDDEN PROBLEMS

In years past, sellers have tended to be fairly forthcoming about disclosing problems with their homes—they didn't want to be sued when buyers discovered problems later. Today desperate sellers are as likely to hide problems as disclose them.

The situation is even worse if you buy a property owned by a bank. Banks almost never disclose problems with their properties, because they usually don't know about them.

Hire an experienced home inspector and accompany him/her on the inspection. Ask questions about anything you don't understand. Read his report carefully. Some inspectors bury potential problems deep in the report, rather than explicitly warning buyers of them, to avoid getting sued by sellers for overstating problems...and to avoid developing a reputation among real estate agents for quashing deals.

Example: A home inspector mentioned in passing in his report that he found a sump pump in HVAC ducts located below ground level. The inspector did nothing to highlight this fact, even though a sump pump in such a location can signal that a ventilation system has water and/or mold problems.

TIMING TROUBLES

Home buying always has been a lengthy process, but there are some new time line issues to consider...

- **A short sale**—where the sale price is less than the outstanding mortgage—might seem like a great deal, but it can take as much as six or seven months to close. Worse, it's fairly common for would-be buyers to be told at the end of this long process that the bank has decided against the deal.

Self-defense: Make your offer contingent on the lender's acceptance within a time frame that works for you. Hire an agent who has extensive experience with short sales.

- **The FHA mortgage process has become so slow that it could cost you your chance at a home.** If you have FHA financing and another, non-FHA, buyer also is interested in the property, expect the seller to choose the other buyer rather than wait for you.

Self-defense: Obtain non-FHA financing or increase your offer over market price if you don't want to lose a property to a non-FHA buyer.

• **A home purchase contract usually includes a financing contingency**—language allowing buyers to back out if their mortgage loans fall through. Traditionally, this contingency remains in effect until the deal closes, but some agents now push buyers to include financing contingencies of just 14 to 17 days—or slip these shorter contingency periods into contracts without even warning the buyers.

Self-defense: Read the financing contingency section of your contract carefully before signing, and confirm that it remains in effect until the deal is closed.

If a seller insists on a shorter financing contingency window and you do not want to lose the home, avoid taking out any new loans or lines of credit and be sure to pay all bills on time until the mortgage is finalized to minimize the odds that you will accidentally scare off the lender.

Check Your Insurance

Homes bought at bargain prices may be dangerously underinsured. Home buyers typically purchase the amount of insurance that their mortgage lenders tell them they need—but mortgage lenders require buyers to be covered only for the amount that they owe, which might be significantly less than the reconstruction cost of the home. Ask your insurance agent to help determine the replacement cost. Add coverage if your insurance falls short of 80% of this amount.

J.D. Howard, executive director of Insurance Consumer Advocate Network, Springfield, Missouri. *www.ican2000.com*

Larger FHA Loans

Large mortgages are easier to get under recent rule changes. Congress has authorized the Federal Housing Administration (FHA) to guarantee mortgage loans as large as $729,750 from private lenders in the most expensive regions of the US, up from a limit of $625,500. An FHA-backed loan can require a down payment as low as 3.5% but charges insurance premiums that add to borrowers' costs. To find an FHA lender in your area, go to *www.hud.gov/buying/loans.cfm.*

Greg McBride, CFA, senior financial analyst at Bankrate.com, North Palm Beach, Florida, which provides personal finance and financial-rate information.

Shop Carefully for a Mortgage

Mortgage expenses are jumping, even though interest rates are only fluctuating.

Reasons: New federal rules that reduce flexibility on loan-officer compensation, which is likely to raise borrowers' costs...adjustments to risk-based pricing structures implemented by Fannie Mae and Freddie Mac for borrowers with middling credit scores and/or relatively small down payments...higher annual mortgage insurance premiums for FHA-insured mortgages.

What to do: Shop around for the best deal. Consider putting down more money when taking out a mortgage to get a lower interest rate. Be sure you have the best possible credit score before applying for a mortgage.

Bankrate.com

Older Homes Preferred

New homes are selling more slowly than existing ones. New houses cost an average of 29% more, and some have features that postrecession buyers do not want, such as larger rooms that cost more to heat and cool. And many new homes were built far from cities—but buyers now are looking for close-in housing that will reduce commuting times and costs.

What to do: Evaluate the pluses and minuses of new and existing homes before making a decision—for example, some new houses cost more to buy but are more energy-efficient, reducing maintenance expenses.

Walter Molony, spokesperson for the National Association of Realtors, Washington, DC. *www.realtor.org*

Low Appraisals Prevent Home Sales

In a recent survey, 10% of real estate agents said that they have had sales canceled because appraisals came in below the prices buyers agreed to pay. Another 15% said contracts had to be renegotiated. And one-third of home builders say that they have lost sales because of low appraisals. Lenders and appraisers say home values continue to fall, so appraisals are down. But some real estate agents and buyers object to appraisers' inclusion of foreclosed properties when estimating the value of nondistressed homes in the same area. And new rules designed to reduce lenders' influence over appraisals have led to the use of many appraisers who are not familiar with the neighborhoods they are evaluating.

USA Today citing surveys from the National Association of Realtors and National Association of Home Builders and information from American Bankers Association and Securities and Exchange Commission.

Simpler Way to Weigh Refinancing

With mortgage rates at the lowest levels in decades, it is tempting to refinance. But closing costs typically are 2% of the mortgage value and can eat up the savings.

What to do: Use Laibson's free online calculator at *http://zwicke.nber.org/refinance.*

Example: A home owner with $300,000 and 20 years left on a 30-year-fixed rate mortgage at 4.85% may not find it cost-effective to refinance unless rates are 3.38% or below.

David Laibson, PhD, economics professor at Harvard University, Cambridge, Massachusetts, and coauthor of a study on the optimal interest rates for refinancing.

Mortgage Lenders Cutting Fees

To remain competitive amid plunging mortgage rates, lenders are reducing fees.

Recent examples: Capital One is erasing an average of $3,300 in closing costs for refinancing into a 30-year mortgage in New York, Texas and the metro Washington, DC, area. The Navy Federal Credit Union is offering to lower closing costs by $2,500. Citi is lowering so-called discount points (which require a prepayment of interest in exchange for lowering the interest rate over the life of the loan) by 0.75% of the loan amount and Bank of America by 0.25 percentage point in 20 states.

Caution: Consider the total cost of the loan, including the mortgage interest rate as well as special incentives, when comparing mortgage offers. Also, in some cases a lending institution requires that you have a large amount of cash in an account with the institution.

SmartMoney.com

Sale Strategy

Selling a house in a rent-to-own arrangement can help you move out in a stagnant market. But buyers interested in rent-to-own are likely to have poorer credit than ones who can buy outright.

What to do: Check out the potential renter-buyer carefully, with credit and background checks and employment verification. Write a lease that clearly spells out the total deal—both the rental and purchase agreements. (You can compose a lease agreement at *www.lawdepot.com*, with a free one-week trial.) Make the provision for eviction for late payment airtight so that you can remove the tenant right away if even a single payment is missed. Set the rent higher than the going rate for comparable homes, but consider crediting a portion toward the eventual sale. Make it clear what happens to that portion if the tenant decides not to buy. Be sure to spell out clearly who is responsible for maintenance and improvements during the rental period. Generally, the landlord should pay for maintenance such as repairing a broken furnace or air conditioner, but if the tenant wants to remodel the kitchen, the tenant should pay.

MarketWatch.com

Estimate College Costs

Online calculators for true college costs make it easier to figure out the price of particular schools based on your personal situation. Each college and university now is required to provide a net price calculator that lets families figure out the true cost of attending a college.

What to do: Use the calculators carefully. Be sure the information that you enter is accurate—you will need your income and other financial data. Be cautious about results that include loans and work-study funds—they may not be truly comparable to results at other schools. Some calculators may be based on two-year-old cost and aid data, so treat the net price results as ballpark estimates.

Mark Kantrowitz, publisher, Fastweb.com and Fin Aid.org, financial-aid Web sites, Cranberry Township, Pennsylvania.

Education Accounts

More flexible than college-savings 529 plans—Coverdell Education Savings Accounts. Coverdells can be set up at most banks, brokerage firms and mutual fund companies, and the money in them can be invested in bank CDs, mutual funds, individual stocks and individual bonds. This makes Coverdells much less restrictive than 529 plans, which are state-sponsored and offer limited investment options. Under the bill that extended Bush-era tax cuts, up to $2,000 can be invested in a Coverdell in 2012.

What to do: Consult your financial adviser for details and tax treatment of the accounts.

Bankrate.com

Get More College Financial Aid With This Simple Strategy

Kalman A. Chany, founder and president of Campus Consultants, Inc., a New York City–based company founded in 1984 that has helped thousands of families maximize their financial aid. He is author of *Paying for College Without Going Broke* (Princeton Review). *www.campusconsultants.com*

How much income parents have when their child is in the junior year of high school can be crucial in determining eligibility for financial aid. That's because the calendar year that begins in the middle of the junior year is the base year for determining the parents' income on college financial aid forms.

Strategies to minimize income during the base year and to maximize financial aid…

- **Don't convert a traditional IRA to a Roth IRA that year** because the converted amount may count as income.
- **Defer workplace bonuses.**
- **Avoid selling highly appreciated assets such as stocks that would generate capital gains.** Also avoid cashing in US savings bonds that would generate income (unless you've been paying taxes on the interest each year as it was generated).

• **Postpone distributions that you are not required to take from retirement plans such as 401(k)s.**

• **If you own a business, make capital investments in the business during the base year.** Time your invoices so that as much income as possible arrives during the prior year rather than the base year.

• **If you have dependent children other than the college-bound high school junior** and those children have taxable investment income, file separate tax returns for them. That keeps those kids' investment income off your tax return and out of the college-aid equation.

• **Avoid taking on significant margin debt—borrowings secured by stocks or bonds.** College-aid formulas won't allow you to subtract the interest expense from your investment income when calculating your income.

Leftover Money in a 529 College Savings Plan?

If the intended beneficiary decides not to go to college, the money can be used to pay for postsecondary vocational or technical training at schools eligible for financial-aid programs administered by the US Department of Education. (Check the "Tools and Calculators" section of *www.savingforcollege.com* to see if a school is eligible.) If there is money left after the beneficiary graduates, you can use it for graduate-school expenses...or change the beneficiary to another family member. As a parent who funded the account, you can use the money to pay for part-time college courses for yourself. If money is left over because your child got a big scholarship and you want to withdraw cash for nonqualified expenses, the 10% penalty usually imposed for nonqualified expenses is waived as long as withdrawals don't exceed the scholarship amount, but the money withdrawn is subject to tax on the earnings.

The Wall Street Journal

529 Tax Loophole

You can put money into a 529 college savings plan, withdraw it immediately for tuition if your child is in college, and still receive a state tax deduction up to the allowable annual limit. A 529 plan is an education savings plan designed to help families set aside funds for future college costs. Thirty-four states and Washington, DC, allow a deduction on state income taxes for 529 contributions and do not specify how long contributions must sit in the plan.

Joseph Hurley, founder of SavingForCollege.com, Pittsford, New York, which provides information on paying for higher education costs.

The Student Loan Crisis—What to Do If You or Your Child Can't Make the Payments

Deanne Loonin, an attorney who serves as director of the nonprofit National Consumer Law Center's Student Loan Borrower Assistance project, Boston. *www.studentloanborrowerassistance.org*

Sky-high tuition and the weak job market have left many recent college grads with student loan debt that they cannot afford to pay. More than 11% of student loans are at least 90 days past due, according to the Federal Reserve Bank of New York, and that figure is rising.

How to solve your student loan problems...

FEDERAL LOANS

If you are having trouble repaying a student loan made by the federal government—or by a private lender through the Federal Family Education Loans program—there are a number of solutions. Explore these options as soon as it becomes clear that you will have trouble making payments. There can be severe consequences, such as having your loan sent to a collection agency, for defaulting on federal student loans.

• **Loan discharge completely cancels remaining debt.** *This could be available in the case of...*

• Public service careers. Some federal student loans can be fully or partially discharged if the former student works full-time for at least five years as a teacher in certain low-income regions or 10 years in public service.

• Bankruptcy. It is very difficult, but not impossible, to discharge federal student loans through student or parent bankruptcy. A judicial hearing is required to show that repaying the loan would cause "undue hardship."

• Death or disability. To qualify, a borrower's disability must be permanent and severe enough to prevent any substantial gainful activity. In the case of a federal PLUS loan made to a parent, discharge can be based on the disability of the parent (but not the student)...or on the death of the student or the parent. If two parents sign a PLUS loan and one becomes disabled or dies, the other remains responsible.

• **Loan deferment lets borrowers postpone paying back federal student loans without penalty and,** in the case of subsidized federal loans, without accruing interest during the deferment period. Loan deferment could be available to you if the loan is not in default and you are unemployed...or you receive public assistance...or you are working full-time and your income is below 150% of the federal poverty line...or you are in the military...or you obtain a graduate fellowship or return to school for at least half-time study.

Details: Visit *www.studentaid.ed.gov*, click on "Tools and Resources," followed by "Federal Student Aid Forms," then scan down to "Managing Your Student Loans."

• **Income-Based Repayment (IBR) lowers your monthly student debt payments to levels that are manageable.** Your loan servicer will be able to determine if you qualify, based on how high your debt is relative to your income and family size. The new payments are likely to be reduced to less than 10% of your total income. Any balance remaining after 25 years is forgiven. IBR is available on most federal student loans, though not loans in default.

Alternative: Extended Repayment reduces your monthly payments by stretching repayment out to 25 years.

Details: Visit *www.studentaid.ed.gov*, select "Repay Your Loans," then "Repayment Plans and Calculators."

• **Forbearance allows delayed repayment without penalty,** though unlike with deferment, interest accrues during this delay. Lenders have considerable discretion in deciding when to offer forbearance, which can be granted a year at a time for up to three years. It tends to be easier to obtain than a deferment and can be offered even if the loan is in default.

Details: Contact the lender to request forbearance.

PRIVATE LOANS

There are fewer options for repaying a private student loan...

Read your loan agreement for any mention of loan modification or forbearance. A small percentage of private loan agreements has these options built in.

Call the lender...describe your financial situation...and request loan modification or forbearance even if these are not written into your contract. Lenders occasionally agree to this temporarily if both the borrower and all the loan co-signers are experiencing serious financial problems.

Discharging the loan could be an option if the former student has died or become permanently disabled. A small percentage of private student loans include this provision. Read your student loan contract for details. Private student loans are difficult, but not impossible, to discharge through bankruptcy.

OTHER FINANCIAL OPTIONS

Some student debt solutions apply to federal and private loans. Some universities forgive debt for students, especially law students, who take public service jobs. Some employers have programs to help employees repay student loans. Check with your employer's human resources department.

If You Divorce After 50—Watch Out for the Big Financial Traps

Janice L. Green, JD, an attorney specializing in divorce and family law. She is a partner with Farris & Green in Austin, Texas, and author of *Divorce After 50: Your Guide to the Unique Legal & Financial Challenges* (Nolo). *www.janicelgreen.com*

Divorce rates among those age 50 and older more than doubled between 1990 and 2008, according to researchers at Bowling Green State University. These older couples now account for one-quarter of all US divorces.

Splitting up after age 50 can be particularly problematic for those with limited assets and limited time to recover financially. And those who divorce after age 50 but before Medicare eligibility kicks in at age 65 may struggle to obtain affordable health insurance.

Here's what you or someone close to you might need to know to get the best possible settlement in a divorce after age 50...

RETIREMENT PLANS

An IRA or a 401(k) might be in the name of just one spouse, but the other spouse has a legal right to claim a share in a divorce. In community property states, both partners are considered joint owners of these accounts. In noncommunity property states, these assets will be divided according to the divorce agreement. A divorce decree can include language that spells out how the retirement plan's sponsors should divide the benefits. It's crucial that older divorcees obtain a fair share of this money—retirement savings often are an older couple's most valuable asset.

Four things that older people should consider before agreeing to a division of retirement plan assets...

- **Taxes.** Divorce attorneys tend to pay little attention to future taxation of retirement plan withdrawals. Remind your attorney that these taxes must be taken into account when dividing assets.

Exception: Money can be withdrawn tax-free from Roth IRA accounts in retirement.

- **Fluctuating asset values.** It typically takes months for a divorce to be finalized. If the divorce agreement is poorly written, a sharp swing in asset values during this time could result in an unintended and unfair division of assets.

Example: A divorce agreement gives the wife $100,000 from her husband's $400,000 401(k), plus the couple's house. The value of that 401(k) falls by $120,000 in a market downturn before the divorce is finalized, leaving the wife with 38% of its value rather than the intended 25%, and the husband with no house and only $180,000 in savings with retirement looming.

Ask your attorney to explain how the proposed division of assets would be affected if your portfolio were to rise or fall by 25% or 30% before the agreement is finalized. If the result seems unfair, suggest dividing retirement savings by a percentage rather than specifying that one partner receive a certain dollar amount.

- **Pension plan rules.** Many older Americans still have traditional defined-benefit pensions—pensions that pay a steady monthly income during retirement. Former spouses typically are entitled to a share of this money, but the rules are complicated. A divorce court can issue a "qualified domestic relations order" (QDRO) to the retirement plan's sponsor spelling out how benefits are to be divided. If your spouse has a defined-benefit plan, obtain a copy of the summary plan description from the employer or plan administrator.

Plan rules sometimes specify that an ex cannot claim benefits as an "alternate payee" until the plan member retires, even if the plan member works for many years beyond normal retirement age. If so, ask your attorney to attempt to negotiate for alimony or some other compensation to make up for your lost pension income should your ex work past normal retirement age.

Also, if your former spouse's pension pays joint and survivor benefits, scan the plan rules to determine whether the original spouse or a later spouse is considered the survivor if the plan member remarries. If it's the new spouse, have your attorney take this into account when dividing assets.

If you're the divorcing spouse who has the pension plan and you intend to remarry, be aware that your new spouse might not receive the survivor benefits you expect—check the plan rules for details.

• **Transfer of assets.** Make sure that any money shifted from your partner's IRA or 401(k) to your IRA when assets are divided is handled as a trustee-to-trustee transfer. You could incur penalties and taxes if these assets pass through your hands.

LIFE INSURANCE

Many older couples have been paying into life insurance policies for years, and such policies can be valuable assets. But when couples appear headed toward divorce, partners who are insured sometimes stop paying these premiums—they see little reason to pay for a policy that only benefits the soon-to-be ex.

If you are the spouse who is insured, do not stop paying these premiums. This policy can be a useful bargaining chip in your divorce. Agreeing to continue funding it might let you obtain a larger share of other assets or reduce your future alimony payments.

If you are the spouse who is not insured, explain to your spouse that he/she can use this policy as a bargaining chip, as discussed above, and seek an agreement that it will continue to be funded.

If the relationship is too strained for such an agreement, obtain a court order to this effect. You want an agreement in place before the next premium is due—even one missed payment could forfeit the coverage.

Alternative: Suggest that the policy be altered to benefit the children, not the ex.

If your divorce agreement dictates that your ex continue to fund a life insurance policy, instruct your attorney to be certain that you will have some way to confirm that these premiums continue to be paid.

HEALTH INSURANCE

It has become extremely difficult and expensive for people in their 50s or early 60s to obtain individual health insurance. Contact issuers immediately to find out just how expensive it will be as soon as possible. Take these costs fully into account in the settlement.

Among the potential options...

• **COBRA rules let divorcees continue to receive coverage through an ex-spouse's employer group plan for up to 36 months.** Contact the plan administrator within 60 days after the divorce is finalized. Your divorce agreement should specify whether you or your spouse is responsible for paying the COBRA premiums.

Warning: Obtain an agreement—or, if necessary, a court order—from your spouse agreeing not to drop you from the employer's group plan.

• **Delay finalizing your divorce until you turn 65 and qualify for Medicare**—or until you turn 62 if COBRA is available to bridge the remaining 36-month gap. Read your health insurance plan's rules carefully before attempting this, however. Some plans require that spouses live under the same roof to qualify for coverage.

THE HOME

Some older divorcees decide, I just want the house...he/she can have the 401(k). That may be a bad idea, given the real estate market's recent uncertainty. You could get stuck in a home that is larger than you need and that you cannot sell at a reasonable price. It's wiser to seek a diversified portfolio of assets in the divorce, even if that means selling the home and splitting the proceeds. *If it cannot be sold at a reasonable price or in a timely manner in this real estate market, you and your ex could agree to...*

• **Rent the house out until prices rebound.** The divorce agreement should specify how this rent will be divided, who will pay home-related expenses until it is sold and how the proceeds of the eventual sale will be split.

• **Have one spouse continue to live in the home until it is sold.** This spouse could pay rent to the other and pay home owner expenses.

BENEFICIARY DESIGNATIONS

Update the beneficiary designations in your investment accounts and estate plan as soon as divorce seems inevitable. Ex-spouses are automatically removed as beneficiaries in some states, but this won't occur until the divorce is finalized.

Exception: Some states issue automatic restraining orders preventing the alteration of beneficiary designations until the details of the divorce are agreed upon. In other states, attorneys might obtain restraining orders preventing this.

RELOCATION

Older couples often move to different states or even different countries when they retire. If you suspect that your marriage could be headed for divorce, speak with a family law attorney before relocating. Divorce laws in the new state or country might be less advantageous to you than the laws where you currently reside. If so, it might make sense to postpone or refuse relocation.

Watch Your E-Mail

Hacked e-mail can lead to pillaged financial accounts. The FBI recently issued a fraud alert about high-tech thieves who gain access to victims' e-mail accounts and search for messages to or from banks, brokers or investment companies. Then—posing as the account holder—the scammers send e-mails to those financial companies asking that money be withdrawn and wired to them. Warn your financial institutions immediately if you receive bounced e-mails that you didn't send... or if your e-mail password is altered.

Gerri Walsh, JD, vice president for investor education at the Financial Industry Regulatory Authority, Washington, DC. *www.finra.org/investors*

Beware Promise of Unclaimed-Property

Thieves claiming to be from the National Association of Unclaimed Property Administrators are sending e-mails telling people that they can claim substantial amounts of property but need to provide identification to obtain it. The scammers ask for bank account, credit card and Social Security numbers.

Self-defense: Delete e-mails about unclaimed property—and hang up if you get an unsolicited phone call about it. Check for property to which you may be legitimately entitled by going to *www.unclaimed.org.*

Consumer Reports Money Adviser, 101 Truman Ave., Yonkers, New York 10703. *www.consumerreports.org/bookstore*

Identity Scams

Criminals pose as someone you know or trust to get personal data for identity theft.

Examples: The grandchild scam involves sending an instant Facebook message from a supposed grandchild, asking for immediate help because his/her money was stolen or he has been wrongly imprisoned. The sender actually is a thief who has hacked into a Facebook account. Another scam uses online links—supposedly from friends—to send you to sites that install malware.

What to do: Never respond to money requests immediately—take the time to check out the claims. Do not click on links to sites recommended in an e-mail unless you call the sender and are sure his/her account has not been hacked.

Federal Trade Commission Consumer Alert. *www.ftc.gov*

Don't Send Money

Beware of any sweepstakes that require you to wire money or accept a check in return for wiring money. These are scams. Never pay insurance, taxes or shipping to claim what you are told that you won—legitimate sweepstakes do not require this. Ignore claims that a government agency is sponsoring a sweepstakes—federal agencies do not sponsor or oversee these types of contests. Never agree to act immediately—any legitimate offer allows you to take time to consider what to do.

Federal Trade Commission, Washington, DC. *www.ftc.gov*

Ads That Infect Computers Turn Up on Legitimate Web Sites

Crooks are hijacking the distribution system used by advertising networks, putting phony ads in among legitimate ones. These malvertisements may attack a computer when a user goes to an infected site...cause phony security warnings that go away only when users pay for fake antivirus protection...or cause a user's computer to lock up.

Best: Run an updated antivirus program at all times. Install the latest updates for Web browsers and applications, especially Adobe Flash and Adobe Reader. These updates often will feature security enhancements. Use the Firefox browser with the NoScript add-on (in the browser, click on "Tools," then "Add-ons," then search for NoScript).

Paul Stephens, director, policy and advocacy, Privacy Rights Clearinghouse, San Diego. *www.privacyrights.org*

Bar Code Alert

Don't get scammed by the new bar codes. Quick response (QR) bar codes, which look like square checkerboard patterns and appear in ads, contain text messages or links to Web sites that can be accessed with a smartphone camera. But scammers are creating QR codes that steal ID information or send text messages urging you to call a number that puts big charges on your account. Some cybercriminals even are sticking fake QR code labels over legitimate ones.

Katherine Hutt, national spokesperson at Council of Better Business Bureaus, Arlington, Virginia. *www.bbb.org/us*

New Twist on Internet Car Scams

Criminals who pretend to have cars to sell on sites such as Craigslist or eBay use a live-chat feature in e-mail correspondence to answer questions and assure buyers that deals are safe. They claim that safeguards are in place to reimburse buyers for any loss and assure them that sales are protected by liability insurance coverage up to $50,000. The criminals also will push for a quick completion of the sale through a wire transfer.

Beware: Many scammers use real company names and third-party transfer services, such as Western Union, to appear legitimate.

Federal Bureau of Investigation, Washington, DC. *www.fbi.gov*

Protect Your Social Security Identity

1. An identity thief contacts you by phone, e-mail or letter and claims to be a Social Security employee checking records and asks for personal data such as your Social Security number and mother's maiden name.

2. A scammer claims to be able to get you a higher benefit if you pay a filing fee.

3. Someone claims that you will get a lump-sum payment to compensate for the recent lack of Social Security cost-of-living adjustments if you pay to file a new tax return.

What to do: Before providing any personal information or responding to a suspicious offer, call the Social Security Administration at 800-772-1213 to make sure that the contact is legitimate.

AARP.org

8

Your Insurance

What Health Insurance Companies Don't Want You to Know

America's health insurance system is ailing in ways that hurt many consumers despite the federal government's efforts to overhaul it. That's the view of a former industry executive who spent 20 years trying to protect the image of major health insurers and now is willing to reveal their secrets in an effort to help consumers.

We asked Wendell Potter to explain how consumers can protect themselves from sneaky insurance company practices. *Here's what health insurance companies don't want you to know...*

1. We don't want your business...not unless you're young and completely healthy, that is. Insurers routinely reject one-third or more of people who apply for individual coverage. It isn't just the chronically ill and out of shape who are turned away by insurers, either. It's frequently anyone who has any upcoming or ongoing medical expenses—even something as minor as corns or cataracts might be grounds for disqualification.

Also, health insurance applications inevitably ask whether the applicant has been previously rejected by another insurer—and they tend to reject anyone who has been. So once one health insurance company turns you down, it can be extremely difficult or impossible to obtain coverage anywhere.

What to do: Before applying for individual health insurance, try a membership organization or association that provides benefits to its members. Or visit *www.healthcare.gov* to find a list of private insurance plans for individuals,

---

Wendell Potter, who spent 20 years in charge of the corporate communications departments of leading health insurance companies, including Cigna and Humana, before leaving the industry in 2008. He is author of *Deadly Spin: An Insurance Company Insider Speaks Out on How Corporate PR Is Killing Health Care and Deceiving Americans* (Bloomsbury). *www.wendellpotter.com*

families and small businesses in your region. Submit applications to most or all of these companies at the same time. That way, if you are rejected by one or more insurers, the rejections will come only after you have submitted applications to other insurers, eliminating the need to disclose prior rejections.

If multiple members of your family need coverage, submit applications together as a family and individually to increase the odds that at least some of you will be offered reasonable coverage.

Because of the new federal legislation, all states now offer high-risk-insurance pools for those who are not healthy enough to obtain health insurance on the open market. Unfortunately, you won't qualify for these pools until you have been without health insurance for at least six months.

If you want help navigating your health insurance options, contact your state's insurance department and ask if there is someone on staff who can assist you. If there isn't, contact an insurance broker that specializes in health insurance.

2. If your premiums are not going up this year, it is because we've come up with sneakier ways to make your coverage a lot more expensive. Insurers increasingly are slipping through price increases by keeping premiums relatively level but significantly increasing co-pays and deductibles or eliminating specific types of coverage. Most people don't look much past the monthly premium when they evaluate their options during open enrollment or read about changes to their coverage. So they often don't even realize that their coverage has been gutted until they get sick and find out that they're responsible for much or all of the bills.

Examples: A Blue Cross/Blue Shield policy in Indiana now imposes a stunningly high 50% co-pay for network providers. Many insurers are dropping large numbers of medical-care providers from their coverage networks—plan holders might go to the same doctor they always have only to be hit with a huge bill for using what is now an out-of-network provider with a co-pay of 70%. Some insurers have quietly removed coverage for mental health and/or substance-abuse treatment and other health-care categories from certain policies entirely.

My own son recently was informed that his health insurance plan had been discontinued but that a new plan was available for a similar premium. This new plan had a $5,000 deductible—10 times the size of his previous plan's $500 deductible.

What to do: If you're in an individual plan, carefully read all updates and handbooks that you receive from your health insurance company and pay special attention to changes in co-pays, deductibles and excluded categories and services.

If you are not certain, call your insurer to confirm coverage of the particular services and providers that you use. If you are told that a drug or procedure that your doctor has recommended is not covered, ask your doctor to write a letter to the insurer explaining why it is medically necessary for you to have it.

If you're in a group plan, ask the plan administrator to help you understand the potential out-of-pocket costs associated with each plan offered during the open-enrollment period.

Also ask if your employer will cover any of these out-of-pocket expenses—some do, but employees don't always know this.

3. We would rather decline coverage for a legitimate claim than risk paying a claim that we don't have to. Health insurance companies routinely, and sometimes arbitrarily, reject claims that should be covered based on such things as clerical errors, missing information and unclear language about covered benefits. Some of these rejections are done by computer with no human reviewing the claim at all.

What to do: Always appeal rejected claims. It is your legal right, and these appeals very often are successful—in some states, the claims-appeal success rate is greater than 50%. The insurers know this, but they go right on rejecting legitimate claims because they know that many policyholders don't bother to appeal.

If you are in a group plan, bring the matter to the plan administrator. If you have an individual plan, read the policy to find out how to appeal, or contact your state's insurance regulator and ask for instructions. Also ask the agency how to file a complaint with the insurance commissioner. Let the insurer know that you have done so.

If your appeal fails, contact your state insurance department to ask about additional appeal options. Also contact consumer reporters in the local media and ask if they are interested in a story about a health insurance company that is treating a policyholder unfairly. The media is most likely to be interested if it is a life-or-death matter or if a child's health is at stake. Insurers often relent when the press picks up the story.

You also could ask a lawyer, even if it's a friend or family member, to write a letter to the insurance company on your behalf.

4. A national health-care system might be headed our way, but residents of your state might not fully benefit. Starting in 2014, each state will have an insurance exchange where individuals and small businesses can compare the policies available to them. But while some states intend to actively negotiate rates and vet these policies to ensure that each offers value to consumers, other states do not. In states that don't, there easily could be language hidden in a policy's small print that makes the coverage far less appealing than it seems.

What to do: When the exchanges are up and running, call your state's insurance agency and ask if the state is an "active purchaser"—that's the official term for states that play an active role in negotiating rates and terms. California and Massachusetts intend to be active purchasers, for example.

If your state is not an active purchaser, you'll have to play detective, carefully picking through the policy language in search of copays, deductibles, exclusions and limits before signing up—exactly the sort of challenge that the exchanges were supposed to eliminate.

Some Good News On Insurance

Health insurance has become more affordable for some people with preexisting conditions. The Department of Health and Human Services slashed premiums for its Pre-Existing Condition Insurance Plan by up to 40% in many states. This plan is available only to US citizens and legal residents who have been without insurance for at least six months. Some states run their own preexisting condition insurance plans. For information, go to *www.pcip.gov.*

Ankeny Minoux, president of the Foundation for Health Coverage Education, a nonprofit organization based in San Jose, California. *www.coverageforall.org*

What Does "Explanation Of Benefits" Really Mean?

Charles B. Inlander, consumer advocate and health-care consultant based in Fogelsville, Pennsylvania. He was the founding president of the nonprofit People's Medical Society, a consumer advocacy organization credited with key improvements in the quality of US health care in the 1980s and 1990s, and is author of 20 books, including *Take This Book to the Hospital With You: A Consumer Guide to Surviving Your Hospital Stay* (St. Martin's).

Think back to the last time you received one of those forms from Medicare or your health insurer that's marked "THIS IS NOT A BILL." Chances are you stuck it in a pile or even tossed it in the garbage, never really looking at it. But if you take the time to understand and review these forms, you may save a lot in out-of-pocket expenses. I once saved $9,500 because of an error on the form—more on that later.

• **What's the form all about?** This form is called your "Explanation of Benefits," or "EOB" for short. By law, Medicare or your insurance company must send it to you every time a medical practitioner or hospital submits a claim for services provided to you. Sometimes, a single form will include a long list of services rendered—especially if you were hospitalized. While the form does not go into detail about the services listed, the EOB is for you, the patient, to review and know what portion, if any, of the charges you will have to pay out-of-pocket—and to spot errors.

• **What should you look at first?** Every EOB must have the policyholder's name (which may be your spouse if he/she has the insurance through his/her employer)...the patient's name...and the patient's insurance ID number (the number on the patient's insurance or Medicare card). It will also name the doctor, the practice or the hospital that submitted the claim. Don't worry about every column on the form. Pay particular attention to "Total Charges," which is what the hospital or doctor submits to the insurer, and "Allowable Amount" (or "Medicare or Insurance Approved"), which is the amount the doctor or hospital has agreed to accept as full payment. Also check the columns under "Patient Responsibility" that explain what you may have to pay as part of your insurance deductible or copayment. For example, if a hospital submits a bill for a total charge of $10,000, and your insurer or Medicare lists an allowable charge of $4,000, that means the hospital has agreed to accept $4,000 as total payment. If your policy requires that you pay 20% of the bill, the EOB will show that the hospital is allowed to bill you for up to $800 (20% of $4,000)—and no more. If you get a bill for more than that, call your insurer—and do not pay it until the situation is resolved.

• **What can go wrong?** In my case, my insurer had disallowed a $9,500 charge on the EOB because it claimed that my one-night hospital stay had not been preapproved. But I knew that it had. I called the insurer and pointed out the mistake. The representative told me the error would be corrected and not to pay any bills from the hospital until it was. Other common mistakes include mixing up patients who have similar names, so make sure that your name and identification number are both correct. Also check the EOB for charges from doctors or hospitals that you don't recognize and look for duplicate charges—such as the use of two operating rooms on the same day. These simple steps can save you a bundle!

Latest Trend in Coverage

High-deductible health insurance plans are growing in popularity. The plans shift more costs to employees but reduce monthly premiums. In 2011, almost one-third of companies with 500 or more employees offered these plans—up from 23% a year earlier. The plans often are combined with health savings accounts, into which workers can deposit up to $3,100 for self-coverage or $6,250 for family coverage tax-free to pay deductibles.

Survey of 2,844 private and public employers by Mercer LLC, benefits consultants, New York City. *www.mercer.com*

HSA Loophole

Paul Fronstin, PhD, director of the health research and education program at Employee Benefit Research Institute (EBRI), a private, nonprofit based in Washington, DC. Dr. Fronstin also oversees the institute's Center for Research on Health Benefits Innovation. *www.ebri.org*

Deadlines for Health Savings Account (HSA) contributions are later than many people realize. For instance, you have until April 15, 2013, to make HSA contributions that can be tax-deductible for 2012. To make sure that the contributions are applied to the 2012 limit, indicate the amount on the appropriate line of IRS Form 8889, Health Savings Accounts. And it's best to make any such HSA allocations before filing your taxes owed for 2012 to avoid having to file an amended return.

As a basic requirement, holders of an HSA must have a high-deductible health insurance plan (HDHP). This year, individuals with HDHP coverage can contribute up to $3,100 to their HSAs, while those on a high-deductible family plan can put in up to $6,250.

However, people age 55 and older and not receiving Medicare can make additional catch-up HSA contributions of up to $1,000 per person per year.

Choosing a Medicare Advantage Plan? Common Mistakes Can Be Very Costly

Frederic Riccardi, MSW, director of programs and outreach with the Medicare Rights Center, a nonprofit consumer rights organization with offices in New York City and Washington, DC. *www.medicarerights.org*

The choice of a Medicare Advantage plan can be a crucial one when it comes to the cost and quality of your health care.

Trap: People who are eligible often overlook important factors when considering the many plans that are offered by private health insurers.

Sometimes called Medicare Part C, the plans are alternatives to traditional Medicare. (See next page for descriptions of each Medicare option.) Medicare Advantage plans sometimes cost less than combining traditional Medicare coverage with a Medigap supplemental plan and Medicare Part D drug coverage, depending on the level and type of health care you need. And they often offer a wider array of benefits, perhaps including dental, vision and hearing. That's why about 11.7 million Americans—about 25% of all Medicare recipients—choose Medicare Advantage plans.

The Medicare Plan Finder (*www.medicare.gov/find-a-plan*) is useful for comparing the Advantage plans available in your area.

Important: This year, the open-enrollment period runs from October 15 through December 7 (not to year-end).

As you make your decision, be wary of these eight common mistakes...

- **Signing up for a plan that doesn't include your doctor.** Just because a doctor's office (or hospital or skilled nursing facility) accepts Medicare doesn't guarantee that it will accept your Medicare Advantage plan. If it doesn't, you may have to pay substantial out-of-network costs (or switch doctors). Check with all your health-care providers before choosing an Advantage plan.

Warning: If you split your year between homes in different parts of the country, be particularly wary of plans that impose hefty out-of-pocket costs for seeing out-of-network providers.

- **Failing to check the drug list.** Before signing up for any plan, scan its formulary—the list of prescription drugs covered—to confirm that all of the medications you currently take are included without excessive co-pays or a requirement that you try less expensive drugs first. If an otherwise appealing plan does not include one of your medications, ask your doctor whether another drug that is covered by the plan would work as well for you.

- **Failing to confirm the quality of dental, vision and hearing coverage.** Medicare Advantage plans often include dental, vision and hearing benefits—coverage that traditional Medicare lacks. Unfortunately, these benefits often are much less valuable than they seem, sometimes offering little more than basic eye and hearing exams or discounted dental cleanings.

What to do: Don't rely solely on the plan's brochure. Look for the plan's "Evidence of Coverage" on its Web site for details. Use the Medicare Plan Finder to determine which plans have the best coverage for a reasonable cost.

- **Ignoring the kinds of cost differences that aren't obvious.** Rather than comparing just premiums and deductibles—the two costs that most people focus on—also compare out-of-pocket maximums set by various plans, plus co-payments and coinsurance charged for doctor office visits...hospital stays...diagnostic tests...visits to specialists...emergency care...ambulance services...the cost of purchasing medications you take on an ongoing basis...and other medical services. These can be found in descriptions available at *www.medicare.gov.*

• **Ignoring the annual notice of change.** If you already belong to an Advantage plan, you should receive an update each year explaining how your plan is changing in the coming year. Read this carefully—plans can change substantially from one year to the next.

• **Accidentally voiding retiree coverage from a former employer.** If you have retiree health coverage, speak with your former employer's benefits manager before signing up for a Medicare Advantage plan. Some retiree coverage may be voided if participants sign up for a Medicare Advantage plan or Part D.

• **Overlooking Part B premiums when calculating a plan's cost.** Part B covers doctor's services, outpatient care and home health services, among other medical services. If you opt for an Advantage plan, it will provide these services, but you still will have to pay the Part B premium, in addition to any premium charged by an Advantage plan.

• **Ignoring the downside of Medicare Advantage disenrollment.** The Medicare system offers an escape route for those who quickly become disenchanted with their Medicare Advantage plans. They can disenroll from their plans between January 1 and February 14 and rejoin traditional Medicare. But depending on your state's laws, that might be too late for you also to sign up for a Medigap policy—an insurance policy offered by a private company that pays co-insurance and deductibles associated with traditional Medicare. Without a Medigap policy, you might have to pay significant medical costs out of pocket, perhaps for the rest of your life. It's wiser to make an informed choice during the annual election period than to depend on disenrollment.

More from Frederic Riccardi, MSW...

Understanding Medicare Options

Medicare's many options can be quite confusing. *What each is...*

• **Medicare Part A** helps cover the cost of inpatient care in hospitals, skilled nursing facilities and hospices, plus certain home health-care costs. For most people, there is no premium because they paid Medicare taxes while working.

• **Medicare Part B** helps cover the cost of doctors' services, outpatient care and certain other medical services. There usually is a premium for Part B that is deducted from your monthly Social Security check.

• **Traditional Medicare,** sometimes called original Medicare, consists of Medicare Part A and Part B.

• **Medicare Part D** helps cover the cost of prescription medications. It is offered by private Medicare-approved companies. Part D plans vary somewhat in premiums, co-pays, coinsurance and deductibles.

• **Medicare Advantage plans,** also called Medicare Part C, are an alternative to traditional Medicare. Unlike traditional Medicare, which lets participants choose virtually any health-care provider, many Advantage plans operate like HMOs or PPOs, using financial incentives to steer members toward in-network providers. Advantage plans often charge premiums (beyond those for Medicare Part B).

• **Medigap policies,** also called Medicare Supplement Insurance, help pay health-care costs not covered by traditional Medicare, including co-payments, coinsurance and deductibles. While Advantage plans replace traditional Medicare, Medigap policies just supplement it. Costs and coverage details depend on the Medigap plan selected.

Unraveling the Medicare Insurance Maze

Charles B. Inlander, consumer advocate and health-care consultant based in Fogelsville, Pennsylvania. He was the founding president of the nonprofit People's Medical Society, a consumer advocacy organization credited with key improvements in the quality of US health care in the 1980s and 1990s, and is author of 20 books, including *Take This Book to the Hospital With You: A Consumer Guide to Surviving Your Hospital Stay* (St. Martin's).

Having turned 65 this month, I am now officially on Medicare. Enrolling was a snap. I did it on the Medicare.gov

Web site in less than five minutes. This can also be done by mail or at your local Social Security office. What wasn't a snap was deciding whether I should purchase a Medigap policy to supplement my traditional Medicare coverage or opt for a different type of program known as a Medicare Advantage Plan.* *To select the right plan for you...*

• **Know the pros and cons.** Medigap is a type of private health insurance that helps pay some of the health-care costs ("gaps") that traditional Medicare doesn't cover, such as co-payments and deductibles. However, Medicare Advantage Plans do not just fill in the gaps. While also sold by Medicare-approved private insurance companies, they provide all of the usual Medicare-approved services within their own network of doctors and hospitals. To attract members, most Advantage plans offer some additional services, such as dental and vision benefits. Advantage plans substitute for traditional Medicare, so you do not carry a Medigap policy if you join.

When Medigap may be better: If you travel a lot or spend several months each year in another state, traditional Medicare supplemented with a Medigap policy is probably the better choice for you. This combination allows you to use any doctor or hospital in the country that accepts Medicare without any financial penalty. In contrast, with a Medicare Advantage Plan, if a doctor or hospital is not in the plan's network, you must pay an often hefty out-of-network charge.

Insider tip: Premiums for Medigap policies can differ significantly from company to company—even for the exact same coverage. Carefully compare the premiums to ensure you're getting the most for your money.

When an Advantage plan may be better: Medicare Advantage Plans are good for people who are most concerned about finding the lowest possible premium—even if they have to switch doctors to find one within the plan's network.

Insider tip: Be sure to call the company whose plan you're considering (or check its Web site) to confirm exactly which doctors and hospitals are included in the network.

• **Consider getting help.** Many insurance brokers sell Medigap and Medicare Advantage Plans and can be extremely helpful in comparing programs and prices. Contact your state insurance department for a list of licensed brokers in your area. To do your own research, go to the Medicare.gov Web site and click on the "Compare Drug and Health Plans" (for Advantage plans) and "Compare Medigap Policies" tabs. Each will display the Medicare-approved plans and policies available in your zip code and allow you to compare benefits and prices. Or call Medicare at 800-MEDICARE (633-4227), and ask for the information to be sent to you.

*If you're already enrolled in Medicare, you can switch your Medigap or Advantage plan once annually (usually mid-October to early December). This means you can buy a different Advantage or Medigap plan or jump from a Medigap to an Advantage plan (or vice versa).

Medicare Covers More Screening Tests

With the intention of preventing diseases and conditions that cost much more to treat if allowed to develop, Medicare offers more than two dozen preventive services without co-payments or deductibles. They include mammograms and Pap smears for women... PSA tests for men...and a free colonoscopy to screen for colon cancer for everyone. Additional free screenings are available for people whose doctors consider them at risk for aortic aneurysms, diabetes and other conditions.

Medicare Rights Center, New York City. *www.medicarerights.org*

How to Research Costs

Compare the cost of medical services through state-sponsored Web sites that collect payment information and make it available online. A few states, including Maine and New Hampshire, have Web sites showing medical costs based on actual claims. Other states are expected to set up similar sites. You can see if your state has a Web site on the site of the All-Payer Claims Databases Council (*www.apcdcouncil.org*).

If your state does not have a site yet: Try *www.fairhealthconsumer.org,* which offers typical figures for various locations...or *www.healthcarebluebook.com,* which provides what it calls a fair price for services in a given area.

Also helpful: The American Medical Association's Medicare-reimbursement information (*www.amacodingonline.com*) shows what Medicare pays for services. You then can call providers in your area to find out how their charges compare.

The Wall Street Journal

Less Disability Insurance

Employees are losing disability coverage as employers cut back on high-cost benefits. Companies that are not dropping the coverage often are raising employees' cost of obtaining it while reducing the benefits paid by the disability policies.

What to do: Find out if you can buy additional coverage through your employer at your own expense...or buy an individual policy. Buying through your employer costs less but may provide narrower coverage—analyze the options carefully.

SmartMoney

Manage Disability Payments

Defend yourself against disability insurance cutbacks. Find out how much you would collect on an after-tax basis from an employer-paid policy. If that is not enough, ask whether you can buy more coverage through your employer at a discount. If your assets would be severely strained in the event of a disability, consider buying insurance on your own. Read policies carefully—many pay only if you can't do any work, and some pay only if you are fully, not partially, disabled.

To reduce costs: Delay the time when payments begin. If you have six months of emergency cash, you can handle a 180-day elimination period instead of the standard 90 days.

Helpful: The National Association of Health Underwriters Web site (*www.nahu.org*) will refer you to a licensed agent who can help you compare policies.

Gary Schatsky, JD, The Objective Advice Group, personal financial advisers, New York City. *www.objectiveadvice.com*

Earthquake Insurance Loopholes

Most earthquake policies will pay for losses only to the extent that they exceed a deductible that is figured as a percentage of the replacement value of the structure.

Example: If the replacement cost of your home is $300,000 and you have a 5% deductible, you could make a claim for reimbursement only if your losses exceed $15,000—and only for the amount that exceeds $15,000. Also, most earthquake policies impose many exclusions.

Examples: A deck may not be covered unless you have to use it to enter and exit the house...a decorative facade may not be covered at all. And coverage for your home's contents varies based on whether you have taken proactive steps, such as strapping down a boiler or bolting your house to the foundation.

CBS MoneyWatch.com

Do the Research Yourself

Don't trust car insurers' price comparisons. Visit competitors' Web sites directly to get quotes from them.

Example: Progressive offers a name-your-own-price option for auto insurance at its Web site. It does not actually let you go as low as you want to but does offer a wide range of plans at different costs—and compares them with other companies' plans. But Progressive's quotes for other firms' insurance are not necessarily the same as those companies' own quotes.

What to do: Shop around by visiting multiple sites even if it seems easier to go to a single site and use its comparison tool.

Consumer Reports, 101 Truman Ave., Yonkers, New York 10703. *www.consumerreports.org*

Don't Be Fooled

Vanishing car insurance deductibles are costly.

Examples: Nationwide Insurance is promoting a new feature that reduces your deductible by $100 in every year that you don't make a claim, up to a maximum reduction of $500—but the feature typically costs an extra $60 or more per year. Similarly, The Hartford reduces your deductible by up to $150 initially if you have a clean record and then $50 per year if your record stays clean—but the premium is 6% higher than that of the basic policy.

J.D. Howard, executive director of Insurance Consumer Advocate Network, LLC, Springfield, Missouri. *www.ican2000.com*

Accident Scams

Staged auto accidents are used to defraud insurance companies—and can cause your insurance rates to rise. Crooks look for drivers of nice cars. Then one crook drives ahead of you slowly while another tailgates you. The car behind swoops past you...the accomplice slams on the brakes so that you hit that car... and you are liable.

Or: You are merging into traffic, and the crook waves you into a tight spot ahead of him. Then, as you speed up to merge, he does, too, so that you hit his car...then he claims never to have waved you in.

What to do: Leave plenty of room between your car and the one in front...ignore pressure to tailgate...resist distractions, which means turning off your cell phone while driving... stay aware of cars around you. If you do have an accident, use a camera or smartphone to take pictures of both cars and the other car's occupants.

CBS MoneyWatch.com

Car Insurance Discounts

Some insurers lower rates for teenage drivers who are on the honor roll. And if a teen goes to college and does not take the car, premiums can drop by as much as 25%. For drivers age 55 and above, taking a defensive-driving course can lower rates by 10% to 15%. If you do not drive your car to work, you may get a discount of up to 15%—and you may get one if you buy both auto and homeowners insurance from the same company.

What to do: Look over your auto policy every year to be sure you need the same coverage and are getting all discounts to which you are entitled.

Madelyn Flannagan, vice president of agent development, education and research, Independent Insurance Agents & Brokers of America, Alexandria, Virginia. *www.iiba.com*

Customers Rate Insurers

A survey of more than 4,500 insurance customers ranked the 20 largest insurers by customer satisfaction. Among car insurers, USAA, Auto-Owners Insurance and The Hartford ranked highest, in that order, while Esurance, MetLife, Mercury General, Progressive and American Family ranked at the bottom. For home insurance companies, USAA, Amica Mutual and Chubb ranked highest, while Citizens Property Insurance, Fireman's Fund, Universal Property & Casualty, American Family and Auto-Owners Insurance ranked at the bottom. The highest-ranked health insurance companies were Blue Cross Blue Shield of Illinois, Horizon Blue Cross Blue Shield of New Jersey and Kaiser Permanente, and the worst were Blue Shield of California, Assurant, Health Net, Aetna Life and Coventry Health Care. The study asked about customer service, claims experience, value for the price paid for insurance, whether customers plan to renew their policies and whether they would recommend the insurance company to a friend. To see the entire list, go to *www.insure.com* and search for "Best Insurance Companies."

Insure.com

Ways to Save

Cut your auto insurance bill with a device that monitors your driving. Available devices vary by insurance company.

Examples: GMAC Insurance and State Farm Insurance give low-mileage discounts to some owners of GM cars equipped with OnStar service who allow their mileage to be monitored. Progressive Insurance has a program called Snapshot that uses a plug-in device to monitor driving habits for 30 days—including how many miles a day you drive and at what time. These and other firms' programs then adjust your insurance rates if you fit the profile of a lower-risk driver. Other insurers are working on similar programs.

The Wall Street Journal

Life Insurance Warning—Your Paid-Up Policy May *Not* Be Paid Up After All

Thomas J. Henske, CFP, CFS, a chartered life insurance underwriter, certified in long-term care, and a partner in the wealth-advisory firm Lenox Advisors, Inc., which has offices in New York, Chicago, San Francisco and Stamford, Connecticut. *www.lenoxadvisors.com*

Today's low interest rates mean that many people who think they have fully paid-up whole and universal life insurance policies will one day receive some distressing news in the mail—there are insufficient funds in their accounts to keep their policies in effect.

When consumers purchase whole or universal life insurance, they typically are told that if they make payments of a certain size for a certain number of years, their policies will be fully paid up, with no additional payments required for a lifetime of coverage and death benefits for their heirs.

Trouble is, those payment schedules are not guarantees—they're just estimates based on the returns that insurance companies expect to earn by investing policyholders' payments in low-risk investments. The ultra-low interest rates paid by those low-risk investments in recent years have left many whole and universal policies that were written more than 10 years ago well short of their projected investment returns and therefore underfunded. (Less-than-stellar stock market returns mean many variable life policies written in the mid-to-late 1990s have fallen well short, too.) When that happens, any cash value that the policy has built up begins to erode—eaten away by the need to fund new premium payments.

Policyholders who receive notices of insufficient funds typically are given two options—make sizable additional payments or allow the policy to lapse, requiring no more payments but voiding the coverage. If a policy is allowed to lapse, the policyholder and beneficiaries will receive nothing despite all the money previously poured into the policy. Many of these policyholders now are retired and living on fixed incomes. The additional payments required to keep original coverage amounts can take a massive bite out of their nest eggs.

Example: A 72-year-old man who thought his $3 million universal life policy was completely paid up decades earlier, ensuring that his heirs would receive $3 million when he died, instead received a notice warning that he would have to pay an additional $50,000 per year for 10 years.

Helpful: There might be a third option—some policies allow policy-holders facing this situation to keep their policies in effect with a lower coverage amount. But insurance companies often do not mention this option unless policyholders know to ask.

What policyholders need to know now to protect their policies...

DON'T WAIT FOR NOTICE

Insurers typically send policyholders notices of insufficient funds only when their policies are on the verge of default. The companies have no incentive to send them out sooner—they would prefer that the policies lapse so that they never have to pay out the death benefits. The earlier that you identify such a problem, the smaller the annual payments required to keep your policy in effect.

What to do: Don't wait. Call or send a letter to your life insurance company's policyholder service department requesting your policy's "In Force Policy Pages." (A form or written request signed by the policy owner may be required.) You will receive paperwork projecting what the future looks like for your policy, including whether additional annual payments are likely to be required. Contact the agent who sold you your policy or the insurance company's policyholder service department for help interpreting this complex document.

MAKE AN INVESTMENT DECISION

If your paid-up status is in danger, you may feel angry about it, but resist the urge to allow the policy to lapse because of this anger. Instead, assuming that you can afford to make the additional payments, think of them as the cost of a new investment and the amount that the policy eventually will pay out as the investment's return. Compare that return to what you could earn from other safe investments. A financial planner can help with this analysis if necessary.

Example: If you must pay $40,000 a year for 10 years to keep a $1 million policy in effect, your $400,000 essentially is earning a 150% return ($600,000) over the remaining years of your life, which might be far better than you and your heirs could do with any other low-risk investment.

If you cannot afford to make the annual payments required, give your heirs the option of making them for you. As the beneficiaries of the policy, it might be in their financial interests to do so.

TRUSTEE TROUBLES

You are at risk if you are a trustee for a trust that contains an insufficiently funded life insurance policy. You could be sued if this policy lapses—even if you agreed to be a trustee only as a favor for a friend. Do not assume litigation is unthinkable because the trust belongs to a friend who would never sue you. You still could be sued by your friend's adult children, the future beneficiaries of the trust.

Bring the policy to a well-credentialed insurance expert, such as a Certified Life Underwriter (CLU), Chartered Financial Consultant (ChFC) or Certified Financial Planner (CFP), for review. Doing this should fulfill your fiduciary duty as trustee. This expert might charge $500 to $1,000 for his/her time—a fee that typically is paid by the trust—or he might audit the policy for free to build a relationship with a potential new client.

9

Tax Tune-Up

These Taxpayers Fought The IRS...and Won! Loopholes for Us All

The IRS constantly is challenging what taxpayers do on matters ranging from property tax to medical payments. Sometimes the taxpayers beat back those challenges. *How you can benefit big-time from some recent taxpayer victories...*

DEDUCTIONS FOR BILLS

In one recent Tax Court case, the mother of a home owner named Judith Lang had paid the city the $6,840 in property taxes that Judith owed. The mother also paid Judith's medical expenses of $27,776 directly to her doctors. Judith included the real estate taxes and medical costs among her itemized deductions in filing her federal income tax forms. The IRS rejected the deductions, and Judith challenged that rejection in Tax Court.

IRS Position: Judith cannot deduct the payments because she did not make them—someone else (her mother) did.

Tax court ruling: Judith can deduct the expenses paid by her mother. The court views the situation as if the mother made a gift to the daughter, who then paid her taxes and medical costs herself.

Note: In this case, the mother was not subject to any gift tax, because the amount of the real estate tax was less than the annual gift-tax exclusion ($12,000 at that time...$13,000 in 2012). Payments of medical expenses directly to doctors and hospitals in any amount are free of gift tax.

Better way: To avoid any IRS challenge, anyone who wants to help a friend or relative pay taxes is advised to make a gift of cash to

---

Barbara Weltman, Esq., an attorney in Millwood, New York, is author of *J.K. Lasser's 1001 Deductions and Tax Breaks* (Wiley). She is publisher of *Big Ideas for Small Business*, a free monthly e-newsletter at *www.barbaraweltman.com.*

the friend or relative, who then can use the money to pay his/her taxes.

(Judith F. Lang, Tax Court Memo 2010-286)

REPAIRS FOR DRYWALL

For a number of years, home owners have been complaining about corrosive drywall (called "Chinese drywall" because much of it was imported from China between 2001 and 2009). The drywall destroyed wiring and other building components, as well as appliances, and produced sulfur gas odors.

The issue for taxpayers who are not fully covered by homeowners insurance for the damage: Should this be considered a tax-deductible casualty loss, which would require that it involve a sudden, unexpected event (such as a fire or storm)...or a nondeductible loss from progressive deterioration (such as termite damage)?

IRS Position: Initially, the IRS said that it would not allow a deduction, but eventually it reconsidered. Bowing to pressure from taxpayers and congressional leaders in 23 states, the IRS decided that damage from corrosive drywall is a casualty loss. Home owners who pay for repairs can use the cost of repairs as the amount of their loss and can take the deduction in the year that they pay for the repairs.

If home owners sued or plan to sue the manufacturer or other party, then under a special "safe harbor" provision created by the IRS, they can deduct 75% of the unreimbursed repair costs right away—they do not have to wait until litigation is finished.

What to do: Home owners must check whether their drywall is "problem drywall" (see guidelines from the Consumer Product Safety Commission and the Department of Housing and Urban Development at *www.cpsc.gov/info/drywall/interimidguidance012810.pdf*). When claiming the deduction for corrosive drywall, complete IRS Form 4684, Casualties and Thefts, and write "Rev. Proc. 2010-36" across the top.

Note: Only taxpayers who itemize can benefit from this ruling. According to the IRS, the taxpayer must first reduce the loss by $100 ($500 if repairs were made in 2009 and an amended return is filed for that year). Also, the taxpayer must reduce the total cost of the loss by 10% of adjusted gross income. Only the excess over the $100 and 10% limit is deductible.

NO SOCIAL SECURITY OR MEDICARE TAX ON SEVERANCE

In a case that could benefit employees, the bankruptcy trustee for Quality Stores, Inc., challenged the IRS in bankruptcy court in Michigan seeking a tax refund of more than $1 million of Social Security and Medicare (FICA) taxes. The chain of stores, which sells agriculture-related merchandise, had paid the tax on severance benefits that it gave to former employees when it closed 63 stores and nine distribution centers. After the bankruptcy court backed the trustee's challenge, the IRS appealed to a Federal District Court.

IRS Position: The severance payments are "wages" that are subject to Social Security and Medicare payroll taxes under the Federal Insurance Contributions Act (FICA).

District court ruling: These severance payments are not wages. Instead, the court ruled that the severance payments are akin to Social Security payments made to retired or disabled employees—these payments are not subject to FICA.

What to do: Ex-employees who received severance payments within the past three years and had FICA taxes withheld from their checks can ask their former employers whether the company has received a refund of these taxes and then ask for a rebate of their portion of FICA taxes. If a business does not share its refund, affected employees can request in writing a refund from the IRS.

(Quality Stores, Inc., District Court, Michigan. February 23, 2010)

SINGLES GET BREAK ON PROFITABLE HOME SALES

Sung Huey Mei Hsu, who was single at the time, co-owned a home with another single person, and they sold it for a total gain of about $530,000, splitting the profits in half. She claimed a $250,000 tax exclusion on her half of the profit and reported a taxable gain of less than $15,000.

The amount of the allowable exclusion is up to $250,000 for singles and $500,000 for married couples if the owners have owned and used the home for at least two of the five years before the sale date.

IRS Position: Home owners who are single are restricted to a total profit of $250,000 per home, not per owner, before they have to pay the tax, so a single co-owner's limit would be $125,000, not $250,000.

Tax court ruling: The Tax Code does not restrict the total exclusion to $250,000 when there are two single co-owners. IRS regulations even contain an example of unmarried joint owners, both holding a 50% share, who are each allowed a tax-free limit up to $250,000.

What to do: Unmarried home owners who have sold their residences and reported a taxable gain based on their belief that they were required to share the $250,000 exclusion can file an amended return requesting a $250,000 exclusion for each. Generally, they need to act within three years of the due date of the federal tax return on which the sale was reported.

(Sung Huey Mei Hsu, Tax Court Summary Opinion 2010-68)

What to Do Now to Cut Your Bill

Greg Rosica, CPA, CFA, a partner with Ernst & Young in the firm's personal financial services and tax-consulting practices, Tampa. He is a contributing author for the *Ernst & Young Tax Guide 2012* (Ernst & Young). *www.ey.com*

Congressional gridlock has had one slightly beneficial impact on federal income tax filers. There aren't many big changes in the tax rules. But that is likely to change later this year—Congress will need to grapple with the fact that Bush-era tax cuts from a decade ago are scheduled to disappear in 2013. And new rules that are being phased in require brokerage firms to report more details of your investment purchases and sales.

Among the key changes and potential changes that could affect how much you pay for tax year 2013 and beyond...

CAPITAL GAINS RULES

In an effort to detect inaccuracies on investment gains and losses reported on tax returns, the IRS is requiring brokerage firms to report additional information directly to the IRS.

When you sell certain investments, the brokerages will issue 1099-B forms that show the amount you paid for the investments (known as the cost basis)...any capital gains or losses (calculated by subtracting the cost basis from the sale price)...and some "wash sales," which occur when an investor buys the same investment within 30 days before or after a sale. In the event of a wash sale, you cannot declare a capital loss on that investment for tax purposes.

Last year, the IRS started requiring brokerage firms to report the new details to the IRS on individual stocks bought on or after January 1, 2011.

Starting this year, the new brokerage reporting rules apply to shares of mutual funds and exchange-traded funds (ETFs) held in taxable accounts, but only those you purchased on or after January 1, 2012.

Next year, brokerage firms will be required to start reporting the same information on bonds, options and private placements bought on or after January 1, 2013.

What to do: Keep detailed records of all transactions because the IRS could challenge you if your reported capital gains or losses differ from what the brokerage firm reported. Remember that any dividends and capital gains that you reinvest can alter the cost basis.

If you buy shares at various times and eventually sell a portion of your stake rather than all of it at once, you will need to tell your brokerage firm which cost-basis method you want to apply to any sales.

If you don't pick a method for sales of shares in a fund, the brokerage firm may use the average-cost basis in its report to the IRS—that is, the average price you paid for all the shares you own in the fund. It might be of greater advantage for you, however, to use one of several other methods that identify how much you paid for individual shares. Once you choose a method, it must be used for all future sales of shares in a particular investment.

For stocks, if you don't pick a method, the brokerage firm will use the first-in, first-out (FIFO) method, which assumes that the first shares you sell are the first shares you bought.

For more information, speak with your accountant or see IRS Publication 550, *Investment Income and Expenses*, at *www.irs.gov*.

IRA DONATIONS TO CHARITIES

This year, IRA owners who are 70½ or older no longer have the option of donating up to $100,000 in withdrawals from an IRA directly to a qualified tax-exempt charity to avoid federal and/or state taxes on the withdrawals. That's because a provision allowing this tax-free withdrawal expired at the end of 2011 and has not yet been reinstated by Congress, although it still is possible that Congress will reinstate the provision retroactive to the beginning of the year, as it did in 2010.

What to do: Consider waiting until it is clear what Congress will do before you make your IRA withdrawal and charitable contribution. However, even if Congress does not reinstate the tax-free provision and you are taxed on your IRA withdrawal, you will be able to take a deduction for the charitable gift, offsetting part or all of the tax on the withdrawn amount.

WHAT TO DO NOW FOR 2013

If Congress does not act this year on the expiration of the Bush tax cuts, the top rate on ordinary income in 2013 will rise to 39.6% from 35% and rates for other brackets also will jump....all dividends will be subject to ordinary income tax rates...and the highest capital-gains tax rates will rise from 15% to 20%. Also, there will be a new Medicare surtax for singles with income of more than $200,000 and joint filers with income of more than $250,000—it is 3.8% on investment income and 0.9% on earned income. In addition, the lifetime limit on an individual's exemption from the federal estate tax would drop from $5.12 million this year to $1 million, while the tax rate on estate assets over the limit would rise from the current 35% to 55%.

It is widely believed that Congress will come up with some kind of compromise to avoid at least some of the tax increases, but it is unlikely to happen until very late in 2012.

What to do: Have your accountant and investment adviser run projections based on various scenarios—one under much higher taxes in 2013...the other keeping taxes at current rates. Then be ready to execute money-saving tax strategies as soon as we get more clarity. *If tax rates do go higher next year, you may want to...*

- **Identify long-term stock and mutual fund holdings that might make sense to sell this year.** For instance, you might want to sell investments that have had big long-term gains to avoid a higher capital-gains tax in the future.

If possible, shift some ordinary income from 2013 to 2012. This might include payments for contract work, bonuses or nonqualified stock options that you can exercise this year.

- **Push deductions such as charitable contributions into 2013,** because they are more valuable when tax rates are higher.
- **Consider municipal bonds.** Munis may become more attractive because they are exempt from federal taxes and, in some cases, state and local taxes. That exemption becomes more valuable when tax rates rise.
- **Consider switching to tax-managed mutual funds.** These funds use specific strategies, such as limiting turnover of stocks and deferring gains, to enhance the after-tax returns that they produce.

Seniors, Take Note

Consider itemizing deductions after age 65 if your medical expenses, including Medicare premiums, are more than 7.5% of adjusted gross income. Many seniors simply claim the standard deduction because they pay little or no mortgage interest and do not pay much in state and local income and property taxes. But medical deductions cover more expenses than many seniors realize. Premiums for Medicare Part B, Medicare Part D for prescription drugs and Medicare Advantage policies count as medical expenses. So do premiums for Medigap policies and, within limits, qualified long-term-care insurance. Out-of-pocket copayments, deductibles, and dental and vision costs also count, and expenses paid for relatives may count under some circumstances.

SmartMoney.com

Friendlier Tax Brackets For 2012

George Jones, JD, senior federal tax analyst and managing editor, CCH, a global provider of tax, accounting and audit information and services, Riverwoods, Illinois. *www.cch.com*

The incomes that will be subject to each of the federal income tax brackets shifted upward for the 2012 tax year as the result of adjustments for inflation. The top income that falls into the 10% tax bracket is $17,400 for married taxpayers filing jointly, up from $17,000 in the 2011 tax year. For single taxpayers, it is $8,700, up from $8,500.

For other tax brackets: 15% bracket, $70,700 for joint filers, up from $69,000 (and $35,350 for singles, up from $34,500)...25% bracket, $142,700 for joint filers, up from $139,350 (and $85,650 for singles, up from $83,600)...28% bracket, $217,450 for joint filers, up from $212,300 (and $178,650 for singles, up from $174,400)...33% bracket, $388,350 for both joint filers and singles, up from $379,150. The 35% bracket applies for incomes higher than those above.

Also: The standard deduction is $11,900 for joint filers, up from $11,600 (and $5,950 for singles, up from $5,800)...and the personal exemption is $3,800, up from $3,700. The adjustments are based on the inflation rate of 3.8% for the 12 months ended August 31, 2011, which is a sharp jump from the 1.4% inflation rate that had been used for the 2011 tax year adjustments.

Correct Filing Errors

Fix tax-filing mistakes with form 1040X (*Amended US Individual Income Tax Return*). The simple form allows you to correct a mistake going back up to three tax years. It asks how much adjusted gross income you reported before...what you are now reporting...and how much the number has changed. But many tax breaks relate to income and are not allowed at certain income levels, so filing a 1040X may invalidate some parts of your original 1040 or make you ineligible for deductions that you could previously claim.

What to do: If your return is complex or if there is any doubt, it may be better to redo your entire form 1040, adjusting all calculations that could give or take away deductions based on income, and include this with your 1040X, even though the IRS does not require you to do that.

The Los Angeles Times

Education Rules

Employment-related tax deductions for higher education vary widely based on circumstances. Undergraduate costs cannot be written off as business expenses, but you may be able to take the American Opportunity Credit or Lifetime Learning Credit. Those tax credits are for different amounts, are available based on different time periods spent in school and have different requirements for course loads. Deductibility of MBA costs is uncertain—the IRS generally disallows them, but some Tax Court cases have permitted deductions if MBA training maintains or improves skills used in your current job. Laws and regulations are very complex—consult a knowledgeable tax adviser.

SmartMoney.com

Tax Deductions for Damage from Natural Disasters

Barbara Weltman, Esq., is author of *J.K. Lasser's 1001 Deductions and Tax Breaks* (Wiley). Based in Millwood, New York, she is publisher of *Big Ideas for Small Business*, a free monthly e-newsletter at *www.barbaraweltman.com.*

If you have suffered damage to your home, furniture and/or other property from a natural disaster you may be able to take a tax deduction for your losses that would lower your taxable income. *Here's how...*

- **Take inventory of your damaged property.** Go room by room and all around the outside of the house to determine what has been damaged or destroyed. Use IRS publication *Casualty, Disaster, and Theft Loss Workbook* to help (Publication 584 for personal-use property and 584-B for business or income-producing property, such as rental property, available at *www.irs.gov*). Damage to your car, fences, trees and bushes and other property can be included.

- **Calculate your loss.** If you repair property and restore it to precasualty condition, use the cost of repairs as the amount of your loss. Otherwise, estimate the current fair-market value of the damaged and destroyed property, then subtract that from the fair-market value before the disaster. This may require the services of a qualified appraiser—in which case his/her fees can be separately deducted as a miscellaneous itemized deduction. IRS Publication 561, *Determining the Value of Donated Property*, can help you determine fair-market value for property.

The amount of the loss cannot exceed your adjusted cost basis, which typically is what you originally paid plus the cost of any capital improvements that you made. Sentimental value of items, such as a photo album or costume jewelry inherited from a grandparent, does not factor in. *The amount you calculate as a loss must be adjusted based on IRS rules...*

Subtract insurance payments or other reimbursements, such as federal disaster relief grants made to you. If you have insurance coverage, you must put in a claim to be eligible for any tax deduction.

From the total loss related to each disaster, subtract $100. Do this only for personal-use property, such as your home—not income-producing property.

Also subtract 10% of your adjusted gross income (AGI) from the total loss—only for personal-use property.

Figure your loss on IRS Form 4684, *Casualties and Thefts.*

- **Decide the year in which to take the loss.** Usually, you deduct your loss for the tax year in which it occurred. However, if you're within an area eligible for federal disaster relief, you can choose to deduct the loss on the prior year's return. Determine which year will give you the bigger write-off.

If your loss is more than your income for the year, you may have a net operating loss (which can apply whether it is for personal-use or business-use property) that entitles you to carry the loss back to offset income in up to two prior years (five years for losses in a federally declared disaster area).

To see whether you are in a disaster area, go to *www.fema.gov.* Find more information about casualty losses in IRS Publication 547, *Casualties, Disasters, and Thefts.*

Domestic Matters

"Innocent-spouse" tax rules have been eased by the IRS. Taxpayers unaware of a spouse's tax misdeeds—who signed a joint return but were innocent of any wrongdoing—have been required to file for relief within two years of a collection notice. But many innocent spouses—especially domestic-abuse victims—were unaware of the notices and could not file within two years. Now the IRS says that it will waive the deadline both for future cases and for ones currently pending.

What to do: If you have a qualifying innocent-spouse case that has been rejected because of a filing after the two-year deadline, have it filed again. Consult your attorney and accountant for details.

Internal Revenue Service.

IRS Cracks Down on Rental Losses

The tax agency is looking more carefully at rental real estate since the Government Accountability Office reported three years ago that 53% of taxpayers who rent out real estate misreported their activity during 2001—with total misreporting of $12.4 billion. New IRS forms require much more detailed reporting about rental properties, and the IRS plans extra scrutiny of people who claim to be real estate professionals. Expect to report much more detail on rentals, such as what type (condos, single-family, etc.), the number of days that the property was rented, as well as the amount of time it was used for personal purposes.

What to do: Keep highly detailed records of all real estate transactions, and be sure all IRS forms are carefully filled out. Consult with your accountant to make sure you are following the IRS regulations properly.

Investor's Business Daily, 12655 Beatrice St., Los Angeles 90066. *www.investors.com*

Audit Rates Have Risen for the Wealthy

About 12.5% of people who earn $1 million or more a year were audited by the IRS in 2011—up from about 8.4% in 2010 and about 6.4% in 2009. The audit rate has remained steady for people making less than $200,000—at about 1%.

Internal Revenue Service. *www.irs.gov*

Careful With Charities

Verify a group's tax-exempt status before making a donation. The IRS Web site maintains a list of charities eligible to receive tax-deductible contributions. The list used to be published on paper but now is available only online.

What to do: Go to *www.irs.gov/charities*, and click "Search for Charities" at left to find eligible charities. For a list of charities that have had their tax-exempt status revoked, click "Recent Revocations of Determinations of Section 501(c)(3) Status."

Internal Revenue Service.

Protect Yourself

Keep tax information secure and safe. Use only an e-filing service that you find through the official IRS Web site, *www.irs.gov*. Do not file using Wi-Fi—file from a computer that is plugged into your network hub with an Ethernet cable. Be sure your antivirus software is the latest version and has been fully updated. Ignore and delete any e-mails supposedly coming from the IRS—they never are legitimate. The IRS communicates with taxpayers through US mail.

CBSNews.com.

Tax Talks May Not Be Confidential

The IRS has successfully argued in some court cases that accountants working with a lawyer for a client are not protected by lawyer-client privilege.

Example: In a case involving securities fraud and tax evasion, a court said that the so-called Kovel Rule—a 50-year-old principle of extending attorney-client privilege to experts working with lawyers—did not protect talks between a lawyer and an accountant.

What to do: Don't assume that conversations are protected. Address the confidentiality issue with your lawyer, and ask what can be done to protect communications with accountants and other experts.

The Wall Street Journal

When You Inherit An IRA...Avoid These Mistakes That Can Cost You Big

Ed Slott, CPA, president of Ed Slott and Company, LLC, an IRA advisory company based in Rockville Centre, New York. He is host of the PBS special *Ed Slott's Retirement Rescue*, editor of the IRA Planning section of *The CPA Journal* and author of *The Retirement Savings Time Bomb and How to Defuse It* (Penguin). *www.irahelp.com*

An inherited IRA can provide a lifetime of tax-deferred or tax-free investment growth. But as you try to build your nest egg, strict IRS rules make inherited IRAs as fragile as eggshells. Mishandle them, and they will crack, with all of their tax benefits spilling out and going to waste.

Example: A man inherited a $600,000 IRA from his father. Had he left the money in that IRA, the continued tax-deferred investment growth might have provided him with millions of dollars of income over his lifetime. Instead, he transferred the money to his own IRA account, instantly ending the tax-deferred growth and making all of those tax-deferred assets count as taxable income in a single year, pushing him into a very high tax bracket. Only $360,000 remained after the IRS took its share.

Here's how to avoid costly missteps if you inherit an IRA...

TRANSFERRING AN IRA

If you are designated as the beneficiary of an IRA from your spouse, you can simply roll the money over into your own IRA without penalty. But if the IRA belonged to anyone other than your spouse, the IRS has very specific rules that you must follow—and very steep penalties for breaking those rules.

Here's what to do...

- **First, make sure that you have formal proof you're the beneficiary.** You may already know or suspect that you have been designated as the beneficiary. And if you locate a copy of the signed beneficiary form in the files of the deceased, there should be no problem. If not, the IRA custodian—the institution that manages the IRA, such as a bank or mutual fund company—may have a copy. But such paperwork sometimes gets lost, particularly when financial institutions merge.

If no copy can be found, the IRA likely will become part of the deceased person's estate, which could greatly inhibit your ability to stretch out required minimum distributions (RMDs) from the account.

IRS rules do not allow heirs to stretch out these withdrawals from IRAs based on their own projected life spans if the IRA has passed through the estate. When this occurs, heirs instead generally must withdraw all assets by the end of the fifth year following the year of the IRA owner's death.

Exception: If it is a traditional IRA rather than a Roth IRA and the original owner was at least 70½ when he/she died, the five-year rule does not apply. Instead, the heir must make withdrawals based on the deceased's required withdrawal rate.

- **Contact the IRA custodian and retitle the IRA**—but do not retitle it under your own name. To retain its tax-advantaged status, an inherited IRA must be retitled in a specific format—"John Smith IRA, deceased (insert the date of death), F/B/O (for benefit of) John Smith, Jr., Beneficiary." The precise wording varies slightly from custodian to custodian.

When an inherited IRA is simply retitled under the beneficiary's name, the IRS considers it no longer valid. Not only does the heir lose the right to stretch out withdrawals over the remainder of his projected life, but all of the money in the IRA is treated as income in the year that the retitling occurred, potentially pushing the heir into a very high tax bracket.

Rolling the inherited IRA into your own existing IRA would produce similar results—plus it's likely to trigger a 6% penalty for making excess IRA contributions.

Warning: IRA custodians sometimes delegate IRA retitlings to poorly trained low-level clerks who might not understand the nuances of titling and handling inherited IRAs. Every time you speak with an IRA custodian, ask the following—"Do you understand that this is an inherited IRA? Are you familiar with how an inherited IRA must be handled?"

If you have any doubts about the custodian's competence, review the forms carefully before you sign off and/or ask your financial adviser or accountant to contact the custodian on your behalf and confirm that the IRA is being handled properly.

In some cases, it might be possible to correct a mistitled IRA, particularly if the problem is spotted quickly—but not if the assets have become comingled with the heir's non-inherited IRA.

• **Take any required minimum distribution.** Once the owner of a traditional IRA reaches age 70½, the IRS requires that he take annual withdrawals. (This does not apply to Roth IRAs.)

If you inherit a traditional IRA from someone older than this, check with the custodian to see whether sufficient withdrawals already were taken during the year of the person's death. If not, it's up to you to do so by year-end.

Failure to make this withdrawal will result in a steep 50% penalty on the amount that should have been withdrawn. Use IRS Publication 590, Individual Retirement Arrangements, to determine the size of the required withdrawal, or ask the IRA custodian or a tax professional for help.

This is a different table from the one you use to calculate required withdrawals from your own IRA—a potential source of confusion.

• **Consider disclaiming the inherited IRA if it makes sense to allow the assets to pass to "contingent" beneficiaries**—that is, beneficiaries who inherit if the primary beneficiary does not. This could be prudent if you do not need the money...if you are in a profession where lawsuits are common...or (in some states) if you wish to protect the money from your creditors.

If there are multiple beneficiaries, divide up the IRA by the end of the year following the year of the IRA owner's death, if not sooner. Fail to do so, and the IRS will insist that each heir calculate all future required withdrawals based on the age of the oldest beneficiary, reducing the ability of younger beneficiaries to stretch out their withdrawals.

MAINTAINING THE IRA

Even after the inherited IRA is set up, it still is different from your personal IRA in some important ways. *What to do...*

• **Request a direct trustee-to-trustee transfer if you wish to shift the inherited IRA to a different custodian.** If the money is ever in your hands, the IRS will consider it permanently withdrawn from the IRA.

Some heirs believe that as long as they redeposit inherited IRA money with a different IRA custodian within 60 days, they can take possession of it without damaging its tax-deferred status or incurring taxes. That's incorrect—this 60-day window exists for our own IRAs but not for inherited IRAs.

• **Never make contributions to an inherited IRA or roll your own IRA assets into it.** The IRS will consider the inherited IRA no longer valid if you do this, ending its tax-deferred growth and potentially triggering a big tax bill.

• **Make annual withdrawals from the inherited IRA starting in the year after the year of the IRA owner's death.** Heirs sometimes assume that they do not need to make withdrawals until they themselves turn 70½...that they don't need to make minimum withdrawals from an inherited Roth IRA...or that withdrawing money prior to age 59½ will result in early withdrawal penalties. These rules apply to your own IRAs but not to inherited IRAs.

With the exception of spouses who roll inherited IRA assets into their own IRAs, those who inherit IRAs generally are required to make annual withdrawals regardless of their age and regardless of the age at death of the IRA's original owner. (But those required to make all withdrawals by the end of the fifth year following the death can make withdrawals however they like during that span and need not remove money every year.)

This applies to Roth IRAs as well as traditional IRAs. There are no early withdrawal penalties for inherited IRAs.

If you have failed to take required withdrawals from an inherited IRA in years past, file IRS Form 5329, *Additional Taxes on Qualified Plans (Including IRAs) and Other Tax-Favored Accounts*, for each year that you should have done so. Request a waiver of the 50% penalty for each year—if it was an honest mistake, the IRS might be lenient.

New Gift Tax Rules Can Save You Big

Martin Shenkman, CPA, JD, is an estate- and tax-planning attorney with offices in New York City and Paramus, New Jersey. He is author of *Estate Planning for People with a Chronic Condition or Disability* (Demos Health). *www.laweasy.com*

Traditionally, taxpayers with big estates have made large gifts to family members to reduce the eventual tax on their estates. But Congress raised the exemption from the federal estate tax so high last year that most taxpayers figure they don't have to bother giving away assets as gifts to shrink their taxable estates. Despite that, for some taxpayers, there still are advantages to gifting, especially since Congress also increased the lifetime exemption from the federal gift tax, whose rate currently is a hefty 35%.

HOW THE RULES WORK

The current gift tax rules allow you to give away $5 million ($10 million for couples) over your lifetime without ever paying any federal tax on those transfers of assets. That's up from a far lower $1 million ($2 million for couples) under the 2010 rules.

It's important to decide quickly whether you want to take advantage of the new rules, since there's no guarantee that the higher gift tax and estate tax exemptions will be in effect beyond 2012.

Because the estate tax exemption could be substantially lower in future years, it isn't just people with more than $5 million or $10 million in assets who should consider making large gifts to heirs before the end of 2012. Anyone with a few million dollars should consider doing so.

Extra bonus: In addition to the higher lifetime cap on gift tax exemptions, you can continue to entirely exclude the first $13,000 per year—$26,000 for a couple—that you give away to each of your beneficiaries. That amount does not even count against the lifetime gift tax or estate tax totals. If you feel that your heirs are not yet responsible enough to be trusted with large assets, you could instead give assets to a trust, with your heirs named as beneficiaries.

WHEN GIFTING MAKES SENSE

Gifting assets to heirs (or trusts that name heirs as beneficiaries) in 2012 makes particular sense if you…

- **Live in a state with a low state estate tax exemption.** Locations with estate tax exemptions of $1 million or less include Maine, Maryland, Massachusetts, Minnesota, New Jersey, New York, Ohio, Oregon, Rhode Island and Washington, DC. Four other states—Connecticut, Illinois, Vermont and Washington—have estate tax exemptions above $1 million but below the federal levels. The more you gift, the less likely you will be subject to estate taxes. (Be aware, however, that Connecticut and Tennessee impose state gift taxes.)

- **Own a family business.** Anyone over age 50 who owns a multimillion-dollar family business should put succession plans in place before the end of 2012. Transferring shares in this business to heirs today could prevent a massive tax bill later. A trust could be helpful if you do not yet wish to cede control of the business.

- **Need asset protection.** Physicians, lawyers, investment advisers, business owners, large-scale real estate owners and others at high risk for lawsuits can shift assets to heirs or trusts to keep those assets away from future plaintiffs.

• **Have a life partner who is not your legal spouse.** Married couples can transfer unlimited amounts of assets any time between themselves without gift tax or estate tax consequences, but unmarried couples may face such consequences if they exceed the limit.

Tax Stats

US firms pay the second-highest taxes among major industrial nations. The top combined rate imposed under the US federal tax code and by states is 39%. After deductions and exclusions, the average "effective" corporate rate is 22.5%. That is still higher than the corporate rate in any industrialized nations, except for Japan, where the rate is 33.5%.

Analysis by *Barron's*, 200 Liberty St., New York City 10281.

Small Businesses

Two-thirds of US firms pay no corporate income tax because of the way they are organized. About 69% of firms were set up as "pass-through entities" as of 2008 (latest figures available). These companies pay no federal corporate income tax because all of their profits are passed through to owners—who then pay taxes on their individual returns.

Internal Revenue Service data, reported in *The Wall Street Journal.*

Federal Tax Credit For Hiring Veterans

Business owners, take note. The size of the credit depends on how long the veteran was out of work and whether he/she has service-related injuries. For vets who were jobless for at least six months of the year before hiring, the credit is 40% of the first $14,000 of pay. For vets out of work from four weeks to six months, it is 40% of the first $6,000. The amount for unemployed vets with service-related injuries is even larger—40% of the first $24,000.

Barbara Weltman, Esq., attorney and tax expert in Millwood, New York. *www.barbaraweltman.com*

New Scam

Prisoners cheated the IRS out of $39 million by filing fraudulent tax returns. Tricks used by prisoners to claim false refunds included searching the Internet for businesses that filed for bankruptcy. Prisoners used those companies as employers on their tax forms because it is difficult for the IRS to confirm the claims.

J. Russell George, Treasury Department Inspector General for Tax Administration, Washington, DC.

10

Investment Insights

Stocks Under $10 That Are Worth Much More

I love seeing a stock slip below $10 a share. *Reason*: That's the threshold at which many major investment firms sell or ignore a stock. Some mutual funds and pension funds actually are prohibited from owning shares that are trading below $10 because they are too hard to sell in large quantities.

That means these low-priced stocks provide the small investor with a rare edge because you can snatch up bargains while Wall Street is looking the other way.

A low stock price does not mean that you necessarily are investing in an unproven company. Nearly two dozen profitable corporations in the Standard & Poor's 500 stock index recently were trading in the sub-$10-per-share range. Nor does a low price necessarily mean that the company is headed toward bankruptcy, although in some cases—as with Eastman Kodak's bankruptcy filing in January 2012—it does mean that.

Many of my biggest winners over the past decade started out as stocks that were trading under $10 per share when I began investing in them. That includes Priceline, which has topped $664...and Starbucks, which has topped $53.

Two types of low-priced stocks that I look for...

UNDISCOVERED GROWTH

These are great small businesses with stock prices that are low simply because many investors have never heard of the companies or have yet to realize their enormous potential.

These companies may be in unglamorous industries or tapping into growth trends that

Hilary Kramer, New York City, editor in chief of the subscription newsletters *GameChangers* and *Breakout Stocks Under $10*. Formerly, she was CIO of a $5 billion global private equity fund. She is author of *The Little Book of Big Profits from Small Stocks* (Wiley) and *Ahead of the Curve: Nine Simple Ways to Create Wealth by Spotting Stock Trends* (Free Press). *http://gamechangers.investorplace.com*

the public hasn't recognized yet. They typically are small-cap companies experiencing fast growth in revenues.

Characteristics I look for...

Likelihood of at least 15% annual growth in revenues over the next five years based on a variety of positive signs.

A highly fragmented industry in which the company can keep gaining market share year after year, not just from increasing revenue but also by acquiring small competitors.

My favorites now...

• **Casual Male Retail Group (CMRG)** is a big-and-tall men's retailer that operates 500 Casual Male stores in the US and Canada. Wall Street has regarded the extra-large menswear category as a marginal retail niche, but the burgeoning waistlines of American men have made it into a $7 billion-a-year industry. Casual Male is the top retailer in its category but still has room for enormous growth with only a 7% share of that market.

Recent share price: $3.63.*

• **Magic Software Enterprises (MGIC).** Magic Software is an information technology, consulting and software company based in Israel. It specializes in "cloud-computing" applications that help workers at large companies use their smartphones and other mobile devices to connect to their offices and to remote data servers wherever they are. The company, whose global network of business partners includes IBM and Microsoft, has increased revenue by double-digit percentages for eight consecutive quarters. This year, the company is rolling out support for iPhones and Android phones and is making acquisitions of small consulting and staffing-services firms to gain more access to Asian markets.

Recent share price: $5.55.

• **Metalico (MEA)** is a scrap metal processor that buys discarded base metals (steel and iron) and more valuable ones (copper and platinum) from demolition contractors, then recycles and refabricates them. No one thinks of junkyards and waste disposal as a fast-growth business, but global steel mills are showing strong interest in US metal recyclers as low-cost suppliers. Recycling accounts for 2% of the nation's gross domestic product (GDP). That means billions of dollars in potential revenues. Metalico, which operates 30 locations across the US, is more diverse than many of the hundreds of small competitors that make up this industry, providing protection from price volatility in any one metal. It produces metal products for a range of uses, including radiation shielding, stained-glass windows, bridges and US Navy ships.

Recent share price: $2.20.

FALLEN ANGELS

Once-mighty or high-profile companies that have proved they can succeed sometimes encounter problems that send their stock prices plummeting to single digits. The reasons range from accounting scandals and management mistakes to the economic slowdown. The companies may be fixing their problems out of the spotlight and still have great potential—but fickle investors often want no more to do with them.

Questions I ask when considering a promising fallen angel...

• **Is the company profitable, and is it growing its revenues?**

• **Does the company have a clear and effective solution for what went wrong?** For instance, if the company expanded into areas where its executives have no expertise, have they acknowledged this and changed direction?

• **Are there specific catalysts that can jump-start the business again?**

My favorites now...

• **Cowan Group (COWN)** is a diversified financial services firm in New York City run by one of Wall Street's best-known deal makers, Peter Cohen, the former CEO of Shearson Lehman Hutton. It focuses on investment banking, asset management and brokerage services. Cowan shares lost 45% last year amid a meltdown of financial institution stocks. But revenue is likely to grow by 10% annually over the next five years, and a likely increase in mergers-and-acquisition activity should boost Cowan's investment banking business.

Recent share price: $2.66.

*All prices in this chapter are quoted as of July 2012, and are subject to market fluctuations.

• **Ruth's Hospitality Group (RUTH).** The owner of the largest upscale steakhouse chain in the US, Ruth's Chris Steak House, has seen its stock price drop by 72% since 2007 as the economy tanked and investors feared that wealthy diners and business executives would cut back on prime-grade steaks and $75-per-guest checks. But even in this tepid economic recovery, the company, with its exceptionally loyal customers, has managed to increase sales over the past two years. Many of its competitors have gone out of business, and consumer spending by the wealthy is rebounding. Its main competitor, Morton's Restaurant Group, was recently acquired at a 34% premium to its stock price, a sign that Ruth's shares are very undervalued.

Recent share price: $6.60.

The Shrewdest Money Moves You Can Make Now

Interest rates on savings are painfully low…and the stock market is frighteningly volatile. But there still are wise things that investors can do to protect their money and take advantage of financial opportunities.

We asked six top money experts what single thing readers can do to improve their finances.

BETTER BOND YIELDS

• **Use Ginnie Mae bonds instead of US Treasuries as a very low-risk way to invest for income.** The Government National Mortgage Association (GNMA, known as Ginnie Mae) is a federal government–owned corporation that buys mortgages from lenders. Like Treasuries, Ginnie Mae bonds have no real risk of default, only interest rate risk, which means that sharply rising interest rates could make existing bonds worth less until they mature. However, Federal Reserve officials say they expect short-term interest rates to remain "exceptionally low" at least through mid-2013—and Ginnie Maes are paying significantly more interest than Treasuries.

My favorite way to invest now: Vanguard GNMA (VFIIX) is a fund with ultralow expenses that invests primarily in Ginnie Maes, and its performance ranks in the top 10% of its category over the past decade.

Recent yield: 3.1%.

Performance: 7.1%.* *www.vanguard.com.*

Robert M. Brinker is editor of *Brinker Fixed Income Advisor*, Littleton, Colorado. *The Hulbert Financial Digest* ranked it among the five best-performing newsletters over the past five years. *www.brinkeradvisor.com*

• **Use a "mixed risk" strategy to balance higher yields and reduced risk.** Allocate 60% of the bond portion of your portfolio to safe, short-term government and corporate bonds that yield about 2%, and allocate 40% to riskier longer-term, corporate "junk" bonds that yield about 6%. I've found that this strategy provides slightly better returns over time with less risk than investing in an intermediate-term bond fund.

Two attractive funds to create this mix: Vanguard Short-Term Bond ETF (BSV), an exchange-traded fund, *recent yield*: 1.8%. *www.vanguard.com*…Fidelity Capital & Income, a high-yield bond fund (FAGIX), 6.4%. *www.fidelity.com.*

Jonathan D. Pond, president of Jonathan D. Pond, LLC, an investment advisory firm in Newton, Massachusetts, with $170 million in assets under management. He is host of *Money Smarts with Jonathan Pond,* a TV program airing on PBS stations, and author of *Safe Money in Tough Times: Everything You Need to Know to Survive the Financial Crisis* (McGraw-Hill). *www.jonathanpond.com*

• **Invest in the world's most undervalued major asset class now.** The best bargain now by far is the higher-quality bonds of emerging markets, which recently were yielding about 4% to 6% annually. They sound much more exotic and risky than they are, and they will become a standard part of investors' portfolios in the future. Currently, they represent an extraordinary opportunity because anxiety over Europe has unfairly dragged down investment-grade bond prices from both emerging-market

*Fund performance figures in this article are annualized returns for the five years through June 29, 2012.

corporations and foreign governments with booming economies and little debt.

Example of an emerging-market bond fund: iShares JPMorgan USD Emerging Markets Bond (EMB), an exchange-traded fund (ETF) that invests in a mix of about 100 government and corporate bonds, the majority of which are rated BBB or higher, from countries such as Brazil, Peru and the Philippines.

Recent yield: 4.8%.

Recent share price: $114.72.

Robert D. Arnott, chairman and CEO of Research Affiliates, an investment strategy and management firm in Newport Beach, California. He also is manager of the PIMCO All Asset Fund (PASAX), which has outperformed the S&P 500 stock index by an average of four percentage points annually over the past five years. *www.researchaffiliates.com*

BETTER STOCK RETURNS

• **Invest in large-cap growth-stock funds.** Fast-growing US corporations such as Priceline and Whole Foods have adapted well to the new slow-growth economic environment.

Most attractive fund now that invests in this kind of stock: Wells Fargo Advantage Growth Fund (SGROX). The fund's ability to pick winners in both good and bad economic times has led to returns that rank in the top 1% of its category over the past decade, outperforming the Standard & Poor's 500 stock index by an average of 4.4 percentage points a year.

Performance: 7%. *www.wellsfargo.com/advantagefunds.*

Janet M. Brown, president of DAL Investment Co. and managing editor of the *NoLoad FundX* newsletter, both in San Francisco. The Hulbert Financial Digest ranked it among the five best investment newsletters over the past 15 years. *www.fundx.com*

• **Reduce volatility with a fund that can bet against stocks.** The continued deterioration of the European financial system and Congress's struggle with US budget deficits will keep the S&P 500 stock index surging and plunging throughout 2012. I expect daily movements in the index of 1% or greater about 30% of the time, compared with 18% of the time in a normal year. If these scary swings keep you up at night, reduce your risk by putting 5% of your portfolio into a so-called long/short fund. A long/short strategy often is used by hedge funds and allows the manager to not only buy stocks but also to short (bet against) those that he/she expects to decrease in value.

My favorite fund now: Caldwell & Orkin Market Opportunity (COAGX) lost just 4.7% in the market collapse of 2008, compared with a loss of 37% for the S&P 500, and it has managed to beat the stock index over the past 15 years by about one-half a percentage point annually, on average, with half as much volatility.

Performance: 3.4%. *www.caldwellorkin.com.*

Louis P. Stanasolovich, CFP, president of Legend Financial Advisors, a fee-only financial advisory firm with $360 million under management, Pittsburgh. He has been chosen 12 consecutive times by Worth magazine as one of "The Top 100 Wealth Advisors" in America. *www.legend-financial.com*

• **Keep plenty of cash in reserve and stop worrying about the markets.** Wall Street traders will use any news, whether it produces terror or euphoria, to try to make a buck off the rest of us. Yes, our economy has problems, and Europe is a mess, and Congress is dysfunctional—but I'm very optimistic. All that bad news still can't stop US corporations from continuing to report great profits, and it doesn't merit these crazy stock market swings up and down day after day. Long-term investors should keep one-third of their portfolios in cash so they don't panic and do something silly, such as sell stocks when prices plunge, and so they can use some of the cash to buy investments at bargain prices. Put the rest in the Vanguard Total World Stock ETF (VT). It's the simplest low-cost way to get exposure to the entire world and maintain your sanity.

Ben Stein, economist, attorney and a former speech writer for presidents Richard Nixon and Gerald Ford. He is coauthor of *The Little Book of Bulletproof Investing: Do's and Don'ts to Protect Your Financial Life* and author of *What Would Ben Stein Do?* (both from Wiley). He lives in Beverly Hills, California. *www.benstein.com*

More Ways to Get a 7% Yield...Or Even 9%

Neil George, editor of the financial sites Stocks That Pay You and Pay Me Strategy, based in Alexandria, Virginia. Formerly, he served as chief economist for Mercantile Bank and Mark Twain Bank (now part of US Bank). *www.stocksthatpayyou.com*

Roger Conrad, editor of the newsletter *Utility Forecaster,* whose model portfolio has beaten the Standard & Poor's 500 stock index by more than five percentage points a year, on average, over the past decade. He also is editor of the newsletters *Canadian Edge* and MLP Profits and author of *Power Hungry: Strategic Investing in Telecommunications, Utilities & Other Essential Services* (Wiley). *www.utilityforecaster.com*

Increasing your income from investments has become a difficult task in this era of extremely low interest rates. *Two experts tell us their favorite ways...*

Two ideas from Neil George...

EMERGING-MARKET INCOME

Ten-year government bonds from countries such as Brazil, Indonesia, Peru and Turkey can yield more than four times as much as 10-year US Treasury notes, and these countries all have faster-growing economies, stronger balance sheets and far less debt than the US.

Biggest risks: A stronger US dollar could lower the value of your dividends, which are paid in emerging-market currencies and then converted into dollars. Also, whenever there are fears of a slowdown in global growth, many bond investors and bond mutual fund holders are quick to abandon their emerging-market exposure first.

This can drive down share prices and force fund managers to liquidate holdings at a loss just to have enough cash to pay shareholders who are selling their shares.

For these reasons, I often recommend closed-end mutual funds that offer a set number of shares and trade directly on US stock exchanges. Because shares aren't directly redeemed from the fund, the manager can maintain a more stable dividend payment.

My favorite closed-end funds now...

• **AllianceBernstein Global High Income** (AWF) is an aggressive fund that has suffered only one down year in the past 10 while producing superb long-term total returns—15% annualized over the past decade and 12% annualized since 1997. The fund has more than 700 holdings.

Recent yield: 8%.

Recent share price: $14.99.

• **Western Asset Emerging Markets Debt** (ESD), a less aggressive fund, returned an annualized 12.3% over the past five years.

Recent yield: 7.0%.

Recent share price: $20.66.

MINI BONDS WITH MAXI YIELDS

Many corporate bond offerings require investors to buy thousands or millions of dollars worth of bonds at a time, so they are difficult for small investors to purchase. But you still can gain access to some of these high-yielding bonds by purchasing "mini bonds."

Mini bonds typically are long-term corporate bonds that are issued by a single company and packaged as a trust. Their shares are traded on the New York Stock Exchange just like stocks.

Yields are in the 7%-to-12% range, which is possible because the IRS permits the company to treat the dividends as debt. That allows the company to reduce its tax liabilities. Instead of paying $1,000 per bond, you typically pay about $25 per share.

Because mini bonds are not publicized, have confusing names and don't sell in large enough lots to attract institutional buyers, mini bond share prices tend to be relatively steady even in volatile markets.

Important: The dividends that investors receive from mini bonds are taxed at regular income tax rates, so I suggest them only for tax-deferred retirement accounts.

Biggest risks: Possible default, just like any other bond, if the company issuing the mini bond runs into financial trouble. Also, mini bonds are not rated by firms such as Standard & Poor's and Moody's, unlike most corporate bonds, so you have less of a sense of how risky they are. That's why I invest only in mini bonds offered by blue-chip companies that have highly dependable and enormous annual cash flows.

My favorites now...

• **Structured Products Corp 8.50% CorTS Ctfs (KSA)** is a mini bond maturing in 2038 from Unum Group, the nation's largest disability insurer, which generates more than $7 billion in annual premiums, mostly through employer plans.

Recent yield: 7.7%.

Recent share price: $27.58.

• **Synthetic-Fixed-Income Securities Inc. STRATS News America Inc. Call Cl A-1 Series 2006-4 (GJV)** is a mini bond maturing in 2095 from News Corp., the global media empire controlled by Rupert Murdoch that includes *The Wall Street Journal* and Fox News Channel. This company, with its low debt load and vast free cash flow, has very little risk of defaulting on its interest payments. The recent scandal involving phone hacking that caused the demise of the Murdoch-owned British tabloid, *News of the World,* has done little to hurt News Corp.'s financial health.

Recent yield: 6.8%.

Recent share price: $25.82.

Two ideas from Roger Conrad...

PIPELINES TO PROFITS

Some of the steadiest sources of hefty dividends are asset-rich companies in the energy industry, specifically oil and gas pipeline companies and processing facilities. These businesses are essentially toll collectors on the energy expressway with long-term contracts that guarantee rate increases each year, regardless of price fluctuations in oil and gas. They face limited competition because new pipelines and facilities are expensive to build and need lots of regulatory approvals.

Even better, they are structured as master limited partnerships (MLPs), which require them to distribute most of their cash flow to shareholders in exchange for tax-advantaged status. MLPs, which trade like stocks on the major exchanges, typically offer annual yields of 6% to 10%.

Biggest risk: Because MLPs distribute so much cash, they must raise money frequently in order to grow their businesses. If the US enters another recession, it could be much harder and more expensive to raise capital.

My favorites now...

• **Energy Transfer Partners LP (ETP)** is one of the largest MLPs, with more than 17,500 miles of energy pipelines in Texas and surrounding states. It also is the third-largest retail marketer of propane in the US.

Recent yield: 8.2%.

Recent share price: $44.19.

• **Regency Energy Partners LP (RGP)** is a small MLP that operates natural gas pipelines and transportation services in the Gulf Coast region. The company should continue to grow rapidly, thanks to major investments in pipelines servicing the gas-rich Haynesville Shale fields in Northern Louisiana.

Recent yield: 8.0%.

Recent share price: $23.77.

CANADIAN COMPANIES

Foreign stocks often offer higher dividends than comparable US companies do because they are perceived as riskier. But Canada's economy and companies, especially those focused on energy and real estate, are thriving. The Canadian government has very little debt and has had a budget surplus in 12 of the last 13 years.

Biggest risk: Canada is not immune to problems with the US economy. If the US falls back into a recession, Canada is likely to suffer economically, but I expect the effects will be less severe and its eventual recovery will come more quickly.

My favorites now...

• **Enerplus Corp. (ERF)** is a Canadian oil and gas exploration and production company with proven reserves of more than 200 million barrels.

Recent yield: 17.6%.

Recent share price: $12.87.

• **Extendicare REIT (EXETF)** is one of North America's largest nursing-care providers, operating more than 250 senior-care centers for about 30,000 residents in both Canada and the US. By 2020, the number of people ages 65 to 84 will increase dramatically in both the US and Canada.

Recent yield: 12.2%.

Recent share price: $7.17.

Secrets of a Bargain Hunter

Brian Barish, president and director of research at Cambiar Investors, LLC, which manages $5.8 billion, Denver. He oversees the firm's four funds, including the Cambiar Aggressive Value Fund (CAMAX which has returned 16.0% over the past three years). *www.cambiar.com*

Fund manager Brain Barish looks for bargain stocks that have explosive potential.

Evidence that his strategy works: The Cambiar Aggressive Value Fund, launched in 2007, has performed in the top 13% of large-cap value funds over the past three years.

How Barish explained his approach and how it can pay off…

MY TWO MOST IMPORTANT CRITERIA

Every stock I own must live up to two very hard-to-meet criteria. First, like every value investor, I love finding cheap stocks, but I don't do it the traditional way—trying to figure out what the total value of the company should be. That involves too much guesswork. Instead, I hunt for companies whose stocks are cheap compared with their own long-term valuations, based on earnings, book value, cash flow and sales. (Typically they are in the bottom 25% of their historical range.) Alternatively, I look for stocks selling at low valuations, such as price-to-earnings ratio (P/E), relative to their peer group in industries that have favorable prospects.

Second, I don't have the patience to wait years for the company to turn around. I need to see a substantial catalyst, such as a blockbuster new product or expansion into a lucrative market, that convinces me the stock can rise by about 50% or more in the next 12 to 18 months.

My favorite stocks now that meet these two criteria…

• **Archer Daniels Midland Co. (ADM).** Billions of consumers around the globe are raising their standards of living, a trend that is pushing up prices of commodities such as grains. Shares of this 100-year-old agribusiness, which provides hundreds of food ingredients including grains, cooking and salad oils and corn sweeteners, still are cheap. That's because investors are overlooking its massive commodity transportation and storage business, including grain elevators and port warehouses, totaling hundreds of facilities on six continents. Also, it has been rumored that Warren Buffett is considering the company as a takeover prospect.

Recent share price: $29.52.

• **Harman International Industries, Inc. (HAR).** The stock of this high-end audio-equipment designer and manufacturer was recently 66% below its five-year high. Investors aren't accounting for its dominance in a lucrative part of the industry—more elaborate and sophisticated entertainment systems in vehicles—that I think is about to soar, thanks to the fascination with digital products. Harman is the leading provider of high-tech audio and videographics equipment for major automakers such as BMW, Hyundai, Lexus, Mercedes-Benz, Toyota and Volkswagen.

Recent share price: $39.60.

• **Hess Corp. (HES).** Oil prices will stay high for years, thanks to the huge growth in demand from emerging markets as well as the difficulty and expense of finding new sources of oil. But Hess is a US oil exploration and production company that has not benefited from high oil prices as much as its peers because of recent disruptions at its sites in war-torn Libya. The stock is 66% below its five-year high. Hess's stock price deserves to be much higher because it has several promising oil-and-gas projects, including recent discoveries in Australia and Brazil, as well as expansion plans for existing wells in North Dakota and the Norwegian North Sea.

Recent share price: $43.45.

• **The Western Union Co. (WU).** This company runs the largest money-transfer service in the world, with more than 450,000 agents and a 20% share of international remittances (which includes money sent by foreign workers back to their home countries). Western Union suffered during the global recession as fewer immigrant jobs meant fewer money transfers and less revenue. But as the employment situation improves, the company will use its dominance in the industry to charge lower prices than smaller competitors and gain even more customers, especially in huge, untapped markets such as the Asia-Pacific region, where the firm now derives less than 10% of its total revenue.

Recent share price: $16.84.

BENEFIT FROM EMERGING MARKETS

In addition to the strict valuation criteria I use to narrow down the universe of stocks I choose from, I look for companies that tap into two powerful trends...

Companies in the developed world that can profit from the faster-growing economies in emerging markets. I started my career as an emerging-markets analyst and have watched those developing economies outperform the more mature developed world for many years. But emerging-market stocks have grown so expensive that I currently have no direct exposure to them at all. Instead, I'm finding the best values in US and European companies that have bright futures because they derive much of their revenue from emerging-market economies. *My favorite now...*

• **Vodafone Group PLC (VOD).** The wireless telecommunications giant is headquartered in England but operates in more than 40 countries around the world and is expanding aggressively into emerging-market countries such as Albania, Ghana, Kenya and Malaysia. Vodafone will benefit in the future from new products such as M-PESA, a mobile phone that allows users without bank accounts to load money onto their phones and pay bills via text message.

Recent share price: $28.12.

BULL-MARKET SECTORS OF THE STANDARD & POOR'S 500

The index has nearly doubled from its 12-year low in March 2009, but this is the least-loved bull market I've ever seen. Investors have embraced the "New Normal," an economic theory that the deep recession and real estate bubble in the US will take many years to fully unwind, during which time we can expect below-average economic growth and subpar stock returns.

I think that's true for certain industries, such as housing, construction, commercial real estate and the financial companies that extended home buyers far too much credit.

However, other parts of the economy, such as technology, are doing much better than is generally perceived. They have experienced a typical recovery and already are in a new phase of expansion. *My favorites now...*

• **Corning, Inc. (GLW).** Corning is the leading designer and manufacturer of specialty glass and ceramics found in liquid crystal displays and fiber-optic cables. It will benefit from the massive demand this year for portable tech products such as smartphones, as well as flat-panel TVs with integrated computer-like capabilities.

Recent share price: $12.93.

• **Flextronics International Ltd. (FLEX).** This Singapore-based manufacturer and supplier for dozens of leading electronics firms helps design and assemble products ranging from BlackBerry smartphones to Xbox video game consoles. Its stock is 50% below its five-year high, but this is one of my favorite companies positioned to take advantage of increased consumer spending on high-tech gear as the economy improves.

Recent share price: $6.20.

Get a Better Yield—Secrets of America's "Dividend Detective"

Harry Domash, publisher of Dividend Detective, a Web site specializing in dividend investing. Based in Aptos, California, he is author of *Fire Your Stock Analyst: Analyzing Stocks on Your Own* (FT Press) and frequent contributor on major financial websites including *MarketWatch*, *MSN Money* and *Morningstar* and print publications. *www.DividendDetective.com*

Finding attractive yields on investments today has become more of a treacherous scavenger hunt than a routine financial exercise. US Treasury notes that mature in 10 years pay a measly 1.6%. Even many bonds issued by corporations pay less than 4%. But if you are willing to take some risks, you can find yields topping 7%.

We asked seasoned stock analyst Harry Domash, known as the "Dividend Detective" for his favorite ways to boost an investment portfolio's yields to 7% or better. Domash employs both fundamental and technical stock analysis, together with a sophisticated understanding of the global economic outlook.

Here he suggests stocks ranging from phone companies to real estate investment trusts.

How to boost your yields now...

LOCAL PHONE PROVIDERS

Companies that provide landline phone service in less populated areas of the US seem like dinosaurs in a world of dazzling smartphones and superfast Internet. Their revenues are contracting by about 3% a year overall, but they have significant strengths that many investors overlook—fairly stable stock prices...enormous annual cash flows...low overhead and expansion costs because most of the infrastructure to run their services already is in place...minimal competition from cable companies in rural markets that they serve...and best of all, annual dividend yields of 7% to 9%.

Biggest risk: Limited opportunity for stock price gains. These companies won't offer the kind of growth that will push up their stock prices very much in the coming years, but for many investors, the dividends make up for that.

My favorites now...

- **CenturyLink (CTL)** is the third-largest landline phone company in the US, providing local phone service to 15 million customers and high-speed Internet access to more than five million customers across 37 states. Its recent acquisition of Qwest Communications substantially increased its customer base.

Recent share price: $39.49.

Recent yield: 7.5%.

- **Windstream Corp. (WIN)** provides landlines to three million customers and Internet access to more than one million people in the Southeast and Midwest. It has supplemented its declining core business with acquisitions that enable it to deliver high-speed Internet, digital phone and high-definition TV services.

Recent share price: $9.66.

Recent yield: 10.7%.

SPECIALTY LENDERS

With banks and other traditional lenders still reluctant to extend most forms of credit, many midsized businesses that are too small to go public are desperate for financing. That's a lucrative environment for Business Development Companies (BDCs), which are able to borrow money cheaply and then lend it to firms at higher rates and/or take an equity stake and provide managerial expertise.

Because BDCs enjoy a tax-advantaged status, they are able to pay annual yields typically in the range of 8% to 12%.

Biggest risk: Another recession. A BDC's stock price and the stability of its dividends depend on making shrewd investments in smaller companies. The financial crisis of 2008 hurt BDCs severely. Credit markets froze, and BDCs were forced to cut their dividend distributions as many of the companies that they invested in went out of business. I think the possibility of slipping back into a recession is now remote, but it is wise to buy only the most stable and well-financed BDCs.

My favorites now...

- **Ares Capital (ARCC)** is one of the nation's largest BDCs, with a $5 billion portfolio invested in about 150 companies.

Recent share price: $15.96.

Recent yield: 9.3%.

- **Triangle Capital Corporation (TCAP)** is a well-managed BDC that focuses on companies with annual revenues under $100 million in the Southeast and mid-Atlantic regions.

Recent share price: $22.78.

Recent yield: 8.8%.

MORTGAGE REITS

There is a special type of corporation that invests in government-issued securities backed by bundles of thousands of residential mortgages. These so-called mortgage real estate investment trusts (REITs) use short-term borrowed money to fund these investments. Interest rates on short-term loans now are so low that these mortgage REITs can make big profits on the difference between the interest they earn on their investments and the interest they pay on the borrowed money. As a result, mortgage REITs—which pay no federal income tax because they pay out most of their income as dividends to shareholders—are generating yields as high as 20% on those dividends.

Biggest risks: The Securities and Exchange Commission has begun a review on whether to tighten regulation of mortgage REITs, which could limit their ability to use large amounts of borrowed money to make investments. This caused mortgage REIT stock prices to plunge in September 2011 and could continue to stir up trouble. Another risk is that if higher interest rates push up the cost of borrowed money, mortgage REITs would have to cut their dividend payouts, although it is unlikely that interest rates will jump anytime soon, given that the Federal Reserve is intent on keeping them low to bolster the economy.

My favorites now...

- **American Capital Agency (AGNC),** with $57 billion in assets under management, is one of the highest-yielding mortgage REITs.

Recent share price: $33.61.

Recent yield: 15.0%.

- **Annaly Capital Management (NLY),** which is the largest mortgage REIT, has more than $110 billion in assets under management and a strong 14-year track record.

Recent share price: $16.78.

Recent yield: 13.2%.

How to Find Insider Information

For advance warning of company problems, study the company's audit fees. The fees are reported in a firm's Securities and Exchange Commission filings. If audit fees grow suddenly, that could mean the auditors have found something requiring additional accounting attention...or see risks of future problems.

What to do: Examine similar-sized companies in the same industry. If one has a much higher audit fee than others, look carefully at the reasons before investing in that firm.

Jonathan D. Stanley, PhD, CPA, assistant professor of accounting, College of Business, Auburn University, Auburn, Alabama, and leader of a study of SEC filings from 2000 to 2007, published in *Auditing: A Journal of Practice & Theory.*

Expert's Stock Strategy

Low-volatility stocks beat high-volatility stocks. Despite conventional wisdom that investors get rewarded for taking risks, an index of the 100 least volatile stocks in the Standard & Poor's 500 stock index beat the overall index by significant margins over the past 10- and 20-year periods.

Lee's favorite fund now: PowerShares S&P 500 Low Volatility Portfolio (SPLV).

Samuel Lee, financial analyst specializing in exchange-traded funds at Morningstar, Inc., Chicago, which tracks about 400,000 investment offerings. *www.morningstar.com*

Software Stock Opportunity

The smartphone and computer-tablet wars are likely to benefit several software makers that serve a variety of competitors, according to analyst Scott P. Sutherland.

His favorites: Unwired Planet (UPIP) provides software and services used by telecommunications network operators to give customers wireless access to e-mail, Web navigation and messaging services. Synchronoss Technologies (SNCR) software enables service activation and changes to service plans.

Scott P. Sutherland, CFA, telecommunications software and wireless equipment analyst and a managing director at Wedbush Securities, Inc., an investment banking firm in Los Angeles. *www.wedbush.com*

Pawn Stores

Pawnshop companies provide a strong stock opportunity, according to analyst David Burtzlaff. High unemployment rates and credit card companies slashing credit lines have forced more middle-class households to turn to pawnshops for loans. At the same time, high prices for gold and silver are leading more people to pawn jewelry—the most profitable type of item for pawnshops.

His favorites, each with more than 1,000 pawn and loan stores: Cash America International (CSH) and EzCorp (EZPW).

David Burtzlaff, Dallas-based consumer-finance analyst at Stephens Inc., which offers wealth-management and analytic services. *www.stephens.com*

Computer Security Stocks

Cyber-security companies are attractive investments, says Stephen Leeb. Demand is soaring for the services of these companies, which create and maintain software that protects businesses' online commerce, data and communications from cyber-attacks and viruses.

Stocks likely to benefit: CACI International (CACI), a leading provider of information-technology services to the federal government...and Citrix Systems (CTXS), which manages data systems that allow employees to access their companies' central computer servers.

Stephen Leeb, PhD, president of Leeb Capital Management, New York City, and author of *Game Over: How You Can Prosper in a Shattered Economy* (Business Plus).

Less Risky Investment Idea

Look into emerging-market companies that pay dividends, says Cliff Remily of Thornburg Investment Management. These allow you to invest with less risk in fast-growing developing countries.

His favorites now: Advanced Info Service, a Thai telecommunications provider (*recent yield:* 4.6%)...Ceske Energeticke Zavody, a Czech utility company that provides electricity to central and southeastern Europe (6.5%), available through some brokers.

Cliff Remily, CFA, managing director at Thornburg Investment Management, Sante Fe, New Mexico, and co-portfolio manager of the Thornburg Investment Income Builder Fund (TIBAX). *www.thornburginvestments.com*

Investment Opportunity

Look for companies that improve energy efficiency in buildings, reports analyst Shawn Severson. About 30% of a typical commercial building's annual operating costs go toward electricity. So property owners are retrofitting existing buildings with sophisticated systems that automatically turn off lights or adjust energy usage in sunnier areas of a building.

Likely to benefit: Acuity Brands (AYI), a leader in high-tech lighting-control systems...Cooper Industries (CBE), a maker of electrical and industrial products.

Shawn Severson, managing director of Industrial Cleantech Research at ThinkEquity LLC, a financial advisory firm, San Francisco. *www.thinkequity.com*

Bank Stocks

Look at regional banks that have survived the mortgage and credit crisis. Some of them operate in areas of the US with rapid population growth, such as the Sunbelt states, and they may not be affected as much by the extensive regulations and capital requirements of national banks. Nevertheless, many investors have lumped them in with the rest of the banking industry.

Most appealing: BB&T Corp. (BBT), which operates in the southeastern states and Washington, DC...Dallas-based Comerica (CMA)... and PNC Financial Services (PNC), a conservative Pittsburgh bank.

Erik Oja, US bank analyst for Standard & Poors Equity Research, New York City. *www.standardandpoors.com*

Investment Opportunity

Look into small companies making military drones and associated equipment, we hear from defense stock expert Brian W. Ruttenbur. For fiscal 2012, the military has budgeted $4.8 billion for drones—unmanned, low-flying spy planes with high-powered cameras that have played an important role in the wars in Iraq and Afghanistan.

Attractive: Drone maker AeroVironment (AVAV)...electronics equipment maker L-3 Communications Holdings (LLL).

Brian W. Ruttenbur, formerly defense analyst for Morgan Keegan & Company, one of the largest regional investment firms, Nashville. *www.morgankeegan.com*

Spin-Off Boom

Corporate spin-offs are booming, says Joseph W. Cornell. Recently, 40 spin-offs have been announced, including announcements by Kraft Foods, Marathon Oil, Motorola, Sara Lee and Tyco International.

Reasons: These moves are meant to create more focused companies that can grow faster, benefiting stock prices. Spun-off companies also often are acquired by other companies, further pushing up stock prices.

Cornell's favorite recent spin-offs: Fortune Brands Home & Security (FBHS) and Golar LNG Partners LP (GMLP).

Joseph W. Cornell, CFA, principal of Spin-Off Advisors, LLC, a Chicago-based independent equity research firm, and author of *Spin-Off to Pay-Off* (McGraw-Hill).

Use "Loss Robots" to Offset Capital Gains, Save on Taxes

These new automated programs are available through financial planners and at Fidelity Investments. Loss robots find losers among individual stocks you own, sell them to balance your profits from gainers and replace the losing shares with similar securities. This makes "loss harvesting" easier and less emotional and minimizes taxes. The cost of the service generally starts at about 0.3% of assets a year, in addition to the fee of 1% a year or more charged by financial planners.

Forbes, 60 Fifth Ave., New York City 10011. *www.forbes.com*

Is It Time to Ditch Your Ailing Mutual Funds?

Leonard Goodall, PhD, CFP, co-editor of *No-Load Portfolios*, a monthly newsletter specializing in mutual funds. The newsletter is ranked by *The Hulbert Financial Digest* among the top five newsletters over the past decade. Based in Las Vegas, Goodall is former president of University of Nevada. *www.no-loadportfolios.com*

A mutual fund can go from red-hot to ice-cold seemingly overnight. That can happen even when the overall market is strong, let alone when a market crash adds to the fund's problems. The fund can be among the top performers for years, attracting billions of dollars in assets—then, without warning, its performance can collapse. The reversal of fortune may prompt many investors to run for the exits, while others may hang in, figuring that the weakness is a mere blip and the manager will guide the fund to a strong recovery.

To help you decide whether you should stick with a "superstar" fund that fell on hard times even before the stock market experienced its recent gut-wrenching drops, we spoke with leading fund expert Leonard Goodall, PhD, CFP…

WHY FUNDS FAIL

There can be many reasons for a fund's returns to lag other than the economic problems that have pummeled the performance of most funds lately. The fund may have changed managers or grown too big to continue its once-nimble maneuvering among investments. Its style of investing—whether it's focused on growth- or value-oriented stocks or on large or small companies—may just be temporarily out of favor. The fund may have made big bets on a few sectors—a strategy that may pay off big at certain times but fail dismally at other times. Or it may always have been more volatile than you thought…or than you can handle. Before you decide whether to abandon a fund, it is critical that you understand what has led to its shift in performance and how it fits in with your overall portfolio and risk tolerance. Also consider whether you can use any capital loss on the sale of an ailing fund to offset capital gains on your income taxes.

Examples of once stellar funds that have stumbled…

FAIRHOLME FUND (FAIRX)

Reflective of the Fairholme Fund's consistently impressive performance in the past, including during the 2008 market crash, Bruce Berkowitz was named US stock fund manager of the decade for the 2000s by research firm Morningstar, Inc. But from 2010 to 2011, the fund's performance went from the top 1% of the large-cap value fund category to the bottom 1%—losing 32.4%—and gone from more than $17 billion in assets to less than $8 billion.

What went wrong: Berkowitz built up stakes in financial and real estate stocks that many investors considered too shaky to own, including American International Group, Bank of America, Citigroup and St. Joe Co., the largest land owner in northern Florida. (St. Joe named Berkowitz as chairman after he fought with and then ousted its management.) Berkowitz says that the financial sector has the potential for large returns, once investors start realizing how deeply undervalued the stocks are.

Ten-year performance: 9.0%.

Year-to-date: –24.7%.*

Outlook: I think investors have gotten too pessimistic and shortsighted about the financial sector.

This ultra-concentrated fund, which recently held shares in fewer than 20 companies, probably isn't a good fit for very conservative portfolios. But moderately aggressive and aggressive investors with longer time horizons can expect Berkowitz's holdings to improve in performance in the next few years and help this fund rebound.

My bottom line: Keep it.**

CGM FOCUS FUND (CGMFX)

This large-cap blend (growth and value) fund run by maverick manager Ken Heebner ranked in the top 1% of its category as recently as 2007, and even now it ranks in the top 23% for the past decade, topping the Standard & Poor's 500 stock index by one percentage point a year, on average. That is due to Heebner's concentrated portfolio of two dozen or fewer stocks, his rapid turnover style—a stock rarely is held more than three months—and his brilliant instincts. Heebner made a fortune for fund shareholders by betting against technology stocks as the dotcom bubble burst in 2000–2001 and again in the mid-2000s by investing in home-builder stocks as the real estate bubble inflated.

What went wrong: In 2008, the highly concentrated fund had a return of –48%, compared with –37% for the S&P 500. Because of ill-timed bets on financial and auto stocks, the fund has sunk to the bottom of its category for the past three-year period (trailing the S&P 500 by an average of 15 points per year). Assets have shrunk to a mere $1.5 billion.

**If you don't own this article's "keeper" funds, consider buying shares incrementally over the next six months if you are willing to hold them for three years or longer.

Ten-year performance: 6.2%.

Year-to-date: –1.8%.

Outlook: Investors in this wildly unpredictable fund must endure stomach-churning losses and hope that profits during hot streaks make up for them. In the past, Heebner has regained his market-timing mastery after cold spells, but with the current market so directionless, owning shares in this fund feels more like gambling than investing.

My bottom line: Sell it.

JANUS TWENTY FUND (JAVLX)

This fund was chock-full of large-cap growth stocks that dominated their industries and generated lots of cash. These carefully researched picks pushed the fund into the top 7% of its peers over the past decade.

What went wrong: The fund has struggled since its manager was changed in 2008, and it has underperformed 96% of the funds in its large-cap growth category over the past three years, returning an average of two percentage points less per year than the S&P 500.

Ten-year performance: 8.2%.

Year-to-date: –13.8%.

Outlook: Even great funds have bad streaks. Current manager Ron Sachs had great success with a similar large-cap growth style at the Janus Orion Fund. He has loaded up on mega-cap stocks in recent years because he believes that stocks of giant companies offer the best values. After several years in which small-cap stocks outperformed large-caps, I think his strategy is a wise one, albeit adopted too early. The fund is a solid choice for aggressive investors.

My bottom line: Keep it.

LEGG MASON CAPITAL MANAGEMENT VALUE FUND (LMVTX)

Bill Miller beat the S&P 500 every year from 1991 to 2005, earning him the manager of the decade award from Morningstar for the 1990s. Miller accomplished this feat by making bold, contrarian moves during bear markets, scooping up bargain-priced stocks when most investors were panicking.

What went wrong: Miller's large-cap blend fund began to show cracks in 2006 when it missed the rally in energy stocks. Then in 2007, the fund returned –6.6%, partly due to losses in home-builder stocks. Miller lost 55% in 2008. Since then, returns have been mediocre at best.

Ten-year performance: –1.1%.

Year-to-date: –6.1%.

Outlook: Miller's approach feels out of step with the slow-growth, hard-to-predict environment that we're in now. He has mellowed his approach in the past few years, increasing the number of stocks in the portfolio and working with a younger manager who will succeed him, but the results have been mixed.

My bottom line: Sell it.

FIDELITY MAGELLAN FUND (FMAGX)

Magellan achieved legendary status under manager Peter Lynch, who was at the helm from 1977 to 1990, and it became the largest mutual fund in the world, thanks to its stellar performance. It closed to new investors in 2000 with a staggering $110 billion in assets.

What went wrong: Even some of Fidelity's smartest and most talented managers have been unable to steer this behemoth. This was especially true in 2008, when the value of Magellan's shares dropped by an abysmal 49% after the fund loaded up on beaten-down financial stocks. When that sector crashed, the fund could not sell the stocks quickly enough to avoid major damage. Over the past decade, Magellan performed worse than 96% of funds in its category. The fund, which now is reopened to new investors, has shrunk to less than $14.5 billion in assets.

Ten-year performance: 2.5%.

Year-to-date: –10.3%.

Outlook: This relic still is too large to be able to invest in enough shares of fast-growing mid- and small-cap stocks to make a significant difference in returns. Moreover, Magellan's long-term performance numbers are so poor that shareholders are likely to continue to exit, putting pressure on the fund to sell stocks in order to meet redemptions.

My bottom line: Sell it.

*All performance figures are annualized returns through June 29, 2012.

Bank Loan Mutual Funds

Bank loan mutual funds can help reduce volatility in your bond portfolio as interest rates rise. These "floating-rate funds" invest in loans that banks make to corporate borrowers. The yields on the bank loans reset every 90 days, keeping pace with short-term rates.

Caution: You can lose money if the economy weakens and borrowers default on their loans, so these funds shouldn't constitute more than 5% to 10% of the bond portion of your portfolio.

Attractive now: Fidelity Floating Rate High Income (FFRHX), which avoids the riskiest bank loans.

Recent yield: 3.23%.

Eric Jacobson, director of fixed-income research at Morningstar, Inc., Chicago, which tracks about 380,000 investment offerings. *www.morningstar.com*

New Predictive Tool

New Morningstar ratings predict which mutual funds will outperform others in their category. The ratings will supplement Morningstar's star ratings, which measure only a fund's past performance. The new system gives each fund a rating of AAA, AA, A, neutral or negative, based on various factors not included in the star ratings—such as the record and tenure of fund managers and the culture and resources of a fund's parent company. The new ratings will be available free at *www.morningstar.com*.

What to do: Use these ratings and the star system, as well as other research, to help you select the best funds for your investment needs.

CBS MoneyWatch.com

"Ladder" Your Bond Mutual Funds

New bond mutual funds let you create "ladders" to maximize yields and protect your principal. Defined Maturity Funds from Fidelity Investments offer municipal bonds that mature on June 30 of 2015, 2017, 2019 and 2021. By buying several of the funds, you can "ladder" your investments across several years. iShares offers exchange-traded funds (ETFs), such as the iShares 2012 S&P

AMT-Free Municipal Series (MUAA) can serve a similar purpose.

Russel Kinnel, director of fund research at Morningstar, Inc., Chicago. *www.morningstar.com*

Higher Yields from Emerging-Market Bond Funds

For investors willing to take moderate risks, funds that hold government and corporate bonds with ratings that average above BBB+ from countries with fast-growing economies such as Brazil, Indonesia, Mexico and Russia offer yields of about 5% to 7%.

Attractive now: TCW Emerging Markets Local Currency Income Fund (TGWNX)... T. Rowe Price Emerging Markets Local Currency Bond Fund (PRELX).

Mark Salzinger, chief investment officer of Salzinger Sheaff Brock, LLC, a money-management firm in Indianapolis. He is editor and publisher of *The Investor's ETF Report* and *The No-Load Fund Investor*. *www.noloadfundinvestor.com*

Copper Could Rise 50%—How to Invest

Frank Holmes, CEO and chief investment officer at US Global Investors, San Antonio. *www.usfunds.com*

You need look no further than the penny in your pocket for a metal that is an attractive alternative to gold or silver for investors. Copper is experiencing some of the greatest global demand of any industrial metal due to two strong catalysts that should continue to drive up prices. First, increasingly popular hybrid automobiles use about two to three times as much copper as older nonhybrid cars. Second, emerging-market countries are in the midst of a decades-long infrastructure buildout that depends on copper for electrical wiring. Copper prices could easily rise by 50% over the next few years.

How to invest: Many precious metals dealers have started selling copper bullion in the form of bars or coins, much like gold. But storing copper bullion is not realistic for most people.

Better: Consider buying shares of iPath Dow Jones-UBS Copper Subindex Total Return ETN (JJC), a fund that buys futures contracts to track the world price of copper. You also can invest in copper-mining stocks, which are riskier but have the potential for faster appreciation.

Global X Copper Miners ETF (COPX) is an exchange-traded fund that holds shares in about 30 large copper-mining companies.

Freeport-McMoRan Copper & Gold (FCX) is the world's largest publicly traded copper miner.

Volatility warning: Copper prices plunged 30% during a three-month period last year over fears that China, one of the world's biggest industrial-metal purchasers, was facing a significant economic slowdown. Prices have since recovered about 25%.

Protect Yourself Against Investment Fraud

Protect yourself against investment fraud by visiting Web sites that help you identify and avoid scams. The Alliance for Investor Education offers links to top antiscam resources at *www.investoreducation.org/highriskinvestments*.

The featured resources include the Financial Industry Regulatory Authority's "The Grass Isn't Always Greener—Chasing Return in a Challenging Investment Environment"...the American Association of Individual Investors' "Outrageous Advertising: A Survival Guide for Investors"...and the Certified Financial Planner Board of Standards' "Consumer Guide to Financial Self-Defense."

The Wall Street Journal

Advisor Check-Up

Check up on your financial adviser at BrightScope, which has data on the backgrounds of nearly 450,000 financial professionals. You can go to *www.brightscope.com*, and enter your adviser's name to gain access. Information on advisers has been public for some time through the SEC and Financial Industry Regulatory Authority (FINRA) but often has been difficult to find or confusingly presented. BrightScope, an independent rater of 401(k) plans, makes data available more easily and clearly.

The Wall Street Journal

Tricky Scams Even Smart Investors Fell For

Pat Huddleston, founder and CEO of Investor's Watchdog, LLC, an investor protection firm based in Kennesaw, Georgia. He served from 1990 to 1996 in the enforcement division of the US Securities and Exchange Commission (SEC), where he became an enforcement branch chief in 1992, leading investigations of cases involving insider trading, brokerage-firm misconduct and Ponzi schemes. He is author of *The Vigilant Investor: A Former SEC Enforcer Reveals How to Fraud-Proof Your Investments* (Amacom).

For more than two decades, Pat Huddleston has roamed the dark side of the investment world, turning the spotlight on reckless stockbrokers, wily con artists, sophisticated Ponzi schemers and other scammers who drain investors of their life savings. *We asked the former Securities and Exchange Commission (SEC) investigator how readers can guard against becoming victims of fraud...*

DON'T SKIP THE BASICS

Investors could avoid many (although not all) financial scams by taking relatively simple precautions. These include things such as researching the investment provider's name and background using an online search engine such as Google. But whenever I talk to victims, even financially savvy ones, they admit to skipping the basic steps.

Reason: When it comes to investing, our brains trigger powerful biases that can make us overly trusting and gullible. Scam artists are aware of these biases, which they turn to their advantage.

Example: Because investors have become skeptical of outlandishly high returns in the wake of so many recent Ponzi schemes, scammers are more likely to claim that they can safely provide returns that are just a few percentage points above what you could earn in legitimate investments.

Here, lessons for us all from several recent cases...

EMPTY GUARANTEES

John Clement told investors that he ran a San Diego–area hedge fund called Edgefund Capital, which bought and sold growth stocks. Through word of mouth, Clement, who worked out of his home, recruited wealthy investors by promising the fund would deliver returns of at least 12% annually with very limited risk. Clement told them that he could limit losses by using a "stop-loss" policy that would automatically trigger the sale of any asset that declined in value by 5%. In May 2011, the SEC shut down Edgefund Capital, claiming Clement had misappropriated and misspent $2.1 million of investors' money rather than investing it.

Lesson: Be wary of any stock strategy that promises you won't suffer large losses. While "stop-loss" has become a buzzword for safety, it's a red flag for me because there is nothing that prevents the manager from removing a stop-loss order or never even placing one.

BAD MEDICINE

Attorney David G. Stern, an entrepreneur based in Newport, Rhode Island, persuaded investors through his Web site and word of mouth to put up money for an information technology service called Online Medical Registries (OMR). It enabled online subscribers to digitally store and share their confidential medical information with emergency room doctors and other medical professionals at crucial times. Stern told investors that he had built up a database of thousands of users, successfully tested the service with a major hospital and set up a partnership deal with Google that could be worth as much as $100 million. Investors bought $170,000 worth of private stock before the SEC stepped in and charged Stern with fraud. The SEC said OMR actually had only a dozen users, and Stern hid the fact that he was a felon who had served more than two years in jail and had been disbarred in Massachusetts for using assets from client trust funds to pay off personal debts.

Lesson: Ask "dumb" questions. The smarter the investor, the more embarrassed he/she often is to show ignorance by making simple inquiries. I wouldn't expect most potential investors to ferret out Stern's disbarment, but they could have asked and checked the name of the hospital that his system had purportedly been tested in (there was none) and asked for the name of someone to call at Google to confirm the partnership with OMR. It turned out that all Stern did was fill out an application on a Google site to become a third-party service provider, something that scores of companies have done and that means little.

FRIENDLY FIRE

For many years, Sam Otto Folin was a trusted Philadelphia-based investment adviser. He oversaw stock and bond portfolios for wealthy clients and for his friends and family members. When the stock market turned perilous in recent years, Folin started Safe Haven Investment Portfolios, a group of funds that he said emphasized investments in private companies with "socially responsible" goals. Many investors had been with Folin for so long that they never asked questions about Safe Haven's investments. In 2011, Folin was charged with misappropriating $8.7 million from Safe Haven. He allegedly used most of the money to pay back the initial investors and pay his own multimillion-dollar salary and expenses.

Lesson: There has been a growing trend of portfolio investment advisers who start their own funds. Even if the new funds seem attractive, you need another professional without a conflict of interest to evaluate whether such a fund is likely to succeed and is suitable for your needs.

POWER PLAY

A. Paul Reynolds of Simpsonville, South Carolina, raised millions of dollars from 500 investors by selling interests in three investment programs.

In the biggest program, he projected risk-free rates of return from 10% to 480%. The SEC said that his company, Success Trust and Holding, played on investors' desires to pay off their mortgages and own their homes outright. At conferences around the country, Reynolds promised investors that in exchange for a fee of $3,000 to $7,500 and power of attorney to pledge their residences as collateral for loans, he would make enough money to cover their monthly mortgage payments. He would do this through profits he earned buying and selling low-risk "bank guarantees." These are international letters of credit between banks to insure payment for goods in international trade.

In reality, the SEC said, Reynolds, who called himself Dr. Reynolds even though he didn't have any doctorate, was running a Ponzi scheme and planned to use money from new investors to distribute assets to older ones. He spent nearly $1 million of investor money on maintaining his own luxurious lifestyle.

When I interviewed some of the victims, they said that Reynolds gained their confidence when they visited his office and he pointed out a photograph of himself receiving an award from then President George W. Bush.

Lesson: Claims of connections with the rich and powerful should not be interpreted as a sign of credibility. It turns out that Reynolds hadn't received a presidential award and he was not a friend of Bush's. In fact, the photo opportunity with the president was something most anyone could get for making a sizable contribution at a campaign fund-raiser. The truth is that legitimate investment promoters respect their relationships with famous businessmen, politicians and the like too much to use them in sales pitches.

POOR PROMISES

Florida energy impresario Ronald F. LeGrand informed investors through e-mail solicitations and real estate investment seminars that he needed to raise a quick $7 million to purchase the land and other assets of a West Virginia oil and gas company at a federal bankruptcy auction. LeGrand said that just selling off the timber on the land would be worth an estimated $5.5 million. In addition, he cited geographical reports indicating that oil and gas reserves eventually would be worth several hundred million dollars. Investors were told that they could be confident of getting paid because LeGrand was issuing short-term promissory notes in exchange for the loans. These are loan agreements lasting less than nine months that pay interest. Most promissory notes must be registered with the SEC, which gives investors an added layer of safety, but very short-term notes are considered so safe that the government often exempts them from the registration requirement. LeGrand, however, neither registered the notes nor got an exemption. Also, according to the SEC, Le-Grand deceived investors by vastly overstating the value of the assets in the West Virginia energy company. Most investors never recovered their money.

Lesson: Skip investments involving promissory notes altogether. I tell my clients to just walk away from the deal. Promissory notes are the number-one vehicle for financial scams today because they are so easy to misrepresent that even professionals get fooled.

11

Consumer Smarts

Sneaky Ways Companies Trick You Into Buying

The tricks and traps marketers use to get us to buy things are more widespread and manipulative than ever before. They range from advertising ploys and clever language to audio and visual cues. *How they do it…*

THE GOOD OLD DAYS

When the economy falters, companies try to sell us memories of happier times. Nearly 35% of brands now are using nostalgia in their ad campaigns.

Examples: Mountain Dew, Doritos and Pepsi are among the products currently available in packaging designed to look like the packaging of decades ago.

Psychologists believe our minds paint rosy pictures of the past to help us continue to move forward during hard times—we're more likely to believe today's problems are just temporary if we remember most of our life as being pretty enjoyable. It's why we're likely to buy products with labeling that recalls the past, even if we weren't really in love with that product back then.

People over age 50 are particularly likely to be hit with nostalgic sales pitches—the older we get, the more intense our longing becomes for the past.

What to do: When you find yourself reaching for a product that has a label or slogan designed to evoke past decades, pause and ask yourself, Do I really need this product…or am I trying to buy a happy memory of the past? If it is the latter, don't buy the product—you already have that happy memory for free.

Martin Lindstrom, a consumer advocate and marketing expert based in New York City. His clients have included McDonald's, Microsoft and Proctor & Gamble. He was named one of the World's 100 Most Influential People in 2009 by *Time* magazine and is author of *Brandwashed: Tricks Companies Use to Manipulate Our Minds and Persuade Us to Buy* (Crown Business). *www.martinlindstrom.com*

A GOOD "INVESTMENT"

Stand in front of a new luxury car, high-end HDTV or pricey piece of jewelry in a showroom these days, and a salesperson is likely to assure you that the item is "a good investment" or "an investment you can enjoy." The salesperson is likely to avoid entirely words such as "purchase, "spend" and "cost."

Fewer shoppers will splurge on pricey products in this economy, but retailers have discovered that shoppers' minds become less resistant to forking over large amounts of cash when the word "investment" is used. Trouble is, consumer products are not investments. Investments are things likely to increase in value—virtually all consumer products decline in value.

What to do: When you hear the word "investment" from a retail salesperson, mentally replace it with the word "purchase."

HARD-TO-FIND BARGAINS

Department stores now make it intentionally difficult to locate certain products on their shelves. These hard-to-find items might include heavily advertised discounted items or staples that many shoppers need. Hiding these products in unexpected sections of the store forces shoppers to spend more time searching aisles, which increases the odds that they will buy other items, too.

Hiding discounted items also gives the sales staff a chance to lead customers to these deals, which makes those customers feel good and included, increasing their loyalty to the store.

More store-layout and time-management tricks…

- **Various stores, including supermarkets, are installing speed bumps**—textured sections of flooring. They have discovered that shoppers pushing carts slow down and pay more attention when they roll over bumpy flooring, increasing sales of nearby products by up to 6%. Stores often place premium products and things that shoppers don't really need on the shelves near these speed bumps.

Self-defense: When your shopping cart rolls over textured flooring, consider it a reminder that the store is trying to manipulate you into noticing and buying the products placed nearby.

- **Most supermarkets now have their entrance on the right to encourage customers to move counterclockwise through the store.** Research has found that counterclockwise shoppers spend up to 7% more, possibly because most people are right-handed and counter-clockwise shopping makes it slightly easier to grab items with the right hand.

Self-defense: If the store entrance is on the right, cut across the store immediately after entering and shop left to right.

- **Muzak is getting slower.** The slower the beat of background music, the longer shoppers stay in the store and the more they spend. Some businesses are even customizing their background music to specific areas within the store to subtly influence shoppers.

Example: Some supermarkets add subtle sound effects that evoke pleasant memories of the products found in that particular aisle—ice clinking in a glass in the beverage section or steak sizzling in the meats section.

Self-defense: Wear headphones and listen to fast-paced music while shopping. If you really want to save money, choose music that you don't like very much—your shopping trips will be faster and less expensive.

NOT THAT FRESH

Many foods in the typical supermarket—ranging from marmalade to fish—are older than we are led to believe. Even produce isn't necessarily as fresh as we think—the typical supermarket apple has been off the tree for 14 months. But supermarkets know that our minds tend to associate freshness with healthfulness and goodness, so they have developed strategies to trick us into believing that their food actually is very fresh…

- **Products closely associated with freshness, such as fresh-cut flowers and fresh fruit, are placed right by the entrance.** Seeing fresh-looking things when we first walk in the door primes our minds to associate the whole store with freshness.

• **Produce prices are displayed on what appear to be chalkboards.** This gives the impression that new produce arrives so often that the prices must be updated frequently. But these "chalkboards" usually are just preprinted signs designed to look as if they were written in chalk.

• **Seafood is displayed on crushed ice**—even though modern refrigerator cases don't need ice to keep seafood at the right temperature. Our minds associate ice with a lack of spoilage.

• **Packaged products are placed near fresh products,** creating a sense of freshness by association in our minds.

Example: A display of high-end salsas or salad dressings might be placed in the fresh-produce section of a supermarket, creating the possibly false impression that these are fresher or healthier than cheaper salsas and salad dressings found elsewhere in the store.

Self-defense: If freshness is something you value, shop at farmers' markets. Do not pay premium prices for freshness at high-end supermarkets such as Whole Foods—you may be paying for the illusion of freshness there, too.

Paying Extra for Better Service

Several firms are offering benefits such as shorter wait times, easier returns, faster airline boarding or the promise of contact with real people instead of a machine.

Costs vary widely: Time Warner Cable offers priority service with a premium package starting at $180/month...American Airlines charges $9 to $19 per flight segment for faster boarding...Best Buy extends its 30-day return period to 45 days for customers who spend at least $2,500 per year.

What to do: Balance costs and benefits. Many companies use the same service centers for all callers but simply pick up more quickly for those who pay.

SmartMoney.com

Keep It Confidential

You don't have to provide your zip code, phone number or other personal information to cashiers. The only time this information is required is when a salesclerk can't compare your signature to the one on your credit card, such as at the gas pump or when making purchases online.

Kiplinger's Personal Finance, 1729 H St. NW, Washington, DC 20006. *www.kiplinger.com*

How to Tell an Honest Evaluation from a Phony One

Jeffrey Hancock, PhD, associate professor in Cornell University's department of communications. He recently worked with graduate students Myle Ott and Yejin Choi and professor Claire Cardie, PhD, to analyze online hotel reviews and develop a software program that can identify deceptive reviews with about 90% accuracy. The team's results were presented at the annual meeting of the Association for Computational Linguistics in 2011. *www.reviewskeptic.com*

"This is the hotel of your dreams." "This oven will explode when you turn it on." "This restaurant has the best, most tender steak I ever ate." That's the kind of commentary you can find from consumers who review a range of products and services on Web sites, but how do you know whether you can trust them? They may appear to be honest critics, but many are tricksters intentionally misleading you.

Some sparkling reviews actually are posted by people who work for the businesses that are being reviewed...by marketing companies hired by those businesses...or by consumers who have been bribed with free merchandise.

Negative reviews are not always legitimate either. Some are posted by competing businesses...by disgruntled former employees... and by others who have axes to grind.

This is troubling because about 80% of Internet shoppers change their minds about purchases based on online reviews from other consumers, according to a 2011 survey by the market analysis firm Cone Communications.

We asked Cornell associate professor Jeffrey Hancock, PhD, who led a study of online reviews, how we can distinguish honest ones from phony ones...

• **Trust reviews that feature numerous references to space, size and distance.** When we use a product or a service such as a hotel or restaurant, our minds make note of things such as size and distance. When we later describe the experience, these spatial aspects inevitably come out.

Examples: We might note that a hotel room seemed too small to fit a suitcase...that a popular restaurant was just a block east of our hotel...or that a product was larger than we expected.

In contrast, our team's research suggests that people tend to make significantly fewer references to space, size and distance when they fabricate reviews. Their descriptions of hotels or restaurants generally say little about where they are or how to reach them...and their descriptions of products generally say little about the size of the products.

Helpful: It's tricky to judge just how many spatial references are sufficient to suggest an honest review, so our team created a free online tool to help. Copy and paste a review into Review Skeptic (*www.reviewskeptic.com*), and it will tell you whether it's truthful or deceptive with about 90% accuracy, based on a test run conducted on 800 reviews of Chicago hotels that had been validated as real or fake. Review Skeptic currently is designed to vet only hotel reviews, but we expect to expand the site over the course of 2012 to include evaluations of online product reviews and doctor reviews.

• **Trust reviews of the reviews.** Web sites that feature user reviews sometimes let other consumers rate the usefulness of each posted review.

Example: On Amazon.com, reviews often are preceded by a statistic reporting how many other shoppers "found the following review helpful."

Reviews that receive high scores from other users generally are honest. A fake review might be convincing enough to fool those who are unfamiliar with the product in question, but few fake reviews can overcome the collective wisdom of all shoppers on a Web site.

True, someone who writes a fake review also could fake a good score for that review by logging onto the site many times under different names and reporting the review helpful—but that would be very time-consuming, so it doesn't happen often.

• **Seek confirmation from other sites.** Enter the name of the product or service that you're considering and the word "reviews" into a search engine to find other sites that offer user reviews or professionally written reviews of it. Be suspicious if different review sites offer substantially different opinions. A fake reviewer might have targeted one site but not another.

• **Beware of reviews offering strong opinions but few specifics.** Reviews that provide little detail beyond over-the-top adjectives extolling or panning a product or service often are fake. And even if these reviews are honest, they're not very useful—without specifics, there's no way to know whether the reason for the strong opinion is something that is important to you.

• **Trust reviews from verified customers.** Some Web sites that feature online user reviews specify which of those reviews come from shoppers who actually purchased the product or used the service through the Web site. Reviews that come from verified customers are very likely to be honest.

Example: On Amazon.com, reviews labeled "Amazon Verified Purchase" are written by people who bought the item from Amazon.com.

Some hotel review Web sites, including Hotels.com and Orbitz, do not allow users to post reviews unless they have booked a room at the hotel through the site, greatly decreasing the odds of fake reviews. Other sites, including TripAdvisor.com, let anyone post a review, making fakes more likely.

• **Read the negative reviews even if they're outnumbered.** A product or service that receives mostly very positive reviews still might have a few very negative reviews. True, those harsh reviews might be written by cranks—but they also might be the only honest reviews. Someone might be trying to bury the honest negative reviews under a flood of fake raves.

If the bad reviews point to similar, specific and significant problems, there could be cause for concern. Maybe the raves are fakes or maybe there's a serious problem that only crops up in some cases. Either way, proceed with caution.

Example: An elliptical trainer received great user reviews—except for a handful of negative reviews, each of which mentioned that a particular metal bar on the device snapped, a sign of a serious flaw.

• **Trust the product's or service's overall score if there are at least 50 or so reviews of it on the site.** When there are a large number of reviews, it's hard for fakers to skew the score. It would take too much time and effort to substantially alter it.

• **Do not be convinced by "balanced" reviews.** There's a widespread belief that online user reviews must be honest if they make any attempt to be balanced—a score of four stars rather than five, perhaps, or a mention of some small feature that they say could have been better but was not terrible. Unfortunately, savvy fake reviewers have figured out that shoppers trust balanced reviews, and some now intentionally include a touch of balance to add credibility.

• **Be particularly leery of reviews of doctors.** Our preliminary research into online reviews of medical providers suggests that the deception rate can be high, likely in part because medical provider review Web sites do not yet attract the heavy volume of legitimate reviews that product, hotel and restaurant review sites often do, making it easier for fake reviews to skew the results.

The sites that provide doctor reviews—most notably RateMDs.com—are aware of this problem and are trying to correct it. But for the time being, I would not recommend selecting a health-care provider based solely on online reviews. Instead, obtain recommendations from your other health- care providers or from people you know and trust.

• **Be suspicious of rave reviews from "top reviewers."** Some sites identify certain reviews as coming from elite reviewers who are particularly active on the site.

Example: On Amazon.com, some reviewers are described as "Top 500" or "Top 1,000" reviewers.

Consumers tend to assume that reviews from these elite reviewers must be particularly trustworthy. But a recent survey of 166 of Amazon's top 1,000 reviewers (whose names and/or e-mail addresses often are publicly available) by Cornell professor of science and technology studies Trevor Pinch, PhD, suggests that these top reviewers often are not as independent as they seem.

It turns out that product marketers know that opinions from top reviewers carry a lot of weight, so they shower the top reviewers with free merchandise in hopes of getting these products reviewed. The top reviewers understand that the free stuff will stop arriving if they are critical in their reviews, so many of them write overwhelmingly or exclusively positive reviews.

Before trusting a review written by a "top reviewer," scan other reviews written by this person. Make sure that there's a full range of positive, neutral and negative scores—not all raves. On Amazon.com, this is done by clicking "See all my reviews."

Helpful: Also be wary of reviews labeled "Amazon Vine." This means that the reviewer received the product for free from Amazon.com.

Layaway Rules

When purchasing an item on a layaway plan, read the fine print. Many large stores, such as Walmart, Toys R Us, Sears, Kmart, Best Buy and TJ Maxx/Marshalls, offer layaway plans during the holiday season. Layaway lets customers put items on hold and pay for them in installments. Typically, stores allow products to be held on layaway for up to three months. However, the restrictions and exclusions can be confusing and are not consistent from store to store. Read the fine print, and pay close attention to the service and cancellation fees for each plan.

Christine Frietchen, editor in chief of product review site ConsumerSearch. *www.consumersearch.com*

Downside of a Digital Wallet

If you use your smartphone to make purchases, your protection against fraud may be limited. Digital-wallet programs let you wave your phone at a cash register or tap a retailer's reader to make a payment with a credit or debit card, gift card or bank account...or charge what you buy to your mobile-phone account. If you use it to pay by credit or debit card, you get the protection offered by those cards—usually a maximum liability of $50. But if you use the phone to buy something with a prepaid card or gift card or on your mobile-phone bill, you will be liable for all purchases until you report a problem, such as a lost or stolen phone.

Kiplinger's Personal Finance Magazine, 1729 H St. NW, Washington, DC 20006. *www.kiplinger.com*

Search for Savings

Qualifying for free shipping from online merchants is becoming more difficult, partly because of high oil prices. To save money, try doing an Internet search for "Promo Code" and the store's name to see if there are any discounts or promotions available.

Money, Time-Life Bldg., Rockefeller Center, New York City 10020. *www.money.com*

Always Compare

Don't judge an online deal by the "list price." Many Web sites misrepresent products' list prices in order to make their prices seem like good deals.

Example: SuperDuperClub.com listed an HP printer at $66.99—$19.01 off the manufacturer's $86 list price. But HP's list price actually was $69.99, so the discount was only $3.

Best: Ignore a site's comparison to a manufacturer's list price, and instead, comparison shop at similar sites to determine whether a deal is good.

Consumer Reports Money Adviser, 101 Truman Ave., Yonkers, New York 10703. *www.consumerreports.org/bookstore*

The Dark Side of Coupons

Farnoosh Torabi, a financial journalist who has been an anchor for *CBS MoneyWatch* segments, a reporter for *Money* magazine and a contributor to Wall Street Confidential video podcasts. Based in Brooklyn, New York, she is author of *Psych Yourself Rich* (FT Press). *www.farnoosh.tv*

Clipping coupons can be an effective way to save money—or a trap that costs us money, time and even our health.

Among the ways these ostensible money savers actually work against us...

- **Coupons can convince us to buy overpriced or unneeded products.** Most coupons are for pricey brand-name goods, not cheaper generic or store-label items. Coupons for brand-name goods are legitimate money savers only if they reduce the price enough that these items are cheaper than their generic alternatives or if the brand-name products truly are better than the generic ones. Often neither is the case.

Frequently coupons steer us toward obscure or recently unveiled products that we wouldn't have considered at all without a coupon. It's perfectly reasonable to try new foods and household products that seem interesting. Just don't be fooled into thinking you are saving money. Unless you cross something more expensive off your shopping list each time you use a coupon for an item that you would not otherwise have purchased, you could be coming out behind.

Warning: Be especially wary of coupons that feature the word "free" in large typeface, such as "Buy two, get one FREE." Consumer-products companies have discovered that shoppers tend to significantly overestimate how attractive a deal is when they see the word "free," a fact confirmed by MIT researchers in a study published in *Marketing Science.* The study found that consumers are far more likely to accept the offer of a free candy than the offer of a candy at a price so low—one cent—that it is essentially free. The authors of the study also noted that Internet retailer Amazon.com had come to the same conclusion about the powerful effect of the word "free." When Amazon.com tested free shipping, orders increased dramatically, but when it reduced the cost of shipping to a negligible amount (the equivalent of 10 cents), orders hardly picked up at all.

• **Coupons can persuade us to eat unhealthy foods.** Among the most common coupon categories are prepackaged sugary or salty snacks, cookie dough and soda.

These "junk food" coupons encourage shoppers to mistake irresponsible behavior, such as purchasing and consuming junk food, for responsible behavior—saving money with coupons. This psychological trap undercuts some shoppers' ability to skip the supermarket snack and soda aisles and can foster poor eating habits and weight gain.

Besides, junk food coupons are not really money savers at all. As the term implies, junk food is food that we don't really need, so any money spent on junk food always is money poorly spent. If a 25-cents-off coupon convinces us to buy a $1 bottle of soda, we haven't saved 25 cents—we've misspent 75 cents. And because junk food makes us less healthy when consumed regularly, it could increase our long-term health-care bills as well.

• **We tend to fritter away any money that we save with coupons.** Shoppers often reward themselves for their coupon-clipping frugality by allowing themselves to splurge on a luxury item or two. These splurges sometimes are greater than the amount that was saved in the first place, an observation confirmed by a 2008 working paper by Harvard Business School researchers. The authors of that paper found that shoppers at an online grocery Web site who redeemed a $10-off coupon spent an average of $1.59 more than shoppers who didn't use a coupon. The financial reward for using a coupon is a lower bill, not an extra purchase.

• **Some people see coupon clipping as a substitute for a job.** Jobs are hard to find these days, and some frustrated job hunters are turning to coupon clipping as a productive way to use time previously spent in the workplace. This thinking received a boost from a well-publicized 2010 *Wall Street Journal* article that concluded that couponers earn the equivalent of $86.40 per hour, tax-free, for their efforts.

Unfortunately, coupon clipping is not a reasonable substitute for a job. While a few minutes per week flipping through the Sunday circulars or visiting coupon Web sites in search of savings on items that you would have purchased anyway can indeed yield solid financial returns, the per-hour earning rate from coupon clipping declines dramatically the more time that is devoted to it. Those who are unemployed would be better served spending their time obtaining new job skills or searching for a new job, as frustrating as that can be.

How America's Cheapest Family Eats Great Food On $12 a Day

Steve and Annette Economides, best-selling authors of *Cut Your Grocery Bill in Half with America's Cheapest Family* (Thomas Nelson). The couple, who lives in Scottsdale, Arizona, have become recognized internationally as family finance experts. *www.americascheapestfamily.com*

It's tough to feed a five-member household on a shoestring, but that's what we do. Two of our kids have left the nest, but three still are at home, ages 17 to 26. They all are athletes, and each is a bottomless pit. But we still manage to spend less than $350 a month on groceries—that's about $2.30 per person per day—without giving up our favorite foods or couponing till we drop. You probably won't want to use all our techniques, at least not right away. But even the smallest action can save you money. *You've got nothing to lose but your escalating grocery bill...*

• **Plan more, shop less.** Making weekly menus, complete with recipes, may sound tedious, but when you map out what you'll eat when, your shopping list will be so focused that your cart won't bulge with expensive impulse items.

What to do: Take a detailed inventory of your pantry and freezer...check the sales circulars from nearby grocery stores...choose one or two stores with the best loss-leaders (items at no-profit prices to lure customers into the store)...decide the menus for the week...and then go shopping.

If you run out of an ingredient or forget an item, substitute something else or make a different meal—just don't go back to the store. Once you are able to limit your trips to the store to once a week, try taking the next step and stretch your trips to once every two weeks. The less you shop, the more you save. We go shopping only once a month, with one mid-month run to restock fruits and vegetables.

Also, one day a month, we batch cook, making family favorites such as shepherd's pie, cheese enchiladas and baked ziti, which we freeze in family-sized portions. We bought a nine-cubic-foot freezer from a friend, so we have plenty of room for our frozen foods.

• **Go outside the box.** When Annette discovered that a local dollar store sells deeply discounted day-old bakery items, she asked what day and time the truck comes in so that she can meet it and stock up. Restaurant-supply outlets can be a hidden source of bargains—for example, the one near us sells 25 pounds of carrots (which keep for weeks in the refrigerator) for $5.99.

However, we avoid warehouse clubs. They're a haven for expensive impulse buying. We call them the "$200 clubs" because you usually can't get out of those warehouses for less than $200. You go in for some produce and meat and come out with an air-hockey table or a new gazebo.

• **Coupon sanely.** We fall somewhere between the coupon maven who buys $374 worth of groceries for 50 cents and the not-now-not-ever crowd. You don't have to be an avid couponer to do very well on your grocery bills. If you're too tired, too busy, too overwhelmed, skip it or be selective. Ideally, you'll use coupons when they can be applied to items already on sale. The best coupons come from newspaper inserts—ask friends and neighbors to save theirs for you. You also can find good ones online at SmartSource.com and GroceryCouponGuide.com. Keep in mind that some stores will accept coupons a few days after the expiration date because there is a grace period for processing.

• **Grind your own.** We grind our own beef from boneless cuts bought on sale. After experimenting, we learned to leave in a little fat because the taste is better and meatballs and meat loaf hold together better. Even so, our end product is as lean as the 97% fat-free from the store but still cheaper than the 80% hamburger. We use an attachment designed for our heavy-duty KitchenAid mixer.

• **Be smart about stocking up.** Buy extras of nonperishables on sale—but buy only what you know you'll use. We once found a great deal on mayonnaise and bought six jars. When we got around to opening the last one, it had gone bad and was so gross that we had to pitch it. On the other hand, we love cocoa for cold nights, so when it's on sale, we buy three months' worth—by the time our supply runs out, it'll probably be on sale again. We always snap up the loss-leaders for the pantry or the freezer, then use a big permanent marker to mark the expiration date on the top of each package.

• **Snack wisely and well.** Between meals, we eat fresh fruit in season, hard-boiled eggs, celery with peanut butter, nuts bought on sale, homemade trail mix (made with various combinations of nuts, seeds, soy nuts, M&Ms and granola), pickles (we buy them by the gallon), popcorn, pretzels, plain yogurt with fresh fruit added, smoothies, string cheese and salsa with tortilla chips. (Steve's folks, despite our advice to the contrary, have a warehouse membership, so we ask them to buy us tortilla chips in five-pound bags.) And we hardly ever drink juice and never drink soda—water is healthier and considerably less expensive. We do have a filter on our kitchen tap.

• **Buy quality equipment.** If you are going to save money by doing more cooking from scratch, you'll be more efficient and motivated if you have the proper tools. We have a good set of pots and pans. And we don't use nonstick—we have found that the nonstick ones just don't last. Our meat grinder attachment, which cost only about $40, has long since paid for itself. Fill in gaps in your equipment by watching for sales on good knives, ceramic CorningWare and Pyrex casserole dishes, storage containers, stainless cookie sheets, a slow cooker and the like.

• **Strategize take-out meals.** Even with the best planning, sometimes you're too tired or too grumpy to cook. We keep our eyes open for take-out specials—for example, a nearby grocery with a prepared food counter frequently discounts fried or roasted chicken. With two chickens at $3.99 each, a loaf of bread and a bag of salad, you've got a meal for five for around $10 or $12. Another favorite option is Chinese buffet carryout—we go at midday to take advantage of the lunch prices. We fill up four large square Styrofoam containers to the top, which easily feeds us all. (We cook our own rice, to leave more room for the tastier options.)

• **Save restaurants for special occasions.** When we have sit-down restaurant meals for anniversaries and birthdays, we bring coupons from Restaurant.com or the Entertainment book (*www.entertainment.com*). Once we're there, we drink water to save on beverages, split a large portion between two people (you may be charged a bit for the extra plate), and when the server suggests adding things such as cheese, mushrooms or avocado, we always ask, "How much does that cost?" If it is too much money, we skip it.

Another great way to celebrate is to go out just for dessert. There's a restaurant near our house that serves an incredible mud pie—sharing one giant slice is a sweet night out for the two of us. (To be fair to your server, go when the eatery is not busy and there are plenty of tables.) Or you can plan ahead, and save up for an extravagant meal even if it takes you three months. The anticipation will make the occasion that much more special. At least that's how it works for us.

Get the Most Savings

Add discounts to your supermarket loyalty cards before you shop so that the discounts will automatically be credited to your bill.

How to do it: Before shopping, visit the Web sites associated with your favorite stores, enter/register your savings card and add "electronic coupons" to the card. The coupons are automatically redeemed when you use the card at checkout. Customers of Kroger and Safeway can go to Shortcuts.com. Customers of Shoprite, Tom Thumb, Randalls and Vons can go to Cellfire.com. A&P, Waldbaum's and Superfresh customers can check Zavers.com. Procter & Gamble has its own online program for its many products at PGESaver.com.

Better Homes and Gardens, 1716 Locust St., Des Moines 50309. *www.bhg.com*

Consumer Alert on Beef Prices

Retail beef prices likely will rise by 5% to 10% this year. The US is suffering from the lowest cattle supply since the 1950s because of severe droughts in Texas and Oklahoma that produced little grass for grazing and created drinking water shortages. Also, beef exports have increased as global demand has grown and the US dollar has weakened.

Good Choice: Pork, with flat prices likely this year, looks like the most economical alternative for consumers. And retail poultry prices should rise no more than 5%.

John S. Nalivka, president of Sterling Marketing, an agricultural economic research and advisory firm specializing in the livestock and meat industry, Vale, Oregon.

Save Money by Buying Grocery Basics at the Best Times

March is the industry's "Frozen Food Month," so it is a good time to stock up on frozen fruits, vegetables and frozen dinners. May ends with Memorial Day, so sodas and hot dogs often are on special. June through August, you'll find deals on ice cream. August and September feature discounts on cereal and peanut butter because kids are returning to school. November through December is baking season, so flour, sugar, chocolate chips and other ingredients often are on sale. January is National Oatmeal Month and thus the best time to buy oatmeal and, because of upcoming Super Bowl parties, chilies and canned tomatoes.

USA Today

House Brands Rising

Store brands are gaining popularity as food prices rise and the effects of the recession continue. Private-label brands made up 17.4% of the US dollar share of food products last year, compared with 15.2% in 2006.

"The Rise of the Value-Conscious Shopper," The Nielsen Company, a global information and measurement company, headquartered in New York City. *www.nielsen.com*

Small Fast-Food Chains Rank Higher

In a recent survey, In-N-Out Burger, Chipotle Mexican Grill, Chick-fil-A and Papa Murphy's Take 'N' Bake Pizza ranked at the top of their categories for food quality and service. Larger chains, such as McDonald's, Pizza Hut and Taco Bell, ranked near the bottom.

Consumer Reports, 101 Truman Ave., Yonkers, New York 10703. *www.consumerreports.org*

Save on Wine

Use social media and limited-time sales sites to buy wine for less. Many wineries use Web sites such as Twitter and Facebook to offer discounts up to 30% and to waive tasting fees for people who visit their wineries in person. These tasting fees typically are $5 to $7, though they may be as high as $40, for a tasting of four to six wines—so the savings can be substantial. Also, look for limited-time wine sales at sites such as Gilt Groupe (*www.gilt.com*) and Lot18 (*www.lot18.com*).

George Christie, founder and president, Wine Industry Network, Healdsburg, California. *www.wineindustrynetwork.com*

New Homes to Have Energy Labels

Home builders are starting to tout the energy efficiencies of their homes with labels estimating monthly utility costs and highlighting Energy Star ratings.

Jeffrey T. Mezger, president and CEO, KB Home, one of the first home builders to include an Energy Performance Guide (EPG) on its homes, Los Angeles. *www.kbhome.com*

Compare Your Energy Usage

Energy reports compare your usage with that of 100 similar-sized homes in the same area. The reports from Opower are available through 25 US utilities, including six of the 10 biggest. Many companies offer ways to help consumers manage power use, but Opower looks at the home's age and construction type, which may tell how well-insulated the home is, and whether it has a pool, which drives up energy usage.

What to do: Ask your power company if Opower reports or similar personalized information is available. If they are, and if yours shows above-average energy use, ask the power company for an energy audit to help find ways to reduce consumption.

Teresa Mastrangelo, analyst, Smart Grid Trends, a research firm in Roanoke, Virginia.

Save on Winter Heating Bills

Buy bronze-strip weather stripping for exterior doors, and cut it to size with metal snips—avoid self-adhesive foam, which will soon work loose. Get spring-loaded automatic door sweeps for outside doors—they lift up as the door opens and press down to form a tight seal when it closes. Insulate the attic hatch with an attic tent—a fabric "hut" you install over the hatch, staple to the attic floor and zip open when you need to climb through. Seal cracks where pipes penetrate the wall under sinks and where baseboards meet the floor with spray insulating foam or caulk.

Money, Time-Life Bldg., Rockefeller Center, New York City 10020. *www.money.com*

Cut Costs With Wind Turbine?

According to the US Department of Energy, anyone can have a wind turbine, which is used to generate electricity from wind power. And having one can potentially lower your electric bills by 50% to 90%.

However, a wind turbine is best-suited for rural areas, where zoning considerations are less likely to impede its setup. For example, a home owner in a residential area may be barred by zoning rules from setting one up on his/her front lawn. Also, wind conditions in the area influence whether wind power makes sense.

The US Department of Energy has a guide to help home owners, ranchers and small businesses decide if wind energy will work for them at *www.energysavers.gov* (search for "Small Wind Electric Systems").

Tom Welch, a press officer at the US Department of Energy, Washington, DC.

Before You Travel Overseas

Avoid the high cost of smartphone roaming when you are abroad by signing up for an international data package before you leave.

Example: An AT&T package costs $200/month for 200 MB—which would cost nearly $4,000 at standard AT&T rates.

Also: Track your data use to avoid going over the allotment. On an iPhone, go to "Settings," then "General," then "Usage"...on an Android phone, download the free Stats app from Marketplace.

Condé Nast Traveler, 4 Times Square, New York City 10036. *www.cntraveler.com*

Mobile Phone Alert

Warnings before mobile-phone users hit usage limits will soon be provided by wireless carriers. Under an agreement between the government and the wireless industry, companies will alert users before they exceed whatever talk, text and data limits they have paid for. There also will be alerts for international roaming charges. Alerts must start to be phased in by October 17, 2012, and must all be available by April 17, 2013. Some carriers already provide some alerts.

Federal Communications Commission, Washington, DC.

Save Money by Unplugging Appliances

Among those that use significant amounts of energy in standby mode are desktop and laptop computers, TVs, DVD players, VCRs, modems, cable-TV boxes, stereos, radios, coffeemakers, lamps and toasters. This accounts for 5% to 10% of a home electric bill. To avoid the annoyance of turning off multiple appliances every night, connect several to a power strip and turn off the strip when going to bed...then turn it back on the next day.

DailyFinance.com

Power Savings

Cable- and satellite-TV boxes are costing you money even when you are not using them. The devices do not power down when they are not in use.

Result: The 160 million set-top boxes cost $3 billion to operate last year—and $2 billion of that was wasted because the boxes were connected but not being used. The average household with two set-top boxes spends about $50 a year on electricity to power the boxes.

What to do: Ask your pay-TV provider for boxes with Energy Star approval—they use at least 30% less power than traditional boxes. Boxes can be unplugged, but then you can't tape programs and the boxes take a long time to reboot.

Noah Horowitz, senior scientist, Natural Resources Defense Council, an environmental group based in New York City. *www.nrdc.org*

Rabbit Ears?

Rabbit-ear antennas are making a comeback. The old-fashioned TV antennas allow free access to over-the-air programming from noncable stations, such as affiliates of CBS, NBC and ABC. Because of the recession and high pay-TV bills, the number of Americans relying solely on over-the-air TV has risen to 46 million from 42 million in the past year. A roof antenna can cost as little as $50 and may fit into the same brackets as a disconnected satellite dish. Indoor antennas can cost even less—RadioShack's Budget TV Antenna is priced at $13—and any old ones lying around still may work.

Helpful: Be prepared to experiment with positioning both roof and indoor antennas. When using an antenna, connect it to the antenna input on your TV—not the cable input.

DailyFinance.com

Every Man Can Pick The Perfect Perfume

Victoria Frolova, editor of the independent perfume Web site Bois de Jasmin, based in Princeton, New Jersey. The Web site won a FiFi award for Editorial Excellence from The Fragrance Foundation, a leading industry organization. Frolova also has written for *Perfumer and Flavorist Magazine* and has received perfumery training from leading scent producer International Flavors & Fragrances. *www.boisdejasmin.com*

The right perfume is alluring and can lift the spirits—especially if a loved one is wearing it. But perfumes smell different on different people. *Here's how to boost the odds that the person you love will love the perfume you buy...*

GIFT IDEAS

If you want the gift to be a surprise, scan the recipient's perfume shelf. Then jot down names from bottles. The safest course is to buy a perfume that this person already uses and is nearly out of.

If you wish to choose something new, take your list of perfumes to a store—a skilled salesperson can make recommendations based on the perfumes that someone already wears. Technology can help here. For example, Sephora's in-store touch-screen "Scentsa" system and online "Fragrance Finder" tool (on *www.sephora.com*, select "Fragrance" then "Fragrance Finder" at left) make suggestions based on perfumes currently enjoyed. The free smartphone apps iPerfumer (*www.givaudan.com/iperfumer*) and OsMoz (*www.osmoz.com*) also do this.

Another gift idea is to put several perfume samples in a gift box so that the recipient can try them. *You can order samples over the Internet...*

- **Aedes de Venustas,** a wonderful New York City fragrance shop, offers samples in vials of any seven fragrances in stock for a $15 shipping charge (*www.aedes.com*, click on "Complimentary Samples" at left).
- **LuckyScent,** an Internet fragrance retailer, sells samples of a wide range of fragrances, most for $3 or $4 apiece, plus $4 shipping per order (866-931-8297, *www.luckyscent.com/samples.asp*).

SHOPPING TOGETHER

A surprise is fun, but the best way to pick perfume is to take the recipient with you. *What you need to know...*

- **Choose the right store.** Among the major chains, Nordstrom has perhaps the best-trained perfume-counter sales staff and a good perfume selection (to find a store, go to *www.nordstrom.com*). Sephora (*www.sephora.com*) has a fine selection, too.
- **Make the fragrance counter your first stop.** Sense of smell is sharpest immediately after leaving fresh, outdoor air.
- **Have your loved one sample just three or four perfumes at a time.** The olfactory system will be too fatigued to note the differences after that. If you must sample more, take a walk outside before continuing. I also find that taking a sip of water helps.
- **Have perfumes sprayed a good distance from one another on the skin so they don't mingle**—one scent on each wrist and one near each elbow if sampling four. Let the perfumes dry for a few seconds before smelling them. Then sniff in short, quick inhales with the nose a few inches from the skin—long, deep inhales could oversaturate your sense of smell, limiting your ability to appreciate additional scents.
- **Do not make your purchase immediately.** Perfumes often smell different when initially applied than after they have been on the skin for a while. Wait at least 30 minutes and preferably an hour or longer, then sniff again.
- **Be wary of pushy salespeople.** They often receive larger commissions for selling new products.

Vintage Values

High-quality vintage costume jewelry can be valuable. Rhinestone and Bakelite jewelry can fetch hundreds of dollars now.

One undiscovered category: Carved wood jewelry from the 1940s and 1950s. Good examples still can be purchased in vintage jewelry shops and at estate sales for less than $50.

Terry Kovel has written more than 100 books about collecting and has a syndicated column that appears in more than 150 newspapers. Based in Cleveland, she is coauthor of *Kovel's Antiques & Collectibles Price Guide* (Black Dog & Leventhal). *www.kovels.com*

Electronic Textbook Rentals

Amazon.com has announced that it is starting a program to rent electronic versions of college textbooks on its Kindle e-reader platform. The company says that students can save as much as 80% when renting instead of buying. Books can be rented for periods of 30 to 360 days, and Kindle reader software is available for PC and Mac computers as well as many mobile devices.

Don't Get Taken by One Of These Health Scams

Charles B. Inlander, health-care consultant and founding president of the People's Medical Society, a consumer advocacy organization active in the 1980s and 1990s. He is author of 20 books, including *Take This Book to the Hospital with You: A Consumer Guide to Surviving Your Hospital Stay* (St. Martin's).

Health-care fraud is big business. Various studies suggest that Medicare alone is bilked out of more than $60 billion a year in fraudulent and questionable claims. The federal government has been rooting out these fraudsters over the past decade, but they're still out there—and much of this cost is passed on to you, the consumer, in the form of higher copayments or even full payment for the service or product if not approved by Medicare or your insurer. *Common scams and what you can do to avoid them...*

- **"Free" medical equipment.** Beware of offers for free medical equipment such as canes, scooters or walkers. Many of these offers come via phone calls, door-to-door salespeople or e-mails from equipment manufacturers. The equipment is free, they tell you, because Medicare or insurance will pay for it, and the company will take care of all the paperwork. They then ask for your Medicare or insurance number. They may send you the product but then bill Medicare or an insurance company (and you for a copay) for other products that you never received.

My advice: Never give your Medicare or insurance number over the phone or on the Internet unless you know that you're dealing with a nationally recognized company or it's someone you've done business with before.

- **Doctors who sell medical products.** The American Medical Association has a very strong policy discouraging doctors from selling supplements or any other such products and cautioning doctors not to make unproven claims about products they do sell. No studies show that doctors sell higher-quality products than those available elsewhere.

My advice: If your doctor tries to sell you a product, be especially leery of anything that you could easily buy at your local pharmacy.

- **Expensive "discount cards."** Have you seen those commercials or ads claiming to save you up to 70% on doctor visits, hospital stays, eyeglasses and medications? If you can read the very small print, you'll find out that these promises are not coming from health insurance plans, as many consumers mistakenly believe. Instead, the programs are really for "discount cards" that bill your credit card $19.95 a month or more. The Federal Trade Commission has put out a warning that while some of these programs are legitimate, others charge much more than you'll ever save.

My advice: Before you sign up, check to see if your doctor, pharmacy or local hospitals will accept the card. Also, find out exactly what the discount is at those places that accept it. Consider the card only if you're sure that you will save more than what you'll pay annually.

• Padded bills. Over the years, consumers and insurers have been frequently billed for health-care services that were never received. This is a growing problem with nursing homes, home-care agencies and even hospices.

My advice: Carefully review all of your health-related bills and insurance statements. Challenge the provider on any charges that seem questionable. If you have any concern about the legitimacy of a charge, call your insurer or the Inspector General's Fraud hotline (800-447-8477).

Clark Howard Shows How to Save on Doctor Bills...Prescription Drugs ...Phone Bills...More

Clark Howard, host of *The Clark Howard Show*, a syndicated radio program about saving money. He also is host of a cable-TV show on CNN's HLN network. Based in Atlanta, his latest book is *Clark Howard's Living Large in Lean Times: 250+ Ways to Buy Smarter, Spend Smarter, and Save Money* (Avery). *www.clarkhoward.com*

We all are trying to stretch the dollars that we earn as far as we can. Among the best opportunities for big savings are two very different necessities that often are huge drains on a household budget—health care and telecommunications. *Ways to cut costs without sacrificing quality of life...*

HEALTH-CARE SAVINGS

Three ways to trim health-care costs...

• Get health-care providers and pharmacies to bid for your business online. If you require a medical, dental or vision procedure that is not covered by your insurance, enter it into the free Web site PriceDoc.com (*www.pricedoc.com*, registration required). Health-care professionals offer lower-than-normal prices through this site to bring in new clients.

PriceDoc.com tends to be most useful for finding low prices for dental and cosmetic procedures. Many people are postponing these expenses in this weak economy, forcing providers to scramble to fill open hours. It's sometimes possible to obtain discounts of 25% to 30% or more.

Similarly, enter prescription medications that you need into the free Web site BidRx.com (*www.BidRx.com*, registration required), and pharmacies will offer you their lowest prices. Only reputable US pharmacies are allowed to participate. If you cannot wait for a medication to arrive by mail, the site can restrict the search to local pharmacies. Savings of as much as 50% are possible.

• Buy eyeglasses for very low prices online. Zenni Optical (*www.zennioptical.com)* offers good prescription eyeglasses online for less than $20—lenses, frames and shipping included. That's a fraction of what you would pay a local provider. Eyeglasses with special features such as progressive lenses can cost $50 or more.

Zenni's lenses are ground in China and its frames are not brand names, but Zenni offers a quality product. My family and I have been buying from this company for five years without a problem, and an investigative report by an Atlanta TV journalist concluded that Zenni's glasses are just as good as glasses purchased locally. The Web site allows you to upload a picture of yourself and "try on" frames. The major downside is that there is no customer service after the sale, so you'll have to fiddle with the glasses yourself if they don't fit your face perfectly or bring them to a local optician for adjusting.

To help get the fit right, make sure that your eye doctor checks and records on your prescription your pupillary distance (PD)—the distance between the centers of your pupils.

• Enroll in a hospital gym. Many hospitals have clean, well-equipped fitness centers that are not crowded much of the time. These usually are rehab-based or geared to the hospital staff. Most sell memberships to the public, often for much less than what comparably equipped gyms charge and typically without long-term contracts. Call local hospitals to see if they have a gym, then ask if gym memberships are available to the public.

TELECOM SAVINGS

Three ways to cut calling costs...

• **Opt for prepaid cell-phone service instead of standard plans.** Standard cell-phone plans typically cost $40 or more per month for a limited amount of use...require you to sign a two-year contract...and impose steep fees. Although such contract plans typically include a free or low-priced cell phone, the extra costs often outweigh the savings. There's no need to sign high-priced contracts unless you absolutely need the latest phone. Instead, consider one of the following prepaid options...

If you use a cell phone only occasionally, try Net10 (*www.net10.com*), which offers several low-priced packages ranging from 200 minutes of calls to anywhere in the US (and/or Web access) over 30 days for $20 to 900 minutes over 90 days for $60. Phones cost between $30 and $80.

If you do a lot of calling, texting and/or surfing the Internet, try Straight Talk, a prepaid wireless service from Walmart (*www.walmart.com*), which offers 30 days of unlimited use with no contract for $45. Phones cost $30 to $200.

If you (or your teenager) use a cell phone mostly for texting, try Kajeet (*www.kajeet.com*), which offers unlimited text messages plus 60 minutes of calls per month for $15 with no contract and an option for parental controls. Phones start at $45.

• **Escape a cellular service contract without a termination fee.** Cellular service providers often impose fees in the hundreds of dollars when customers cancel service before their contracts expire. Before paying this fee, try to hand off your phone and contract to someone who is willing to take them over.

The Web site CellTradeUSA.com (*www.celltradeusa.com*) facilitates these handoffs for a fee of about $20. You're most likely to find a taker if you're trading in a popular smartphone, such as an Android or iPhone.

Conversely, taking over someone else's cell phone and contract can be a good way for you to get cell-phone service without paying an activation fee...without paying for the cell phone itself...and without locking yourself into a full two-year contract. There often is significantly less time remaining on the contracts being traded in. It's a particularly smart way to obtain a recently introduced smartphone.

• **Downgrade or cancel your landline phone service if you don't use it often.** If you have a cell phone and/or an Internet-based phone, you might not use your old-fashioned landline much anymore. Canceling the landline could save you hundreds of dollars a year. If you don't want to cancel it—or you need a landline for your security system—at least get the cheapest possible rate.

Every state requires local phone service providers to offer an inexpensive "lifeline" or "tariff" rate based on income eligibility. Details vary by state, but these rates are typically $7 to $18 per month. They might not include free local calls, but that doesn't matter if you place calls from your cell or Internet-based phone instead.

Alternative: If you have high-speed Internet service and don't need a landline, Internet-based phone service Ooma Telo (*www.ooma.com*) is an attractive option. For $250 (possibly less at retailers such as Amazon.com and Best Buy), you get a device that links your corded or cordless phones to your Internet connection, providing unlimited domestic calling for life (although Ooma has the option to impose a 5,000-minute-per-month limit). You can use your existing home phones as always, and in most cases, you can keep your current home phone number.

Ooma Telo is very easy to set up and use...the call quality is excellent...it includes voice mail and caller ID...and the only ongoing charges are government fees and taxes, typically $3 to $5 per month. As with any lifetime service plan, there is some danger that the company will go out of business, rendering its service plans worthless. However, Ooma Telo service should pay for itself in well under a year, greatly reducing any financial risk.

Compare Medical Costs

Compare the cost of medical services through state-sponsored Web sites that collect payment information and make it available online. A few states, including Maine and New Hampshire, have Web sites showing medical costs based on actual claims. Other states are expected to set up similar sites. You can see if your state has a Web site on the site of the All-Payer Claims Database Council (*www.apcdcouncil.org*).

If your state does not have a site yet: Try fairhealthconsumer.org, which offers typical figures for various locations…or Healthcare-BlueBook.com, which provides what it calls a fair price for services in a given area.

Also helpful: The American Medical Association's Medicare-reimbursement information (*www.amacodingonline.com*) shows what Medicare pays for services. You then can call providers in your area to find out how their charges compare.

The Wall Street Journal

Considering Pet Insurance?

Think carefully before buying pet insurance. The policies often exclude preexisting illnesses and hereditary conditions linked to specific breeds, such as hip dysplasia in many dogs. Routine care is not covered or requires high-priced wellness riders. Newborn pets usually are not covered. Policies can cost $300 to $1,000 or more a year—and may pay only 60% of expenses.

Also: You generally must pay the bill in full and then submit it for reimbursement.

SmartMoney, 1755 Broadway, New York City 10019. *www.smartmoney.com*

Beware Online Pet Meds

Online pet pharmacies may sell counterfeit, outdated or mislabeled medicines…or medicines that have been improperly stored and so are less effective.

Self-defense: Avoid online sites that do not require veterinary prescriptions…do not have a licensed pharmacist to answer questions…lack a physical business address and phone number…are located outside the US…aren't licensed by the state board of pharmacy where the business is based. Licensed pet pharmacies are listed at *www.nabp.net*.

Food and Drug Administration's Center for Veterinary Medicine, Silver Spring, Maryland. *www.fda.gov/animalveterinary*

Online Help with Consumer Complaints

The federal government Web site *www.usa.gov* lists state and local consumer agencies and the types of issues that each one handles. Find agencies in your state by going to *www.usa.gov/directory/stateconsumer*. For a list of federal agencies, go to *www.usa.gov/directory/federal*. For product complaints, go to the Consumer Product Safety Commission site, *www.cpsc.gov/federal.html*.

What else to do: Contact your local Better Business Bureau through *www.bbb.org* to find out what additional help may be available.

Consumer Reports Money Adviser, 101 Truman Ave., Yonkers, New York 10703. *www.consumerreports.org/bookstore*

Robocalls Rules Getting Tougher

The Federal Communications Commission (FCC) is set to approve additional protections against unwanted auto-dialed or prerecorded calls to home phone lines. Under the new rules, a telemarketer will have to get written consent before calling a home phone even if the consumer already has done business with the company. Telemarketers also will have to provide an automated means of opting out of future calls during each robocall.

Federal Communications Commission, Washington, DC. *www.fcc.gov*

Watch Care

Never change the date setting of a watch between the hours of 10 pm and 2 am—this can break the calendar wheel.

Also: Be careful when pulling the crown outward to adjust the hands—some watches adjust with a simple pull of the crown...others require you to unscrew the crown in order to adjust the hands. After you have adjusted the time, be sure to screw the crown back tightly (if unscrewed) in order to keep out moisture.

Nagi Osta, certified gemologist appraiser, Nagi Jewelers, Stamford, Connecticut.

Shopping May Be Healthy

Recent study: About 1,800 adults age 65 and older were asked how often they went shopping—with options ranging from "never" to "every day." Researchers found that those who shopped every day had a 27% lower risk for death than those who shopped less frequently. Daily shopping was especially beneficial for men—their mortality reduction was 28%, compared with 23% for women.

Theory: Shopping, even window shopping, allows you to get out of the house, socialize and be physically active—factors believed to extend life.

Yu-Hung Chang, PhD, researcher, Institute of Population Health Sciences, Taiwan.

12

Richer Retirement

How to Spend More In Retirement Without Running Out of Money

It's one of the most important questions you face in retirement—how much of my nest egg can I spend each year? If you choose too high an amount, you eventually could run out of money. Choose too small an amount, and you may feel that you are depriving yourself. At a time when a volatile stock market and paltry bond returns have made it difficult to gauge whether your nest egg is sufficient, relying on standard methods to pick a withdrawal rate may not work.

HOW THE 4% RULE WORKS

Using the standard approach, in the first year of retirement you withdraw 4% of your savings and investments to help cover living expenses. Every year after that, you increase the dollar amount by the previous year's rate of inflation. The strategy is meant to sustain a retirement of about 30 years whether you start with $100,000 or a few million dollars, but there are no guarantees.

Example: If you start with a nest egg of $1 million, you withdraw $40,000 in year one. Then if annual inflation is running at 2.5%, you withdraw $41,000 in the second year...$42,025 in the third year...and so on. With this strategy, if you have invested your money in a standard mix of 60% large-cap US stocks and 40% US intermediate-term bonds (and rebalance each year to maintain that mix), there is only a 10% chance that if you retire at age 65 you will run out of money by age 95, according to a study by T. Rowe Price.

Scott Burns, chief investment strategist at Asset Builder, Inc., an investment-management firm in Plano, Texas, with more than $455 million under management. He is coauthor with economist Laurence J. Kotlikoff of *Raising Your Living Standard in Today's Economy and When You Retire* (Simon & Schuster). *www.assetbuilder.com*

But the best withdrawal strategy for you depends on factors such as how well you are able to stomach volatility...how long you expect that you and your spouse will live...how much you will receive from other sources of income, such as Social Security, pension benefits and part-time work...and whether you want to leave a sizable inheritance to your heirs.

Here, assorted alternatives to the 4% rule, as designed by several experts...

CONSERVATIVE: THE 4%-PLUS ANNUITY STRATEGY

Asset-allocation authority Ibbotson Associates uses annuities to increase the odds that you won't run out of money. This strategy guarantees that you will have enough money for basic expenses for as long as you live, even if the market plunges, while allowing your nest egg to grow over the long-term.

How it works: Use a portion of your assets to buy an immediate annuity, and use a percentage formula, such as the 4% rule, for the rest of your assets so that they will continue to grow over the long-term. The annuity's payouts should be just big enough to cover the estimated costs of your essential monthly living expenses, such as mortgage payments, utility bills, basic food costs and health insurance premiums. In exchange for handing over a lump sum for the annuity, you get steady monthly income that can be adjusted for inflation.

Caution: The lump sum that you initially hand over will not be available for your heirs, and the payouts typically stop when you die.

Example: A 65-year-old man living in Connecticut who has $1 million available for investments and savings needs to generate $1,300 a month for basic living expenses. He can purchase an immediate annuity with a cost-of-living rider (assuming an average of 3% inflation each year) for about $350,000. With the remaining $650,000, he can use the 4% rule, allowing withdrawals of an additional $26,000 per year, with adjustments for inflation.

Withdrawals can be used for optional expenses, such as a big trip overseas or a new car, and for emergency expenses, such as unexpected health-care costs. Even in the unlikely event that he exhausts his remaining portfolio in less than 30 years, he still can count on his annuity checks in later years.

For more information on annuities and price quotes, go to *www.immediateannuities.com* or *https://personal.vanguard.com/us/funds/annuities*.

AGGRESSIVE: THE 5% MULTI-ASSET STRATEGY

Brigham Young professor Craig L. Israelsen, PhD, found that increasing diversification raises returns and allows a higher withdrawal rate. This strategy allows you to withdraw 5% per year, instead of 4%, without running out of money and without greater risk, but it's much more complicated than other strategies and requires a greater variety of investments.

How it works: Withdraw 5% of your initial nest egg in the first year of retirement instead of 4%...increase the amount for inflation each year...and rebalance your investment portfolio annually. Instead of a 60% stocks/40% bonds split, divide your portfolio evenly among 12 asset classes (about 8.33% of your portfolio in each).

You can do this by investing in exchange-traded funds (ETFs), which track specific sectors and typically have lower expenses than mutual funds, to focus on the following segments—large-, mid- and small-cap US stocks...foreign stocks in developed markets...emerging-market stocks...global real estate...natural resources (energy, precious metals)...commodities (agriculture)...US bonds...US Treasury Inflation-Protected Securities (TIPS)...foreign bonds...and cash. Although there are no guarantees, extensive research and computer simulations indicate that you are likely to be safe withdrawing more each year than with the 60/40 portfolio because over the past 40 years, this kind of multi-asset portfolio has generated an additional percentage point in annual returns.

VERY AGGRESSIVE: THE 6.2% FLEXIBLE STRATEGY

Financial adviser Jonathan Guyton, CFP, has focused on "sustainable" withdrawals and how they are affected by volatility. This strategy allows you to withdraw even higher amounts if you are willing to face sharp ups and downs in the value of your portfolio.

How it works: You withdraw 6.2% of your portfolio's initial value in the first year...you increase the dollar amount of the withdrawals each year based on the inflation rate but within strict limits...and you rebalance each year.

To make this higher withdrawal rate work and keep up with inflation, you will need higher returns.

That means taking more risk by raising the stock portion of your overall portfolio to 80% rather than 60%. It also means a mix of stock ETFs that includes 30% US large-caps...20% US small-caps...20% foreign stocks...and 10% REITs...as well as putting 10% of your overall investment portfolio in US intermediate-term bonds and 10% in cash.

The biggest danger with an aggressive portfolio and high withdrawal rates is that you might face sharp market drops in some years and periods of very high inflation. So you need to follow some strict rules if you want your money to last for at least 30 years.

Rule 1: Regardless of the inflation rate or how much your portfolio grows, you cannot increase the dollar amount of your withdrawals by more than 6% in any year. So if you withdraw $62,000 from a $1 million portfolio in your first year, the most that you can increase the withdrawal in the next year is $3,720 (6% of $62,000), even if inflation soars beyond 6%.

Rule 2: If the value of your portfolio shrinks in any year, you cannot increase your annual withdrawal at all the next year to compensate for inflation, and there is no "catch-up" for that missed increase in subsequent years.

Rule 3: At the end of each year, raise the money you need to fund next year's withdrawal by selling shares of your ETFs in a very disciplined way. First, trim back your stock ETFs that have appreciated the most so that they are in line with your original target percentage allocations.

Next, if necessary to finish making the year's withdrawals, trim back your bond ETFs that have experienced the greatest appreciation to their target allocations. If those profits aren't enough, dip into your cash. The idea is to avoid being forced to sell shares in any asset class that has temporarily lost money. That way, the shares have an opportunity to recover.

Trade Annuities?

Trading in a variable annuity usually is a bad move—but insurance agents may pressure you to do so. Brokers get large commissions if you trade in an old annuity for a new one. But older annuities often have benefits that new ones lack...while new features come at a high cost and require you to lock up your money for a longer term.

What to do: Analyze any proposed trade-in carefully—not with the insurance agent but with an independent and knowledgeable financial adviser. Compare features, costs and tax consequences of a trade-in very thoroughly.

Kiplinger's Retirement Report, 1729 H St. NW, Washington, DC 20006. *www.kiplinger.com*

Are These Retirement Mutual Funds Right for You?

Roger Wohlner, CFP, cofounder of Retirement Fiduciary Advisors, which provides direct investment and retirement-planning advice to 401(k) plan participants around the country. He also oversees $100 million in assets as the head of the Chicago office of the investment advisory firm Asset Strategy Consultants. *www.retirementfiduciaryadvisors.com*

When target-date funds were introduced nearly a decade ago, they were touted as a simple and relatively safe way to invest for retirement. A target-date fund is composed of shares in several other individual mutual funds—and your fund typically has a "target date" close to the year that you plan to retire. Then, as the years go by, the fund company scales back the riskier components of your fund each year as you prepare for and enter retirement. The benefit for you, in a nutshell, is that you don't have to figure out how best to divide and adjust your investments every year.

Problem: In the 2008 market crash, some target-date funds suffered losses as high as 50%, blindsiding target-date fund investors who were close to retirement. The resulting outcry forced fund companies to tinker with their target-date funds' long-term strategies and take steps to make the funds safer. Target-date funds have rebounded strongly in the past two bullish years, and more than 80% of all 401(k) plans now offer them. But should you trust these newer versions, and could they pass another severe test?

We asked retirement plan investment expert Roger Wohlner, CFP, what issues our readers must consider—and what dangers there still may be—if they want to put money into today's target-date funds...

• **What steps have target-date funds taken to be safer?** Fund companies have taken a variety of steps to diversify their target-date portfolios, adding nontraditional asset classes and higher allocations to bonds. These changes could help lower the risk for large losses in another stock market collapse and smooth your ride over the years. For example, many of the T. Rowe Price Retirement funds now include shares of an international bond fund. Both T. Rowe Price and Fidelity use a commodity-related stock fund, a Treasury Inflation-Protected Securities (TIPS) fund and an emerging-markets debt fund. An emerging-markets debt fund may sound risky on its own but should actually make the target-date funds safer because of strong economic growth in those markets.

• **So would you consider the funds safe now?** Even with the changes that fund companies have made, you should not consider target-date funds to be "safe" or low-risk. In fact, most have long-term growth-oriented portfolios that easily could suffer double-digit annual losses in the future. Even bond-heavy target-date funds remain relatively risky because inflation and interest rates are likely to rise over the next several years, which means prices of many types of bonds could suffer.

• **Personal retirement plans offered by most employers include target-date funds from only one fund family. Does the fund family matter?** It matters because each of the more than 40 target-date fund families has a different philosophy about retirement investing. Just because your plan is with a well-known fund company doesn't mean that it's right for you. For instance, the Retirement Strategy funds from AllianceBernstein are very aggressive—they typically have about 65% of assets in stocks when their funds reach their target dates. In contrast, John Hancock offers funds that are designed to have less than 10% in stocks at their target dates.

In addition, the pace at which similar funds grow more conservative as you age (by shifting your money from stocks to fixed-income investments and cash) varies enormously by family. T. Rowe Price funds don't become ultra-conservative (mostly bonds and cash) until 30 years past their target dates. Vanguard reaches a similar allocation just 10 years past the fund's target date.

My advice: Study the prospectuses of target-date funds available to you and understand what you're investing in. To compare allocations, risk measures and returns between different families' funds, you can type in their ticker symbols at *www.morningstar.com.*

• **Is it always best to choose the fund that corresponds closest to the year you want to retire?** Not necessarily. Fund companies space their target-date funds five years apart (2015, 2020, etc.), but these are just broad recommendations for what the average investor might find suitable. So first, it's best to decide what kind of investment portfolio is most appropriate for your situation and risk tolerance. Then choose the target-date fund that fits these needs, regardless of your retirement date. For example, if your spouse has a guaranteed pension in retirement that can cover your living expenses...or if you have substantial assets, are in good health and feel confident about your job...you might want to be more aggressive. Instead of the age-appropriate 2020 fund, you might switch to the 2030 fund. It will own more stock because it's designed for people who are younger than you. The fund will be more volatile than a 2020 fund, but it also is likely to reward you with higher returns.

• **Is it best to put all of your 401(k) investments into a target-date fund?** Maybe. The key is not to invest in a vacuum. Step back and see how the fund fits into your overall investment portfolio, including multiple retirement savings accounts, such as traditional IRAs and Roth IRAs, as well as 401(k)s (and possibly even 529 college savings plans). For instance, if you have most of your IRA assets in short-term bonds, you may want to put your 401(k) money into a fund with a distant target date, meaning that its allocation mix is relatively aggressive.

The five years before you retire are critical because you have accumulated a lifetime of savings and have the most to lose in a bear market. If you have other sources of income and won't need to touch that money for several years, target-date funds can serve nicely as the growth portion of your portfolio. However, if that's all, or nearly all, the money you have, you'll want very little risk and should seek a more conservative, personalized strategy. Ask your 401(k) plan sponsor if financial advice services are available. Some are free, while others charge a fee.

• **Once I do retire, what if I need my target-date fund to provide monthly income?** Then sticking with it may not be your best option. A typical 2005 fund, meant for people already in retirement for several years, has an annual yield ranging from 1.3% to 2.5%. Once you are in full retirement, you may want some very conservative or steady income-producing investments. You could take out a portion of the money in your target-date fund, and shift it to dividend-yielding stocks, bonds, real estate investment trusts (REITs), even annuities, that will produce adequate annual income for you to live on. It generally is a good idea for retirees to keep a portion of their nest eggs easily accessible in savings accounts, money-market funds, short-term bond funds and the like. That way, during market drops, they can avoid selling stocks to fund their ongoing cash needs.

Review Target Date Funds

Target-date mutual funds underperformed the major US stock and bond benchmarks last year. The average retirement-oriented fund with about four to eight years until its target date gained 1.3%, while the S&P 500 gained 4.7% and the Barclays Capital Aggregate Bond Index rose by 7.4%.

Reason: The target-date funds hold a broad array of investments, but only a few of those, including blue-chip stocks and long-term government bonds, have done well lately.

What to do: If you choose to invest in target-date funds, make sure that you understand what the individual funds are investing in and that those investments match your preferences and risk tolerances.

Josh Charlson, fund analyst, Morningstar Inc., Chicago. *www.Morningstar.com*

Appeal Social Security Decisions Within 60 Days

Nancy Shor, executive director, National Organization of Social Security Claimants' Representatives, an association of more than 4,000 attorneys and other advocates who represent Social Security and Supplemental Security Income claimants, based in Englewood Cliffs, New Jersey. *www.nosscr.org*

You can file an appeal if you receive a decision from Social Security denying your claim (for example, your claim for disability benefits or other benefits is denied)...you believe that an agency employee made an error...or you did not get credit for certain working years. The general rule is that you have 60 days from the date you receive a decision, but in some cases, you may need to act sooner. On Social Security's Web site, review *Your Right to Question the Decision Made On Your Claim* (*www.ssa.gov/pubs/10058.pdf*). The pamphlet explains the different appeals levels, how to file an appeal and what to expect if you appeal.

If you appeal: Be sure to assemble all the documents and facts that support your claim. If your first appeal is denied, you can appeal to the next level and will be able to file additional paperwork. The process can take considerable time, but initial negative decisions can be reversed if you have the facts on your side.

Social Security Scam Warning

Social Security scams are on the rise because of the cost-of-living allowance (COLA) increase last year. Thieves are posing as Social Security Administration (SSA) employees and calling or e-mailing seniors to get personal information, supposedly to guarantee that seniors get the COLA boost.

But: Genuine SSA employees do not make unsolicited phone or e-mail contact with Social Security recipients...and the COLA increase is automatic.

AARP.org

The COLA Increase

Social Security checks rose by 3.6% in 2012. This is the first cost-of-living increase for seniors since 2009. But many retirees will not see all of the increase because Medicare Part B premiums will rise by $3.50 a month, to $99.90, in 2012 for most seniors. Those payments are deducted from Social Security checks.

Steve Vernon, FSA, member, executive faculty and research fellow, California Institute for Finance at California Lutheran University, Thousand Oaks. *www.restoflife.com*

What Your Employer Doesn't Want You to Know About Your Retirement Benefits

Ellen E. Schultz, a New York City–based investigative reporter for *The Wall Street Journal*. In 2003, she was part of a team that won the Pulitzer Prize for a series of articles on corporate scandals. She is author of *Retirement Heist: How Companies Plunder and Profit from the Nest Eggs of American Workers* (Penguin). *www.retirementheist.com*

Your retirement finances might not be as secure as you would like to think—and your employer might be to blame. This could apply to you if you are one of the 44 million Americans who have a defined benefit pension plan at a private company...and/or are one of the tens of millions who have been promised retirement health benefits. Unfortunately, many employers have spent the past two decades exploiting loopholes in pension laws and retiree health plan agreements so that they could slash these promised benefits. *Eight secrets your employer doesn't want you to know about your retiree benefits...*

1. When we "restructure" our pension plan, it's often a way to slash older workers' pensions. Many employers have been converting their traditional pension plans into "account style" or "cash balance" plans that superficially resemble 401(k)s. Employers often have claimed that the change will benefit employees. What they won't say is that it's younger employees with limited tenure who stand to benefit, while older, longer-tenured employees can lose as much as 20% to 50% of their pensions because of changes in the formula used to calculate benefits.

2. Those "skyrocketing" pension costs that we complained about when we froze your pension might be from money owed to upper management. In Securities & Exchange Commission (SEC) filings, employers are allowed to bundle pensions in with the companies' general pension liabilities.

Example: Unisys froze its pension plan in 2006, shortly after its CEO blamed higher pension expenses for recent losses. He didn't mention that much of the company's pension expense increase stemmed not from the regular pension plan, but from supplemental pension and savings plans provided only to top executives.

3. Lump-sum pension payouts provide smaller lumps than they should. Employers often act as though lump-sum pension payouts are a special perk. They know that most people are predisposed to prefer money now to money later. The employers may neglect to mention that the lump-sum payouts may be worth significantly less than the present value of the monthly pension checks they replace because of the way formulas are calculated.

Example: An IBM employee was offered a $71,500 lump sum in lieu of her pension. Before accepting, she took the offer to a financial adviser—who calculated that the true value of her pension based on her life expectancy was $101,000.

Lowball lump-sum offers may not violate federal laws that are designed to protect employees from illegal pension reductions when employees voluntarily choose the lump-sum option.

4. We're the reason your pension plan is underfunded. Employers with underfunded pension plans often blame stock market losses, low interest rates and retirees' longer life spans for the plans' predicament. In truth, many pension plans are underfunded partly because employers have siphoned billions of dollars out of the plans over the years and/or failed to fully fund the plans.

Examples: Numerous employers, including Delta Air Lines, United Airlines, General Motors and Ford Motor Company, have used pension-plan assets to fund buyouts and pay termination benefits when cutting their workforces. Some other companies even used pension money to pay for executive parachutes (compensation for executives who lose their jobs).

5. We can break the law with near impunity when we slash your retiree benefits. Pension law does not allow retirees and employees to sue for punitive damages or compensation for pain and suffering when their retiree benefits are illegally denied to them. They can sue only to reclaim the improperly eliminated benefits—and pension lawsuits tend to be so lengthy and expensive that these cases are rarely pursued.

6. We might transfer your pension to a company that you never worked for. Pension obligations sometimes are transferred from one company to another when a unit is sold. Companies that acquire pensions feel no loyalty to retirees who never worked for them and often cut their benefits. And many companies look for potential overpayments, and if they find overpayments, they don't just reduce future benefits—they typically demand repayment of the prior overpayments.

Example: A retired corporate jet pilot suffering from cancer received a letter from the company that had recently acquired his pension claiming that he had been overpaid and owed $31,904. When the pilot died two years later, the company made his widow repay his remaining debt.

7. Our retiree health-care promises can't be trusted. Many retirees who were promised retiree health insurance covering ages 55 to 65—or coverage to supplement Medicare after age 65—now are receiving excuses instead of insurance. Employers are eliminating retiree health benefits or forcing retirees to pay huge premiums to obtain it.

Example: General Motors cut its retiree health coverage even though it had given its employees brochures specifying that this coverage would be provided "at GM's expense for your lifetime."

Companies can get away with this because they bury "reservation of rights" clauses deep in the legalese of benefit plan documents. These clauses say that the company reserves the right to make changes to the plan. The plan description takes legal precedence over any verbal or written promises about future benefits made to employees.

8. We have a life insurance policy on you and will profit when you die. Hundreds of employers, including Nestlé, Walt Disney, Walmart and Bank of America, bought billions of dollars of life insurance covering millions of workers. Many companies claim that they use the policies to pay for retiree health benefits, but in fact, they use the policies to finance executive pay and pensions.

WHAT YOU CAN DO

Individual employees are powerless to stop much of what's happening, but there are some things they can do...

- **Request a copy of the Summary Plan Description from the employer's benefits department.** This document lays out the details of the pension plan.
- **Contact the Pension Rights Center,** a nonprofit based in Washington, DC, if you experience a problem with your pension plan (202-296-3776, *www.pensionrights.org*). Explain your problem, and ask if someone there can put you in contact with a pension expert in your area who can supply free advice.
- **Hire an actuary to examine your options before accepting a lump-sum pension offer.** Select "Find an Actuary" on the Web site of the American Academy of Actuaries (202-223-8196, *www.actuary.org*).

Know Your Plan

Pension-plan changes may entitle employees to compensation if a company misrepresents the effects of the changes in a way that makes them seem beneficial when in fact they reduce benefits for some workers. The US Supreme Court says employees may be awarded damages that will bring them up to the level they were told to expect. But if there is a conflict between the summary of a pension plan, which is given to all employees, and the plan document itself, which employees rarely see, the plan document's terms remain in effect.

What to do: Be sure you thoroughly understand any plan changes that your employer makes or proposes. Consult a knowledgeable attorney if necessary.

The Wall Street Journal

Sneaky Fees Can Reduce Your 401(K) by 10%—But These New Rules Will Help You Fix That

Peter Philipp, CFP, CFA, who specializes in employee benefits and investment management for businesses and individuals at Cambridge Investment Research, Inc. Based in San Francisco, he is an instructor in wealth management with the UC Berkeley Personal Financial Planning program. *www.cambridgesf.com*

Employee retirement plans have drawbacks as well as advantages. Several new rules from two departments of the federal government—Labor and Treasury—are designed to reduce some of the drawbacks and provide new opportunities.

Here's a closer look at how your retirement plan is about to change and what you can do...

FEE DISCLOSURES

An AARP study last year found that 71% of 401(k) participants are unaware that they are paying any fees at all in their 401(k) plans, even though those fees can have a major impact on their retirement nest eggs.

Example: Paying an extra 0.5% in annual fees throughout a 30-year career can reduce the amount in a 401(k) at retirement by 10%, according to the fund company Vanguard.

The Labor Department has issued new rules that start within the next few months that are meant to make it easier to figure out how much you're paying in fees and expenses in 401(k) plans and in 403(b) plans that are covered by the Employee Retirement Income Security Act (ERISA). *Here are some of the fees you'll be hearing about...*

- **Administrative fees are what you pay just to participate in your 401(k) plan.** These include recordkeeping and accounting expenses, among other costs. Although employees at large companies often are not charged these fees, employees at smaller companies typically are. An employee at a company with 10 employees might be charged an amount ranging from $50 to $200 per year.

What's new: Any administrative fees imposed on plan participants now must be revealed in the annual disclosure statement. When plan providers debit these fees from participant accounts, they also must be clearly listed in the "account activity" section of the next quarterly statement.

What to do: If you're charged significantly more than $50 per year (perhaps $100 if you work for a company that has fewer than 10 employees), encourage your employer to explore lower-cost 401(k) providers. Suggest that your coworkers make the same request.

• **Asset-based fees are what you pay to invest in specific mutual funds (or other investments) in your 401(k).** They are a percentage of the amount invested and can vary significantly. When insurance companies manage 401(k) plans, they typically impose a "wrap charge"—sometimes called an "asset charge"—of as much as 1% or 2% annually on top of mutual fund fees. That charge often has not been disclosed to plan participants.

What's new: The fees and expenses charged in each investment now must be clearly disclosed in a chart for easy comparison. Annual expenses also must be listed both as a percentage and as a dollar figure per $1,000 invested. Any wrap charges must be included. Shareholder fees, such as up-front sales commissions and redemption fees, also must be listed.

What to do: Try to avoid investments that impose annual fees in excess of 1%. (It's reasonable to adjust that down to 0.5% for bond funds...or up to 1.5% to 2% for foreign stock funds.) Index funds should charge much less. Unfortunately, 401(k) plans typically offer very limited investment options, and there might not be any options appropriate for your goals that fall below these fee levels. If so, request that your employer seek out a 401(k) provider offering lower-cost investments. Also, check whether your 401(k) offers a "brokerage window" that allows you to invest in mutual funds or other investments that are not specifically included in the plan. If so, you can use this window to invest in lower-fee investment options.

Warning: You generally cannot arrange automatic contributions through a brokerage window, so you will have to make each share purchase yourself. Some 401(k) providers charge either a flat fee or a per-trade commission for using the brokerage window. Find out if yours does.

• **Individual service fees are charged when you take advantage of optional 401(k) plan services,** such as borrowing money from your account or requesting a check via overnight mail.

What's new: These fees now will be summarized in a straightforward table.

What to do: Refer to this table before requesting any special services.

NEW ANNUITY OPTIONS

In decades past, it was common for traditional pensions to provide retirees with a check each month for as long as they lived. Now most retirement plans are 401(k)s, which offer no guarantee of income for life. And even retirees who still have traditional pensions often opt for the flexibility of a lump-sum payout rather than monthly checks.

That lack of guaranteed retirement income—together with longer life spans, low bond interest rates and recent declines in the value of homes—has greatly increased the odds that retirees will outlive their savings.

The Treasury Department has proposed rules to reduce that risk...

• **Longevity annuities would be allowed in 401(k)s and IRAs.** Longevity annuities provide an income stream that starts when the buyer reaches a fairly advanced age—usually 80 or 85—and continues for the remainder of the buyer's life (or the life of the buyer and his/her spouse, in the case of a joint-life longevity annuity). These can be a lot more affordable than an immediate annuity that begins making payments soon after your initial investment.

Example: A 65-year-old might have to pay $277,500 to purchase an annuity that pays $20,000 per year starting immediately...or just $35,200 for a longevity annuity that pays out $20,000 per year starting at age 85, according to a report issued by the President's Council of Economic Advisers.

Trouble is, it currently is difficult or impossible to purchase a longevity annuity in a 401(k), 403(b), 457 plan or IRA—they run afoul of required minimum distribution (RMD) rules that force investors to begin taking money out of tax-deferred accounts starting at age 70½.

What's new: The proposed rules would exempt assets invested in longevity annuities from RMD calculations—as long as the annuity costs no more than 25% of the account balance...and as long as the cost of the annuity is no more than $100,000...and starts making payments no later than age 85.

What to do: A longevity annuity might be a viable option in certain cases—say, if you're healthy and come from a long-lived family. But that doesn't mean you should jump at the one offered in your 401(k).

While the plan provider might have used its market power to obtain better annuity terms than you could obtain on your own, it also is possible that you could find a better longevity annuity on the open market, outside your 401(k).

• **Compare the costs and monthly payments offered by several insurers before making any choice.** Consider the financial health of the insurance company offering the annuity, too. If this company goes out of business, the value of your investment could be severely diminished—protections for annuity investors in the case of insurance company insolvency vary by state but often do not exceed $100,000, which might be much less than what you expected your longevity annuity to provide. (See *www.ambest.com* and *www.standardandpoors.com* for ratings of insurers.) Married people should strongly consider a joint-life longevity annuity, which makes payments until both spouses pass away.

Be aware that today's low interest rates mean longevity annuities currently are relatively expensive. There's something to be said for delaying a purchase or seeking out another way to ensure that you don't outlive your retirement savings, such as delaying the start of Social Security benefits, which increases your monthly checks by 7% to 8% for every year you delay from age 62 to age 70.

• **Those with traditional pensions will be allowed to take two forms of payment.** Currently, employees with old-fashioned pensions are offered a choice upon retirement—either monthly payments or a lump-sum payout.

What's new: The Treasury proposal would make it simpler for employers to offer the option of taking part of the pension as a monthly check and part as a lump sum, something that currently is difficult and rare.

What to do: Taking part of your pension as an annuity for safety and part as a lump sum for flexibility could make some sense. But it's wise to hire an actuary to examine the plan's lump-sum offer first to make sure that it is as large as it should be. There's a lot of money on the line, and it is very hard for the average person to gauge whether he/she is getting a good deal. Unfortunately, the lump sums offered by pension plans sometimes are significantly lower than the present value of the monthly pension checks surrendered to acquire them.

401(K) Plan Participants Gaining More Access to Cost Details and Options

Under new rules from the US Labor Department, mutual fund firms and other 401(k) retirement plan administrators must disclose more details about fees and performance. That should allow employers to negotiate better deals and employees to request more cost-efficient plans, saving them substantial amounts of money over the years. Also, the Treasury Department has proposed rules to make it easier for the plans to offer participants "longevity" annuities that would allow them to get a guaranteed income stream beginning at an advanced age, say 80 or 85. Another proposed rule would make it simpler for traditional "defined-benefit" pension plans to offer new retirees a combination of a lump-sum cash payout and a fixed-income lifetime annuity.

The Wall Street Journal

When to Consider a Roth

Consider converting now to a Roth IRA to save on taxes. When you convert a traditional IRA to a Roth, you pay income tax on the entire amount converted. By converting at a time when stock prices have plunged, as they have recently, you likely will pay less in taxes. Then you never have to pay taxes again on assets in the Roth. To maximize your flexibility, set up at least two separate Roth accounts, dividing them into more conservative assets, such as bonds, and more aggressive investments. That way, if one asset class—say, stocks—continues to fall after the conversion, you can undo, or "recharacterize," that particular Roth back into a traditional IRA and then, after a waiting period, convert it again to a Roth with an even lower tax bill.

Ed Slott, CPA, founder and president of Ed Slott & Company, a financial consulting firm specializing in IRAs, Rockville Centre, New York. He is author of *Parlay Your IRA into a Family Fortune* (Penguin). *www.irahelp.com*

IRA Limits

Higher income limits were established for tax-deductible IRA contributions in 2012. Single filers and heads of household who participate in retirement plans at work can deduct the maximum IRA contribution if their modified adjusted gross income is $58,000 or less…and receive a partial deduction if income is up to $68,000. In 2011, those income limits were $56,000 for a full deduction and $66,000 for a partial deduction. For both years, the maximum contribution you can make is $5,000—or $6,000 if you are at least 50 years old by the end of the year. Rules for married couples filing jointly, when only one is covered in the workplace, are complex. If the spouse making the contribution is covered, the deduction is phased out when income is between $92,000 and $112,000. If the IRA contributor is not covered at work but the spouse is, the deduction is phased out when income is between $173,000 and $183,000. For more information, search for "2012 IRA Contribution" at *www.IRS.gov* or call 800-829-1040.

Barbara Weltman, Esq., an attorney in Millwood, New York, and publisher of *Big Ideas for Small Business*, a free monthly e-newsletter. *www.barbaraweltman.com*

Reverse Mortgage?

Be sure to name both spouses on a reverse mortgage. In a reverse mortgage, the home owner gets regular monthly payments by borrowing against the equity in the home. Naming only one spouse puts the other at risk if the named spouse dies, because death is one trigger for the mortgage to immediately come due. If a surviving spouse who is not named on the reverse mortgage wants to keep the home, he/she must pay off the full loan—even if it is higher than the house's appraised value.

Kiplinger's Retirement Report, 1729 H St. NW, Washington, DC 20006. *www.kiplinger.com*

New Rules

Reverse mortgages are now harder to get because two big providers stopped making the loans. Wells Fargo and Bank of America cited rising risk because of declining home values and higher property taxes and insurance costs. Also, the US Department of Housing and Urban Development (HUD) is expected to propose new rules allowing lenders to reject more applications. For a list of HUD-approved reverse-mortgage lenders, call 800-569-4287 or go to *www.hud.gov.*

Robert Siefert, CFP, wealth adviser and principal at Modera Wealth Management, Boston. *www.moderawealth.com*

Elder Abuse

Financial abuse of the elderly now costs seniors $2.9 billion a year—a 12% increase since 2008. Crimes involving strangers make up half the reported cases...crimes involving family, friends and neighbors account for one-third...and exploitation by businesses is 12%. Most victims are ages 80 to 89, live alone and need some help with health care or home maintenance. Women are nearly twice as likely as men to be victims. Crimes range from purse snatching to forged checks, stolen credit cards and asset transfers.

What to do: Pay close attention to the financial affairs of parents and elderly relatives to reduce the chance of abuse.

MetLife Mature Market Institute, Westport, Connecticut.

Tax Deduction

There are tax breaks for residents of continuing-care retirement communities, such as assisted-living facilities. Such costs, including onetime entrance fees and monthly fees, can be written off with other medical deductions. A percentage of these costs counts as medical expenses even if the resident lives independently and does not require medical care. Taxpayers are allowed to write off medical expenses only to the extent that they exceed 7.5% of adjusted gross income, but because the cost of continuing-care communities can be quite high, this can be a significant deduction.

SmartMoney.com

Amazing Discounts If You're 50 or Older

David Smidt, founder and president of SeniorDiscounts.com, a Web site based in Albuquerque, New Mexico, that tracks discounts available to those age 50 and up.

Discounts for older consumers have become more common, more generous and more available, even to people in their 50s.

Example: Most Banana Republic stores offer 10% off for those 50 and older who request a senior discount at the register, although some individual stores may have different policies (*www.bananarepublic.com*).

In many cases, you have to ask whether so-called senior discounts are available. Most stores don't have signs or brochures featuring senior discounts. And only rarely do employees volunteer the information, perhaps because they don't want to offend customers. With discount offers frequently reaching 10%, 20% or more, it's worth asking in most places if a discount for seniors is available.

Caution: Hotel chains, car-rental agencies and other travel-related companies frequently offer senior discounts, but lower prices often can be obtained by going through a travel deals Web site such as Orbitz.com or Hotels.com.

Here's a look at some of the best, newest and most widely available senior discounts. Confirm the details with an employee before shopping because discount programs occasionally change, sometimes require preregistration and might not be offered by all stores in a chain or on every product in a store.

SUPERMARKETS

An increasing number of supermarket chains now offer senior discounts, in part to lure older shoppers away from low-priced chains such as Walmart. Many local food co-ops offer senior discounts as well. *Among the chains with discounts...*

- **Earth Fare organic supermarkets** typically offer a 5% discount on "select days" to those either age 55 and older or 60 and older. *www.earthfare.com.*

• **Fred Meyer stores** offer those age 55 and older 10% off select goods on the first Tuesday of each month. *www.fredmeyer.com.*

• **Fry's Food Stores Senior Rewards Program** offers customers age 55 and older a 10% discount on most purchases on the first Wednesday of each month. *www.frysfood.com.*

• **Harris Teeter's program** offers those age 60 and older a 5% discount on Thursdays. *www.harristeeter.com.*

• **Kroger supermarkets** in selected areas often offer customers who are at least 60, depending on each store's version of the policy, such as 10% off most purchases on the first Wednesday of every month. *www.kroger.com.*

• **Shop 'n Save supermarkets** often offer a 10% discount one day a week to shoppers age 55 and older. *www.shopnsave.com.*

AUTO MAINTENANCE

Several major auto-care chains offer seniors discounts in at least some of their branches...

• **Jiffy Lube service centers** often offer a 10% senior discount on parts and/or service. At some Jiffy Lubes, the discount is available to those as young as 50, but at others, customers must be at least 60. *www.jiffylube.com.*

• **Midas service centers** in many locations offer 10% senior discounts on parts and/or service. The minimum age requirement ranges from 50 to 60. *www.midas.com.*

• **STS Tire & Auto Centers Silver Club** provides a 5% discount on tires, services and accessories to customers age 55 and older. *www.ststire.com.*

DINING AND ENTERTAINMENT

Many movie theaters have long offered excellent senior discounts, often 25% or more. But they're not the only entertainment option for seniors in search of discounts.

• **Symphonies, ballets and plays** often offer wonderful senior discounts, in some cases more than 50%.

Example: Tickets to the Houston Ballet that ordinarily cost $88 (Grand Tier) or $148 (Orchestra Center) cost just $17 or $40 for those 65 or older during the 90 minutes prior to select shows, availability permitting. *www.houstonballet.org.*

• **Museums, zoos and aquariums** almost always offer seniors a few dollars or more off standard admission rates.

Examples: Those 65 and older get $4 off at the Museum of Modern Art (*www.moma.org*) in New York City...$6.50 off at the Guggenheim (*www.guggenheim.org*)...and $3 off at the San Francisco Zoo (*www.sfzoo.org).*

• **Sporting events occasionally provide senior discounts.** This is most common with minor league sports, but a few major league baseball teams and NHL hockey teams have senior discount programs, too.

Example: The New York Yankees Senior Citizen Games Ticket Special offers fans age 60 and up $5 tickets in designated-seating areas for select Monday through Thursday games, a fraction of what Yankees tickets normally cost. These tickets must be purchased at stadium ticket windows in the two hours preceding the game and are subject to availability. *http://newyork.yankees.mlb.com.*

Call ticket offices or explore team Web sites for details. Be aware that senior discounts are very rare with NBA basketball and unheard of with NFL football.

• **The US National Park Service America the Beautiful Pass provides access to all national parks and federal recreational lands.** It normally costs $80 per year, but those at least 62 years old can obtain a lifetime Senior Pass for just $10 plus a $10 document processing fee. This Senior Pass also provides discounts on park services such as camping and boat launching, and it even lets you bring up to three other adults into the park in your car at no additional fee, even if those other adults are younger than 62. Senior Passes can be obtained in person at a park or by calling 888-275-8747, extension 1, or at *www.store.usgs.gov/pass*.

Note: Many state parks offer senior discounts for admission, although some states are under pressure to reduce the discounts.

Example: Colorado recently increased the cost of an Aspen Leaf senior citizen annual pass to $60 from $35 and to $300 from $175 for a lifetime pass.

- **Restaurant chains typically give senior discounts of 10% or so.** This is most common in cheaper restaurants, but attractive discounts are available at some nicer establishments, too.

Examples: Elephant Bar, an appealing "global grill" restaurant with dozens of locations in California and elsewhere, offers a Senior Explorer VIP Card that provides 20% off food purchases to those 60 or older. Beverages, lunch specials and certain other purchases are not included (*www.elephantbar.com*). If you are 60 or older, Applebee's Neighborhood Grill & Bar may give you a 10% or 15% discount. These discounts are not available at all Applebee's, however. *www.applebees.com*.

RETAILERS

Certain retail chains offer senior discounts on specific days of the week...

- **Kohl's stores typically offer 15% discounts** every Wednesday to shoppers age 60 or older, but they may not cover marked-down items. *www.kohls.com*.
- **Bealls stores offer discounts to people as young as age 50.** *www.beallsflorida.com*.
- **Dressbarn stores typically offer 10% off to those age 62 and older,** often on Tuesday or Wednesday. *www.dressbarn.com*.
- **CJ Banks plus-size women's clothing stores offer 10% off** to those age 60 and older every Wednesday. *www.cjbanks.com*.
- **Ross Dress for Less stores,** which sell clothing and footwear, offer 10% off every Tuesday to those age 55 and older. *www.rossstores.com*.

MUNICIPAL SERVICES AND UTILITIES

Some municipalities now offer senior residents discount rates on services such as water, sewer or trash pickup. A few regions even have negotiated lower rates for seniors on utilities provided by private companies, such as electricity, natural gas, phone service and cable television.

Call the phone number listed on your utility and municipal services bills, and ask if there is a senior discount program.

Examples: El Paso residents age 65 and older can obtain a 20% discount on garbage pickup (*www.elpasotexas.gov*). Chicago residents age 65 and older often qualify for a Senior Citizen Sewer Service Charge Exemption, eliminating the sewer portion of their water bills (*www.cityofchicago.org*).

In some regions, older residents can obtain a discount on their property taxes, too. Call your city assessor—or whatever city agency is listed on your property tax bills—to ask if any such program exists in your area.

Senior Fare Savings

Airfare discounts for seniors still are available despite cutbacks. Though not always the cheapest fares, discounted senior fares typically carry few restrictions...are fully refundable any time before the flight...and often can be obtained at the last minute. Only Southwest Airlines offers discounts on all domestic routes to passengers age 65 and older. American, United and Delta offer senior discounts on some flights. Call the airlines directly to find these fares.

Tom Parsons, cofounder and CEO of BestFares.com, a Web site that monitors travel-related discounts, Arlington, Texas.

How to Enjoy Life Until 100 (and Beyond!)

Roy Rowan, 91, former correspondent for *Time*, *Life* and *Fortune* magazines. His latest book is *Never Too Late: A 90-Year-Old's Pursuit of a Whirlwind Life* (Lyons). He lives in Greenwich, Connecticut. *www.royrowan.com*

At 91, Roy Rowan is reconciled to the fact that young women offer him their seats on the bus—but that doesn't mean he's ready to accept those offers. He's still steady on his feet and living an active, productive, exciting life. He doesn't run marathons anymore, but he does still enjoy surf casting for fish. He's not a war correspondent any longer, but he's still answering fan mail from readers of *Chasing the Dragon*, a book about the Chinese Revolution that he wrote when he was in his mid-80s.

We interviewed Rowan on how we can stay young. He says that as long as you are still in reasonable health, you can continue to enjoy a lively life at any age. *Here's how...*

ACT YOUNG

Among the activities that help keep me young...

• **Working.** There's no substitute for work, even if you don't need the money and even if it's just part-time. Work provides a sense of accomplishment and usefulness that keeps us feeling young and relevant.

I'm fortunate to have a job—writing—that I can continue into my 90s. Those whose careers are not so easily extended postretirement still can seek out ways to continue the elements of their career that they found rewarding. Those elements might include working with a team toward a goal...solving problems...providing a useful service to the community...or receiving thanks from satisfied customers.

Volunteering often is an excellent way to obtain these things. A part-time job—even in a low-level position—is another option.

• **Staying in contact even with those you have no obvious reason to stay in contact with.** We tend to leave most of our professional contacts behind when we retire and many of our personal contacts behind when we relocate. Don't. Save your old address books, and keep in touch via e-mail, phone calls, letters and cards. The network of contacts we establish over the decades is among our most valuable possessions.

The larger our circle of acquaintances, the more opportunities we have to socialize and the lower the odds that we will wind up lonely when our close friends pass away or retire to different regions. Our contacts even could provide future opportunities for adventure or projects.

Example: Though we were not close friends, I remained in contact with David Kennerly, the Pulitzer Prize–winning photographer. We had worked together covering the Vietnam war for *Time* magazine. He later threw me a party to help cheer me up after a bout with cancer.

• **Being dignified.** Remain fit, dress well and shave every day. Looking our best helps us feel better about ourselves and our place in the world as we age. It also improves how others see us and treat us. Old people who seem dignified get treated with dignity. Those who let themselves go tend to be ignored or avoided.

• **Remaining abreast of current events.** Knowing the latest news allows us to contribute something interesting to conversations, reducing the odds that we will fall into the old-age conversation traps of complaining about our health or endlessly rehashing the past. When old people fall into these traps, young people avoid them. That's unfortunate, because interacting with the young is an excellent way to continue to feel youthful.

Making friends with younger people has an additional advantage as well—it allows us to remain social if we outlive most of those in our own generation. These days, many of my wife's and my best friends are a generation younger than we are.

THINK YOUNG

How we think about the world in our later years helps determine whether we remain young in spirit...

• **Be optimistic and resilient.** A major part of remaining youthful is believing that happiness and success lie ahead. That can be a challenge for older people. It's easy to fret that our best years are behind us and to feel crushed by setbacks from which we lack the time and/or earning potential to recover. But setbacks are inevitable as we get older—old people suffer health problems, and our friends die—so thinking that way is a sure path to unhappiness.

The secret is to reframe setbacks so that they seem like reasons for gratitude. There is always more than one way to look at a situation. I try to choose the most positive way.

Examples: I've had cancer twice. Rather than become distraught about my situation, I was thankful that I didn't have even worse health problems that others face. I've also lost many close friends. Rather than wallow in despair, I was grateful for the years that I had with those people and for the many friends I still have.

In China, they don't ask, "How old are you?" They ask, "What is your glorious age?" That's a wonderful example of reframing old age in a positive light.

• **Make plans.** Drifting through day after day without plans or obligations might sound relaxing, but it's a dismal, uninspiring way to live. Plans give us a reason to get up in the morning and do something with our day. They keep us motivated and give us purpose, which keeps us young.

Example: Comedian George Burns made plans to perform on his 100th birthday years in advance. "I can't die," he quipped. "I'm booked." And he did continue to work until shortly before his death in 1996 at the age of 100.

• **Stop being so analytical.** Older people are prone to paralysis by analysis. We often fail to act until we have thought through every possibility. Maybe this is because we've seen over the years that decisions can have long-lasting repercussions and not always good ones. But worrying about every decision does not generally lead to better decisions—it leads only to more anxiety. And the more we think before acting, the more likely we are to think ourselves out of the sorts of new experiences and new challenges that can help keep us young.

That doesn't mean that we should make rash decisions, but it does mean that once we have mulled things over a bit, we should trust our instincts. By the time we reach old age, our instincts have decades of experience to draw upon and usually steer us toward what we really want if we let them.

Example: An 89-year-old engineer from Florida named Charles Smith followed his gut and visited both the North and South poles, a youthful adventure that most older people would think themselves out of.

• **Let yourself reflect.** Time spent thinking about the past is not wasted time. It's an opportunity to remind ourselves of everything we have accomplished and everything we are capable of accomplishing. Thinking about past successes can bring happiness to sad times. Our past even can provide ideas for the future. Just don't let the past absorb too much of the present. I get up every morning at 5:30 or 6:00, make a cup of tea, sit in an easy chair and think about the past. It's one of my favorite times of the day, and it usually leaves me more appreciative for all that I have done and all that I have. But once this morning ritual is over, I stop thinking about the past and I move on to my current plans for the rest of the day.

The Easiest Computers Ever—Simple to Use, Right Out of the Box

Jim Miller, an advocate for senior citizens, writes Savvy Senior, a weekly information column syndicated in more than 400 newspapers and magazines nationwide. Based in Norman, Oklahoma, he also offers a free senior news service at *www.savvysenior.org.*

For seniors and other people who want a home computer that is easier to use than most models available today, there are several user-friendly machines designed specifically for you. These computers provide simplified and senior-friendly software applications...extra-large keys and type...and a range of customer-assistance plans.

The very best options now...

TELIKIN TOUCH-SCREEN

By simply touching the clearly labeled on-screen option of your choice with your finger (you don't need a mouse to navigate), you can get instant access to the Web, e-mail, games, video chat, photo sharing, news, weather and more.

• **The Telikin desktop computer** is available in two sizes—an 18.6-inch LCD touch-screen with a 320-gigabyte hard drive that costs $699...and a 20-inch LCD touch-screen with 500 gigabytes (useful to store lots of videos and pictures) for $999. All Telikin computers come with built-in speakers, a Web camera, microphone, keyboard and mouse. They also offer a unique "tech buddy" (remote access) feature that allows a designated friend or family member to access your Telikin from his/her computer, so that he can help guide you through any questions or problems that you might have.

Running on the Linux operating system instead of Windows or Mac OS, the Telikin is more virus-resistant than standard computers and comes with a 60-day trial period, a one-year warranty and free customer support for the first 30 days ($9.95 per month afterward). 800-230-3881, *www.telikin.com.*

Note: Telikin has a partnership with first-STREET (800-704-1209, *www.firststreetonline.com*), a direct marketing company specializing in products for seniors, which also is selling the 20-inch Telikin for $999 but has rebranded it as the "WOW! Computer for Seniors."

SENIOR PC

• **HP SeniorPC** is a brand of Hewlett-Packard computer that comes completely set up and ready to use right out of the box—no need to configure software settings to get it going. It comes equipped with software called OnTimeRx that can remind users to take medications and keep appointments. The desktop version includes a mouse, a 17-inch monitor and speakers. It also includes the Keys-U-See keyboard, a high-contrast keyboard with bright yellow large keys on a black background and one-touch Internet and media control buttons. Both the desktop and laptop versions come with a color printer. 888-640-1999, *www.enablemart.com.*

There are several models...

• For ease of use and speech controls, the Autopilot desktop computer offers speech-to-text capabilities that let you write letters, e-mails and documents by speaking into the computer's microphone (sold separately)...and text-to-speech capabilities that will read e-mails, documents and Web pages to you aloud. The PC costs $1,125. EnableMart also offers an Autopilot computer in a laptop edition for $1,165.

• For those with impaired vision, there is the Vision Plus model. It comes preconfigured with screen-magnification software, a high-visibility Keys-U-See keyboard (for the desktop model) and an all-in-one printer/scanner for scanning in books, e-mail and other reading materials to be magnified. $1,255 for the Vision Plus desktop or $1,895 for the laptop version.

APPLE IPAD

While the iPad 3 tablet computer is not designed specifically for seniors, its simple iOS operating system makes it easy to understand and use. The 9.5-inch screen has such high resolution that it is great for aging eyes, and its thin (0.37 inches) and lightweight (1.44 lb.) design makes it easy to hold and convenient to carry. And everything is done simply by touching the screen—there's no mouse or external keyboard.

All Apple iPads come with an array of built-in accessibility tools (see *www.apple.com/accessibility)* that can help seniors with vision and/or hearing impairments. Apple includes a one-year warranty and phone technical support for the first 90 days. Prices range from $499 to $829 (for models that come with 4G connectivity). 800-692-7753, *www.apple.com.*

Your Heirs Will Lose Money If You Don't Take These Steps Now

Chad J. Norfolk, CFP, principal and lead adviser with Financial Advantage, Inc., a financial-planning, retirement-planning and investment-management company based in Columbia, Maryland. *www.investfail.com*

If your spouse and/or other heirs cannot quickly figure out your financial affairs after you pass away or become incapacitated, you won't just leave them frustrated—you might leave them with less money. Accounts and other assets could be overlooked...and financial penalties could be incurred, such as those for not taking required distributions from tax-deferred retirement accounts.

State treasuries and other government agencies currently hold more than $32 billion in unclaimed financial assets, including brokerage and bank accounts, insurance policy proceeds and unredeemed savings bonds. Much of these proceeds belonged to now-deceased account holders whose heirs were unaware that the accounts existed.

In the past, organizing affairs for heirs usually meant little more than telling them where your will and the key to the safe-deposit box were stashed. It has become more complicated in today's world of online accounts...automatic withdrawals and bill payments...and dozens of passwords and PIN codes.

Compiling financial information for heirs can make for a dull day, and many people are reluctant to tackle death-related issues—but most people sleep a little easier when the task is complete. It feels good to know that we've done all we can to ensure our families will be able to carry on when we are gone.

SEVEN LISTS YOUR HEIRS WILL NEED

Below are seven lists you need to compile that will make your surviving heirs' lives easier and help preserve your wealth for your family. Create these lists, staple them together, store them in a home safe if you have one and update the lists at least once each year.

If you don't have a home safe, you can store them in a desk or a file cabinet. But don't put them at the very top or front of a drawer where a burglar or an untrustworthy family member might find them. Bury them deep among other paperwork, then share the file's name and location with your spouse and multiple dependable heirs to ensure that it is found when needed.

Alternatively, you could ask a trusted family member or two to store copies of your lists for you—but lists held outside your home are inconvenient to update.

Warning: A bank safe-deposit box is not an ideal storage place for these lists. Your heirs might be denied fast access to this box after your death.

The seven lists...

1. Your financial accounts, including investment, bank and credit card accounts. Include the name of each institution, the type of account, the account number, contact phone number and password for each. Explain where account statements and checkbooks are stored.

2. Your financial professionals, including financial planners, insurance agents, estate-planning attorneys, investment advisers and tax preparers. Provide contact information for each and a brief explanation of what he/she does for you and how he could assist heirs.

3. Your recurring bills, such as bills for utilities and insurance, as well as loan payments. Otherwise your heirs might miss payments, triggering penalties, repossessions or policy cancellations. Make special note of any recurring bills that arrive in your e-mail inbox rather than your mailbox—heirs are particularly likely to miss these.

Also list any recurring automatic withdrawals taken directly from your bank accounts so that your heirs don't close these accounts or draw down balances without making other arrangements to pay.

This list of recurring bills and automatic withdrawals also will help your heirs cancel any that are no longer needed.

Include a note on this list recommending that after your death your heirs contact providers of any no-longer-needed insurance policies. The heirs should check whether your estate is entitled to a refund for the unused portion of the most recent payment. Refunds can reach into the hundreds, particularly with expensive long-term-care insurance policies and any premiums paid annually or semiannually rather than monthly. Your heirs also should ask about refunds when they cancel any prepaid utility accounts.

4. Every e-mail address you use, along with account passwords. This will help your heirs access any online bills and account statements and notify acquaintances of your incapacitation or death.

5. Money that should come in during your life and/or after your death. This includes pensions, annuities, Social Security benefits, veterans benefits, payments on loans that you have made and life and disability insurance policy benefits.

6. Minimum annual distributions that you are required to take from your retirement accounts. Each year, note on this list when you take these distributions. Your estate might face steep penalties if your heirs fail to take these distributions from your accounts on your behalf in the year of your death or incapacitation if you have not done so already.

7. Locations of your important documents, including your will and other estate-planning documents, recent tax returns, mortgage and other loan documents, deeds and titles to vehicles and other property, vehicle registrations, insurance contracts, birth certificate, military discharge papers, marriage licenses and divorce decrees. List any safe-deposit boxes as well, along with the location of the keys.

Plan Carefully

Seniors expect to help their kids financially. Half of those age 55 or older expect to give family members financial assistance—and 70% of those think they will have to aid their adult children. This reverses previous patterns in which older adults expected their children to take care of them in later years.

Also: Multigenerational living arrangements are becoming more common.

What to do: Think through your retirement goals in light of the possibility of having to help other family members or having them live with you.

Ken Dychtwald, founder, Age Wave, which specializes in aging issues, Emeryville, California. *www.agewave.com*

Establish Trust

Although IRAs and other retirement accounts are protected from creditors under federal bankruptcy law and bankruptcy laws in most states, once they are inherited, they might not be protected anymore. A number of recent court decisions have held that these accounts are not protected, and several state legislatures are currently considering this issue.

A more protective approach would be to establish a "conduit" trust, whose assets are protected as long as they are in the trust. Such a trust must be established during your lifetime, and the trust must be named as the beneficiary of your retirement accounts. Your son then can be the beneficiary of the trust and can receive the Required Minimum Distribution (RMD) that each retirement account generates each year. However, such distributions, once received by the beneficiary, might not be protected from creditors anymore.

Gideon Rothschild, Esq., partner, Moses & Singer, LLP, New York City, and adjunct professor in estate planning, University of Miami School of Law. *www.mosessinger.com*

13

Travel Secrets

The Secrets Hotels Don't Want You to Know

Hotels are supposed to be restful oases away from the stresses of the road. Instead, they often are sources of stress for travelers. Some hotels are not as appealing as their ads or Web sites suggest...many pad their bills...and/or they suffer from security problems or bedbug infestations.

What hotel guests need to know...

WATCH OUT

• **Online hotel reviews and descriptions often are not what they seem.** Hotel managers—and the marketing companies they hire—sometimes pretend to be travelers and write phony rave reviews about their own hotels on travel Web sites such as TripAdvisor.com.

Negative hotel reviews are not necessarily on the level either. They sometimes are written by competing hotels or guests less interested in accuracy than in exacting revenge for perceived problems during their stays.

The descriptions and photos provided on hotels' own sites can be deceptive as well. Hotels that claim to be "minutes from the airport" or "steps from the beach" might be much farther away than those phrases imply. Photos of rooms might have been taken with lenses that make those rooms seem much larger than they are...and photos of views might crop out nearby highways or buildings.

What to do: Compare reviews by unbiased professional reviewers at LonelyPlanet.com, Oyster.com and my family's site, Frommers.com.

Pauline Frommer, creator of the *Pauline Frommer Spend Less, See More Guidebooks* (Wiley) and cohost of *The Travel Show,* a nationally syndicated radio show. She is two-time winner of the North American Travel Journalists Association's "Best Guidebook of the Year" award. The daughter of Arthur Frommer (founder of the famed Frommer's travel guides), she has been traveling extensively since she was four months old. For more, go to *www.frommers.com/pauline.*

• **High-end hotels now are the most likely to nickel-and-dime guests with excessive fees.** Travelers tend to assume that low-cost hotels are where excessive fees are likely. Nicer hotels seem above such tactics. In reality, most economy chains have learned that their budget-minded customers won't come back if they are charged too many fees, while luxury chains have learned that their guests tend not to complain about fees.

Example: WiFi is now free at most mid-priced and budget hotels, yet it often costs $10 to $12 per day at luxury hotels, sometimes even more.

In fact, luxury chains are dreaming up new fees all the time. Among the latest are porterage fees for carrying your bags to your room (on top of the tip you likely already paid the porter)...bag-check fees for asking the hotel to hold your luggage...groundskeeping surcharges...energy surcharges to cover the hotel's electricity bills...increasingly strict reservation-cancellation policies...and steep early check-in fees if you arrive before 3 or 4 pm. These fees often are not even disclosed when the service is provided.

What to do: Check the fine print, and/or call the hotel. Before making a reservation, ask whether any surcharges, such as resort fees or groundskeeping surcharges, will be added to your daily room rate, particularly when you are staying at an upscale hotel. Ask about fees before requesting any hotel service. Scan your bill upon checkout, and question fees that you don't understand or that you were not warned about in advance. Upscale hotels sometimes waive fees when guests politely complain about them, particularly when this complaining is done in the lobby in the presence of other guests.

If avoiding such fees is your top priority, skip the luxury hotels and stay at chains such as Microtel Inns & Suites (800-337-0044, *www.microtelinn.com*), an economy chain with hotels throughout the US that does extremely well in customer satisfaction surveys, in part because it keeps fees to a minimum. Microtel even offers free domestic phone calls.

• **Your luggage faces a greater bedbug danger than you do.** Bedbug bites can cause itchy red welts, but those welts will heal. The more substantial risk is that hotel bedbugs could hitch a ride back to your home on or in your luggage, then feast on you and your family again and again.

What to do: Place your luggage on a folding luggage rack with metal legs from the moment you enter your hotel room—never on a hotel bed, carpet or upholstered furniture. Bedbugs cannot climb metal. If there are not enough folding racks of this type for all of your luggage, a tile bathroom floor or entryway is the next best alternative. Dressers or desks are safer spots than beds or carpets, but bedbugs do sometimes infest hotel dressers or hide behind pictures or mirrors hung above this furniture.

The good news is that despite well-publicized recent bedbug outbreaks, the odds of encountering these pests in a US hotel room remain very low. *To improve your odds even further...*

• **Pull back a corner of your bedding when you first check in, and scan the seams of the mattress for tiny bugs or pepper-like droppings.** If you see any, immediately request a new room. Inspect the mattress in that room, too.

• **Inspect your luggage carefully inside and out when you return home.** Ideally, do this in the garage before the bags enter the living area of your home. Even if your hotel room was not infested, bedbugs might have climbed onto your bags in an airplane luggage compartment or carry-on compartment. For tips on spotting bedbugs and what to do if you find them, go to the Web site BedBugCentral.com.

• **Insider advice from a hotel concierge might not be on the level.** Hotel concierges sometimes steer guests to certain restaurants, bars and/or tourist attractions because they receive kickbacks from those establishments, not because they are the best in the region.

What to do: Check guidebooks and/or ask locals who seem knowledgeable.

• **Identity thieves have targeted hotel chain computers.** Major hotel chains, including Wyndham, Westin and Destination hotels, have experienced security breaches in recent years. High-tech crooks have learned that if they break into the computer system of one hotel in a chain, they often can access the entire chain's reservation records, obtaining the credit card and debit card data of tens of thousands of current and former guests.

What to do: Use a credit card, not a debit card, when you book a hotel room. Debit cards do not always provide the same level of consumer protection for fraudulent charges. Use just one credit card for all hotel reservations, if possible, so that only one card is at risk. Call that card's toll-free number, or pull up your account online, to check for suspicious account activity as soon as you return home, and scan subsequent statements carefully.

ON THE BRIGHT SIDE

• **Hotel loyalty programs are quietly improving as airline frequent-flier programs spiral downward.** Frequent-flier programs get all the attention, but good luck redeeming your miles for a ticket these days. Meanwhile, many hotel loyalty programs are adding perks for frequent guests such as breakfast, WiFi, room upgrades and later checkout times. It is rarely a problem to get a free room when you earn enough points in a hotel program. In fact, programs sometimes offer special deals that provide free rooms much sooner than you might expect.

Example: Choice Hotels recently offered program members a free night after just four nights as long as those four nights included stays in at least two locations.

What to do: Remain loyal to one or two chains when you travel, and sign up for their loyalty programs. Consider applying for these chains' cobranded credit cards, too, if they are offered—such cards often provide an accelerated path to loyalty program perks. Marriott's loyalty program receives high rankings in surveys, but the best hotel loyalty program for you is the one offered by the chain that you like the most, assuming that it has locations in the places you travel to most frequently.

Luxury Camping for Nature Lovers

David Troya, CEO of GlampingHub.com, a Web site that provides links to glamping sites and information about glamping-equipment manufacturers. Splitting his time between Sevilla, Spain, and San Francisco, he previously was general director of DiscoverSevilla, a Spanish travel company. *http://GlampingHub.com*

Some people dream of vacations at posh resorts...others of camp sites in the wild. "Glamping"—short for glamour camping—offers both.

On a glamping trip, your days might be spent hiking or rafting in the backcountry, but your nights could be spent sleeping on fresh sheets in a soft bed. Though you might be many miles from civilization, your meals could be prepared by an elite chef, and there might be hot water for your morning shower.

Here's what you need to know before you give glamping a try...

WHAT TO EXPECT

There's little consensus about what level of luxury the term "glamping" implies, which can make it difficult for travelers to know what they're getting. Some glamping facilities and tour operators truly offer amenities on par with high-end resorts. Guests enjoy maid and butler service, four-star chefs and opulent accommodations. But others really are just camping facilities that throw in a few extras such as a real bed and a private bathroom.

Prices vary greatly, too, from $100 a night to well into the thousands—and might or might not include meals.

Warning: Some campground owners are trying to cash in on the glamping trend by using the term for extremely rustic facilities that barely qualify as comfortable, much less glamorous. Before booking a stay with any glamping facility or tour operator, confirm that you will have a real bed, not just a sleeping bag. That's the absolute minimum requirement for true glamping.

Also, check the company's Web site or call to ask the following questions to get a feel for the level of luxury provided...

Is there electricity? Just a few lights, or can I plug in other devices as well?

Is there running water? Hot water? A private shower? A private bathroom?

Is there maid service?

Is there heating?

Is there Internet access?

Are meals provided? Which meals? Are they included in the base price? What's the chef's background? If the chef has well-regarded restaurants on his/her résumé, it's a good sign that this is truly a luxury camping experience.

What are the accommodations? If it's a tent or a teepee, how large is it? Glamping tents should be as spacious as a small room, perhaps 10-foot-by-10-foot or larger. And they should be on wood platforms, not pitched directly on the soil. Other acceptable glamping accommodations include tree houses, cabins and yurts—a yurt is a circular tent, typically made from felt or skins.

How private are the accommodations? If guests sleep in tents, it's worth knowing how far these tents are from one another—canvas walls don't provide much privacy.

Should I bring a sleeping bag? A tent? Be concerned if the answer to either is yes—unlike a basic campground, a true glamping facility should provide guests with tents and beds.

Are sheets, blankets and towels provided? Most glamping facilities provide these, but some basic ones do not.

What do you recommend guests bring? Guests might or might not be expected to bring their own camping basics such as flashlights and bug spray.

GREAT GLAMPSITES

Four of the best places to go glamping in the US and Canada…

• **Treebones Resort** in Big Sur, California, is located on a bluff 400 feet above the Pacific Ocean offering spectacular views. Guests stay in spacious, fully furnished yurts with comfortable beds and hot and cold running water. The facility also features a pool and hot tub with an ocean view, an outdoor sushi bar and an on-site restaurant.

Downside: Showers and toilets are located in the main building, not in each yurt.

Rates: Typically $160 to $250 per night, but more for larger yurts. 877-424-4787, *www.TreebonesResort.com.*

• **Paws Up** in Greenough, Montana, 35 miles east of Missoula, is the most famous luxury camping facility in North America. Guests stay in spectacular tents set among pine groves or along the Blackfoot River on Paws Up's 37,000-acre wilderness property. Most tents feature king-sized beds, en-suite bathrooms and art hanging on the walls. Guests eat in great restaurants and enjoy stellar service. Paws Up truly defines the glamping experience.

Downside: It's extremely expensive.

Rates: $1,000 to $1,800 per night, which includes three meals a day. 800-473-0601, *www.PawsUp.com.*

• **WildExodus** in Ontario, Canada, offers luxurious lakeside camping in the Boreal Forest of Ontario's Wilderness Region. Guests stay in tents styled after "prospector" tents, only with modern amenities such as comfortable beds and electricity. They dine on fish caught the same day and prepared by a skilled chef. WildExodus excels at providing outdoor activities such as canoeing and fishing.

Downside: Parties must be between four and 12 guests.

Rates: For a seven-day stay, $950 to $1,900 per person. Rates include three meals per day, professional guide services and use of sporting equipment. 705-266-1555, *www.WildExodus.com.*

• **The Martyn House** in Ellijay, Georgia, is a bed-and-breakfast that also offers luxury tents set in the forested foothills of the Appalachian Mountains, about an hour and a half north of Atlanta. Though Georgia's weather can get very hot, The Martyn House's mountain location and open-tent design keep its tents relatively cool. There are heaters for cold nights. Each tent has its own bathroom with hot and cold running water, a shower and toilet. In addition to outdoor activities such as fly-fishing, rafting and hiking, the region features numerous art galleries, antiques shops and restaurants.

Downside: This isn't a glamping facility where guests explore a remote wilderness—The Martyn House is just two miles from downtown Ellijay.

Rates: $180 to $220 per night, with a minimum two-night stay. Prices include breakfast. 706-635-4759, *www.TheMartynHouse.com.*

City Discount Cards

The cards, which are available for New York, San Francisco and Miami, allow you to bypass long lines at busy attractions. New York Pass cards range in price from $80 per adult and $55 per child for one day to $200 per adult and $160 per child for seven days. Free attractions include several museums, ferry rides, bike rentals (half-day rental), botanical gardens and tours, plus discounts at retail stores, such as Macy's and Bloomingdale's, and several restaurants. The Go San Francisco Card costs from $55 per adult and $40 per child for one day to $145 per adult and $95 per child for seven days. The Go Miami Card costs from $65 per adult and $50 per child for one day to $198 per adult and $167 per child for seven days.

Information: *www.SmartDestinations.com.*

Nancy Dunnan, editor, *TravelSmart* newsletter. *www.travelsmartnewsletter.com*

For Group Travel

Use the Web to plan and manage your trip. If you are traveling with many people, Travelstormer.com gives you a place for a group to plan and book a trip—and an expense tracker to show who owes what to whom. If you like to take friends' suggestions, Gtrot.com, used with a Facebook account, lets you get travel advice from Facebook friends who live where you want to travel, who have traveled there before and/or who are going to be there when you are. If you are not sure where to go, enter your budget, departure city, interests and travel dates at Wanderfly.com for suggestions.

What to do: After using these free sites to help plan your trip, visit other travel Web sites, such as Expedia.com or Orbitz.com as well as individual airline sites, to find the lowest prices and make your bookings.

Nancy Dunnan, editor, TravelSmart newsletter. *www.travelsmartnewsletter.com*

New Travel Web Sites

InsideTrip helps you choose the best airline by comparing flights using 12 criteria, such as legroom, on-time record and aircraft age. Hipmunk helps users identify flights that might be agonizing because of layovers and an abnormally long trip time. GogoBot lets users get trip recommendations from their friends on Facebook and Twitter. TripIt uses your flight itinerary to build a custom report with maps and the weather forecast. Jetsetter gives members discounts of up to 50% on travel to exotic locales and upscale resorts. Room 77 helps you choose the best hotel room by ranking rooms by variables such as price, bed size and distance from the elevator.

Bloomberg Businessweek, 1221 Avenue of the Americas, New York City 10020. *www.businessweek.com*

Free Travel Apps

RoadAhead, for iPhone only, tells you where you are on an interstate highway, what direction you are going and what services are available at upcoming exits. It also can compare gas prices among upcoming exits and get customer reviews for nearby restaurants, shops and other amenities. GoHow Airport, for iPhone, Android and BlackBerry, links to more than 50 domestic and 30 foreign airports. It warns you about flight delays and tells you departure and arrival gates—and what restaurants and shops are near your gate.

The New York Times

Fliers' Favorites

Airlines that rank highest with travelers: Low-cost carriers that have newer planes and that focus on service, such as JetBlue and Southwest, consistently outrank more established, higher-cost airlines, such as US Airways, United, Delta and American, on customer-satisfaction surveys.

Analysis of government and consumer-survey data by *USA Today.*

Watch Your Miles

Consensus of frequent travelers, reported online at USNews.com.

Automatically track your airline miles online to match them to the best available deals—and to be sure that they do not expire.

Sites that offer tracking: AwardWallet (*www.awardwallet.com*) syncs with hundreds of rewards programs and offers a free regular account and a premium account with flexible pricing. Tripit Pro (*www.tripit.com*) sends you alerts about flight delays, cancellations and gate changes and lets you share itineraries with others—free for 30 days, then $49/yr. Mileage-Manager (*www.mileagemanager.com*) searches for flights and hotels and can calculate the cost in cash or number of points needed—free for 30 days, then $14.95/yr. Milewise (*www.milewise.com*) tracks more than 300 rewards programs and calculates the cash value of points or the number of frequent-flier points needed—free. GoMiles (*www.gomiles.com*) tracks hotel and airline rewards programs, plus dailydeal sites such as Groupon—free.

How to Get More Mileage from Your Frequent-Flier Miles

Tim Winship, contributing editor, SmarterTravel.com. He has spent nearly 25 years in the travel industry and helped develop and manage frequent-travel programs for Singapore Airlines, All Nippon Airways and Hilton Hotels.

Cashing in frequent-flier miles for the flights that you want can be devilishly difficult. *Ways to overcome the barriers...*

• **Use different airlines for different legs of the journey.** In the past, frequent-flier trips essentially had to be round-trips between two destinations on one airline or its partners—that's how the programs offered awards tickets. Today most airlines offer awards tickets per flight. So if you can't find both the outbound and return awards seats you want at the frequent-flier price you want on one airline, you can search for a flight for each leg separately on two different airlines, assuming that you have enough miles on both airlines.

• **Add a third leg.** On some airlines, you might be able to add an extra destination without increasing the number of required frequent-flier miles. For instance, on Delta you could fly from New York City to London, then a few days later, from London to Paris on the same airline or one of its partner airlines, and then from Paris back to New York City. However, airlines are increasingly phasing out this practice.

• **Participate in the Southwest, JetBlue or Virgin America frequent-flier program.** These airlines do not impose limits on the number of available awards seats on a flight. Any seat that is available for cash also is available for frequent-flier miles.

There is a downside—the number of miles required for an awards ticket increases with the cash price of the ticket. Still, participating in one of these three programs is a great way to ensure that you can get an awards ticket even to popular destinations and/or during busy travel times.

• **Call a reservations agent.** Airlines now impose fees for booking awards tickets over the phone—usually around $25 per passenger for the entire trip—but calling an agent can make sense when you're having trouble finding the best ticket.

Good reservations agents not only know the ins and outs of the awards seat booking system, they also often have options available to them that are not available to customers through the airline's Web site. These include cobbling together trips using partner airlines...changing planes in less obvious airports...or perhaps even unlocking seats that are not listed on the site as awards seats.

You pay nothing if the reservations agent can't find a solution that satisfies you and you don't book a ticket.

• **Book early, book late or book holiday flights.** The single best time to find an awards seat is 330 days before the flight, when these seats first enter the system. However, additional awards seats often enter the system within two weeks of departure. Awards seats also tend to be plentiful for people willing to travel on Christmas or Thanksgiving Day rather than during the week before or after.

• **Redeem British Airways miles on the airline's partner, American Airlines.** British Airways (BA) now charges extremely steep fuel surcharges. A "free" round-trip flight between the US and London could cost upward of $500—on top of the frequent-flier miles required. That includes unavoidable taxes, but it's mostly the fuel surcharge. Many other foreign airlines charge fuel surcharges, too, though most are nowhere near as steep as those of BA. To avoid these massive surcharges, redeem BA miles for flights on American Airlines, a BA partner airline that does not impose fuel surcharges.

Don't Let Your Frequent-Flier Miles Expire

Tim Winship, publisher of FrequentFlier.com, an independent travel Web site, and contributing editor at SmarterTravel.com. He has spent nearly 25 years in the travel industry and helped develop and manage frequent-travel programs for Singapore Airlines, All Nippon Airways and Hilton Hotels.

Unused frequent-flier miles can expire in 18 or 24 months in most airline programs if there is no activity in the account. *Fortunately, it usually is possible to extend the expiration dates by another 18 or 24 months—and you don't even have to fly or cash in miles to do it...*

TRACK EXPIRATION DATES

Make sure that each frequent-flier program you belong to has your up-to-date e-mail address. If you handle the frequent-flier miles for your whole family, use your e-mail address for your spouse's and children's accounts, too. Web sites such as Mileage Manager ($14.95/year, *www.mileagemanager.com*) and MilePort (free, *www.mileport.com*) can help track expiration dates in multiple frequent-flier programs all in one place—but none of them is perfect, so don't rely exclusively on these sites.

EARN MILES

Major airline programs have hundreds of corporate partners. Adding a few miles this way can extend the expiration date for all miles. *Options...*

• **Restaurants and bars.** Buying a meal—or even just a drink—at a restaurant or bar that has partnered with your frequent-flier program will earn you miles. Register one or more of your credit or debit cards with an airline's dining rewards program, then simply pay with this card when you dine or drink at any of the eateries on the partner list.

Helpful: If you belong to several frequent-flier programs or have multiple accounts in different family members' names, consider assigning each of your credit and debit cards to a different frequent-flier dining program account so that you can pay with different cards to extend expiration dates as needed.

• **Online retailers.** These partners often include the sites of large, well-known companies that you might have bought from anyway, such as WalMart.com, Sears.com, Borders.com and Staples.com. A few frequent-flier programs now also allow members to earn miles by making purchases in certain stores.

• **Airline-branded credit cards.** Each time you use one of these cards, you push back your frequent-flier expiration date for that airline. But annual card fees can be hefty, ranging from $40 for an American Express JetBlue card to $375 for a United Mileage Plus Club Visa card.

• **Marketing companies.** Some marketing companies will reward you with frequent-flier miles if you watch a few ads online or take a short survey.

Example: e-Miles offers miles in the Delta, US Airways, Alaska Airlines, Frontier and AirTran programs to those who watch a few online marketing videos and answer follow-up questions (*www.e-miles.com*).

SUBTRACT MILES

Reducing the miles in your account also automatically extends expiration dates. *Among the options...*

Subscriptions and other small purchases paid with miles, including magazine and newspaper subscriptions, flowers or gift cards.

Charitable donations of miles to a participating charity. The minimum donation typically is 1,000 miles.

Mile transfers from one member's account to another's will reset the expiration dates of the donor account and perhaps the recipient account as well. But be aware that programs tend to charge significant transfer fees—$30 to $60 or more.

Best Ticket Shopping

To get the best price on an airline ticket: Use TripAdvisor.com's fee estimator to determine the real cost of a flight, including baggage and other fees. Sign up for e-mail alerts at your favorite travel Web sites, such as Orbitz.com and SmarterTravel.com, and follow your favorite airline on Twitter to find out about special deals and sales. Act quickly—buy a ticket if you see that ticket prices are going up. Use Bing.com's price predictor tool to see which way fares are headed.

Best time to buy tickets to get the best price: Tuesday at 3 pm eastern standard time because most discounted sales campaigns start late Monday evening.

Money, Time-Life Building, Rockefeller Center, New York City 10020. *www.money.com*

Fly in Style

You may be able to fly on a private jet for the cost of a commercial first-class or business-class ticket. London-based charter broker Air Partner (*www.EmptySectors.com*) helps fill seats when planes fly back to base or are between jobs. JetSuite, in California (www.JetSuite.com), offers SuiteShare, which lets customers charter a four-passenger aircraft and offer unneeded seats through Facebook to reduce the cost. Social Flights (*www.SocialFlights.com*), a collective-buying company in Tennessee, uses social networking to help charter companies fill seats.

The New York Times

For the Best Seats

To find comfortable airplane seats and avoid the worst ones, go to *www.seatguru.com*. The site offers more than 700 layouts and ratings for nearly 100 airlines. It uses its own research plus feedback from travelers to rate seat desirability. Individual airlines' cabin configurations vary, and different carriers will have different good and bad seating options.

Examples: American Airlines 767-300 has extra legroom in seats 17A, B, H and J...Southwest Airlines 737 has exit row seats that lack extra legroom and that have limited recline.

Airline Customer Favorites

Major airlines get low grades for seat comfort. In a survey, eight of 10 got poor scores—only JetBlue scored above average, and Southwest got middling seat-comfort scores. Those two airlines topped the list for overall customer satisfaction in areas such as check-in ease, cabin-crew service, cabin cleanliness, baggage handling and in-flight entertainment. Southwest earned praise for letting travelers avoid a variety of tacked-on fees. The bottom-ranked major airline was US Airways, which also received the lowest ranking the last time this survey was done, in 2007.

Consumer Reports, 101 Truman Ave., Yonkers, New York 10703. *www.consumerreports.org*

Protect Your Luggage

Checked bags may be left outside in rain, snow, sleet and hail, especially at small airports, before they eventually make it onto the aircraft.

Self-defense: Put your best clothes in the middle of your luggage, and keep clothing and valuables in airtight plastic bags. You should be able to get appropriate clothing bags from your local dry cleaner for 50 cents to $1 apiece.

Nancy Dunnan, editor, *TravelSmart* newsletter. *www.travelsmartnewsletter.com*

Lock It Up!

Lock your luggage to the luggage rack on a train or a bus with a cable lock that wraps around the racks. That will keep it safe if you fall asleep—or if you get up to go to the restroom or to a train's dining car.

Nancy Dunnan, editor, *TravelSmart* newsletter. *www.travelsmartnewsletter.com*

For Weather Alert

If you suspect bad weather may interfere with your flight...sign up for flight-status notifications at FlightStats.com and TripIt.com so that you will receive e-mails and text updates to your phone about delays. Book nonstop morning flights when possible—this lowers the chance of flight cancellations or delays at intermediate airports. If you get to the airport and your flight is canceled, search for ones on other airlines—some may still be flying—and ask your carrier to endorse your ticket for use on the other airline. This is not required, but many airlines will do it—although you may have to pay more for the new seat. Pack carry-on bags with delays in mind—keep amenities, such as toiletries, reading materials, water, snacks, a light sweater or jacket and a change of clothing handy. Check the weather forecast before heading home, and consider rebooking if there is a chance that your flight may be canceled. Call the hotel's front desk to extend your hotel stay.

Travel + Leisure, 1120 Avenue of the Americas, New York City 10036. *www.travelandleisure.com*

Turn It Off!

Many airline passengers are keeping electronics turned on even after cabin crews warn them to turn off the equipment. Passengers often do not believe crew warnings about use of electronic devices—but the devices' radio signals can interfere with flight systems and cockpit instruments. The probability of interference is small, but some incidents have been reported by pilots.

USA Today

Don't Drink the Water

Many airlines don't stock enough bottled water. When they run out, attendants may resort to the plane's water system. The EPA found that the water in 15% of planes contained coliform bacteria. Stick with drinking canned beverages on your next airplane flight...or buy your own bottled water at the airport before boarding.

AARP The Magazine, 601 E St. NW, Washington, DC 20049. *www.AARP.org/bulletin*

Health Precaution

Avoid using airplane restrooms. They are rarely sanitized during flights and often are infected with E. coli and other harmful bacteria. If you have to use the bathroom, use a paper towel to open and close the toilet lid... turn faucets off and on...and open the door. When you get back to your seat, use sanitizer to disinfect your hands.

Peter Sheldon, vice president of operations and development, Coverall Health-Based Cleaning System, franchisor of commercial cleaning businesses, Boca Raton, Florida. *www.coverall.com*

Free Apps for Air Travelers

GateGuru lists restaurants, shops, lounges and services at more than 120 airports. It has more than 20,000 ratings and reviews and more than 4,000 photos. It does not provide prices or information on operating hours. Flysmart gives flight status and gate information, plus lists of restaurants, shops, ATMs and restrooms. It links to airline Web sites and provides points of interest—but has data for only 26 airports. GoHow Airport lists restaurants, shops, ATMs, restrooms, flight and parking status, and security wait times for 80 airports, although not all information is available for all airports and the maps can be hard to read.

Healthy Airport Eating

At 15 major US airports, an average of 83% of restaurants now have at least one vegetarian item on the menu—compared with 57% a decade ago. In Detroit, every one of the airport's 59 restaurants offers at least one low-fat, low-cholesterol meal. In San Francisco, 96% of restaurants offer a healthful choice...at Washington/Dulles, 92%...at Minneapolis/St. Paul, 86%...at Dallas/Fort Worth and Las Vegas, 83%. Even at the lowest-scoring major airport, Atlanta, 71% of restaurants offered healthful food.

Susan Levin, MS, RD, nutrition education director, Physicians Committee for Responsible Medicine, Washington, DC. *www.pcrm.org*

Need a Nap?

Napping rooms at US airports may make layovers easier. The small rooms are available at Atlanta's Hartsfield-Jackson Airport and Philadelphia International Airport for $30 per hour. They include a daybed sofa, pillows with disposable covers, blankets, a desk, Internet access and a flat-screen 32-inch monitor. Similar rooms are available at Heathrow and Gatwick airports in the UK...Schiphol in Amsterdam... Sheremet-Yevo in Moscow...Munich airport... and Indira Gandhi International in India.

New York Times

Best Tech Airports

Dallas-Fort Worth had the overall best score in a study of airports' Wi-Fi quality, cell-phone reception and number of electrical outlets. It was followed by New York's JFK International...Atlanta's Hartsfield-Jackson... Detroit Metro...Sacramento International... Oakland International...New York's LaGuardia...Salt Lake City International...Baltimore-Washington International...and San Francisco International.

Study of technical quality of the 40 busiest airports in the US by researchers at *PC World.*

Crime Rates Higher Near Big Airports

Your risk of being robbed or assaulted is four times greater than the national average in areas close to the nation's largest airports.

Cities with the riskiest areas near airports: Philadelphia...Ontario, California...Portland, Oregon...Houston...and Phoenix. Your risk of being robbed or assaulted near certain train stations is more than double the national average.

Cities with the riskiest train station neighborhoods: Houston...Los Angeles...Chicago...Portland, Oregon...and Philadelphia.

CAP Index, a crime data and solutions consulting company, Exton, Pennsylvania. *www.CAPIndex.com*

Renters' Picks

Car-rental firms with the highest scores for customer satisfaction: Enterprise, National and Hertz.

Lowest scores: Payless, Thrifty, Dollar and Budget. This is according to a recent survey ranking car-rental firms on customer satisfaction for costs and fees, pickup process, the rental car itself, return process, reservation process and shuttle bus or van service.

Stuart Greif, vice president, JD Power and Associates, Westlake Village, California. *www.jdpower.com*

Best Car Rental Rates In Europe

Use a regional firm such as Sixt Rent a Car (*www.Sixt.com*) or Europcar (*www.europcar.com*).

Alternative: Join Zipcar (*www.zipcar.com*) in the US, and pick up a car in London or another European city. If your trip is longer than three weeks, check Auto Europe (*www.AutoEurope.com*) or RenaultEuro drive (*www.renaultusa.com*)—both offer cost-efficient short-term auto leases. Choose a small car to save on fuel and maneuver more easily through Europe's narrow streets.

Travel + Leisure, 1120 Avenue of the Americas, New York City 10036. *www.travelandleisure.com*

Car Rental Safety

Research the safety of the rental car you want—or that the rental company wants to give you. Most vehicles in rental fleets were rated "good" for safety in head-on crashes, but many didn't fare as well in side, rear and rollover collisions.

Safest rental cars: Among small cars—Honda Civic, Kia Forte and Subaru Impreza... midsized cars—Ford Fusion, Chevrolet Malibu and Dodge Avenger...large cars—Lincoln MKS, Chrysler 300 and Cadillac CTS...SUVs—Subaru Forester, Ford Explorer and Jeep Grand Cherokee.

USA Today

Consider Travel Insurance

Travel insurance can cover prepaid hotel costs. Some hotel rates are deeply discounted but nonrefundable. They are offered by Expedia, Travelocity, Orbitz and hotel Web sites. Without travel insurance, you might have to forfeit your advance payment if you cancel. Travel insurance allows you to cancel for such reasons as illness, injury, bad weather, canceled flights and sometimes for work-related reasons.

Nancy Dunnan, editor, *TravelSmart* newsletter. *www.travelsmartnewsletter.com*

Big City Savings

Save money on weekend leisure travel by staying in big-city hotels that cater to business travelers. Vacation-oriented hotels raise rates on weekends—but business-oriented ones lower their prices. The savings are biggest in large cities.

Examples: The InterContinental San Francisco recently charged $235/night for a standard room on the weekend—while the tourist-oriented Hyatt near Fisherman's Wharf charged $359. In New York City, a weekend night at the Millennium Hotel in the Wall Street area recently cost $219, compared with $309 for a room in a comparable hotel near Times Square.

Money, Time-Life Bldg., Rockefeller Center, New York City 10020. *www.money.com*

Gas Discounts

Hotels are offering gas discounts. Many US hotels are promoting fuel-related discounts to entice travelers. Promotions include free gas gift cards, discounts on rooms when you provide gas receipts and special deals for people who carpool or take mass transit.

Recent examples: At Affinia Manhattan in New York City, guests can get a $20 gas gift card if they show a mass transit ticket and receipt. Napa Old World Inn in Napa, California, gives guests who carpool a two-bedroom suite for the price of a standard room. At the Barefoot Resort in Myrtle Beach, South Carolina, guests can receive a $50 gas gift card and a free night if they book a seven-night stay and check in on a Saturday.

USA Today

Late-Breaking Bargains

Last-minute hotel deals are being offered to people who book them on impulse or in emergencies.

Examples: Commuters working late, people without electricity, travelers whose flights are canceled.

Use your smartphone to save on same-day hotel bookings: Use the Hotel Tonight app, which shows hotels that offer daily deals of at least 20% off (*www.hoteltonight.com*)...or check Priceline's mobile app, which features same-day hotel deals.

Alternative: Contact hotels directly for last-minute discounts. Be sure to call the hotel's local number, not the 800 number. Also, if you are unsuccessful at first, ask to speak to the general manager. On average, 40% of hotel rooms go unsold each night.

Nancy Dunnan, editor, *TravelSmart. www.travelsmartnewsletter.com*

Clean It Yourself

Clean your hotel room's TV remote, alarm clock and ice bucket before using them. These items are rarely cleaned by housekeepers.

Also likely to be covered in germs: The steering wheel and gearshift of a rental car.

Peter Sheldon, vice president of operations and development, Coverall Health-Based Cleaning System, a franchise of commercial cleaning businesses, Boca Raton, Florida. *www.coverall.com*

Don't Be Tempted to Take a Souvenir

Hotels are tracking linens. At a small but growing number of hotels, radio-frequency chips are being sewn in robes and linens to prevent guests from taking them. The tags can be read by sensors up to six feet away and trigger an alarm.

Economist.com

Chemicals That Kill Bedbugs Can Cause Illness

More than 100 people were sickened by the insecticides between 2003 and 2010—and one person died.

Reasons for the illnesses: Overuse of the insecticides...failing to wash or change bedding that had been treated with the insecticides.

Self-defense: Call in a certified professional to handle a bedbug problem.

Naomi L. Hudson, DrPH, Epidemic Intelligence Service Office, Centers for Disease Control and Prevention, Atlanta, and coauthor of a study published in *Morbidity and Mortality Weekly Report.*

Hotel Safety Tip

Do not use the "Please Clean Room" sign when staying at a hotel. It tells people that the room is vacant—a possible invitation to thieves. Instead, call housekeeping and request that the room be cleaned—and explain that you are hanging the "Do Not Disturb" sign on the door and leaving on the TV.

Nancy Dunnan, editor, *TravelSmart. www.travelsmart newsletter.com*

At Your Service

You can use a hotel's concierge services even when you are not staying at the hotel. Most concierges will arrange for transportation, tickets to entertainment events and references to English-speaking doctors. Tell the concierge that you are not a guest but would appreciate his/her help, and tip generously when you receive it.

Condé Nast Traveler, 4 Times Square, New York City 10036. *www.CNTraveler.com*

New Program

Loyalty rewards program has started at many airports. The free program Thanks Again (*www.ThanksAgain.com*) offers between two and five airline miles for every dollar spent shopping, dining and using parking facilities at 160 airports.

Nancy Dunnan, publisher of the monthly newsletter *TravelSmart*, New York City, and author or coauthor of more than 30 books, including *Recession-Proof Your Financial Life* (McGraw-Hill). *www.travelsmart newsletter.com*

Who Needs a Hotel? Swap Homes Instead

John Mensinger, cofounder of HomeExchangeUniversity.com, which offers advice on vacation home exchange. He is author of *The HomeExchangeGuru.com Guide to Trading Your Home* (BookSurge) and has personally exchanged his Modesto, California, home 13 times.

Home-exchange programs dramatically cut travel costs and often make excursions more enjoyable. Program members agree to trade homes for days, weeks or longer, saving the cost of lodging and cutting down on restaurant bills. Cars are exchanged in about half of home exchanges, eliminating vehicle rental costs as well.

You can participate in a home exchange even if your home is not in or near a popular vacation destination—you'll just have to exchange homes with others whose homes are in less popular areas. My hometown of Modesto, California, is not popular enough for me to find a great home in a great neighborhood in London or Paris, but we could find a modest home in a less popular neighborhood in those cities. Or we can trade our home for a wonderful home in a lesser known area such as the British midlands.

TOP AGENCIES

The easiest way to exchange a home is through an agency that specializes in this. There are now dozens of home-exchange agencies. The yearly membership fees allow you to list your home, look at other listings and contact fellow members to propose an exchange. The largest agencies tend to be the best by virtue of their size alone—more members mean more potential trade partners.

Agencies include...

- **HomeExchange.com** is the largest agency, with more than 40,000 members. It is particularly strong in the US, which is great if you travel domestically, but it increases your competition for trades when you travel internationally. $120/year.
- **HomeForExchange.com** has about 13,600 members. It's strong in France, Australia and the US, and its membership fee is relatively low. $59/year.
- **HomeLink International** (*www.homelink.org/usa*) is one of the oldest agencies and has about 13,000 members. It has regional affiliates with English-speaking employees in many foreign countries, so members often have a local contact if problems develop during a home exchange. HomeLink International is particularly strong in Australia, France, Germany, Great Britain, the Netherlands and the US. $119/year.
- **Home Base Holidays** (*www.homebase-hols.com*) is not as large as the agencies listed above, with just 2,300 members, but it is very strong in the UK and a reasonable choice for Americans hoping to travel there. £29/year (approximately $47).

GETTING STARTED

Once you join an agency, follow its instructions to list your home on its Web site. These sites let members upload numerous photos of their homes, but the first photo usually is the most important—that's the photo that will be displayed when other members browse listings. It doesn't have to be a picture of the front of your house. If your home is on a beach or has a pool, consider making that your first picture.

If you do not live in a city that's popular with vacationers, include in your description of the property the names of all cities and vacation destinations within a few hours' drive of your home so that your listing pops up when other members search those keywords.

Example: The listing for my home in Modesto notes that we are two hours from San Francisco and Yosemite.

Next, use the Web site's search tools to locate program members who have homes in places you wish to visit and who have expressed an interest in visiting your region (or who say they will travel anywhere). Typically, it is best for families with kids to trade with other families with kids. Their homes will be set up for children, with toys, video games and fewer breakable items.

MAKING A TRADE

When you find a potential trade partner, send an e-mail asking if he/she would be interested in exchanging with you. Explain when and for how long you would like to trade and where your home is located. If your home is in a desirable region, you'll probably find a partner quickly. If it's in an ordinary region, send out 10 to 20 e-mails at a time and see who responds.

Warning: If you're trying to arrange a trip during your kids' summer vacation, start sending out e-mails 10 to 12 months in advance. Families with school-age kids often select vacation exchange partners very early.

Home exchangers typically coordinate travel dates so that they are in each other's homes at the same time. Travel dates do not have to match up when second homes are being exchanged.

Communicate with potential trade partners at least two or three times by e-mail or phone before finalizing the agreement. Ask any questions you can think of about the home and neighborhood. These interactions won't just help you decide if the home is right for you—they also can give you a feel for the home's owner. If someone is not friendly and responsive, this might not be someone you want to trust with your home.

Two questions I particularly like...

Can we meet prior to the exchange? Most home exchangers don't do this, but I've found a face-to-face meeting builds trust on both sides. The meeting could be a quick hello at an airport or one family could travel a day before the other and share a home briefly. You also could try to set up a video chat using Skype or Apple's Facetime.

Could you arrange introductions with a few of your friends or neighbors so that I have local contacts? Not only is it nice to know people in the places you visit—this also makes you a part of the home owner's social circle, and that increases the odds that he will treat your home with respect.

REDUCING THE RISKS

Those new to home exchange sometimes fear that they will accidentally invite burglars into their homes. I've never heard of that happening with a home exchange—there are much easier ways for burglars to access homes.

There is some risk that guests accidentally will damage your home, so confirm with your home owner's insurance provider that damage would be covered. Make it clear to the insurer that these are nonpaying guests.

Trading cars adds to the financial risk of home exchange. Confirm with your auto insurance provider that both you and your guest would be covered if your guest has an accident. Also confirm that your exchange partner has sufficient insurance to protect you if you crash his car.

One often overlooked risk in home exchange is that differing expectations will lead to dissatisfaction with the trade. *Topics worth raising with potential trade partners include...*

- **Cleaning.** Different people have different opinions about what constitutes "clean." Discuss the level of cleanliness expected. Suggest that each of you brings in your own local cleaning company or maid service at the end of the trade if this seems like a potential point of contention.

- **Food.** Can home exchangers consume the food and liquor they find in the home? Lean toward answering yes—sharing one's food sets a friendly tone for the exchange.

- **Phones and computers.** Are guests allowed to use these as much as they please? Within certain limits? Not at all? In a long-term exchange, will guests pay their own utility bills?

Helpful: Put together a user's manual for your home, explaining how to use anything that isn't obvious...how to contact you, your friends and local service people in an emergency...and offering insider guidance on the area, such as recommended restaurants or strategies for avoiding rush-hour traffic. This will help your guests enjoy their visit, and it will help them get to know you a little better, in written form, increasing the odds that they will consider you a friend and treat your property with respect.

Room Reservation Up for Bids

A new hotel-booking site, BackBid (*www.BackBid.com*), lets you post an existing reservation made on another hotel or online travel agency Web site and then receive e-mail bids from competing hotels. Create a free profile, then enter your hotel reservation information, including check-in and check-out dates and your confirmation number. Next you will receive e-mails from hotels trying to woo you.

Caution: Use BackBid only if your existing reservation doesn't require prepayment and can be canceled without penalty.

USA Today

Hidden Cruise Costs

Cruises may claim to be all-inclusive, but they often are not. Beverages such as alcohol, bottled water and soda usually are not included. But most cruises let you bring your own soda and bottled water aboard—or you may save by buying an unlimited-drinks package. Gratuities for the crew typically are added automatically to your bill, at $10 to $12 per passenger per day. Bar bills often include an automatic 15% gratuity. You usually can adjust amounts at the purser's desk. Shore excursions are high-priced if booked through the cruise line—you can save by booking through an independent local operator. Food is included at casual buffets, but gourmet offerings can cost an extra $10 to $75. Avoid them, or budget for them.

AARP.org

Safety on Board

Cruise ship emergencies can be complicated by language barriers. On the Costa Concordia, which struck a reef off the Italian coast in January 2012, a range of mistakes led to many deaths. Adding to the confusion was that announcements were made in Italian, German, French, Spanish and English. English-speaking travelers may want to stick with cruise lines that use English primarily, such as Princess and Royal Caribbean.

Paul Motter, editor of the cruise guide CruiseMates.com, Los Angeles. He previously worked on cruise ships, where he received training in evacuation procedures. *www.cruisemates.com*

Cruise Ship Illnesses

There were 14 outbreaks of gastrointestinal illnesses such as norovirus on ships operating out of US ports in 2010—down from 15 outbreaks in 2009 and 2008...21 in 2007...and 34 in 2006. Several major cruise lines, including Princess Cruises and Norwegian, had no outbreaks at all during the year. To see the full list of cruiseship lines and the number of outbreaks, go to *www.cdc.gov/nceh/vsp*.

Study by the Centers for Disease Control and Prevention, Atlanta. *www.cdc.gov*

Safe Travel In Risky Times

Christopher Falkenberg, president, Insite Security, New York City. *www.insitesecurity.com*

Luggage: Skip locks for your luggage, and use plastic ties instead. Baggage thieves are less likely to try to steal from a bag that is locked in any way, but a broken tie will alert you and security personnel that someone has been inside your luggage.

Airports: Many European terror alerts identify presecurity sections of the airport, including the duty-free shopping areas, as possible terrorist targets.

Best: Check in, and go through security as quickly as possible.

Hotels: Stay at a local hotel rather than a high-profile one. Most terrorists target the highest-profile place. Pack a flashlight in case of power failures or other emergencies.

Most important: Plan your response ahead of time in case you are involved in a dangerous situation—plan your escape route from your hotel...listen to safety instructions in the plane, identify the exits and visualize your escape.

Free Language Translation App

Using Google's voice-recognition technology, iPhone and Android users now can speak or type an English phrase into the phone and the free app Google Translate will translate it into one of more than 50 foreign languages. Once the word or phrase is translated, you can press a button to hear it spoken.

Charge It Wisely Overseas

Reduce foreign transaction fees by carefully choosing the credit cards you use overseas. The average fee is 3% for banks and 1% for credit unions. Cardholders are charged the fee when they purchase items overseas.

What to do: Look into cards that do not charge or pass on currency conversion fees, such as American Express Platinum and Centurion cards...cards issued by Capital One and Discover.

Caution: Simmons and TD do charge fees for credit card use.

Consensus of frequent travelers, reported in *USA Today. www.usatoday.com*

Taking Your Smartphone Abroad?

Contact your service provider before traveling to ensure that the phone is activated for international use. Disable the data portion of your connection or turn it on only when you need to access e-mail to avoid high pay-per-use rates. Use free Wi-Fi spots as much as possible. Know roaming rates, especially in European countries, where it's easy to cross from one country to another.

Example: The AT&T roaming rate for calls in Finland is $1.39 a minute, while calls in neighboring Russia are $4.99 a minute.

The Wall Street Journal

14

Time Off Tips

Tricks to Improve Your Golf Game (Without Leaving Home)

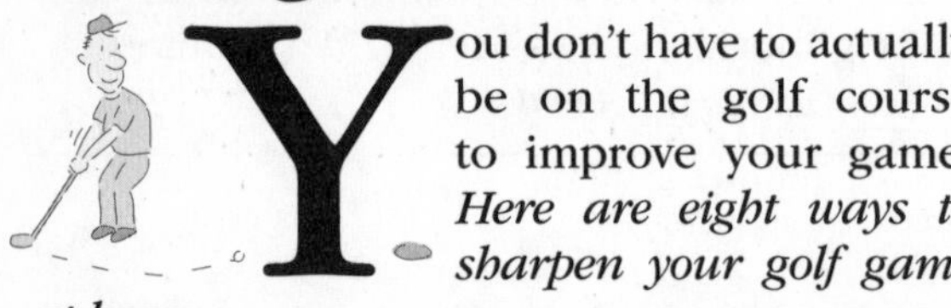

You don't have to actually be on the golf course to improve your game. *Here are eight ways to sharpen your golf game at home...*

• **Improve your grip.** It is said that the legendary golfer Ben Hogan, who early in his career fought a pronounced hook shot, once spent an entire winter just learning how to affix his hands to the club properly, doing nothing more than holding the club. This makes sense because the only connection a player's body has to the club is through the hands. You can purchase a form-fitting grip, or training grip, at any golf shop and attach it to any golf club. Let your hands get familiar with the proper positioning on the club, and it will be comfortable to replicate when you're on the course. Hold the club for five to 10 minutes a day, four to five times a week.

• **Strengthen your hand muscles.** Strengthen your wrists and the dozens of tiny muscles in your hands and fingers by laying a dishrag flat on a hard surface, then crumpling it into a tight ball, letting it go and repeating a dozen times with each hand. Do this three or four times weekly. You also can use one of those spring-loaded grip-strengthener devices, although it won't use all the tiny muscles as effectively as the dishrag.

• **Use an exercise ball.** Oversized exercise balls (Swiss Ball is a well-known brand) assist with balance, stability, flexibility and core strength. Beginners simply can sit on the ball with their feet on the floor for a few minutes a day. This helps with balance and core strength,

Joel Zuckerman is a freelance golf and travel writer who has played nearly 800 golf courses around the world, written for more than 100 publications and is author of five books. His most recent, *Pete Dye Golf Courses—Fifty Years of Visionary Design* (Abrams), was named Book of the Year by the International Network of Golf. *www.vagabondgolfer.com*

both key components of the golf swing. Lying back on the ball puts the spine into extension, as opposed to the flexion we experience all day long sitting at desks, driving, etc. This helps to lengthen and stretch the spine, making it much more comfortable to get into the forward-bending posture required for a golf swing. For more exercises, go to *www.swissballexercises.org*.

• **Increase clubhead speed.** The faster you swing the club, the more you also compress the golf ball and, assuming a solid (as opposed to off-center) strike, the straighter and longer that ball will fly. A great new product that helps to increase clubhead speed is called the Speed Whoosh (about $80, *www.momentusgolf.com*, click on "Speed Whoosh"). It is a long, skinny, flexible antennae-like apparatus that can be swung much faster than a conventional club. Swing it a dozen times a day when you can't play golf, and then when you pick up a club on the course, you will be swinging it several miles per hour faster than before.

• **Use therapeutic bands.** These stretchy bands are good for stretching and strengthening shoulder and chest muscles in ways that expensive and cumbersome gym equipment does not. Shoulder muscles, particularly rotator cuffs, are easily injured and will keep you off the golf course for extended periods if they become injured. A strong chest is needed for an effective golf swing. Hold the band overhead with both hands so that you feel some tension in the band. You can increase or decrease tension in the band as needed by gripping it widely or narrowly. Slowly bring the band behind your back, then back up over your head and down to your belt line. You can even tie a band securely to a doorknob and practice your golf swing. Hold the position at both backswing and follow-through for a beat or two to build strength.

• **Work on flexibility.** A more flexible body allows a golfer to make a bigger, more powerful turn from the hips and torso to generate the tension in the body to hit the ball a long way. There are any number of effective ways to increase flexibility, but one of the best is the program devised by Roger Fredericks. A former PGA professional turned flexibility guru, Fredericks offers beginner, intermediate and advanced stretching programs on DVD that help golfers learn to get their bodies into positions that will allow them to play the game more effectively, with less stress on the body and a reduced chance of injury (*www.fredericksgolf.com*).

• **Sharpen your mental focus.** It's long been said that the most important six inches in golf are between the ears. To that end, there are a number of relevant books that help the golfer sharpen his/her mental focus and perform better under pressure. These books include the best-selling *Golf Is Not a Game of Perfect* by Bob Rotella, PhD, which offers some excellent visualization techniques. *Easier Said Than Done* by Rick Jensen, PhD, emphasizes how to move your effectiveness on the driving range right to the course itself. *Every Shot Must Have a Purpose* and *The Game Before the Game* by Pia Nilsson and coauthor Lynn Marriott also offer valuable information on effective practice techniques and how to use mental focus to play your best.

• **Daydream about golf.** Daydreaming about the game has been proved to have a positive effect on performance. Recent scientific studies have shown that while physical practice is the most beneficial technique, mentally practicing your swing and desired ball flight and outcome is more beneficial than doing nothing at all. Picture the sound and feel of solid contact from the tee, the flight of the drive, the club you choose for your approach shot, the contour of the green, the speed of the putt, etc. Play the first several holes in your mind until you start to lose focus. Then try again the next day.

Dining Tip

To get a great table at a restaurant, make your reservation for either 6:45 pm or 8:15 pm—not 7:30 pm.

Reason: Seating a party at 7:30 means that the restaurant probably won't be able to seat that table again after you leave—so your party is less likely to get one of the better tables.

Marino Monferrato, general manager of Cecconi's, West Hollywood, California. *www.cecconiswesthollywood.com*

Casinos You Can Bet On

Steve Bourie, who has been publishing the *American Casino Guide* annually since 1992 (Casino Vacations). Based in Dania, Florida, he has more than 35 years of experience in the gambling industry. *www.americancasinoguide.com*

Each year, roughly one in four Americans over age 21 gambles in a casino. Which of them walks away a winner depends in part on which casinos they select.

Here's how to choose casinos in the major American gambling centers of Las Vegas, Atlantic City, Reno and Mississippi, where you are likely to win the most when playing four popular games.

Helpful: Although Connecticut has two popular casinos, Foxwoods and Mohegan Sun (technically, three, because there are two casinos at the Foxwoods complex), they offer very similar odds. Occasionally, however, there is reason to choose one over the other, as noted below.

BLACKJACK

Play blackjack only in casinos and at tables offering 3-to-2 payouts when you make a blackjack (21 on the first two cards)—$7.50 on a five-dollar bet, for example—never at those paying 6-to-5. Also, favor casinos where the dealer must stand on a soft 17—that is, the dealer does not take an additional card when the house has a 17 that includes an ace being counted as an 11. Blackjack played with a single deck offers better odds than six- or eight-deck games, but if the payout is just 6-to-5, it's not worth playing, even with a single deck.

Great casinos for blackjack include...

In Las Vegas: El Cortez features single-deck games with $5 minimums, 3-to-2 payouts when you make a blackjack and other player-friendly rules that reduce the overall house edge to just 0.2%—that is, the house makes an average of about two cents for each $10 bet—compared with up to 1.5% at other casinos. *www.elcortezhotelcasino.com.*

In Atlantic City: Dealers at some tables, generally indicated by a placard, stand on soft 17 at Borgata (*www.theborgata.com*) and Trump Plaza (*www.trumpplaza.com*), lowering the house advantage to around 0.4%, compared with the standard 0.7% in Atlantic City.

Warning: Avoid a $1-minimum blackjack table if it charges a 25-cent-per-hand fee—common in Atlantic City.

Near Reno: The Alamo, a small casino in Sparks, Nevada, just east of Reno, offers perhaps the most favorable casino blackjack in the US. It features single-deck, 3-to-2 games with a wide range of player-friendly rules, including the right to split and resplit any pair (turning one hand into two and doubling your bet when you have two cards of the same number)...late surrender (the option of discarding a hand inexpensively when the dealer does not have a blackjack)...and even a six-card Charley (an automatic win for players who reach six cards without busting). Play well, and the house advantage is just 0.1%. *www.thealamo.com.*

In Mississippi: The Isle of Capri in Biloxi offers double-deck 3-to-2 games where dealers stand on a soft 17, for a house advantage of just 0.2%. *www.biloxi.isleofcapricasinos.com.*

VIDEO POKER

Video poker machines display their pay tables—the number of coins returned if specific hands are made. Gamblers who learn how to interpret these tables, which are displayed right on the screens, can find the casinos and machines that offer the best odds. *Two types of video poker machines particularly worth seeking out...*

- **9/6 Jacks or Better.** With these machines, players win if they get at least a pair of jacks, and the payout is nine coins for every coin bet when the player gets a full house and six coins for a flush, among other payouts. Play well, and the casino's edge is less than 0.5%.
- **Full-Pay Deuces Wild.** Deuces Wild video poker machines are considered full pay if they

pay three coins for a full house, five for four of a kind, nine for a straight flush and 15 for five of a kind, among other payouts. Play well, and you have an edge of nearly 0.8%—one of the rare times when the gambler has an advantage over the casino.

The Web site vpFREE2 (*www.vpfree2.com*) offers feedback from gamblers about the video poker games and odds offered by casinos around the US.

Warning: In New York State and Washington State, video poker is not a game of skill at all, merely a game of chance, like a lottery scratch-off ticket. The machines simply spit out winning hands a certain percentage of the time.

Among the best casinos for video poker...

In Las Vegas: Sam's Town (*www.samstownlv.com*), Cannery (*www.cannerycasino.com*) and South Point (*www.southpointcasino.com*) have some full-pay Deuces Wild machines.

In Atlantic City: Borgata and Bally's (*www.ballyslasvegas.com*) have some 9/6-Jacks-or-Better machines that can be played for as little as 25 cents.

In Mississippi: Island View (*www.islandviewcasino.com*) and the Isle of Capri offer some 9/6-Jacks-or-Better machines that accept bets as low as a quarter.

In Reno: John Ascuaga's Nugget in Sparks (*www.janugget.com*) and Peppermill (*www.PeppermillReno.com*) have 9/6-Jacks-or-Better machines that take bets as low as a penny. Silver Legacy (*www.silverlegacyreno.com*), a nice downtown casino, has 9/6-Jacks-or-Better machines that take bets as low as a quarter.

Warning: Even casinos that offer 9/6-Jacks-or-Better or full-pay Deuces Wild machines usually scatter these among other Jacks-or-Better or Deuces Wild machines that offer lower odds.

SLOTS

Slot machines tend to pay out at least 85% of the money they take in, but higher-denomination slots tend to pay a greater percentage, as much as 97% for some $25-and-up machines. See my Web site for statistics on payouts (*www.americancasinoguide.com*, click on "Slot Payback Info").

In Atlantic City: Borgata offers the city's highest slots payouts, at an average of 91.7% of the total money bet.

In Connecticut: Mohegan Sun offers a slightly higher payout than Foxwoods—92.0% to 91.7%. Both match or exceed any casino in Atlantic City for slots odds.

Outside Atlantic City and Connecticut, slots players should favor casinos that offer the best odds to video poker players. Anecdotal evidence strongly suggests casinos that provide the best odds to video poker players tend to offer relatively good odds to slots players, too.

ROULETTE

The best way to improve your odds at roulette is to find a wheel that has just a single 0, not a 00 space as well. That reduces the casino's edge from nearly 5.3% to 2.7%. Unfortunately, single-0 wheels are becoming extremely hard to find in the US outside of high-limit rooms, where minimum bets typically are $100 per spin. When single-0 wheels do appear on the main casino floor, they usually have still-steep $25 minimums. *Recently I did find one single-0 wheel with a modest minimum...*

In Las Vegas: The Riviera offers a single-0 wheel with a $5 minimum on occasion (*www.rivierahotel.com*).

Also...

In Atlantic City: Make even-money bets, such as red/black, even/odd or high/low, rather than bet on a specific number. Under Atlantic City's roulette rules, the casino takes only half of the money lost on even-money bets when the ball lands on 0 or 00, halving the house advantage, compared with casinos elsewhere in the country.

OTHER LOCATIONS

Three rules of thumb for choosing a casino when gambling outside Las Vegas, Reno, Atlantic City or Mississippi...

- **The fewer casinos in the area, the worse the odds.** Competition drives down prices at casinos just as it does in most other businesses. The farther an Indian casino, a riverboat casino or a racetrack slots and video poker parlor are from other casinos, the worse the odds gamblers likely face there. Cruise ship casinos tend to offer poor odds, too.

• **The more a state taxes casino revenue, the worse the odds.** Casinos facing steep taxes pass this expense along to gamblers through poor odds.

Example: Pennsylvania takes 55% of gambling revenues, so gamblers there generally face terrible odds. In comparison, Nevada claims 6.75%.

• **The more glamorous a casino, the worse the odds.** It is gamblers' losses that pay for all those sparkling chandeliers. Relatively plain casinos often rely on business from locals, not tourists, and often offer better odds to encourage repeat business.

Cook the Perfect Burger

Jonathan Waxman, chef and owner of Barbuto, a popular restaurant in New York City's West Village. Waxman's legendary restaurant Jams first introduced California cuisine to New York in the 1980s, and famed chef Bobby Flay considers Waxman a mentor. Waxman is author of *A Great American Cook* (Houghton Mifflin) and *Italian, My Way* (Simon & Schuster). *www.barbutonyc.com*

Hamburgers are among America's favorite foods, but most people don't know how to cook them so that they're juicy on the inside with a great outer crust. *Here's how anyone can make the perfect burger...*

Mind the meat: Use ground chuck that is 80% lean/20% fat. Beef that's leaner than this makes a dry, less tasty burger. Ask the butcher at the supermarket to grind the meat for you fresh. Your burger is doomed to be flavorless if you use old, tired ground beef.

Prepare patties: Use seven ounces of meat per burger—that's a little less than a half-pound. Slap the meat down onto a flat, cold surface (a cold plate will work), and quickly but gently form it into a patty approximately one-inch thick in the center with gently rounded edges. Season both sides with freshly ground pepper and a dash of coarse salt. If you are not cooking the patties immediately, return them to the fridge (do not freeze).

Warning: Excessive kneading or squeezing packs the meat too tight, resulting in dry, tough burgers.

How to cook the burgers: If you're cooking burgers in the kitchen, use a well-seasoned cast-iron skillet. Stainless steel is the second-best option.

Add a little bacon fat or olive oil to the skillet, and preheat the pan over a medium-to-medium-high flame for three to four minutes.

Using a spatula, gently slide the patties into the skillet, then just leave them alone. Do not touch them! Moving the patties reduces their chances of developing that wonderful outer crust that the perfect burger requires.

After three to four minutes, use your spatula to flip the burgers.

Helpful: Check whether the pan appears dry before flipping the burgers to cook on the second side. If so, add a very small amount of fat or oil—perhaps one-quarter teaspoon—to the spot where each flipped burger is about to be placed. Skip this step if you see fat in the pan already.

If you want a rare burger, cook for two minutes on the second side...for medium rare, cook three minutes...for medium, cook four to five minutes...and if you like your burgers well-done, six to seven minutes.

If you're cooking outside on a grill, buy a cast-iron solid griddle insert for your barbecue grill instead of using a grate, then cook the burgers on this using the process described above. This way, you'll get that great outer crust that you can get only from a skillet or griddle. This approach also prevents the burgers from sticking to the bars of the grill. If your grill has a lid, keep it open.

Topping and buns: If you're going to add cheese, do so immediately after cooking the burgers on one side and flipping them. I love Gruyère on a burger, and cheddar and Monterey jack are fine choices, too. Ideally, if you put cheese on a burger, you should put a metal cover over the burger until the cheese melts properly. A cooking store might stock something specifically for this purpose, but even a metal loaf pan could do the trick. Make sure that whatever you use does not seal the pan—your burger will wind up steamed, which won't taste as good.

Great buns for hamburgers include potato rolls, kaiser rolls, soft baguettes and English muffins. Buns can be toasted briefly on the skillet/griddle, then lightly buttered.

I like to skip the ketchup in favor of mayonnaise and slices of tomato. Add sliced Vidalia onions, too.

Borrow eBooks

Borrow ebooks from the library with a free app for iPads, Android tablets and smartphones. OverDrive Media Console, available at Apple's App Store and the Android Market, lets you borrow ebooks by searching for a local library...browsing titles...entering your library card number...and downloading books. The ebook expires in seven, 14 or 21 days, depending on the library.

But: If the book you want is checked out, you still have to join a list to wait for someone to return it before you can borrow it. There are no fines or late fees because digital access to the book expires on a set date.

Also: Recently, OverDrive and Amazon.com announced that you can borrow ebooks for your Kindle. Go to your library's site, and search for "Kindle Books."

Hidden Treasures at Yard Sales

Cari Cucksey, an antiques dealer and liquidator who owns RePurpose Estate Services in Northville, Michigan. She is host of *Cash & Cari*, a program about vintage merchandise appraisals and estate sales that airs on HGTV. *www.hgtv.com*

A team of photography experts and investigators announced last year that a set of glass negatives purchased at a California yard sale for $45 likely were the work of Ansel Adams and potentially worth $200 million. Others have since disputed that conclusion, but if it turns out to be true, it wouldn't be the first million-dollar yard sale find.

A Pennsylvania man found an early copy of the Declaration of Independence behind a framed picture he purchased for $4 at a flea market in 1989. It sold at auction in 1991 for $2.42 million. A painting purchased at a Wisconsin rummage sale in the late 1990s for around $20 turned out to be by 19th-century artist Martin Johnson Heade. It sold at auction for $1.35 million.

Very few yard sale shoppers will stumble across a million-dollar discovery, of course. But you can make yard sale shopping profitable by learning which common items still have value to collectors or others. Such things might cost a few dollars apiece, so there's no huge financial risk, even if some of your finds turn out to be worthless.

Web sites such as eBay (*www.ebay.com*), eBay Classifieds (*www.ebayclassifieds.com*) and Craigslist (*www.craigslist.org*) make it relatively easy to resell yard sale purchases. If you have questions about an item you have purchased, there are chat rooms and fan pages on the Internet for virtually every type of collectible. Type the name of the collectible into a search engine to find these.

Among the products that often are worth considerably more than they sell for at yard sales...

- **Fisher-Price toys from the 1980s or earlier.** Kids who grew up in the 1970s and 1980s now are old enough to collect the toys that they once played with. Fisher-Price toys in good condition are particularly desirable.

  Example: A vintage Fisher-Price Little People Castle from the 1970s in excellent condition with all of its accessories could be worth $150 or more. Even castles in lesser condition or the reissued castle from the 1980s can bring significant amounts. (The pennant on the side of the 1970s version says "Play Family Castle"...the one on the reissue has a sleeping dragon.)

- **Marantz stereo equipment.** Decades-old electronics tend to be very inexpensive at yard sales, and some audiophiles prefer the sound from the elite stereo equipment of the past to today's audio electronics. If you come across an amplifier, receiver or speakers made by a company called Marantz in reasonable condition for a small sum at a yard sale, buy it, even if it looks out of date. It could be worth hundreds of dollars or more.

Example: A Marantz Model 2385 receiver in excellent condition from the late 1970s recently sold for close to $2,000 on eBay.

Some vintage Pioneer receivers are valuable as well. And any old amplifier or radio that contains vacuum tubes rather than transistors could be worth a gamble of a few dollars. Audiophiles sometimes buy old vacuum tubes to keep their own vintage stereos running. It's not uncommon for old tubes to sell for $10 to $20 or more apiece.

• **Old hardware.** Doorknobs, doorknob plates, hinges, locking mechanisms, doorstops, drawer pulls and other hardware from the 1950s or earlier frequently turn up at yard sales for a few dollars apiece. These can be highly valued by designers and home remodelers.

Hardware that has an Arts & Crafts, Art Nouveau or Art Deco look is particularly likely to be valuable—but as long as a piece of hardware is old, attractive and in decent condition, it's likely that someone will pay more than yard sale prices for it. You typically can tell the difference between reproduction hardware and the real thing by the patina and construction. Older pieces tend to be heavier and show significant wear.

Example: A single chrome drawer pull from the 1950s can bring $10 to $20. Matching sets are particularly likely to get a good price.

• **Old paper items.** Sometimes you can buy a stack of old magazines, pamphlets or other printed items at a yard sale for just a few dollars, yet many printed materials from the 1950s or earlier are worth at least several dollars to collectors, if not more. As a rule of thumb, if it's pre-1960, made of paper and features eye-catching graphics or a picture of an iconic product or person, there probably is a collector out there who is willing to pay for it. Among the pre-1960 magazines that typically bring a good price are *Popular Mechanics*, *Life*, *Mad* and *Jet*, as well as almost any well-illustrated train magazine, World War II–focused magazine or women's magazine.

Examples: Issues of *Ladies' Home Journal* from the 1920s or earlier with appealing cover art in good condition often sell for $20 or more apiece on eBay. Issues of the World War II publication *Signal* magazine often sell for $50 to $75 or more.

Even paper items from the 1960s and 1970s can have some value if they are related to a highly collectible topic. It often is worth paying a dollar or two for an obscure car magazine from the 1960s or 1970s if it features eye-catching pictures of classic muscle cars...or a music magazine if it contains attractive full-page ads for famous rock acts or a cover story on a music icon, such as Michael Jackson.

• **Vintage needlecraft items.** Sewing and knitting are experiencing a major revival among young people, boosting the resale market for vintage sewing and knitting goods. Vintage knitting needles and crochet hooks often are worth $1 or more apiece, sometimes considerably more. Old spools of thread and knitting yarn can have value, too. That can really add up if you come across a sewing kit containing dozens of these things.

A sewing pattern from the 1980s and earlier can be worth some money, particularly if the garment still is considered fashionable. Patterns for iconic or attractive dresses from decades past tend to be worth the most.

Example: A 1960s Vogue Paris Original dress pattern brought $73. A vintage 1930s Simplicity dress pattern recently sold on eBay for about $50.

• **Barbie's old clothes.** If you come across a bin of doll clothes at a yard sale, search through it for any with styles that suggest the 1950s, 1960s or 1970s. If you find these, check inside for a Mattel Barbie tag (or the tag of one of the other Mattel dolls in the Barbie collection, such as Francie, Ken or Skipper). Old Barbie clothes sometimes are more valuable than the dolls themselves.

Example: I recently sold a 1960s Barbie raincoat, rain boots and umbrella set for $150.

• **Musical instruments.** Yard sale instruments often can be resold for much more than yard sale prices, either through one of the Web sites listed earlier or through a local music shop. High school-band–quality woodwind or brass instruments in good condition often bring $100 or more. String instruments in good shape usually bring at least $50 and potentially significantly more. Antique instruments can fetch thousands.

Example: My old high school clarinet is nothing special, yet it has a resale value of around $250.

• **Vintage picture frames.** It might be worth paying a few dollars for an old painting even if the picture is unappealing—if it is in an old hand-carved wood frame. Such frames can be worth $50 or more.

Pick up the frame—a vintage hand-carved wood frame should be heavier than you expect. The more ornate the frame, the more it is likely to bring.

Example: Ornate gold-colored frames in good shape often are worth $50 to $100 and up.

• **Designer clothing from the 1980s.** Many young people are wearing retro styles—and they consider the 1980s retro. Garments from the 1980s that have famous designer labels are the best bets. High-end designers such as *Dior* and *Gucci* generally are most valuable, but even mass-market Izod clothes from the 1980s can have resale value if their look is iconic to that decade.

Example: Izod sweaters from the 1980s can bring $25 to $40 on eBay.

Planting Help

When planting bulbs in the fall, place each bulb in a hole that is three times deeper than the height of the bulb. If you want flowers that bloom and multiply every year, look for bulbs that "naturalize," such as daffodils. Plant bulbs before late December to improve their chances of survival, and avoid storing bulbs in the basement or garage, where they often get soft and moldy. It is better to plant bulbs and take your chances. They won't survive out of the ground indefinitely.

Better Homes and Gardens, 1716 Locust St., Des Moines 50309. *www.bhg.com*

No More Slugs

To get rid of slugs in your garden, sprinkle fresh chopped garlic around areas where you see slugs.

Danny Ledoux, pest control expert and consultant, Fort Pierce, Florida, and author of *Pest Control Simplified for Everyone: Kill, Repel, or Mitigate Pests With or Without Pesticides* (Universal).

Lyme Disease Alert

If you live in the Northeast or upper Midwest of the US (where deer ticks infected with Lyme disease are most prevalent) and find a tick attached to your skin, you should consult a doctor. He/she will decide whether to prescribe antibiotics to treat possible Lyme disease, taking into account the duration of tick attachment and your medical history and risk factors. If not, you will be monitored for the next few weeks for symptoms such as a red "bull's-eye" rash at the bite site, fever, headache, aching muscles and joints, and fatigue. If you develop these symptoms, your doctor may reevaluate your condition and do blood tests to detect the presence of Lyme disease antibodies. When possible, save the tick to bring in for analysis.

Aaron Glatt, MD, professor of clinical medicine, New York Medical College, Valhalla, New York, and president and CEO, St. Joseph Hospital, Bethpage, New York.

15

Car Care

How to Beat a Traffic Ticket

A friend of mine recently got a speeding ticket. She's not alone. Many police forces have been issuing unusually high numbers of tickets, says Gary Biller, president of the National Motorists Association. People aren't driving faster—municipalities are using ticket revenue to close budget gaps.

My friend, who admits she was speeding but had never gotten a speeding ticket before, wondered if she should contest her ticket. Biller says that it's usually worth a try. Drivers sometimes are offered plea bargains that keep their driving records clean and auto insurance rates low. That's what happened to my friend. She contested the ticket and was invited to make a "pretrial appearance" at the court. When she arrived, the prosecuting attorney had already looked up her record, and because it was her first offense, she got off with no points on her license and the cost of the ticket was cut in half. She didn't have to take a driving class, which sometimes is a condition of a reduced fine.

Delay tactics can work, too. Someone my friend knew got a speeding ticket that had a box to check off if he wanted a written report of the traffic stop. He sent the ticket back with the box checked but never got a report. When he called, he was told that the case had been dismissed because legally the court had been required to send a report within 30 days.

Postponing the court appearance is another option. The officer who wrote the ticket might not show up, and the ticket will be dismissed.

Now, don't get me wrong. I'm not advocating speeding. As my friend said, getting stopped by the police was a good thing. She's been hugging the speed limit ever since.

Karen Larson, editor, *BottomLine* newsletters, Boardroom Inc., 281 Tresser Blvd., Stamford, Connecticut 06901.

Emergency Move

To ***gain control of a car if the driver passes out:*** Shift the transmission into neutral if you have plenty of room to stop. This will allow you to steer easily as the car rolls to a stop. Pull the hand brake to slow the car faster. If that doesn't work, try to reach over the driver to apply the brake with your left foot. If all else fails, slam the transmission into the lowest gear. Doing so will slow the car faster than putting it in neutral.

What not to do: Turn off the engine—the car will lose its power steering and power brakes, making it very difficult to maneuver.

CarTalk.com

Stuck-In-Snow Strategy

If your car gets stuck in snow, keep the front wheels straight and rock the car by shifting between drive and reverse and pressing the accelerator lightly. Change directions as soon as your wheels start spinning. Then spread sand in your tracks in front of and behind the car and try to drive out. If you don't have sand, planks or even your car's floor mats or trunk liner can work. If the car won't move at all, do not spin the wheels—that will just dig them in more deeply. You may need to jack up the car—if you can do it safely—and put some form of traction under the drive wheels.

Consumer Reports, 101 Truman Ave., Yonkers, New York 10703. *www.consumerreports.com*

Mechanics' Pick

Cars that cost the least to repair: Toyota models have the fewest and least costly repairs of all cars surveyed. The 2009 Toyota Corolla is the top-ranked model for all cars made between 2001 and 2011, with infrequent trips to the shop and an average repair cost of only $45.84. Second to Toyota is Hyundai, followed by Honda, Ford and General Motors. The rankings include all of a manufacturer's brands—for example, Lexus and Scion are included for Toyota. Rankings are based on data from mechanics.

Analysis of data from 3,000 US mechanics by CarMD, a company that sells a diagnostic tool that lets car owners know what is wrong with their cars and what it should cost to have the problem fixed, reported online at CBSNews.com.

Easy Way to Save On a New Car

Use the buying service Zag—which manages car-purchase offerings for affinity groups such as American Express, USAA and AAA members. The Zag service provides pre-negotiated prices on new cars from participating dealers. Go to the Web site of the affinity group you belong to or go directly to *www.Zag.com.*

Alternative: Pay a negotiating service to find you the best price on the car you want.

Example: CarBargains charges $200 to get bids on the model you want with the options you choose in the area you specify. You get detailed pricing from at least five dealers and can go to any of them to make the purchase.

Kiplinger's Personal Finance, 1729 H St. NW, Washington, DC 20006. *www.kiplinger.com*

Trading In Your Car?

An offer from the dealer to give you the original manufacturer's suggested retail price (MSRP) is probably not as good a deal as it sounds.

Reasons: The fine print likely lists many deductions that would be subtracted from the

MSRP, such as 25 cents for each mile driven… a "reconditioning" charge…and the amount of any rebates or incentives that were available when the vehicle was purchased. Even more deductions could be taken based on your car's condition or history.

Consumer Reports, 101 Truman Ave., Yonkers, New York 10703. *www.consumerreports.org*

Leasing a Car May Be Better Than Buying if You Avoid These Traps

Jesse Toprak is vice president of industry trends at TrueCar.com, which tracks prices paid by car buyers. Based in Santa Monica, California, he previously operated several auto dealerships and served as executive director of industry analysis for the car-pricing site Edmunds.com.

Leases accounted for more than 20% of new-car sales in March of this year—the highest rate since 2005—as consumers took advantage of increasingly attractive lease terms from automakers. Leasing isn't for everyone, but it can make sense for drivers who buy new cars every few years and put less than 15,000 miles on those cars per year…or for business owners, for whom leasing can have tax advantages.

Trouble is, leasing is unfamiliar to most car shoppers and lease contracts are complex, creating an opportunity for dealerships to promote lease deals that cost customers more than they should.

Car-leasing traps to watch out for…

Trap: "You're leasing, so we don't have to haggle over price." Dealerships sometimes try to convince lessees that their monthly lease payment is set in stone by the automaker's lease terms.

What you need to know: Automakers advertise specific lease terms, but that doesn't mean you can't do better. There is a purchase price built into your contract, even though you are leasing, not buying. Unless the vehicle is in very high demand, that purchase price likely is negotiable, just as it would be if you were buying. Use a site such as mine, TrueCar.com, to find out what buyers in your area are paying for the vehicle that you wish to lease. If the price in your contract is higher, point that out. You then might be able to get a monthly payment below the advertised rate.

Trap: "I can get you an amazingly low monthly payment—just don't worry about how many payments you will have to make or how many miles you'll get to drive."

What you need to know: Dealerships often try to get lessees to think only about their monthly payment so that they can slip in unattractive terms elsewhere in the lease contract. The lease's length and mileage limits are two potential trouble spots. If the term of a lease has been stretched beyond three years, the deal probably isn't as attractive as its monthly payment makes it seem. For one thing, the vehicle's warranty might last only three years, which means that you could end up responsible for expensive repairs. Also, be wary of lease contracts that have mileage limits of less than 15,000 per year. That could result in thousands of dollars in overage fees. But if you don't drive much, be sure to ask the dealer if you can lower your monthly payments if you accept a very low-mileage lease program.

Trap: "Lease a new car, and we'll get you out of your upside-down loan on your current vehicle," where you owe more than the car is worth. That might sound like a great idea, but beware of the fine print.

What you need to know: A dealership that makes this offer likely will imply that it is absorbing a loss on your old vehicle. More likely, though, it intends to roll the amount owed on the used vehicle above its trade-in value into the new monthly lease payment without telling you that this is what's being done.

That isn't necessarily a terrible way to get out from under an upside-down auto loan if the interest rate on the new lease is lower than the one charged on the old loan. Just don't let the dealership claim that it can't negotiate other parts of the lease, such as purchase price or trade-in value, because it already is absorbing your upside-down loan. It likely is doing no such thing.

Similar trap: Be wary if a dealership offers to let you out of an existing auto lease early if you agree to lease a new vehicle. Automakers occasionally make these offers, but they typically are mailed directly from the automaker to the lessee. Dealerships have no legal standing in lease contracts and cannot terminate existing leases early even if they wish to. A dealership that makes this offer might intend to roll the remaining lease payments on the old vehicle into the new lease without telling you…or perhaps it simply intends to return your old vehicle to the automaker early, incurring penalties that you will have to pay. If you want to get out of a lease early, the best bet often is swapping it for another leased vehicle through LeaseTrader.com or LeaseSwap.com.

Trap: "There's no way to avoid acquisition fees with a lease." Automakers (and third-party lease companies) inevitably impose an acquisition fee, sometimes called an assignment or a bank fee, when they set up a new lease. This ranges from a few hundred dollars to more than $1,000, depending on the automaker. Attempts to negotiate this fee away inevitably are shot down.

What you need to know: The dealership is being honest when it says that lease acquisition fees are imposed by the automaker and can't be avoided. But there's a chance that the dealership is neglecting to mention that this fee could be reduced. An ever-increasing number of dealerships are inflating automaker acquisition fees and keeping the excess for themselves.

Before visiting a dealership to lease a vehicle, locate the advertised lease terms for that vehicle on the automaker's Web site. The acquisition fee will be disclosed somewhere in the small print. If the acquisition fee in your lease contract is higher, the dealership is inflating it and you might be able to negotiate away some or all of the excess.

Trap: "You have to buy life and disability insurance with this lease—it's the automaker's rule, not ours."

What you need to know: Dealerships sometimes try to force lessees to buy extras such as life and disability insurance or rust-proofing, insisting that the automaker requires it. Automakers never require such things.

The Best Used Cars Under $6,000

Karl Brauer, who has 17 years of experience as an automotive journalist, including a recent stint as editor-in-chief and a senior analyst at the car information site Edmunds.com. Based in Santa Monica, California, he was the first Web-based journalist to be named to the jury of the prestigious North American Car and Truck of the Year award.

Demand for some used cars increased recently as disruptions in Japanese auto and parts production led buyers to seek alternatives. But you still can find good deals for around $6,000 or less—if you choose carefully and negotiate well.

HOW TO FIND BARGAINS

- **Check the mileage.** Search for used vehicles that were driven significantly less than the typical 15,000 miles per year. Asking prices tend to be more highly correlated with a used car's age than its mileage, but it is lower mileage that tends to be the better indicator that a car still has a lot of life left in it.

- **Sign up with Carfax for background checks on particular cars** (*www.Carfax.com*, $44.99 for reports on up to five vehicles). Carfax compiles data on vehicles from more than 34,000 sources, including service centers, mechanics, insurance companies and motor vehicle agencies based on the vehicle identification number. This service is not perfect, but it can help you weed out many problem vehicles that have been involved in accidents or have lengthy repair histories, odometer rollbacks or other red flags.

Helpful: Be wary of used vehicles that Carfax says have been registered in more than one state over the years. Sellers sometimes move cars from state to state to hide serious problems in their history, such as salvage titles, which typically are issued when a vehicle has such major problems that an insurer has deemed it a total loss.

• **Get the vehicle's maintenance records.** Car owners who have comprehensive maintenance records tend to be car owners who take good care of their cars. Ask for maintenance records even if you buy from a dealer.

• **Get a prepurchase inspection.** Expect to pay a mechanic $100 to $200 per inspection. Make sure it includes a road test. If you don't already have a mechanic you trust, ask friends for recommendations.

Among the most reliable used car options for around $6,000 or less...

HATCHBACK

• **2003 Pontiac Vibe/Toyota Matrix.** The Vibe and Matrix are sister cars, built in the same factory and differing only in the nameplates attached to them. Whatever it is called, this is a reliable, fuel-efficient five-door hatchback with so much interior room that it sometimes is referred to as a small station wagon or even a mini-SUV.

Price: Base models in good condition from 2003 are selling for an average of $5,880, compared with an original manufacturer's suggested retail price (MSRP) that started at $14,670.

Fuel economy: 25 miles per gallon (MPG) city/30 highway.*

COMPACT SEDAN

• **2005 Hyundai Elantra.** The Elantra has been a terrific high-reliability, low-problem car ever since its 2001 redesign. It offers excellent fuel economy with a smooth ride and well-designed interior relative to other cars in its class. The 2005 Elantra is perhaps the newest well-made vehicle that is likely to sell for less than $6,000 with reasonably low miles.

Price: The base model sedan is selling for $5,520 on average, compared with an original MSRP that started at $13,599.

MPG: 21 city/29 highway.

*All fuel economy figures in this article reflect the Environmental Protection Agency's estimates for new vehicles. The fuel economy of a used vehicle could be significantly lower.

MIDSIZED SEDAN

• **2002 Toyota Camry.** Despite some recent well-publicized Toyota recalls, arguably no vehicle matches the Camry when it comes to offering solid build, quality, dependability and a quiet ride at a reasonable price. A 2002 redesign brought additional interior space, a more powerful engine and a smoother transmission, among other improvements.

Price: Base model 2002 Camrys now average $5,930, compared with an original MSRP that started at $18,970.

MPG: 21 city/29 highway.

LARGE SEDAN

• **2003 Ford Crown Victoria.** Crown Vics provide the comfortable, safe driving experience that big-car buyers crave. They hold up very well as they age, and they were made in such large numbers in the past decade that there are plenty of used ones available, keeping resale prices and parts prices relatively low. Many Crown Victorias are used as police cars and taxis. That's a testament to their durability, but you probably don't want to own one that was driven as hard as cabs and police cars tend to be, so check the Carfax report to confirm that the one you select has always been in private hands.

Price: Currently, 2003 base model Crown Victorias sell for an average of $5,610, down from an original MSRP that started at $23,705.

MPG: 16 city/23 highway.

SPORTS CAR/CONVERTIBLE

• **2001 Mazda Miata.** The sporty two-seater Miata offers possibly the most fun top-down driving experience you can find for a reasonable price. It also is quite reliable and relatively fuel-efficient. Many Miatas have been sold, so there typically are plenty of used ones to choose among. They hold their value well, however, so you might have to buy a car that's more than 10 years old to get a Miata in good shape for under $6,000. (For around $8,000, you should be able to find a Miata that's a few years newer.)

Price: Base model Miatas from 2001 are selling for an average of $5,270, down from an original MSRP that started at $21,180.

MPG: 20 city/25 highway.

MINIVAN

• **2002 Honda Odyssey.** The Odyssey has been the best minivan on the market since its 1999 redesign. It is well-made, reliable and roomy. Its crash safety scores are hard to beat, and its hideaway third-row seats are very easy to fold and unfold. The only downside is that 1999 through 2004 Odysseys experienced automatic transmission problems at a higher-than-normal rate, leaving some owners with repair bills in excess of $3,000. Before buying a 2002 (or 2003 or 2004) Odyssey, confirm through service records or Carfax reports that it received the recall procedure meant to address this problem. (Honda offered an extended transmission warranty on 1999 through 2001 models, but it is no longer in effect.)

Prices: The 2002 Odyssey LX base model currently averages $6,140, down from an original MSRP that started at $24,250.

MPG: 16 city/23 highway.

MINI SUV

• **2004 Hyundai Santa Fe.** The extremely reliable, well-designed Santa Fe stands out as the clear bargain in the pricey SUV pack. The only downside is that models with the 2.4-liter base package engine are a bit underpowered. They might struggle to tow a trailer or carry a full load of passengers up a steep incline.

Price: A 2004 base model Santa Fe is likely to cost around $6,060, but expect to pay perhaps $1,000 more for one with the larger 3.5-liter engine. Base models had an original MSRP starting at $17,999.

MPG: 18 city/25 highway.

PICKUP TRUCK

• **2003 Ford F150.** The versatile, durable F150 has been the best-selling truck for many years, so there usually are plenty of used ones to choose among at competitive prices. Its ride and handling are better than those of most pickups, too. Trucks are designed to endure rough use, but it's best to seek out one that has been babied.

Examples of how to spot problems: If there's little life left in a pickup's rear springs and shocks, it will sag when parked on a level surface. If it drifts rather than holding a straight line during your test drive, or if there are significant dents or scrapes along the lower bodywork and/or the major underbody components, it could mean that the truck has had a hard life of hauling or off-road driving and is best avoided.

Price: The F-150 has been offered in a wide range of different configurations, but the 2003 XL base model is among the most recent that is likely to be available in good shape for less than $6,000, with an average sales price of $5,230, down from an original MSRP that started at $19,125.

MPG: 14 city/19 highway.

Car Shoppers: 31,000 Miles Better Than 29,000

The price of a used car drops by about $200 each time the odometer rolls over a 10,000-mile mark. But there is little if any difference, mechanically, between a well-maintained car with 31,000 miles and a similar one that has 29,000 miles…or 41,000 miles compared with 39,000.

What to do: Look for a used car that is just above a 10,000-mile odometer reading.

CNNMoney.com

Your Used Car Could Be Worth Big Bucks

Phil Reed, senior consumer advice editor at Edmunds.com, an automotive information Web site. Based in Santa Monica, California, he is author of *Strategies for Smart Car Buyers* (Edmunds).

Cars traditionally keep declining in value from the moment they are driven off the dealership lot. But the resale value of many used cars has climbed significantly in the past year. Fuel-efficient used compact cars have done especially well, with prices rising by 19.2% in 12 months—but even gas-thirsty used cars have risen in value.

• **Blame the weak economy, which has altered the usual used-car supply/demand balance.** Cost-conscious car buyers increasingly are opting for used cars rather than stretching their budgets for new ones...while equally economical car owners are driving their current vehicles longer before replacing them, reducing the number of used cars on the market.

Other factors include the government's Cash for Clunkers program, which pulled hundreds of thousands of used cars off the market a few years ago, and the tsunami that struck Japan in March 2011, disrupting the supply of new cars and further increasing the demand for used ones.

Used-car values are likely to retreat slightly from their current lofty levels this fall but they probably will remain high by historical standards for at least a few years.

Taking advantage of high used-car prices can be tricky, however. New-car prices are high these days, too, so selling a used car and then buying a new one isn't necessarily a smart move. *Three smart ways car owners can cash in...*

1. Get by with fewer cars. Retired couples and families who live near good public transit systems or car-sharing programs such as Zipcar (866-494-7227, *www.zipcar.com*) often don't need a separate car for every driver. Such households could sell a vehicle for top dollar now and put off buying a replacement until prices pull back or even not replace it at all. They also will save money on auto insurance and vehicle registration costs in the interim.

Example: My family had an extra car because my wife now walks to work and one of my teenage sons is overseas for a year. We sold our 2007 Honda Fit Sport for $11,500—just $4,200 less than we had bought it for new five years earlier.

Selling strategy: Sell a fuel-efficient vehicle if possible, because these are fetching the best prices.

However, used-vehicle values are changing so rapidly these days that setting an appropriate asking price can be tricky. If you live near one of the more than 100 outlets of the car-selling and car-buying chain CarMax (800-519-1511, *www.carmax.com*), bring in the car and ask what CarMax would pay for it. Then list the car for sale in the local newspaper or in eBay's free classifieds (*www.ebayclassifieds.com*) for $1,000 or so more than CarMax offered.

If no one offers more than CarMax within a week, return to CarMax and accept its offer, which is valid for seven days. If you don't live near a CarMax, check what similar vehicles are listed for in the local newspaper or on eBay.

2. Trade up to a larger vehicle. If you want a larger car, this might be a good time to get one. While fuel-efficient used cars have increased in value, demand for used gas guzzlers is relatively weak. You might be able to sell a small car and buy a big one without kicking in much extra cash. If you don't drive this vehicle very much, the reduction in fuel efficiency won't cost you much, either. At current gas prices, if you drive only 5,000 miles annually, the difference between a car getting 20 miles per gallon (mpg) and one getting 30 mpg is about $300 per year.

Examples: Big, well-built gas guzzlers, such as the 2007 GMC Yukon (original manufacturer's suggested retail price of $34,675 and up) and 2007 Chevrolet Suburban ($37,000 and up), now can be found for less than $20,000. Yukons and Suburbans from 2004 and earlier often can be found for about $10,000.

3. See if it makes sense to buy the vehicle you have been leasing. Lease contracts give lessees the option of purchasing their vehicles at the end of their lease terms at some predetermined price. Traditionally this purchase price is not very attractive, but with today's high used-car prices, it might be less than the car is worth on the open market, particularly if it is a fuel-efficient vehicle. If you have maintained your leased car well, it might be a safer choice than buying a stranger's used car.

Warning: Lease contracts often make it difficult to decipher the total cost of purchasing the vehicle at the lease's end. There frequently are "acquisition fees" or other hard-to-spot add-on charges. Call the financing company, say that you're considering buying the vehicle at the end of your lease term and ask the total amount of the check that you would have to write to do this, fees included. Also, ask what financing terms the financing company could offer. It might provide a below-market loan if it wants your continued business or wants a quick sale on the vehicle.

Best Rated

B***est overall-value car brand:*** Toyota. Total ownership costs include maintenance, repairs, fuel, fees, financing, insurance and depreciation.

Nine of its models have the lowest total ownership costs in their categories: Compact crossover/wagon (Matrix), compact pickup (Tacoma), crossover/wagon (Prius v), full-sized crossover/wagon (Highlander), full-sized pickup (Tundra), minivan (Sienna), passenger car (Prius), sporty/coupe (Yaris) and SUV (FJ Cruiser).

Other cars that scored tops in their categories include Honda Insight, MINI Cooper convertible, Chevrolet Tahoe, Infiniti FX35 and M37, Audi A3 and A5 convertible and coupe and Buick LaCrosse four-cylinder. For a complete list, go to *www.intellichoice.com.*

IntelliChoice's Best Overall Value of the Year Awards, identifying the vehicles with the lowest cost to own and operate over the first five years of ownership.

Dangerous Trend

One in five drivers admits to surfing the Internet on a cell phone at least once a week while driving. More than 70% made or received calls...35% sent or received text messages while driving.

Cindy Garretson, director, auto technology research, State Farm Insurance, Bloomington, Illinois, and leader of a survey of 912 drivers.

Save $150 (or More) A Year on Gas With the Right Credit Card

Bill Hardekopf, CEO of LowCards.com, which helps consumers compare credit cards and provides rankings and reviews for each card, Birmingham, Alabama. He is coauthor of *The Credit Card Guidebook* (Lulu). *www.lowcards.com*

Credit cards that offer rebates of as much as 5% for purchases of gasoline are especially appealing in this era of high fuel prices. But beware—not all such credit cards are as attractive as their marketing materials make them seem.

Some advertise hefty rebates that shrink dramatically after 60 or 90 days. Others cap rebates at as little as $20 per month or even less in some cases...or they void accumulated rebates if cardholders are even one day late with a payment. And most rebate cards charge very high interest rates that make them inappropriate for people who carry balances.

Still, cards with hefty rebates on gas purchases can be money savers for careful consumers, trimming annual transportation costs by perhaps $100 to $150 for the typical driver and potentially more for those who drive their cars a lot.

Note: None of the credit cards in this article charges an annual fee...and offers are subject to change.*

UNBRANDED GAS-REBATE CARDS

Some credit cards provide sizable rebates for purchases at most or all gas stations, not just stations that sell a particular brand of gas. *Worth considering...*

If you have excellent credit: PenFed Visa Platinum Cashback Rewards Card offers a tough-to-top 5% rebate on gas purchases paid for at the pump, with no rebate cap. It also offers a 1% rebate on other purchases, and its 13.99% variable annual percentage rate (APR) is quite low by rebate card standards. (800-247-5626, *www.penfed.org*)

Downside: This card is available only to extremely qualified applicants. Even those with high credit scores sometimes are rejected if the notoriously conservative PenFed spots something in particular on the credit report that it considers a reason for concern, such as a high debt-to-income or credit-utilization ratio. Only members of the PenFed Credit Union can apply for this card, but anyone can join this credit union by paying a onetime $15 fee to join Voices for America's Troops, a nonprofit (see PenFed's Web site for details). This membership fee will not be refunded if your credit card application is rejected.

If you are a Costco member: True Earnings Card from Costco and American Express offers 3% back on gas purchases of up to $3,000 per year at domestic stand-alone gas stations and Costco gas stations and 1% thereafter. It also offers 3% cash back at restaurants, 2% on many travel-related purchases and 1% on other purchases. (800-223-2670, *www.americanexpress.com*)

Downside: It is available only to Costco members. Rebate checks are distributed just once a year and can be cashed only at a Costco.

If you like things simple: Capital One No Hassle Cash Rewards MasterCard is a reasonable choice for those who want cash back for buying gas at almost any station without membership requirements, rebate limits or other tricky rules. (800-410-0020, *www.capitalone.com*)

Downside: The gas rebates aren't the highest—cardholders receive 2% cash back. (The card also provides 2% cash back at major grocery stores and 1% on most other purchases.)

GAS COMPANY–BRANDED CREDIT CARDS

Most major gasoline brands are linked to credit cards. Applications usually are available at the branded stations or through the brands' Web sites.

If it's convenient for you to buy a single brand of gas, there may be good reason to consider branded gas-rebate credit cards. Their rebates sometimes are larger than those of most general gas cards, often 4% or 5%. Many gas-company credit cards provide these rebates as credits against future gas purchases, not as cash, but that's nearly as good.

The best card for you might be the one linked to the brand of gas most convenient for you to buy even if its rebate is not the biggest. Otherwise you're likely to waste more time and gas driving out of your way to obtain the discount than it's worth. *Cards to consider...*

- **BP Visa offers a 5% rebate at BP and Amoco stations, with no rebate cap.** It provides a 2% rebate on most travel-related purchases, such as airline tickets, car rentals, lodging and dining, and a 1% rebate on almost everything else. New cardholders receive double rebates for the first 60 days (*www.bp.com*, then from the "Products and Services" menu, select "Gas and Fuel Cards").
- **ExxonMobil MasterCard offers 15 cents back per gallon at Exxon and Mobil stations with no rebate cap.** That's the equivalent of slightly more than a 4% rebate with gas at $3.70 per gallon, or 5% should gas prices slip back to $3 per gallon. There's a 0.5% to 2% rebate on most other purchases (800-554-6914, then say "Apply" when the automated system asks for your account number, *www.exxonmobilcard.com*).
- **Sinclair Platinum Edition Visa offers a 4% rebate on up to $7,500 per year in purchases made at Sinclair stations.** Cardholders earn 1% on Sinclair purchases that exceed this amount and on most other purchases. New cardholders receive 8% cash back at Sinclair during their first two billing cycles (866-552-9812, *www.sinclairvisa.com*).
- **Citi Platinum Select Citgo MasterCard offers 4% at Citgo stations and 0.5% to 1% on most other purchases.** Rebates are capped at $50 per month (800-241-8356, then say "Apply" when the automated system asks for your account number, *www.citgo.com*).
- **Gulf Platinum MasterCard offers a 3% rebate at Gulf stations and 1% on most other purchases, with no rebate limits** (800-307-0341, *www.gulfmastercard.com*).

• **Chevron and Texaco Visa offers 10 cents cash back per gallon at Chevron and Texaco stations.** That's the equivalent of a relatively unimpressive 2.7% rebate with gas at $3.70 per gallon, though it would climb to a more competitive 3.3% if gas fell back to $3 per gallon. Fuel credits are capped at $300 per year. The card also provides a 3% discount on nonfuel purchases at Chevron and Texaco stations and a 1% rebate on nonfuel purchases made elsewhere (866-448-4367, *www.chevrontexaco cards.com*).

Note: The Shell Platinum MasterCard recently stopped being available, so watch Shell stations or the Shell Web site for applications and details of a new Shell-branded card (*www.shell.us*). The Sunoco MasterCard provides Thank You rewards points redeemable for merchandise, not a straightforward gas rebate (800-238-1437, *www.gosunoco.com*).

Buy Groceries, Save On Gas

Several major grocery chains have made arrangements with Shell Oil—one of the biggest gasoline marketers in North America—to redeem the chains' reward points for discounts at the pump. In most cases, $50 of grocery purchases produces a gas discount of five cents a gallon...$100 in grocery purchases gives a discount of 10 cents a gallon. Participating stores include Bi-Lo, Giant, Kroger, Save Mart, Stop & Shop and Winn-Dixie, as well as many regional convenience stores.

Jeff Lenard, spokesperson, National Association of Convenience Stores, Alexandria, Virginia. *www.nacs online.com*

Share Your Car to Make Money

Peer-to-peer car-sharing services let you make money from your car when it would sit idle...or drive someone else's car instead of renting from a rental company. The Internet-based services connect people whose cars sit for hours in parking lots or are unused on weekends with people who need cars during those periods. Renters pay $5 to $15 per hour for a car, including insurance—the peer-to-peer company buys the policy. Right now, almost all the companies are operating only in parts of California.

What to do: Contact firms such as Getaround in San Francisco and parts of San Diego, *www.getaround.com*...Spride Share, San Francisco, *www.spride.com*...RelayRides, San Francisco and Cambridge, Massachusetts, *www.relayrides.com*...and JustShareIt, San Francisco and Los Angeles, *www.justshareit.com*.

USA Today

Most Likely...to Be Stolen

Five vehicles most likely to be stolen: Cadillac Escalade SUV...Ford F-250 crew cab pickup...Infinity G37...Dodge Charger HEMI...and Chevrolet Corvette Z06.

Least likely to be stolen: Volvo S80...Saturn Vue...Nissan Murano...Honda Pilot...and Subaru Impreza.

Kim Hazelbaker, senior vice president, Highway Loss Data Institute, part of the Insurance Institute for Highway Safety, Arlington, Virginia, and leader of a study of theft-claim rates for 2007 through 2009 model years.

Tell Your Auto Mechanic "NO" When He Tells You This

Tom Torbjornsen, host of America's Car Show with Tom Torbjornsen on the SSI Radio Network. He spent nearly two decades as an automotive technician, service manager and auto service center manager. Based in Jamestown, New York, Torbjornsen is maintenance editor for AOL Autos and author of *How to Make Your Car Last Forever* (Motorbooks). *www.americascarshow.com*

Even the smartest people sometimes feel foolish when speaking with car mechanics. We often say yes to maintenance services because we figure that the auto mechanic knows what is best for our cars.

However, car owners sometimes overspend because less-than-honest auto repair shops talk them into services that their cars don't really need. They also may not understand that today's vehicles have different needs than those of decades past.

Among the most common money-wasting mistakes car owners make...

FLUID FLUSHES

Some quick-lube shops, independent mechanics and car dealerships pressure car owners into replacing automotive fluids that still are perfectly fine. In some cases, this will mean draining the fluids...in others, they might recommend actually flushing the system out completely, cleaning out virtually every drop of the old fluid. In either case, these services can cost $70 to $150 or more apiece.

• **Brake fluid flushes.** Don't trust a shop that recommends you flush your brake fluid regularly. Brake fluid can last as long as your vehicle. There are exceptions, however. Your brake fluid might legitimately need to be flushed if moisture gets into the system or the brake fluid has overheated.

What to do: Visually inspect your brake fluid once or twice a year, or ask a mechanic you trust to do so when you stop by for some other service. Brake fluid should be clear or translucent. If the fluid is rust-colored, moisture might have gotten in and a flush might be warranted. If your brake fluid is black or has a burnt smell, your braking system likely has a problem that requires a mechanic's attention, not just a flush. If it is below the recommended level, it might have a leak.

If the brake fluid is clear or translucent, does not smell burnt and is at the correct level, agree to a flush only if your vehicle's maintenance schedule calls for it, which is rare.

• **Power steering fluid flushes.** Power steering fluid can last the life of a vehicle, too, unless otherwise noted in the vehicle's maintenance schedule.

What to do: Inspect the fluid once or twice a year, or ask a trusted mechanic to do so for you. It should be flushed and replaced if it smells burnt or you see black grime or metal flakes in the fluid—shining a light into the reservoir can help you spot these flakes. There could be an underlying problem that requires a mechanic's attention as well. Otherwise there's no need for the flush.

• **Transmission fluid flushes.** Automatic transmission fluid should be flushed occasionally—but some disreputable quick-lube shops recommend these flushes to seemingly every customer who comes in for an oil change. Most of those flushes are completely unnecessary and in some cases might even hurt the transmission.

What to do: Have your transmission fluid flushed every 35,000 miles or so. Make sure that the shop replaces the filter when it changes the fluid. Some automakers say a transmission fluid flush isn't necessary until perhaps 100,000 miles, but transmission fluid is an oil and oil can break down over time, so this is one situation where it makes sense to err on the side of caution.

• **Engine oil flushes.** Ask some quick-lube shops and mechanics for a $25 oil change, and they will try to sell you a $100 to $200 engine oil flush. They'll claim this is the only way to clear years of sludge out of the engine. Trouble is, any sludge that an oil flush does dislodge could clog the oil pump pickup screen, causing more problems than it solves.

What to do: Have your oil changed, not flushed. Get oil changes according to your vehicle's maintenance schedule—that's likely every 5,000 miles or 7,500 miles, not every 3,000 miles, the old rule of thumb. Lean toward a high-quality synthetic oil, such as AMSOIL or Mobil 1, assuming that synthetic oils are recommended as an option in your vehicle's owner's manual. These cost a few dollars more but do a far superior job protecting your engine.

UNNEEDED CLEANINGS

Keeping a car clean might seem like a wise investment, but in some cases it's money misspent.

• **Brake system cleanings.** This typically involves taking the brakes apart and washing or even sandblasting the components, usually at a cost upward of $100. It's probably unnecessary. Modern braking systems are designed to pretty much take care of themselves without this treatment.

What to do: Don't agree to this unless it is recommended by a mechanic you trust and your vehicle has experienced a braking problem, such as a high-pitched squealing even though the brake pads are not yet worn out, which could be a sign that glazing has developed on the brake parts.

• **Fuel system cleanings.** Quick-lube shops sometimes recommend these every 5,000 or 10,000 miles. They inevitably claim that this $100-to-$150 service will pay for itself in improved gas mileage. That's true only if the fuel injectors were badly clogged. Fuel injectors can become clogged and require cleaning, but this generally happens slowly.

What to do: Get a fuel system cleaning every 35,000 miles or so. Anything more is overkill. Have this work done by a mechanic in a fully equipped shop that appears very well-stocked with modern-looking computerized equipment. Doing fuel system cleanings properly requires specialized equipment, tools and know-how that many shops lack.

• **Any service offered by a car wash beyond the wash itself.** The paint sealants, protectants, under-car sealant and color waxes that car washes offer tend to be virtually worthless. They're likely to wash away the first time the car is out in the rain.

What to do: The only service worth paying for at a car wash is a car wash.

BUT DON'T CUT CORNERS

Sometimes not spending enough on vehicle maintenance ends up costing car owners. *Examples....*

• **Buying generic brake pads or delaying brake pad replacement.** Low-quality brake pads will wear out faster than higher-quality pads. That means you'll have to return to the shop sooner to replace them, more than offsetting any money saved by buying the cheaper part.

Delaying brake pad replacement or using low-quality brake pads also can increase the wear on the brake rotors. That could force you to replace both the pads and rotors, which could easily double or triple the cost of the brake job. Using worn-out or low-quality brake pads also could reduce your ability to bring your vehicle to a stop in an emergency.

What to do: Replace your brake pads as soon as they have worn down to less than one-quarter inch in depth. It might be time to replace the pads if your brakes consistently screech, too—perfectly good brake pads might screech on wet days, but if the brake pads are still good, that screeching likely will not persist throughout a long trip or once the weather dries up. Opt for high-quality brake pads, such as those made by Wagner (800-325-8886, *www.federalmogul.com*) or Bendix (*www.bendixbrakes.com*). These typically cost $15 to $20 more per pad than the generics, but that's a small price to pay for longer pad life, longer rotor life and greater safety. The original-equipment brake pads sold by dealerships likely are fine, too, but might be expensive.

• **Not replacing the air filter regularly.** There's no good excuse for not replacing your vehicle's air filter every 10,000 to 12,000 miles. Air filters are inexpensive—usually $15 to $20—and putting in a new one is a simple do-it-yourself job in most vehicles. If you don't want to do this yourself, a mechanic should be able to do this for you for the cost of the filter and a half-hour's labor or less. Continue to use a dirty air filter, and you cost yourself money by reducing your car's fuel efficiency.

What to do: If you want to minimize the long-term cost and hassle of replacing air filters, buy a K&N air filter (800-858-3333, *www.KNFilters.com*). These typically cost $40 to $60, but unlike conventional paper air filters, they can provide excellent fuel efficiency and filtration for the life of your vehicle. Just clean them every 50,000 miles using a K&N cleaning kit designed for the purpose. The kits cost around $10 to $12 and last for many cleanings.

• **Washing your car with household soap.** Common household soaps, such as dishwashing soap, might remove the wax coating from a vehicle or otherwise damage its finish.

What to do: Wash your car only with pH-neutral wash solutions specifically designed for use on vehicles. These are available in auto-parts stores and in the auto sections of discount stores. Or take the car to a car wash.

16

Family Life

Are You Parenting Your Parents?

Teenagers aren't the only ones who argue with their parents. Full-grown adults sometimes disagree with their aging parents. When these conflicts involve a parent's safety or financial security, the adult children often refuse to yield despite the parent's wishes.

These disagreements can grow so heated that it almost seems as if a referee needs to be called in to avoid ruining the relationship.

Here are ways to increase the odds of a peaceful resolution when grown children and their parents disagree...

• **Include close family members in the conversation with the parent, and meet with those family members beforehand.** Family members who are close to this parent are more likely to oppose your position if they feel excluded from the decision-making process. Also, parents are more likely to respect an opinion shared by many family members than that of just one adult child.

• **Schedule the conversation for morning or early afternoon if the parent experiences "sundowning"**—reduced mental clarity as evening approaches. People in the early stages of dementia often are mentally sharpest and best able to contribute to important conversations early in the day.

Have ready specific examples of why you believe something needs to be done. Examples can increase the odds that the parent and other relatives will agree that action is required.

Example: "It's not just my opinion that your driving skills have slipped. You've had three fender benders in the past year."

John Bertschler, PhD, a mediator, licensed psychologist and co-owner of Northcoast Conflict Solutions, a mediation practice based in Seven Hills, Ohio. He also trains mediators and is coauthor of *Elder Mediation: A New Solution to Age-Old Problems* (NCS). *www.ncsmediation.com*

• **Raise an issue by saying it might be time to discuss the available options, not by saying it's time to take the specific action that you, personally, consider best.** Pushing your opinion at the outset only increases the odds that the parent will dig in his/her heels.

Example: Say, "I think it's time we discussed what sort of help you might need in the future," rather than, "I think it's time we thought about moving you into a nursing home"—even if you think a nursing home is the best choice.

Once a parent agrees to take part in the discussion, it is more likely that he will listen when you provide evidence that the option you favor is worth a look.

• **If family discussions about elder issues become rancorous, find a mediator.** The National Eldercare Mediator Network (*www.EldercareMediators.com*) or the Association for Conflict Resolution (*www.acrnet.org*) can help you locate a professional mediator in your region who has experience dealing with elder issues. Mediators typically charge from $150 to $500 an hour, depending on the region and their experience. If this is cost prohibitive, perhaps the family can agree on a respected family member, family friend or religious counselor to serve as a mediator.

Among the issues involving elderly parents that often become sources of family strife...

HOW MUCH CARE

Conflict: Some family members believe an elderly parent needs more assistance from professional caregivers, possibly even a nursing home—but the parent disagrees.

Strategy: Cite the specific dangerous incidents that are causing your concern—falls or ovens being left on, for example. Keep the term "nursing home" out of the conversation—it carries too much negative baggage in many people's minds. Instead, explain that there are many other possible care options, ranging from having someone look in on the parent regularly...to an assisted-living facility. Say that your goal is to find the option that gets the parent the amount of assistance needed to live the life he wants.

If that fails—or if you are the elderly parent and you truly believe that your current living arrangements are appropriate—suggest that the family arrange a geriatric assessment. This provides an unbiased, informed evaluation of what level of assistance is appropriate for a senior. It is typically offered through hospitals and geriatric care centers. The parent's doctor might be able to recommend someone. If not, your state's Adult Protective Services department might be able to help you find one. (Put "Adult Protective Services" and your state's name into any search engine to find contact information for this government agency.)

SHOULD THE PARENT DRIVE?

Conflict: An aging parent's driving seems unsafe to one or more family members, but the parent won't surrender the car keys.

Strategy: Do not just ask a parent to give up the car keys—present a plan for how the parent will get around without a car. If you are the parent, explain that you might be willing to discuss giving up driving if such a plan could be arranged. Research the region's public transit, senior shuttles and taxi services. Or explore whether family members and friends who live in the region could provide rides when needed.

Example: A man agreed to sell his car when his son suggested that some of the money from this sale be put into an account with a local cab company.

If the parent still considers himself a safe driver, suggest that he retake the driving test through the state department of motor vehicles to settle the matter objectively...and/or suggest that he take driving lessons designed for aging adults given by organizations such as Keeping Us Safe (877-907-8841, *www.KeepingUsSafe.org*)...and AAA (202-638-5944, *www.SeniorDrivers.org*).

LIVING TOGETHER

Conflict: Family members may get under one another's skin when an elderly parent moves in with an adult child.

Strategy: Neither parent nor child should attempt to impose "house rules." Instead, say that everyone will have to work together to develop a system that keeps family members from annoying one another. Propose that the first month be treated as an adjustment period, and choose a date and time of month in the future for family members to discuss what policies need to be implemented.

Example: An older man often got up in the middle of the night for a snack, then left his son's kitchen a mess. During the follow-up meeting, he agreed to clean his dishes before returning to bed. He hadn't realized this was annoying because his late wife had never complained about it.

If the parent has diminished mental capacity and cannot help but do things that annoy the rest of the family, search for ways you could alter the living arrangements to minimize these annoyances. Perhaps the parent could move into a room in the basement so that his late-night noise is less disruptive. If no solution presents itself, the adult child must decide whether the behavior can be endured or whether it is so disruptive that the only solution is to find alternate living arrangements for the parent.

Stay Connected to A Loved One with Alzheimer's

Marjory Abrams, president, *BottomLine* newsletters, Boardroom Inc., 281 Tresser Blvd., Stamford, Connecticut 06901.

The news that a friend or relative has Alzheimer's disease is not only devastating—it also can be intimidating, as I've heard so often from friends. Most people don't quite know what to say or do when they are with the person. Yet there are specific ways you can stay close with the loved one and contribute to his/her ongoing comfort and serenity, says medical social worker Nancy Pearce, author of *Inside Alzheimer's: How to Hear and Honor Connections with a Person Who Has Dementia* (*www.InsideAlzheimers.com*). She offers the following guidelines, which work whether the person was recently diagnosed or is now quite impaired...

- **Decide to connect.** Before every visit, think about what might be getting in the way of interacting with this person. Often it's our innermost feelings, such as, "This is just so sad" or "This is too hard". Such thinking distracts us from being truly present.

- **Another obstacle to connection is how you communicate nonverbally.** A person with dementia still can feel your tensions, distractions or apathy because these are broadcast through your stance and voice. Before you go into the room, take a moment and breathe deeply to release tension.

Let go of rigid thinking, and think about what is best for the person.

Case in point: Pearce once worked with a 92-year-old man who every day anxiously asked for his mother—and every time was told that she had died. Each day, he grieved anew. His caregivers meant well, but their concern with accuracy actually was cruel. When his caregivers realized what really was behind the request—the need to feel taken care of—they were able to make the patient's life much more peaceful. For example, when he wanted his mother to do something for him, his caregivers let him know that she could not be there at that time, but that they would help him instead.

- **Open your heart and enter the person's world, rather than getting caught up in the nuts and bolts of the disease by asking about symptoms and so on.** Pearce knew a man with dementia whose longtime golf buddy picked him up every week to play. When the man could no longer hit the ball, his friend found other things for him to do at the golf course—drive the cart or clean the balls—so they still could happily share their mutual interest. There was another woman whose beloved grandmother had Alzheimer's, and as a result, the grandmother often was angry. After much trial and error, the woman learned that what opened both their hearts was to watch old movies together.

- **Embrace silence.** When it comes to talking, less can be more, especially for people who may be frustrated about losing their ability to speak and comprehend. You don't have to fill every silence with conversation.

• **Express gratitude.** No matter how advanced the disease, notice and thank the person for all the little things you appreciate about being with him. You might simply thank him for allowing you the time spent together.

Advice for Caregivers

Beth Kallmyer, MSW, senior director of Constituent Services, Alzheimer's Association, Chicago.

Empathy is especially important when you are interacting with people with Alzheimer's disease.

Example: If an Alzheimer's patient starts talking about his/her long-dead mother as if she were still alive, the caregiver should not try to correct him. Instead, say something like, "It sounds as if you really miss your mom." Learning how Alzheimer's progresses and how to handle it can help family members develop empathy—go to *www.alz.org* for details. Paid caregivers can be taught to have more empathy, too. Tell caregivers what the patient is used to doing—share his interests and patterns with them.

Example: If the person with Alzheimer's is used to taking showers only at night, he/she may become distressed if caregivers try to help him shower in the morning.

Helpful: Fill out the "Personal Facts and Insights" form at *www.alz.org* (search for "Personal Facts and Insights"). The form, which asks questions about the person with Alzheimer's, can be given to all caregivers.

Social Networking For Elder Care

Several free Web sites now make it easier for families to coordinate care for older adults—and even to save money doing so. The sites help caregivers communicate with many people at once, using messages, blogs and photos to keep people up to date on the status of the person under care while asking for assistance when it is needed. Some sites have set up networks in which people can volunteer caregiving help. Popular sites include Lotsa Helping Hands (*www.lotsahelpinghands.com*)... CarePages (*www.carepages.com*)...Caring Bridge (*www.caringbridge.org*)...eCareDiary (*www.ecarediary.com*)...CareCentral (*www.carecentral.com*)...and CareFlash (*www.careflash.com*).

Anne Tergesen, "Family Value" columnist, *The Wall Street Journal.*

Spouses Affect Each Other's Health

Recent study: When researchers followed more than 1,700 couples (ages 76 to 90, many who were married for more than 40 years) over a 15-year period, they found that the couples often shared depressive symptoms, such as unhappiness and loneliness, and functional limitations, such as the inability to perform basic tasks, including climbing stairs and cooking.

Christiane Hoppmann, PhD, assistant professor of psychology, The University of British Columbia, Canada.

Don't Like Your Child's Friends?

Don't bad-mouth them. Instead, find out why he/she is drawn to them by getting to know them yourself. You may find that they aren't so bad. Be honest about your concerns. Have a heart-to-heart talk with your child about the influence you think his friends may have. Don't forget your own childhood and teen years. You likely had friends your parents didn't approve of as well. Think about what you wish your parents had done or said.

Jenny Runkel, cofounder and director of content, The ScreamFree Institute, a not-for-profit organization dedicated to helping families stay connected, Norcross, Georgia. *www.screamfree.com*

Lack of Sun Hurts Young Eyes

Recent finding: Studies in the US, Singapore and China have found a consistent link between the time spent outdoors and myopia (nearsightedness). Children who spent the most time outdoors—10 to 14 hours a week—were half as likely to have myopia as children who were outdoors only three to six hours a week. Avoiding the outdoors causes a lack of retinal dopamine, which can lead to myopia.

Kathryn Rose, PhD, associate professor, Faculty of Health Sciences, University of Sydney, Australia, and coauthor of a study of 4,132 children, published in *Ophthalmology*.

"Green" Danger

New "green" plastic water bottle caps can be a choking hazard. The smaller caps save plastic but can be dangerous for children under three years old. After opening a bottle of water, immediately throw away the bottle cap if young children are in the area.

Richard O'Brien, MD, attending emergency physician at Moses Taylor Hospital, and associate professor of emergency medicine at The Commonwealth Medical College of Pennsylvania, both in Scranton.

Croup Can Be Fatal

Bacterial croup is a severe childhood illness that may require hospitalization and can lead to death if not treated immediately. The telltale symptom is a cough that sounds like a seal barking.

Important: Croup that starts in the daytime is potentially more dangerous than croup that starts at night. See a pediatrician immediately if croup starts in the daytime and is accompanied by fever. Croup that starts at night and does not involve fever typically resolves without lasting effects, but it is still wise to place a call to your pediatrician.

James Cherry, MD, professor of pediatrics at David Geffen School of Medicine, University of California, Los Angeles.

Radiation Concern For Children

The average American child is exposed to medical radiation more than seven times by age 18. X-rays and other medical tests that use radiation increase risk for cancer. Of particular concern are CT scans, which use more radiation than X-rays.

Adam L. Dorfman, MD, assistant professor, departments of pediatrics and radiology, University of Michigan Medical School, Ann Arbor, and leader of a study of 355,088 children, published in *Archives of Pediatrics and Adolescent Medicine*.

Rx Not Necessary

Antibiotics may not be necessary for most kids' ear infections. Eighty percent of children with ear infections get better on their own in about three days, according to a recent study. Antibiotics may cause side effects such as rash or diarrhea. And overuse of antibiotics may be responsible for the increase in stronger, drug-resistant bacteria.

Helpful: Ask your pediatrician to write a prescription for antibiotics to be filled only if your child gets worse or if the infection has not cleared up within two to three days. Give your child *ibuprofen* or *acetaminophen* to help relieve pain.

Tumaini Coker, MD, pediatrician, Mattel Children's Hospital, University of California, Los Angeles, and leader of a systematic review of 135 studies on acute ear infections, published in *The Journal of the American Medical Association.*

Meningitis Shots For Teens

A vaccine for meningococcal meningitis is recommended for children ages 11 or 12—the disease is common in adolescents and spreads readily in crowded places, such as camps and dorm rooms. The shot was originally thought to last for at least 10 years.

But: Recent research shows that the vaccine may last for less than five years—so a federal advisory panel now recommends a booster shot at age 16. The recommendation has recently been adopted by the Centers for Disease Control and Prevention. Ask your doctor for details.

James Turner, MD, executive director, department of student health, University of Virginia, Charlottesville.

Teen Hearing Loss

One in five US teens has hearing loss, according to studies.

Recent finding: From 1988 to 1994, 14.9% of 12- to 19-year-olds had hearing loss...in 2005 to 2006 (most recent data available), 19.5% of teens of the same ages had hearing loss—a 31% increase. Adolescent males were more likely to have hearing loss than females...and children from families living below the federal poverty threshold had higher rates than those above that threshold. More study is needed to understand the causes of teens' hearing loss.

Josef Shargorodsky, MD, otolaryngologist, Massachusetts Eye and Ear Infirmary, Harvard Medical School, Boston, and leader of a review of two databases of hearing loss, published in *The Journal of the American Medical Association.*

Depression on the Net

Depression is more common among teens who spend excessive time online.

Recent finding: Teens identified as severe and moderate pathological Internet users, as assessed by the Internet Addiction Test (*www.netaddiction.com*, click on "Self-Test"), were two-and-a-half times more likely to develop severe depression than normal Internet users. Depression has been identified as a risk factor for excessive Internet use, but this study suggests that the reverse also may be true.

Lawrence T. Lam, PhD, associate professor of pediatrics and child health, School of Medicine, The University of Sydney, Australia, and the University of Notre Dame Australia, Fremantle, and leader of a nine-month study published in *Archives of Pediatrics & Adolescent Medicine.*

Life After High School

Marjory Abrams, president, *BottomLine* newsletters, Boardroom Inc., 281 Tresser Blvd., Stamford, Connecticut 06901.

I know of several high school students who are struggling to figure out what they want to do after high school—including whether to go to college. And their parents are struggling because their kids don't want to talk about it with them.

"Discussions about the future should be a series of conversations, not just one or two drawn-out sessions that turn into battles," says psychologist Lawrence Kutner, PhD, author of *Making Sense of Your Teenager* and executive director of the Jack Kent Cooke Foundation (*www.jkcf.org*), which helps promising students reach their potential through education. "Start by sharing your own struggles in choosing your path(s), and be sure to demonstrate that decisions don't have to be final. Talk about the choices that other people have made—but without passing judgment. Acknowledge your child's insights and emotions. Create an environment that is safe for him/her to test things out. A listening, objective, noncritical parental ear will go a long way in helping a confused child figure things out."

Lindsey Pollak, a "Generation Y" career consultant and author of *Getting from College to Career,* finds that young people often are overwhelmed by the abundance of options. Exposure to the possibilities can help them zero in on what truly interests them—for example, with an after-school job, volunteering or simply looking at job listings, as well as talking with slightly older people about the choices they've made.

Helpful resource: Shatterbox (*www.shatterbox.com*), an online video-based community that features 20-somethings talking about their careers.

Top Colleges for Kids with Learning Disabilities or ADHD

Imy Wax, MS, LCPC, CEP, licensed psychotherapist and educational consultant in Chicago and Deerfield, Illinois. She is coauthor of the *K&W Guide to Colleges for Students with Learning Disabilities or Attention Deficit/Hyperactivity Disorder* (ADHD) (Princeton Review). *www.imywax.com*

If you have a child with a learning disability (LD) or attention-deficit/hyperactivity disorder (ADHD), you may wonder how he/she will make it through college. Schools are required to offer support if they accept federal funds, but the amount and type of support vary dramatically.

Here, eight schools with strong programs for LD/ADHD students...

• **Curry College** is a four-year private college in Milton, Massachusetts, just minutes from Boston. Its Program for Advancement of Learning (PAL) is for LD/ADHD students. Students applying through PAL are not required to submit SAT or ACT scores. The program includes a special three-credit three-week summer session to help ease incoming LD/ADHD students' transition to college. PAL students receive extremely strong support during their first year of college in particular, including regular meetings with specially trained instructors and help with homework. It's a great program for students who need extensive support but could be too much for more independent LD/ADHD students. (Around 2,000 undergraduate students. $30,700 tuition plus $12,285 room and board. 617-333-0500, *www.curry.edu.*)

• **Dean College** is a private college in Franklin, Massachusetts, about 35 miles southwest of Boston and 20 miles north of Providence. The college provides a range of excellent support options for LD/ADHD students. Its Personalized Learning Services offers extensive tutoring...its Arch Learning Community offers intensive academic skill development...and its Pathway Learning Community offers small class sizes and individual attention. Additional fees of $800 to $4,000 per semester apply to these programs. The college offers mostly two-year programs, but it has an agreement with other colleges and universities that allows Dean College students who meet certain academic requirements to transition seamlessly and earn four-year degrees. (Around 1,000 full-time undergraduate students. $30,570 tuition plus $13,050 room and board. 877-879-3326, *www.dean.edu.*)

• **Landmark College** is a two-year private college in the rural small town of Putney in southern Vermont. It is one of the few accredited colleges in the country specifically designed for LD/ADHD students. Rather than simply provide students with accommodations and resources that minimize the impact of their LD/ADHD, Landmark focuses on teaching students to overcome their disabilities so that they can transfer to four-year schools for their last two years of college. Landmark also is notable for its very small class sizes and customized tutorial and coaching programs. (Around 450 undergraduate students. $48,210 tuition plus $8,620 room and board. 802-387-6718, *www.landmark.edu.*)

• **Lynn University** is a four-year private university in Boca Raton, a town on Florida's Gold Coast, roughly an hour north of Miami—the campus is about three miles from the ocean. It offers its excellent Comprehensive Support

Program to LD/ADHD students. The program provides individual tutoring, study strategy sessions, specialized classes and numerous other resources and accommodations. (More than 1,600 undergraduate students. $30,200 tuition plus $11,950 room and board. 800-888-5966, *www.lynn.edu.*)

• **Southern Illinois University Carbondale** is a four-year public school in Carbondale, two hours southeast of St. Louis in southern Illinois. The campus is on the edge of the Shawnee National Forest. It offers its Achieve Program to LD/ADHD students. This program begins with a two-day diagnostic evaluation that helps the school fully understand participants' learning disabilities and ensure that the students receive appropriate support. There is a $300 fee for this evaluation. Participants also receive extensive tutoring and access to resources including note takers, textbooks in audio format and remedial classes. (Around 16,500 undergraduate students. $7,794 in-state tuition, $19,485 out-of-state plus $8,648 room and board. 618-453-2121, *www.siuc.edu.*)

• **The University of Arizona** is a four-year public university in downtown Tucson. The campus offers beautiful views of the nearby Santa Catalina Mountains. It also offers support for LD/ADHD students through its Strategic Alternative Learning Techniques (SALT) program and Disability Resource Center (DRC). These programs provide extensive facilities, resources and support, but potential applicants should be aware that this is a huge school with very large class sizes. Thus Arizona is appropriate for LD/ADHD students who require only a few accommodations and some extra tutoring, but not for those who need extensive hand-holding, such as regular one-on-one time with professors. (Around 29,700 undergraduate students. $9,286 in-state tuition, $25,496 out-of-state plus $8,540 room and board. 520-621-2211, *www.arizona.edu.*)

• **The University of Denver** is a four-year private university south of downtown Denver. It offers support customized to each LD/ADHD student's specific needs through its wide-ranging Learning Effectiveness Program (LEP). Program participants receive ongoing one-on-one attention from counselors. These services come with an added fee of $3,000 per year. (Around 5,300 undergraduate students. $36,936 tuition plus $10,440 room and board. 303-871-2000, *www.du.edu.*)

• **The University of Indianapolis** is a four-year private university in a suburban neighborhood close to downtown Indianapolis. The university offers a program called Baccalaureate for University of Indianapolis Learning Disabled (BUILD) to its LD/ADHD students. BUILD participants receive a minimum of two hours of individualized tutoring per week. Special math and English courses are offered to students who otherwise might struggle to meet the university's requirements in those areas. (Around 4,000 undergraduate students. $22,790 tuition plus $8,270 room and board. 800-232-8634, *www.uindy.edu.*)

WHAT TO ASK BEFORE APPLYING

Before your LD/ADHD student starts applying to colleges or at least before he/she makes a final choice, contact the disabilities support services (DSS) departments at schools being considered to investigate whether the services provided are appropriate for your child's needs. *Among the questions to consider asking...*

• **Are LD/ADHD students allowed extra time on exams and provided with a distraction-free exam environment upon request?**

• **Do LD/ADHD students have access to private tutors?** Is there a fee for these tutors?

• **Are LD/ADHD students offered single-occupancy rooms?** Under what circumstances? Some LD/ADHD students have trouble studying with the distraction of a roommate.

• **Does the school have a structured program designed specifically for LD/ADHD students?** What does this program include?

• **Are LD/ADHD students given priority registration for classes?** This greatly increases LD/ADHD students' odds of getting into classes taught in styles and by professors that mesh well with their learning styles.

• **Does the DSS department have anyone on staff with expertise in my child's disability?**

• **Are Kurzweil readers (devices that convert written text to audio) and smart pens (pens that make audio recordings of lectures and sync them with written notes) available?**

• **Does the school take LD/ADHD into consideration during the admissions process?** If so, consider telling the student to include a cover letter with the application describing the disability and citing academic achievements made since his diagnosis. Include a copy of the diagnosis.

• **Are any scholarships available specifically for students with disabilities?** Ask this of the college financial-aid office as well.

• **What courses are required for graduation?** Are these requirements waived for LD students?

Example: If your student's learning disability makes it unlikely that he could pass a college-level math course, a school that requires math for graduation could be a poor fit.

• **Is note-taking assistance available for LD/ADHD students?** Some disabilities make it difficult to listen and take notes at the same time.

• **Are LD/ADHD students offered accommodations on specific types of exams that give them trouble?**

Example: Some learning disabilities include visual/spatial problems that make it challenging to fill in the circles on standard Scantron computer-graded exams.

• **What documentation is required to qualify for the benefits offered to LD/ADHD students?** Many schools require a psychological assessment made by a licensed professional within the past year or two. The Individualized Education Program (IEP) that qualified your child for comparable services in high school probably is insufficient.

Back Home

If a college-graduate child moves back home, put the young adult on a budget to help him/her prepare for financial independence. Create rules that make it clear that the move home is temporary—which means charging rent and something for utilities, groceries and other services. Set deadlines for repayment of loans, and enforce them. Do not go into debt or damage your credit to help a child, and do not tap retirement funds to pay off college debt.

What else to do: Understand that your child's moving back home is not an indication that he or you have failed—about 80% of recent graduates move back in with their parents, and almost half get financial help from them.

Bill Hardekopf, CEO, LowCards.com, Birmingham, Alabama, and coauthor of *The Credit Card Guidebook* (Lulu).

Natural Flea Control For Dogs and Cats

Shawn Messonnier, DVM, veterinarian and owner of Paws & Claws Animal Hospital in Plano, Texas. He hosts the award-winning radio program Dr. Shawn Messonnier, The Natural Vet and is author of *The Natural Health Bible for Dogs & Cats: Your A-Z Guide to Over 200 Conditions, Herbs, Vitamins, and Supplements* (Three Rivers). *www.PetCareNaturally.com*

Chemical flea collars, sprays, topical products and dips can be effective, but the toxic compounds used in these products can linger in your dog's or cat's body and can potentially cause respiratory problems, nausea and other side effects, including convulsions.

Natural forms of flea control can be just as effective with no risk of poisoning. *What to do...*

• **Treat the house before you treat your pet.** Fleas don't spend all their time on your pet. They also are present in the yard, in damp corners, on carpets or under couch cushions. It doesn't help to treat your pet unless you treat the environment as well.

• **If your home has fleas, steam-clean carpets and upholstery.** Then, every day, vacuum and/or mop the areas where your pet spends time. This will eliminate most fleas and their eggs. Also, wash your pet's bedding and clothing in hot water daily.

• **Dust with diatomaceous earth.** This chalklike form of fossilized algaelike plants kills fleas by penetrating their waxy coating. It is available at pet and garden stores and on the Internet. Follow the directions on the label. Sprinkle it outside on areas where your pet spends time, such as a favorite spot in the garden. In the house, you can sprinkle it in corners or on carpets and area rugs (and later vacuum it up).

• **Treat the yard with nematodes.** If your pet spends time outside, you'll need to treat the entire yard with nematodes in addition to a sprinkling of diatomaceous earth. Nematodes are microscopic worms that feed on fleas in their preadult and larval stages. Nematodes typically come on a small sponge, which contains a million or more microorganisms. They're applied with a lawn sprayer and available at most garden stores. Follow the directions on the label.

• **Give your pet a citrus bath.** Shampoos and sprays that contain the citrus oils D-limonene and linalool kill adult fleas as well as their eggs. They are available at pet-supply stores and on the Internet.

Important: Products that are safe for dogs can be dangerous or even fatal to cats. If you have a cat, read labels carefully to make sure that the product is cat-safe.

• **You can make your own citrus rinse by putting lemon slices in hot water and letting them steep overnight.** Remove the lemon slices from the water, then sponge the liquid on your dog's or cat's skin. It will give your pet a pleasant citrus scent that will help repel fleas.

• **Avoid pyrethrin.** This type of natural pesticide is derived from chrysanthemums. Veterinarians used to recommend it because it is safer than synthetic pesticides. It is safer but not as safe as natural oils.

Keep Your Puppy Calm

To keep your dog calm during a storm: Offer treats. Offer the dog treats during storms so that over time the noise becomes associated with goodies. This is best started when the dog is a puppy. Dampen the noise. Put cotton balls in the dog's ears during the storm (be sure to take them out later). Let the dog hide in its crate or other enclosed area. Having a hiding place is comforting and a natural psychological defense for dogs. It also helps mute the sound. Leave the crate door open so that your dog does not feel trapped. Keep the dog away from the noise. Put the animal in an enclosed room, and play the radio or TV as a distraction. Play thunderstorm CDs when there isn't a storm so the dog becomes accustomed to the sounds.

If nothing else helps: Ask your veterinarian about medications and natural therapies, such as Bach flower extract and lavender, to relieve your dog's anxiety.

Jon Geller, DVM, diplomate, American Board of Veterinary Practitioners, Veterinary Emergency and Rehabilitation Hospital, Fort Collins, Colorado. *www.dogchannel.com*

Dental Disease In Dogs Is On the Rise—And It Can Kill Your Pet

Jean Joo, DVM, dental and oral surgeon at Tufts Veterinary Emergency Treatment and Specialties clinic in Walpole, Massachusetts, and an assistant clinical professor in the department of clinical sciences at Tufts University Cummings School of Veterinary Medicine, West Grafton, Massachusetts.

Dental disease is the most common disease in dogs. It affects 59 out of every 100 dogs seen by vets, according to researchers at Banfield Pet Hospital in Portland, Oregon. And it's on the rise—since 2006, it has increased by more than 12%. The reason for the increase isn't known.

Dogs with dental disease may have difficulty chewing. They can lose their teeth. But the biggest danger is that they face a higher risk for other diseases because the bacteria that are responsible for dental disease can enter the bloodstream and infect the heart, kidneys and/or other organs.

Here's how to protect your dog from dental disease...

IT STARTS IN THE GUMS

The most common form of dental disease in dogs is periodontal disease. Periodontal disease in dogs is similar to periodontal disease in humans. It is an ongoing inflammation of the gums that can cause bleeding and tenderness.

Dogs with gingivitis—the earliest stage of periodontal disease—usually will have tooth discoloration near the gums. The gums will be red and swollen. Without treatment, gingivitis can progress to periodontitis, a more severe form of inflammation that can damage the underlying bone and lead to tooth loss, as well as more dangerous conditions.

Example: A Perdue University study, published in *Journal of the American Veterinary Medical Association,* found that dogs with periodontal disease had a higher risk for congestive heart failure, as well as endocarditis, an inflammation of the heart valves.

WHICH DOGS ARE MOST AT RISK?

Any dog can develop dental disease. Some breeds are more prone to it, however. The breeds most likely to develop dental problems are toy poodles, Yorkshire terriers, Maltese, Pomeranians and Shetland sheepdogs. These breeds tend to have more severe problems because they have large teeth relative to the size of the jaw. This causes tooth-crowding that traps food and hair, along with plaque, the sticky substance that leads to gum disease.

Also at increased risk: Bulldogs, pugs, boxers and other brachycephalic breeds with "pushed-in" faces. Because of the shape and size of their jaws, the teeth are crowded.

DANGER SIGNS

If your dog has a few discolored teeth, it may indicate dental disease. If all the teeth are uniformly discolored, it's probably just normal staining. If just one or a few teeth are discolored, your dog needs to get checked.

In addition, any change in your dog's breath—particularly if it is accompanied by gum redness or apparent mouth discomfort—should be checked by a veterinarian. Veterinarians routinely do mouth-and-gum examinations when you bring your dog in for a checkup. You should take your dog to the veterinarian at least once a year, although dogs that already have dental disease may need to be checked every six months.

DOGGIE DENTAL CARE

Important steps to protect your dog...

- **Brush your dog's teeth at least every other day.** Daily brushing is ideal. Dogs need to have their teeth brushed for the same reasons that people do—it removes bacteria-laden plaque before it has a chance to harden and turn into tartar.
- **Use a toothbrush your dog likes.** There are toothbrushes made for dogs, including finger brushes, which go on the end of your index finger. But a child's toothbrush can work...and some dogs will accept electric toothbrushes.
- **Never use human toothpastes for your pet.** These contain ingredients such as xylitol that are not safe for dogs. Pet stores sell a variety of toothpastes in dog-friendly flavors, such as liver or poultry.
- **Feed dogs dry food.** Wet foods leave a sticky coating on the teeth that makes it easier for plaque to accumulate. Dry foods don't leave as much of this film. Also, the crunching that's required to eat dry food can help clean the teeth.
- **Some foods promote dental cleaning.** These include Hill's Prescription Diet t/d and Purina's DH Dental Health foods. They have larger-sized kibbles that help clean the teeth.

Also helpful: Dry dog foods from Iams/Eukanuba. They're coated with substances that prevent minerals in saliva from accumulating and hardening on the teeth.

- **Provide tooth-friendly toys.** A variety of chew toys are promoted for dental benefits. There's no real evidence that these work better than other chews, but they might help.

I like sturdy rubber toys because they have a little "give"—dogs can chew them without the risk of breaking a tooth. A company called Kong makes good ones. Special rawhides, such as Tartar Shield Soft Rawhide Chews, also are a good choice for many dogs.

Important: Look for the foods and treats that have been awarded the Veterinary Oral Health Council (VOHC) seal. It's displayed on products that have been proved to help control plaque and tartar.

• **Spike their water.** You can add liquid products to your dog's water that reduce the concentration of oral bacteria and inhibit the formation of plaque. Products such as Dog Essential HealthyMouth, made by HealthyMouth, can reduce plaque by more than two-thirds.

PROFESSIONAL CLEANING

If you have a dog that has never or rarely had its teeth cleaned, you may want to schedule a professional cleaning. This is particularly important if tarter is already present, since it can't be removed by brushing alone.

What's involved: The procedure is done under general anesthesia. The teeth are "scaled," or scraped, to remove tartar. The veterinarian also will clean under the gums where infections and periodontal disease originate.

Cost: Generally between $100 and $500.

More Dognapping

Dognapping is on the rise. Reports of stolen dogs increased by 49% in the US in the first seven months of 2011. Dogs have been taken from homes, pet stores, shelters, cars and parks. Some thieves sell the dogs. Others pretend to have found them after the owner offers a reward. Small breeds are abducted more often than others, but dogs of all sizes have been taken.

Self-defense: Always keep your dog on a leash...never leave a dog unattended outside a store...do not brag about a dog's breed or price...take photos that you can give to police, neighbors and shelters if your dog goes missing...ask your vet about having a pet-identifying microchip implanted in your dog.

Lisa Peterson, director of communications, American Kennel Club, New York City. *www.akccar.org*

Pet Precautions

Pets can transmit dangerous bacteria. The bacteria staphylococcus aureus was detected in oral swabs taken from cats and dogs—2% of the cats in the study carried the bacteria and 10% of dogs. It can be transmitted to humans if pets come in contact with food prepared for humans and also can be transmitted via direct contact. This bacteria can cause food poisoning and skin infections.

To prevent an outbreak of food poisoning: Wash hands after touching pets and before preparing food. Keep animals off kitchen counters.

Ahmed Samir, PhD, lecturer of microbiology, faculty of veterinary medicine, Cairo University, Egypt, and coauthor of a study published in *Vector-Borne and Zoonotic Diseases.*

Coyote Alert

Protect cats and dogs from coyotes by keeping pets inside at night, dawn and dusk—the times when coyotes most often hunt. Even outdoor cats should be inside at those times. Ordinary yard fences will not deter coyotes. Never leave food or water outside for pets—if you must feed them outside, remove all uneaten food immediately.

Also: Bird feeders attract rodents—which attract coyotes.

Carol Cartaino, author, based in Seaman, Ohio, of *Myths and Truths about Coyotes: What You Need to Know About America's Most Misunderstood Predator* (Menasha Ridge).

Missing Pet Registry

Register a missing pet online at *www.PetAmberAlert.com* or by calling 877-875-7387. The site reports an 85% success rate in finding lost animals and reuniting them with their owners if the alert goes out in the first week. It uses automated recordings to call neighbors...sends faxes to shelters and veterinarians...and posts notices on Facebook and Twitter.

Cost: $50 and up for onetime use.

Best Toys for Your Cat

Avoid toys that have strings, ribbons or plastic eyes attached—the cat may accidentally swallow one of these, which could cause choking or intestinal blockage. Look for child warnings—if a toy could be hazardous to a child, then it also could be hazardous to your cat. Buy toys that stimulate your cat mentally and physically.

Catnip, Box 5656, Norwalk, Connecticut, 06856. *www.tuftscatnip.com*

Shelter Dog Help

To help a dog from a rescue shelter adjust, do basic obedience training. Dogs with a history of neglect or abuse can be timid and easily frightened, so it is important to start with the "stay" command. (You can find simple instructions with a search on the Internet.) It teaches the dog confidence, self-control and security. Once the dog understands the command, move farther and farther away. Try playing hide-and-seek—run off while repeating the "stay" command, then come back and praise the dog highly for staying. This shows that you can be out of sight without abandoning the dog.

Also helpful for any puppy: Provide chew toys to prevent damage to furniture and shoes. To avoid accidents indoors, give water and food only at set times and give the dog frequent walks.

Alexandra Allred, dog trainer for more than 20 years, based in Dallas and author of *Teaching Basic Obedience: Train the Owner, Train the Dog* (TFH).

Your Medications Can Poison Pets

Jon Geller, DVM, Diplomate, American Board of Veterinary Practitioners, Fort Collins, Colorado.

Many medicines that are safe for people are not safe for pets so keep all medications out of reach. *Examples...*

- **Nonsteroidal anti-inflammatory drugs (NSAIDs),** such as Advil and Aleve, can cause kidney failure and serious ulcers in dogs, cats, birds and other pets.
- ***Acetaminophen,*** such as Tylenol, can severely damage cats' red blood cells and may cause liver failure in dogs.
- **Antidepressants** are sometimes used in pets in small doses, but human-strength pills can cause tremors, seizures, elevated heart rate and other dangerous conditions.
- **ADD/ADHD medicines** can cause life-threatening tremors, seizures and heart problems.
- **Medical marijuana** can affect a dog's heart and cause a comalike stupor, loss of bladder control and more.

Other human medicines that are dangerous to pets: Sleep aids, birth-control pills, heart medicines, thyroid hormones and more. Ask your veterinarian for details. If you think your pet has swallowed any human medicine, immediately call your vet or the Pet Poison Helpline, 800-213-6680.

17

Household Helpers

Quick Cures for Clutter—All You Need Is 10 Minutes or Less

You may be putting off clearing out clutter because the task seems daunting and tedious—but it doesn't have to be. Simply by breaking clutter-clearing into smaller projects, you can make progress in as little as five to 10 minutes at a time.

And you'll be glad you did. Your living or working space will become much more pleasant and efficient almost before you know it.

Important: Be sure that each "mini-project" you do can be completed in the allotted time. The satisfaction and sense of control you gain will keep you motivated for the next mini-project and the next one.

Here, quick clutter-clearing steps for common clutter problems. *You can do each step in 10 minutes or less...*

KITCHEN

• **Organize your storage containers.**

10 minutes: Cull and sort. Pull everything out of the container cupboard. Sort through what you have. Keep only the containers that you use most often and that have lids. Put the rest in discard/giveaway bags.

Put the keepers back in the cupboard. To save space, nest containers that are the same shape.

10 minutes: Organize the lids. Double-check that every lid in your collection has a container that it fits. Toss any stray lids. If you have more than one lid for a container you love, you can keep the extra, but don't keep more than two lids for any container.

Stack lids of similar shape underneath their nested containers, or place all lids together on

---

Julie Morgenstern, internationally renowned organizing and time-management expert, consultant and speaker based in New York City. Her books include *The New York Times* best seller *Organizing from the Inside Out* (Holt), which was developed into a popular special for PBS. *www.JulieMorgenstern.com*

their sides in a single storage container so that they stand up vertically and are easy to pull out.

• **Clean the refrigerator.**

10 minutes: Clean just one shelf or drawer. By working in 10-minute chunks, you soon will get through the whole refrigerator.

Pull all items out of the section you've chosen, and place them on the kitchen table or counter. Throw out all food that is past its printed expiration date...any produce that is going limp...leftovers whose age you are unsure about...and anything that causes you to ask, Is this still good?

Wipe the shelf or drawer with a clean, damp sponge sprinkled with baking soda, then dry with a dish towel. Replace the fresh items.

BATHROOM

• **Organize the cabinet under the sink.**

5 minutes: Measure and order. The inside of the typical under-sink cabinet is just a big, inefficient space.

Solution: Fit your cabinet with stacking drawers. First, measure the inside of the cabinet. Then order stacking drawers online in plastic or metal mesh. Each stack should be at least two drawers high and narrow enough to fit on either side of the sink's drainpipe. If you keep tall cleaning supplies such as glass or toilet bowl cleaners under the cabinet, allow space for those.

Recommended source: The Container Store, *www.containerstore.com.*

10 minutes: Assemble and assign. Unpack and assemble the drawers, and decide what category of object will go in which drawer.

Example: One drawer could hold cleaning supplies such as sponges, scouring powder and rubber gloves...one drawer could hold extra toilet paper and facial tissues...another could hold a hair dryer and accessories.

10 minutes: Toss and install. Pull everything out of the cabinet. Discard any used sponges, old razors and toiletries you no longer use. Place the drawers inside the cabinet, and put all objects into their new locations.

HOME OFFICE

• **Tidy papers.**

10 minutes: Sort. The papers cluttering the surface of your desk represent to-dos. Quickly divide the papers into stacks, with one stack for each type of to-do.

Examples: Call...write...pay...return...order...check with family member...brainstorm...file.

Label each stack by writing the category name on a sticky note and putting the note on top of the stack.

Remind yourself to do nothing else but sort in this session. Do not stop to read any of the papers or do any of the tasks. Otherwise you will never get through the clutter.

5 minutes: Set up a simple action system. Put each stack into its own manila folder. If you are a highly visual person, use colored folders. Write the task category on the front of the folder in large bold letters and on the side tab.

Keep the folders handy and visible. Either stack them on the corner of your desk, put them in stacking trays or place them in a vertical rack.

Whenever you have five or 10 minutes between other activities, you can go through one of the folders and take action. Often you can get through an entire folder in 10 minutes when you are focused.

BEDROOM

• **Clear your night table.**

5 minutes: Choose what will stay. Decide what few objects you want/need on your bedside table.

Examples: Reading lamp...alarm clock or mobile phone...book...small basket that holds reading glasses, bookmarks, highlighter, pen, small notepad.

10 minutes: Cull. Remove everything else from the table—many items will be objects that have found their way in from other rooms. Discard trash, and put items that belong elsewhere into a basket with handles, a small plastic tub or other portable container.

10 minutes: Carry the container around the house, and deliver anything that belongs elsewhere to its appropriate spot.

FAMILY ROOM

• Organize CDs and DVDs

10 minutes: Choose categories. On a piece of paper, list the broad categories of your video and music collections. Use terms that you and your family would be most likely to think of when looking for a CD or DVD.

Examples: Your movie categories might include action...comedy...kids...drama. Your music might be sorted by genre such as jazz or classical, or by mood, task or time of day you would be likely to listen to it, such as relaxing on Sunday afternoon...cleaning the house...working out...entertaining guests.

10 minutes: Sort and retrieve. Quickly go through all the cases—whether or not they contain their CDs or DVDs—and sort them by category. Then gather all loose CDs and DVDs, and put them back in their cases. Return the cases to their storage shelves, separated by category. If you like, label the categories.

If your collection is large, you can spend five to 10 minutes at a time alphabetizing each section to make titles or artists easier to find. However, don't bother alphabetizing unless the rest of your family values the convenience and will commit to replacing recordings in alphabetical order every time.

Cheaper Way to Enlarge Your Home

Build a bump-out instead of an addition. A bump-out is extra space that hangs off the side of a house. It usually can be up to three feet from the existing exterior wall and can run almost the whole length of your home. It does not require a foundation, as a full addition would, so it costs much less to build—usually about $6,000 to $12,000. This could be enough space to allow an eating area or large closet, for example.

Money, Time-Life Bldg., Rockefeller Center, New York City 10020. *www.money.com*

Save When You Remodel

Use specialty Web sites. Find heavily discounted castoffs from other remodeling projects—everything from doors to cabinet hardware, bricks and lumber—at *www.diggerslist.com.* If you need a small countertop, search for a stone remnant through *www.thestonebroker.com.* Purchase high-end lighting fixtures directly from a top manufacturer, and save 20% to 30% of what you would pay at a specialty shop at *www.rejuvenation.com.*

Money, Time-Life Bldg., Rockefeller Center, New York City 10020. *www.money.com*

Moldy Basement

Jeffrey May, CEO, May Indoor Air Investigations LLC, Tyngsborough, Massachusetts, and author of *The Mold Survival Guide* (Johns Hopkins University).

How do you know if you have mold? If there's a musty smell, you have mold, which can trigger conditions such as allergies and asthma. Even if there's no smell, you might not be in the clear—many molds produce very little odor. If the relative humidity anywhere in your basement has ever been over 80% for more than a few days, you probably have mold. To measure humidity levels, hygrometers are available at hardware stores for about $25.

To find mold on smooth surfaces, in dim light, shine a bright flashlight almost parallel to the surface and look at the bottom of the walls and the legs of any basement furniture. You may see colonies of white, yellow, green or black mold that are not readily visible under normal light.

To remove small areas of mold, use one-eighth cup of laundry detergent in a gallon of water with a cup of bleach. Open windows and doors for ventilation, and wear protective gloves and eyewear. Never combine bleach with ammonia—this will create toxic fumes.

Throw out rugs/carpets that have been wet for more than 24 hours—mold cannot be cleaned from the fibers. Mold can also grow in upholstery, floor and ceiling tiles, wallpaper, clothing, leather, wood, paper and food items. These should also be discarded if they cannot be thoroughly cleaned and dried.

Mold can grow in drywall, insulation and the dust on masonry walls. Have a professional inspect finished interior walls if they have been wet for more than 24 hours.

Home Repairs You Should Not Put Off

Annual heating and air-conditioning inspection costs around $200 to $300, but it could save you thousands by providing maintenance before you need to replace major components. Chimney inspection costs about $65 to $150 and could prevent a fire—or show that you need minor repairs to stop water leaks that can cause mold. Termite inspection costs $75 to $200 or more—termites can cause far more than $200 of damage. Power washing and sealing of a wood deck cost $100 to $300 for a 200-square-foot deck and get rid of algae and mold that can make the deck dangerously slippery.

What else to do: Have dryer vents cleaned every year to avoid lint buildup...clean carpets at least once a year to reduce pollen, bacteria and dirt in your home.

Bankrate.com

Dishwasher Danger

Dishwashers may harbor toxic fungi. Biologists tested for organisms in 189 dishwashers in homes around the world.

Result: Thirty-five percent contained two strains of *Exophaiala*, a potentially deadly black yeast fungi.

Theory: The fungi thrive in moisture and extreme temperatures like those found in dishwashers and are not affected by detergents. The fungi may appear as a black, slimy smear but are often too small to be visible. Diluted bleach is known to kill fungi, so you may want to use it to clean the dishwasher's rubber door seal.

Nina Gunde-Cimerman, PhD, associate professor of microbiology, University of Ljubljana, Slovenia.

Radiation From Your Washing Machine? Hair Dryer? These Secrets Will Help Keep You Safe

David O. Carpenter, MD, director of the Institute for Health and the Environment and a professor of environmental health and toxicology at the University at Albany, New York. He is a member of the editorial board of *Environmental Health Perspectives*, published by the National Institute of Environmental Health Sciences, and an editorial adviser for *Cellular and Molecular Neurobiology*.

You've probably heard about the scientific studies linking cell phones to a variety of tumors, including brain cancer. The World Health Organization has now classified cell phones as a "possible carcinogen."*

What's being largely overlooked: *Electromagnetic radiation*—from electrical appliances, such as hair dryers, microwave ovens and washing machines...as well as that from wireless signals for computers—also may contribute to cancer risk independent of cellphone use.

What you need to know...

INVISIBLE POLLUTION

Every electrical appliance in your home emits electric and magnetic fields (EMFs) of

*A team of 31 scientists from 14 countries analyzed peer-reviewed studies before classifying radiofrequency electromagnetic fields from wireless cell phones as "possibly carcinogenic to humans" based on an increased risk for glioma, a type of brain cancer.

energy. An appliance that is plugged in has an electric field even when it is turned off. The appliance produces a magnetic field when it is turned on and the electrical current is flowing. However, the EMFs from appliances are considered extremely low frequency (ELF), meaning that the radiation flows at very low levels.

Still, some studies show that regular exposure to even low levels of ELF electromagnetic radiation, such as 3 milligauss (mG), may increase the risk for leukemia in children—and possibly, to a lesser degree, in adults. Preliminary research has also linked this form of energy to Alzheimer's disease and Lou Gehrig's disease, but this association is still being debated.

Some experts maintain that the electromagnetic radiation from cell phones and electrical appliances is too weak to cause the types of cell damage that can lead to cancer. But evidence is emerging that even weak forms of energy may interfere with normal cell functions, perhaps contributing to the development of cancer and other diseases.

SAFER POWER

Appliances that use the most electrical current, such as handheld hair dryers, emit the highest levels of ELF radiation. But even small appliances, such as coffeemakers, produce some. (See chart below for other examples.)

Important: ELF fields are strongest at the point where the electrical wires enter the device. The fields diminish to almost nothing within a foot or two.

To test electromagnetic radiation around your appliances: Use a gauss meter—available online for about $150 to $500.

Important: ELF fields are *directional*—if you hold the meter to the right of a washing machine, for example, the reading might be zero, but it may be much higher a foot to the left. For accurate readings, test in different locations around the electrical appliance within a radius of a few feet.

Electrical wiring in the walls also can be an issue.

What I've found: In my son's bedroom, most of the wiring that carries electricity to lights and electrical outlets is in one of the walls. When we tested with a gauss meter, the EMFs were highest near his bed, so we moved his bed to the other side of the room.

In general, electrical wiring in walls generates high ELF only when the current is flowing or there is a ground current created by faulty wiring. However, the ELF exposure from wiring adds to the total exposure from appliances.

RADIATION FROM APPLIANCES IN YOUR HOME...

The following table lists the median electromagnetic fields for household appliances as measured from varying distances in milligauss (mG)*...

	Distance from Source			
Source	**6 inches**	**1 foot**	**2 feet**	**4 feet**
Electric shaver	100	20	–	–
Hair dryer	300	1	–	–
Microwave oven	200	40	10	2
Electric range	30	8	2	–
Television	n/a	7	2	–
Air conditioner	n/a	3	1	–
Washing machine	20	7	1	–
Vacuum cleaner	300	60	10	1
PC with color monitor	14	5	2	–

*The dash (–) means that the magnetic field at this distance was indistinguishable from background measurements taken before the appliance was turned on. *Source:* Environmental Protection Agency.

To reduce exposure...

• **Don't linger near appliances when they're running.** Even though the ELF levels are typically highest at the back of an appliance where the electrical cord plugs in, the magnetic field directly in front of a typical washing machine can reach 20 mG. You'll be exposed to only normal background levels by moving a foot or two away.

Important: Even the best microwave ovens leak some of the radiation they use to heat the food, so stand at least four feet away from the front of the oven when it's running. Microwave ovens also produce high levels of ELF electromagnetic radiation from the electricity used to power the oven, so there's a double risk.

• **Towel-dry your hair.** Hair dryers are among the most dangerous sources of magnetic fields because they use a lot of power and the motor/heater is held close to the head. Although using a low-fan and/or low-heat setting helps some, it's better to avoid hair dryers altogether.

If towel-drying is not convenient, consider using a low-EMF hair dryer such as the Chi Ceramic Low EMF Ionic Hair Dryer available for about $100 online...or a low-EMF wall-mounted hair dryer for $89.95 from the EMF Safety Superstore, *www.lessemf.com*.

• **Use the electric blanket before you get into bed.** Electric blankets don't draw a lot of electrical current, but they expose your entire body to ELF radiation for the entire night if you leave them on. If you want a warm bed, turn on the blanket half an hour before bedtime, then turn it off when you get into bed.

• **Get a new bedside clock.** Old-style alarm clocks—analog clocks with lighted dials—produce surprisingly high levels of electromagnetic radiation.

My advice: Get a digital bedside clock, which emits almost no ELF.

• **Throw out your cordless phones.** Cordless phones emit electromagnetic radiation whether or not they are being used. That's why I recommend replacing cordless phones with corded phones.

SAFER COMPUTER USE

Most computers give off electromagnetic radiation. If you use a desktop model, position it toward the back of your desk. Most monitors, which produce lower levels of electromagnetic radiation than computers, have conductive screens to block the ELF exposure. But it's still wise to position your monitor as far away from you as possible.

What I've found: I once measured the fields near my secretary's desk. The reading was about 10 mG, which is extremely high. I realized that the high-powered electrical wiring used by the computer was behind the wall closest to her. We had to move her desk 10 feet to get out of range.

Also, virtually every modern computer (including laptops) is designed to receive wireless signals. If you have a wireless router, which connects to a cable and wirelessly "routes" this connection to one or more computers in your home, your exposure to electromagnetic radiation is constant.

To be safer...

• **Hardwire the computer to the modem.** Use cables to connect computers to your modem rather than using a wireless signal, so you can forgo the router. If more than one person uses a computer at home, however, this approach may not be practical.

• **Turn off the router when it's not in use.** If you do use a router, turn it on only when you need the signal for using the Internet, streaming video to the TV, etc.

• **Disable Wi-Fi settings on your computer if you don't use a router.** Otherwise, the computer—or any device that operates wirelessly, such as some printers—will constantly emit electromagnetic radiation as it tries to find the nearest wireless source. Shut down your computer when it's not in use to reduce ELF radiation in your home.

For Cleaner Dishes

Dishwasher detergents don't clean as well as they used to. New detergent formulas lack phosphates, chemicals that were good for cleaning but bad for the environment.

For cleaner dishes: Tablets or packets tend to clean better than gels or powders. Run the hot water tap for a minute before turning on the dishwasher—the dishwasher will start out with hot water, which will dissolve the detergent at the start of the cycle.

To remove the white film left by phosphate-free detergents: Put two cups of vinegar in a bowl on the bottom rack of the dishwasher with the film-covered dishes and let the machine run a cycle without detergent before washing dishes with detergent to get rid of the remaining vinegar.

USA Today

Cookware Care

Treat nonstick cookware with care. Pre-season nonstick pots and pans before the first use by rinsing and drying them and then rubbing them with a little cooking oil on a paper towel. Each time you use a nonstick pan, rub about a teaspoon of oil or butter on the cold pan. Despite the name "nonstick," most need a little lubricant. Don't use cooking sprays that contain soy lecithin, such as Pam—they build up in the areas where the heat doesn't burn off the spray, such as the sides of a frying pan, and the pan will become sticky. If you want to use a spray, try Baker's Joy, which contains flour as well as oil and won't leave the pan sticky. Do not cook on high heat—it will cause the nonstick coating to crack. Don't use metal or sharp objects to stir food. They can puncture the coating. Hand-wash nonstick cookware—harsh detergents and heat from the dishwasher can ruin the coating. Place a cloth or paper napkin between stored pots and pans to prevent scratches.

The New York Times

Secrets from America's Lawn Geek

John (Trey) Rogers III, PhD, professor of turfgrass management at Michigan State University, East Lansing. He was a turf consultant and project leader for the 2004 and 2008 Summer Olympic Games and 2008 UEFA World Cup, and is author of *Lawn Geek: Tips and Tricks for the Ultimate Turf From the Guru of Grass* (New American Library). *www.briggsandstratton.com/yardsmarts*

Spring's arrival signals the start of lawn-care season across much of the US. But while most home owners try to take care of their grass, they don't always do it properly. Lawns don't come with instruction manuals, and lawn-care folk wisdom often is wrong. *Answers to 10 important lawn-care questions...*

- **Last winter was relatively warm and snow-less winter across much of the country. Does that affect the way I should be caring for my lawn?** Your grass might start growing sooner than usual. If so, it might be wise to tackle spring lawn chores such as overseeding or aerating in April rather than leaving them for May (see below for details).

- **Does it matter how short I cut my grass when I mow?** It matters a lot. "Scalping" a lawn—mowing off more than one-third of the grass's height—is the number-one lawn-care mistake that home owners make. Doing this sends grass into physiological shock, which leaves the lawn prone to invasion by weeds and less able to cope with drought and other environmental stresses.

The more often you mow—and the less grass you remove with each mowing—the thicker and healthier your lawn is likely to become. If the grass gets so long that you can't get it down to proper length in one mowing, wait a day or two and mow again.

For St. Augustine and bahia grasses and for cool-season grasses, such as Kentucky bluegrass and perennial rye, three to four inches is generally best...for most Bermuda and zoysia, one to two inches. Various Web sites, such as *www.american-lawns.com,* can help you identify what type of grass you have.

- **Should I mulch or bag my lawn clippings?** Definitely mulch. Grass clippings are full of nitrogen and other nutrients. Removing them deprives the lawn of free fertilizer. Modern mulching mowers do an excellent job of grinding up grass into mulch, particularly when you mow off less than one-third of the grass's height, as described previously.

Helpful: Research has shown that mulching grass does not create excessive thatch and thus does not make lawns more susceptible to disease or drought.

• **My lawn feels hard-packed. Should I aerate? And if so, what's the best way to do that?** It is worth aerating if your soil is hard-packed. It's difficult for grass roots to grow properly when the soil is compacted.

Rent a core aerator (about $40 to $50 for two to four hours), or pay a lawn-care professional to aerate for you. The aerator used should pull plugs of soil from the ground, not just slash the soil, which is far less effective.

Aerate when grass is actively growing. With the cool-season grasses of the northern US, such as bluegrass, fescue and ryegrass, that generally means April or September (and perhaps the months that precede or follow these, depending on temperatures). With the warm-season grasses of the South, such as bahia, Bermuda, buffalo or zoysia, it typically means May through July or August. Aerating once each year for three years usually solves compaction problems.

Warning: If the distance between the holes created by the aerator is greater than three inches, you almost certainly need to make another pass with the aerator.

• **I know that there are dangers to fertilizing too often, but how often is best?** Excessive fertilizer can "burn" grass, causing severe dehydration that could kill the lawn. Or extra fertilizer might cause grass to grow quickly, making it difficult to keep up with the mowing and increasing the odds that you will scalp the grass, as described on page 282.

Best strategy: Fertilize on the "holiday plan"—on or around Memorial Day, the Fourth of July, Labor Day and Halloween. Four times a year is all a lawn really needs. Do not exceed the dosages recommended on the fertilizer's packaging.

Warning: Do not fertilize your lawn if it has not rained recently and local water-use restrictions prevent watering. Some home owners faced with this situation think, Well, if I can't water my lawn, I can at least feed it fertilizer. Unfortunately, this makes a bad situation worse—recently fertilized lawns require even more water than those that have not been fertilized.

• **My lawn is discolored where my dog relieves itself. How can I keep these patches of lawn healthy?** Dog urine contains high concentrations of ammonia salts (nitrogen), just like fertilizer. And like fertilizer, it's good for a lawn in modest amounts but causes problems when too much is supplied. Trouble is, dogs often relieve themselves in roughly the same areas of the lawn every day, causing "burn spots" of dehydrated or dead grass just as if you were overfertilizing these areas.

The best solution is to saturate the affected area thoroughly with a hose every week, particularly when there hasn't been much rain. Or pour a pail of water on the area right after the dog urinates. An alternative is to train the dog to urinate in a section of the lawn that is landscaped with gravel or wood chips rather than grass.

Warning: Do not alter the dog's diet in an attempt to solve this problem. Despite folk wisdom, regularly feeding a dog tomato juice or other fruit juices is unlikely to significantly improve the lawn's problem and it could cause health problems for the dog.

• **How much should I water my lawn?** A good rule of thumb is to give your lawn around one inch of water per week, perhaps a bit more during a stretch of very hot days. That guideline includes rainfall. There are new wireless devices on the market that monitor soil moisture and prevent automated irrigation systems from watering when additional water isn't needed. That's not just good for your lawn...it's also good for your water bill.

Examples: Toro Precision Soil Sensor ($140, *www.toro.com*)...UgMO ProHome Soil Sensor System ($499 for a two-sensor system, *www.ugmo.com*).

Water early in the morning so that the grass blades aren't unnecessarily damp come nightfall—lawns are particularly susceptible to disease when they're damp on humid summer nights.

Overwatering is much more common than underwatering except when local drought restrictions ban watering. Signs of an overwatered lawn include the growth of mushrooms or nutsedge (grasslike weeds)...significant runoff from the lawn into the street during watering...or a mushy feeling when walking across the lawn hours after watering. Signs of an underwatered lawn include footprints remaining visible in the grass long after you have walked across it.

• **Burrowing animals are digging holes in my lawn. Is that bad for the grass? What's the best way to get rid of those animals?** It won't significantly harm your grass. The lawn might get upheaved a bit in places, but you usually can push it back down easily with your foot.

Research suggests that traps are the most reliable way to rid a lawn of burrowing animals. No one has ever shown that burrowing animals are significantly deterred by blocking their holes or by folk-wisdom solutions such as placing chewing gum in their holes.

• **There are thin patches in my lawn every year after the snow melts, but overseeding never seems to work. What's the secret to overseeding?** First, always overseed when your grass is actively growing. With the cool-season grasses of the North, that generally means April or September (and perhaps the months that come before and after these, depending on local climate). In the South, it typically means May through July or August.

Second, don't use a nonselective pre-emergent herbicide if you're overseeding. Such herbicides don't just prevent the growth of weed seeds, they prevent the growth of all seeds, including grass seed. If you're overseeding and you want to use a preemergent herbicide, choose one with siduron that allows grass seed to grow. Most major herbicide companies offer a siduron-based product.

Third, take a close look at the thinned patches. If the grass seems matted down and you notice a white, gray or pink growth on the grass blades, snow mold might be the source of your problem. Fluff up this matted-down grass with a rake to allow more sunlight and air circulation to reach these blades.

• **My kids play on my lawn. Is there any way I can stop using herbicides without winding up with weeds?** Weeds thrive only when there are gaps in the lawn large enough for them to get the sun they need to grow. If you water, mow and fertilize, your lawn should be thick and healthy enough so that weeds won't be a problem even without herbicides.

Clean Crystal Candleholders

To remove melted wax from crystal candleholders, fill a basin with hot water and immerse the holders in it—put them in upside down if the bases are cloth-covered. Let the holders soak for several minutes, then peel off the wax. Use a soft-scrub sponge for any stuck-on pieces. Then wash the candleholders in hot, sudsy water, rinse and dry.

Alternative: Put the holders in the freezer for two to three hours. This makes the wax brittle so it can be chipped off.

Caution: Don't put thin-walled glass candleholders in the freezer—they may break.

Good Housekeeping, 300 W. 57 St., New York City 10019. *www.goodhousekeeping.com*

"Nutty" Solution to Cover Scratches

To cover scratches on a wood floor, break the meat of a pecan or walnut in half and rub it into the scratches—going with the grain of the wood. Do this until the meat of the nut is warm. Then buff with a soft cloth. Repeat several times for deep scratches.

If this does not work: Find a crayon that matches the floor color. Rub it into the scratch until the crayon gets warm, then buff with a soft cloth.

Heloise, internationally syndicated lifestyle columnist, San Antonio, and author of *Handy Household Hints from Heloise* (Rodale). *www.heloise.com*

Beautiful Houseplants That Clean Indoor Air

B.C. Wolverton, PhD, president of Wolverton Environmental Services, Inc., an environmental consulting firm in Picayune, Mississippi. He previously spent more than 30 years working for the US military and the National Aeronautics and Space Administration (NASA) as a civilian scientist developing systems to protect against toxic chemicals and pathogenic microbes. He is author of *Plants: Why You Can't Live Without Them* (Roli) and *How to Grow Fresh Air* (Penguin). *www.wolvertonenvironmental.com*

Homes and office buildings are being built and remodeled tighter than ever today to save energy. But sealing out drafts can mean sealing in dangerous chemicals such as benzene and formaldehyde, which are off-gassed by many things, from carpet to pressed-wood furniture. Cleaning products used at home and the office also may release chemicals, including ammonia and chlorinated solvents.

Prolonged breathing of chemicals such as these can cause headaches, throat irritation, congestion, even cancer. The Environmental Protection Agency (EPA) now ranks indoor-air quality among the five top threats to human health. The problem is worse in winter, when we spend the most time sealed in our homes and offices.

Expensive air-filtration systems are not the only solution. When I worked at NASA, we discovered that simple houseplants can filter many dangerous chemicals out of indoor air. The plants' leaves absorb and destroy certain volatile organic compounds, while the microbes that live around the plants' roots convert chemicals into a source of food and energy for themselves and their host plant.

Some houseplants are much more effective at air filtration than others. *Ten that do a great job cleaning the air and are easy to grow…*

THE TOP FOUR

The following four plants are exceptionally effective at cleaning the air.

- **Areca Palm** (*Chrysalidocarpus lutescens*) also is known as yellow palm or butterfly palm.

Care: Keep its root-ball damp, and mist the leaves with water often. Feed monthly with liquid fertilizer except in winter. Remove dead branches promptly.

- **Lady palm** (*Rhapis excelsa*) is one of the most effective houseplants for improving indoor-air quality, and it is highly resistant to most insects. It has fans, six to 12 inches wide, made up of shiny green leaves.

Care: Water generously, especially during spring and summer. Feed monthly with liquid fertilizer per label instructions. Leaf tips can be trimmed with pinking shears if they turn brown.

- **Rubber plant** (*Ficus robusta*) is a hearty plant with thick, leathery, dark green leaves. It will tolerate limited light and cool temperatures and is very effective at removing chemical toxins from indoor air—the best of the ficus genus yet tested.

Care: Water regularly from mid-summer through autumn, but let the soil dry slightly between waterings. Water sparingly during the rest of the year—rubber trees struggle when overwatered. Feed monthly with liquid fertilizer during the summer only.

- **Peace Lily** (*Spathiphyllum sp.*), produces beautiful white flowers, making it one of a relatively small number of plants that bloom reliably indoors.

Care: Keep the soil evenly moist, and feed monthly with liquid fertilizer from spring through autumn. Discontinue feedings, and keep the soil slightly drier in winter. Wash the leaves occasionally with a damp cloth to reduce the odds of infestation by insects such as spider mites.

THE RUNNERS-UP

These plants work well, too, but not quite as well as the first four…

- **Dracaena "Janet Craig"** (*Dracaena deremensis "Janet Craig"*) is a pest-resistant leafy plant that can live for decades. It will tolerate poorly lit areas, though its growth will be slowed. Favor the "Compacta" variety, which grows to one to three feet in height, not the regular variety, which requires more care and can reach 10 feet if not pruned.

Care: In spring and summer, keep soil evenly moist so the root-ball does not dry, but never water so much that the soil becomes soggy. Feed with liquid fertilizer twice a month. In autumn and winter, water less often and do not feed. Spray with a water mist.

• **English Ivy** (*Hedera helix*) is best-known as a ground cover, but it also grows very well in indoor hanging baskets. And it adapts well to a wide range of indoor conditions—though it does benefit from some time outdoors in spring or summer. English Ivy does not like high temperatures.

Care: Water well, and feed once a month with liquid fertilizer in spring and summer. Discontinue feedings, and allow to dry slightly between waterings in fall and winter. Mist regularly in winter.

Warning: English Ivy contains chemicals that can irritate the skin or cause illness if consumed. Wear gloves when handling, and keep out of reach of pets and young children.

• **Golden Pothos** (*Epipremnum aureum*) tolerates neglect and low light and is extremely resistant to insects. Golden Pothos's name refers to the splashes of gold or cream color on its green, heart-shaped leaves. It usually is grown in hanging baskets, but it also can climb.

Care: Allow the soil to dry slightly between waterings. Feed with diluted liquid fertilizer weekly in spring and summer. Clean the leaves occasionally with a damp cloth.

• **Corn Plant** (*Dracaena fragrans "Massangeana"*) is so named because its leaves look like those of corn stalks, not because it actually produces corn. It tolerates low light, though it prefers bright light.

Care: Keep soil moist but not soggy from spring through autumn, then drier in winter. Feed monthly in spring and summer with liquid fertilizer. Mist often. Brown leaf tips can be trimmed.

• **Syngonium** (*Syngonium podophyllum*) produces visually appealing, arrow-shaped, green-and-white or green-and-silver leaves.

Care: Keep soil evenly moist but not soggy from spring through autumn. Allow the soil to dry between waterings in winter. Feed monthly with a liquid fertilizer except in winter. Syngonium appreciates frequent mistings. Pinch back shoots if you want a thicker, bushier plant.

• **Snake Plant** (*Sansevieria trifasciata*) is about 50% less effective at cleaning indoor air than the other plants on this list, but it is so hard to kill that it's worth including as an option for those who struggle to keep other houseplants alive. The snake plant has visually appealing, spearlike leaves that stand upright, typically two to four feet in height. It occasionally produces small greenish-white flowers.

Care: Water sparingly, allowing the soil to dry between waterings. Overwatering is one of the few ways to kill a snake plant. Feed with diluted liquid fertilizer once a month. Remove flowers if they appear, or they might release a sticky, hard-to-clean substance.

HOW MANY PLANTS?

As a rule of thumb, one to two good-sized plants from the list above per 100 square feet of interior space tend to be sufficient. There's no health downside to having more plants than this as long as mold doesn't develop in the potting soil.

Helpful: Our latest research suggests that growing plants in hydroculture significantly increases their ability to clean the air. With hydroculture, plants are grown in watertight containers and rooted not in potting soil, but in expanded clay pebbles sold for this purpose at some garden stores.

All of the plants listed above will grow in hydroculture, and the Peace Lily, in particular, thrives when grown this way. Hydroculture also reduces the risk that fungal spores, mold and soil-borne pests will develop on houseplants. Plants grown in hydroculture need a complete fertilizer that contains micronutients. Ask your garden store for details.

7 Things to Do With Dental Floss (Besides Floss)

Joan Wilen and Lydia Wilen are authors of *Bottom Line's Household Magic* and *Bottom Line's Treasury of Home Remedies & Natural Cures.* You can receive a useful tip daily by signing up for their free e-letter at *www.bottomlinepublications.com/free-e-letters.*

While good oral health is the reason dental floss was invented, you can use unflavored floss in many more ways...

• **Fix eyeglasses.** Ever lose one of those tiny screws that attaches the earpiece to the front of the frame? As a quick fix, thread a piece of dental floss through the holes that the screw goes through. Then knot the floss, and cut off the excess. The floss will allow you to wear your glasses until you can replace the screw.

• **Sew a button.** Children's clothes and some types of work clothes often test the endurance of cotton thread. Sew buttons on with dental floss, and they will pass the test with flying colors.

If you have buttons floating around in a drawer, use dental floss to string all the same-color buttons together. Next time you need a button, you'll be glad they're organized that way.

Floss also can be used to repair any kind of fine netting, such as some fishing nets and mosquito netting.

• **Relieve the dripping sound.** Dental floss will not stop a faucet from leaking, but it will stop the sound of the drip-drip-drip until the plumber arrives. Cut a piece of floss long enough to tie around the spout of the faucet, and let it hang down into the drain. You may have to use tape to position the floss so that the drip is touching the floss, enabling each drop to slide down the length of the floss into the drain, eliminating the annoying noise it makes when it falls from the faucet to the sink.

• **Cut cake and more.** Dental floss will cut a cheesecake better than most knives. Take a piece of floss that's a few inches longer than the diameter of the cake. Hold an end in each hand, making the floss taut. Then maneuver the floss through the cheesecake to cut it in half. Slide the floss out from the bottom of the cake. Now that there are two halves, you can cut slices—one at a time—using the same taut-floss method.

You also can use this floss method to cut soft cheese, some kinds of bread, hard-boiled eggs and canned cranberry jelly.

Having a hard time taking freshly baked cookies off the cookie sheet? Holding a piece of floss tautly, gently slide it under each cookie, coaxing the cookie off the pan.

• **Clean furniture.** If you have furniture with hard-to-get-at crevices, take about 12 inches of floss, tie or wind the ends on your index fingers (loose enough to keep the circulation going, of course) and clean out the furniture's wedged-in dirt. Floss also may be used to clean between cracks or crevices around the stove, sink, counter and wherever else dirt gets imbedded.

• **Tie it up.** When a shoelace tears and you have no string around, use floss to keep your shoe tied until you replace the lace.

If you lose your luggage lock while traveling, keep the luggage zipper closed by tying it with floss.

• **String a roast.** Some recipes for roasts call for the meat to be tied with cotton butcher string to make it more uniformly shaped, preserve moisture, keep any stuffing in place and ensure even cooking. If you have the meat but no string, use unwaxed dental floss. Rest assured, it won't burn or melt!

It is recommended that poultry (chicken, turkey, duck) also be tied (trussed) before roasting. Once again, unwaxed dental floss can be used as a string substitute.

18 Winning Ways

How to Get Anyone To Like You In Two Minutes or Less

If you want to make new friends or land new clients or a new job, you need to make a great first impression—fast. People form permanent opinions of those they meet within just a few minutes of setting eyes upon them.

A study published in *Journal of Experimental Psychology: General* reported that the first impression someone has of a new acquaintance is likely to always dominate the way he/she views this acquaintance. Any later evidence that this first impression might have been erroneous tends to be dismissed as nothing more than an exception to the rule.

The trouble is, making a good first impression can be tricky. Our words, actions, facial expressions and body language all send subtle messages, often without our even realizing that we are doing it.

Below are 11 tricks for making a great first impression. Pick just one or two to try at a time, and add more when those become second nature.

YOUR BODY AND FACE

Facial expression and body position can make you seem more likable to those you meet...

1. Use a slow-flooding smile. Obviously it's a good idea to smile when you meet someone, but instantly switching on a 100-watt smile can make you seem phony. Instead, let your smile build slowly when you make eye contact. This sends the message that there is something about this person in particular that you like.

Leil Lowndes, a communications consultant and corporate trainer based in New York City, whose clients have included The Walt Disney Company, Kodak and the US Peace Corps. She is author of *How to Instantly Connect with Anyone* (McGraw-Hill). *www.lowndes.com*

2. Have "sticky" eyes. People are inclined to like and trust those who make strong eye contact. If you are not a natural at maintaining eye contact, make it a habit to note specific characteristics about new acquaintances' eyes—what color are they...what shape...how far apart...how long are their lashes...how often do they blink...how often do they look away while talking to you? Answering these questions will force you to make strong eye contact with the other person.

Do break eye contact occasionally—staring too intently can make people uncomfortable—but don't do it abruptly. Break eye contact slowly, as if your gaze were stuck on this person and you find it difficult to pull it away.

3. Select an open, welcoming body position. Arrange yourself so that your torso is mostly but not completely facing the person whom you just met. During the first minute of conversation, very slowly and slightly rotate your body to completely face this person.

Exception: A man meeting a woman for the first time should stop a few degrees short of angling his upper body directly toward hers. That stance seems overly aggressive to some women.

If you are holding a drink or plate of hors d'oeuvres, either find a spot to set it down or hold it down by your side. If you hold it up in front of your chest, your arm will block off your body, making you seem less open. If you are self-conscious about what to do with your hands, use gestures when you talk or even put your hands in your pockets—just don't cross your arms across your chest, which makes you seem closed off.

4. Stand with one foot a few inches forward of the other. Put most of your weight on the forward foot. This stance suggests that you're an energetic person and are interested in the person with whom you are speaking.

YOUR ACTIONS

Even seemingly inconsequential actions can affect how you are viewed during an initial meeting...

5. Find your conversation partner's personal-space comfort zone. Stand too close to a new acquaintance, and you will make him feel uncomfortable. Stand too far away, and the odds increase that he will not feel a connection with you. What's the proper distance? For the average American, it's around 24 inches. Trouble is, that's just an average—everyone is a little different.

The best strategy is to start a conversation with a new acquaintance by placing yourself 26 to 28 inches away. Move toward this person imperceptibly slowly until you see discomfort in his eyes. Then ease back very slightly until that discomfort disappears.

6. When you shake hands, very gently touch your forefinger to the other person's wrist. Aim for the spot on the underside of the wrist where you would take a pulse. This is a very sensitive spot, and gently touching it tends to foster a feeling of warmth and closeness, even though your light contact might not be consciously noticed by the other person. Attempting this wrist touch also forces a deep handshake, which encourages a sense of closeness, too.

7. Treat business cards with respect. A business card symbolizes someone's professional accomplishments. Showing respect for the card shows respect for the person. When you are handed a card, imagine that it is a delicate and precious gift. Hold it gently in your hands. Pause to read it, then carefully place it into your briefcase or purse or, at the very least, your wallet. Never just jam a card into a pocket.

YOUR WORDS

A few tips for an initial conversation...

8. Begin with a conversation starter question or two. Questions that make great icebreakers include, "What do you do?" followed by "How did you decide that you wanted to do that?"...Or (to couples) "How did you two meet?"

9. Slowly nod while people speak. This sends a message of acceptance and encouragement, which makes people feel more in sync with us.

Important: Be aware that men and women can have different interpretations of nodding. Do not nod if a man is saying something with which you completely disagree. Your nodding might be interpreted as agreement. Women, however, tend to interpret nodding as meaning, "I understand," not "I agree."

10. Listen for words that suggest people's interests. The words that people use and the topics that they reference, even in passing, often provide hints at their true areas of interest. If you can spot these words and topics, you can redirect dull, forgettable small-talk conversations toward things that people actually want to talk about.

Examples: If the small talk is about the weather and someone says, "At least the rain is good for my plants," seize on the word plants and ask, "Do you have a garden?" If someone says, "It's been too hot to walk my dogs," seize on the word dogs and ask "What kind of dogs do you have?"

11. Use the same terms as your conversation partner. This is particularly important when discussing topics that tend to matter to a lot of people, such as their families or careers.

Examples: If a parent refers to her "child," you should ask about her "child" as well, not her "little one" or "baby." If someone refers to his "profession," you should refer to it as his "profession," not his "job" or "career."

People tend to use the terms that their family members or closest friends use. If you use the same terms, it increases the odds that this person will feel comfortable with you.

Go With the Flow

Don't try too hard to be happy. Making happiness a personal goal actually makes it harder to achieve.

Recent finding: Women who actively strive for happiness tend to set higher goals for themselves and fall short more often...and thus are likely to be more depressed.

Iris Mauss, PhD, assistant professor of psychology, University of Denver, and leader of two studies published online in *Emotion.*

To Boost Happiness, Grab a Pen and Paper

R***ecent study:*** Eighty-five adults were surveyed on their gratitude and happiness levels, then half were asked to write letters of gratitude to people in their lives. Six weeks later, letter writers reported a significantly higher sense of gratitude and happiness compared with those who did not write letters.

Theory: Well-being improves when people express positive emotions in letters.

Best: Write three such letters every six weeks.

Steven Toepfer, PhD, associate professor of family and consumer studies, Kent State University, Ohio.

How to Complain to People You Know... So That You Get Results

Guy Winch, PhD, a licensed psychologist in private practice in New York City. He is author of *The Squeaky Wheel: Complaining the Right Way to Get Results, Improve Your Relationships, and Enhance Self-Esteem* (Walker & Company). He writes the Squeaky Wheel blog on PsychologyToday.com. *www.GuyWinch.com*

You may be good at resolving complaints with store managers or customer service reps, but complaining to people you know and see regularly—neighbors, colleagues, friends and relatives—is trickier.

Reason: It's about more than being right and getting satisfaction. You're trying to preserve the bonds of respect, friendship and/or love. Rather than risk starting an argument, some of us repress our complaints, which builds up frustration and deepens the cycle of miscommunication.

We interviewed communications expert Guy Winch, PhD, about how to complain to friends and family members in a way that produces results instead of headaches...

DON'T BE A SQUEAKY WHEEL

• **Most people complain like squeaky wheels.** They vent their emotions as they tick off a list of problems in a tense, annoyed tone. Venting may provide you with cathartic relief and can be effective in situations when you're complaining about a product or service because it proves that you mean business, and the squeakiest wheels do get results. However, it rarely works with friends and family. No matter how justified your anger or how culpable the other parties are, venting is interpreted as an unfair attack and triggers defensive behaviors, including angry denials, retaliatory complaints or shutting down and tuning you out.

USE A "COMPLAINT SANDWICH"

This is my favorite way to ease past the defense systems of people you know. Sandwich your complaint in between two positive statements.

The top slice of bread is a compliment that gets the person's attention and makes him/her more receptive to your complaint.

Case study: I had a patient who was throwing a party and was worried that her overbearing mother-in-law would try to take charge as she had done in the past. My patient was a bit intimidated by this woman and did not want to hurt her feelings.

Her top slice went this way, "You throw amazing parties, and I know this one would probably be a snap for you. But I wanted to talk to you about something." This last sentence framed what she had to say as a benign "talk" rather than a complaint.

The meat of the sandwich is a single, specific complaint. More than that just overwhelms people. My patient told her mother-in-law, "You've taken charge of things in previous parties, which I've appreciated, but it hasn't allowed me to test my own party-throwing abilities."

The bottom slice of bread is a friendly expression of appreciation combined with a request for a favor that motivates the other person to take some positive action. My patient said, "You really enjoy party planning, so I know that I'm asking a lot, but I would really appreciate it if you would let me fly solo on this one and let me handle the party myself."

AVOID CRITICIZING

Complaints focus on particular behaviors in particular situations and seek beneficial change. Criticisms are generalized accusations about the other person's character. They can cause long-lasting wounds and be toxic to a relationship.

Case study: I heard from a man whose wife was always on her iPhone. She even checked it at the dinner table and during movies at the theater. He complained to her that she was an "iPhone addict." Not surprisingly, their exchange escalated into a big fight. "Addict" was too highly charged a word to be productive in resolving his complaint. Instead, I suggested he try saying, "I got frustrated in the movie theater the other night when you had to respond to that message from work, because I really look forward to spending time with you. If we could designate movies as a time when we both turn off our phones, I would feel much less annoyed."

What got through to the wife was when the husband said that her iPhone use bothered him because he really looked forward to spending time with her. She agreed to negotiate times that they would turn off their phones—the list included movies/shows, dinner together and "relationship talks."

USE THE WORD "DISAPPOINTED"

When dealing with issues of trust, "disappointment" is a powerful word that exudes vulnerability and puts the burden on the other person to accept some blame and make amends. Use it instead of more aggressive, hostile words such as "violated" or "betrayed," which often push the other person to lash out with complaints about you.

Example: You confide in a colleague at work about your husband's medical condition. Though you've asked her not to tell anyone else, the colleague tells the receptionist. Instead of saying, "How could you violate my trust?" say, "I was so disappointed to hear that you mentioned Michael's diagnosis to the receptionist." Your friend's likely reaction is to say, "I'm sorry." But if your friend responds with a countercomplaint of her own ("You've talked about my family"), resist getting defensive yourself. Give your colleague an incentive to keep listening to you. Say, "That's worth discussing. Let's go back to what I initially brought up, then I promise we will talk about what you said."

BE SELECTIVE

If you voice every small annoyance and irritation to people you know, you become a chronic complainer whom no one takes seriously.

My rule of thumb: Ask yourself, Will this incident still bother me a month from now and have a negative effect on my life and self-esteem? If not, let it go.

DECIDE ON THE OUTCOME

Select the outcome that will be satisfying and meaningful to you. Otherwise, the person may fulfill your request but still leave you feeling frustrated.

Case study: A wife complained bitterly about her husband eating ice cream in bed at night. I asked her if she would feel better if he stopped bringing ice cream to bed. Perhaps he could eat it in the kitchen instead? Or he could eat something healthier? Or bring a dish for her? The wife realized that none of those alternatives would feel satisfactory. What she really was complaining about was the lack of physical and emotional intimacy in bed with her husband.

PUT ON A DUCHENNE SMILE

Much of what people react to when you complain is the unhappy, tense look on your face and the condescending tone in your voice. The easiest and simplest way to make a person more receptive is to make eye contact and smile as if you mean it. Guillaume Duchenne, a 19th-century French neurologist, was the first to recognize that a truly authentic smile involves the eye and cheek muscles, not just the mouth and lips. So don't just give a tense little smile. Give a big smile when you have a complaint to voice. This not only transmits emotion that makes you seem calm and open-minded, but it also makes it less likely that you will maintain a tone of anger and condescension in your voice.

Secrets of People Who Excel Under Pressure

Paul J. Sullivan, a journalist who writes the "Wealth Matters" column for *The New York Times* business section. Based in Stamford, Connecticut, he is author of the book *Clutch: Why Some People Excel Under Pressure and Others Don't* (Portfolio/Penguin). *www.PaulJSullivan.com*

Certain people always seem to come through in pivotal, make-or-break moments when many of us would buckle under the stress. *The New York Times* reporter Paul J. Sullivan wanted to figure out how these "clutch performers" do it—and whether it's a skill that can be learned.

As a reporter, he has access to the greatest clutch performers around, including star athletes, corporate titans, military officers and top trial attorneys. He discovered that the ability of clutch performers to remain calm and confident under fire doesn't come naturally. *They work hard to develop it by using specific coping techniques—techniques that you can use, too, to make sure that you come through when the heat is on...*

PRACTICE PRESSURE SITUATIONS

The more experience you have performing under pressure, the better you will do because it becomes familiar and less intimidating. The trick is to prepare for your own personal high-stakes situations by approximating the pressure you will experience. Make your practice as close to the real thing as possible. For instance, when I go to the golf range to practice my game, I typically hit 20 shots with my driver, 20 with my four wood, 20 with my three iron and so on. But that's not how the pros practice. Every shot they take is part of an imaginary scenario that they might face in real competition—I'm in the rough on the 14th hole, two strokes off the lead, trying to clear the bunkers to the left of the green. The pros experience the reality of these scenarios so intensely that when they are faced with similar shots in a real tournament, they're confident because they've "been there" before.

USE A SIMPLE ROUTINE

Pressure situations cause our physiological responses to quicken. The heart beats faster…muscles tense…but the ability to think rationally declines. In such situations, clutch performers use brief routines to slow down and regain their composure. It doesn't matter what your personal routine is—a mantra you whisper to yourself…a brief prayer…even just readjusting your tie—but it's important to repeat it regularly, even in practice, so that it becomes ingrained.

Example: The US Olympic riflery team hired a world-renowned psychiatrist, Dr. Ari Kiev, back in the 1970s to help them understand why they couldn't shoot as well in competition as they did in practice. Dr. Kiev (who died in 2009) realized that the athletes needed a routine they could concentrate on to give them an ongoing sense of discipline and control. He focused on their breathing and suggested that they pull the trigger in the stillness between breaths. Shooting between breaths improved their scores in competition and has become widely adopted by competitive shooters.

STAY FOCUSED

People make mistakes under pressure because they get distracted by a flood of thoughts, causing them to lose concentration on the task at hand. They typically obsess about their performance so far or about how this performance was better or worse than previous efforts or about how they will look to others if they succeed or fail.

Clutch performers realize that all this extraneous emotion raises internal stress levels, so they make a conscious decision to stay in the present. They decide what's most important to focus on at that moment and let all other distractions recede.

Example: I spent time with David Boies, the renowned trial attorney who participated in some of the most scrutinized court cases of the past two decades, including Bush versus Gore during the 2000 presidential election and the federal government's antitrust case against Microsoft. Once a trial starts, Boies's focus puts him into a bubble. He spends little time worrying about whether he's winning or losing the overall trial, and he never stops to congratulate himself on a particularly deft cross-examination or berate himself over mistakes. His concern is the task at hand—is the current argument working? Will it hold up to scrutiny from the opposing lawyer? This helps him ignore his nervousness and not be compromised by the crushing intensity surrounding his high-profile trials.

ADAPT

Stubborn pride is an often overlooked reason for why we fail under pressure. It acts like a smoke screen, keeping us from making the right choice at the right time. Look at how CEO Tony Hayward dealt with oil giant BP's catastrophic spill in the Gulf of Mexico. When initial plans to stem the spill didn't work, Hayward appeared to have choked. He seemed to blame others and seemed to refuse to admit the magnitude of his mistakes and be slow to take a new direction.

Clutch performers don't worry about being right or wrong—they focus on being effective, and they quickly readjust their plans when pressure renders them ineffective.

Example: The US Marines pride themselves on resilience and flexibility. I met a colonel, Matthew Bogdanos, who earned a Bronze Star in combat. Back in 2003, Bogdanos took an elite group of 100 soldiers to Iraq to stop the looting of the National Museum of Iraq. His plan was to round up the culprits, but he soon realized that that was a foolish priority, compared with recovering the thousands of stolen rare pieces, many of them dating back more than 5,000 years.

Bogdanos swallowed his pride as a military man and decided to let the thieves off the hook. He put the word out that no questions would be asked and that no one would be prosecuted when items were returned. An Iraqi came forward and returned a Syrian vase and a copper bas relief of a bull from 800 BC. Bogdanos arranged for the man to be interviewed on local television, hoping that this would show the Iraqis that American soldiers kept their word. It worked. Many of the artifacts eventually were recovered.

STUDY YOUR FAILURES

Most of us would rather forget how we messed up in pressure-filled moments and not relive the embarrassment or disappointment. But you need to examine your performance to gain perspective about what happened. In fact, clutch performers are obsessive about reviewing videotapes of themselves under pressure and asking knowledgeable observers for their opinions. That's because we tend to choke in the same way again and again.

Understanding how you personally react to pressure can help you break these patterns. It's important to reach out to others for feedback, in addition to analyzing your own performance, because we often misperceive what we did wrong.

How to Get a Yes From Anyone...Fast

Michael V. Pantalon, PhD, a psychologist, motivational coach and member of the faculty at Yale School of Medicine, New Haven, Connecticut. He is author of *Instant Influence: How to Get Anyone to Do Anything—Fast* (Little, Brown). *www.michaelpantalon.com*

Tell people what they should do, and there's a very good chance that they won't do it. Threaten them with dire consequences if they fail to act, and they often just dig in their heels.

Words spoken by others tend not to spur people to action. If you want to convince family members, coworkers, acquaintances or strangers to do something, the secret is to get them to say why they should want to do these things.

Example: A 2003 study published in *Journal of Consulting and Clinical Psychology* found that the number of times a counselor tells an addict that he needs to change has no effect on the addict's future behavior...but the more the addict himself speaks of his desire to change, the greater the odds are that he will overcome his addiction.

I've developed a series of six questions that we can pose to those we hope to influence to encourage them to voice their reasons for doing whatever we want them to do. These questions are based on a well-established counseling approach known as motivational interviewing.

This isn't mind control, and it's unlikely to work if someone is 100% against your idea, but in most other situations, it can be very effective.

Example: Asking these six questions increased by 250% the odds that inner-city hospital patients would return for scheduled follow-up visits.

"IT'S YOUR DECISION"

My strategy is most likely to be effective if the person you are attempting to influence feels free to make up his/her own mind and is not backed into a corner. So liberally sprinkle in phrases such as, "It's completely your decision"..."No one can force you to do anything"...or "You're your own person and can do what you want."

To further encourage this person's sense of autonomy, ask permission to ask a question before launching into the questions below, then ask permission to ask follow-up questions.

Set aside any temptation to vent at this person about problematic behavior...to interject your own opinions...or to explain the dire consequences of not doing what you suggest. Such actions on your part detract from the other person's sense of autonomy.

Overall, the person asking the questions (the influencer) should reiterate any positive reasons for change that he hears from the "influencee" and ignore (and definitely not argue against) any reasons he might hear against change.

THE SIX QUESTIONS

Ask these questions, in order, to bring someone around to your way of thinking...

QUESTION 1

Why might you do this? Fine-tune this question so that it fits the specific situation at hand.

Examples: "If you were to decide to drink less—and I'm not saying you have to, it's completely your decision—what would be the reason?"..."Hypothetically, why might it be beneficial to you to work with me on this project?"..."If you were to give me a discount, what would you get out of it?"

This encourages people to consider their motivations for doing what you want them to do.

Helpful: Cite a small, incremental change, such as "drink less," rather than "quit drinking."

If the person you are attempting to influence responds with a personal benefit that he would derive, move on to question 2.

Potential complications: People sometimes respond that they would get no benefit from doing what you suggest. If so, point to a statement or action that this person previously made or took that indicates he does have some motivation to do something along the lines of what you said.

Example: "Earlier in this conversation, you told me that you wished that there was something I could do to help you. Why did you wish that if you get nothing out of being helped?"

You might receive a response that reflects your goals or some third party's goals, not the goals of the person you are trying to influence. If so, ask, "But what would you, personally, get out of it?"

Example: If the initial response is, "It would make my wife happy if I quit smoking," ask follow-up questions until you hear something more personal such as, "I wouldn't wake up coughing"..."I would save money"...or "I feel good when I make my wife happy."

Occasionally people will decline to answer this question because they are not considering doing what you suggest. If this happens, explain that the question is purely hypothetical and ask for a response.

QUESTION 2

How ready are you to do this, on a scale of one to 10, where one means "not ready at all" and 10 means "totally ready"? Replace "do this" with the specific action that's being discussed, such as "How ready are you to back my candidacy?"

Most people pick a number higher than one if only because saying "one" sounds unreasonable and closed minded. The trick is that when these people answer with a number above one, they hear themselves admit that some part of them is open to the idea.

Potential complication: Occasionally someone will answer "one." When this occurs, repeat the question using a less daunting incremental step.

Example: "Dad, if you're at one, then I get that you are really not ready to discuss moving to an assisted-living facility. But on the same one-to-10 scale, how ready are you to visit a few assisted-living facilities with me just to see what they're actually like?"

QUESTION 3

Why didn't you pick a lower number? Asking this forces people to confront the fact that they have at least a sliver of desire to do what you wish them to do.

Potential complications: People occasionally respond, "Well, my number was pretty low." If so, counter, "Sure, but it wasn't one. Why not?" Sometimes people even attempt to revise their earlier two or three down to one when asked this question. If so, say, "Maybe now it's one, but a second ago, you said two. Why was it above one then?"

QUESTION 4

Imagine that you already did this. What would the positive outcomes be for you? Unlike Question 1, where you asked why you might do this, this question assumes the action is already done. *Replace "did this" with the specific action being discussed, such as "Imagine you've already started exercising..."*

When people consider taking action, they tend to focus on the challenges that they face and the possibility of failure. This question encourages them to mentally skip ahead to a time when those difficulties and risks are in the past and they are enjoying their success. Imagining success makes ideas under discussion seem real rather than pie-in-the-sky dreams. It also makes people more optimistic and excited.

Potential complication: The person you are trying to influence might mention how other people would benefit. If so, ask, "But how would you benefit?"

Example: Your employee says that coming in on time would be good for his department's productivity. Press him until he says it also would be good for his performance reviews...or that it would allow him to get his work done earlier so that he could get home to see his kids in the evenings.

QUESTION 5

Why are those outcomes important to you? This question encourages people to really reflect upon the positive outcomes they mentioned in response to question 4. Continue asking, "And why is that important to you?" to each ensuing response until you reach something concrete and deeply personal. Specific, personal goals are much better motivators than vague desires.

Example: If the answer to question 4 is "Because I'd be healthier," ask, "Why is it important for you to be healthier?" Then continue asking "why?" to each ensuing response until you get something very personal, such as, "If I were healthier, I could play with my grandkids in the park."

QUESTION 6

So what's your next step, if any? This final question asks the individual to identify a specific, near-term action that he will take toward the larger goal you have been discussing. Saying this step out loud can help bridge the crucial gap between motivation and action.

Don't let the "if any" at the end of this question fool you—obtaining an answer here is not optional. The "if any" is included to reinforce this person's sense of autonomy by conveying that you are not ordering him to do anything—it is his decision to take this next step. People are more likely to follow through and take action when they feel that doing so is their decision.

The Prophetic Power Of Your Dreams

Judith Orloff, MD, a psychiatrist in private practice and an assistant clinical professor of psychiatry at the University of California, Los Angeles. She is author of *Emotional Freedom: Liberate Yourself from Negative Emotions and Transform Your Life* (Three Rivers). *www.drjudithorloff.com*

Most people don't believe it, but our nighttime dreams are a powerful source of insight that can help us lead more fulfilling lives. In fact, by working with your dreams, you can move past obstacles, cope better with anxiety, heal old hurts and make better decisions. We spoke with Judith Orloff, MD, author of the book *Emotional Freedom,* about how we all can use our dreams to make our lives better...

HOW TO REMEMBER YOUR DREAMS

Everyone dreams, but not everyone remembers dreaming. You can train yourself to recall your dreams.

• **Keep a notebook and pen by your bed.** Before you go to sleep each night, say to yourself, I will remember a dream tonight. You also may wish to write down a question at bedtime about an emotional dilemma, such as How can I be happier?

When you wake up in the morning, don't jump out of bed. Instead, spend a few minutes with your eyes closed, relaxing in the peaceful state between sleeping and waking.

Then, open your eyes and write down anything you remember about your previous night's dreams. Don't try to interpret them right away—this could interfere with your recall. You don't have to record every detail, but don't shy away from the embarrassing, frightening or otherwise distressing parts. Those elements often contain the most valuable information.

You may need to follow these steps for a week or more before you form the habit of remembering your dreams.

Once you remember your dreams and have written them down, you can begin to analyze them. You will find that they fall into three categories—psychological, predictive or guidance.

PSYCHOLOGICAL DREAMS

Psychological dreams are the most common type, offering a window into your emotional life. Some psychological dreams point out a problem that needs your attention.

Examples: Dreams about being chased...being naked in public...taking a test for which you are completely unprepared. These dreams usually arise from a fear or insecurity that is holding you back.

Other psychological dreams celebrate your strengths, achievements and transitions.

Examples: Dreams about flying...triumphing over odds...getting married.

TO USE PSYCHOLOGICAL DREAMS...

Focus on the most emotionally intense part of the dream, whether upsetting or uplifting. Identify the issue that the dream is referring to by asking, How does this dream seem to relate to my life? Write any answers in your dream notebook.

If your dream brings up a problem or issue, brainstorm ways of dealing with it. Write down the steps that you can take to address it. Take action, and see whether your situation or attitude improves.

Example: You dream that you are being chased by a bandit. Ask yourself, Who in my life is pursuing me? Where am I feeling unsafe? Perhaps the pursuer reminds you of a coworker who is intruding on your project. Explore the ways in which you are feeling pressured by this person, and examine your options. Perhaps you need to find other allies at work or to say "no" more assertively.

Enjoy the positive emotions a dream brings up, such as scenes or feelings of accomplishment or encouragement. Too often we breeze past our successes and focus immediately on the next goal. Instead, ask yourself what situation in your life the dream is celebrating, and do something special or inspirational to savor this milestone.

Examples: Throw a party...or call a friend to talk about it.

PREDICTIVE DREAMS

Predictive dreams give you information that you would otherwise have no way of knowing. These dreams might portray you in a career, relationship or other life circumstance you had not considered or depict a health problem that you have not been consciously aware of.

Example 1: When I was in my 20s, I had a dream in which I became a doctor. At that time, I was a college dropout working contentedly in a department store. The dream opened my eyes to potential I had not seen in myself. A few months later, I reenrolled in college, went on to get my medical degree and became a psychiatrist.

Example 2: One of my patients dreamed that he saw fire around his neck. He woke up with a calm sense of certainty that he had cancer. His doctor didn't feel anything unusual during a physical examination, and tests were normal. The patient persisted until he found a specialist willing to do a scan. The scan indicated a thyroid tumor, which was successfully treated.

How is a predictive dream different from a psychological dream? Whereas psychological dreams involve strong emotions, predictive dreams are emotionally neutral. Images and scenarios are crisp and clear in predictive dreams, and information is conveyed in a detached way. You feel more like a witness than a participant, as if you're in a theater watching a movie.

TO USE PREDICTIVE DREAMS...

Ask yourself, What is the dream trying to tell me? Use your common sense as you apply the information you receive. Dreaming about illness does not necessarily mean that you are ill. Dreaming about divorce does not necessarily mean that your marriage is in trouble. Do not feel compelled to take sudden, drastic action if it feels wrong. Take gradual steps, and observe their effects. As you respond to the message in a predictive dream, you will feel lighter emotionally.

If you wake up racked with worry about a dream involving the future, it was more likely a psychological dream than a predictive dream. In that case, work with it as a psychological dream—identify the problems that it relates to so that you can clear out your anxiety about the issue. Then you will be able to listen more clearly to any intuition.

Example: If you have recurring dreams in which you develop a terrifying disease, ask yourself questions such as, Where is this anxiety about health coming from? Does this have to do with my mother, who frets about my health? What steps can I take to separate my own attitude toward my health from my parents'? Where have I been neglecting my health, and what can I do to be healthier?

GUIDANCE DREAMS

Guidance dreams contain answers to waking dilemmas. They dispel confusion so that you can make good choices.

Example: A friend of mine wondered whether he should get involved in a real estate venture with his sister. She had never been dependable but had recently been acting more stable. Before he went to sleep, he asked for guidance about the potential partnership. He dreamed that he was in a car with his sister at the wheel. She was driving recklessly and almost crashed. He realized that the stress of partnering with her was not worth the risk.

How do guidance dreams differ from predictive dreams? Guidance dreams sometimes contain an element of prediction. However, predictive dreams arise spontaneously, whereas guidance dreams occur in response to a question. Guidance dreams also produce a physical response, such as a tingle, when you start to analyze them in contrast to the neutral tone of predictive dreams.

Guidance dreams are especially helpful when you have been overanalyzing a situation and feel stuck.

To use guidance dreams…

At bedtime, write a question in your dream notebook about a problem or decision you are struggling with.

Examples: Why do my spouse and I argue so often?…Should I say yes to this job opportunity? When you wake up, record your dream. Look for a scene, word or image that grabs your attention and generates a physical response, such as a flush or chill.

Explore what this element of the dream tells you about the situation. Listen for a feeling of "rightness" in your body and a sense of emotional release. Act on your dream's advice, and observe the results.

Connect! Social Networking Fosters Stronger Friendships

Digital communication may encourage greater honesty, faster intimacy in relationships and an increased sense of belonging. The idea that technology enhances real-world relationships runs counter to the notion of lonely people sitting at computers and not interacting with others. In fact, new and established friendships are reinforced.

Nancy Baym, PhD, communications studies professor, University of Kansas, Lawrence, and leader of a study published in *Information, Communication & Society.*

How to Gracefully End A Bad Relationship

Henry Cloud, PhD, a leadership coach and clinical psychologist based in Los Angeles. He is author of *Necessary Endings: The Employees, Businesses, and Relationships That All of Us Have to Give Up in Order to Move Forward* (HarperBusiness). *www.DrCloud.com*

Endings can be as important as beginnings in personal and professional relationships. But people often are reluctant to face the awkwardness and pain—on both sides—of ending a bad relationship.

Why it's crucial: Although it may sound harsh, the time and energy that we waste on bad relationships could be more enjoyably or profitably devoted to people and pursuits that we prefer. Worse, when we spend time with people who have bad attitudes, bad habits or chronic bad moods, we dramatically increase the odds that we will suffer from these, too—a phenomenon called "social contagion."

Example: A study published in *The New England Journal of Medicine* found that our odds of becoming obese increase by 57% if one of our friends becomes obese. The same research team also found that having a single unhappy friend increases the odds that we will be unhappy by about 7%.

Yet most people rarely, if ever, end bad relationships, aside from failed romantic relationships. They continue putting up with unpleasant, unproductive or even toxic associations because they don't want to hurt anyone's feelings...they don't want to endure the difficult conversation required to end a relationship... they don't realize the price they're paying for having this person in their life...they view ending relationships as a form of failure...and/or they think only mean people intentionally cut other people out of their lives.

• **Ending bad relationships is not selfish.** If we don't end them, we have less time and energy for the friends, loved ones and business associates who need and deserve our attention. And we risk dragging those people down with the bad habits and moods that we pick up from our troubled relationships. It is perfectly natural for relationships to end. What's not natural is maintaining relationships that bring more bad than good to our lives.

PICKING PEOPLE TO DROP

Consider what you want your life and career to be like. Now consider each of your personal and professional relationships. Which are not helping you move toward this vision? Which are pulling you away from it? These are the relationships that may have to end.

Exception: It might be worth continuing a difficult relationship if there are overriding reasons, such as a marriage worth salvaging, and especially if there is a reason to believe that this person and relationship could improve in the near future. Perhaps the relationship used to be better and turned sour only because this person is going through a difficult phase...or perhaps this person recently has begun taking action to address his/her problems.

SECOND CHANCES

If someone you're considering eliminating from your life is wise enough to respond positively to feedback, that is reason to have hope that the relationship could improve. *Before ending any relationship...*

Discuss with the other person the trouble that you are having with the relationship.

Example: "Lately, when we are together, you complain about something the entire time. I need friends who will help me grow in life, solve problems and feel good about life. I would like you to be one of those friends. If you can do that, I would love to continue to spend time with you. If not, I'm not going to be able to socialize with you anymore."

Be open about your own faults, too, during this discussion. Try to frame your concerns as issues that you bring to the relationship as well, not just complaints about the other person's behavior.

Use a soft and caring tone of voice, and say how much the positive aspects of the relationship have meant to you.

If this person listens to your concerns and strives to correct the problems you raise, the relationship could be worth continuing. If he/she becomes defensive, angry or combative when faced with these problems, there's much less hope for the relationship. *What to do...*

Lay out the specific, painful consequences this person will incur because of his misbehavior.

Example: "Because you keep getting drunk and belligerent when the family gets together, you're no longer invited when there might be alcohol present."

This might sound tough, but being direct could be the only way to get this person's attention and help him understand the urgency of the situation.

If this person still fails to see the light, place the fate of the relationship in his hands. Explain what you expect from a friend...employee...professional contact...or romantic partner. Then say, "I'd like that to be you, but if it isn't, we can't spend time together anymore."

Leave it to this person to decide whether he can do what is necessary to continue the relationship.

Presented with an ultimatum, this person might try to improve or he might quietly disappear from your life. If neither of these things occurs, proceed to the section below, and do so without guilt—you are not the one ending this relationship. Your former acquaintance is ending it by declining to do what is necessary to save it.

HOW TO PREPARE

To make a break in a way that lets you feel it is a positive step, you have to prepare yourself in various ways...

• **Keep your vision for your life in front of you.** Position photos of the people you love spending time with where you'll see them frequently. This should continually remind you what you're sacrificing when you waste time on toxic relationships. Budget time for the relationships you value and make them a priority.

• **Increase your interactions with the problem person.** We normally attempt to limit our interactions with those we don't like so that we can avoid facing the problem. But by distancing ourselves from bad relationships, we make it possible to pretend that they're not really so bad. Stop screening calls from people you don't want to talk to, and stop coming up with excuses to cut conversations with them short. The more you face the pain that the relationship causes you, the greater the odds that you'll reach the point where you're willing to end it.

Helpful: When you speak with these people, picture yourself dealing with them not just today but next month, next year and for the rest of your life.

• **Seek out new, fulfilling relationships.** Your desire to end bad relationships is likely to climb dramatically if you have numerous enjoyable, productive relationships and activities vying for your time.

Helpful: Volunteer with a variety of nonprofit causes that you care about. This should increase your awareness that your time is valuable and help you meet new people who have a positive outlook on life.

HOW TO END IT

To minimize hurt feelings and raised tempers, place the blame for the failed relationship on the way you and this person interact with each other, not solely on the other person's shoulders.

If the other person becomes angry, express empathy, then return the conversation to the issue.

Example: "I know this is hard to hear. It's hard for me to say. But this really is an issue, and it isn't getting any better."

This is not fun, but it's the only way you can spend your time with people you have decided to invest in—and the only way that those people will get as much of you as they deserve.

Banish Guilt!

Study participants wrote about rejecting someone, then submerged their hands in ice water for as long as possible or warm water. The ice-water group reported feeling half as much guilt as the warm-water group.

Theory: Self-punishment helps alleviate remorse.

Psychological Science

Multitasking May Hurt Your Self-Control

Ryan Hamilton, PhD, assistant professor, department of marketing, Goizueta Business School, Emory University, Atlanta, and leader of a study published in *Organizational Behavior and Human Decision Processes.*

Recent study: People who shift focus between two or more activities that require different mind-sets may have trouble with concentration and self-control in other areas of their lives.

Example: Checking your BlackBerry while helping children with their homework requires you to switch back and forth between two different tasks. Consistent multitasking such as this taxes the executive function of the brain, which regulates self-control and discipline. That may make it difficult for you to control your temper, stick to a diet or keep up with an exercise routine.

Self-defense: Try to group similar activities together...or recognize that you may be prone to self-control failures after multitasking, so plan accordingly.

• **No matter your approach, make creative time a priority.** Schedule it on your calendar. The payback can be truly magnificent.

Creativity Boosters

Marjory Abrams, president, *BottomLine* newsletters, Boardroom Inc., 281 Tresser Blvd., Stamford, Connecticut 06901.

I am at my most creative when I'm just waking up. The challenge is to keep my creative juices flowing the rest of the day. *Two of the more provocative ideas I have come across...*

• **Randomly select a word from the dictionary.** Make as many connections as you can between the word and the problem at hand.

• **Reverse brainstorm.** Think about ways to make a problem worse. Create your solution by doing the opposite of these "anti-solutions."

Gail McMeekin, president of Boston-based Creative Success and author of several books on the topic, including *The 12 Secrets of Highly Successful Women: A Portable Life Coach for Creative Women,* makes a business out of encouraging creativity. *Her favorite suggestions, which apply equally to men and women...*

• **Record yourself talking about a problem**—what it is, what you want, where you seem stuck, etc. Then listen to the recording. Hearing it can provide clarity.

• **Visit a toy store.** Search for metaphors and connections that may stimulate solutions.

Example: A toy caterpillar with interlocking segments helped McMeekin realize that the training program she was developing would work best if divided into individual, daylong segments.

• **Keep track of what fascinates you**—a dew-laden spiderweb, a meaningful quotation, an unusual sign, a splashy car. Write them down, or photograph them and review every few weeks. You never know what solutions they may lead to, consciously or unconsciously.

New Type of Translator

If you've been confused by Internet slang, check out *www.noslang.com.* There you can find the meaning of common abbreviations and acronyms used in message boards, blogs and texting.

Examples: rofl ("rolling on the floor laughing")...ftfy ("fixed that for you")...ymmv ("your mileage may vary"). Just enter the abbreviation, and click "Translate Slang." The site also has information on common Twitter abbreviations, instant messaging etiquette and more.

David Boyer, research editor, *Bottom Line/Personal.*

Clever Phone Tricks to Get Through to Anyone

Leil Lowndes, a communications consultant and corporate trainer based in New York City, whose clients have included The Walt Disney Company, Kodak and the US Peace Corps. Based in New York City, she is author of *How to Instantly Connect with Anyone* (McGraw-Hill). *www.lowndes.com*

Knowing a few phone tricks can make life easier—and even make you more successful...

• **When you can't place the name of a caller who seems to know you and you're embarrassed to admit it, say, "I'm right in the middle of something**—give me your number, and I'll call you right back." Then hang up, and rack your memory to figure out who the caller is. Then call back.

• **Use an air of familiarity to increase the odds that a secretary will put you through to a big shot.** If you can create the impression that you are on close terms with the big shot, the secretary might put you through rather than risk offending a good friend of the boss. Identify yourself only by your first name, say "he" or "she" rather than the big shot's name and use the secretary's first name if you know it.

Example: "Oh, hi, Lisa. This is Jim. Is he in?"

• **Inject pep into phone calls.** Phone conversations tend to be less engaging than face-to-face chats because the caller can't see your facial expressions and hand gestures. Add perhaps 30% more than your usual energy to your voice on the phone to make up for this pep deficit. Expect it to feel a little unnatural at first.

• **Call when you know no one is there to answer if you don't want a long or awkward conversation.** Leave a voice mail message, and say there's no need to call back.

Helpful: You can't just call when someone's out if you're calling a cell phone—people carry their cell phones with them when they go out. Instead, use a service called slydial (*www.slydial.com*) to leave a message in a cell phone's voice mail. Call 267-759-3425, then enter the number you wish to reach when prompted. Your call will go right to the cell-phone's voice mail without the cell-phone's owner having a chance to answer. Slydial is free, but you will have to listen to a few advertisements and your standard long-distance rates apply.

• **Keep your tone restrained when you first answer your phone**—then shift to a very pleased tone to say, "Oh, Mary, great to hear from you," when the caller identifies herself. This tone shift sends a message that you are happy to hear from this particular person, which is likely to encourage callers to have warm feelings toward you, too.

• **Use your conversation partner's first name more frequently than you would when speaking in person.** People perk up when they hear their names, so this can increase the call's energy and sense of engagement.

Examples: "That's a good point, Steve," or "You know what I think, Steve..."

• **Plan what you'll say if voice mail picks up...or if a person picks up.** Anticipating one and getting the other is among the most common causes of phone fumbles.

• **Give your phone number twice when you leave a message.** This saves listeners from having to replay your message if they miss a digit the first time.

Helpful: Speak your number in two different groupings, such as "five-five-five-nine-two-nine-one," then "five-fifty-five...ninety-two...ninety-one." This doubles the odds that you've said it in a way that the person you called will remember.

• **Let people see you turn off your cell phone when you meet with them face to face.** This sends a powerful message that you consider these people important.

Memory Aid

Instead of trying to remember a specific thing that you have to do—such as repaying money borrowed from a coworker—visualize a scene in which you actually are doing it.

Example: Imagine taking the money out of your pocket or purse and handing it to the coworker at a specific location, such as the break room. Create the visualization before going to sleep—your brain will strengthen the image overnight, and you will be more likely to do the task the next day.

Mark McDaniel, PhD, professor of psychology, Washington University in St. Louis.

For a Sharper Memory

Recent study: Researchers examined dietary and memory-test data on nearly 1,400 adults (average age 61) over a three- to 10-year period.

Result: People whose diets contained the highest levels of the nutrient choline performed better on memory tests than those who consumed the least amount.

Theory: Choline is a precursor to a brain chemical called acetylcholine, which plays a key role in cognition.

Good sources of choline: Eggs, poultry, saltwater fish, liver and kidney beans.

Rhoda Au, PhD, associate professor of neurology, Boston University School of Medicine.

Break Free from Habits That Hold You Back

Rebecca Gladding, MD, staff psychiatrist with the Veterans Administration California Healthcare System. She recently served as a clinical instructor and medical director of the UCLA Adult Inpatient Eating Disorders Program. She is coauthor of *You Are Not Your Brain: The 4-Step Solution for Changing Bad Habits, Ending Unhealthy Thinking, and Taking Control of Your Life* (Avery).

Habits are hard to break because of the way the brain is wired. Each time you repeat a harmful behavior—overeating, overspending, procrastinating or something else—the brain circuits involved in that action become stronger. The brain associates the action with the situation that gave rise to it, such as being under stress. Over time, the brain becomes hardwired to choose that behavior automatically any time a similar situation arises.

Example: If you reach for a sugary snack whenever you are worried about a project at work, after a while, you may crave sugar the moment that you start feeling anxious about anything anywhere.

That's the bad news.

The good news: You can rewire your brain to choose constructive habits...

Step 1: **Relabel**

Negative habits are triggered by *deceptive brain messages*—thoughts, beliefs and impulses that run counter to your positive, healthy intentions. These thoughts and urges are accompanied by unpleasant emotions or physical sensations such as anger, sadness, anxiety or fatigue. Because the discomfort is so intense, you are driven to get rid of it as fast as you can, usually by indulging in an unhealthy habit. This brings temporary relief but in reality makes the situation worse—each time you give in, you further strengthen the brain pathways that connect the thought or urge with the bad habit.

Relabeling means recognizing your impulses and negative thoughts as deceptive brain messages and calling them what they are. It means simply noting to yourself what is happening, such as, *I am having a craving even though I just ate 30 minutes ago* or *My boss just yelled at me, and because of that, now I need some chocolate.* The more you are aware of these habits, the more opportunities you have to stop acting on them.

Becoming aware of these messages can be challenging at first. *To develop your ability to relabel...*

- **Practice making mental notes.** Any time you feel "off" or uneasy in some way, notice what is going on in your body or mind, and pick a simple word or phrase to describe it. For example, if you notice that you are thinking about a conversation with a friend that went awry—when you really need to be working—say to yourself, *Mind wandering.* If you are having physical symptoms, such as heart pounding, shakiness, feeling a pit in your stomach, note this as *anxiety.* The key is to snap yourself back into awareness—which is the first step toward doing something about the situation in a healthy, productive way.
- **Focus on your breathing.** One way to enhance your ability to notice what's happening in a moment-to-moment way is by focusing on your breath. For five minutes, sit in a quiet place, close your eyes and simply pay attention to your breath as you inhale and exhale. What you will find as you try to do this is that your brain is constantly running, thinking about plans for later in the week or stressing about what you have to do today. Whenever you realize that you have become lost in thought in these ways, say to yourself, *Thinking* or *Planning* or *Wandering,* then gently turn your focus back to your breathing.

Do this focused breathing exercise once a day, and gradually extend the length of time to 20 or 30 minutes.

Step 2: **Reframe**

As you become aware of deceptive brain messages, you can begin changing your perception of their importance. You do this by reframing—challenging your default response.

Reframing does not mean denying the existence of a thought or impulse or judging yourself for having it. Instead, you look at the thought from a new perspective and diminish its importance so that you do not automatically react in your habitual way.

Example: *I feel upset right now, but that doesn't mean I have to have a cigarette (or that I am a bad person because I am craving one).*

To change your perspective...

• **Use distancing phrases.** When you notice a deceptive brain message, say to yourself, *That's not me, it's just my brain...or Oh, that's just mental chatter*...or *I'm having a bad brain day.*

• **Look for thinking errors.** We often make inaccurate assumptions about difficult situations and painful feelings. To uncover these erroneous, unhelpful thoughts, ask yourself nonjudgmental questions, such as, *What is it about this situation that is upsetting me? What am I telling myself about what is happening? What are some other interpretations?*

Common thinking errors include...

All-or-nothing thinking: Seeing situations and people in extremes, such as perfect or hopeless, all good or all bad.

Worst-case thinking: Assuming that something terrible inevitably is going to happen.

Discounting the positive: Ignoring your good qualities and failing to notice or take seriously other people's positive reactions toward you.

• **Be compassionate with yourself.** Write down the deceptive brain message—the thought, sensation or impulse—that is bothering you. Then ask yourself what a kindhearted friend would advise or think.

• **Use the 15-minute rule.** When you experience an especially powerful impulse, try to wait 15 minutes before you act. Then if you still cannot resist the urge, slowly and mindfully engage in the activity that your deceptive brain message is insisting upon.

Important: Do not try to talk yourself out of an uncomfortable feeling. Simply examine it. You are training yourself to be less frightened of discomfort, to learn that it will pass and that it is not such a big deal.

Step 3: **Refocus**

Once you have relabeled and reframed a deceptive brain message, you may find it surprisingly easy to actively shift your attention to a healthy, constructive activity—even as your deceptive thoughts are urging you to act in your old, habitual way. By refocusing repeatedly, you weaken the brain circuits associated with your cravings and retrain your brain to choose healthier responses when you are stressed or sad.

The best refocusing activities are ones that engage and interest you. If they require strategy or learning something new, they will be even more effective, but any wholesome activity that you enjoy is fine.

Examples: Do a crossword puzzle...read...exercise...call a friend...play with a pet...sing a song...pursue a hobby...cook a healthy recipe.

If you are at work, refocus on a task that you can accomplish quickly or that is less demanding.

What makes this step powerful is that you allow uncomfortable sensations and impulses to be present...but then you act constructively anyway. You are learning that the messages do not have to dominate your attention or control your actions. You are training your brain to create new associations between thoughts and healthy actions. This takes patience.

Step 4: **Revalue**

The final step is really about gaining perspective and the strength to believe in yourself. Each person gets there at his/her own pace, and when you do, you can look at the deceptive brain message and unhelpful impulses and simply say to yourself, *This is nothing more than the feeling of a deceptive brain message. I do not have to act on it, and it does not define me.* The more you are able to relabel, reframe and refocus, the more empowered you will be to dismiss those deceptive brain messages and move on with your life in a positive direction—one that you define. That's the essence of revalue and the goal of the four steps.

19

Working Life

Good Professions for People Without a Degree

The recent recession has taken its toll on many working people, but those who lack college degrees have fared the worst. The unemployment rate among Americans whose education ended with a high school diploma recently was 10.3%, nearly twice the 5.4% rate for those who have bachelor's degrees, according to the US Bureau of Labor Statistics.

Going back to school to earn a college degree is one potential path for these unemployed individuals—but not everyone has the time, temperament and/or bankroll for college. Another option is seeking out a profession that is hiring now and has bright prospects for the coming years but doesn't require a college degree. Such professions are rare these days, but they do exist. *Among the best prospects…*

• **Emergency medical technicians (EMTs)** are dispatched by 911 operators to assist people in need of immediate medical attention or transport to a medical facility. Demand for EMTs should increase as the aging US population has more medical emergencies.

Wage range: $24,070 to $39,590.

Training and requirements: Job requirements vary by state, but EMTs typically must complete courses at a technical school to earn a certificate, then pass a state exam. For more information, visit the Web site of the National Registry of Emergency Medical Technicians (*www.nremt.org*, select "Become an EMS

Laurence Shatkin, PhD, who has spent more than 30 years in the career information field. He is senior product developer with JIST Publishing, a publisher of career-related books, and previously was a researcher and developer at Educational Testing Service. Based in Titusville, New Jersey, he is past president of the Association of Computer-Based Systems for Career Information and author or coauthor of numerous books on career topics, including *300 Best Jobs Without a Four-Year Degree* (JIST). *www.shatkin.com*

Professional"). You need to be a good driver and be able to perform under pressure.

• **Insurance sales agents** sell insurance policies and related financial products. It's one of the few desk jobs that does not require a college degree (though some employers in this field do prefer college-educated candidates). Insurance salespeople remain in strong demand even as the economy has struggled—insurance typically is one of the last expenses people sacrifice during tough times.

Wage range: $33,330 to $71,620 (some of which may be based on commission).

Training and requirements: In most states, insurance agents must be licensed. This usually involves taking a course and passing an examination, but rules vary by state and category of insurance. Contact your state's insurance bureau for details (*www.naic.org*, then click "States & Jurisdiction Map" to find contact information for your state) or discuss licensing requirements with an insurance agency that is hiring. Very strong interpersonal skills are essential, and a background in sales is a plus.

• **Pharmacy technicians** fill prescriptions and assist customers under the supervision of a pharmacist. Demand for pharmacy techs is expected to continue to increase as America's aging population fills an ever-increasing number of prescriptions.

Wage range: $23,370 to $34,560.

Training and requirements: Employers prefer applicants who have formal training or certification. Training programs are offered by community colleges and technical schools and run from six months to two years. Some hospitals, as well as the armed forces, also offer training. The Pharmacy Technician Certification Board (PTCB) and the Institute for the Certification of Pharmacy Technicians (ICPT) offer national certification exams.

• **Private detectives and investigators** might spend their days surreptitiously following unfaithful spouses or insurance cheats... helping lawyers track down information for cases...or conducting background checks for employers. Demand currently is strong because of heightened security concerns and increasing litigation rates. In addition to private detective work, jobs in the field are offered by insurance companies, law firms, retailers and hotels.

Wage range: $32,630 to $58,130.

Training and requirements: There are no formal training requirements, though many private detectives and investigators have experience in police work, security or accounting. Computer skills are helpful—private detectives often do much of their legwork online.

A license is needed in most states. Contact the agency that handles licensing in your state for details. That's often the State Department of Public Safety or the State Police. Or try typing the name of your state and the words "private detective license" into a search engine.

• **Athletic coaches and scouts** are in demand these days as baby boomers enter retirement and hire golf and tennis instructors in increasing numbers...and as parents increasingly view sports as a potential path to college athletic scholarships for their kids. Also, professional teams hire coaches and scouts to recruit and train athletes.

Wage range: $18,800 to $43,930.

Training and requirements: No formal training or certification is required for most coaching and scouting positions, but that doesn't mean just anyone can step into this profession. Extensive background in the sport is required, as is physical fitness. Jobs in this field often go to those who have a strong network of contacts in the sports community.

• **Pest-control workers** remedy insect and rodent problems. It's a recession-resistant profession, and recent bedbug outbreaks have only spurred demand.

Wage range: $24,960 to $37,850.

Training and requirements: Most training is on the job. Many states require that pest-control workers pass an exam to prove that they understand how to safely handle the dangerous chemicals used in the profession, but pest-control companies typically provide their employees with the training needed to pass this exam.

Some agility and physical fitness are necessary, too—pest-control workers sometimes must climb high ladders, venture into tight crawl spaces and carry heavy tanks.

• **Fitness trainers and aerobics instructors** lead classes in gyms and provide private workouts. Americans' increasing attention to health and fitness has helped keep demand strong for these professionals.

Wage range: $19,870 to $46,130.

Training and requirements: No formal training is required (unless you're teaching a specific discipline such as Pilates or yoga), but familiarity with aerobics techniques and/or modern gym equipment is a must, as, of course, is physical fitness.

• **Septic tank servicers** pump out full septic tanks. Some also repair broken septic systems or sewer lines. It's dirty, smelly work, but it's a profession that is always in demand—septic tanks aren't used any less during recessions.

Wage range: $26,670 to $42,630.

Training and requirements: All necessary training typically is provided on the job. Reasonably good physical fitness is required—as is a strong stomach.

Where the Jobs Are

Laurence Shatkin, PhD, who has spent more than 30 years in the career information field. He is senior product developer with JIST Publishing, Titusville, New Jersey, a publisher of career-related books, and previously was a researcher and developer at Educational Testing Service. He is past president of the Association of Computer-based Systems for Career Information and author of numerous books on career topics, including *2011 Career Plan* (JIST). *www.shatkin.com*

The job market finally seems to be on the road to recovery. Unfortunately, that road still looks long and rocky in many sectors. But there are professions that have job openings today and excellent prospects for the coming decade, based on Department of Labor projections.

A career transition need not take long. There are jobs with good prospects that require two years or less of specialized training.

Among the hottest low-barrier-to-entry professions...*

HEALTH-CARE CAREERS

Most health-care careers require many years of training, but not all...

• **Radiologic technologists help doctors perform diagnostic exams,** such as X-rays, CT scans and MRIs. They work in hospitals, clinics and physicians' offices.

Median wage: $53,000.

Job requirements: State licensing rules vary, but most radiologic technologists have just a two-year associate degree from a community college or technical college or have graduated from a 21- to 24-month certificate program.

To learn more: Visit the Web site of the American Registry of Radiologic Technologists (*www.arrt.org*) or the American Society of Radiologic Technologists (*www.asrt.org*).

• **Physical therapist assistants help patients implement therapy programs developed for the patients by physical therapists.** Job growth in this field should be very strong because America's aging population is likely to require additional physical therapy in the years ahead.

Median wage: $48,000.

Job requirements: In most states, a two-year associate degree from an accredited program is required and a licensing exam must be passed. A reasonable amount of strength and physical fitness is needed as well.

To learn more: Visit the Web site of the American Physical Therapy Association (*www.apta.org*). The site of the Commission on Accreditation in Physical Therapy Education (*www.capteonline.org*) can point you to accredited programs in your area.

Note: Physical therapist assistants are different from physical therapist aides, who are unlicensed and whose job prospects and earnings potential are not considered as strong.

• **Medical assistants provide office support and clinical assistance for medical practices.** This might include updating patients'

*All median wages listed in this article are annual wages based on full-time employment.

medical records, filing insurance forms and preparing patients for exams. Salaries are not great, but the field does offer strong job prospects and good health insurance benefits.

Median wage: $29,000.

Job requirements: Clerical and people skills are essential. One- and two-year programs in medical assisting are offered by many vocational schools, community colleges and junior colleges. These are not always required but will make it easier to land a job.

To learn more: Visit the Web site of the American Association of Medical Assistants (*www.aama-ntl.org*).

• **Dental hygienists provide dental cleanings and exams in dentist's offices.** The career offers excellent wages relative to the amount of education required, great job prospects and flexibility—many dental hygienists work part-time.

Median wage: $67,000.

Job requirements: A two-year associate degree in dental hygiene usually is required, and a written licensing exam must be passed. Manual dexterity and strong people skills are necessary, too.

To learn more: Visit the Web site of the American Dental Hygienists' Association (*www.adha.org*). The American Dental Association's Web site features links to accredited programs (*www.ada.org/267.aspx*, then click "Search Dental Assisting, Hygiene and Lab Technology Programs").

• **Veterinary technicians operate the advanced diagnostic equipment that is increasingly found in veterinary offices and provide other assistance to vets.** Demand for veterinary technicians is growing rapidly as pet owners spend more money on their pets' health.

Median wage: $29,000.

Job requirements: You'll need a two-year associate degree in veterinary technology and will have to pass a state licensing exam.

To learn more: Click the "Veterinary Technicians" link under the "Careers" heading on the Web site of the American Veterinary Medical Association (*www.avma.org*).

NON–HEALTH-CARE CAREERS

Not everyone wants to enter the health-care sector. *Among the other careers that offer solid job prospects without much specialized training…*

• **Personal financial advisors construct plans to help clients reach financial goals.** Many financial advisors are self-employed, though some work for investment companies, banks or other planners. Demand for financial advisors is expected to be strong as the aging population prepares for and enters retirement.

Median wage: $68,000.

Job requirements: It takes several years of training to earn a Certified Financial Planner credential from the Certified Financial Planner Board of Standards, but this credential—while beneficial—is not required. In most states, no specific degrees or licenses are needed to become a financial advisor. A test must be taken, and licensing is required to directly sell investment or insurance products, but not all advisors sell these products. Analytical, interpersonal and sales skills are important for financial advisors, and a bachelor's degree or better in a field such as accounting, finance or economics will be helpful. Success depends on establishing a track record that creates favorable word of mouth.

To learn more: Visit the Web site of the National Association of Personal Financial Advisors (*www.napfa.org*) or the Certified Financial Planner Board of Standards (*www.cfp.net*).

• **Financial examiners monitor compliance with financial laws and regulations.** Most work for state or federal government agencies, though some work for the companies that must comply with the financial regulations. Public sector hiring has slowed in recent years, but demand for financial examiners remains strong in the private sector.

Median wage: $72,000.

Job requirements: No specialized degree or license is needed, but you will need a bachelor's degree or a master's degree in a field such as accounting, finance or business administration. Those take more than two years to earn, but many people already have them.

To learn more: Search the government jobs Web site *www.usajobs.gov* for "financial examiners."

• **Survey researchers conduct opinion polls and analyze data for polling companies, marketing companies and corporations.** Job growth in this field is projected to be very strong, though the best jobs and salaries typically go to those with advanced degrees.

Median wage: $35,000.

Job requirements: You'll need strong math skills and a bachelor's degree or better in a relevant field such as statistics, marketing, economics, sociology or mathematics.

To learn more: Visit the Web site of the Marketing Research Association (*www.mranet.org*).

• **Adult literacy education providers teach English as a second language or remedial English classes,** often at community colleges. Demand now is stronger than in most other teaching fields.

Median wage: $46,000.

Job requirements: Requirements vary by state and program. Some positions require a degree in education and a teaching license, but others require only a bachelor's degree in any field and strong communication skills.

To learn more: Go to the Web site of the Center for Adult English Language Acquisition (*www.cal.org/caela*).

• **Adult education for self-enrichment providers teach classes on nonprofessional and often nonacademic subjects,** such as pottery or woodcarving. This is expected to be a fast-growing field as baby boomers retire and take classes to fill their free hours. Classes might be taught on a part-time basis through night schools or marketed to the public through newspaper ads or flyers on community bulletin boards. Because most providers are self-employed or work limited hours, this career is not a good way to get health insurance benefits.

Median wage: $17 per hour.

Job requirements: You'll need to be an expert in the topic you're teaching and have strong communication skills.

To learn more: Take a class on the topic you are considering teaching, perhaps in a neighboring region, to gauge interest and find out how your skills stack up against others marketing themselves as teachers.

Some Industries Eager to Hire

Online ads recently increased by 20% or more for industrial engineers, managers of mechanics, auto specialty technicians, mechanical engineers and financial-services sales agents. Advertising also rose significantly for retail salespeople, electrical engineers, loan officers, computer software engineers and accountants.

The Wall Street Journal

Don't Let Interviewers Steal Your Ideas Or Your Clients

Alan L. Sklover, attorney specializing in employment law and executive compensation and severance agreement negotiation. He is founding partner of Sklover & Donath, LLC, New York City, and author of *Fired, Downsized, or Laid Off: What Your Employer Doesn't Want You to Know About How to Fight Back* (Holt). *www.skloverworkingwisdom.com*

A job interviewer who asks about your ideas might be trying to evaluate your potential—but may end up using your ideas even if you're not hired for the job. Employers sometimes use the job interview process not only to vet potential hires but also to gather good ideas, client lists and insight into the competition.

Example: A graphic artist mentioned her idea for an online "virtual try-on room" during a job interview with a fashion-sector Web site. The interviewer asked her to put together a detailed digital workup of the idea before her second interview. She didn't get the job, but the firm used her work anyway.

Anecdotal evidence suggests that job interview theft is on the rise as companies struggle to remain competitive in these difficult economic times.

Defending against job interview theft can be tricky. *Here are seven prudent ways to reduce your odds of becoming a victim...*

1. Decide before the interview what ideas, information and efforts you will share at this stage. Thinking this through in advance greatly reduces the odds that you will blurt out more than you should during the interview.

Consider how much you can say about your ideas without inadvertently giving them away. Identify which of your current employer's plans and projects are confidential and which have been reported in the media.

2. Prepare a polite way to steer discussions away from a current employer's (or your own) confidential plans and projects. Such queries usually can be redirected toward information in the public domain or information about the company's past projects without offending the interviewer.

Example: "That's a good question, but one that I can't answer fully without divulging confidential information. What I can discuss is what's publicly known on the subject. *Fortune* did some excellent reporting about this..."

3. Treat clearly over-the-line requests for confidential corporate information as tests. Tell yourself the interviewer is attempting to find out if you are trustworthy and savvy enough to look out for your employer's interests. This might or might not be the case, but it is a good way to reduce any temptation to say more than you should.

4. Mark your creative efforts as your property. If you provide samples of your work, clearly mark these "For interview purposes. Not to be reproduced or used for any purpose without prior written consent of (YOUR NAME)." If you provide writing samples, such as marketing copy, mark each page "© 2012 (YOUR NAME). All Rights Reserved."

These phrases provide a measure of legal protection and send a strong signal to the interviewer that you know your rights and intend to protect your work.

5. Request a payment agreement for substantial creative efforts. If an interviewer asks you to prepare a detailed sample of your work that will take many hours of your time, say, "I'd be happy to do that for you, but I'd like to get an agreement that I'll be compensated if I'm not hired and you use my work." That's a reasonable request that a well-intentioned interviewer is likely to agree to and is unlikely to hurt your chances of getting a job. If the interviewer does agree, send an e-mail confirming the terms of this agreement after the interview.

6. Obtain an informal nondisclosure agreement before you submit valuable ideas. If a small number of big ideas are the core of what you have to offer a potential employer, you might have to share some of these during the interview process to prove your worth. If that's the case, send your contact at the company an e-mail prior to the interview asking for an agreement that the company will not use your ideas or disclose them to others if you are not hired. Ask your contact to respond to this e-mail with an e-mail, stating, "I agree." Submit your ideas in writing at some point during the interview process so that there is no question later what ideas you provided.

7. Confront interview theft issues with confidence. Confidence sells. If you hem and haw about whether you can answer a question during an interview, you will appear weak and uncertain. If you confidently explain why a piece of information isn't something you can divulge, a reasonable employer is likely to see your point and not hold the lack of an answer against you.

LinkedIn Basics

Join LinkedIn when looking for a job. Recruiters and hiring managers do keyword searches on LinkedIn when looking for qualified candidates. The site lets you highlight employment experience, achievements, awards, technology skills, publications, professional and community affiliations and more. Be sure your profile includes all important keywords for your industry and profession, showcases your achievements and is expertly written.

Wendy S. Enelow, author, trainer and career consultant, Coleman Falls, Virginia. *www.wendyenelow.com*

LinkedIn Strategy

Better use of LinkedIn.com: Create a headline statement that describes your talents and expertise—not a vague one that just gives your job title.

Example: "Hospitality executive with expertise in franchise, operations and change management." Keep your profile active—regularly reach out to potential contacts, and use their status updates as opportunities to congratulate them on their successes. Expand your network, for example, by joining a LinkedIn Group to connect yourself with someone new.

What else to do: Network all the time—not just when you need something. And give recommendations when asked—giving more recommendations will get you more recommendations in return.

Kimberly Schneiderman, founder, City Career Services, New York City. *www.citycareerservices.com*

Where to Look for Jobs

Look for a job in the lowest-unemployment areas in the US. Not all states have depressed job markets now.

Example: North Dakota's unemployment rate is just 3.5%, compared with the US rate of 9.1%. Jobs are available in a broad range of fields, from oil service and construction to education and office work. After North Dakota, the states with the lowest unemployment rates are Nebraska (4.2%), South Dakota (4.6%) and New Hampshire (5.4%).

Tony Weiler, North Dakota labor commissioner and an attorney based in Bismarck. *www.nd.gov/labor*

Facebook Strategy

Make your Facebook page professional to use it as a way to promote yourself for a job. Hire a photographer to take a good head shot. Post pictures of yourself in a work environment, and use captions to emphasize your professional qualifications. Include any work-related testimonials you have. Provide professional contact information, such as a link to your LinkedIn profile or Web site. Use Facebook to network by joining the Facebook groups of professional associations. But keep details of your job search off your Facebook page—your current employer may check the page from time to time.

J.T. O'Donnell, CEO, CareerHMO.com, Portsmouth, New Hampshire.

Bad News

Being unemployed reduces your chances of being hired. Some job listings on Monster, CareerBuilder and other sites state that all applicants must be currently employed. Some ads even say, "No unemployed will be considered."

Reasons: Employed candidates are seen as more qualified than those who have been laid off...and many employers assume that those who are unemployed were let go for performance reasons.

AARP Bulletin, 601 E St. NW, Washington, DC 20049. *www.aarp.org/bulletin*

For People with Disabilities

If you are job hunting and have a disability... address your disability early in the interview if it is visible. Point out that the disability will not impact your ability to do the job or that it will require only minimal accommodations. If your disability is not visible, wait until after a job offer is extended and a start date is established. Then you can disclose the disability and mention any workplace accommodations that you may need.

Daniel J. Ryan, PhD, author of *Job Search Handbook for People with Disabilities* (JIST).

Smokers, Beware

Smoking may prevent you from being hired. Many hospitals and other organizations are enacting anti-tobacco policies for employees. Job applications may ask if you're a smoker, and answering "yes" could be reason for you not to be hired.

But: It is not yet clear if such policies are lawful in all states. Employers can prohibit employees from smoking on company property or time, but many states don't allow employers to discriminate against employees for smoking during off-duty time away from work premises.

The New York Times

Salary Strategy

How to negotiate salary in today's tough job market: Job candidates often are so happy to be offered a job that they accept a lower salary than they should.

Self-defense: When asked for your salary requirement on applications, leave it blank or write "Open." During interviews, if you are asked about your previous salary, ask about the range for the job you are discussing. Don't negotiate salary in the interview. Say that you are interested and will seriously consider any offer that the company makes...or say that once you get a clear understanding of the job requirements and advancement potential, you'll be better prepared to discuss salary. When you receive an offer, ask if there is any flexibility. You may not be offered a higher salary, but you might get an extra week of vacation or a signing bonus.

Bill Humbert, professional recruiter, Park City, Utah, and author of *RecruiterGuy's Guide to Finding a Job* (Corridor Media). *www.recruiterguy.com*

Beauty Does Pay

Attractive people earn more. A person whose facial features put him/her in the top one-third of what people consider attractive earned about 5% more than most similarly qualified people with less attractive features... and 15% more than the worst-looking one-eighth of workers.

Daniel S. Hamermesh, PhD, economist, University of Texas, Austin, and author of *Beauty Pays: Why Attractive People Are More Successful* (Princeton University).

Good Investments

College with the best return on investment—MIT. Over 30 years, an MIT grad makes \$1,688,000 more in wages than a typical high school graduate earns. California Institute of Technology is second, at \$1,644,000...Harvard, third at \$1,631,000...Harvey Mudd College, fourth at \$1,627,000...Dartmouth, fifth at \$1,587,000.

Study by PayScale, a Seattle company that collects wage information, reported in *Bloomberg Businessweek.*

What to Ask a Job Candidate

What is something you are passionate about? Look for an enthusiastic, upbeat answer.

What weakness has had the most effect on your ability to succeed? This helps determine the candidate's self-awareness.

Do you volunteer within the community? You can't ask what nonprofessional organizations the applicant belongs to because it could reveal information about national origin or religious affiliations, but if he/she is a volunteer and tells you about it, that can reveal useful traits—such as physical strength or fund-raising ability.

Describe a situation in which you had to work with a difficult person. Find out what the job seeker did—and follow up with a question about the outcome.

What can I tell you about what we do here? Look for intelligent questions that focus specifically on your company, not general ones that would indicate the applicant is looking for any possible job.

Inc.com, a Web site based in New York City offering advice, tools and services to help businesses start, run and grow.

Consider Paying Your Interns

Be careful when hiring unpaid interns. Interns must meet multiple criteria to be considered trainees and not employees—be sure your corporate counsel knows the rules. Internships must focus on training for the intern, not on benefits for the company. The employer is not supposed to receive immediate benefits from the intern's work.

What to do: Consider paid internships. Paying an intern may motivate him/her to do more and better work...and paid internships do not have to adhere to the same Department of Labor criteria as unpaid ones. Ask your attorney for details.

Matthew Zinman, founder, The Internship Institute, a nonprofit dedicated to promoting the best practices in internships, and CEO of Internship Success, Newtown, Pennsylvania. *www.internshipsuccess.com*

Easier Transition for Veterans

Several states are cutting job-related red tape for returning members of the military.

Examples: New York plans to help soldiers who drove trucks while in the service get commercial licenses more easily. Wyoming is making it easier for military medics to qualify for work as emergency medical technicians. Texas and Minnesota are lowering credential requirements for veterans who can do plumbing, pipe-fitting and electrical work. Ohio and Indiana are encouraging veterans trained in biochemical preparedness to take civilian jobs in the field.

The Kiplinger Letter, 1729 H St. NW, Washington, DC 20006. *www.kiplinger.com*

Are You Using 'QR' Codes?

"Quick response codes" are scanned at least two million times a month—up from 80,000 a month in 2009. An information-packed variation on bar codes, these square patterns that resemble abstract art or Rorschach tests are found on ads, billboards, product displays, price tags and even outdoor seating. When scanned by a smartphone or tablet computer, they open a Web page or play a video. Also known as QRs, they are inexpensive and easy to set up and convey information designed to make a sale easier—for instance, how-to guides at a home-improvement store.

What small businesses can do: Try using QRs yourself to determine how they could boost your business.

Colin Gibbs, analyst, GigaOm Pro, research firm, San Francisco. *http://pro.gigaom.com*

Get the Word Out

Get more and better referrals for your business. Talk to other people in your network and tell them just what kind of customer you are looking for. And ask satisfied customers themselves for referrals—request that they tell their friends, family and their own networks about your company.

What else to do: Consider teaming up with another company that targets the same kind of customer—sharing databases and customer lists can expand both your businesses.

FoxBusiness.com

Business Owner Concerns

Nine out of 10 small-business owners are concerned that the US could slip back into recession—but 79% say they are prepared to deal with another downturn.

What to do: Be very cautious about hiring—78% of small-business owners say they will keep the same number of employees.

Raj Seshadri, head of small-business banking, Citibank, New York City, which surveyed 1,000 small businesses with revenue over $100,000 and no more than 100 employees.

Clever Ways to Make Money on the Internet (Anyone Can Do It!)

Marc Ostrofsky, an Internet entrepreneur most famous for selling the domain name "Business.com" for a record $7.5 million. Based in Houston, he owns several Internet-based businesses, including Blinds.com, CuffLinks.com and SummerCamps.com. His new book is *Get Rich Click! The Ultimate Guide to Making Money on the Internet* (Free Press). *www.getrichclick.com*

In today's "Internet Economy," anyone can make money online. Certain Internet business models offer the potential for profit with limited up-front investment and financial risk. And you don't have to be a computer expert—many technologies and Web sites exist that can help the average person make money online.

Here, four business models to consider...

ZERO-INVENTORY SALES

You don't need to pay rent for an expensive storefront when you sell merchandise through the Internet. With a "zero inventory" strategy, you don't even need to put money down to purchase the goods ahead of time.

How to do it: Use a digital camera or a cell-phone camera to take in-store pictures of items for sale in your region that seem like great deals—they must be better deals than shoppers are likely to find elsewhere. Use these pictures to post the items for sale on eBay, even though you don't own them. Set a high enough minimum sale price to cover the price of buying the item, including sales tax, eBay's fee and a profit large enough to compensate you for your time and effort. Set shipping fees high enough to cover your mailing costs, too. Don't bother listing the item if it doesn't still look like a great deal when all these costs are totaled.

Return to the store and purchase the item only after someone buys it from you on eBay.

There usually is a fee for posting items on eBay even if they do not sell, but this typically is just a few dollars, often much less if the minimum price you set is low.

A zero-inventory sales strategy works only with goods that you can purchase for significantly less than other people can. These might include items on which you can negotiate a special, lower-than-retail rate through a local producer or wholesaler, perhaps by promising repeat business. *Two examples...*

Example 1: My company Blinds.com does not have any inventory. Instead, we have an arrangement with a manufacturer to make custom window blinds whenever we receive an order and ship them directly to the customer.

Example 2: A Houston couple found a firm that sells automotive car mats in bulk. The couple makes a nice profit reselling the mats on eBay.

Do not attempt zero-inventory sales of an item that is in very limited supply. Such goods might go out of stock before you return to buy what you already have sold.

The clarity of your photos and the detail and accuracy of your item descriptions can dramatically affect the amount your products fetch on eBay. Put some effort into getting these right. Read the descriptions of similar products that have sold for high prices on eBay...or vary your item descriptions and pictures when you relist items that you sell repeatedly and see which bring the highest bids.

Alternative: Ask friends and neighbors if they have possessions that they would like to sell and how much they would want for these things. With their permission, take pictures of the items and post them on eBay. If an item fetches more than the friend wants, you can keep the difference as a profit or you can take a commission from the sale.

SELL AN eBOOK

If you are an expert on a topic—any topic—write an eBook about it. Or maybe you know an expert—a doctor, lawyer, researcher, professor, psychologist—whom you could interview for a book. You then could split the profits.

The most challenging aspect of making money from eBooks has always been marketing them to potential buyers. Unlike conventional books, self-published eBooks don't have a publisher's marketing team promoting them or a place on bookstore shelves where browsers can find them. But a Web site called ClickBank.com offers a potential solution—it lets other people market your eBook for you.

List your eBook on ClickBank.com, set a sales price, and choose how large a commission you are willing to pay "affiliates" who help you sell it—commissions of 50% or more tend to draw the greatest affiliate interest. If your eBook is well-written and useful and your commission is attractive, affiliates who have blogs, Twitter feeds and/or Facebook accounts that cover topics related to your eBook might post favorable reviews of your book and include a link to a Web site from which it can be downloaded.

Example: A man named Jacob Hiller has made more than $1 million through ClickBank.com selling *The Jump Manual*, a guidebook designed to help amateur athletes increase their vertical leap.

ClickBank.com charges a onetime $49.95 activation fee and a commission of 7.5% plus $1 on each sale it generates. In addition to eBooks, ClickBank.com sells digital videos, software, recordings of original songs and other digital content.

Helpful: If you decide to interview an expert, consider videotaping it. Then you can offer the videotape along with the eBook. This gets even more attention.

FREELANCE LABOR

Web sites such as Guru.com, Elance.com, ODesk.com and 99Designs.com connect writers, graphic designers, programmers, translators and other freelance contractors to businesses that need their services. More and more businesses are turning to these Web sites to locate skilled contract labor because the range of talents available through them is much broader than it is in most local regions, and the rates charged often are substantially lower.

This presents a low-cost business opportunity to people who have skills that translate well to outsourcing. Offer your services on one or more of these Web sites or bid for assignments posted on them.

It also creates an opportunity for those whose background is in management or deal making. Approach businesses in your region that seem to be in need of the freelance services offered through these Web sites. If a business agrees to work with you, bid out the job through one of these Web sites, leaving yourself a nice profit for serving as the middleman. Why would a business work with you when it could just hire a contractor itself through one of these Web sites? Not every business owner knows about these sites, and even those that do might prefer to deal with someone local whom they can work with face-to-face.

Example: A local small business has a low-quality Web site or an unappealing logo. Check how much the freelancers on these Web sites typically charge for Web site or logo design. Next, approach the business and offer to find a professional to create a better one and then manage the project for the business owner.

TRADE IN DOMAIN NAMES

In 1995, I bought the Internet domain name Business.com for $150,000. Four years later, I sold it for $7.5 million. Paying six figures for a domain name might be risky, but dozens of companies will help you register a currently unclaimed domain name for less than $10. Just type "domain names" into Google to find these companies.

True, most of the domain names with the greatest profit potential were snapped up years ago. But new domain names can become valuable when current events, new phrases and new products catch the public's attention. When you read about a new and potentially popular innovation that's on the way or hear a catchphrase or newly coined term in the movies or on TV that you suspect might become trendy, use WhoIs.net or another domain-name registry Web site to see if the ".com" version of this term still is available. Snap it up if it is.

Once you own a domain name, you can list it for resale at a profit through a domain-name resale Web site such as SEDO.com or BuyDomains.com. Or if you have some basic Internet skills, you can create a Web site that steers Internet users to another site that will pay you a commission for sending customers its way, such as Amazon.com.

Example: A man bought the domain name "PresidentsBook.com" when he heard President Clinton was working on his memoirs some years ago. He created a simple Web site that featured his review of the book and a link to the book's page on Amazon.com. The Amazon Associates program pays commissions as high as 15% when Internet browsers click links such as these and make purchases.

Borrowing Basics

Improve your chance of a bank loan for a small business. Look for better-capitalized banks—avoid ones being pressured by regulators to improve their assets. You can go to the Web site of the US Small Business Administration (*www.sba.gov*), and search for local lenders with high loan volume. Search online for articles on banks that recently funded small firms. Get someone to vouch for you—a recommendation from a lawyer, accountant or business owner who has received a bank loan can help you with a lender.

If banks turn you down: Ask for a referral to a microlender—a firm that makes smaller loans (with limits up to $100,000 or much less, depending on the lender) and often coaches entrepreneurs so they will be able to get larger loans later. The largest microlender in the US is Accion Network (*www.accionnetwork.org*), but a local banker may know of others that are better choices in your community.

Money, Time-Life Bldg., Rockefeller Center, New York City 10020. *www.money.com*

"Crowdfunding" for New Projects

The word refers to a method of getting money in small amounts from many people online—often, friends, family members and members of the community. The money does not have to be repaid, but those managing a project usually show appreciation by giving contributors products or services. Web sites typically require those starting a project to set a goal and time frame for contributions and explain why they are seeking them. And the sites generally keep a small percentage of the funds raised. Visit IndieGogo (*www.indiegogo.com*), Kickstarter (*www.kickstarter.com*), Peerbackers (*www.peerbackers.com*) and Rocket Hub (*www.rockethub.com*)—the four best-known crowdfunding sites—to find out how each works and what each requires.

Consensus of entrepreneurs and site operators, reported in *The Wall Street Journal.*

The Amazing Things Humble Jobs Can Teach

Little jobs can teach us big lessons. We asked successful people to reflect on humble jobs that they once held and share the lessons they learned from those jobs that contributed to their later success...

DEBORAH NORVILLE

It's your job to understand your customer. One of my summer jobs in high school was as a cashier and stock girl at Dalton Farm and Garden Supply in Dalton, Georgia. It was a real farm-supply store where actual farmers bought seed, not just a garden shop for home owners.

One day after work, I complained to my mother that I couldn't understand what the farmers were saying. To me, it seemed as if they barely opened their mouths to talk. My mother was not sympathetic. She told me that I was being a snob and that it was my job to understand the customers, not their job to be understood by me.

She was right. From then on, I devoted myself to understanding those farmers—and I became a far better employee by doing so. At the end of the summer, my boss told me I was one of the best teenagers he had ever hired, something that certainly hadn't been true when I started.

That became an important brick in the foundation of my journalism career. I never made the mistake of thinking of myself as better than the viewers. They're my customers. It's my job to understand and serve them.

Deborah Norville, two-time Emmy Award–winning anchor of the television news magazine *Inside Edition*. Based in New York City, she is author of several books, including *The Power of Respect* (Thomas Nelson), and creator of the Deborah Norville Collection of knitting and crocheting yarns. *www.dnorville.com*

LESLIE D. MICHELSON

Intuition is great, but data is better. As a student in the early 1970s, I took a job at a university hospital inputting data from medical studies into a computer. The work was drudgery, but the studies were compelling. I saw that it was surprisingly common for studies to show that the widely held beliefs of medical professionals were wrong. Ever since then, I've made it a point to question individual opinions until there's data to back them up. Time and again, that has paid off.

Examples: When I was CEO of the Prostate Cancer Foundation, almost everyone in the field believed PSA testing made sense for all men until a study found that that wasn't always true. Many physicians believed that certain antioxidants would lower the risk for prostate cancer until a study found that they made no difference.

Leslie D. Michelson, chief executive officer of Private Health Management, a health-care services company, Los Angeles. He previously served as CEO of the Prostate Cancer Foundation, the leading source of philanthropic support of prostate cancer research, and as Special Assistant to the General Counsel of the US Department of Health and Human Services.

FREDERIC MALEK

Teams can be more powerful than individuals. One of my earliest jobs was at a Chicago beer-bottling facility, lugging cases of beer from the line to the warehouse. It was repetitive work and physically taxing, but I learned that any job can be enjoyable if you enjoy the people you are working with. My fellow employees and I developed a camaraderie that made the work more pleasant—and, in the process, made us more productive. When there's a collaborative spirit in a workplace, the sum of a group's efforts is greater than the parts.

Bosses who never worked in the trenches don't always grasp this. They don't always understand how to foster a spirit of teamwork among employees or know how to spot problem employees who hold teams back by not working well with others.

Frederic Malek, founder and chairman of Thayer Capital Partners, a corporate buyout firm based in Washington, DC, as well as Thayer Lodging Group, a private equity firm that acquires and operates hotels. He previously served as president of Marriott Hotels and Northwest Airlines. Last year, Malek received the Horatio Alger Award, a prize given to those who achieve remarkable success through hard work and perseverance over adversity.

JANE BRYANT QUINN

Let others know your goals. I began my career in journalism in 1961 with a very humble job—sorting and delivering mail at *Newsweek*. Soon I switched to the still humble job of clipping articles for the magazine's files. It seemed unlikely that I would climb much higher—at the time, *Newsweek* did not promote women to writing positions. Still, I worked extremely hard, and I made it very clear to the *Newsweek* writers and editors I came to know that writing was what I wanted to do.

One *Newsweek* colleague soon helped me locate and land my first writing job with a consumer newsletter. That job launched my writing career.

A humble job is not a bad job as long as it provides access to people who have the connections or clout to help you secure a better job. Just do the humble job much better than is required—that way, there's no question that you have the capacity to do more—and let those around you know exactly what you want your next step to be.

Jane Bryant Quinn, financial journalist whose syndicated column ran in more than 250 newspapers before she retired from writing it after 27 years. She also worked for *CBS News* for more than a decade and wrote a column for *Newsweek* for 30 years. She now writes a biweekly column for CBS MoneyWatch.com and a monthly column for *AARP Bulletin*. She is author of *Making the Most of Your Money Now* (Simon & Schuster). *www.janebryantquinn.com*

RICHARD NELSON BOLLES

It's not the attempt that counts—it's the result. Throughout my career, I've encountered people who believe that as long as they're working hard, they are doing their jobs. When things don't go their way, they say, "Well, I tried" or "It was a good idea...it just didn't work out." Thanks to a humble job that I had decades ago, I never fell into that trap.

After graduating from high school, I laid concrete sidewalks and built concrete walls in Teaneck, New Jersey. Concrete is a great teacher. It taught me that hard work alone is not enough in the real world. It's also crucial to pay attention to each step of the process and get every last detail right. Fail to do this, and concrete will set poorly. People don't look at a poorly set concrete sidewalk and think, "Someone tried hard." They think, "Someone screwed up." Hard work isn't the goal—it's just one ingredient. The goal is to produce results.

Richard Nelson Bolles often is called the founder of modern career development. Based in the San Francisco Bay Area, he is author of *What Color Is Your Parachute?* (Ten Speed), the best-selling job-search book of all time. Among his recent books is *The Job-Hunter's Survival Guide: How to Find Hope and Rewarding Work, Even When "There Are No Jobs"* (Ten Speed). *www.jobhuntersbible.com*

HUMA GRUAZ

Small offices can be big training grounds. When I was in my late 20s, I had to move to Holland for personal reasons. I had to leave my job at Ogilvy & Mather, one of the world's most prominent advertising firms, and look for work in a country where I wasn't a citizen and didn't speak the language. The only job I could find was as an assistant to a small-time entrepreneur. I was the second person in a two-person office.

As it turned out, it was a wonderful opportunity. When you're the only employee other than the boss, you learn every aspect of running a business. I did accounting...I drafted business letters...I met clients. I did it all. It was like getting paid to go to business school. That humble assistant's position did more to prepare me to launch my own company than any other job I ever had.

Huma Gruaz is president and CEO of Alpaytac, Inc., a public relations and marketing communications company based in Chicago. She was named Brand Marketer of the Year by the trade publication *PR News* in 2010. *www.alpaytac.com*

GREG DOLLARHYDE

A humble job in a field you know well trumps a better job in a new sector. It can be tempting to see a major career setback as a sign that it's time to change professions and try something new. Unless your sector is in permanent decline, however, that's probably a mistake.

Your sector is what you know best, so you can perform a humble job in that area very well and earn promotions quickly if you just take the philosophy of "working your patch." This is where you have developed a network of contacts who can help you locate better opportunities. A job available to you in a different sector might be a step higher or better paying, but you could be stuck on that step much longer as you learn the ropes.

I was managing a successful restaurant in Lake Tahoe in the 1970s when the gas crisis hit. Suddenly no one wanted to drive to Lake Tahoe. The restaurant closed, and I was forced to take very humble jobs, waiting tables and cooking food just to pay the rent. More appealing jobs were available to me outside the restaurant sector, but I persevered. As long as I kept working my patch, a good opportunity would turn up. Sure enough, a few years later, one did—an opportunity to enroll in Cornell's elite hotel and restaurant administration program fell into my lap, which wouldn't have happened if I had left restaurants behind.

Greg Dollarhyde, CEO and equity partner of Veggie Grill, a 100% plant-based restaurant chain in California. He has been chairman or chief executive officer of seven restaurant companies in his career, expanding Baja Fresh from 30 to 280 locations before selling it to Wendy's for $275 million in 2003, and overseeing the growth of successful chains, including Zoës Kitchen and TGIF. *www.veggiegrill.com.*

How to Enchant Others With Your Ideas, Plans Or Products

Guy Kawasaki, former chief evangelist of Apple Computer, who often is credited with shaping that high-tech company's image. He is cofounder of Alltop.com, an index of online articles sorted by categories, and founding partner of the venture capital fund Garage Technology Ventures. Kawasaki is author of *Enchantment: The Art of Changing Hearts, Minds, and Actions* (Portfolio). *www.guykawasaki.com*

In a world where style often counts as much as substance, having a strong idea is often not enough when you try to launch a company, drum up support for a cause or land a job. You also must present your project and yourself in an enchanting way. Your plan or product must be irresistible, not just reasonable. You must seem likable and trustworthy. You must delight.

Unfortunately, it's easy for us to become so caught up in our own opinion of what we do that we fail to see how others perceive it—or us. *Six things you can do to maximize the odds that you will enchant and succeed...*

1. Knock down any "fences" that stand between the people you are trying to reach and the place you are trying to lead them. Common fences include the time it will take people to do what you would like them to do and the money it will cost them. Do everything in your power to completely remove any potential barriers, even those that seem inconsequential to you. Never underestimate how little it takes to convince people that something isn't worth the time, trouble or expense, particularly when they have not yet fully committed to the product or cause.

Example: A Web site forces visitors to fill out a long registration form before it allows access. Many visitors leave without registering and never return.

If you're not sure whether an inconvenience, fee or step will deter interest in your cause, ask mothers who have three or more young children if it would deter them. These women have so many competing demands on their time, attention and finances that they generally have an excellent sense of what is and is not worth the trouble.

2. Make your pitch short, simple and credible. The easier an idea is to deliver, believe and pass along, the more likely it is to find support. *Among the ways to do this…*

• Use "tricolons" as slogans. These contain three sections of about equal length. Their cadence makes them catchy and powerful.

Examples: Republican presidential candidate Herman Cain's "9-9-9" economic plan…or "Location, location, location." Caesar's "Veni, Vidi, Vici" (I came, I saw, I conquered) is widely remembered 2,000 years later. President Barrack Obama opened his inaugural address with "I stand here today humbled by the task before us, grateful for the trust you have bestowed, mindful of the sacrifices borne by our ancestors."

• Use similes and metaphors to link your cause to a strong mental image or familiar, trusted starting point.

Example: An effective Band-Aid ad stated, "Say hello to your child's new bodyguard," linking the company's new product to the powerful, reassuring image of a bodyguard.

• Stay positive. Scare tactics often backfire. People are warned about so many things these days that new warnings tend to be ignored—sometimes even mocked when a threat does not seem significant or credible.

Example: Anti-alcohol and anti-marijuana campaigns aimed at teens sometimes warn that those who indulge are more likely to engage in premarital sex. Not surprisingly, few teens seem to consider this a risk worth avoiding.

• Be succinct. Keep your e-mails to no more than six sentences…PowerPoint presentations no more than 10 slides…and business plans no more than 20 pages.

• Create a simple name for your cause or company. The simpler the name, the easier people will find it to consider your project and discuss it with others.

Example: Researchers at New York University's Stern School of Business found that the stocks of companies with easy-to-pronounce names tend to outperform those of companies with hard-to-pronounce names.

3. Conduct a "premortem." Postmortems are commonly conducted when ideas and projects fail, to determine what went wrong. It is better to conduct a premortem to catch problems before they undermine your efforts.

Before launching, ask team members or others with knowledge of the project to assume that it has failed and identify reasons why they think this imaginary failure occurred. Instructing people to assume failure frees them to point out potential trouble spots—otherwise, they might keep their mouths shut even if they do see potential problems, for fear of appearing negative or unsupportive.

Example: Faced with this premortem question, an employee says that he thinks delays from a particular parts supplier could ruin a crucial product rollout. The boss locates a backup supplier capable of stepping in on short notice if necessary.

4. Set specific goals. People with clear goals tend to seem centered, organized and driven to those they meet, increasing their personal appeal.

Detailing specific goals also greatly increases the odds that people will be viewed as trustworthy. It makes them seem as if they have their cards on the table and thus no hidden agenda.

5. Compose an enchanting story about yourself and your cause. The best stories often reveal people's motivations rather than just describe what they're offering. *Four story formats that tend to enchant…*

• Great aspirations. Describe how the underlying goal of your efforts is to help make the world a better place in some specific way.

• David vs. Goliath. Explain how you are taking on a big, powerful foe—and succeeding.

• Profiles in courage. Recount how you have struggled to accomplish great things despite the injustices or obstacles that have been heaped upon you.

• One person's success. Hearing about one individual's positive results is more likely to sway listeners than hearing statistics that summarize thousands of people's positive results.

Example: "We gave a sample of our product to a 90-year-old bedridden grandmother in Hoboken, and she told us it changed her life" is more enchanting than "87% of people who try our product report favorable results."

6. Create a checklist—with the first few steps already checked off. Checklists help people organize, analyze and later implement their plans. As a bonus, they increase the odds that others will see you as organized and action-oriented, traits people tend to find enchanting.

Don't make your checklist just a list of the steps that remain to be tackled, however—include one or two that already have been accomplished. This instills in others a sense of momentum and investment in the cause, increasing the odds that they will join.

Example: A car wash replaced its buy-eight-get-one-free loyalty card with a buy-10-get-one-free card that had the first two washes already checked off. Customer retention nearly doubled, even though it was essentially the same deal.

Five Things Never to Say at Work

Alan Axelrod, PhD, leadership and communications consultant based in Atlanta who has worked with organizations ranging from Siemens AG to the Metropolitan Museum of Art. Writing under the pseudonym Jack Griffin, he is author of *How to Say It: Be Indispensable at Work* (Prentice Hall).

A few poorly chosen words in the workplace can damage an employee's reputation and cripple his/her career. Even smart, well-meaning employees sometimes say the wrong things. *Among the thoughts never to voice at work...*

1. "Looks like I'm working late again." Employees often are eager to be seen as hard workers who put in long hours—particularly in tough economies such as this one, when layoffs seem to lurk around every corner. While showing up early and working late can indeed further your career, talking about doing so could hold you back. When you verbalize that you're putting in long hours, you risk giving the impression that you're complaining about your workload or that you're struggling to get your work done. That might lead a boss to view you as ungrateful or as a potential burnout candidate. And it might dissuade your employer from seeing you as a candidate for promotion—if you're struggling to keep up in your current job, how could you possibly handle more responsibility?

2. "I'll get to it when I can." Avoid saying anything that might be interpreted as questioning an assignment's importance—even if you don't think it is a high priority. The project might be a higher priority for the person with whom you are speaking than you realize. Even if it isn't, you risk giving the impression that you don't take the assignment seriously.

3. "I can do it better alone." Employees sometimes say things such as this in hopes of seeming self-sufficient or in hopes of avoiding working closely with a colleague they don't like. But telling a boss that you work best alone can lead to a career-damaging "poor team player" reputation.

If you are assigned a teammate you simply cannot work with effectively, express your reservations in terms of the company's goals, not personal feelings about this person.

Example: Point out that this teammate has a lot on his plate already, and say that you would be happy to tackle this task alone if it would help the company.

4. "I did it." Most workplace victories are team victories. Failing to share the credit with colleagues and underlings who contributed reduces the odds that they will work as hard for you in the future. That doesn't mean you should give away all the credit or downplay your role—just that when you accept thanks, you also should mention and praise the specific roles played by others.

5. "The way I've always done it works just fine." If you voice resistance to new ideas without giving them a shot, you risk being viewed as someone unwilling to embrace any change. From there, it's only a short hop to being seen as obsolete and thus dispensable.

Justifiably or not, older workers are particularly likely to be stuck with this label.

Instead, express enthusiasm for exploring new methods and technologies when they are suggested. Voice your doubts only after the idea has been attempted or at least analyzed in greater depth. As long as you initially express enthusiasm for a new idea, you later can question it without seeming hostile to change.

If you do later raise reservations, frame them in terms of specific company goals, not personal preferences.

Example: "It's an interesting approach that was worth exploring, but the results seem to suggest that it's detracting from our department's turnaround time."

Easier E-mails

If you can communicate your message in a few words, do so in the subject line, followed by EOM for "end of message." That way, the recipient does not have to open the e-mail. If you need to put text in the body of the message but don't need a reply, end with NNTR for "no need to respond."

School of International and Public Affairs at Columbia University, New York City. *www.sipa.columbia.edu*

Don't Waste Time Organizing E-mail

A recent study found that people searching through unfiled correspondence located what they wanted more quickly than people who set up elaborate file systems.

Best: Try leaving your e-mail unsorted, and see whether the change boosts your productivity.

Study by IBM researchers, San Jose, California.

Get Better Voice-Mail Messages

Ask callers to leave their name...phone number...the nature of their call...and a good time to reach them. Specifically ask them to speak their phone number slowly to avoid messages in which the number is difficult or impossible to hear.

Christine Holton Cashen, MAEd, CSP, motivational speaker, Dallas, and author of *The Good Stuff: Quips and Tips on Life, Love, Work and Happiness* (D.C. Murphy). *www.christinecashen.com*

Productivity Booster

Let employees use their own personal electronic devices at work to boost productivity. People who regularly do business on laptops, personal smartphones, tablets and other devices that they own often will work after hours and even on vacation.

Caution: Outside devices can be stolen or lost and may compromise data security or transmit viruses.

What to do: Set clear usage policies, including a requirement for passwords to protect data and an employee agreement to let employers remotely erase hard-drive data if necessary. Talk to your lawyer for details.

The Kiplinger Letter, 1729 H St. NW, Washington, DC 20006. *www.kiplinger.com*

Keep a Young Outlook

Strategies for older workers surrounded by younger colleagues and supervisors—don't get defensive. If someone says you look good for your age, just say thanks and change the topic. Avoid negative self-talk, such as asking yourself whether you are too old for your job—consider yourself a highly experienced professional with much to contribute. Learn social media—have a Facebook page, and consider Twitter. Adjust your communication style so that you fit in better—for example, if your boss likes to text, learn to text. Do not date yourself by repeatedly mentioning the past.

Barbara Pachter, business etiquette specialist based in Cherry Hill, New Jersey, and author of *Greet! Eat! Tweet! 52 Business Etiquette Postings to Avoid Pitfalls & Boost Your Career* (CreateSpace). *www.pachter.com*

Extra Perks

Some firms are offering unusual perks to keep employees motivated at a time of heavy workloads and small salary increases.

Examples: Theme-park tickets, cell-phone-plan discounts, at-work massages, auto-insurance discounts.

John Bremen, managing director, Towers Watson, employer consultants based in New York City.

On the Move

Companies are relocating employees again. Nearly one-third of firms plan worker relocations this year—the highest percentage in six years. The Midwest is the top area to which transfers are being made.

But: Reimbursements for moving costs are often lower than in past years...temporary housing is being provided for shorter periods...and many employers are making only high-level workers whole for losses on home sales.

What to do: If you are going to be transferred, negotiate the terms just as you would negotiate for salary or benefits.

The Kiplinger Letter, 1729 H St. NW, Washington, DC 20006. *www.Kiplinger.com*

Read the Fine Print

Pension-plan changes may entitle employees to compensation if a company misrepresents the effects of the changes in a way that makes them seem beneficial when in fact they reduce benefits for some workers. The US Supreme Court says employees may be awarded damages that will bring them up to the level they were told to expect. But if there is a conflict between the summary of a pension plan, which is given to all employees, and the plan document itself, which employees rarely see, the plan document's terms remain in effect.

What to do: Be sure you thoroughly understand any plan changes that your employer makes or proposes. Consult a knowledgeable attorney if necessary.

The Wall Street Journal

Protect Yourself

Communication with your lawyer on your company's computer may not be private.

Recent case: A California court said that a woman who used a company computer and e-mail account to communicate with her attorney about a pregnancy-discrimination claim could not claim attorney-client privilege.

Self-defense: Assume that communications using company computers and accounts will not be private. Use a personal computer, wireless phone or BlackBerry for confidential communication.

Jonathan B. Orleans and Daniel A. Schwartz, attorneys, Pullman & Comley LLC, Bridgeport, Connecticut. *www.pullcom.com*

Criticism of Bosses May Be Protected Speech

Bosses who discipline workers who criticize them on the social-networking site can be reported to the National Labor Relations Board, which has said that negative Facebook comments may be protected activity similar to water cooler comments if they are part of a discussion of employment conditions.

What bosses need to do: Update the company's social-media policies, and train supervisors who have disciplinary power so that they do not attempt to prevent or interfere with protected activities.

The Kiplinger Letter, 1729 H St. NW, Washington, DC 20006. *www.kiplinger.com*

Apologies Can Help Mend Fences

An apology must be separated from an explanation or any attempt to share blame.

What to do: Apologize directly. Once the other person has accepted your apology, you can try to explain or excuse yourself. Offer to discuss the problem further, but do not insist on it. Make the apology face-to-face if possible or at least on Skype or by phone—do not use e-mail unless there is no alternative. Offer options to make things right, but do not assume that you know the best way to do so. Close by focusing on next steps. If the other person brings the matter up again, say that you consider it closed because you have offered an apology and he/she has accepted it.

Tom Searcy, founder and CEO of Hunt Big Sales, consultancy firm, Fishers, Indiana. *www.huntbigsales.com*

Be Mindful

Your employer may check out your online profile to make sure that you're not bashing the company or acting in a way that reflects on it poorly. Even when your privacy settings are tight, you never know who might see your profile, so never post inappropriate or potentially offensive photos, videos, wall posts, updates or other content on Facebook or other social networks.

Consensus of human resources executives, reported online at CBS MoneyWatch.com.

Business Travel Hurts Your Health

Businessmen and -women who travel more than 20 nights a month were almost three times as likely to report that they were in poor or fair health, compared with those who traveled one to six days a month. The same workers also were about twice as likely to be obese, which can lead to serious health problems such as diabetes and heart disease. Researchers believe that the stress of business travel, limited availability of healthy eating options and no time for or access to physical exercise make it difficult to stay healthy while traveling.

Andrew Rundle, DrPh, associate professor, department of epidemiology, Mailman School of Public Health, Columbia University, New York City, and senior author of a study of 13,057 people, published in *Journal of Occupational and Environmental Medicine.*

On the Rise

Nearly three in 10 US workers called in sick with fake excuses last year. Calling in sick without a legitimate reason has consequences—15% of companies have fired people for this, and 28% check up on employees. When employers were asked to share the most unusual excuses that they had heard for missing work, these are some of the examples given—bitten by a deer during hunting season...got bats in hair...12-year-old daughter stole car...refrigerator fell on him...was in line at coffee shop when truck carrying flour backed up and dumped flour into her convertible...drank antifreeze by mistake and had to go to the hospital.

Online survey of 2,696 hiring managers and human resources professionals, and 4,384 full-time private-sector workers, by Harris Interactive on behalf of CareerBuilder.com, reported online at CareerBuilder.com.

Long Work Hours May Harm Your Heart

Recent study: People who worked more than 11 hours a day had 67% higher risk for heart disease than people who worked seven to eight hours a day.

If you work long hours: Decrease your risk for heart disease in other ways, such as eating a healthy diet, exercising and maintaining healthy blood pressure, blood sugar and cholesterol levels.

Mika Kivimaki, PhD, professor, department of epidemiology and public health, University College London, England, and leader of a study that followed 7,095 workers for 11 years, published in *Annals of Internal Medicine.*

Be Healthy

Financial rewards for staying healthy are being offered by an increasing number of companies, and more firms plan to start penalizing employees who don't follow healthful habits. Although only 12% of the firms surveyed said they currently use rewards or penalties based on outcomes—such as cholesterol levels or body mass index—a further 16% plan to adopt this approach for 2012.

Survey of 335 companies by Towers Watson and the National Business Group of Health, reported online at MedicalNewsToday.com.

Home Work Attractive

Surprising: Eighty-six percent of employees say they work more productively at home than in the office. And 40% would be willing to take a pay cut to be able to work from home.

Staples Advantage, the business-to-business division of Staples, Inc., Framingham, Massachusetts. *www.staplesadvantage.com*

More Bikes

Bike-sharing programs in US cities are helping to ease traffic congestion while cutting pollution and improving cyclists' health.

How it works: You pay a fee, often monthly or annually, to get a key that you can use to retrieve a bike at one of the many docking stations in a city. Additional fees based on time spent riding apply after the first half hour, which usually is free, and the bike can be returned to the same station or one closer to the person's destination. Cities with bike-sharing programs include Minneapolis...Washington, DC...Chicago...Denver...Miami Beach...Boston...and Des Moines. San Francisco and New York City are planning to launch programs soon. For more information, do an online search for "bike sharing" and the city name.

Andy Clarke, president, American League of Bicyclists, a national bicycle advocacy group. *www.bikeleague.org*

20

Safety Matters

The Whistle-Blower's Guide to Doing What's Right While Protecting Yourself

In November 2011, shocking allegations emerged that Jerry Sandusky, a former defensive coordinator of the Penn State University football team, had sexually molested young boys whom he befriended through a charity he started. Sandusky's alleged actions were not the only appalling part of the story. Also disturbing were the allegations that other Penn State coaches and employees knew of the crimes for years but failed to notify police.

According to the nonprofit Ethics Resource Center, about half of all American employees have witnessed a boss or colleague engage in illegal or unethical conduct in the workplace. That misconduct usually involves something like fraud, ignoring safety or environmental laws or underpaying taxes—not child abuse—but whatever the crime, employees who witness it are in a difficult position. They typically want to stop the misbehavior, but calling attention to misconduct can damage or even ruin the whistle-blower's career or, in some cases, get him/her sued.

Though the decks are stacked against whistle-blowers, you still can do what's right and protect yourself. *Here's what you need to know before you speak up about an ethical or legal lapse in your workplace...*

THE DANGERS OF DOING RIGHT

Most whistle-blowers don't set out to be whistle-blowers—they just come across potential problems that they want to warn others

Stephen Kohn, executive director of the National Whistleblowers Center, a nonprofit, nonpartisan organization, and an attorney with the law firm Kohn, Kohn & Colapinto, LLP, both in Washington, DC. Kohn has testified before Congress about whistle-blower reforms and worked with the staff of the Senate Judiciary Committee drafting the Sarbanes-Oxley whistle-blower law. He is author of *The Whistleblower's Handbook: A Step-by-Step Guide to Doing What's Right and Protecting Yourself* (Lyons). *www.whistleblowers.org*

about. But not all bosses are grateful for these warnings. Some consider employees who call attention to ethical or legal lapses disloyal troublemakers—particularly if management is involved or if the situation would be expensive to correct.

Other employers decide that the best solution is to bury the problem—which could include burying the career of the employee who called attention to it. The employer will dig up or fabricate a black mark on the work history of this well-meaning employee, then use that mark as an excuse for termination. That way, if the employee later reports the misconduct to the police, government regulators or the media, the allegations can be dismissed as coming from a disgruntled ex-employee with an axe to grind.

Example: When Enron employee Sherron Watkins sent a heads-up memo about accounting issues to her boss in 2001, her employer investigated whether Watkins could legally be fired. (She ended up resigning.)

Three recommendations if you're thinking of blowing the whistle...

- **Be wary of employer ethics hot lines.** Most large employers now have corporate compliance departments that maintain phone numbers specifically for employees to report ethical and legal concerns. But before dialing, try to find an organizational chart that shows to whom the corporate compliance department reports. If it reports to the board of directors or the company's audit committee, the hot line likely is a safe way to voice concerns. But if it reports to the company's general counsel or you cannot determine to whom it reports, beware. The general counsel's goal likely will be to minimize the company's legal and financial risks, not to do what's right by you.

- **Consider making your report anonymously if you have doubts about how your employers will treat you when you call attention to an ethical lapse.**

Helpful: Under the Dodd-Frank Act, employees can file complaints concerning securities and commodities fraud anonymously and still qualify for large financial rewards. The procedures for anonymously blowing the whistle are spelled out in new regulations published by the Securities and Exchange Commission (SEC) and mandate that the whistle-blower obtain legal counsel to ensure that an anonymous claim is properly filed and that the whistle-blower is fully protected.

Information: *www.sec.gov/whistleblower.*

- **Consult with a lawyer experienced in whistle-blower law before calling your boss's attention to workplace misconduct,** not after your career has been harmed by coming forward. This attorney can help you understand the risks and offer guidance about using whistle-blower laws to minimize those risks. Paying for that attorney's guidance beforehand is likely to be substantially cheaper than hiring an attorney to sue for wrongful termination later.

Helpful: The nonprofit National Whistleblower Legal Defense and Education Fund can provide attorney referrals. (Go to *www.whistleblowers.org*, select "Services," then "Attorney Referrals.")

THE BEST WHISTLE-BLOWER LAWS

There are dozens of federal and state laws that protect the jobs of whistle-blowers and allow them to sue for back pay and legal fees if they are unfairly terminated. But each of these laws applies only in specific circumstances, and it's easy for whistle-blowers to make missteps that deprive them of legal protection.

Example: A construction engineer discovers that his employer has used an inadequate grade of concrete to build a bridge. When his supervisor ignores his concerns, he speaks to the press. The company fires the engineer and sues him, arguing that its concrete mix is a trade secret that he had no right to disclose. Had this engineer consulted a lawyer, he would have been advised to voice his concerns to the Department of Justice rather than the press. This would have allowed him to take advantage of whistle-blower laws that could have shielded him from liability.

Some whistle-blower laws offer financial rewards to whistle-blowers—typically 10% to 30% of any money collected by the government in the form of fines or funds recovered from those who defrauded the government. *Among the laws that offer rewards...*

• **The False Claims Act covers fraud in federal procurement and contracting.** Whistle-blower cases sometimes can be linked to the False Claims Act even when the federal government is not the primary victim as long as a federal government program is affected.

Example: Whistle-blowers caught pharmaceutical company Eli Lilly using illegal marketing techniques to increase sales of Zyprexa, a drug used to treat schizophrenia and bipolar disorder. The case qualified under the False Claims Act because some patients obtained Zyprexa through the federal government programs Medicare and Medicaid. The whistle-blowers received nearly $79 million in rewards in 2009.

• **Section 406 of the Internal Revenue Code,** enacted in 2006, covers major tax fraud and underpayment. It applies only if the underpayment is in excess of $2 million, among other restrictions. Whistle-blowers need not work for the guilty corporation or individual to qualify for rewards.

Helpful: To report tax fraud, complete IRS Form 211, *Application for Reward for Original Information* (*www.irs.gov*).

• **Section 21F of the Securities Exchange Act covers stock fraud,** attempts to rip off shareholders and other corporate misdeeds policed by the SEC.

• **Section 23 of the Commodity Exchange Act,** enacted in 2010, covers illegal trading in commodities such as oil, minerals and agricultural products.

Many states have whistle-blower protection laws, but these typically offer less protection than comparable federal laws.

Exceptions: State whistle-blower protection laws are very strong in California and New Jersey.

GATHERING EVIDENCE

Whistle-blowers are more likely to be believed if they have evidence to back up their allegations. But gathering evidence can be a legal minefield. *What you need to know...*

• **Secretly recording conversations generally is legal under federal law** as long as the person doing the recording is party to the conversation being recorded.

Exceptions: Recording conversations without the knowledge and consent of all parties involved usually is illegal under state law in California, Connecticut, Florida, Illinois, Maryland, Massachusetts, Michigan, Montana, Nevada, New Hampshire, Pennsylvania and Washington. Ask a lawyer about the recording laws that pertain to your situation.

• **Copying or taking documents belonging to an employer in order to blow the whistle on illegal activities** typically is legal as long as the whistle-blower has lawful access to those documents. It is illegal for would-be whistle-blowers to rifle through offices or files that they do not have permission to access in search of evidence.

Warning: Companies increasingly are suing whistle-blowers who copy or remove valuable documents, such as those that spell out trade secrets. These companies argue that because the documents have value, whistle-blowers who take them are guilty of theft. Courts usually side with whistle-blowers in these cases—particularly when the whistle-blower has good reason to believe that the documents will be destroyed if not removed. Still, when valuable information is involved, the safest policy for whistle-blowers is not to remove or copy the documents, but instead to determine precisely where these documents are located in the office, then provide government regulators with instructions on how to find them.

Early Warning System

Text messages warning of tornadoes, hurricanes and other disasters are sent through the FCC's Personal Localized Alerting Network (PLAN). Emergency officials will be able to send geographically targeted messages to cell phones. The free service was launched nationwide in April 2012.

USA Today

Protect Your Documents

Keep a fireproof safe at home for valuables and crucial documents, such as wills, passports and insurance policies.

Reasons: Valuables in a bank safe-deposit box rarely are insured, but ones in a home safe are covered by home-owner's insurance. Bank boxes often are fireproof but not waterproof—you can buy a home safe that is both. And bank boxes are sealed upon receiving a death notice, so estate representatives must provide court papers to gain access.

CBS Moneywatch.com

If Your Home Phone Is Wireless

Homes with only wireless phones make up more than one-quarter of all US households. In the state with the highest wireless-only percentage, Arkansas, more than 35% of homes have no landlines.

Caution: If you have only a wireless phone, be sure local emergency departments can find you if you need help.

USA Today

Ordinary People Who Foiled Terrorists

Marjory Abrams, president, *BottomLine* newsletters, Boardroom Inc., 281 Tresser Blvd., Stamford, Connecticut 06901.

Every time I see William McCarthy, PhD, CPP, president of Threat Research, Inc. (*www.threatresearchinc.com)*, and former commanding officer of the NYPD Bomb Squad, I find myself wanting to share with you additional safety precautions against terrorism.

Most recently, Bill was the strongest I had heard him in his assertion that we should expect more terrorist attacks to occur here in the US. It is simply too difficult to stop all of the crazies, whether they are homegrown or "imported." Awareness remains our best defense. *Ordinary people following their instincts foiled would-be terrorists in these recent events...*

- **In New York City's Times Square, vendors reported to the police a parked vehicle with the engine running,** flashing lights and smoke coming out near the backseat. The area was evacuated. Fortunately, the car bomb failed to detonate.
- **A driver's behavior—including checking under his car and moving away when he saw a uniformed officer**—stirred up suspicion at a New Jersey rest stop. It turned out that he was carrying three powerful homemade bombs in his vehicle.
- **A plot to kill soldiers at Fort Dix was foiled** when a salesperson told police that customers had asked him to convert to a DVD video footage of them firing assault weapons.

The key to awareness: Knowing what "normal" looks like—which cars are regularly in your neighborhood, who makes deliveries at work, etc.—and then paying attention to what is eccentric or out of place. Most people know to report peculiar packages that arrive in the mail and unattended bags. *Other red flags...*

- **People who are overdressed for the weather.**
- **People who move off quickly when seen or approached.**
- **People in restricted areas or other places they don't belong.**
- **Vehicles that appear to be carrying heavy weight...**are abandoned...illegally parked...leaking fluid other than from engines or fuel tanks.
- **Unusual requests for information about physical access to a home,** hospital, sports arena, workplace, etc.
- **Surveillance activity at government buildings, other key facilities and crowded,**

high-profile places. Is someone scanning with binoculars? Taking photos?

• **On trains, watch for people who place items in a luggage compartment and then move to a different car.**

• **People using watercraft should be alert to missing fencing or lighting near dams...** boats anchored in areas not typically used for anchoring...unusual diving or night operations...signals flashing between boats.

Many people fail to report suspicious activities because they are afraid of being criticized if it is not a real threat. But if you sense something suspicious, report it right away. You never know when a threat will be real. We all have a role in keeping ourselves and our nation safe, so continue to be very vigilant.

Be Careful in Big Crowds

Big crowds can be dangerous, even resulting in deadly stampedes.

Here's what you can do to protect yourself and your loved ones when you have to be in a crowded area...

• **Pick a side**—never be in the middle of a crowd, even at a concert or sports event. Sit or stand to one side so that you can move away quickly.

• **Don't be curious**—if you see a crowd gathering, walk the other way as fast as you can. Spontaneous crowds are a major danger outside the US and also can be a big domestic risk. If you feel that security forces are not doing their job in any crowded area, including sports stadiums and at parades, leave immediately—it is not worth risking your safety to see a parade, concert or sports event.

• **Do your homework**—never go anywhere that has only one entrance and exit.

• **Know where exits are at all times**—look around and memorize the exact location of several of them.

Dale Yeager, CEO, Seraph, a consulting firm for legal, liability and security problems, Phoenixville, Pennsylvania. *www.seraph.net*

Involved in a Lawsuit?—Watch Out for These Attorney Tricks

Dan Brecher, JD, counsel to the New York City and New Jersey law firm Scarinci Hollenbeck, LLC. He recently obtained eight-figure judgments in two separate cases based largely on information obtained during depositions. *www.scarincihollenbeck.com*

If you are ever involved in a lawsuit, it's likely that you will be asked to give a deposition.

Exception: Depositions usually are not taken in small-claims court cases.

Giving a deposition means answering questions posed by the opposing counsel prior to the trial in the presence of your own attorney and a court reporter who transcribes the proceedings. The primary purpose is to record your version of the facts in advance of trial so that it can be used to challenge a change in your testimony. The opposing lawyer also tries to trick you into saying things that work against your interests or make you seem dishonest. *The lawyer might try one or more of the following...*

• **Remain silent and stare at you after you answer a question.** Long silences make people uncomfortable. The attorney is hoping that you will fill this awkward silence by saying more than you should. Remind yourself that it's a trick, and keep your mouth shut once you've said what you need to.

• **Ask questions subtly different from what you expect.** If you fail to pay close attention, you won't notice these subtle differences and will damage your case by providing answers that don't fit the questions in crucial ways.

Example: A lawyer asks, "Were you driving at the speed limit when you went through that red light?" If you're not paying close attention, you might not realize that answering yes makes it seem that you're admitting to running a red light.

• **Insist that you answer certain questions either "yes" or "no."** You are not required to follow this yes-or-no-only instruction. You can respond, "That's not a question that can be answered with just a yes or no."

• **Ask what you have done to comply with the lawyer's request for documents and e-mails relevant to the case.** If your response seems vague or unusual, an attorney might decide to dig deeper into your affairs. If you answer, "I handed everything over," this could be used to make you look dishonest if there's something you accidentally forgot to provide. The best response is to very briefly discuss your process.

Example: "I searched my e-mail files for your client's name, printed out everything that came up and gave the printouts to my attorney."

• **Cut you off with a new question during your response.** Insist that the lawyer give you a chance to finish answering the previous question.

• **Frame questions in a way that you must choose between making statements against your interests and being dishonest.** When you feel trapped between hurting your case or lying, consider whether it's appropriate to answer, "I'm not certain."

If the attorney follows up by asking for your best guess or estimate, repeat that you don't know—do not guess.

• **Try to make you angry.** This could include baiting you with sneers or a patronizing tone. Deposition transcripts include only what is said, not how it's said. If you get mad, you might say something that will make you look bad during the trial.

Alternative: The opposing attorney might instead be very friendly. This also may be a trick. He's hoping that you'll let down your guard and say something that you shouldn't.

• **Ask you if you spoke with someone other than your lawyer to prepare.** Don't say anything about the case to anyone prior to your deposition. This person might be subpoenaed.

Beware of Free Charging Stations

These stand-alone electronics-charging stations found at malls, airports and other public places are outfitted with charging cables for popular portable electronics such as smartphones and iPads. However, these kiosks can be tampered with by people who want to steal the data on your device.

Better: Bring your own charging cable, and plug it directly into an outlet.

KrebsOnSecurity.com, security news and investigations Web site.

Invisible Stalkers Track Your Online Moves

Linda Criddle, president of Safe Internet Alliance, a nonprofit group that encourages Web sites to improve user privacy, Kirkland, Washington. She also is president of LookBothWays Inc., an online safety software and consulting company that works with corporations and law-enforcement agencies. She previously spent 13 years with Microsoft as an online safety expert. *www.safeinternet.org*

Identity thieves aren't the only prying eyes on the Internet. Mainstream Web sites and their advertising partners track our digital doings as well. Some of this tracking is innocent and even beneficial—for example, an Internet merchant might record which items we browse so that it can suggest related products the next time we visit. Unfortunately, online tracking can cross the line from welcome feature to worrisome invasion of privacy. Sites often sell information about us to other companies…install tracking files onto our computers without our permission…and allow ad-tracking companies to lurk unseen on their sites, gathering information about us.

WHO'S DOING IT

It isn't just shopping sites that are tracking us. Media companies sell information about which articles we read online. Charities sell information about the causes we seem interested in. Even government sites might share information about visitors.

Example: A man who registered to visit the Grand Canyon on the National Park Service site was immediately deluged with advertisements from companies selling hiking gear.

Much of this information is recorded, analyzed and shared with anyone willing to pay for it, all without our consent. If it falls into the wrong hands, such data potentially could be used for ID theft. Even if that doesn't happen, it's likely to be used to determine whether we are approved for loans and insurance and to target us with solicitations designed to take advantage of our opinions and weaknesses.

Examples: If we visit the site of a political organization or charity, disreputable companies that want our business might portray themselves as sympathetic to this cause in the online ads we see, even if they are not. If you buy a book from an Internet merchant about overcoming gambling addiction, you might receive a flood of ads from poker Web sites.

The sharing of our private data also could cause us embarrassment if a friend or family member who uses our computer sees that we receive an unusually large number of ads for dating sites, debt-reduction services or treatments for potentially embarrassing health conditions.

WHAT TO DO

There are many ways to make your online activities more private. Some are complex, expensive or inconvenient—*but there are some simple, free online privacy options that most Internet users find worth the trouble...*

1. Make an intermediate stop at Yahoo.com. Generally, each Web site we visit knows which site we were visiting before we dropped in and which site we head to when we leave. Unfortunately, a disreputable site could use this information for nefarious purposes. What we can do to help prevent this is visit a safe, innocuous site such as Yahoo.com both before and after we visit any site that we would prefer to keep private, such as the site of a financial company with which we do business. The fact that we visit Yahoo.com tells others almost nothing about us.

2. Use an ad-tracker tracker. These programs don't stop the online spies, but they do warn us when we are being watched by them, so you can make an informed decision regarding whether you want to visit certain sites.

Example: TrackerScan is available for free at *www.privacychoice.org/trackerscan.*

3. Opt out of ad tracking. Many online advertisers and companies that sell data to online advertisers allow Internet users to opt out of Internet tracking by signing up with opt-out services.

Examples: Opt-out services include *www.aboutads.info...www.privacychoice.org*...and *www.networkadvertising.org.*

Also, several Web browsers, including Mozilla Firefox and Google Chrome, are beginning to offer users ways to permanently opt out of ad tracking. However, less ethical advertisers do not participate in these opt-out programs.

4. Periodically clear your cookie cache. Cookies are computer files stored by Web sites on our computers that remind the sites who we are when we return or that track our movements around the Internet. As a result, marketers may know more about us than we want to share. We can delete most of these cookies from our computers in a few simple steps—but be aware that doing so will cause some sites to lose information that we want them to have. We might have to retype passwords, mailing addresses, user profiles and other information the next time we visit. *Examples of how to clear your cookies...**

- In Internet Explorer 8, select "Internet Options" from the "Tools" menu, select the "General" tab, then click "Delete." Next, select "Cookies," then click "Delete" again.
- In Mozilla Firefox, select "Options" from the "Tools" menu, click "Privacy," then "Show Cookies," followed by "Remove All Cookies."

5. Adjust your browser settings for greater privacy. In addition to deleting the cook-

*For more details on removing cookies and adjusting privacy settings on various browsers, see your browser's "Help" file.

ies that already are on our computers, we can instruct our browsers to permit fewer cookies in the future.

Most browsers also have a "Private Browsing" option (Internet Explorer calls it "InPrivate Browsing") for when we want our browsing to be especially private.

6. Avoid sites that do a poor job protecting user privacy. Don't use a site if its "Privacy Policy" or "Privacy Terms" states that information about you can be shared with third parties. Avoid a site if a security-rating program, such as MacAfee's SiteAdvisor, warns you that the site could expose your computer to malicious software, which could put your personal information at high risk. For a free version of MacAfee's SiteAdvisor, go to *www.siteadvisor.com.*

Cyber Bandits Could Strike Anytime

Robert Siciliano, a personal and corporate security consultant based in Boston. He is chief executive officer of IDTheftSecurity.com and a member of the consumer advisory board of security software designer McAfee.

They know where you are. And wherever you are, cyber bandits can invade your privacy, steal your identity and even take your money through the seemingly safe electronic gadgets that you use every day.

SMARTPHONE TRACKING

How cyber bandits get you: Smartphones feature GPS applications that provide driving directions and, often, geolocation applications that share your whereabouts with friends.

The location-tracking systems of Apple iPhones and iPads and of Google Android handsets recently came under criticism from members of Congress who expressed concerns about the potential for criminal activity.

The danger is that if a hacker gains access to your location information, he/she could stalk you, kidnap you or even figure out when you're out and burglarize your home.

Example: Police in Nashua, New Hampshire, broke up a three-man burglary ring that had stolen more than $100,000 in valuables by breaking into the homes of more than 50 people who had shared their whereabouts with friends online.

What to do: Don't post your location on services such as Facebook and Twitter. Also, skip geolocation services such as Foursquare, Gowalla and Facebook Places. For maximum security, look in "Settings" for instructions on disabling your smartphone's location services entirely. Mapping, weather and other location-based apps still should work in most cases, but you will have to enter your location manually.

MOBILE COMMERCE ACCOUNT THEFT

How they get you: As smartphones become more common, banks, credit card companies and retailers are likely to allow consumers to use their smartphones to make payments and other financial transactions. The trouble is, testing suggests that with today's technology, these smartphone payments might not be completely secure. Hackers could steal account information wirelessly...or pickpockets could steal your smartphones and make transactions using your accounts.

What to do: At a minimum, if you use mobile commerce applications, you should password-protect your smartphone and check your credit card and bank accounts frequently for any unauthorized transactions. Better yet, do not use your smartphone for mobile commerce at all—at least until it is in very wide use and has been proved safe.

CELL-PHONE EAVESDROPPING

How they get you: You receive a text message that appears to come from your bank—or some other trusted institution—warning of a problem with your account. But when you click a link in this text message, it actually downloads software onto your phone that lets a criminal listen in on future calls, read your text messages, see photos taken with the phone, track your location or even listen to in-person conversations when the phone is nearby. The criminal could gain access to your e-mail and computer files, too, or even your credit card or bank account information if you use the phone to make online purchases.

What to do: Never click a link in a text message unless you are certain that the message was sent by someone you trust. Keep your cell phone on your person whenever you are away from home, reducing the odds that a criminal will find the phone unguarded and load malicious software onto it.

Example: In 2007, a stalker is believed to have gained access to the cell phones used by three families in a suburb of Tacoma, Washington, and used that access to record the families' private conversations. He then called the families anonymously, played those conversations back as proof of his access to them and made death threats.

CAMERA VIRUSES

How they get you: You connect your digital camera (or video camera) to a public computer in a hotel lobby or an Internet café to upload pictures to a Facebook page or photo-sharing Web site. But while you're uploading your pictures, a virus is secretly loading itself onto your camera. When you return home and connect the camera to your personal computer, the virus will infect it, too, giving the hacker access to every file stored on the computer plus a record of everything you type on the computer from then on—potentially even account passwords and credit card or bank account numbers.

Hackers have even managed to infect digital picture frames with viruses before they left the factory. The virus reported everything typed on any computer that the frame was attached to.

What to do: Never attach your digital camera or video camera to a public computer. Use your computer's security software to run an antivirus scan the first time you connect a new digital photo device to your computer. (Look in your antivirus software's "Help" file for details.) Run another scan after you let a friend attach his/her camera to your computer or after you attach your camera to a friend's computer.

COPIER COPYING

How they get you: You make a copy of your tax return at a local copy shop or you print out a copy on your workplace printer. Many copy machines and high-end printers now have digital memory that saves digital records of documents printed. Anyone with access to this device could print out a duplicate copy.

What to do: Avoid copying sensitive documents on workplace or public copiers. If you must do this, leave particularly sensitive data—such as your Social Security number or credit card number—blank until after you make the copy, then fill it in. Do not sell or donate a printer that has document memory if it has been used to print sensitive information. Contact the manufacturer or look in the manual or on the Internet to see how you can erase what is on the hard drive.

GPS DETOURS

How they get you: You connect your GPS navigation device to your computer to download a software update. This new software secretly reports your travels to a criminal, who could use the information to stalk you or determine when you go out so that he can burglarize your home. Security experts say that this is possible, although we have not yet heard of any actual cases.

What to do: If you want to be extra cautious, download GPS software updates only from the Web site of the company that made your GPS unit.

Index

A

ACE (*angiotensin-converting enzyme*) inhibitors, 7
Acupressure, facial, 54–55
ADHD (attention-deficit/hyperactivity disorder), 269–271
Adolescents. *See* Children/teenagers
Aging, 43, 76, 77. *See also* Longevity
Air travel. *See also* Travel
  airport security tips, 233, 235
  apps for, 234
  bargains in, 232
  best seats for, 232–233
  canceled and delayed flights, 233
  fees and perks in, 232, 233
  first-class, 232
  with frequent flier miles, 230–232
  getting sick after, 46–47
  hand-washing during, 234
  meals at airports, 234
  napping rooms, 234
  onboard meal safety, 234
Alcohol consumption
  wine, 197
  by women, 5
Allergies, 52, 55
Aluminum bottles, 12
Alzheimer's disease
  apple juice for symptoms of, 108
  diagnosis guidelines for, 19
  family members with, 265–266
  maternal link to, 19
  prevention advice, 20, 21
Anesthesia, 43–44. *See also* Surgery
Anger, 88
Angina, 5
Annuities, 207, 208. *See also* Investing
Anorexia nervosa, 68
Antibiotics, 17, 23–24, 121, 267–268
Anticoagulants, 3–4, 89–90
Antidepressants, 10, 21, 39, 42, 102, 275. *See also* Depression
Antioxidants, 87, 90–92, 96, 101
Antipsychotics, 38–39
Antiseizure drugs, 39
Apples
  for lowering cholesterol, 85
  organic, 25
Appliances
  money-saving tips for, 199
  tips on caring for, 279–281
Appraisals, 139
Apps
  for air travel, 234
  language translation, 241
  travel, 229–230
Arginine, for better sex, 84
Arthritis, 83–84, 96, 101
Aspirin, 7, 9, 15, 22–23, 87, 95, 112
  See also NSAIDs
Asthma, 45, 48, 51, 78
Atherosclerosis, 81, 85, 104, 110
Athletic performance, 106
Attention-deficit/hyperactivity disorder (ADHD), 269–271
Audits, tax, 164
Automobiles. *See* Cars

B

Back pain, 35, 98–100
Bacteria
  in airplane water, 234
  from animal bites, 249
Bananas, 58
Banking. *See* Money
Barley, 91–92
BED (binge-eating disorder), 68
Bedbugs, 226, 237
Beef prices, 197
Berries, 100
Beta-blockers, 7
Bike-sharing programs, 325
Binge-eating disorder (BED), 68
Biofeedback, 108
Biopsies, 112, 119
Bisphenol A (BPA), 12–13
Blood clots, 9, 89–90
Blood glucose, 43
Blood pressure, 1–2, 4, 81, 82, 83, 85–86, 101–102
Blood sugar, 11–12, 79. *See also* Diabetes
Blood tests, 35, 108, 112
Blood thinners, 3, 89–90
Blueberries, aiding in weight loss, 64
"Body Clock," 77–79
Body image, 68
Bonds, investing in, 126–127, 130, 171–172. *See also* Investing
Bone health, 36, 75, 96
BPA (bisphenol A), 12–13
Brain health, 13–14, 20, 59, 82. *See also* Memory; Stroke
Bread, 74–76
Breast cancer, 17, 112, 113
Broccoli, 95
Bulimia nervosa, 68
Bunions, 57
Burnout, of doctors, 32–33
Burns, natural treatment for, 83
Businesses. *See also* Work
  employee perks, 323
  free publicity for, 314
  growing, 313–316
  Internet, 314–316
  interns, 313
  interviewing job candidates, 313
  money matters for small, 132
  quick response codes, 313–314
  starting your own, 319–321
  travel, 324
Bypass surgery, 70

C

Caffeine, small doses of, 70. *See also* Coffee; Tea
Calcium, 5, 75
Calcium channel blockers, 4
Calendula, for cataracts, 101
Calmare pain therapy treatment, 16–17
Canada, investments based in, 174. *See also* Investing
Cancer. *See also specific types*
  attic insulation link to, 16
  formaldehyde link to, 12
  grilling link to, 83
  HPV test, 107
  reduction from surgery in, 113
  rosemary for, 83
  tea in preventing, 95
  treatment for, 93–95
  WWP2 for, 12
Capital gains tax, 160–161
Carbohydrates, 74–76
Cardiovascular health. *See* Heart attacks; Heart health; Stroke
Cardiovascular screening, 35
Careers. *See* Businesses; Work
Carpal tunnel syndrome (CTS), 48–49
Cars
  accidents involving, 257
  buying and selling, 251–252, 253–257
  gas mileage of, 261
  hybrid, 184
  insuring, 155–156
  maintenance on, 251, 260–262
  renting and leasing, 235, 252–253
  safety tips, 251
  sharing, 259
  traffic tickets, 250
Casinos, 244–246
Cataracts, 77, 93, 101
Catheters, 8, 23, 37, 45
Cats. *See* Pets
CDs (certificates of deposit), 125–126. *See also* Investing
Celery, 83
Celiac disease, 75
Cell phones. *See* Telephones
Cereal, 87–88
Certificates of deposit (CDs), 125–126. *See also* Investing
Cervical cancer, 15, 107, 113

Chapped lips, 55
Charities, 164
Check cashing, 128
Chemotherapy, 17, 112–113
Children/teenagers
  career discussions with, 268–269
  friends of, 266–267
  health problems of, 267–268
  money issues involving, 271. *See also* College
  social networking addiction in, 268
  vaccines for, 268
Chinese food, 64
Chiropractors, 48–49
Chocolate, 73
Cholesterol, high, 20, 36, 85
Chromium, 84
Chronic pain, 16–17
Cigarettes, 7. *See also* Smoking
Cimetidine, 95
Cinnamon, 92
Cleaning, 276–278, 284
Coffee
  in cancer prevention, 116
  fighting depression with, 100
  for hair loss reduction, 54
  as stroke reducer, 90–91
Cognitive behavioral therapy, 69
COLA, 211
Cold, exposure to, 67
"Cold cap," 17
Colds, natural prevention of, 50. *See also* Infections
Cold sore treatments, 20
College
  defaulting on loans, 141–142
  estimating costs, 139
  financial aid for, 140–141
  for learning disabilities or ADHD, 269–271
  saving for, 140
Colon cancer, 116, 122–123
Colon cleanses, 116
Colonoscopies, 43, 114–116, 117, 123
Communication, nonverbal, 265
Complaining, 290–292
Computers. *See also* Internet
  security for, 331-334
  for seniors, 221–222
Constipation, 47, 115, 122
Contact lenses, 56
Contractors, finding best, 316
Copper, 184
Coronary artery disease. *See* Heart disease
Cough, 50–51
Coupons, 193–194, 195
Cranberry juice, 85
Cravings, meaning of, 65–67
Creativity, 301
Credit cards
  credit score and, 132
  fees, 132–133
  foreign transaction fees, 241
  for gas, 257–259
  gold cards, 132–133
  incentives for, 130–132
  prepaid, 132–133
  refunds, 132–133
  for small businesses, 132
  travel tips for using, 131
Credit scores, 132, 134
Crime. *See also* Fraud
  accident scams, 155
  at airports, 235
  car theft, 259
  of the elderly, 217
  health scams, 201–202
  identity theft, 145
  Internet, 146
  Social Security scams, 211
  traffic ticket advice, 250
  unclaimed-property, 145
  via Wi-Fi connections, 164
Croup, 267
Crowdfunding, 316–317
Cruises, tip for taking, 240. *See also* Travel
CTS (carpal tunnel syndrome), 48–49
CT (computed tomography) scans, 36–37
Curcumin, 89–90
Cyberchondriacs, 27–28

D

Death. *See* Estate planning
Debt. *See also* Money
  credit card, 133
  defaulting on, 130
  Social Security in paying off, 224
Deep vein thrombosis (DVT), 47
Dehydration, 59–60
Dementia, 20. *See also* Alzheimer's disease
Dentists, 56
Depression. *See also* Mental health
  antidepressants, 10, 21, 39, 42, 102, 275
  coffee for fighting, 100
  in the elderly, 21
  medication side effects, 38–40
  risks from, 9
  saffron for, 102
  seasonal affective disorder (SAD), 77
  suppressing appetite, 68
  in teenagers, 268
  trans fats and risk of, 21
Diabetes, 11–12, 75, 78, 84, 91–92, 93, 104, 116. *See also* Blood sugar
Diet. *See also* Food and drink
  healthy grilling tips, 83
  for lowering cholesterol, 85
  for men, 117
  for pH balance, 56
  for weight gain, 62–64
  yo-yo, 67
Digestive health, 122. *See also* Constipation; Heartburn
Digital-wallet programs, 193
Disabilities, work for people with, 312
Disability insurance, 154
Dishwashers, 279, 282
Diuretics, 4, 18, 60, 101
Diverticulitis, 122
Dividends, stocks providing, 173–178
Divorce, 68, 143–145. *See also* Marriage
Doctors
  burnout of, 32–33
  misdiagnoses by, 30–31
  oncologists, 31–32
  visits to, 28–30
Dogs. *See* Pets
Dreams, 296–298
Dreams, predicting disease, 21
Driving. *See* Cars
Drowsiness, 79
Drugs. *See* Medications; *specific conditions*; *specific drug groups*
DVT (deep vein thrombosis), 47

E

Earthquake insurance, 154
Eating disorders, 67–69
E-books, 201, 247
E-mail etiquette, 322
E-mail scams, 145–146
Empty-nest syndrome, 68
Encouraging people, 294–296
Endometrial cancer, 110
Energy bars, 72–73
Energy labels, 198
Energy stocks, 182
Energy usage, 198
Erectile dysfunction, 108, 120–121
Estate planning. *See also* Investing; Money; Retirement
  avoiding will challenges in, 223–224
  IRA beneficiaries in, 165–167
  post-death issues in, 165
  tax update on, 161, 167–168
Estate taxes, 161, 167–168
Estrogen, 108–111
Europe, investments based in, 172, 176, 179
Exercise
  for back pain, 98–100
  for better sex, 105, 107–108
  health and longevity link to, 76, 92
  hydration and, 70
  like a kid, 71–72
  as mood booster, 58
  pedal machines, 86
  sitting versus, 4, 70
  stress affecting, 79
  in stroke rehabilitation, 9
  swimming as, 70
Exfoliating, 15
Eye health
  buying glasses, 202
  cataracts, 77, 93, 101
  contact lenses, 56
  dark leafy greens for, 93
  eyebrows, 17
  glaucoma, 23
  reading glasses, 56
  sun and, 267

F

Facebook, 106, 311
Facial acupressure, 54–55
Falls, 97–98
Family. *See* Children/teenagers; Marriage; Men; Relationships; Women
Fantasies, 105
Fast food, 197
Fat, belly, 22
Fennel seed, 102
Fiber, 76, 86
Fibromyalgia, 19, 49
Fire safety, 329
First aid, 61
Fish, 25, 49, 63, 76, 88, 92. *See also* Omega-3 fatty acids
Fish oil, 89, 93
529 college savings plans, 141
Flatulence, 102
Floss, 87
Flowers. *See* Herbal treatments; Plants
Flu, 24–25, 50–51. *See also* Infections
Folates, 83. *See also* Vitamin B
Food and drink. *See also* Diet; *specific foods and drinks*
  beef prices, 197
  cravings for specific, 65–67
  curbing appetite, 67

cures, 82–84
eating disorders, 67–69
fast food, 197
for fighting inflammation, 96
hamburgers, 246–247
organic food, 16, 25, 92, 217–218
portion control, 65
promoting weight loss, 62–64
restaurants, 196, 219, 231–232, 234, 243–244
satisfaction with, 65
senior discounts on, 218
shopping for, 195–196, 197
Formaldehyde, 12
401K accounts, 143, 165, 166–167, 210, 213–216. *See also* Estate planning; Investing; Retirement
Fraud. *See also* Crime
credit card, 227
digital wallet and, 193
investment-based, 184
Friends, making, 288–290
Fruit, 91

G

Gambling, 244–246
Gardening, 249, 282–284
Garlic, 90, 102
Gas discounts, 236
Gastrointestinal tract (GI) disorders. *See* Digestive health
Germs, 45. *See also* Bacteria; Infections
GI (gastrointestinal tract) disorders. *See* Digestive health
Gift cards, 193
Gifts, tips for giving, 200
Gift tax, 167–168
Ginger, health benefits of, 89–90
Ginkgo, 90
Glamping, 227–229
Glaucoma, 23
Gold, investing in, 184
Golf, 242–243
Grapefruit, aiding in weight loss, 64
"Green" plastic water bottle caps, 267
Greens, 93
Grief, heart attacks after, 8
Grilling, healthy tips on, 83
Guilt, 300
Gum, chewing, as heart disease prevention, 87
Gym, memberships at hospitals, 202–203

H

Habits, breaking, 303–304
Hair loss, 54, 107, 112–113, 117
Hamburgers, 246–247
Hamstring, treatment for injury, 57
Hand washing, 56
Happiness, 105, 290
Headaches, 49, 53–54
Health. *See also* Doctors; *specific health issues*
myths about, 46–47
scams, 201–202
Health-care savings, 202–203
Health insurance, 144, 147–154
Health savings accounts (HSAs), 150–151
Hearing, sense of, 20, 22–23, 268
Heart attacks, 6–7, 8–9, 10, 77–78, 89–90
Heartburn, 58, 59
Heart disease, 5, 75, 80–82, 87–89, 106. *See also* Heart health
Heart health
long work hours affecting, 325
nuts for, 84
stent and carotid surgeries for, 8
Heat
as diabetes risk, 11
for weight loss, 70
Heating costs, 198
Heel pain, 56–57
Hepatitis C, 18
Herbal treatments, 50, 89–90. *See also* Natural treatments; Supplements
HFCS (high-fructose corn syrup), 91
Hiccups, 52
High-fructose corn syrup (HFCS), 91
Hip replacement, 19
HIV, 106–107
Home life, 325. *See also* Marriage; Relationships
Homeowners insurance, 138
Home remedies. *See* Natural treatments
Homes. *See also* Mortgages
appliance-saving tips, 279–281
appraisals, 139
cleaning, 276–278
cookware, 282
DIY projects for, 284–285, 287
property taxes on, 161, 219
purchasing, 135–138
refinancing, 139
remodeling, 278
selling, 139–140
swapping, 238–239
Honey, for better sleep, 83
Hormone levels, 104
Hospitals. *See also* Surgery
gym memberships, 202–203
patient safety tips, 43, 44–45
reducing stays by walking, 42
robotic surgery claims, 45
Hotels, saving and safety at, 225–227, 237
Hot flashes, for reduction in breast cancer, 112
Housework, 276–278
HPV (human papillomavirus), 15, 107
HSAs (health savings accounts), 150–151
Human papillomavirus (HPV), 15, 107
Hypertension, 81, 83, 85–86, 88, 101
Hyperthyroidism, 36
Hypothyroidism, 17
Hysterectomy, kidney cancer link to, 111

I

IBS (irritable bowel syndrome), 122
Ibuprofen, 21
Ice bath, 72
ICU (intensive care unit), 23. *See also* Hospitals
Identity theft, 145, 226–227
Immune system, 3, 23, 76, 95. *See also* Infections
Incontinence, after prostate cancer, 121
Indigestion, 102
Individual Retirement Accounts. *See* IRAs; Retirement
Infections. *See also* Immune system
from hospital stays, 44–45
probiotics in preventing, 63–64
staph, 17, 274
tips for avoiding, 61
urinary tract, 23, 121–122
Infidelity, 106
Inflammation, 5, 9, 23, 36, 96, 273
Inflation, 162, 206–208
Inhalers, 45
Inheritance, 207. *See also* Estate planning; Retirement
Insomnia, 5, 60. *See also* Sleep
Insulation, 16
Insulin resistance, 75
Insurance
appeals process, 148–149
auto, 155–156
disability, 154
earthquake, 154
health, 144, 147–154
high-deductible, low-cost, 150
homeowners, 138
life, 144, 156–157
long-term care, 162, 224
for pets, 204
travel, 236
Intensive care unit (ICU), 23. *See also* Hospitals
Interest rates, 126–127, 131–132
Internet. *See also* Computers; Social networking
patient diagnoses on, 26–28
security, 331–334
slang, 301
Interns, 313
Interviews
for job candidates, 313
tips for, 309–310. *See also* Work
Investing. *See also* Estate planning; Money; Retirement
annuity types, 207, 208
bargain stocks, 175–176
in bonds, 171–172
in Canadian markets, 174
in European markets, 172, 176, 179
in gold, 184
mutual funds, 208–210
in US stock market, 169–171, 172
yield-increasing tips, 173–174, 176–177
IRAs. *See also* Estate planning; Investing; Retirement
beneficiaries of, 165–167
Roth IRAs, 143, 165, 166–167, 210, 216
traditional versus Roth, 216
Irritable bowel syndrome (IBS), 122
IRS. *See* Taxes
IUDs, 113

J

Jewelry, 200–201
Jobs. *See* Work
Joint health, 23, 24, 49–50, 51–53

K

Kegel exercises, 107–108
Kidney health, 17, 18, 111
Knees, 52, 57

L

Laughter, health and longevity link to, 76
Lawsuits, 330–331
Learning disabilities, 269–271
Leasing cars, 252–253
Libido, 103–105
Licorice gargle, 43–44
Life insurance, 144, 156–157
LinkedIn, 311
Lips, chapped, 55
Loans, 133, 134, 140–142, 316
Longevity, 75–76, 86, 100–101
Losses, tax reporting of, 160–161

Lubricants, 104
Lyme disease, 249

M

Maggots, 44
Magnesium
benefits of, 84, 93
depletion of, 18
Magnetic resonance imaging (MRI) scans, 9, 34, 37
Mammograms, 114
Marijuana, 21–22, 275
Marinating, for safer grilling, 83
Marketing tricks, 188–192
Marriage. *See also* Children/teenagers; Divorce; Relationships
health and longevity link to, 266
life insurance affected by, 144
Massage, 55
Masturbation, 104
Meat
healthy grilling tips, 83
red, 66, 76
tips for eating, 92
Medical bills, comparing costs, 204
Medical tests, 35–36
Medicare, 151–154
Medications. *See also specific conditions; specific drug groups*
antibiotics, 267–268
common mistakes with, 40–41
home health care and, 42–43
off-label, 38–40
for pets, 204, 275
prescription errors, 41–42
side effects of, 104
swallowing pills, 42
Melatonin, 85–86
Melon, 25, 85
Memory, 79–80, 302–303. *See also* Brain health
Men. *See also* Marriage
diet for, 117
HPV and, 107
Menopause, 108–111
Mental health, 21–22. *See also* Depression
Mercury, in tuna, 25
Metabolic syndrome, 87
Migraines, 54, 84. *See also* Headaches
Milk
chocolate, 73
congestion link, 47
organic, 16
Mold, 278–279
Money. *See also* Debt; Estate planning; Investing; Retirement; Shopping
bank fees, 128–129
for business start-ups, 132
cable TV savings, 203
cell phone savings, 203
check cashing, 128
for college, 140–141
credit cards, 130, 132–133
credit scores, 134
credit unions, 124–125
debt score and identity risk score, 130
digital-wallet programs, 193
health-care savings, 202–203
identity theft protection, 145
interest rates, 126–127
joint accounts, 129
layaway, 193
loans, 133
marital problems and, 143–145
marketing tricks, 188–192
medication prices. *See* Medications
overdraft protection, 125–126
pawnshops as source of, 179
for pet care, 204
savings bonds, 130
senior discounts, 217–219
for small-business borrowers, 132
supermarket loyalty cards, 196
switching bank accounts, 127–128
teaching teens about, 271
tips for saving, 126, 199
using coupons to save, 193–194, 195
vacation planning on less, 229–232, 240. *See also* Travel
Mortgages. *See also* Homes
choosing duration of, 137
fees for, 139
rates on, 137
REITs, 177–178
reverse, 216–217
Mosquitoes, 60
Mozart, 43
MRI (magnetic resonance imaging) scans, 9, 34, 37
MRSA (methicillin-resistant *Staphylococcus aureus*), 17
Multitasking, 300–301
Muscles
excess sitting affecting, 86
relieving aches, 72
Music, 43, 47–48, 119
Mutual funds, 208–210

N

Napping, benefits of, 234. *See also* Sleep
Nattokinase, 90
Natural treatments. *See also* Herbal treatments; Supplements
for arthritis, 83–84, 101
for back pain, 98–100
biofeedback, 108
blood thinners, 89–90
Nearsightedness, 23
Nervous system, 48
Nicotine patches, 16
Nonverbal communication, 265
"Nordic" diet, 77
Nosebleed treatments, 47
NSAIDs (nonsteroidal anti-inflammatory drugs). *See also* Aspirin
diverticulitis link to, 122
erectile dysfunction link to, 108
risks from, 8
Nurse, 34
Nutrition. *See* Diet; Food and drink; *specific vitamins and minerals*
Nuts
for the heart, 84
as snacks, 92

O

Obsessive-compulsive disorder (OCD), 22
OCD (obsessive-compulsive disorder), 22
Olive oil, for arthritis, 83–84
Omega-3 fatty acids, 3, 76, 83, 84, 89, 92, 93, 117. *See also* Fish
Oncologists, 31–32
Onion, 101–102
Oral health, 56
Orange juice, 85
Oregano, 101
Organic foods, 16, 25, 92, 217–218
Organization, reducing stress with, 80
Osteoarthritis, 84, 101. *See also* Arthritis
Osteoporosis, 22, 36, 96
Ovarian cancer, 113

P

Pacemakers, 9
Pain, 16–17, 43–44, 51, 79, 81, 98–100
Pancreatic cancer, 15
Parents, parenting your, 263–265
Parkinson's disease, 21, 100
Pawnshops, 179
Pensions, 143–144, 211–213, 323
Peppers, aiding in weight loss, 64
Pets
cat toys, 275
costs of caring for, 204
coyotes, 274
dental disease in, 272–274
dognapping, 274
dry food warning, 273
flea control for, 271–272
health issues from, 274
insurance for, 204
medications for, 275
microchip identification for, 274
missing, 275
online medications for, 204
shelter dogs, 275
during storms, 272
pH balance, 56
Physicians. *See* Doctors
Pistachios, lowering cholesterol, 96
Plants, 285–286. *See also* Herbal treatments
Plant sterols, 96
Popcorn, curbing appetite, 67
Popping ears, 52–53
Post-traumatic-stress-disorder (PTSD), 38–39
Posture, 51
Potassium, 3, 58
Potatoes, purple, 82
Prescriptions. See Medications
Pressure, being under, 292–294
Probiotics, 63–64
Profits, tax reporting of, 159–160, 168
Property taxes, 161, 219
Prostate cancer, 117, 119–121
Prostate-specific antigen (PSA) tests, 117–118
Protein, 69, 75–76, 92
Prunes, 96, 122
PSA (prostate-specific antigen) tests, 117–118
Psychosocial factors, 104
Psyllium, for constipation, 122
PTSD (post-traumatic-stress-disorder), 38–39

Q

Quercetin, 96, 101–102
Quick response codes, 313–314

R

Radiation, sources of, 14, 37, 119, 267, 279–281
Rebates, 131, 257–259
Red yeast rice, lowering cholesterol, 95
Reflux drugs, 18
REITs, 177–178
Relationships. *See also* Marriage; Social networking
ending, 298–300
health and longevity link to, 88–89

with older relatives, 263–266
partners cheating in, 106
with younger generation, 266–267
Research
on car mechanics, 260–262
before investing, 183–184
before vacations, 229–233
Restaurants, 196, 219, 231–232, 234, 243–244
Restless legs, 5
Retirement. *See also* 401K accounts; Estate planning; Investing; Money
divorce and, 143–144
employers and, 211–213
inheritance and, 207
IRA beneficiaries, 165–167
mutual funds, 208–210
nest eggs, 206–208
Roth IRA accounts for, 143, 165, 166–167, 210, 216
Social Security and, 210–211
volunteering after, 220, 266, 300, 313
Reverse mortgages, 216–217
Reviews, of companies, 190–192
Rice, 95
Robocalls, 204–205
Robotic procedures, 45
Rosemary, 83
Roth IRAs, 143, 165, 166–167, 210, 216
Rye bread, 77

S

Saccharin, 12
SAD (seasonal affective disorder), 77
Saffron, 102
Salt, reducing intake of, 1–3
Savings bonds, 130
Scams. *See* Crime; Fraud
Scents, 200
Sea salt, 50
Seasonal affective disorder (SAD), 77
Senior discounts, 217–219
Seniors
computers for, 221–222
enjoying life, 220–221
Sepsis, 23–25
Severance packages, 159
Sex, 103–105, 106
Shoes, 97–98
Shopping. *See also* Money
best days of week for, 197
for cars, 253–257
coupons, 193–194, 195
discounts, 193, 259
for food and drink, 195–196, 197
gift cards for, 193
health benefits of, 205
organic food, 16, 25, 92, 217–218
rebates and, 131, 257–259
retail store bonus deals, 197
senior grocery discounts, 217–218
supermarket loyalty cards, 196
at yard sales, 247–249
Short sales, 135–136, 137
Singing, 47–48
Sinus infections, 36, 51
Sitting, health risks from, 86
Skin cancer, 15, 21. *See also* Sun protection
Sleep
colon cancer link to, 122–123
dreams during, 296–298
fighting stress with, 80
health and longevity link to, 88
honey for, 83
television and, 58–59
treatment for lack of, 60. *See also* Insomnia
Sleep apnea, 51
Sleepiness, 79
Slugs, 249
Smell, sense of. *See* Scents
Smoking
hair loss and, 54
heart attack risks of, 7, 8
looking for work and, 312
marijuana, 21–22, 275
nicotine patches, 16
quitting, 16
Social networking. *See also* Relationships
for elder care, 266
Facebook, 311
fostering friendships with, 298
identity theft link to, 145
LinkedIn, 311
teens addicted to, 268
Social Security, 146, 210–211. *See also* Retirement
Soda consumption, 91
Sodium, 1–3
Software. *See* Computers
Soy, 111
Special needs, 105
Spices, benefits of, 95, 96, 101–102. *See also specific spices*
Spinach, for mood improvement, 83
SSRIs (selective serotonin reuptake inhibitors), 21, 42, 104
Statins, 3, 7, 11, 36
Stents, 8
Steroids, 42
Stock investments, 169–171, 172. *See also* Investing
Stress
biofeedback in controlling, 81
dancing reducing, 57
exercise injury link to, 79
laughter reducing, 76
symptoms of, 79–80
tips for managing, 58
weight gain link to, 80
Stroke
coffee in reducing, 90–91
diagnosing, 10
fruit in reducing, 91
magnesium in reducing, 93
reducing risk of, 89–90
rehabilitation after, 10
risk of, 9, 10, 54
surgery in preventing, 8
Suicide, 32. *See also* Depression; Mental health
Sun protection, 15, 267
Supplements. *See also* Herbal treatments; Natural treatments; *specific supplements*; *specific vitamins*
drugs interacting with, 89
for migraine prevention, 84
Surgery. *See also* Hospitals; *specific conditions*
anesthesia during, 43–44
bypass, 70
recovery from, 44
reduction in cancer risk from, 113
Sweepstakes, 145–146
Sweeteners, 12
Swimming, 70

T

Target-date mutual funds, 210
Taxes
2012 tax brackets, 162
audit tips, 164
capital gains, 158–160
confidentiality of, 164–165
for continuing-care retirement community residents, 217
deductions for natural disaster damage, 163
in e-mail scams, 145–146
employment-related deductions for higher education, 162
on estates, 223–224. *See also* Estate planning
filing errors, 162
gift, 167–168
for hiring veterans, 168
'innocent-spouse' rules, 163–164
itemizing deductions, 161–162
loopholes, 158–160
profit and loss reporting, 159, 160–168
property, 161, 219
rental losses, 164
for small businesses, 168
Taxes charities, 164
Tea
black, 86, 87
green, 60, 63, 95
for heart disease prevention, 87
kidney stone risk and, 17
Teenagers. *See* Children/teenagers
Teeth, 56
Telephones
alerts for usage limits, 199
brain tumor risk from, 13–14
home security systems using, 203
money-saving tips, 203
radiation from, 18–19
tinnitus from using, 22–23
tips for, 301–302
travel tips, 198–199, 241
voice-mail, 322
wireless for home, 329
Television
cable costs, 199
exercising while watching, 69
heart health link to, 25
sleeping to, 58–59
Tendonitis, 53
Tendons, healing technique for, 57
Terrorism, 329–330
Tetanus, 61
Texting tendonitis, 53
Therapy, types of, 16–17, 59, 69, 112–113
Thyroid gland, 17
TIAs (transient ischemic attacks), 10
Tinnitus, 22–23. *See also* Hearing, sense of
TM (transcendental meditation), 80–82
TMD (temporomandibular joint disorder), 49
Tomato juice, 96
Towels, bacteria on, 56
Transcendental meditation (TM), 80–82
Trans fats, and depression risk, 21
Transient ischemic attacks (TIAs), 10
Travel. *See also* Air travel
bargains for, 229–232, 240
bedbugs, 226, 237
for business, 324
car rental and, 235
cell phone services, 198–199
credit card tips, 131

glamping, 227–229
group, 229
home swapping, 238–239
hotel reviews, 225–227
hotel savings, 227
insurance, 236
language translation app, 241
last-minute deals, 236
safety tips, 237
senior discounts, 219
tips for successful, 236–237, 240–241
Trusts, 224
Tuna, 25
Turmeric, 95

U

United States, investments based in. *See* Investing
University education. *See* College
Urinalysis, 35
Urinary incontinence, 121
Urinary tract health
catheter use, 8, 23, 37, 45
infections (UTIs), 23, 121–122
UTIs (urinary tract infections), 23, 121–122

V

Vacations. *See* Air travel; Travel
Vaccines, 15, 61, 268
Vaginal dryness, 104
Variable annuities, 208
Vegetables
grilling, 83. *See also specific vegetables*
for longevity, 100–101
for reducing infection, 61
Vegetarians, 122
Veterans, 313
Vinpocetine, 90
Vision, 22. *See also* Eye health
Visualization therapy, 59
Vitamin B, 109. *See also* Folates
Vitamin C, 84
Vitamin D, 44, 87–88, 92, 94–95, 121–122
Vitamin E, 94
Vitamin K, 96
Volunteering, 220, 266, 300, 313

W

Waist circumference, 22
Walking, 42, 70
Walnuts, 284
Watches, 205
Water
airplane, 234
cleaning with hot, 282, 284
consumption recommendation, 59–60
Weather, 328
Weight
excess, around waist, 22
prostate cancer link to, 121
stress link to gaining, 80
Weight loss, 62–64
Wheat, 74–76
Whistle-blowers, 326–328
Wills. *See* Estate planning
Wind turbine, 198
Wine, 197. *See also* Alcohol consumption
Women. *See also* Marriage
diabetes risk for, 11
hot flash treatment for, 112
stress management for, 58
Work. *See also* Businesses
defending your ideas at, 319–321
difficult boss at, 324
disabilities and, 312
e-mail etiquette at, 322
heart health link to, 325
interview, tips for, 309–310
looking for, 305–309, 311
relocations, 323
salary negotiations, 312
sleepiness at, 79
words of wisdom on, 317–319, 321–322
Wound healing, 44

Y

Yards, 249, 271–272, 282–284. *See also* Homes
Yard sales, 247–249
Yield, earning higher, 173–174